www.ingramcontent.com/pod-product-compliance
Lightning Source LLC
Chambersburg PA
CBHW030312100426
42812CB00002B/668

9 7 8 1 9 5 2 8 9 5 3 8 8

TIMES
of
ELEVATION

VOLUME 2
Pesach - Ninth of Av

Kabbalah Centre Publishing is a registered DBA of The Kabbalah Centre International, Inc.

For further information:
The Kabbalah Centre
155 E. 48th St., New York, NY 10017
1062 S. Robertson Blvd., Los Angeles, CA 90035

1.800.Kabbalah   www.kabbalah.com

Printed in China, August 2024

ISBN: 978-1-952895-38-8

Times of Elevation, Volume 2, First Edition

Cover Design: HL Design (Hyun Min Lee) www.hldesignco.com
Graphic Layout: Shlomit Heymann

TIMES
of
ELEVATION

Secrets of the Zohar
on the Most Powerful
Days of the Year

Edited by Rav Michael Berg

VOLUME 2
Pesach - Ninth of Av

TABLE OF CONTENTS

PESACH

Bo
9. Leaven and leavened dough...13

Bo
10. Matzah of Judgment 16

Bo
11. Relating the praise of the exodus from Egypt.......................24

Bo
12. The Paschal sacrifice...29

Tetzaveh
9. The bread of the first fruits...36

Emor
24. The two bloods: of the Paschal lamb and of Circumcision........44

Pinchas
105. The Holiday of Pesach...58

106. "Shout down the beast of the reeds"................................90

Vayetze
22. His thought was with Rachel 98

Vayechi
33. The world is judged four times a year................................101

Mishpatim
18. Two Messiahs 103

TETZAVEH
5. Giving a portion to the Other Side 105

SEVENTH DAY OF PESACH

BESHALACH
11. "And the Angel of God... moved" 109

BESHALACH
14. "And moved…, And it came…, And stretched out…" 113

BESHALACH
16. "Then sang Moses" 133

COUNTING OF THE OMER

TETZAVEH
7. Matzot and the Counting of the Omer.............................. 153

EMOR
29. The Counting of the Omer 161

EMOR
31. The Counting of the Omer and the Holiday of Shavuot......... 165

LAG B'OMER

PROLOGUE
10. The vision of Rav Chiya 181

PROLOGUE
20. Rav Shimon's departure from the cave............................ 188

VAYECHI
19. Rav Yitzchak sat sadly 192

NASO
5. A wife suspected of adultery (Sota) 202

NASO (IDRA RABBA)
1. The Foreword to the Holy Idra Raba 203

NASO
51. The passing of the three friends 212

HA'AZINU
6. The day when Rav Shimon wanted to depart from the world 218

HA'AZINU
48. The passing away of Rav Shimon ben Yochai 224

ZOHAR CHADASH: BERESHEET
55. When Rav Shimon became ill 228

SHAVUOT

PROLOGUE
14. The night of the Bride 237

YITRO
13. "In the third month" 296

EMOR
25. Why there are not seven days to Shavuot? 302

EMOR
27. The Festival of Shavuot 306

EMOR
30. Shavuot Night 314

EMOR
31. The Counting of the Omer and the Holiday of Shavuot 319

PINCHAS

113. Shavuot.. 326

114. "But you shall surely let the mother go"............................ 338

115. Israel know how to hunt good game.............................. 339

119. "Also on the day of the First Fruits"............................... 340

127. Shavuot.. 343

YITRO

17. "And it came to pass, on the third day"............................. 346

18. "There were thundering and lightning" 350

19. "And all the people saw the voices" 355

20. "And God (Elohim) spoke" 361

21. "The Tablets were the work of God"............................... 369

YOSEF HATZADIK

VAYASHEV

10. "And a certain man found him" 383

VAYESHEV

19. "And Joseph was brought down to Egypt…"....................... 386

VAYESHEV

20. "And the Lord was with Joseph" 392

VAYESHEV

21. "His master's wife cast her eyes" 397

MIKETZ

5. "Since God has shown you all this" 403

MIKETZ

7. "And Joseph was the governor of the land" 407

MIKETZ

11. "And took from them Shimon"....................................... 412

VAYECHI

77. "Joseph is a fruitful bough"..419

NINTH OF AV

VAYISHLACH

7. The sinew of the vein 433

PESACH

Bo

9. Leaven and leavened dough

A Synopsis

In this discussion, we read that leaven, leavened fermentation, and leavened bread are all the same thing. In response to Rav Yehuda's query about why, if it is so important, Israel is only restricted from eating leaven seven days a year, Rav Shimon replies that this is an annual celebration of the days that they went out of bondage.

Se'or, Chametz, and Machmetzet all allude to the Evil Inclination.

166. וְהַיְינוּ דְּאָמַר רִבִּי שִׁמְעוֹן, מַאי דִּכְתִּיב, אַךְ בַּיּוֹם הָרִאשׁוֹן תַּשְׁבִּיתוּ שְּׂאוֹר מִבָּתֵּיכֶם כִּי כָּל אוֹכֵל מַחְמֶצֶת. אֲנָא הָכִי אוֹקִימְנָא, הַאי שְּׂאוֹר, וְהַאי מַחְמֶצֶת, דַּרְגָּא חַד אִינוּן, וְכֻלְּהוּ חַד. רְשׁוּ אוֹחֲרֵי, אִינּוּן שָׁלְטָנִין, דִּמְמֻנָּן עַל שְׁאַר עַמִּין, וְקָרִינָן לְהוּ יֵצֶר הָרָע, רְשׁוּתָא אַחֲרָא, אֵל נֵכָר, אֱלֹהִים אֲחֵרִים. אוּף הָכִי, שְּׂאוֹר, וּמַחְמֶצֶת, וְחָמֵץ, וְכֹלָּא חַד. אָמַר קוּדְשָׁא בְּרִיךְ הוּא, כָּל הָנֵי שְׁנֵי, קַיְּימְתוּ בִּרְשׁוּתָא אַחֲרָא, עַבְדִּין לְעַם אַחֲרָא, מִכָּאן וּלְהָלְאָה דְּאַתּוּן בְּנֵי חוֹרִין, אַךְ בַּיּוֹם הָרִאשׁוֹן תַּשְׁבִּיתוּ שְּׂאוֹר מִבָּתֵּיכֶם. כָּל מַחְמֶצֶת לֹא תֹאכֵלוּ. וְלֹא יֵרָאֶה לְךָ חָמֵץ.

166. This is what Rav Shimon said: "It is written, '...but on the first day you shall remove leaven (*se'or*) out of your houses; for whoever eats leavened dough (*machmetzet*)....' (Exodus 12:15) I have explained it thus: This leaven (*se'or*) and this leavened dough (*machmetzet*) are one level, and they are all one. The other dominion is the ministers appointed over the other nations, whom we call Evil Inclination, Other Domain, Foreign *El* (God), Other *Elohim* (Gods). Here also, leaven (*se'or*), leavened dough (*machmetzet*), and leavened bread (*chametz*) are all one. The Holy One, blessed be He, said: 'All those years, you were under the authority of others and served another nation. From now on, you are free.' '...but on the first day

you shall remove leaven (*se'or*) out of your houses…' (Exodus 12:15), 'You shall eat nothing leavened (*machmetzet*)' (Ibid. 20) and '…no leavened bread (*chametz*) shall be seen with you….' (Exodus 13:7)"

Leaven is forbidden only on Pesach,
when we need to show ourselves as free.

167. אָמַר רִבִּי יְהוּדָה, אִי הָכִי כָּל יְמֵי שַׁתָּא נָמֵי, אֲמַאי שִׁבְעַת יוֹמִין, דִּכְתִּיב שִׁבְעַת יָמִים שְׂאוֹר לֹא יִמָּצֵא בְּבָתֵּיכֶם, שִׁבְעַת יָמִים, וְלָא יַתִּיר. א"ל, כָּל זִמְנָא דְּאִתְחַיָּיב בַּר נָשׁ לְאִתְחֲזָאָה גַּרְמֵיהּ בֶּן חוֹרִין, הָכִי אִצְטְרִיךְ, כָּל זִמְנָא דְּלָא אִתְחַיָּיב לָא אִצְטְרִיךְ.

167. Rav Yehuda said: "If so, then also all the days of the year we should not eat leaven? Why only seven days, as it is written, 'Seven days… shall there be no leaven found in your houses…' (Exodus 13:7) and not more?" He said to him: "At all times that a person is obliged **to show himself free, it is required** not to eat leavened bread, **but whenever he is not obligated then he does not need** to observe the prohibition of leavened bread.

Every year we need to observe the days we went out of bondage
and into the Holy Authority.

168. לְמַלְכָּא דְּעָבֵד לְחַד בַּר נָשׁ רוֹפִינוֹס, כָּל אִינּוּן יוֹמִין דְּסָלִיק לְהַאי דַּרְגָּא, חַדֵי, וְלָבֵישׁ לְבוּשֵׁי יְקָר, לְבָתַר לָא אִצְטְרִיךְ. לְשַׁעְתָּא אַחֲרָא נָטִיר אִינּוּן יוֹמִין דְּסָלִיק לְיָקִירוּ דָּא, וְלָבֵשׁ אִינּוּן לְבוּשִׁין, וְכֵן כָּל שַׁתָּא וְשַׁתָּא כְּהַאי גַּוְונָא יִשְׂרָאֵל, כְּתִיב, שִׁבְעַת יָמִים שְׂאוֹר לֹא יִמָּצֵא, דְּאִינּוּן יוֹמֵי חֶדְוָותָא, יוֹמִין דְּסָלִיקוּ לִיקָרָא דָּא, וְנַפְקוּ מִשִׁעְבּוּדָא אַחֲרָא. וּבְגִין כַּךְ, נַטְרִין בְּכָל שַׁתָּא וְשַׁתָּא, יוֹמִין דְּסָלִיקוּ לְהַאי יְקָר, וְנַפְקוּ מֵרְשׁוּתָא אַחֲרָא, וְעָאלוּ בִּרְשׁוּתָא קַדִּישָׁא, וְעַל דָּא כְּתִיב, שִׁבְעַת יָמִים מַצּוֹת תֹּאכֵלוּ.

168. "This is comparable to a king who appointed a person to be a minister. He rejoiced and wore clothes of glory all those days that

he was being elevated to this level, but afterwards he did not need it. The following year, he observed those days that he rose to this honor and wore those clothes, and he did so each and every year. Similarly with Israel, it is written, 'Seven days… shall there be no leaven found…' (Exodus 13:7) for they are days of rejoicing, the days that they arose to this honor, and went out of other bondage. Every year, they observed those days when they rose to this honor and went out of another authority and came under Holy Authority. Therefore, it is written, 'Seven days… shall you eat unleavened bread….' (Ibid.)"

Bo

10. Matzah of Judgment

A Synopsis

Rav Shimon talks about the time that the moon was in a decreased state, when Israel had not yet completed the Covenant by the uncovering of the corona. After they were uncovered, God gave them bread from a higher place, from the Heavens. Then Israel observe those days when they entered under the wings of the Shechinah and guarded the bread, the Matzot, that came from its side.

The bonds that Rav Shimon refers to next are those that join the Upper to the Lower levels, and in the observance of the sacrifice those bonds are strengthened, as when the lamb is sacrificed.

Matzah is Holy Judgment.

169. אָמַר רְבִּי שִׁמְעוֹן, מַצַּת כְּתִיב, כמד"א, מַרְאֹת אֱלֹהִים. וְלָמָּה אִתְקְרֵי מַצָּת. דִּינָא. דִּינָא קַדִּישָׁא. דִּינָא דְּאִתְאַחֲדָא בְּשְׁמָא קַדִּישָׁא. דִּינָא דְּלָא הֲוָה תַקִּיפָא כָּל הַהוּא זִמְנָא בְּגַוַּיְיהוּ דְּיִשְׂרָאֵל, דְּהָא קַיְּימָא סִיהֲרָא בִּפְגִימוּתָא. וְעַל דְּקַיְּימָא סִיהֲרָא בִּפְגִימוּתָא, לֶחֶם עֹנִי כְּתִיב.

169. Rav Shimon said: "Matzot (unleavened bread; מצת) is spelled without Vav, as, '...visions (*mar'ot*; מראת) of God (Elohim)' (Ezekiel 1:1) is without Vav, which alludes to Judgment." [He asks:] **"Why were they called *Matzot*?"** [He answers:] **"Because they are Judgment, Holy Judgment, Judgment that is attached to the Holy Name, Judgment that was not strong throughout that time among Israel as the moon was damaged. And since the moon was damaged, it is written, '...the bread of affliction....' (Deuteronomy 16:3)"**

Explanation: At first Nukva was in the secret of "...the two great luminaries..." (Genesis 1:16), where both Zeir Anpin and Malchut were in equal stature. Zeir Anpin clothed the Right Column of Binah and Malchut the Left Side of Binah. Then they were in the aspect of "small face" because they are Mochin of Achorayim that do not shine and they are the aspect of Judgment. Afterwards, through the Female Waters that the Lower Beings elevate, Malchut is diminished and returns to be a dot and then she is rebuilt bigger through Aba and Ima, and they return to have Mochin of Gadlut [Maturity]. [At this point], even though Zeir Anpin and Malchut stand with Mochin of Gadlut [Maturity], the Mochin of Achorayim are not nullified but return to shine in the aspect of Mercy, and all the Illumination of Chochmah in the grade come from these Mochin. Know that the secret of Matzah is these Mochin of Achorayim once they are fixed by the Mochin of Gadlut.

This is: **"Why were they called Matzot? Because they are Judgment,"** which is why it is called Matzah without a Vav, representing Judgment, because they are the Mochin of Achorayim when Zeir Anpin and Nukva are with the Mochin of Katnut [Immaturity]. But it is **"Holy Judgment, Judgment that is attached to the Holy Name,"** because they have already returned and came with the Mochin of Gadlut [Maturity], which are Holy and united in the secret of the Three Columns, which are Yud-Hei-Vav (יהו) of the Holy Name (יהוה). We explained earlier that to come to the Mochin of Gadlut, Malchut needs two corrections: the first to be diminished to a dot, and the second to be built to Gadlut [Maturity]. For this there are two actions to awaken from Below: circumcision (milah) and uncovering (priyah). The Israelites circumcised themselves at that point, so Malchut had already been through the first correction to be diminished to a dot, in the secret of the diminishment of the moon, and thus the Judgment of the Mochin of Katnut in the Matzah was already sweetened. And through the priyah (uncovering the corona), which is the letters of para Yud-Hei (פרע יה; Yud-Hei uncovered), we awaken Above the building of Malchut through Aba and Ima, and the Mochin of Gadlut are revealed.

This is: **"Judgment that was not strong throughout that time among Israel because the moon was damaged"** because they had already circumcised themselves and the moon—Malchut—diminished, and the Judgment force in the Mochin of Katnut weakened. Then, when *priyah* (uncovering the corona) happens, the Mochin of Gadlut will emerge, as it will say later. You may ask: "Why on Pesach do the Mochin of Gadlut already shine even though the Israelites did not yet do *priyah?*" But what we are talking about here is through an awakening from Below, and on the night of Pesach, the Illumination of the Mochin was only from an awakening from Above, and therefore they only shone that night alone. This is: **"And since the moon was damaged, it is written, 'The bread of affliction' (Deuteronomy 16:3)"** because they did not yet draw the Mochin of Gadlut from the aspect of an awakening from Below.

The importance of Priyah.

170. מ"ט קַיְּימָא בִּפְגִימוּתָא. בְּגִין דְּלָא אִתְפְּרָעוּ, וְלָא אִתְגַּלְיָא הַאי אָת קַדִּישָׁא. גְּזִירִין הֲווֹ וְלָא אִתְפְּרָעוּ, אִימָתַי אִתְפְּרָעוּ, בְּשַׁעֲתָא דִּכְתִיב, שָׂם שָׂם לוֹ חֹק וּמִשְׁפָּט וְשָׁם נִסָּהוּ, וְאַע"ג דְּאוֹקִימְנָא הַאי קְרָא בְּמִלָּה אַחֲרָא, כֹּלָּא הֲוָה וְיֵאוֹת.

170. He asks: **"What is the reason** that the moon, which is Malchut, **was diminished?"** He answers: **"Because they did not do *priyah*, and the Holy Sign was not revealed** because through *priyah* we draw the Mochin of Gadlut and thus the moon is in its full state. **Israel were circumcised, but did not do *priyah*. When they did, it is written, '...There He made for them a statute and an ordinance, and there He tested him.' (Exodus 15:25) And even though we have explained this passage as referring to something else, it is all true and is well."**

Once Israel performed Priyah, they ate bread from the Heavens.

171. וְאִי תֵימָא דְּבִימֵי יְהוֹשֻׁעַ אִתְפְּרָעוּ. לָאו הָכִי, אֶלָּא אִינּוּן דִּכְתִיב וְכָל הָעָם הַיִּלוֹדִים בַּמִּדְבָּר בַּדֶּרֶךְ וְגוֹ'. בָּתַר דְּאִתְפְּרָעוּ, אָמַר קוּדְשָׁא בְּרִיךְ הוּא, בְּקַדְמֵיתָא אֲכַלְתּוּן מַצּוֹת, דְּקַיְּימָא סִיהֲרָא בִּפְגִימוּתָא, וְאִקְרֵי לֶחֶם עֹנִי, מִכָּאן וּלְהָלְאָה הַאי לֶחֶם מֵאֲתַר אַחֲרָא לֶהֱוֵי. מַאי הוּא. דִּכְתִיב הִנְנִי מַמְטִיר לָכֶם לֶחֶם מִן הַשָּׁמָיִם. לָא מִן סִיהֲרָא כְּהַהוּא זִמְנָא, אֶלָּא מִן הַשָּׁמַיִם מַמָּשׁ, כְּמָה דִּכְתִיב וְיִתֶּן לְךָ הָאֱלֹהִים מִטַּל הַשָּׁמָיִם.

171. If you ask: "Did they not do *priyah* in the days of Joshua?" This was not so. Only those about whom it is written: "But all the people that were born in the wilderness by the way as they came out of Egypt, them they had not circumcised." (Joshua 5:5) After they did *priyah*, the Holy One, blessed be He, said to them, "Previously, you ate unleavened bread because the moon remained waned, and it was called 'the bread of affliction.' But from now on, bread will be from a different place." And what is it? It is what is written: "... 'Behold, I will rain bread from heaven for you....'" (Exodus 16:4) Not from the moon, which is Malchut, **like at that time** before they did *priyah*, **but literally from the Heavens,** which is Zeir Anpin, **as it is written: "And God shall give you of the dew of Heaven...."** (Genesis 27:28)

Israel observe the days when they came under the wings of the Shechinah.

172. וְיִשְׂרָאֵל קַדִּישִׁין, נַטְרִין אִינּוּן יוֹמִין דְּעָאלוּ תְּחוֹת גַּדְפוֹי דִּשְׁכִינְתָּא, וְנַטְרִין הַהוּא נַהֲמָא דְּאַתְיָא מִסִּטְרָהָא, וְעַ"ד כְּתִיב, אֶת חַג מַצּוֹת תִּשְׁמֹר וְגוֹ', וּכְתִיב וּשְׁמַרְתֶּם אֶת הַמַּצּוֹת. מַהוּ וּשְׁמַרְתֶּם אֶת הַמַּצּוֹת. כד"א, וּשְׁמַרְתֶּם אֶת בְּרִיתִי. וְכֹלָּא בְּחַד דַּרְגָּא סַלְקָא וְאִתְאֲחָד.

172. And Holy Israel observe the days when they came under the wings of the Shechinah and keep the bread that came from its Side, namely the Matzot, **as it is written: "And you shall observe the commandment of unleavened bread...."** (Exodus 12:17) **What is**

the meaning of, "And you shall observe... the unleavened bread...?" (Ibid.) It is similar to: "...and keep My Covenant..." (Exodus 19:5), which is the Covenant of Circumcision. **And it all rises and is attached to the same level,** as mentioned before.

Circumcision without uncovering brings about the bread of affliction.

173. וְאִי תֵּימָא מֹשֶׁה הֵיךְ לָא פָּרַע לְהוּ. אֶלָּא, בְּגִין דְּלָא יִתְעַכְּבוּן יִשְׂרָאֵל תַּמָּן עַד דְּיִתְּסְיאוּ, וְעַל דָּא כְּתִיב, שִׁבְעַת יָמִים תֹּאכַל עָלָיו מַצּוֹת לֶחֶם עֹנִי. מַ"ט לֶחֶם עֹנִי, מִשּׁוּם כִּי בְחִפָּזוֹן יָצָאתָ וְגוֹ' וּכְתִיב וְלֹא יָכְלוּ לְהִתְמַהְמֵהַּ.

173. **One may wonder how it could be that Moses did not uncover them** but let them remain circumcised without being uncovered. He answers, **"So that Israel would not be delayed there until they became healed,** he therefore did not uncover them. **Pertaining to this, it is written, '...seven days shall you eat unleavened bread with it, the bread of affliction....'** (Deuteronomy 16:3) Why was it '**the bread of affliction'?** Because, '**...for you came forth... in haste...'** (Ibid.) and similarly, **it is written, '...and could not delay....'** (Exodus 12:39) Therefore, they were not uncovered, and circumcision without uncovering brings about the bread of affliction.

Priyah was done before entering Israel, for it is a land where Yesod shines.

174. תָּא חֲזֵי, כַּד עָאלוּ יִשְׂרָאֵל לְאַרְעָא, עָאלוּ גְּזִירִין וְאִתְפְּרָעוּ. וּמַה כְּתִיב, אֶרֶץ אֲשֶׁר לֹא בְמִסְכֵּנוּת תֹּאכַל בָּהּ לֶחֶם. מַאי בְמִסְכֵּנוּת. לֶחֶם עֹנִי. אַמַּאי אִקְרֵי לֶחֶם עֹנִי. מִשּׁוּם דְּקַיְימָא סִיהֲרָא בִּפְגִימוּתָא, וְלָא מִתְבָּרְכָא מִשִּׁמְשָׁא, וְלָא מִתְנַהֲרָא מִן שִׁמְשָׁא, כְּמָה דְּאַתְּ אָמֵר, כִּי כֹל בַּשָּׁמַיִם וּבָאָרֶץ, וְלָא אִתְנַהֲרָא מִיּוֹבְלָא. מַאי טַעֲמָא. מִשּׁוּם דְּלָא אִתְפְּרָעוּ. אֲבָל הָכָא, דְּאִתְגְּזָרוּ יִשְׂרָאֵל וְאִתְפְּרָעוּ, לֹא תֶחְסַר כֹּל בָּהּ כְּתִיב, וְעַל דָּא לֹא בְמִסְכֵּנוּת תֹּאכַל בָּהּ לֶחֶם. מַאי טַעֲמָא. מִשּׁוּם דְּלָא תֶחְסַר כֹּ"ל בָּהּ, כְּמָה דְּחַזְרוּ לֵיהּ בְּמִצְרַיִם.

174. "Come and see, when Israel came to the Holy Land, they came circumcised and uncovered, and it is written, 'A land in which you shall eat bread without scarceness….' (Deuteronomy 8:9) And what is 'scarceness'? It is 'the bread of affliction.' And why is it called 'the bread of affliction'? This is because the moon, which is Malchut, is waning and is not blessed from the sun, which is Zeir Anpin, and does not shine from the sun, as it is written, '…for all (kol) that is in Heaven and on Earth…' (I Chronicles 29:11)," meaning that kol (all), which is Yesod of Zeir Anpin, is attached to Heaven, which is Zeir Anpin, and to the Earth, which is Malchut, and receives from the Heavens and gives to the Earth. [He asks:] "What is the reason that it did not shine from the Jubilee, which is Binah?" [He answers:] "This is because they did not uncover themselves, as mentioned before, but now that Israel were circumcised and uncovered upon arriving into the Holy Land, it is written, '…where you shall not lack anything (kol)…' (Deuteronomy 8:9), namely Yesod of Zeir Anpin that illuminates on Malchut and is called kol. [He asks:] "What is the reason for, '…in which you will not eat bread without scarceness…'? [He answers:] "It is because 'You shall not lack anything (kol) in it,' (Ibid.) the way they did in Egypt."

We make a remembrance by eating Matzot on Pesach.

175. וּבְכָל שַׁתָּא וְשַׁתָּא דּוּכְרָנָא דְּמִצְרַיִם קָא עַבְדֵי יִשְׂרָאֵל, וְאַכְלֵי וְלָא אִשְׁתְּצֵי מִדָּרֵי דָרִין. וּבְגִין דְּלָא אִתְפְּרָעוּ הָכָא בְּמִצְרַיִם, חַסְרוּ לֵיהּ לְהַאי כָּל, וְקַיְּימָא סִיהֲרָא בִּפְגִימוּתָא, וְאִקְרֵי לֶחֶם עֹנִי, עֹנִי: כְּתַרְגּוּמוֹ בְּמִסְכֵּנוּת. וּמַאי דְּאַכְלוּ לֵיהּ תַּמָּן בְּאַרְעָא, בְּגִין דּוּכְרָנָא דְּמִצְרַיִם הֲוָה, וְהַאי לְדָרֵי דָרִין, וּלְזִמְנָא דְּאָתֵי כְּתִיב, לֹא יָבֹא עוֹד שִׁמְשֵׁךְ וִירֵחֵךְ וְגוֹ'.

175. And every year, the children of Israel make a remembrance to Egypt and eat unleavened bread and have not interrupted this for generations and generations. Because they did not uncover themselves in Egypt, they lacked this kol, and the moon was waning

and is called "the bread of affliction." **Affliction** means "poverty," as in the Aramaic translation. **The reason they ate the bread of affliction in the Holy Land,** even though they had already uncovered themselves, **serves as a remembrance to Egypt. This is a custom for generations and generations. And for the future to come, it is written: "Your sun shall no more set; nor shall your moon withdraw itself…" (Isaiah 60:20),** meaning that the waning of the moon, which is Malchut, will be no more.

Taking the lamb on the tenth day of the month.

176. תָּנָא א"ר שִׁמְעוֹן כְּתִיב בֶּעָשׂוֹר לַחֹדֶשׁ הַזֶּה וְיִקְחוּ לָהֶם וְגוֹ', וּכְתִיב אַךְ בֶּעָשׂוֹר לַחֹדֶשׁ הַשְּׁבִיעִי הַזֶּה יוֹם הַכִּפּוּרִים הוּא, אִשְׁתְּמַע כְּמָה דְּאִתְּמַר, דִּכְתִיב בֶּעָשׂוֹר לַחֹדֶשׁ הַזֶּה. מַאי קָא מַיְירֵי. אֶלָּא בֶּעָשׂוֹר, מִלָּה דָּא בֶּעָשׂוֹר תַּלְיָא. לַחֹדֶשׁ הַזֶּה בַּחֹדֶשׁ הַזֶּה מִבָּעֵי לֵיהּ. אֶלָּא, כַּד אָתָא נְהוֹרָא לְהַאי דַּרְגָּא, כְּתִיב לַחֹדֶשׁ הַזֶּה דַּיְקָא.

176. We learned that Rav Shimon said: "It is written, '…on the tenth day of this month they shall take…' (Exodus 12:3) and 'Also on the tenth day of this seventh month there shall be Yom Kippur….' (Leviticus 23:27) It is derived from what we learned, as it is written, 'on the tenth day of this month.' (Ibid.)" The Zohar wonders and asks: **"What does it mean by this?"** He answers: **"It alludes to the words, 'on the tenth.' This matter** of taking the lamb **depends on the tenth,"** which is Binah that shines on Malchut, as mentioned. And this is why he first mentions the analogy between the tenth in this context and the tenth of Yom Kippur, which is Binah. And he asks: **"It is written, 'of this month,' (Ibid.) but should it not say, 'in this month'?"** He answers: "It is because **when the Illumination came to this level,** which is Malchut, it is written **'of this month' (Ibid.)** [since] 'of this month' **is exact,** which is Malchut that is called 'month.'"

The lamb represents the Klipot, and we tie it so as to
bind and subdue all the Negative Forces.

177. וְיִקְחוּ לָהֶם אִישׁ שֶׂה לְבֵית אָבֹת שֶׂה לָבָיִת. תָּנָא תְּלַת קָשְׁרִין אִינּוּן,
בְּכוֹר בְּהֵמָה, בְּכוֹר הַשְּׁבִי, בְּכוֹר הַשִּׁפְחָה. דְּכָל שְׁאַר מִתְקַשְׁרֵי בְּהוּ בְּאִלֵּין
תְּלַת גַּוְונֵי דִלְעֵילָא. וּבְהַאי דְּאִתְקְרֵי צֹאן, אִתְקְשַׁר כֹּלָּא, וְכֹלָּא כָּלִיל בַּצֹּאן,
אִתְקְשַׁר צֹאן בַּצֹּאן, וְלָא יָכִיל לְאִתְפָּרְשָׁא מִקְּטִירוֹי, וּבְהַאי כֻּלְּהוּ אִתְקַשְׁרוּ,
וְעַ"ד כְּתִיב, וְהָיָה לָכֶם לְמִשְׁמֶרֶת, קְטִירוּ לֵיהּ בִּקְטִירוּתָא, וְיְהֵא אִתְמְסַר
בִּידֵיכוֹן בִּרְשׁוּתְכוֹן, עַד דְּתִנְכְסוּ לֵיהּ, וְתַעְבְּדוּן בֵּיהּ דִּינָא, וּלְזִמְנָא דְּאָתֵי כְּתִיב
מִי זֶה בָּא מֵאֱדוֹם. וּכְתִיב, כִּי זֶבַח לַיְיָ' בְּבָצְרָה. וּכְתִיב, וְהָיָה יְיָ' לְמֶלֶךְ עַל כָּל
הָאָרֶץ בַּיּוֹם הַהוּא יִהְיֶה יְיָ' אֶחָד וּשְׁמוֹ אֶחָד.

177. "...they shall take to them every man a lamb, according to the houses of their fathers, a lamb for a house." (Exodus 12:3) We learned that there are three bonds: the firstborn of cattle, the firstborn of the captive, and the firstborn of the maidservant. All the other levels of the Klipah are connected to these three aspects Above. They are all bound to the one called "flock," and everything is included in it. It is the highest level among them. The flock Below is connected to the flock Above, and is unable to separate from its bond. So we see that they are all connected to this, to the flock. This is why it is written by it: "and you shall keep watch over it" (Exodus 12:6), meaning bind it with a knot, and it would be given into your hands under your control until you slaughter it and execute Judgment upon it. In the time to come, it is written: "Who is this that comes from Edom..." (Isaiah 63:1) and "...For the Lord has a sacrifice in Botzrah..." (Isaiah 34:6), meaning that He will destroy the entire Other Side from the Earth. And then it is written: "And the Lord shall be king over all the Earth. On that day the Lord shall be One and His Name One." (Zechariah 14:9)

Bo

11. Relating the praise of the exodus from Egypt

A Synopsis

We hear again about the Precept to remove the leaven from the bread. Then we are told that Israel must say the praises of the exodus from Egypt, and when relating that account they will rejoice with the Shechinah in the World to Come. When God hears that praise, His retinue gathers round and rejoices and praises Him, and then His strength and power are increased Above. Just as it is important for a person to relate the miracles of God, it is important for him to relate his own sins; this is because when a person enumerates every one of his sins beforehand, he leaves no open issue for the Accuser to exploit when standing before God to seek retribution. If the person repents, all will be well, but if he does not, the Accuser will return and demand Judgment. Lastly, we hear again of the Precept to eat Matzah on Passover because it is a remembrance for generations and generations of the secret of the Faith.

Chametz alludes to the Evil Inclination,
and Matzah alludes to the good inclination.

רעיא מהימנא

178. וְיִשָּׂא הָעָם אֶת בְּצֵקוֹ טֶרֶם יֶחְמָץ וְגוֹ'. כ"ה פִּקוּדָא דָא, לְבָעֵר חָמֵץ. דְּהָא פִּקוּדָא דָא, אִתְמְסַר לְהוּ לְיִשְׂרָאֵל וְיִשָּׂא הָעָם אֶת בְּצֵקוֹ טֶרֶם יֶחְמָץ. וּכְתִיב שְׂאוֹר לֹא יִמָּצֵא בְּבָתֵּיכֶם, וְהָא אוּקְמוּהָ חַבְרַיָּא, וְרָזָא אוֹקִימְנָא, בֵּין חָמֵץ וּמַצָּה דְּכַמָּה דּוּכְתֵּי, דָא יֵצֶר רַע, וְדָא יֵצֶר טוֹב.

Ra'aya Meheimna (Faithful Shepherd)
178. "And the people took their dough before it was leavened...."
(Exodus 12:34) This (25th) Precept is to remove the leaven. For this Precept was given over to Israel: "And the people took up and carried their dough before it was leavened..." (Exodus 12:34) and

"…shall there be no leaven found in your houses…." (Exodus 12:19)
The friends have already explained it, and we have explained the
secret meaning of the difference between leavened (*chametz*) and
unleavened bread (*matzah*) of the exodus from Egypt in many places;
one is the Evil Inclination and the other is the Good Inclination.

The Precept to tell the story of the Exodus.

179. כ"ו פִּקּוּדָא בָּתַר דָּא, לְסַפֵּר בְּשִׁבְחָא דִּיצִיאַת מִצְרַיִם, דְּאִיהוּ וְיוּבָא עַל
בַּר נָשׁ, לְאִשְׁתָּעֵי בְּהַאי שִׁבְחָא לְעָלְמִין. הָכִי אוֹקִימְנָא, כָּל בַּר נָשׁ דְּאִשְׁתָּעֵי
בִּיצִיאַת מִצְרַיִם, וּבְהַהוּא סִפּוּר חַדֵּי בְּחֶדְוָה, זַמִּין אִיהוּ לְמֶחֱדֵי בִּשְׁכִינְתָּא
לְעָלְמָא דְּאָתֵי דְּהוּא חֶדּוּ מִכֹּלָּא, דְּהַאי אִיהוּ בַּר דְּחַדֵּי בְּמָרֵיה, וְקוּדְשָׁא
בְּרִיךְ הוּא חַדֵּי בְּהַהוּא סִפּוּר.

179. The following (26th) Precept is to relate the praise of the exodus
from Egypt, which is incumbent upon every person always to relate
these praises. We have explained that every person who relates
the exodus from Egypt and rejoices when relating that account is
destined to rejoice with the Shechinah in the World to Come, which
is joy from all sides. For such is a person who rejoices in his Master,
and the Holy One, blessed be He, rejoices in his story.

The Creator and His entourage come to hear
the praise of the exodus on the Seder night.

180. בֵּיהּ שַׁעֲתָא, כָּנִישׁ קוּדְשָׁא בְּרִיךְ הוּא לְכָל פָּמַלְיָא דִּילֵיהּ, וְאָמַר לוֹן, זִילוּ
וּשְׁמָעוּ סִפּוּרָא דִּשְׁבָחָא דִּילִי, דְּקָא מִשְׁתָּעוּ בָּנַי, וְחַדְאן בְּפוּרְקָנִי. כְּדֵין כֻּלְּהוּ
מִתְכַּנְּשִׁין, וְאַתְיָין וּמִתְחַבְּרִין בַּהֲדַיְיהוּ דְּיִשְׂרָאֵל, וְשָׁמְעוּ סִפּוּרָא דִּשְׁבָחָא, דְּקָא
חַדָּאן בְּחֶדְוָה דְּפוּרְקָנָא דְּמָרֵיהוֹן, כְּדֵין אַתְיָין וְאוֹדָן לֵיהּ לְקוּדְשָׁא בְּרִיךְ הוּא,
עַל כָּל אִינּוּן נִסִּין וּגְבוּרָן וְאוֹדָאן לֵיהּ עַל עַמָּא קַדִּישָׁא דְּאִית לֵיהּ בְּאַרְעָא,
דְּחַדָּאן בְּחֶדְוָה דְּפוּרְקָנָא דְּמָארֵיהוֹן.

180. At that time, the Holy One, blessed be He, gathers His entire entourage, and says to them, "Go and listen to the account of My praise that My children are relating and are rejoicing in My redemption." At that time, they all gather and come and join with Israel to hear the story of the praise. They rejoice with the joy of the deliverance by their Master, and come to thank and praise the Holy One, blessed be He, for all these miracles and mighty deeds, and thank Him for the Holy Nation that He has on Earth that rejoices in the joy of the deliverance of their Master.

The Israelites give power to their Master, so to speak, by praising.

181. כְּדֵין אִתּוֹסָף לֵיהּ חֵילָא וּגְבוּרְתָּא לְעֵילָא, וְיִשְׂרָאֵל בְּהַהוּא סִפּוּרָא יָהֲבֵי חֵילָא לְמָארֵיהוֹן, כְּמַלְכָּא, דְּאִתּוֹסָף חֵילָא וּגְבוּרְתָּא, כַּד מְשַׁבְּחִין גְּבוּרְתֵּיהּ, וְאוֹדָן לֵיהּ, וְכֻלְּהוּ דַּחֲלִין מִקָּמֵיהּ, וְאִסְתַּלָּק יְקָרֵיהּ עַל כֻּלְּהוּ. וּבְגִין כָּךְ, אִית לְשַׁבְּחָא וּלְאִשְׁתָּעֵי בְּסִפּוּר דָּא כְּמָה דְּאִתְּמַר. כְּגַוְונָא דָּא, וְחוֹבָה אִיהוּ עַל בַּר נָשׁ, לְאִשְׁתָּעֵי תָּדִיר קָמֵי קוּדְשָׁא בְּרִיךְ הוּא, וּלְפַרְסוּמֵי נִיסָא בְּכָל אִינּוּן נִיסִין דְּעָבַד.

181. Then His strength and power are increased Above. By their recounting, the Israelites give power to their Master, like a king whose strength and power are increased when his strength is praised and he is acknowledged. All fear Him, and His glory rises above all of them. Therefore, it is incumbent to praise and relate this story, as we learned. Similarly, it is the duty of every person to relate before the Holy One, blessed be He, and publicize the miracle with all these miracles that He did.

Publicizing miracles.

182. וְאִי תֵּימָא, אֲמַאי אִיהוּ וְחוֹבָתָא, וְהָא קוּדְשָׁא בְּרִיךְ הוּא יָדַע כֹּלָּא, כָּל מַה דַּהֲוָה, וִיהֵוֵי לְבָתַר דְּנָא, אֲמַאי פַּרְסוּמָא דָּא קָמֵיהּ, עַל מַה דְּאִיהוּ עָבַד, וְאִיהוּ יָדַע. אֶלָּא וַדַּאי אִצְטְרִיךְ בַּר נָשׁ לְפַרְסוּמֵי נִיסָא, וּלְאִשְׁתָּעֵי קָמֵיהּ בְּכָל מַה

דְּאִיהוּ עָבַד, בְּגִין דְּאִינּוּן מִלִּין סַלְּקִין, וְכָל פָּמַלְיָא דִּלְעֵילָּא מִתְכַּנְּשִׁין, וְחָמָאן
לוֹן, וְאוֹדָאן כֻּלְּהוּ לְקוּדְשָׁא בְּרִיךְ הוּא, וְאִסְתַּלָּק יְקָרֵיהּ עָלַיְיהוּ עֵילָּא וְתַתָּא.

182. One may ask: "Why it is obligatory to relate the miracles; does
not the Holy One, blessed be He, know everything, everything that
was and will be in the future? What is this publicity before Him
of what He did, if He knows?" He answers: "Rather, surely one has
to make the miracle known and relate before Him all that He did
because these words ascend and all the entourage Above gather and
see them, and give thanks before the Holy One, blessed be He, and
His glory rises over them Above and Below.

Detailing one's own sins prevents the Accuser from demanding Judgment.

183. כְּגַוְונָא דָא, מַאן דְּאִשְׁתָּעֵי וּמְפָרֵט וְטָאוֹי עַל כָּל מַה דְּעָבַד, אִי תֵּימָא
לְמַאי אִצְטְרִיךְ. אֶלָּא מְקַטְרְגָא קָאִים תָּדִיר קָמֵי קוּדְשָׁא בְּרִיךְ הוּא, בְּגִין
לְאִשְׁתָּעֵי וּלְמִתְבַּע חוֹבֵי בְּנֵי נָשָׁא, וּלְמִתְבַּע עֲלֵיהוֹן דִּינָא. כֵּיוָן דְּאַקְדִּים בַּר
נָשׁ, וּמְפָרֵיט וְטָאוֹי, כָּל חַד וְחַד, לָא אַשְׁאִיר פִּתְרָא דְּפוּמָא לְהַהוּא מְקַטְרְגָא,
וְלָא יָכִיל לְמִתְבַּע עֲלֵיהּ דִּינָא. דְּהָא תָּדִיר תָּבַע דִּינָא בְּקַדְמֵיתָא, וּלְבָתַר
מִשְׁתָּעֵי וּמְקַטְרֵג פְּלוֹנִי עָבֵד כַּךְ. וְעַל דָּא, אִצְטְרִיךְ לֵיהּ לְבַר נָשׁ לְאַקְדְּמָא,
וּלְפָרֵט וְטָאוֹי.

183. "It is the same with he who relates and enumerates his sins
of everything that he has done. If you ask why this is necessary, it
is because the Accuser is constantly before the Holy One, blessed
be He, to recount and seek retribution for the sins of people, and
to demand Judgment against them. However when the person
enumerates each and every one of his sins beforehand, he does not
leave any pretext to the Accuser to exploit. And the Accuser cannot
demand any Judgment against him, for he always demands Judgment
first, and afterwards enumerates and accuses. Therefore the person
should take his own initiative before the Accuser and enumerate his
own sins.

Confession is not enough; it must be followed by Teshuvah.

184. כֵּיוָן דִּמְקַטְרְגָא חָמֵי דָא, לֵית לֵיהּ פִּטְרָא דְּפוּמָא עֲלֵיהּ, וּכְדֵין אִתְפְּרַשׁ מִנֵּיהּ בְּכֹל וָכֹל. אִי תָב בְּתִיוּבְתָּא יֵאוֹת, וְאִי לָאו, הָא מְקַטְרְגָא אִשְׁתְּכַח עֲלֵיהּ, וְאָמַר פְּלוֹנִי דְּאָתָא לְקָמָךְ בְּתוּקְפָּא דְּאַפִּין, בָּעִיט בְּמָרֵיהּ, וְחוֹבוֹי כַּךְ וְכַךְ. עַל דָּא יֵאוֹת לְאִזְדַּהֲרָא בַּר נָשׁ בְּכֹל הֲנֵי, בְּגִין דְּיִשְׁתְּכַח עַבְדָּא מְהֵימְנָא קָמֵי קוּדְשָׁא בְּרִיךְ הוּא.

184. "As soon as the Accuser sees this, he has no pretext to complain against him, and then takes leave from him entirely. If he repents, it is good, but if not, the Accuser rests on him and says, 'So and so, who came before you and confessed unashamedly he kicked his Master, his sins are such and such.' Therefore it is advisable that a person be careful in all this so that he should be considered a faithful servant before the Holy One, blessed be He."

The Precept to eat Matzah on Pesach.

185. כ"ז פִּקּוּדָא בָּתַר דָּא, לְאֶכוֹל מַצָּה בְּפֶסַח, בְּגִין דְּאִיהוּ דוּכְרָנָא לְדָרֵי דָרִין, עַל רָזָא דִּמְהֵימְנוּתָא. וְהָא אוּקְמוּהָ, דְּיִשְׂרָאֵל נָפְקוּ בְּהַהוּא זִמְנָא מֵרָזָא דְּטַעֲוָון אַחֲרָן, וְעָאלוּ בְּרָזָא דִּמְהֵימְנוּתָא. וְהָא אוּקְמוּהָ רָזָא דְּנָא בְּכַמָּה דּוּכְתֵּי.

185. The following (27th) Precept is to eat Matzah on Pesach because it is a remembrance for generations upon generations for the secret of the Faith. It has been explained that Israel went out at that time from the secret of other gods and came into the secret of Faith. This secret has been explained in many places.

Bo

12. The Paschal sacrifice

A Synopsis

The ordinance of the Passover is to slaughter the Paschal sacrifice at twilight of the fourteenth day of Nissan as a remembrance of the Passover in Egypt. The moon becomes complete on the fifteenth day, and the sacrifice should be slaughtered at twilight of the fourteenth day because that is the time that Judgment hangs over the world. The main part of the Precept is to gain pleasure from the scent that spreads from the roasting over the fire. Only one who is circumcised can eat of it. At the time when God came to Egypt and saw the blood marked on the entrances of the houses of Israel, the people used hyssop to spread the blood, since hyssop removes evil spirits and any aspect of a bad odor because it arouses the Supernal Redemption of Israel. In the time to come, God will slaughter the Evil Inclination. Because God slew all the firstborn of the Egyptians, He obligated all the firstborn of Israel to redeem themselves, and He guarded them against everything. Scripture says, about the sacrifice, "…neither shall you break a bone of it" (Exodus 12:46) because the bones were the deities of the Other Side, and the children of Israel threw them out in contempt to express their contempt for the Egyptian deities.

The Precept of the Paschal offering on the fourteenth day of Nissan.

‏186. וַיֹּאמֶר יְיָ' אֶל מֹשֶׁה וְאַהֲרֹן זֹאת חֻקַּת הַפֶּסַח וְגוֹ'. כ"ח פִּקּוּדָא דָא,‏
‏לְמִשְׁחַט פֶּסַח בֵּין הָעַרְבַּיִם, בִּי"ד בְּנִיסָן, דּוּכְרָנָא דְּהַהוּא פֶּסַח דְּמִצְרַיִם. וְדָא‏
‏אִיהוּ חוֹבְתָא עַל כֹּלָּא, כְּמָה דְּאַתְּ אָמֵר, וְשָׁחֲטוּ אוֹתוֹ כֹּל קְהַל עֲדַת יִשְׂרָאֵל‏
‏בֵּין הָעַרְבָּיִם.‏

186. "And the Lord said to Moses and Aaron, 'This is the ordinance of the Passover....'" (Exodus 12:43) This (28th) Precept is to slaughter the Paschal offering at twilight of the fourteenth day

of Nissan, a remembrance to the Passover in Egypt. And this is incumbent upon everyone, as it is written: "...and the whole assembly of the Congregation of Israel shall slaughter it toward evening." (Exodus 12:6)

Keeping the Paschal lamb from the tenth day of the month,
when the moon begins to shine.

187. פֶּסַח דָּא, אִצְטְרִיךְ לְמֶהֱוֵי נָטִיר, מֵעֲשָׂרָה יוֹמִין וּלְהָלְאָה, דִּכְתִיב בֶּעָשׂוֹר לַחֹדֶשׁ הַזֶּה וְיִקְחוּ לָהֶם וְגוֹ'. מַאי טַעֲמָא. בְּגִין דְּהָא כְּדֵין שָׂרִיאת סִיהֲרָא לְאַנְהָרָא, מֵעֲשָׂרָה יוֹמִין וּלְהָלְאָה, עַד דְּאִשְׁתְּלִים בַּחֲמֵיסַר. וְאַרְבֵּיסַר דְּלֶיהֱוֵי נָכִיס, בְּשַׁעֲתָא דְּדִינָא תַּלְיָא עַל עָלְמָא.

187. This Paschal sacrifice has to be kept from the tenth day of the month, as it is written: "...on the tenth day of this month, and they shall take...." (Exodus 12:3) What is the reason? It is because that is when the moon starts to shine, from the tenth day on until it becomes full on the fifteenth day. It should be slaughtered on the fourteenth day at the time that Judgment is impending over the world, namely at twilight.

The members of the Holy Covenant break the power of the Other side.

188. רָזָא דָא, לְאַעְבְּרָא זוּהֲמָא, מִקָּמֵי בְּרִית קַדִּישָׁא, וּלְאִתְהֲנָאָה בְּהַהוּא רֵיחָא דְּנָדִיף טָוֵי נוּר. וְעַל דָּא לָא אַתְיָא אֶלָּא עַל שָׂבְעָא. וְעַל דָּא, וְכָל עָרֵל לֹא יֹאכַל בּוֹ. מַאן דְּאִית בֵּיהּ בְּרִית קַדִּישָׁא, יֵיכוּל בֵּיהּ. מַאן דְּלָא אִית בֵּיהּ בְּרִית קַדִּישָׁא, לָא יֵיכוּל בֵּיהּ. דְּהַאי מִבְּנֵי בְּרִית אִיהוּ לְתַבְּרָא תּוּקְפָּא דְּחֵילָא אַחֲרָא, לְאַעְבְּרָא עָרְלָה מִקָּמֵי בְּרִית. בְּגִין כָּךְ, הַאי בִּבְנֵי בְּרִית אִיהוּ לְמֶעְבַּד, וְלָא בִּבְנֵי עָרְלָה.

188. This secret is to remove the foreskin from before the Holy Covenant and to gain pleasure from the scent that spreads from the meat roasted on fire, meaning that the main part of the Precept

is to enjoy its scent. **Therefore it is only consumed at satiation**, when one does not need to eat anymore. **Thus "...no uncircumcised person shall eat of it"** (Exodus 12:48) but one who has the Holy Covenant may eat of it. This is because one who is of the Covenant breaks the power of the Other Side and removes the foreskin from the Covenant. Therefore, it must be done by members of the Covenant and not by uncircumcised ones.

Hyssop was used to smear the blood on the doorposts
since it removes evil spirits.

189. כַּד אָתָא קוּדְשָׁא בְּרִיךְ הוּא לְמִצְרַיִם, חָמָא דָּמָא דְּהַהוּא פֶּסַח, דַּהֲוָה רְשִׁים עַל פִּתְחָא, וְדָמָא דִּבְרִית, הֵיךְ הֲוֵי קַיְימִין עַל פִּתְחָא, דִּכְתִיב, וּלְקַחְתֶּם אֲגֻדַּת אֵזוֹב וּטְבַלְתֶּם בַּדָּם אֲשֶׁר בַּסַּף וְהִגַּעְתֶּם וְגוֹ'. אֵזוֹבָא, הָא אוּקִימְנָא דְּאִיהוּ מַעֲבַר רוּחִין בִּישִׁין, וְכָל סְטַר רוּחַ בִּישָׁא, מַעֲבַר בְּאִתְעָרוּתָא דִּילֵיהּ, בְּפוּרְקָנָא עִלָּאָה דְּיִשְׂרָאֵל.

189. When the Holy One, blessed be He, came to Egypt, He saw how the blood of the Paschal sacrifice was marked on the entrance and the blood of the circumcision were on the door, as it is written: "And take a bunch of hyssop, and dip it in the blood that is in the basin, and touch with it...." (Exodus 12:22) We have explained that hyssop removes evil spirits, and it removes any aspect of a bad spirit when it is awakened, for the Supernal Redemption of Israel.

The slaughter of the Paschal sacrifice foreshadows
the slaughter of the Evil Inclination.

190. לְזִמְנָא דְּאָתֵי, יֵיתֵי קוּדְשָׁא בְּרִיךְ הוּא לְיֵצֶר הָרָע וְיִכּוֹס לֵיהּ. וְהַשְׁתָּא בְּפוּרְקָנָא דָּא, כְּתִיב וְשָׁחֲטוּ אוֹתוֹ כָּל קְהַל עֲדַת יִשְׂרָאֵל וְגוֹ'. דּוּכְרָנָא דְּזִמְנָא דְּאָתֵי, בְּהַהוּא פּוּרְקָנָא עִלָּאָה.

190. In the future to come, the Holy One, blessed be He, will come to the Evil Inclination and slaughter it. Now in this redemption from Egypt, **it is written: "and the whole assembly of the Congregation of Israel shall slaughter it,"** (Exodus 12:6) **for it is a token of remembrance for the time to come of a higher Redemption** than the one from Egypt.

The blood of the Circumcision and the blood of the sacrifice.

191. עַל שְׁתֵּי הַמְּזוּזוֹת וְעַל הַמַּשְׁקוֹף בְּהַאי רְשִׁימוּ דְּאָת יֹו"ד, וּבְהַאי רְשִׁימוּ דְּאָת יֹו"ד, לְאַחֲזָאָה רְשִׁימוּ דִּבְרִית קַדִּישָׁא, וְאִתְבַּר עָרְלָה מִקַמֵּי דָּמָא דִּבְרִית, רָשִׁים עַל כֹּלָּא, וְאָתָא דָּמָא עַל דָּמָא. כַּד עָבַר הַהוּא מַשְׁחִית, הֲוָה וָזֵי דָּמָא, וְאוֹדְקוֹף מִבֵּיתָא, כְּמָה דְּאַתְּ אָמֵר וְלֹא יִתֵּן הַמַּשְׁחִית וְגֹו'.

191. "...the lintel and the two side posts..." (Exodus 12:22) **They marked the letter Yud** (י) **on the doorposts. They marked the letter Yud** (י) **on the lintel to show** through them **the mark of the Holy Covenant,** which is the Yud, **and the foreskin was broken before the blood of the Covenant that was marked on all. And blood came upon blood,** namely the blood of the Paschal sacrifice on the blood of the Circumcision. **When the Destroyer passed, he would see blood and distance himself from the house, as it is written: "...and will not allow the Destroyer...."** (Exodus 12:23)

The Creator did the killing but the Destroyer tried
to find a pretext to accuse Israel.

192. אִי קוּדְשָׁא בְּרִיךְ הוּא בִּלְחוֹדוֹי קָטִיל, אַמַּאי כְּתִיב וְלֹא יִתֵּן הַמַּשְׁחִית, דְּמַשְׁמַע דְּמַשְׁחִית הֲוָה אָזִיל וְלָא קוּדְשָׁא בְּרִיךְ הוּא. אֶלָּא וַדַּאי קוּדְשָׁא בְּרִיךְ הוּא הֲוָה קָטִיל, וּמַשְׁחִית הֲוָה אָזִיל לְאַשְׁכְּחָא עִילָה לְיִשְׂרָאֵל, כֵּיוָן דַּהֲוָה וָזֵי הַהוּא תְּבִירוּ דְּעָרְלָה, בִּתְרֵין סִטְרִין, הֲוָה עָרִק וְאִתְפְּרַשׁ מִנַּיְיהוּ.

192. He asks: "If the Holy One, blessed be He, Himself was killing, why is it written: "...and will not allow the Destroyer..." (Exodus 12:23), which implies that the Destroyer was doing it and not the Holy One, blessed be He?" He answers: "Assuredly the Holy One, blessed be He, alone was carrying out the killing, and the Destroyer was seeking to find a pretext against Israel to accuse them. As soon as he saw the breakage of the foreskin in two aspects, by the blood of the Paschal Lamb and the blood of circumcision, he would flee and leave them.

The firstborns must be redeemed so that the Other Side
will find no pretext against them.

193. וְעַל דְּקָטַל קוּדְשָׁא בְּרִיךְ הוּא כָּל אִינּוּן בּוּכְרִין דְּהַהוּא סְטְרָא, יָהִיב בּוּכְרִין דְּיִשְׂרָאֵל לְפוּרְקָנָא, דְּלָא יִשְׁכְּחוּ עָלַיְיהוּ סְטְרָא אַחֲרָא עִילָה כְּלָל, וּבְכֹלָּא נָטִיר לוֹן לְיִשְׂרָאֵל קוּדְשָׁא בְּרִיךְ הוּא, כְּאַבָּא עַל בְּנִין.

193. Because the Holy One, blessed be He, slew all the firstborns of that side, He obligated the firstborn of Israel to redeem themselves so that the Other Side will find no pretext against them. The Holy One, blessed be He, guarded them against everything, like a father over children.

The Precept to eat the Paschal sacrifice with Matzah and Maror.

194. בְּבַיִת אֶחָד יֵאָכֵל לֹא תוֹצִיא מִן הַבַּיִת וְגוֹ', פָּקוּדָא כ"ט דָּא, לְמֵיכַל הַאי פֶּסַח. עַל מַצּוֹת וּמְרוֹרִין, מַצּוֹת מַצַּת כְּתִיב. מַאי הַאי לָקֳבֵל הַאי, אֶלָּא לְאַחֲזָאָה גָּלוּתָא דִּשְׁכִינְתָּא עִמְּהוֹן דְּיִשְׂרָאֵל, בְּהַהוּא מְרִירוּ דִּלְהוֹן, דִּכְתִיב וַיְמָרְרוּ אֶת חַיֵּיהֶם בַּעֲבוֹדָה קָשָׁה וְגוֹ'. וְכַד אַכְלִין לְהַאי פֶּסַח, לְאַחֲזָאָה כָּל הַאי דְּעָבְדוּ לוֹן בְּמִצְרַיִם, בְּהַהוּא גָּלוּתָא וּבְהַהוּא שִׁעְבּוּדָא.

194. "In one house shall it be eaten, you shall not take any of the meat outside, out of the house." (Exodus 12:46) This (29th) Precept is to eat the Paschal sacrifice with Matzot and bitter herbs. Matzot is spelled without a Vav (ו). He asks: "What is Matzot with regard to bitter herbs the verse obligates us to eat them together?" He answers: "It is to indicate the exile of the Shechinah with Israel in their bitterness, as it is written, '...and they made their lives bitter with hard bondage....' (Exodus 1:14) When the Paschal sacrifice is eaten, it shows everything that was done to them in Egypt in that exile and that bondage." Therefore, it is eaten with Matzot and bitter herbs.

The bones of the lamb were cast to the dogs in contempt.

195. מַה כְּתִיב וְעֶצֶם לֹא תִשְׁבְּרוּ בוֹ, לְאַחֲזָאָה בֵּיהּ קְלָנָא, וּבְכָל אִינּוּן טַעֲוָון דְּמִצְרָאֵי. דְּהָא גַּרְמִין הֲווֹ רָמָאן בְּשׁוּקָא, וְאָתוּ כַּלְבֵּי וַהֲווֹ גָּרְרֵי לוֹן מֵאֲתָר לַאֲתָר, וְדָא קַשְׁיָא לוֹן מִכֹּלָּא, דְּהָא גַּרְמֵי אִינּוּן תִּקּוּנָא דְּגוּפָא, וְדָמֵי לְגַוְונָא אַחֲרָא, וְיִשְׂרָאֵל רָמָאן לוֹן בְּשׁוּקָא אוֹרַח קְלָנָא, וְע"ד כְּתִיב וְעֶצֶם לֹא תִשְׁבְּרוּ בוֹ, אַתּוּן לָא תִשְׁבְּרוּן, אֲבָל כַּלְבֵּי הֲווֹ אַתְיָין וּמְתַבְּרִין לֵיהּ.

195. [He asks:] "What is the meaning of: '...nor shall you break a bone of it.' (Exodus 12:46)?" [He answers:] "To show contempt to it, and all the deities of Egypt because the unbroken bones were thrown out to the marketplace and dogs would come and drag them from place to place. This was the most difficult thing for them because the bones put the body in order and resemble another side, namely their other deities. The Israelites cast them out into the marketplace in contempt. Therefore it is written, '...nor shall you break a bone of it.' (Ibid.) You must not break them but dogs came and broke them."

The Egyptians were forced to bury their own deity.

196. תּוּ, מִצְרָאֵי הֲווֹ אַתְיָין לְבָתַר, וַהֲווֹ חָזָאן אִינּוּן גַּרְמֵי דַּהֲווֹ נַטְלֵי כַּלְבֵּי מֵאֲתָר לַאֲתָר, וּמַדְקָן לוֹן, וַהֲווֹ מִצְרָאֵי טָמְנֵי לוֹן גּוֹ עַפְרָא, בְּגִין כַּלְבֵּי דְּלָא יִשְׁכְּחוּן לוֹן, וְדָא אִיהוּ בְּטוּלָה דְּעַכוּ"ם, יַתִּיר, מִסִּטְרָא דִּלְהוֹן. וּבְדָא קֻדְשָׁא בְּרִיךְ הוּא אִסְתְּלַק בִּיקָרֵיהּ, וְאִתְכַּפְיָין כָּל חֵילִין אַחֲרָנִין, דְּהָא כְּדֵין אִתְכַּפְיָין

יַתִּיר, כַּד בָּטִילוּ אִשְׁתְּכַח מִסִּטְרָא דִלְהוֹן, וְעַ"ד יִשְׂרָאֵל לָא מְבַטְלֵי לוֹן, דִּכְתִיב וְעֶצֶם לֹא תִשְׁבְּרוּ בוֹ.

196. **Further** we can explain that **the Egyptians came afterwards and saw the dogs dragging these bones from place to place and breaking them. The Egyptians would bury them in the ground so that the dogs could not find them, which was the greatest obliteration of their idols on their side. The Holy One, blessed be He, was elevated in His glory by this. And all the other powers** of the idols **were subdued. When the subjugation of the idols is from their own side, it is even more profound,** namely when they buried bones of their idols in the earth. **Therefore, it is not Israel that voided them, as written: "...nor shall you break a bone of it."** (Exodus 12:46)

Tetzaveh

9. The bread of the first fruits

A Synopsis

We learn that two types of bread were eaten by Israel: when they left Egypt, they ate Matzah, the bread from Malchut; when they were in the wilderness they ate Manna, the bread from Heaven, Zeir Anpin. The question is asked: Why, now that Israel merited the Supernal Bread, was leavened bread not abolished entirely? Why was the offering of the first fruits, leavened bread? Rav Shimon explains that as soon as Israel had eaten Matzah, leavened bread could no longer harm them. The Chametz is burned on the altar and can have no power over Israel. When God gave the Torah to Israel, He had them taste the Supernal Bread, Manna, through which they knew and observed the teachings of the Torah. After these explanations, Rav Shimon and his companions meet an old man holding a boy by the hand.

Two types of bread: bread of affliction and bread from Heaven.

72. תְּרֵין נַהֲמֵי אָכְלוּ יִשְׂרָאֵל, וַד, כַּד נָפְקוּ מִמִּצְרַיִם, אָכְלוּ מַצָּה, לֶחֶם עֹנִי. וְוַד בְּמַדְבְּרָא, לֶחֶם מִן הַשָּׁמַיִם. דִּכְתִּיב הִנְנִי מַמְטִיר לָכֶם לֶחֶם מִן הַשָּׁמַיִם וְעַל דָּא קָרְבָּנָא דְּיוֹמָא דָא נַהֲמָא אִיהוּ. וְעַל נַהֲמָא, אִתְקְרִיבוּ כָּל שְׁאַר קָרְבָּנִין. דְּנַהֲמָא אִיהוּ עִקָּר, דִּכְתִּיב וְהִקְרַבְתֶּם עַל הַלֶּחֶם שִׁבְעַת כְּבָשִׂים וְגוֹ', מִמּוֹשְׁבוֹתֵיכֶם תָּבִיאוּ לֶחֶם תְּנוּפָה וְגוֹ', דְּדָא אִיהוּ נַהֲמָא דְּאַוְכִּימוּ בֵּיהּ יִשְׂרָאֵל, חָכְמָתָא עִלָּאָה דְּאוֹרַיְיתָא, וְעָאלוּ בְּאָרְחָהָא.

72. Two types of bread were eaten by Israel: When they left Egypt, they ate Matzah, the bread of affliction, which is bread from Malchut. **And in the wilderness, they ate bread from Heaven,** which is the bread of Zeir Anpin called Heaven, **as it is written: "... 'Behold, I will rain down bread from Heaven for you....'"** (Exodus 16:4) **Therefore the offering of this day** of the Holiday of Shavuot **is bread, and all**

the other offerings were offered with the bread. The bread is the main part, as is written: "And you shall offer with the bread… seven lambs…" (Leviticus 23:18) "You shall bring out of your habitations two wave loaves…." (Leviticus 23:17) For this is the bread with which Israel became wise with the Supernal Wisdom of the Torah, and entered its ways.

Why do we still eat Chametz after Pesach?

73. הַשְׁתָּא אִית לָן לְאַסְתַּכְּלָא, בַּפֶּסַח נָפְקוּ יִשְׂרָאֵל מִנַּהֲמָא דְּאִתְקְרֵי חָמֵץ, כְּתִיב, וְלֹא יֵרָאֶה לְךָ חָמֵץ, וּכְתִיב כִּי כָּל אוֹכֵל מַחְמֶצֶת מַאי טַעֲמָא. בְּגִין יְקָרָא דְּהַהוּא נַהֲמָא דְּאִתְקְרֵי מַצָּה. הַשְׁתָּא דְּזָכוּ יִשְׂרָאֵל לְנַהֲמָא עִלָּאָה יַתִּיר לָא יָאוֹת הֲוָה לְאִתְבַּטְּלָא חָמֵץ, וְלֹא אִתְחֲזֵיָא כְּלַל. וְאַמַּאי קָרְבְּנָא דָּא, חָמֵץ הֲוָה, דִּכְתִיב סֹלֶת תִּהְיֶינָה חָמֵץ הֵאָפֶינָה. וְתוּ, דְּהַשְׁתָּא בְּיוֹמָא דָּא אִתְבְּטַל יֵצֶר הָרָע, וְאוֹרַיְיתָא דְּאִתְקְרֵי חֵירוּ אִשְׁתְּכַחַת.

73. Now we need to observe. On Pesach Israel went out from the bread that is called Chametz, as it is written: "…and there shall no leavened bread (*chametz*) be seen" (Exodus 13:7), and: "…For whoever eats that which is leavened…." (Exodus 12:19) What is the **reason** that they abandoned Chametz? **It is because of the honor of the bread that is called Matzah.** He asks: "Now that Israel merited **a Supernal Bread,** the bread of Zeir Anpin, **would it not have been proper for the Chametz to be abolished and not be seen at all? Why was the offering** of the first fruits bread, **Chametz as it is written: '…they shall be of fine flour; they shall be baked with leaven….'** (Leviticus 23:17)? Also on this day, the Evil Inclination was negated, which is the secret of Chametz, **as the Torah, that is called freedom, was available."** Why then did they bring Chametz?

Once we eat the Matzah, which is medicine, Chametz is no longer harmful.

‎74. אֶלָּא, לְמַלְכָּא דַהֲוָה לֵיהּ בַּר יְחִידָאי, וְחָלַשׁ. יוֹמָא חַד הֲוָה תָּאִיב לְמֵיכַל, אָמְרוּ יֵיכוֹל בְּרֵיהּ דְמַלְכָּא אַסְוָותָא דָא, וְעַד דְיֵיכוֹל לֵיהּ, לָא יִשְׁתְּכַח מֵיכְלָא וּמְזוֹנָא אַחֲרָא בְּבֵיתָא. עָבְדוּ הָכִי. כֵּיוָן דְאָכַל הַהוּא אַסְוָותָא, אָמַר מִכָּאן וּלְהָלְאָה יֵיכוֹל כָּל מַה דְאִיהוּ תָּאִיב, וְלָא יָכִיל לְנַזְקָא לֵיהּ.

74. He answers: "This is similar **to a king who had an only son who became ill. One day he wished to eat. They said: 'Let the king's son take this medicine but before he eats it, no food whatsoever should be in the house.' They did so. After he had taken the medicine, they said: 'From now on he may eat whatever he desires and it will do him no harm.'**

Matzah is a medicine to come to and know the secret of Faith.

‎75. כַּךְ כַּד נָפְקוּ יִשְׂרָאֵל מִמִּצְרַיִם, לָא הֲווֹ יַדְעֵי עִקָּרָא וְרָזָא דִמְהֵימְנוּתָא, אָמַר קוּדְשָׁא בְּרִיךְ הוּא, יִטְעֲמוּן יִשְׂרָאֵל אַסְוָותָא, וְעַד דְיֵיכְלוּן אַסְוָותָא דָא, לָא אִתְחֲזֵי לְהוֹן מֵיכְלָא אַחֲרָא. כֵּיוָן דְאָכְלוּ מַצָּה, דְאִיהִי אַסְוָותָא לְמֵיעַל וּלְמִנְדַע בְּרָזָא דִמְהֵימְנוּתָא. אָמַר קוּדְשָׁא בְּרִיךְ הוּא, מִכָּאן וּלְהָלְאָה אִתְחֲזֵי לוֹן חָמֵץ, וְיֵיכְלוּן לֵיהּ, דְהָא לָא יָכִיל לְנַזְקָא לוֹן. וְכ"ש דְבְיוֹמָא דְשָׁבוּעוֹת, אִזְדַּמַּן נַהֲמָא עִלָּאָה, דְאִיהוּ אַסְוָותָא בְּכֹלָּא.

75. "Similarly, when Israel left Egypt, they did not know the essence and secret of Faith. The Holy One, blessed be He, let Israel taste medicine but while they take this medicine, no other food should be visible to them, namely Chametz. **As soon as they had eaten Matzah, which is a medicine to come to and know, the secret of Faith,** which is Malchut, **the Holy One, blessed be He, said: 'From now on, Chametz is suitable for them and they may eat it because it can no longer harm them.' And more so on the day of Shavuot, when the Supernal Bread** of Zeir Anpin **is present, which is a complete cure.**

On Shavuot, we offer Chametz to burn the Evil Inclination.

76. וְעַ"ד מְקָרְבִין חָמֵץ, לְאִתּוֹקְדָא עַל מַדְבְּחָא. וּמְקָרְבִין תְּרֵין נַהֲמִין אַחֲרָנִין כַּחֲדָא. וְחָמֵץ, אִתּוֹקְדָא בְּנוּרָא דְּמַדְבְּחָא וְלָא יָכִיל לְשַׁלְטָאָה, וּלְנַזְקָא לוֹן לְיִשְׂרָאֵל. וּבְגִינֵי כַּךְ, יִשְׂרָאֵל קַדִּישִׁין אִתְדְּבָקוּ בֵּיהּ בְּקוּדְשָׁא בְּרִיךְ הוּא, בְּאַסְוָותָא דְּאוֹרַיְיתָא בְּיוֹמָא דָּא. וְאִלְמָלֵי הֲווֹ נַטְרֵי יִשְׂרָאֵל תְּרֵין סִטְרִין דְּנַהֲמֵי אִלֵּין, לָא הֲווֹ עַיְילִין בְּדִינָא לְעָלְמִין.

76. "Therefore we offer Chametz, which is the Evil Inclination, **to be burnt on the altar,** meaning through the offerings that are offered on the altar. **Two other loaves of bread are offered** by waving them **together.** 'Other' means in addition to the offerings. **The Chametz,** which is the Evil Inclination, **is burned in the fire on the altar,** through the offerings, **and cannot have power over, nor harm, Israel. Therefore Israel cleave to the Holy One, blessed be He, on this day through the remedy of Torah. If Israel observed those two types of bread,** namely Matzah and the Holy Supernal Bread of Zeir Anpin, **they would never be under Judgment."**

Explanation of the matter: In general, Nukva has two types of Mochin. The first is from the time She was in the secret of "...the two great luminaries..." (Genesis 1:16), namely before the diminishment, where She was the same stature as Zeir Anpin and did not receive from Him. Rather, both received equally from Ima, where Zeir Anpin clothed its Right Column, Chasadim, and Malchut clothed its Left Column, Chochmah without Chasadim. At that point, the moon complained because without Chasadim Chochmah cannot shine, and her Illumination was extremely limited. Afterwards, She was told, "Go and diminish yourself," and She then descended below the chest of Zeir Anpin, and the Masach in the chest of Zeir Anpin diminished Her until she had nothing of Herself at all, and everything she receives is from Zeir Anpin. In exchange, She is built with great Mochin from Chochmah and Chasadim, until She has unification with Zeir Anpin face-to-face.

However there is not disappearance in the metaphysical, so even though She got diminished and then returned after Her diminishment to be the aspect of face-to-face, She did not lose the Mochin of before the diminishment due to this. But the Illumination of the Mochin, of before the diminishment, is restricted and they are therefore called the Mochin of Achorayim (Back), which is the secret of Matzah called the "bread of affliction." And the Mochin of after the diminishment are called Mochin of Panim (Face or Front) and also "bread from Heaven," as She receives these Mochin from Zeir Anpin called Heaven. They are also considered as containing Chametz, which means Judgments, due to the diminishment She underwent as She descended below the chest of Zeir Anpin, as the Judgments found at the point of the chest of Zeir Anpin is the secret of Chametz. But this Chametz is corrected until it transforms to become Holiness and Mercy because it is revealed that without the diminishment and these Judgments, Malchut would have remained with the bread of affliction and would never receive the great Mochin of face-to-face.

It is found that there are two types of corrections for the two types of Mochin of Malchut. The correction of the Mochin of Achorayim is to burn the Chametz and be distanced from it to not be found or seen, because Chochmah burns away all Judgments. But they do not totally uproot the Chametz from the lower places, as it is still there. It is found that it is a remedy but not completely, which is not the case by the Mochin of Panim, as through them the Chametz transforms and becomes Holiness and Mercy, thus totally uprooting Chametz and leaving it no more room to be awakened. Therefore it is considered a complete remedy.

This is: **"Two types of bread were eaten by Israel: When they left Egypt, they ate Matzah, the bread of affliction,"** namely the Mochin of Achorayim of Malchut, whose Illumination is restricted due to a lack of Chasadim, and it is the bread of affliction. However these Mochin are of Malchut Herself, who received from Binah and not through Zeir Anpin, as mentioned earlier. Therefore the Zohar in verse 64 said that the seven days of Matzot are Below, meaning the Mochin of Malchut Herself, see there. **"And in the wilderness they ate bread from Heaven,"** which is the Manna that was from the Mochin of Zeir Anpin Himself. **"Therefore, the offering of this day is bread,"** namely also bread from the Heaven like the Manna, except that they are from the aspect of the Mochin of Malchut, which she received from Heaven, Zeir Anpin, meaning the Mochin of face-to-face. About them it is said: **"You shall bring out of your habitations two wave loaves..."** **(Leviticus 23:17),** meaning from the Earth, which is Malchut, except that she received them from the Heaven, Zeir Anpin, and they are not her own Mochin like the Mochin of Achorayim.

"The bread is the main part, as it is written: 'And you shall offer with the bread... seven lambs...'" (Leviticus 23:18) because the bread, which is the Mochin of face-to-face that is drawn on Shavuot via the waving of the bread, is the main desired purpose, and the sacrifices we offer are just to complete the bread. Chametz that exists in the Mochin of Panim transforms to be Holiness and Mercy through the sacrifice we offer, where the fire of the altar transforms the Chametz, which is the secret of Judgments that came due to the diminishment, to be the secret of "a pleasant smell of a burnt-offering to the Lord." (Leviticus 1:9) **"... 'You shall bring out of your habitations two wave loaves....'"** **(Leviticus 23:17)** The Zohar brings this verse to specify that it is referring to the bread from the earth that comes "out of your habitations" and not manna like they ate in the wilderness. **"For this is the bread with which Israel became wise with the Supernal Wisdom of the Torah"** since they are the Mochin of Panim that come from Zeir Anpin called Torah to Malchut, and the Israelites who received these Mochin as well merited Supernal wisdom too.

This is how he answers the question: "Since Shavuot is greater than Pesach how are we allowed Chametz; is not Chametz Judgments and Evil Inclination?" He answers that there are two remedies: One is Matzah to distance the Judgments but it does not transform them to Mercy, and the other is the first fruit bread and the sacrifices we offer on the altar, as through the sacrifices, the Chametz is burned on the altar and becomes a pleasant smell, which is a remedy that is complete, until the Chametz becomes Holiness. It says about the wave-offering bread, "baked after leavening" (Leviticus 23:17) and this is (verse 76): **"If Israel observed those two types of bread, they would never be under Judgment"** because through the Matzah and the wave-offering bread with the sacrifices, all the Judgments become Holiness and Mercy in every place they are, as mentioned earlier.

Rosh Hashanah is a Day of Judgment only for those who did not eat the medicine and abandoned the Torah.

77. בְּיוֹמָא דְרֹאשׁ הַשָּׁנָה, דְּאִיהוּ יוֹמָא דְּדִינָא, דְּלָאו אִיהוּ, אֶלָּא לְאִינּוּן דְּלָא נָטְלוּ מֵיכְלָא דְּאַסְוָותָא, וְשָׁבְקוּ לְאַסְוָותָא דְּאוֹרַיְיתָא, בְּגִין מֵיכְלָא אַחֲרָא דְּאִיהוּ חָמֵץ. דְּהָא בְּיוֹמָא דָּא דְּר"ה, הַהוּא חָמֵץ סַלְקָא, וּמְקַטְרְגָא עָלֵיהּ דְּבַר נָשׁ, וְאַלְשִׁין עָלֵיהּ, וְאִיהוּ קַיְימָא בְּיוֹמָא דָּא מְקַטְרְגָא עַל עָלְמָא. וְקוּדְשָׁא בְּרִיךְ הוּא יָתִיב בְּדִינָא עַל כֹּלָּא וְדָאִין עָלְמָא.

77. The day of Rosh Hashanah, which is the Day of Judgment, is only for those who did not take the medicine, which is Matzot, **and abandoned the remedy of Torah,** which is the Mochin of face-to-face from Zeir Anpin called Torah, since through these two remedies **the other food, which is Chametz,** is fixed. **On this day of Rosh Hashanah, that Chametz ascends, accuses the person, slanders him, and stands on this day to be an Accuser over the world. The Holy One, blessed be He, sits in Judgment over everything and judges the world.**

Through the Manna, Israel knew and saw the secrets of the Torah.

‎78. וּבְגִינֵי כַּךְ כַּד יָהַב קוּדְשָׁא בְּרִיךְ הוּא אוֹרַיְיתָא לְיִשְׂרָאֵל, אַטְעִים לְהוּ מֵהַהוּא נַהֲמָא עִלָּאָה, דְּהַהוּא אֲתָר, וּמִגּוֹ הַהוּא נַהֲמָא, הֲווֹ יַדְעִין וּמִסְתַּכְּלִין בְּרָזֵי דְּאוֹרַיְיתָא, לְמֵהַךְ בְּאֹרַח מֵישָׁר, וְהָא אוּקְמוּהָ מִלָּה אִינוּן חַבְרַיָּיא בְּרָזִין אִלֵּין כִּדְקָאמְרָן.

78. Because of this, when the Holy One, blessed be He, gave the Torah to Israel, He had them taste that Supernal Bread, namely the Mochin of Panim of Zeir Anpin, **from that place,** from Malchut called "place" who receives from Him. **Through that bread, they knew and observed the secrets of the Torah to walk in the straight path, and the friends have already explained these matters through these secrets, as we have said.**

EMOR

24. The two bloods: of the Paschal lamb and of Circumcision

A Synopsis

Rav Chiya examines Song of Songs 5:2 that begins, "I sleep, but my heart wakes..." and talks about the exile of Israel, and about the opening one must find to come into God. That opening is the Gates of Righteousness. Rav Chiya talks about the blood marked on the doorposts that was Israel's display of Faith at the time that God killed all the firstborn in Egypt. We read about the time of the full moon, when the Klipot are hidden away and the Holy Union is present. Rav Aba explains about the four cups that correspond to the Four Redemptions, and about the four grades or Sefirot that bond together. He tells Rav Yehuda why the Halel is not recited during the seven days of Pesach.

The Shechinah is both asleep and awake during the exile.

128. וּבַחֹדֶשׁ הָרִאשׁוֹן בְּאַרְבָּעָה עָשָׂר יוֹם לַחֹדֶשׁ וְגוֹ׳. רִבִּי חִיָּיא פָּתַח, אֲנִי יְשֵׁנָה וְלִבִּי עֵר קוֹל דּוֹדִי דוֹפֵק וְגוֹ׳. אָמְרָה כְּנֶסֶת יִשְׂרָאֵל, אֲנִי יְשֵׁנָה בְּגָלוּתָא דְמִצְרַיִם, דַהֲווֹ בָּנַי בְּשִׁעְבּוּדָא דְקַשְׁיוּ. וְלִבִּי עֵר, לְנַטְרָא לְהוֹ דְלָא יִשְׁתֵּיצוּן בְּגָלוּתָא. קוֹל דּוֹדִי דוֹפֵק, דָּא קוּדְשָׁא בְּרִיךְ הוּא, דְּאָמַר וְאֶזְכּוֹר אֶת בְּרִיתִי.

128. "On the fourteenth day of the first month...." (Leviticus 23:5) Rav Chiya opened: "I sleep, but my heart wakes. Hark, my beloved is knocking...." (Song of Songs 5:2) The Congregation of Israel said: "I sleep in exile in Egypt because the exile came from the force of the Left overpowering the Right, and due to the Judgments of the Left the Mochin of Malchut depart, which is the secret of sleep. **My children were there under harsh enslavement, "...but my heart wakes..."** (Ibid.) to keep them so they will not be destroyed in exile. **"...Hark, my beloved is knocking..."** (Ibid.) refers to the Holy One,

blessed be He, who said: "…and I have remembered My covenant."
(Exodus 6:5)

Making an opening for the Shechinah in exile.

129. פִּתְחִי לִי פִּתְחָא כְּחוּדָּא דְּמַחֲטָא, וַאֲנָא אַפְתַּח לָךְ תַּרְעִין עִלָּאִין. פִּתְחִי
לִי אֲחוֹתִי, דְּהָא פִּתְחָא לְאַעְלָא לִי, בָּךְ הוּא, דְּלָא יֵיעֲלוּן לְגַבָּאִי בְּנַי אֶלָּא בָּךְ,
אַנְתְּ הוּא פִּתְחָא לְאַעְלָא לִי בָּךְ, אִי אַנְתְּ לָא תִּפְתַּח פִּתְחָךְ, הָא אֲנָא סָגִיר. דְּלָא
יִשְׁכְּחוּן לִי. בְּגִין כַּךְ, פִּתְחִי לִי. פִּתְחִי לִי וַדַּאי. וְעַל דָּא אָמַר דָּוִד, כַּד בָּעָא
לְאַעְלָא לְמַלְכָּא, אָמַר פִּתְחוּ לִי שַׁעֲרֵי צֶדֶק, אָבֹא בָם אוֹדֶה יָהּ. זֶה הַשַּׁעַר
לַיְיָ', דָּא הוּא פִּתְחָא וַדַּאי לְאַעְלָא לְמַלְכָּא. זֶה הַשַּׁעַר לַיְיָ', לְאַשְׁכְּחָא לֵיהּ,
וּלְאִתְדַּבְּקָא בֵּיהּ, וְעַל דָּא פִּתְחִי לִי אֲחוֹתִי רַעְיָתִי שֶׁרֹאשִׁי וְגוֹ'. בְּגִין לְאִזְדַּוְוגָא
עִמָּךְ, וּלְמֶהֱוֵי עִמָּךְ בִּשְׁלָם דִּעָלְמִין.

129. "…Open to me…" (Song of Songs 5:2) means open to me an
opening as thin as a needle, and I shall open to you the Celestial
Gates. "…Open to me, my sister…" (Ibid.) since the opening to come
to Me is within you, so My children shall enter only through you.
Unless you open your opening, I am closed off and cannot be found.
Hence, "…Open to me…" "…Open to me…" assuredly. Therefore,
when David wished to come to the King, he would say, "Open to
me the gates of righteousness. I will go in to them, and I will praise
the Lord. This is the Gate of the Lord…." (Psalms 118:19-20) This,
the Gates of Righteousness, which is Malchut, is an opening through
which to come in to the King. "…This is the gate of the Lord…"
(Ibid.) to find Him and cleave to Him. Hence, "…Open to me, my
sister, my love for my head is filled with dew…" (Song of Songs 5:2)
to unite with you and be at peace with you forever.

Explanation: Zeir Anpin from His own side is with Chasadim that
are blocked from Chochmah, and Malchut from Her own side is with
Chochmah without Chasadim, as therefore She is called "night" since
Chochmah cannot shine without Chasadim. Therefore there is no

complete abundance for the redemption of Israel except by a unification of Zeir Anpin and Malchut, as then the Chasadim of Zeir Anpin are incorporated with the Chochmah of Malchut, and Israel receive complete abundance from the Upper Three. However when they receive from Malchut alone, the Illumination of Chochmah is very thin since it is the aspect of night, so long as She is not clothed with Chasadim. They also cannot receive from Zeir Anpin alone because as long as the Chasadim are not incorporated with Chochmah they are only in the aspect of the Six Corners, without a head, which have no grasp.

This is what is written that the Holy One, blessed be He, says to Malchut: **"Open to me an opening as thin as a needle…"** namely the Illumination of Chochmah in You, which is as thin as the tip of a needle, since it is without Chasadim, **"…and I shall open to you the Celestial Gates,"** as through My Chasadim that will clothe Your Chochmah, the Celestial Gates will open for You, which are the Gates of the Upper Three, and they will bring the Redemption for Israel. This is: **"…since the opening to come to Me is within you…"** because they cannot come to receive complete abundance from Me except through incorporating My Chasadim with your Chochmah. **"Unless you open your opening, I am closed off and cannot be found"** for if You do not unite with Me with Your Chochmah, then My Chasadim will remain in the aspect of the Six Corners without a head, which are closed off from attainment, and they will not attain Me to cleave to Me. This is: **"'This is the Gate of the Lord…' (Psalms 118: 20) to find Him and cleave to Him,"** meaning that when She has union with Zeir Anpin a Gate to Him is made, by which the Lower Beings can grasp and cleave to Him, through the complete Illumination of the union comprised of Chochmah and Chasadim.

The blood of the Paschal sacrifice and the Circumsicion
showed the mark of Faith.

130. ת"ח, בְּשַׁעֲתָא דְקוּדְשָׁא בְּרִיךְ הוּא הֲוָה קָטִיל לְבוּכְרֵי דְמִצְרָאֵי, כָּל אִינוּן דְקָטַל בְּפַלְגּוּת לֵילְיָא, וְאָחִית דַרְגִּין מֵעֵילָא לְתַתָּא. בֵּיה שַׁעֲתָא עָאלוּ יִשְׂרָאֵל בִּקְיוּמָא דְאָת קַדִּישָׁא, אִתְגְּזָרוּ וְאִשְׁתָּתָפוּ בִּכְנֶסֶת יִשְׂרָאֵל, וְאִתְאַחֲדוּ בָּה. כְּדֵין הַהוּא דָמָא אַחְזִיאוּ לֵיה עַל פָּתְחָא. וּתְרֵין דָמֵי הֲוֹו, חַד דְפִסְחָא, וְחַד דָמָא דְאִתְגְּזָרוּ. וַהֲוָה רָשִׁים עַל פָּתְחָא, רְשִׁימָא דִמְהֵימְנוּתָא, חַד הָכָא וְחַד הָכָא וְחַד בֵּינַיְיהוּ, וְהָא אִתְּמַר, וְנָתְנוּ עַל שְׁתֵּי הַמְזוּזוֹת וְעַל הַמַשְׁקוֹף, בְּגִין לְאַחֲזָאָה מְהֵימְנוּתָא.

130. Come and see, when the Holy One, blessed be He, killed the firstborn Egyptians, namely **all those He killed at midnight, and brought the Upper grades down, at that very time Israel entered the Covenant of the Holy Sign by circumcising and uniting with the Congregation of Israel and joining Her. They then displayed that blood on the lintel. So there were two kinds of blood, the one of the Paschal Sacrifice and the other that of Circumcision, and the mark of Faith was imprinted on the lintel, one on one side, one on the other, and one in between,** the secret of the three Columns: Right, Left, and Central. **And so it says: "…and put it on the two side posts and on the upper door post…"** (Exodus 12:7), **to display Faith.**

Explanation: The Plague of the Firstborn and Circumcision are related to each other because the Plague of the Firstborn happened with the Central Column awakening the Masach of Chirik, which diminishes the Upper Three of the Left, and then all the firstborn, who are drawn from these Upper Three, died. The Judgments of the Masach of Chirik diminished these Upper Three, and this is: **"and brought the Upper Grades down,"** as it diminished the Left from its Upper Three and brought it down to the aspect of Six Corners. Thus the Judgments of the Masach of Chirik nullified the Judgments of the Left. Similarly, the matter of Circumcision is the secret of the Judgments of the Female nullifying the Judgments of the Male. Therefore the Israelites made an awakening from Below at midnight and circumcised themselves, so that the Central Column, along with the Judgments of the Female in the Masach of Chirik, will nullify the Upper Three of the Left. This is: **"So there were two kinds of blood… one on one side, one on the other, and one in between,"** namely to awaken the action of the Central Column to diminish the Upper Three of the Left, and to unite the two Columns together. By the power of this diminishment of the Left Column the first borns of Egypt died, and by the unification of the two Columns the Israelites went out of exile.

How the Israelites merited bread from Heaven.

131. וּבְאַרְבָּעָה עֲשָׂר, הָא אִתְּמַר, דְּהָא כְּדֵין מִבַּטְלִין חָמֵץ וּשְׂאוֹר, וְאִסְתַּלָּקוּ יִשְׂרָאֵל מֵרְשׁוּתָא אָחֳרָא, וְאִתְעֲקָרוּ מִנֵּיהּ, וְאִתְאַחֲדוּ בְּמַצָּה, קְשׁוּרָא קַדִּישָׁא. בָּתַר דְּאִתְגְּזָרוּ, עָאלוּ בָּהּ, עַד דְּאִתְפָּרְעוּ, וְאִתְגַּלְיָיא רְשִׁימָא דִּלְהוֹן, וּכְדֵין יָהַב לְהוֹן קְשׁוּרָא, בַּאֲתַר עִלָּאָה, בִּקְשׁוּרָא דִּמְהֵימְנוּתָא, בַּאֲתַר דִּכְתִּיב הִנְנִי מַמְטִיר לָכֶם לֶחֶם מִן הַשָּׁמָיִם, מִן הַשָּׁמָיִם דַּיְיקָא, וְהָא אוּקְמוּהָ.

131. "On the fourteenth…" (Leviticus 23:5) we learned that then **leavened bread** (*chametz*) **and leaven** (*se'or*) **are nullified, and Israel are gone from another dominion and are uprooted from it and join the Matzah in a Holy bond. After they were circumcised they entered it** by means of the Matzah until after the Giving of the Torah, when **they uncovered the corona and their imprint was revealed. Then He gave them the bond in a High Place in the bond of Faith, the place where it is written: "… 'I will rain bread from Heaven for you…'"** (Exodus 16:4), **"from Heaven" is precise,** namely from Zeir Anpin called Heaven. **This has already been explained.**

Explanation: There are two states in Malchut. The first state is before Her diminishment, when She was in the secret of "…the two great luminaries…" (Genesis 1:16) and was as big as Zeir Anpin. Both received from Binah: Zeir Anpin [received] Chasadim, and Malchut [received] Chochmah. The second state is after Her diminishment, when the Holy One, blessed be He—who is the Central Column in the secret of its Masach of Chirik—said to Her: "Go and diminish yourself." She then descended below the chest of Zeir Anpin, thus not being worthy anymore to receive Chochmah, yet everything She has She receives from Zeir Anpin. The abundance of the first state is called Matzah, and the abudnace of the second state is called "bread from the Heaven" or *chametz*.

There is both an advantage and a disadvantage in the first state, and also in the second state. In the first state there is an advantage in that She has no diminishment and can receive Chochmah, and She receives from the same level that Zeir Anpin receives from, [which is] Binah, and She is therefore as big as Him because They are on the same level under Binah. However there is a great disadvantage there because when she receives from the Left Column of Binah alone, she has in her Chochmah without Chasadim, and Chochmah cannot shine without being clothed in Chasadim. Therefore Her Illumination is restricted and very thin, and therefore the abundance that comes down from Her then is called Matzah or the bread of affliction.

So too, in the second state there is an advantage and a disadvantage. The advantage is that She then receives from Zeir Anpin, and in Him, the Chochmah and Chasadim are included together in the secret of the Central Column, and they shine with great expanse. The disadvantage is that the diminishment lies on Her due to the force of the Masach in the chest of Zeir Anpin, so she is no longer worthy to receive the Light of Binah, but everything She has She receives from Zeir Anpin. Therefore, the abundance She bestows in this state is called "bread from Heaven" because it is not totally Hers; She only receives it from Zeir Anpin called Heaven. So too, in another aspect it is called bread that is unleavened (*chametz*) or leavened (*se'or*) because the Klipot have some grasp on this abundance due to the diminishment that resides on Her from the force of the Masach of the chest of Zeir Anpin.

This is: **"then leavened bread (chametz) and leaven (se'or) are nullified"** because on the night of Pesach, Malchut bestowed to them from the aspect of Her first state, meaning from the level She was on before her diminishment, and all the Klipot that were attached to the diminishment of the moon, which are called leavened bread (chametz) and leaven (se'or), were nullified because their grasp was nullified. And because of this, the Israelites went out from the Egyptian domain. Therefore **"and Israel are gone from another dominion and are uprooted from it and join the Matzah in a Holy bond,"** as all the Klipot and their power to enslave were nullified, and they united with the Holy abundance called Matzah. After they were circumcised and uncovered the corona, the impression was revealed, which is the secret of the Mochin of the second state after the diminishment of Malchut, whose Illumination is broad and big, and is no longer "bread of affliction" since they come from Zeir Anpin, as She is no longer able to receive from Binah since She was diminished, as mentioned earlier. This is: **"Then He gave them the bond in a high place,"** which is Zeir Anpin, **"the place where it is written, '... 'I will rain bread from Heaven for you...'"** (Exodus 16:4), from heaven is precise," namely from Zeir Anpin called "Heaven." And the abundance is no longer considered the abundance of Malchut, since She now has nothing of Herself but it is considered as attributed to Zeir Anpin.

The night of the Seder is a night of watchfulness.

‫132. ת"ו, בְּאַרְבֵּיסַר בְּשַׁעֲתָא דְּוָוגָּא דְּסִיהֲרָא אִשְׁתְּכַח בְּשְׁלִימוּ עִם שִׁמְשָׁא,‬
‫וְכִתְרִין תַּתָּאִין לָא מִשְׁתַּכְּחִין כָּל כַּךְ בְּעָלְמָא, דְּהָא בְּוַדְּתוּתֵי דְּסִיהֲרָא, זִינִין‬
‫בִּישִׁין מִשְׁתַּכְּחִין, וּמִתְעָרֵי לְאִתְפַּשְׁטָא בְּעָלְמָא. וּבְשַׁעֲתָא דְּוָוגָּא דְּסִיהֲרָא‬
‫אִשְׁתְּכַח בִּנְהִירוּ דְּשִׁמְשָׁא בְּשְׁלִימוּ, מִתְכַּנְּשֵׁי כֻּלְהוּ לַאֲתַר חַד, וְקָדוּשֵׁי מַלְכָּא‬

אִתְעָרוּ. כְּדֵין כְּתִיב לֵיל שִׁמּוּרִים הוּא לַיְיָ', דְּהָא זִוּוּגָא קַדִּישָׁא אִשְׁתְּכַח, וְהוּא שִׁמּוּרִים בְּכֹלָּא.

132. Come and see, on the fourteenth day at night, **when the union of the moon,** Malchut, **is in perfection with the sun,** Zeir Anpin, **the lower Sefirot** of the Klipot **are not found so much in the world. For at the time of the renewal of the moon, evil species abound and are roused to expand in the world.** But **when the union of the moon is in the light of the sun completely, all** the Klipot **are gathered into one place** and hide, **while the Holy things of the King are roused. Then, "It is a night of watchfulness to the Lord..."** (Exodus 12:42), since the Holy union is present, which is watchful in every respect.

Preparing the home for Pesach, to prepare
Malchut to unite with Zeir Anpin.

133. ר' אַחָא אָמַר, בְּגִין כַּךְ תִּקּוּנָא דְּכַלָּה בְּהַהוּא יוֹמָא, וּבְלֵילְיָא אִשְׁתְּכַח יְשׁוּבָא דְּבֵיתָא, וַוי לְאִינּוּן דְּלָאו מִבְּנֵי בֵּיתָא נִיְנְהוּ, כַּד אָתָאן לְאִזְדַּוְּוגָא אוֹרַיְיתָא כַּחֲדָא, וַוי לְאִינּוּן דְּלָא אִשְׁתְּמוֹדְעָן גַּבַּיְיהוּ. בְּגִין כַּךְ יִשְׂרָאֵל קַדִּישִׁין מְתַקְּנִין לוֹן בֵּיתָא, כָּל הַהוּא יוֹמָא, וְעַל יְדַיְיהוּ, עַיְילֵי מַאן דְּעַיְילֵי, וְאִינּוּן חַדָאן וַחְמְדָן תַּרְוַויְיהוּ זַכָּאִין אִינּוּן יִשְׂרָאֵל בְּעָלְמָא דֵּין וּבְעָלְמָא דְּאָתֵי.

133. Rav Acha said: "**For that reason the bride,** Malchut, **is made ready on that day,** the fourteenth, **and on the night** of the fifteenth day, **the house is settled,** namely the unification of Zeir Anpin and Nukva. **Woe to those who are not of the household,** who do not cleave to Malchut, **when the two Torahs come to unite**—the Written Torah (Zeir Anpin), and the Oral Torah (Malchut). **Woe to those who are not recognized by them. For that reason, Holy Israel prepare** Zeir Anpin and Nukva **a home,** namely a unification, **all that** fourteenth **day, and through them those who enter will enter,** namely the Mochin necessary for the unification of Zeir Anpin and Nukva. **And they,** Zeir

Anpin and Nukva, **are glad and both sing. Happy are Israel in this world and in the World to Come."**

Watchfulness is written in plural,
alluding to Zeir Anpin and Malchut.

134. אָמַר ר' יוֹסֵי לָמָּה כָּן לְאַטְרְחָא כּוּלֵי הַאי, קְרָא שְׁלִים הוּא, דְּהָא בְּהַאי לֵילְיָא, זִוּוּגָא עִלָּאָה קַדִּישָׁא אִתְעַר וְאִשְׁתְּכַח, הה"ד, הוּא הַלַּיְלָה הַזֶּה לַיְיָ' שִׁמּוּרִים, מַאי שִׁמּוּרִים. תְּרֵי, זִוּוּגָא דְּסִיהֲרָא בְּשִׁמְשָׁא. לְכָל בְּנֵי יִשְׂרָאֵל לְדֹרוֹתָם, דְּהָא מִכָּאן וּלְהָלְאָה, אִתְאַחֲדוּ וְאִתְקַשָּׁרוּ בְּקִשּׁוּרָא דִּשְׁמָא קַדִּישָׁא, וְנָפְקוּ מֵרְשׁוּתָא אָחֳרָא. בְּגִינֵי כַּךְ בְּאַרְבְּעָה עָשָׂר, מְתַקְּנֵי גַּרְמַיְיהוּ, וּמְבַעֲרֵי חָמֵץ מִבֵּינַיְיהוּ, וְעַיְּילֵי בִּרְשׁוּתָא קַדִּישָׁא, וּכְדֵין מִתְעַטְּרֵי חָתָן וְכַלָּה, בְּעִטְּרוֹי דְּאִימָּא עִלָּאָה, וּבָעֵי בַּר נָשׁ לְאַחֲזָאָה גַּרְמֵיהּ דְּאִיהוּ בַּר חוֹרִין.

134. Rav Yosi said: "Why should we bother so much? It is a complete verse that this night the Supernal Holy union is awakened and is present, as it is said: '…that same night is the Lord's, one of watchfulness…' (Exodus 12:42) Why is watchfulness (*shimurim***) with a plural suffix?" He answers: "It alludes to two, relating to the union of the moon with the sun, Malchut and Zeir Anpin. '…for all the children of Israel in their generations' (Ibid.) means that from now on Israel are united and connected with the bond of the Holy Name, and have come out from another dominion. For that reason, they prepare themselves on the fourteenth and burn all the leavened bread (***chametz***) among them and enter into a Holy dominion. Then the groom and bride, Zeir Anpin and Malchut, are crowned with the Crowns of Supernal Ima, Binah, and man should show himself as free," since the Mochin of Supernal Ima are called "Freedom."**

Explanation: The renewal of the moon indicates the diminishment of the moon, which is Malchut, when the Klipot have a grasp on Her, as mentioned earlier. This is [in verse 132]: **"For at the time of the renewal of the moon, evil species abound…"** and this continues until the time of the great unification when Malchut unites with the sun face-to-face to the point where no diminishment is noticeable in her, which is indicated by the fullness of the moon on the fifteenth day of the month, as she has no flaws. This is: **"when the union of the moon is... then, 'It is a night of watchfulness to the Lord...' (Exodus 12:42), since the Holy union is present."** This teaches us that there is a unification of Zeir Anpin and Malchut on the night of Pesach in complete perfection, to the point where She has no diminishment, which is only when Malchut ascends to Supernal Ima and Zeir Anpin to Supernal Aba. This does not happen in any of the Holidays, even during the day. [Rav Yosi] learns this by the Torah calling the fifteenth day of Nissan "a night of watchfulness." This indicates that Malchut is in Her full form like the moon on the night of the fifteenth, and She is protected from all the Klipot due to the great unification of Zeir Anpin and Nukva in the place of Aba and Ima.

Rav Acha learns (in verse 133) that there is a great unification of Zeir Anpin and Nukva on the night of Pesach from the Torah commanding us to remove leavened bread and perform the Paschal sacrifice on the fourteenth, which we do not find on any other Holiday eve. Therefore this teaches us that it is a preparation for the unification of the night. This is: **"For that reason the bride is made ready on that day,"** since we prepare and correct Malchut by removing leavened bread and performing the Paschal sacrifice, **"and on the night the house is settled,"** namely the unification of Zeir Anpin and Nukva. And so **"For that reason, Holy Israel prepare for them a home all that day..."** since from here it is derived that there is a unification on the night of Pesach.

Rav Yosi says: **"Why should we bother so much"** to learn that there is a great unification on the night of Pesach? **"It is a complete verse that this night the Supernal Holy union is awakened and is present... What is watchfulness (shimurim)?"** He learns it by how scripture calls the night "watchfulness" in plural, which indicates **"two, relating to the union of the moon with the sun,"** Zeir Anpin and Malchut. This is:

"Then the groom and bride are crowned with the crowns of supernal Ima," namely that Malchut ascends to Supernal Ima and Zeir Anpin to Supernal Aba, and there is no elevated unification like this except on the night of Pesach alone.

The four cups correspond to Chochmah, Binah, Tiferet, and Malchut.

135. א"ר יוֹסֵי, הָנֵי אַרְבַּע כַּסֵּי דְּהַהוּא לֵילְיָא אֲמַאי. א"ר אַבָּא, הָא אוּקְמוּהָ
חַבְרַיָּיא, לָקֳבֵיל ד' גְּאוּלוֹת. אֲבָל שַׁפִּיר הוּא בְּסִפְרָא דְּרַב יֵיסָא סָבָא, דְּקָאָמַר
הוֹאִיל וְזִוּוּגָא קַדִּישָׁא אִשְׁתְּכַח בְּהַאי לֵילְיָא בְּכָל סִטְרִין, וְזִוּוּגָא הוּא בְּאַרְבַּע
קִשּׁוּרִין, דְּאִינּוּן ד' דַּרְגִּין, וְלָא מִתְפָּרְשֵׁי דָּא מִן דָּא, כַּד זִוּוּגָא דָּא אִשְׁתְּכַח,
וַאֲנָן בְּחֶדְוָותָא דִּלְהוֹן אִתְעַרְנָא, בְּגִין דְּהָא זָכֵינָא בְּהוּ, דְּמַאן דְּאָחִיד בְּדָא, זָכֵי
בְּכֹלָּא. וְעַ"ד אִשְׁתַּנֵּי לֵילְיָא דָּא מִכָּל שְׁאָר לֵילָוָן, וּבָעֵינָן לְמֶעְבַּד שְׁמָא בְּכֹלָּא,
וּלְמֶחְדֵי בְּהַאי לֵילְיָא, בְּגִין דְּחֶדְוָותָא הוּא לְעֵילָּא וְתַתָּא.

135. **Rav Yosi said: "What is the purpose of the four cups on that night?" Rav Aba said: "The friends explained they correspond to the four redemptions:** 'and I will bring... and I will deliver... and I will redeem... and I will take....' (Exodus 6:6-7)" **This is well** explained **in the book of Rav Yesa Saba, who said that since the Holy union abounds that night in all sides,** both in Chochmah and Chasadim, **the union is formed with four bonds, which are four grades that do not separate from each other when this union is present,** which are Chochmah and Binah, Tiferet and Malchut. **And we are awakened by their joy,** and correspondingly drink four cups **because we attained them, since whoever is attached to it,** to the Illumination of the union, **attains all** four grades—Chochmah and Binah, Tiferet and Malchut. **Therefore this night is different than all other nights, and it behooves us to make** and unify **the Name in every way, and rejoice that night since it is joy Above and Below."**

The Four Redemptions.

136. וְעוֹד אָמַר, דְּאַרְבַּע אִלֵּין אַרְבַּע גְּאוּלוֹת קָרֵינָן לְהוּ. מ"ט. בְּגִין דְּהַאי דַרְגָּא בַּתְרָאָה, גּוֹאֵל אִתְקְרֵי, הַמַּלְאָךְ הַגּוֹאֵל. וְלָא אִקְרֵי גּוֹאֵל, אֶלָּא עַל יְדָא דְּדַרְגָּא אָחֳרָא עִלָּאָה, דְּקַיְימָא עָלָה וְנָהִיר לָה. וְדָא לָא לָא אַפִּיק לָה נְהוֹרָא, אֶלָּא בְּאִלֵּין תְּרֵין דַּרְגִּין דְּעָלֵיה. אִשְׁתְּכַח, דְּד' אִלֵּין אַרְבַּע גְּאוּלוֹת נִינְהוּ.

136. **He further said that these four,** Chochmah and Binah, Tiferet and Malchut, **are called Four Redemptions.** [He asks:] **"What is the reason?"** [He answers:] **"It is because this last grade,** Malchut, **is called 'redeemer,'** namely **the redeeming angel. It is only called redeemer through a higher superior grade,** Tiferet, **which is situated over it and shines upon it. It,** Tiferet, **only brings Light upon it by means of the two grades above it,** Chochmah and Binah, from which Tiferet receives. **Thus these four,** Chochmah and Binah, Tiferet and Malchut, **are the Four Redemptions,** since they are connected to Malchut called 'redeemer.'"

Why the Halel is not recited in full all seven days of Pesach.

137. ר' יְהוּדָה שָׁאַל לְר' אַבָּא, הָא כְּתִיב שִׁבְעַת יָמִים שְׂאוֹר לֹא יִמָּצֵא בְּבָתֵּיכֶם, וְחֶדְוְותָא הוּא כָּל שִׁבְעָה, אֲמַאי לָא אִשְׁתְּלִים הַלֵּל כָּל ז' יוֹמִין, כְּמוֹ בְּסֻכּוֹת, דְּאִשְׁתְּכַח ח' יוֹמִין הַלֵּילָא, בִּשְׁלִימוּ דְּחֶדְוְותָא כָּל יוֹמָא וְיוֹמָא.

137. **Rav Yehuda asked Rav Aba: "It says, 'Seven days shall there be no leaven found in your houses...' (Exodus 12:19), and there is joy all those seven. Why do we not recite the complete Halel throughout the seven days** of Pesach **as in Sukkot, where we recite the Halel on each of the eight days with complete joy?"**

The Light of Pesach is not complete until the
Giving of the Torah on Shavuot.

138. אָ"ל שַׁפִּיר קָאֲמַרְת, אֲבָל יְדִיעָא הוּא, דְּהָא הָכָא לָא אִתְקְשָׁרוּ יִשְׂרָאֵל
כָּל כַּךְ בְּכֹלָּא, כְּמָה דְּאִתְקְשָׁרוּ לְבָתַר. בְּגִין כַּךְ בְּהַאי לֵילְיָא, דְּזוּוּגָא אִשְׁתְּכַח
וְחֶדְוָותָא דְּכֹלָּא אִשְׁתְּכַח, וְיִשְׂרָאֵל אִתְקְשָׁרוּ בְּהַהוּא חֶדְוָותָא, עֲבִידְנָא שְׁלִימוּ,
וְהַלֵּילָא אִשְׁתְּלִים. אֲבָל לְבָתַר אע"ג דְּכֻלְּהוּ מִשְׁתַּכְּחֵי, עַד כְּעַן יִשְׂרָאֵל לָא
אִתְקְשָׁרוּ בְּהוּ, וְלָא אִתְפְּרָעוּ לְאִתְגַּלְּיָא רְשִׁימָא קַדִּישָׁא, וְלָא קַבִּילוּ אוֹרַיְיתָא,
וְלָא עָאלוּ בְּמָה דְּעָאלוּ לְבָתַר. בְּגִין כַּךְ בְּסֻכּוֹת שְׁלִימוּ דְּכֹלָּא אִשְׁתְּכַח בֵּיהּ,
וְחֶדְוָותָא דְּכֹלָּא יַתִּיר, אֲבָל הָכָא עַד כְּעַן לָא זָכוּ, וְלָא אִשְׁתְּכַח שְׁלִימוּ בֵּיהּ
כּ"כ, אע"ג דְּאִשְׁתְּכָחוּ כָּל ז', לָאו הוּא בְּאִתְגַּלְּיָא, וְיִשְׂרָאֵל עַד לָא אִתְקְשָׁרוּ
בְּהוּ כַּדְקָא חֲזֵי.

138. He said to him: "Well asked. But it is known that here, on Pesach, **Israel are not bonded as wholly as they were later because on that** first **night—when the union** of Zeir Anpin and Nukva **is present and the joy of all is present and Israel are bonded with that joy—we bring about perfection and the Halel is complete. But later,** throughout the days of Pesach, **even though they,** all seven grades, Chesed, Gevurah, Tiferet, Netzach, Hod, Yesod, and Malchut that shine in the seven days of Pesach, **are all present, Israel have not yet connected to them, nor uncovered the corona for the Holy impression to be revealed in them. Nor did they receive the Torah or enter those** grades: Chesed, Gevurah, Tiferet, Netzach, Hod, Yesod, and Malchut, **as they did later. For that reason, on Sukkot the perfection of all exists and the joy of all** exists **to the utmost. But here** on Pesach **they have not yet attained, and there was not as much perfection in them. Even though all seven are present,** Chesed, Gevurah, Tiferet, Netzach, Hod, Yesod, and Malchut of Zeir Anpin during the seven days of Pesach, **they are not revealed, and Israel were not yet well connected with them,** until after the Giving of the Torah.

On the night of the Seder, there is complete Light
from an awakening from Above.

139. וְעַ"ד חֶדְוָותָא דְּכֹלָּא וּשְׁלִימוּ דְּהַלֵּלָא בְּהַאי לֵילְיָא, בְּגִין הַהוּא חוּלָקָא
דְּאִתְקְשָׁרוּ בֵּיהּ. בְּמַאי טַעֲמָא. דְּכֵיוָן דִּבְהַהוּא לֵילְיָא זִוּוּגָא אִשְׁתְּכַח, כָּל קְשׁוּרָא
דְּכֹלָּא אִשְׁתְּכַח בְּסִטְרָא דְּזִוּוּגָא, וְלָא בְּסִטְרָא דְּיִשְׂרָאֵל, דְּכַד זִוּוּגָא אִשְׁתְּכַח
בָּהּ מִשְׁתַּכְחֵי אִלֵּין תְּרֵין דַּרְגִּין דְּקַיְימִין עָלָהּ. וְכַד אִלֵּין מִשְׁתַּכְחֵי, הָא כָּל גּוּפָא
אִשְׁתְּכַח בְּהוּ, וּכְדֵין שְׁלִימוּ דְּכֹלָּא, וְחֶדְוָותָא דְּכֹלָּא, וְהַלֵּילָא אִשְׁתְּלִים, דְּהָא
כְּדֵין אִתְעַטְּרַת סִיהֲרָא בְּכֹלָּא. אֲבָל לָא לְבָתַר, דְּכָל יוֹמָא וְיוֹמָא אִשְׁתְּכַח,
וְיִשְׂרָאֵל עַד לָא זָכוּ בְּהוּ, הָא לָאו הַלֵּילָא שְׁלֵימָא, כְּמוֹ בְּזִמְנִין אָחֳרָנִין.

**139. Therefore the joy of all and the complete Halel exists on this
first night** of Pesach **because of that portion Israel are attached to.**
[He asks:] **"What is the reason?"** [He answers:] **"It is because on that
night the union is found, and all the bond** of all the grades **is present
from the side of the union,** from the side of the awakening from Above
but not from the side of Israel. When the union of Zeir Anpin **is in
Her,** in Malchut, **the two grades** Chochmah and Binah **are situated
over Her** as well. **When these are present, the whole body,** the whole
stature of Zeir Anpin, **is with them. Then it is the perfection of all
and the joy of all, and the Halel is recited in full,** for then the moon,
Malchut, **is adorned with everything. But this is not so after** the first
night, **since every day** of the seven days, Chesed, Gevurah, Tiferet,
Netzach, Hod, Yesod, and Malchut **are found, and Israel have not yet
attained them. Thus the Halel is not complete as in other times.**

PINCHAS

105. The Holiday of Pesach

A Synopsis

We are told that the Redemption will take place on the fourteenth day of the month of Nissan (Aries).

Redemption during Nissan.

703. וּבַחוֹדֶשׁ הָרִאשׁוֹן, מַאן רִאשׁוֹן. דָּא נִיסָן. תַּמָּן אוֹלִידַת הַהִיא חַיָּה, לְקַיֵּים מַה דְּאוֹקְמוּהָ מָארֵי מַתְנִיתִין, בְּנִיסָן נִגְאָלוּ וּבְנִיסָן עֲתִידִין לְהַגָּאֵל. וּבִי"ד דִּילֵיהּ, וַיֹּאמֶר כִּי יָד עַל כֵּס יָהּ, תַּמָּן אוֹמֵי לְאַעְבְּרָא מֵעָלְמָא זַרְעָא דְּעֵשָׂו עֲמָלֵקְיִים, בְּהַהוּא זִמְנָא מִשְׁכוּ וּקְחוּ לָכֶם צֹאן לְמִשְׁפְּחוֹתֵיכֶם וְשַׁחֲטוּ הַפָּסַח. מִשְׁכוּ: מָשַׁךְ יָדוֹ אֶת לוֹצְצִים.

703. "And in the first month...." (Numbers 28:16) He asks: **"What is the first month?"** He answers: **"It is Nissan, which is when that animal gave birth** to the Lights of the Redemption, **in accord with the teaching of the sages of Mishnah: 'In the month of Nissan they were redeemed, and in the month of Nissan they are destined to be redeemed.' And in its fourteenth,** in the secret of the verse: 'For he said: "Hand (*yad*; 14) on the throne of Yah (the Lord)...."'** (Exodus 17:16) There He swore to remove the seed of Esau, the Amalekites, from the world. At that time: '... **"Draw out and take lambs according to your families, and slaughter the Passover offering"'** (Exodus 12:21) where the meaning of **'draw out'** (*mishchu;* מִשְׁכוּ) is as in the verse: '... he stretched out (*mashach;* מָשַׁךְ) his hand with scorners.' (Hosea 7:5)

At the Redemption, the leaders who went astray will be punished.

704. בְּהַהוּא זִמְנָא, כֹּה אָמַר יְיָ' לָרוֹעִים הַפּוֹשְׁעִים בִּי. וְאוֹמֵר, וְאֶל אַדְמַת יִשְׂרָאֵל לֹא יָבֹאוּ. וְאִלֵּין אִינּוּן רוֹעִים דְּעָנָא, פַּרְנָסֵי דָּרָא. וּבַג"ד אִתְּמַר עֲלַיְיהוּ,

הִנֵּה אָנֹכִי מְפַתֶּיהָ וְהוֹלַכְתֶּיהָ הַמִּדְבָּרָה. וְנִשְׁפַּטְתִּי אִתְּכֶם וְגוֹ', כַּאֲשֶׁר נִשְׁפַּטְתִּי
אֶת אֲבוֹתֵיכֶם דְּקָטִיל לוֹן בְּמַכַּת חֹשֶׁךְ.
ע"כ רעיא מהימנא

704. "At that time, thus said the Lord: 'to the rulers who transgressed against Me: "neither shall they enter into the land of Israel..."' (Ezekiel 13:9), and this refers to the shepherds of the flock, the supporters of the generation. This is why it is said about them: 'Therefore, behold, I will allure her, and bring her into the wilderness....' (Hosea 2:16) [and] '...and there will enter into judgment with you... As I entered into judgment with your fathers...' (Ezekiel 20:35-36), namely whom He killed in the Plague of Darkness."
End of Ra'aya Meheimna (Faithful Shepherd)

A Synopsis
Rav Shimon explains to Rav Elazar how the Upper Days, the Sefirot of Zeir Anpin, will be drawn to the Lower Days, to the Sefirot of Malchut. On the fourteenth day the animal, Malchut, will give birth to the Lights of the Redemption and the Serpent will depart. Then Malchut will be sanctified on high and will be called "Glory."

The fourteenth day of the first month alludes to the correction of Malchut.

705. וּבַחֹדֶשׁ הָרִאשׁוֹן, מַאן חֹדֶשׁ הָרִאשׁוֹן. דָּא אִיהוּ חֹדֶשׁ, דְּהַאי חַיָּה אִתְגַּלְיָיא
בֵּיהּ וְאִתְתְּקָפַת בֵּיהּ, וְנָפְקָא לְעָלְמָא בְּאַרְבְּעָה עָשָׂר יוֹם. בְּאַרְבְּעָה עָשָׂר, אִלֵּין
שְׁאָר חֵיוָותָא, דְּאִינּוּן י' י' לְכָל סְטָר, בַּד' סִטְרִין דְּעָלְמָא. וּבְסִפְרֵי קַדְמָאֵי,
אִיהוּ י', וְחַד לְכָל סְטָר לְאַרְבַּע סִטְרִין, וְאִינּוּן אַרְבַּע עָשָׂר. כֵּיוָן דְּאִינּוּן אַרְבַּע,
מִתְחַבְּרָאן וּמִתְתַּקְנָן עִם אִינּוּן עָשַׂר דִּבְסִטְרָא דִּימִינָא, כְּדֵין י"ד, בְּחֶזְוָה
לְאִתְתַּקְּנָא חַיָּה דָא בְּתִקּוּנָהָא.

705. "And in the first month...." (Numbers 28:16) He asks: "What is meant by the first month?" He answers: "This is the month in which that animal, Malchut, is revealed and strengthened and goes forth into the world, namely emerges from her closure, in the secret of the verse: '...and strip the forests bare...' (Psalms 29:9) on the fourteenth day. The fourteen days refer to the remaining animals, namely Chesed, Gevurah, Tiferet, and Malchut of Zeir Anpin, which illuminate within Malchut, for they are ten in each direction, since Chesed, Gevurah, Tiferet, and Malchut, are the four directions at the four corners of the world, north, south, east, and west, each one of which is composed of Ten Sefirot. And in the ancient books it is stated that she, Malchut, is ten, and that one Sefirah of Chesed, Gevurah, Tiferet, and Malchut, is in each of the four directions of the world, making fourteen. And since these four, Chesed, Gevurah, Tiferet, and Malchut, join in and are established with the ten that are in Malchut from the Right Side, it is thus the fourteenth day of the month to happily establish this animal, which is Malchut, with all her corrections.

Drawing the Solar Days, Zeir Anpin, to the Lunar Days, Malchut.

706. ר' אֶלְעָזָר אָמַר, וַדַּאי הָכִי הוּא. וְת"ח, כְּתִיב מִשְׁכוּ וּקְחוּ לָכֶם צֹאן וְגוֹ', מִשְׁכוּ, מַאי מִשְׁכוּ. כְּמַאן דְּמָשִׁיךְ מֵאֲתָר אַחֲרָא, לַאֲתָר דָּא. מִשְׁכוּ יוֹמִין עִלָּאִין לְגַבֵּי יוֹמִין תַּתָּאִין. יוֹמִין עִלָּאִין אִינוּן ע"ו, כְּחוּשְׁבַּן מִשְׁכוּ. יוֹמִין תַּתָּאִין, וְמְהֵן דְּאִינוּן שנ"ה, וּבְזִמְנָא, דְּאִתְנַהֲרָא סִיהֲרָא בְּאַשְׁלְמוּתָא, סְלִיקוּ לְמֶהֱוֵי אִינוּן יוֹמִין ע"ו, כְּחוּשְׁבַּן מִשְׁכוּ חָסֵר חַד.

706. Rav Elazar said: "This is surely so. But come and see, it is written: 'Draw out and take lambs...' (Exodus 12:21) What is the meaning of 'Draw out'?" He answers: "It is to be understood as one who draws something from another place to this place, namely draw the Upper Days, which are the Sefirot of Zeir Anpin, to the Lower Days, to the Sefirot of Malchut. The Upper Days of Zeir Anpin are 366, like the numerical value of 'Draw out (*mishchu*; משכו; 366),' namely the number of days in a solar year, which is Zeir Anpin. The Lower Days of Malchut are usually 355 days in a

year (*shanah* שָׁנָה; 355). But when the moon, Malchut, **shines at its fullest, the number of its days rises to be 365 days,** as the solar year, which is Zeir Anpin, **namely as the numerical value of** *mishchu* **minus one.**"

The ten days that unite between Zeir Anpin and
Malchut come from the Right.

707. מְשֹׁכוּ יוֹמִין עִלָּאִין לְגַבֵּי יוֹמִין תַּתָּאִין, לְמֶהֱוֵי כֻּלְּהוּ כַּחֲדָא בְּחִבּוּרָא חֲדָא. וּמַאן בָּשִׁיךְ לוֹן. אִינּוּן עֲשַׂר דְּלִסְטַר יְמִינָא, דִּכְתִּיב בֶּעָשׂוֹר. בֶּעָשׂוֹר מִבָּעֵי לֵיהּ, מַאי בֶּעָשׂוֹר. אֶלָּא ט' אִינּוּן לְכָל סְטָר, וּנְקוּדָה חֲדָא דְּאַזְלָא בְּאֶמְצָעִיתָא. כְּגַוְונָא דָּא, 𝄢 וְהַהִיא נְקוּדָה, אַשְׁלִימַת לְעֶשֶׂר. וע"ד בֶּעָשׂוֹר, כְּמָה דְּאִתְּמַר זָכוֹר וְשָׁמוֹר. לְשַׁמּוּשָׁא בַּעֲשָׂרָה, אִינּוּן יוֹמִין תֵּשַׁע, בְּהַהוּא נְקוּדָה. לַחֹדֶשׁ הַזֶּה, יוֹמִין דְּלִסְטַר יְמִינָא, בְּגִין לְאִתְחַבְּרָא זֹאת בְּזֶה, לְמֶהֱוֵי כֹּלָּא חַד.

707. [He asks:] "**Draw the Supernal Days** of Zeir Anpin **to the Lower Days** of Malchut **so that they will be one, all joined together. And who draws them?**" [He answers:] "**It is these ten** of Malchut **when she is on the Right Side,** Chesed, **as it is written: '…on the tenth** (*be'asor*)…' **(Exodus 12:3),** namely Malchut when she is on the Right Side." He asks: "**It is written as** "*be'asor*," **when the verse should have used the more common** *be'asarah*; **what is** *be'asor*?" He answers: "**There are nine in each direction with one point that goes in the middle, like this:** 𝄢 **and this point completes the Ten Sefirot. This is why it is written** *be'asor,* **just as it is written: 'Remember** (*zachor*)…' **(Exodus 20:8) and 'Keep** (*shamor*)…' **(Deuteronomy 5:12),** namely the form of the infinitive absolute of the verb, the meaning of *be'asor* thus being **to use the ten** in such a way **that these nine days** will use **that point. '…of this month…' (Exodus 12:3)** which is Nissan, alludes to Chesed, to show that these **days** that are drawn down **will be on the Right Column,** which is Chesed, **to combine** *zot* (this; feminine), which is Malchut, **with zeh (this; masculine),** which is Zeir Anpin, **for it all to be one.**

When the four days unite with the tenth day,
Malchut gives birth to the Light of Redemption.

708. וּבְזִמְנָא דְּאִינּוּן ד' אִתְקְשָׁרוּ לְד' סִטְרִין בַּהֲדַיְיהוּ. כְּדֵין אוֹלִידַת הַהוּא חַיָּה וְחִוְיָא אָזִיל לֵיהּ וּבְהַהוּא זִמְנָא מִקַדְּשִׁין לְעֵילָּא לְהַאי חַיָּה וְקָרְאָן לָהּ כָּבוֹד. וּכְדֵין אִתְקַדָּשׁ מוֹעֲדָא. מַה דְּלָא הֲוָה עַד הַשְׁתָּא, וּכְעַן קָרְאָן לָהּ כָּבוֹד, הֲדָא הוּא דִכְתִיב וּבְהֵיכָלוֹ כֻּלּוֹ אוֹמֵר כָּבוֹד.

708. "And when these four days that follow the tenth of the month **join up with the four directions,** south, north, east, and west, which are the secret of Chesed, Gevurah, Tiferet, and Malchut, **and combine with them,** with the ten days, **then that animal,** which is Malchut, **gives birth to** the Lights of the Redemption, **and the Serpent departs. And at that time that animal is sanctified on high, and is called "Glory," and then the holiday is sanctified. This had not been the case previously, but now,** on the Holiday, **she is called Glory, as it is written: '..and in His sanctuary, all will proclaim glory.' (Psalms 29:9)"**

A Synopsis

The Faithful Shepherd says that the explanation given is insufficiently clear and requires more Illumination. He tells the Ravs that "on the tenth" means the nine Sefirot are in all directions, and that they parallel the nine months of a pregnant woman's time of gestation. He talks about "Remember" and "Keep" and "Glory," and enumerates the numerology associated with this lesson.

For the wicked, the Lights of the secrets become darkness.

רעיא מהימנא

709. אָמַר רַעְיָא מְהֵימָנָא, מִלִּין אִלֵּין סְתִימִין, וְצָרִיךְ לְמִפְתַּח לוֹן לְגַבֵּי חַבְרַיָּיא, דְּמַאן דְּסָתִים לוֹן גְּנִיזִין דְּאוֹרַיְיתָא, אִיהוּ מְצַעֵר לוֹן. דִּלְרַשִּׁיעַיָּא נְהוֹרִין דְּרָזִין, אִתְחַזְרָן לוֹן חֲשׁוֹכִין. וְאִיהוּ מָתְלָא לְכַמוֹנָא דְּאִיהוּ גָּנִיז, מַאן דְּחָפַר לֵיהּ, עַד דְּגַלֵּי לֵיהּ, וְלָאו אִיהוּ דִּילֵיהּ, אִתְהַדָּר בְּסוּכְלְתָנוּתֵיהּ בַּחֲשׁוֹכָא וְקַבְלָא. וּלְמַאן דְּאִיהוּ דִּילֵיהּ, נָהִיר לֵיהּ. וּבְגִ"ד, אִית לב"ג לְגַלָּאָה רָזִין סְתִימִין דְּבָאוֹרַיְיתָא.

Ra'aya Meheimna (Faithful Shepherd)

709. The Faithful Shepherd said: "These matters that are stated above in the previous paragraph **are opaque, and we need to open them for the friends, since whoever blocks the secrets of the Torah from them causes them pain. For the wicked, the Lights of the secrets become darkness for them. And it is likened to silver that is hidden away. If one digs until he discovers it but it is not his, it becomes like darkness and gloom in his mind, while for one to whom it belongs, it shines to him. This is the reason why a person should reveal the hidden secrets of the Torah** to the friends."

The Dalet receives from the Alef-Chet of echad.

710. בֶּעָשׂוֹר: ט' אִינּוּן לְכָל סְטָר, לָקֳבֵל ט' יַרְחִין דְּיוֹלַדְתָּה, כְּחוּשְׁבַּן א"ח. מַאן יוֹלֶדֶת. ד' מִן אֶחָד. א"ח, אִיהוּ ט', לְד' סִטְרִין דְּאָת ד', וְאִינּוּן אַרְבְּעִים. א"ח זָכוֹר, ד' שָׁמוֹר. הָא אַרְבְּעִין וּתְרֵין.

710. "…on the tenth…" (Exodus 12:3) means that the nine Sefirot are in all directions, corresponding to the nine months of pregnancy of the child-bearer, like the numerical value of [the letters] **Alef-Chet (אח) of** [the word] *echad* (אֶחָד; **one). Who is the child-bearer? She is the Dalet (ד) of** *echad*. **Alef-Chet (אח; 9) are the nine** Sefirot **in the four directions of the letter Dalet (ד; 4), and they are forty. Alef-Chet correspond to "Remember…" (Exodus 20:8) which is Zeir**

Anpin, **and Dalet** corresponds to **"Keep..."** (Deuteronomy 5:12) which is Malchut, and together with them, **they are 42.**

The Dalet of echad completes the 42-letter Name and the 72-letter Name.

711. אִשְׁתְּאַר כָּבוֹד, דְּאִתְּמַר בֵּיהּ בשכמל"ו. וְאִיהוּ כָּבוֹד כ"ב, ד' זִמְנִין לְכָל סְטָר דְּאָת ד', הֲרֵי ס"ד לְד' סִטְרִין, רנ"ו. וְאוֹקְמוּהָ, כָּבוֹד לְעֵילָא, כ"ב לְתַתָּא. ובג"ד מְיַיחֲדִין בְּכָל יוֹמָא תְּרֵין זִמְנִין, דְּאַמְרָן בְּהוּ תְּרֵין זִמְנִין כָּבוֹד, דְּאִיהוּ ס"ד. וּתְרֵין זִמְנִין ד' ד' מִן אֶחָ"ד, הֲרֵי ע"ב. הֲרֵי ד' דְּאֶחָ"ד, עָלִימוּ דְּמ"ב עָלְמָהָן. וְעָלִימוּ דְּע"ב עָלְמָהָן. ובג"ד אַמְרִין בְּמִזְמוֹר לְדָוִד מִי זֶה מֶלֶךְ הַכָּבוֹד יְיָ' עִזּוּז וְגִבּוֹר. וּבְזִמְנָא תִּנְיָינָא מִי הוּא זֶה מֶלֶךְ הַכָּבוֹד.

ע"כ רעיא מהימנא

711. This leaves us with "Glory," as it is said: "Blessed be the Name of the Glory of His kingdom forever and ever." And this is glory *(kavod; 32)* and heart *(lev; 32),* the sum of which is 64. And there are four directions to this letter Dalet (ד), thus 64 to the four sides, which total 256. And it has been taught: Glory Above and heart Below, and for this reason, the recital of the unity of Shema Israel is said twice daily, in which we say [the word] 'glory' *(kavod; 32)* twice, which amounts to 64. And with the two Dalets (4) of *echad* it is 72. Thus the Dalet of *echad* completes the 42-letter Name and also completes the 72-letter Name. And this is why it is said in "A Psalm of David... Who is this King of glory? The Lord strong and mighty..." (Psalms 24:1, 8) and again "Who is this King of glory? The Lord of hosts, He is the King of glory, [Sela]." (Psalms 14:10) End of Ra'aya Meheimna

Explanation of the article: There are two unifications: the Upper Unification and the Lower Unification. The Upper Unification is "... 'let the waters gather to one place, that the dry land may appear'..." (Genesis 1:9), which means, "let all the grades that are below the heaven be gathered into one place, to be complete with the Six Corners" (Zohar,

Prologue 205), which is the secret of Alef-Chet of *echad;* "that the dry land may appear," namely to also connect to these grades of Zeir Anpin that emerged the aspect of the Dalet of *echad,* which is called "dry land" when it is below the chest, where it is blocked and all its Lights are frozen. This unification is the secret of the unity of the six words "Shema Israel…" which reveals the Chasadim for Zeir Anpin. Yet the Dalet of *echad* still does not receive Her correction so that Her Chochmah can shine, until the Lower Unification takes place, which is the secret of "… 'Let the earth sprout vegetation….'" (Genesis 1:11) This unification happens at "Blessed be the Name of the Glory of His kingdom forever and ever (*Baruch Shem Kevod Malchuto le'olam va'ed*)," and then that which was dry land, from the chest of Zeir Anpin and above in the Upper Unification, now becomes fertile soil that can produce fruits and flowers when She descends below the chest in "Blessed be the Name (*Baruch Shem*)…" because the Chochmah in the Dalet (ד) of *echad* (אֶחָד) is revealed from the chest and below. And all the Sefirot of Zeir Anpin, which are Alef-Chet (אח) of *echad* (אֶחָד), fully shine in all the sides of the Dalet of *echad.*

Thus **"the nine Sefirot are in all directions, corresponding to the nine months of pregnancy of the child-bearer, like the numerical value of Alef-Chet,"** namely in the Upper Unification of Shema Israel the Dalet of *echad* receives from the nine Sefirot of Zeir Anpin, who is the secret of Alef-Chet (אח; 9) in the secret of Ibur (Pregnancy), which is 9 months, 9 Sefirot. **"Who is the child-bearer? She is the Dalet (ד) of *echad.*"** In other words, afterwards, when the Lower Unification of the chest and below happens in the "Blessed be the Name (*Baruch Shem*)…" She then births the nine Sefirot, meaning that they become revealed in Her. But in the Upper Unification, the nine Sefirot of Zeir Anpin, which are the Alef-Chet of *echad,* are still covered and concealed in her like a pregnant woman, as then she is in the aspect of dry land, as mentioned earlier.

"**Alef-Chet** (אח; 9) **are...42**" alludes to the Name of 42 since in the chest of Zeir Anpin and above, where the Upper Unification is, the Name of 42 rules, as the Lights of Chochmah are concealed by this name. After this Upper Unification occurs, in the secret of the Name of 42, the Lower Unification of the chest of Zeir Anpin and below still needs to occur, in the secret of "Blessed be the Name (*Baruch Shem*)...." "**This leaves us with 'glory,' as it is said: 'Blessed be the Name of the Glory of His Kingdom forever and ever.'**" Namely now it remains for us to unify this Lower Unification so that the Dalet of *echad* will be birthed and reveal the nine Sefirot that she received on each of her sides in the Upper Unification. This is: "**And this is glory (***kavod***; 32) and heart (***lev***; 32)**" as she is called Glory and the 32 Paths of Wisdom are revealed in her. "**...there are four... which total 256**" alludes to the secret of the 256 Wings of the Living Creatures. And they have established: "**Glory Above and heart Below**" since above the chest Malchut is called Glory. But the revelation of the glory, which is the 32 Paths of Wisdom that are revealed by Malchut, is only below the chest of Zeir Anpin, in the Unification of "Blessed be the Name (*Baruch Shem*)...."

This is: "**and for this reason... the unity... 72.**" In the Lower Unification the Name of 72 is alluded, which is the Name that Chochmah is revealed in. "**Thus the Dalet (ד) of** *echad* **completes the 42-Letter Names and also completes the 72-Letter Names.**" Namely the completion of the Upper Unification from the chest up for the dominance of the Chasadim, which is the secret of the Name of 42, and the completion of the Illumination of Chochmah that is from the chest down, which is the secret of the Name of 72 that comes from the three verses "and moved... and came... and stretched...." (Exodus 14:19-21) This is: "**'Who is this King of glory? The Lord strong and mighty...' (Psalms 24:8),**" namely Glory Above and heart (*lev*; 32) Below, as mentioned earlier, since the first "King of glory" is above the chest, where Malchut is called Glory in the secret of the Name of 42 where there is no revelation of the 32 Paths of Wisdom, and the second "King of glory" where it says **"Lord of Hosts, He is the King of glory"** (Psalms 24:10) refers to the Glory below the chest, the secret of the Name of 72 that has the revelation of Chochmah.

Da'at opening the Right Column, which is the High Priest.

712. מַאן הֵיכָלוֹ. דָא הֵיכָל עִלְאָה פְּנִימָאָה, דְּתַמָּן מִתְקַדְּשָׁא כֹּלָא. תַּמָּן מְקַדְּשִׁין לְמַאן דְּיָחֲזֵי לְאִתְקַדְּשָׁא. הֵיךְ מִתְקַדְּשִׁין לֵיהּ בְּהַהוּא הֵיכָלָא. בְּקַדְמֵיתָא אִתְפַּתְּחוּ תַּרְעִין, וְחַד מִפַּתְחָא סְתִימָא, אִתְקִין וּפָתַח תַּרְעָא חַד, לִסְטַר דָּרוֹם, כְּדֵין עָאל כַּהֲנָא רַבָּא בְּהַהוּא פִּתְחָא, וְאוֹזְדְּרַז בְּהֵימְיָנוֹי, וְתִקּוּנוֹי. וְאִתְעַטַּר בְּעִטְרָא דִּקְדוּשָׁה וּלְבִיעַ חוֹשְׁנָא וְאֵפוֹדָא, וּמֵעֵילָא דְּשִׁבְעִין זַגִּין וְרִמּוֹנִין, דְּאִינּוּן פַּעֲמוֹן זָהָב וְרִמּוֹן. וְצִיץ גְּזֵרָא דְּקוּדְשָׁא עַל מִצְחֵיהּ, דְּאִתְקְרֵי צִיץ נֵזֶר הַקֹּדֶשׁ, וְאִתְקְשַׁט בְּד' בִּגְדֵי זָהָב, וּבְד' בִּגְדֵי לָבָן. וְעַל הַהוּא צִיץ מ"ב אַתְוָון מְכַלָּטָן בֵּיהּ, וּמְנַצְצָן עֲלֵיהּ, וְנָהִיר כָּל הַהוּא הֵיכָלָא בִּנְהוֹרִין עִלָּאִין.

712. It is written: "…and in His Temple everyone speaks of His glory." (Psalms 29:9) He asks: **"What is "His Temple?"** He answers: **"This refers to the inner Upper Temple, where everything,** namely Binah, **is sanctified. Therefore whoever is worthy of being sanctified is sanctified."** [He asks:] **"How is that Temple sanctified?"** He answers: **"Initially the Gates are opened** by Da'at, which is Zeir Anpin." When the Left Column is dominant in Binah, He ascends to Binah to be a Central Column, Da'at, which unites Right and Left, Chochmah and Binah, together. He thus opens the Gates of Binah, meaning that He opens Binah from being closed by the Left Column. Through this, Zeir Anpin also receives Three Columns from [Binah] because since three came out of one, one is found with three. He explains his words: **"One concealed key,** namely Da'at, **fixed and opened one Gate on the south side,** which is the secret of the Right Column. **Then the High Priest,** which is Chesed, **enters into that opening and hurries with his girdle,** which is the secret of Malchut, **and his implements,** namely the four garments of an ordinary priest: Mitre, Tunic, Girdle, and Breeches, which correspond to the four letters Alef-Dalet-Nun-Yud that is Malchut.

Afterwards, **he is adorned with a Crown of Holiness, and puts on a Breastplate and Efod and a robe of seventy bells and pomegranates, which are "a golden bell and pomegranate…"** (Exodus 28:34) the secret of the Mochin of the Illumination of Chochmah that are drawn from the first Hei of the Yud-Hei-Vav-Hei. **And the Plate of the Holy Crown (Mitre) on his forehead is called "the Plate for the Holy Crown"** (Exodus 39:30), namely the Yud of Yud-Hei-Vav-Hei. **And he was embellished with the four garments of gold and with the four garments of white,** which correspond to the eight letters in the Names of Yud-Hei-Vav-Hei and Alef-Dalet-Nun-Yud, **and on that plate 42 letters sparkle and glow,** namely the 42-letter Name, **and the whole of that Temple shines with Supernal Lights.**

Da'at opening the Left Column and Central Column.

713. אִסְתְּחַר הַהוּא מַפְתְּחָא, וּפָתַח סִטְרָא אַחֲרָא דְּבִסְטַר צָפוֹן, כְּדֵין עָאל לֵוִי, מַעְשְׂרָא דְיַעֲקֹב, דְּאַפְרִישׁ לְקוּדְשָׁא בְּרִיךְ הוּא. וְכִנּוֹר דְּעֶשֶׂר נִימִין עִמֵּיהּ, וְאִתְעַטָּר בְּעֶטְרוֹי, וּכְדֵין אִסְתְּחַר מַפְתְּחָא, וּפָתַח בְּהַהוּא הֵיכָלָא חַד תַּרְעָא, הַהוּא תַּרְעָא דְּקַיְּימָא בְּאֶמְצָעִיתָא, עַמּוּדָא דְּלִסְטַר מִזְרַח עָאל וְאִתְעַטָּר בְּשַׁבְעִין עֶטְרִין, וְאִתְעַטָּר בְּאַרְבַּע אַתְוָון, דְּאִינוּן תְּרֵיסָר. וְאִתְעַטָּר בְּגִלּוּפִין דְּמָאתָן וְע' אֲלַף עָלְמִין, וְאִתְעַטָּר בְּעֶטְרִין דְּסַיְּיפֵי עָלְמָא עַד סַיְּפֵי עָלְמָא, בְּכַמָּה לְבוּשֵׁי יְקָר, בְּכַמָּה עִטְרִין קַדִּישִׁין.

713. "That key, which is the secret of Da'at, as mentioned, **turned and opened another side** of Binah, **to the north. Then Levi,** which is the secret of Gevurah and the Left Column, **entered, and he is the tithe of Jacob, whom he set aside** from his sons **for the Holy One, blessed be He, and with him a ten-stringed lyre,** which is the secret of the Ten Sefirot of the Left Column. **And he is crowned with his Crowns,** namely the Mochin of the Upper Three Sefirot called Crowns. **And then the key turned yet again and opened a Gate in that Temple, that gate that stands in the center,** namely the pillar that is on the **eastern side,** which is Tiferet, the Central Column. **It,** namely Tiferet, enters, and is adorned in that Gate **with seventy Crowns, which are** the secret of the Seventy-Two Names. **And it is adorned with four letters, which are twelve,** namely with the twelve permutations of the four letters of Yud-Hei-Vav-Hei, which are the secret of Chesed, Gevurah, Tiferet, and Malchut, each including Three Columns. **And it is adorned with engravings of 270,000 worlds,** namely the place where the Illumination of Chochmah is revealed, which is from the chest and below. The Illumination of Chochmah is called 'thousand,' and in that place is two-thirds of Tiferet, which is 70, and Netzach and Hod that each have 10 Sefirot, thus 270 Sefirot. **And it is crowned with Crowns** that shine **from one end of the world to the other,** namely in Malchut called World, **and in a number of valuable garments and a number of Holy Crowns.**

Da'at opening Malchut and uniting all aspects together.

714. אַסְתְּחַר הַהוּא מַפְתְּחָא, וּפָתַח לֵיהּ כָּל תַּרְעִין גְּנִיזִין, וְכָל תַּרְעִין דִּקְדוּשִׁין טְמִירִין, וְאִתְקַדַּשׁ בְּהוֹ, וְקָיְימָא תַּמָּן כְּמַלְכָּא. מִתְבָּרַךְ בְּכַמָּה בִּרְכָאן, מִתְעַטֵּר בְּכַמָּה עִטְרִין. כְּדֵין נַפְקֵי כֻּלְּהוֹ בְּחוֹבוּרָא חֲדָא, מִתְעַטְּרָן בְּעִטְרַיְיהוֹ כַּדְקָא יָאוֹת. כֵּיוָן דְּנַפְקֵי אִתְעַר לֵיהּ בִּקְשׁוּטוֹי.

714. "That key, which is Da'at, **turned once again and opened all the concealed Gates and all the hidden Holy Gates, and** Zeir Anpin **is sanctified in them and stands there as King,** namely from the aspect of Malchut that is in the Central Column of Binah. **There He is blessed with a number of blessings and crowned with a number of Crowns. Then all of them issue forth** from Binah to their place in Zeir Anpin, namely the Chochmah and Binah of Zeir Anpin from the two Gates that are in the south and north of Binah, and the right half of Da'at from the middle Gate of Binah and the left half of Da'at from Malchut that is in the middle Gate. They all emerge **joined together, and are crowned with their Crowns as is fitting. Once they have left** Binah for the place of Zeir Anpin, **they awaken** Zeir Anpin so that He be adorned **with His adornments,** namely with the four Mochin, as mentioned earlier.

Malchut diminishes Herself due to Her desire for Chasadim.

715. וְהַאי חַיָּה אִתְּעָרָא, וְאַזְעִירַת גַּרְמָהּ, מִגּוֹ רְחִימוּ דְּשִׁירָתָא, הֵיךְ אַזְעָרַת גַּרְמָהּ מִגּוֹ רְחִימוּ דְּשִׁירָתָא, אַזְעָרַת גַּרְמָהּ זְעֵיר זְעֵיר, עַד דְּאִתְעֲבֵידַת נְקוּדָה חֲדָא. כֵּיוָן דְּאִיהִי אַזְעֵירַת גַּרְמָהּ, כְּדֵין כְּתִיב, וַיֵּלֶךְ אִישׁ מִבֵּית לֵוִי וַיִּקַּח אֶת בַּת לֵוִי. בַּת לֵוִי וַדַּאי, מִסִּטְרָא דִּשְׂמָאלָא. הֵיאַךְ אָחִיד לָהּ. אוֹשִׁיט שְׂמָאלָא תְּחוֹת רֵישָׁהּ מִגּוֹ חֲבִיבוּ.

715. "This animal, Malchut, who is still in Her first state and still cleaves to the Left, **awakens and diminishes Herself due to the love of the song,"** meaning due to the desire for Chasadim. Since She is in the Left without the Right, She has Chochmah without Chasadim, which causes Her great pain, and She yearns greatly for Chasadim. Because of this She diminished Herself to the aspect of below the chest so that She can receive Chasadim from Him. [He asks:] **"And how does She diminish Herself?"** [He answers:] **"Due to the love of the song She contracts Herself bit by bit until She becomes a dot** under the Yesod from the aspect of the Lights, and from the aspect of the Vessels, She is a dot under the Chest. **And once she has diminished herself, it is then written: 'And there went a man of the house of Levi...,** which is the secret of the Holy One, blessed be He, **...and took to wife a daughter of Levi...' (Exodus 2:1)** which is Malchut. She is **certainly** called 'a daughter of Levi' because She is from the Left Side." [He asks:] **"How does he hold her?"** [He answers:] **"He puts his left hand under her head out of love,"** namely the left hand of Zeir Anpin becomes for Her the Upper Three Sefirot of Malchut called Head, which is the secret of the verse: "His left hand is under my head...." (Song of Songs 8:3)

In spirituality, the smaller something is the more praiseworthy it is.

716. וְאִי תֵּימָא, כֵּיוָן דְּאִיהִי נְקוּדָה חֲדָא, אֵיךְ יָכִיל לְאַחֲדָא בִּנְקוּדָה זְעֵירָא. אֶלָּא לְגַבֵּי עֵילָּא, כָּל מַה דְּהוּא מִלָּה זְעֵירָא, דָּא תּוּשְׁבַּחְתָּא, וְדָא עִלּוּיָּיא וְרַב בִּרְבוּ עִלָּאָה. מִיַּד כַּהֲנָא רַבָּא אִתְּעַר לָהּ, וְאָחִיד לָהּ, וְחָבִיק לָהּ, דְּאִלּוּ הֲוַות רַבְרְבָא, לָא יַכְלִין לְאַחֲדָא כְּלַל. אֲבָל כֵּיוָן דְּאַזְעִירַת גַּרְמָהּ, וְאִיהִי נְקוּדָה חֲדָא, כְּדֵין אֲחִידִין בָּהּ, וְסַלְקִין לָהּ לְעֵילָּא, כֵּיוָן דְּסַלְּקִין לָהּ, וְיָתְבָא בֵּין תְּרֵין סִטְרִין אִלֵּין, כְּדֵין הַהוּא עַמּוּדָא דְּקָיְימָא בְּאֶמְצָעִיתָא, אִתְחַבָּר בַּהֲדָהּ בִּנְשִׁיקוּ דְּרְחִימוּ דְּחִבּוּרָא חֲדָא. כְּדֵין וַיִּשַּׁק יַעֲקֹב לְרָחֵל, בִּרְחִימוּ דִּנְשִׁיקִין מִתְדַּבְּקָן דָּא בְּדָא, בְּלָא פְּרוּדָא, עַד דְּנַקְטָא נַפְשָׁא דְּעִנּוּגִין כַּדְקָא יָאוּת.

716. And you may ask: "Since She is now a small dot, how could Zeir Anpin unite with a small dot?" He answers: **"Rather, from the perspective of Above, the smaller something is, that is its praise and its value, and it is big in Supernal greatness.** When She is small **the High Priest,** Chesed of Zeir Anpin, **immediately awakens for her and holds and embraces her.** Had She been large, Zeir Anpin and Malchut **would not have been able to unite at all; however since She diminished Herself and is a small dot,** the Sefirot of Zeir Anpin **can hold her and raise her up on high,** between the two arms of Zeir Anpin, Chesed, and Gevurah. **And after they have raised Her up, she sits between these two Sides,** Chesed and Gevurah, **and then the Pillar that stands in the Center,** Tiferet, the Central Column, **joins with her in a love of kisses, a love of uniting as one. And then: 'And Jacob,** Zeir Anpin, **kissed Rachel,** Malchut….' (Genesis 29:11) **since with the love of kisses, they cleave to each other without separation, until she receives a Soul of delights as is fitting."**

Explanation: As long as Malchut is in the first state—in the secret of the two great luminaries, when they both receive from Binah, as Zeir Anpin clothes the Right column of Binah that is Chasadim and Malchut clothes the Left Column of Binah that is Chochmah—Malchut does not want to unite with Zeir Anpin and receive Chasadim from Him, and She is as far from Him as Left is far from Right. For Her to receive Chasadim from Zeir Anpin, She needed to diminish Herself to a dot under the Yesod of Zeir Anpin, namely to a lower grade under Zeir Anpin, and to not be able to receive from Binah but only from Zeir Anpin who is above Her. Therefore when she is a dot under Him She unites with Him as one and receives from Him all the Mochin of Gadlut. Thus **"the smaller something is, that is its praise… Had she been large, they would not have been able to unite at all,"** since as long as Malchut was as big as Zeir Anpin they could not unite because Malchut was in dispute with him like the right column and left column before the central column unites them. **"But since she diminished herself,"** as then She unites with Zeir Anpin with Kisses and Unification and receives all the Gadlut from Him.

The sanctification of the month, namely Malchut.

717. בְּשַׁעֲתָא דְּנַקְטָא נַפְשָׁא דְּעֲנוּגִין כַּדְקָא יָאוּת, וּבַעְיָא לְפַקְּדָא לְחֵילָהָא, מִתְכַּנְּשִׁין כֻּלְּהוּ, וְקָרִין לָהּ מִגּוֹ הֵיכָלָא קַדִּישָׁא, כָּבוֹד כָּבוֹד כָּבוֹד. בְּהֵיכָלָא קַדִּישָׁא אַבָּא וְאִמָּא, פָּתְחֵי וְאַמְרֵי מְקֻדָּשׁ מְקֻדָּשׁ. כְּדֵין יַרְחָא אִתְקַדָּשׁ כַּדְקָא יָאוּת. וּכְדֵין כְּתִיב, וּבַחֹדֶשׁ הָרִאשׁוֹן, רִאשׁוֹן וַדַּאי, וְע"ד מִשֶּׁכּוּ וְגוֹ'. וְע"ד בְּעִשּׂוּר לַחֹדֶשׁ הַזֶּה, דְּאִתְחַבַּר סִיהֲרָא בְּשִׁמְשָׁא, וּמַה דַּהֲוַת נְקוּדָה חֲדָא, כַּד נַחְתָּא אִתְפָּשַׁט וְעִיר וְעִיר, וְאִתְמַלְּיָיא, וְאִתְעֲבֵידַת ה', מַלְיָיא מִכָּל סִטְרִין, מִתְקַדְּשָׁא כַּדְקָא יָאוּת.

717. **"When she receives an appetite of delights, as is fitting, and she wants to visit Her hosts, they all gather together and call Her: 'Glory, glory, glory'** from the Holy Chamber of Aba and Ima. **And in the Holy Chamber itself, Aba and Ima,** Chochmah and Binah, **open and say: 'Sanctified, sanctified.'** In other words, they bestow to Malchut from their Lights called holiness. **Then the month,** which is Malchut, **is sanctified properly. And it is written: 'In the first month, on the…'** (Numbers 28:16) **for it is certainly the first.** Prior to this, when She was attached to the Left without the Right, it was not considered a reality

for Her, since Her Lights were frozen and She could not bestow. Only now, after She diminished to become a dot and was rebuilt by Aba and Ima with the Lights of Holiness so She will be under the grade of Zeir Anpin, is this considered her first reality. Thus then it is written of Her: 'In the first month, on the...' (Numbers 28:16) **And therefore,** Scripture says: **'Draw out and take your lambs...' (Exodus 12:21)** the meaning of which you shall draw down the Supernal days of Zeir Anpin to Malchut, **and** it is **therefore** written: **'On the tenth day of this month' (Exodus 12:3),** meaning **that the moon,** which is Malchut, **has become united to the sun,** which is Zeir Anpin, namely that the nine Sefirot of Zeir Anpin will serve and illuminate in Malchut. **And whereas she was a single dot** after the diminishment**, when she descended** from the Chamber of Aba and Ima, **She now expands bit by bit and fills out and becomes** the final **Hei** of Yud-Hei-Vav-Hei, **which is full of** abundance **from all** four **directions and is properly sanctified."**

A Synopsis

The Faithful Shepherd adds information about how the moon, Malchut, becomes full and is joined to the sun.

Malchut grows by means of the Shema Reading.

רעיא מהימנא

718. אִסְתְּחַר הַהוּא הֵיכָלָא, וּפָתַח תַּרְעָא אַחֲרָא דִּסְטַר דָּרוֹם בְּשַׁבְעִין וּתְרֵין עֶטְרִין. לְבָתַר אַפָּתַח תַּרְעָא תְּלִיתָאָה, לְסְטַר מַעֲרוֹז, בְּחַמְשִׁין נְהוֹרִין, דְּחַמְשִׁין תַּרְעִין דְּבִינָה. לְבָתַר אַפָּתַח תַּרְעָא אַחֲרָא דְּלִסְטַר מַעֲרַב, בְּע"ב עֶטְרִין, וְכָלְהוּ רמ"ח בְּחוּשְׁבַּן חֵיבִין דְּפָרְשִׁיָּין דק"ש. וּמַה דִּבְקַדְמֵיתָא הַהִיא וַיָּה הֲוַת זְעֵירָא, בְּהַהוּא זִמְנָא אִתְרְבִיאַת, הֲדָא הוּא דִּכְתִּיב, מְלֹא כָל הָאָרֶץ כְּבוֹדוֹ, דְּאִיהוּ כָּבוֹד עִלָּאָה וְתַתָּאָה.

Ra'aya Meheimna (Faithful Shepherd)
718. (The beginning of the article is missing). **That Chamber turned and opened another gate on the south side,** the Right Column, **with**

72 Crowns, which is the secret of the Name of 72 that shines in the Right Column. **Later it opens a third Gate on the eastern side,** which is the Central Column, **with fifty Lights of the fifty Gates of Binah.** **Next it opens another Gate on the western side,** which is the secret of Malchut, **with 72 Crowns** of the Name of 72. **All are 248** Chasadim **as the number of words in the portions of the Shema Reading. And whereas this animal,** which is Malchut, **was initially small, at that time,** having received 72 Crowns and 248 Chasadim, **She grows, which is as is written: "…the whole earth is full of His Glory" (Isaiah 6:3) which is the Upper Glory and the Lower Glory,** all of which Malchut receives in the unification of the Shema Reading.

Netzach and Hod are the lips, Yesod is the tongue.

719. כַּד מָטֵי לְחַ"י עָלְמִין, דְּבֵיהּ חַ"י בִּרְכָאן דִּצְלוֹתָא, וּפָתַח בֵּיהּ אֲדֹנָי שְׂפָתַי תִּפְתָּח וּפִי יַגִּיד תְּהִלָּתֶךָ. כְּדֵין עַמּוּדָא דְּאֶמְצָעִיתָא, אִתְחַבַּר בַּהֲדָהּ בִּנְשִׁיקוֹ דִּנְשִׁיקִין דִּשְׂפָוָון, וְאִינּוּן נֶצַח וְהוֹד, וְלָשׁוֹן אִיהוּ צַדִּיק בֵּינַיְיהוּ. לְשׁוֹן לְמוּדִים בְּהַהוּא זִמְנָא, וַיִּשַּׁק יַעֲקֹב לְרָחֵל, כְּדֵין קָרָאן לְהַהִיא חַיָּה, כָּבוֹד כָּבוֹד. אַבָּא וְאִימָּא, מִקְוֹדֶשׁ מִקּוֹדֶשׁ. כְּדֵין יַרְחָא אִתְקַדְּשָׁא כַּדְקָא יָאוּת, כְּדֵין וּבַחוֹדֶשׁ הָרִאשׁוֹן רִאשׁוֹן וַדַּאי.

719. When one reaches the eighteen Worlds, in which are the eighteen blessings of the prayer, the Amidah prayer, **which one starts with "Lord (Adonai), open my lips; and my mouth shall tell Your praise" (Psalms 51:17) then the Central Column,** which is Zeir Anpin, **joins her with affectionate kisses of the lips, which are Netzach and Hod, and the tongue is Righteous,** Yesod, **between them,** in the secret of **the tongue of the learned. At that time "And Jacob kissed Rachel…" (Genesis 29:11),** where Jacob is Zeir Anpin and Rachel is Malchut, **and then that animal,** Malchut, **is called "Glory, glory"** and **Aba and Ima say "Sanctified, sanctified."** Namely Aba and Ima bestow to her their Lights that are called Holiness, **and then the month,**

which is Malchut, **is properly sanctified. And she is then** called **"In the first month, on the..."** (Numbers 28:16); **"first"** precisely.

On the tenth day of Nissan, the Sefirot of Zeir Anpin are drawn to Malchut.

720. וּכְדֵין מִשְׁכוּ. וע"ד בְּעָשׂוֹר לַחוֹדֶשׁ הַזֶּה, דְּאִתְמֵוֹכָּר סִיהֲרָא קַדִּישָׁא בְּשִׁמְשָׁא. דְּאִתְּמַר בֵּיהּ, כִּי שֶׁמֶשׁ וּמָגֵן יְיָ' אֱלֹהִים. וּמַה דַּהֲוַת נְקוּדָה זְעֵירָא, אִתְמַלְּאַת בְּסִיהֲרָא, וּכְדֵין אִיהִי הַחוֹדֶשׁ מָלֵא. וְסִיהֲרָא אִתְמַלְּיָיא מָלֵא כָּל הָאָרֶץ כְּבוֹדוֹ. בְּקַדְמֵיתָא חָסֵר, וּכְעַן בִּשְׁלִימוּ.
ע"כ רעיא מהימנא

720. And then: "Draw out" the Supernal Days of Zeir Anpin to Malchut, **which is why** it is written: **"...on the tenth day of this month..."** (Exodus 12:3), meaning that the nine days of Zeir Anpin shine toward Malchut, namely **that the holy moon,** which is Malchut, **is joined to the sun,** which is Zeir Anpin, **about which it is said: "For the Lord God is a sun and a shield...."** (Psalms 84:12) And whereas Malchut **was a small point, she filled out as the** full **moon, and then the month is full,** namely that **the moon,** Malchut, **is full, and she is: "the whole earth is full of His glory." Initially she was lacking, but now she is complete** in her fullness.
End of Ra'aya Meheimna (Faithful Shepherd)

A Synopsis

Rav Chiya learns that the Paschal sacrifice is a lamb because a lamb was the idol and deity of the Egyptians, and it was hard for the Egyptians to see their idol tied and held prisoner and sacrificed in the fire. In this way the Egyptians saw the power of the God of Israel. Rav Elazar turns the conversation to the prohibition against eating leavened bread, and we learn that anyone who eats leavened bread on Pesach is met with death, and he dies in this world and in the World to Come.

The lamb was the deity of Egypt.

721. ר' חִיָּיא פָּתַח, בְּאַרְבָּעָה עָשָׂר יוֹם לַחֹדֶשׁ פֶּסַח וְגוֹ'. אִימְרָא דְאִיהוּ פִּסְחָא אֲמַאי. אֶלָּא דַּחֲלָא דְּמִצְרָאֵי, וֶאֱלָהָא דִּלְהוֹן, הֲוָה אִימְרָא. בְּגִין דְּמִצְרָאֵי פַּלְחִין לְמַזַּל טָלֶה, וּבַג"כ פַּלְחִין לְאִימְרָא. ת"ח, כְּתִיב הֵן נִזְבַּח אֶת תּוֹעֲבַת מִצְרַיִם. מַאי תּוֹעֲבַת מִצְרַיִם. וְכִי עַל דְּשַׂנְאִין לֵיהּ, כְּתִיב תּוֹעֲבַת מִצְרַיִם. אֶלָּא דַּחֲלָא דְּמִצְרָאֵי, וֶאֱלָהָא דִּלְהוֹן, אִקְרֵי תּוֹעֲבַת מִצְרַיִם. כְּמָה דִּכְתִיב, כְּתוֹעֲבֹת הַגּוֹיִם, דַּחֲלָא דִּשְׁאַר עַמִּין.

721. Rav Chiya opened: "And on the fourteenth day of the first month is the Pesach…" (Numbers 28:16) He asks: "Why is the Paschal sacrifice a lamb?" He answers: "The fear and deity of the Egyptians was a lamb, for they worshipped the constellation of Aries and because of this, they worshipped the lamb. Come and see, it is written: '…for we shall sacrifice the abomination of Egypt….' (Exodus 8:22)" [He asks:] "What is meant by 'the abomination of Egypt?' Could it be that because it is hateful to them it is called 'the abomination of Egypt'?" [He answers:] "On the contrary, it is called 'the abomination of Egypt' because it is the Egyptians' fear and their deity. It is similarly written: '…the abominations of the nations' (Deuteronomy 18:9) meaning the fear of the nations."

Joseph advised his brothers to tell Pharoah they are shepherds.

722. ת"ח וָכְמָתָא דְּיוֹסֵף, דִּכְתִיב וּמִקְצֵה אֶחָיו לָקַח חֲמִשָּׁה אֲנָשִׁים, וְאוֹלִיף לוֹן לְמֵימַר, אַנְשֵׁי מִקְנֶה הָיוּ עֲבָדֶיךָ. וְכִי מַלְכָּא דַּהֲוָה שַׁלִּיט עַל כָּל אַרְעָא, וְאַבָּא לְמַלְכָּא, עָבֵיד כְּדָא, וְעָבֵיד לַאֲחוֹי וְישַׁנֹּאוּן לְהוֹן, וְלָא יַחְשְׁבוּן לְהוֹן. אֶלָּא וַדַּאי תּוֹעֲבַת מִצְרַיִם, דַּחֲלָא וֶאֱלָהָא דִּלְהוֹן אִקְרֵי הָכִי, וע"ד כְּתִיב, הֵן נִזְבַּח אֶת תּוֹעֲבַת מִצְרַיִם.

722. Come and see the wisdom of Joseph, as it is written: "And he took some of his brothers, five men…" (Genesis 47:2), and he taught them to say "… 'Your servants are shepherds….'" (Genesis 47:3) [He

asks:] **"And would a king who was ruler over the country and who was like a father to the king have done such a thing to his brothers to make** the Egyptians **hate them and not show them consideration?"** If you hold the view that "…For all shepherds are an abomination to Egyptians" (Genesis 46:34) this means that the Egyptians hate them. [He answers:] **"But in reality 'the abomination of the Egyptians' is what they would call their idol and their deity. Therefore is it written: 'For we shall sacrifice the abomination of Egypt' (Exodus 8:22)"** meaning their deity.

The Egyptians considered those who tended their idols as idols.

723. אָמַר יוֹסֵף, כָּל מֵיטַב מִצְרַיִם הִיא אֶרֶץ רַעְמְסֵס, וְהַהִיא אַרְעָא אַפְרִישׁוּ לְדַחֲלָא דִלְהוֹן, לְרַעְיָא וּלְמֵיהַךְ בְּכָל עֹנּגִין דְּעָלְמָא. וְכָל מִצְרָאֵי חָשִׁיבוּ לְאִינּוּן דְּרָעָאן לְדַחֲלֵיהוֹן, כִּדְחֲלֵיהוֹן. אֲעֲבֵיד לְאַחַי דְּיַרְתוּן הַהִיא אַרְעָא, וְיִסְגְּדוּן לוֹן מִצְרָאֵי, וְיַחְשְׁבוּן לוֹן כַּדְקָא יָאוּת. וְהַיְינוּ דִּכְתִיב כִּי תוֹעֲבַת מִצְרַיִם כָּל רוֹעֵה צֹאן, מְוַחְשְׁבִין לוֹן כִּדְחֲלֵיהוֹן.

723. **Joseph said: "All the best of Egypt is the land of Rameses, and this part of the land they set aside for their idol,** namely the flocks, **for them to be pastured and walk** there in **all the delights of the world. And all the Egyptians considered those who tended their idols as idols themselves."** He said: **"I shall arrange it so that my brothers inherit that land, and the Egyptians shall bow down to them, and will accord them proper treatment, and this is what is written: '…For every shepherd is an abomination to the Egyptians.' (Genesis 46:34)** Namely **they treat them as their deity."**

Joseph wanted his brothers to have dominion over the deity of Egypt.

724. א"ר יוֹסֵי, וְהָא תָּנֵינָן כַּמָה דְּאִתְפָּרַע קוּדְשָׁא בְּרִיךְ הוּא מֵאִינּוּן דְּפַלְחֵי לע"ז, הָכִי אִתְפָּרַע מע"ז מַמָּשׁ, וְכִי יוֹסֵף עָבֵיד לַאֲחוֹי ע"ז. א"כ, לָא עָבֵיד יוֹסֵף לַאֲחוֹי ע"ז, אֶלָּא עָבֵיד לוֹן לְשַׁלְּטָאָה עַל ע"ז דִּילְהוֹן, וּלְאַכְפְּיָא ע"ז

דִּילְהוֹן תְּחוֹת יְדַיְיהוּ, וּלְרַדָּאָה לוֹן בַּמַּקֵּל. אָמַר יוֹסֵף, אִי יִשְׁלְטוּן אַחַי עַל ע"ז
דִּילְהוֹן, כ"ש דִּישְׁלְטוּן עַל גַּרְמַיְיהוּ, ובג"כ אוֹתִיב לוֹן בְּמֵיטַב אַרְעָא, וְאַשְׁלִיט
לוֹן עַל כָּל אַרְעָא.

724. Rav Yosi said: "Have we not learned, just as the Holy One,
blessed be He, punishes idolaters, so will He punish idolatry itself?
[He asks:] **If this is so, why did Joseph make his brothers into idols**
that the Egyptians should bow down to them as though they were
deities?" **He replied to him: "Joseph did not make his brothers into
idols but into rulers over the idolatry of the Egyptians, subdue their
idolatry under the hands** of his brothers, **and smite it with the rod.
Joseph said: 'If my brothers control their idolatry, how much more
will they rule over them themselves,' which is why he settled them in
the best of the land and made them rulers over all the land."**

Binding the fear and deity of Egypt on the tenth day of Nissan.

725. וע"ד אמרא דְּאִיהוּ פֶּסַח אֲמַאי. אֶלָּא דַּחֲלָא דְּמִצְרָאֵי, וֶאֱלָהָא דִּילְהוֹן
הֲוָה אִימְרָא. אָמַר קוּדְשָׁא בְּרִיךְ הוּא, מִבְּעֶשׂוֹר לַחֹדֶשׁ סִיבוּ דַּחֲלָא דִּילְהוֹן
דְּמִצְרָאֵי, וְתִפְּשׁוּ לֵיהּ, וִיהֵא אָסוּר וְתָפִיס בְּתִפִיסָה דִּילְכוֹן, יוֹמָא חַד וּתְרֵין
וג', וּבְיוֹמָא ד', אַפִּיקוּ לֵיהּ לְדִינָא, וְאִתְכְּנָשׁוּ עָלֵיהּ.

725. [He asks:] **"And so, why is the Paschal sacrifice a lamb?"** The
answer is: **"Because a lamb was the idol and deity of the Egyptians.
The Holy One, blessed be He, said: 'From the tenth of the month,
take the fear of the Egyptians, capture and bind it and let it be
imprisoned and hold it in your keeping one day, and two, and three
days, and on the fourth day carry out its sentence, and assemble
over it.'**

Nothing subdued the Egyptians like the capture and binding of their deity.

726. וּבְשַׁעֲתָא דְּמִצְרָאֵי הֲווֹ שַׁמְעִין קָל דַּחֲלָא דִּילְהוֹן, דְּתָפִיס בִּתְפִיסָה דְּיִשְׂרָאֵל, וְלָא יַכְלִין לְשֵׁזָבָא לֵיהּ, הֲווֹ בָּכָאן, וַהֲוָה קַשְׁיָא עָלַיְיהוּ, כְּאִילוּ גַּרְמַיְיהוּ אִתְעֲקִידוּ לְקָטְלָא. אָמַר קוּדְשָׁא בְּרִיךְ הוּא, יְהֵא תָּפִיס בִּרְשׁוּתַיְיכוּ, יוֹמָא בָּתַר יוֹמָא, אַרְבְּעָה יוֹמִין, בְּגִין דְּיֶחֱמוּן יָתֵיהּ תָּפִיס, וּבְיוֹמָא ד' אַפִּיקוּ לֵיהּ לְקָטְלָא, וְיֶחֱמוּן לֵיהּ מִצְרָאֵי הֵיךְ אַתּוּן עַבְדִּין בֵּיהּ דִּינָא, וְדָא קַשְׁיָא לְהוּ מִן כָּל מַכְתָּשֵׁי דְּעָבֵד לוֹן קוּדְשָׁא בְּרִיךְ הוּא, אִינּוּן דִּינִין דְּיַעַבְדוּן בְּדַחֲלֵיהוֹן.

726. "And when the Egyptians heard the voice of their idol that was being held by Israel, and they were unable to rescue it, they cried, and it was as difficult for them as though they themselves had been tied up for the kill. The Holy One, blessed be He, said: 'Let it be in your possession day after day for four days so that the Egyptians may see it bound and imprisoned, and on the fourth day, bring it out to be killed and let the Egyptians see how you enact judgment on it.' And this, namely these judgments that they performed on their idol, was harder for them to bear than all the plagues that the Holy One, blessed be He, brought on them."

The Paschal offering needed to be roasted so that it could be exposed to all.

727. לְבָתַר דַּיְינִין לֵיהּ בְּנוּרָא, דִּכְתִיב פְּסִילֵי אֱלֹהֵיהֶם תִּשְׂרְפוּן בָּאֵשׁ. אָמַר קוּדְשָׁא בְּרִיךְ הוּא, אַל תֹּאכְלוּ מִמֶּנּוּ נָא, דְּלָא יֵימְרוּן בִּרְעוּתָא וּבְתִיאוּבְתָּא דְּדַחֲלָנָא, אַכְלִין לֵיהּ הָכִי. אֶלָּא אַתְקִינוּ לֵיהּ צָלִי, וְלֹא מְבוּשָׁל, דְּאִלּוּ מְבוּשָׁל יְהֵא טָמִיר, וְלָא יֶחֱמוּן לֵיהּ, אֶלָּא תִּקּוּנָא דִּילֵיהּ דְּיֶחֱמוּן לֵיהּ הָכִי מוֹקְדָא בְּנוּרָא, בְּגִין דְּרֵיחֵיהּ נוֹדֵף.

727. Subsequently, they cast it into the fire, as it is written: "The graven images of their gods shall you burn in fire...." (Deuteronomy 7:25) The Holy One, blessed be He, said: "Eat not of it raw..." (Exodus 12:9) so that the Egyptians will not say: They were so desirous of, and had such a longing for our idol that they

ate it insufficiently roasted. **But it was decreed that it should be eaten roasted and not boiled, for had it been boiled it would have been covered** under the water in the pan, **and they would not have seen it; but the way to deal with it is that they should see it thus being burnt in the fire, since its odor then spreads** far and wide.

The Paschal offering was eaten on a full stomach, to show contempt.

728. וְתוּ רֵישֵׁיהּ עָלֵיהּ כָּפוּף עַל כַּרְסוּלוֹי, דְּלָא יֵימְרוּן דְּחַיָּה, אוֹ מִלָּה אַחֲרָא הוּא, אֶלָּא דְּיִשְׁתְּמוֹדְעָן לֵיהּ, דְּאִיהוּ דַּחֲלָא דִּלְהוֹן. וְתוּ, דְּלָא יֵיכְלוּן לֵיהּ. בְּתִיאוּבְתָּא, אֶלָּא עַל עֲבַדְעָא, אֹרַח קְלָנָא וּבִזְיוֹן. וְתוּ, עֶצֶם לֹא תִשְׁבְּרוּ בוֹ, אֶלָּא דְּיֶחֱזוּן גַּרְמוֹי רַמְיָאן בְּשׁוּקָא, וְלָא יֵיכְלוּן לְשֵׁזָבָא לֵיהּ. וְעַ"ד כְּתִיב, וּבֵאלֹהֵיהֶם עָשָׂה ה' שְׁפָטִים. דִּינִין סַגִּיאִין. תּוּ וּמַקֶּלְכֶם בְּיֶדְכֶם, וְלָא חַרְבָּא וְרוּמְחָא וּשְׁאָר מָאנֵי קְרָבָא.

728. Moreover, its head bent to its legs so that they should not say that it was some animal or other thing but that they should recognize it as their idol. Furthermore, it was not to be eaten out of lust but on a full stomach by way of disgrace and contempt. Additionally, "… nor shall you break a bone of it" (Exodus 12:46) but they should see its bones cast into the marketplace and be unable to rescue it. For this reason it is written: "…whereby the Lord executed judgments on their gods" (Numbers 33:4), namely many judgments. Moreover, "….and your staff in your hands…" (Exodus 12:11) but not a sword, spear, nor any other instrument of war, to demonstrate that you are not afraid of them.

The firstborn of the cattle were actually spiritual grades of impurity.

729. אָמַר ר' יְהוּדָה, הָא אוּקְמוּהָ, דְּבִמִצְרָאֵי פַּלְחֵי לְמַזָּל טָלֶה, וּבג"כ פַּלְחִין לְאִימְרָא. א"ר יוֹסֵי, אִי הָכִי, טָלֶה יִפְלְחוּן, וְלָא אִימְרָא. א"ל, כַּלָּא פַּלְחִין, אֶלָּא בַּזָּל טָלֶה נָחִית וְסָלִיק בְּטָלֶה וְאִימְרָא, וּבג"כ פַּלְחִין לְכֹלָּא. א"ל הָכִי

שְׁמַעְנָא, דְּכָל בְּעִירָא רַבָּא דַּחֲזֵלָא דִּלְהוֹן הֲוָה, וע"ר קָטִיל קוּדְשָׁא בְּרִיךְ הוּא
כָּל בְּכוֹר בְּהֵמָה. וְהָא אִתְּמַר דְּאִלֵּין אִינּוּן דַּרְגִּין דִּלְעֵילָא, דְּאִקְרוּן הָכִי.

729. Rav Yehuda said: "We have already learned that the Egyptians worshipped the constellation of Aries, which is why they worshipped the lamb." Rav Yosi said: "If that is so, they should have worshipped a ram (*taleh*), a baby ram, **rather than a lamb.**" He answered him: "They worshipped them all. But the constellation of Aries descends and ascends, sometimes appearing **as a ram and** at others **like a** large lamb, for which reason they worshipped them all." He said to him: "What I have heard is that every large animal was an idol for them, which is why the Holy One, blessed be He, killed all the firstborn of the cattle. And we have already learned that these were Supernal grades, namely supernal spiritual forces of impurity, **which are so called** 'firstborn of cattle,' and that was why they worshipped them."

Machmetzet is the Female Klipah, and Chametz is the Male Klipah.

730. א"ר אֶלְעָזָר, כְּתִיב כָּל מַחְמֶצֶת לֹא תֹאכֵלוּ, וּכְתִיב לֹא יֵאָכֵל חָמֵץ. אֶלָּא
דָּא דְּכַר, וְדָא נוּקְבָּא. אר"ש, אֶלְעָזָר בְּרִי, בְּדָא כְּתִיב לֹא תֹאכֵלוּ, וּבְדָא
כְּתִיב לֹא יֵאָכֵל, אֲמַאי לָא כְּתִיב לֹא תֹאכֵלוּ. אֶלָּא, נוּקְבָּא דְּאִיהִי אַסְטְיַאת
אָרְחָא, בְּאַזְהָרָה וַדַּאי, דְּכַר דְּאִיהוּ אָוֵיד בְּוַותָא דְּדַכְיוּ יַתִּיר, בְּבַקְשָׁה.
וְעַל דָּא כְּתִיב, לֹא יֵאָכֵל, לֹא תֹאכֵלוּ.

730. Rav Elazar said: "It is written: 'You shall eat nothing leavened (*machmetzet*)...' (Exodus 12:20) and '...no leavened bread (*chametz*) shall be eaten.' (Exodus 13:3) What is the difference between leavened (*machmetzet*) and unleavened (*chametz*)? **The latter (*chametz*) is masculine, while the former (*machmetzet*) is feminine.**" Rav Shimon said: "Elazar, my son, in the former case it is written, '**You shall eat nothing...**' (Exodus 12:20) while in the latter case it is written, '**...no... shall be eaten.**' (Exodus 13:3) Why does is not also say by *chametz*: '**You shall eat no...**'?" He answers: "Rather, with the

female, who corrupts her ways much more, the statement **is by way of
warning:** 'You shall eat nothing...' (Exodus 12:20) Yet in the case of **the
Male** of the Klipot, **who is more inclined to grasp a thread of purity**
than the Female, the statement is **by way of request: '...no... shall be
eaten'** (Exodus 13:3) which is not the language of warning or command.
This is why it is written in the one case **'...no... shall be eaten,'** (Ibid.)
and in the other case **'You shall eat nothing....' (Ibid.)**

The Female Klipah is more severe than the Male Klipah.

731. א"ל אַבָּא, וְהָא כְּתִיב לֹא תֹאכַל עָלָיו חָמֵץ. א"ל, אַסְגֵּי תָּבִין יְתִירִין
לִיקָרָא לְקָרְבְּנָא. אֲבָל בְּקַדְמֵיתָא בְּבַקָּשָׁה לֹא יֵאָכֵל. אֲבָל לְבָתַר בְּאַזְהָרָה,
לֹא תֹאכְלוּ, דְּהוּא קַשְׁיָא מִתַּרְוַויְיהוּ. מַחְמֶצֶת מַ"ט. בְּגִין דְּרֵיחָא דְמוֹתָא אִית
תַּמָּן. חָמֵץ, דְּכַר. מַחְמֶצֶת, נוּקְבָא. רַגְלֶיהָ יוֹרְדוֹת מָוֶת, בְּרֵישָׁא וְסֵיפָא דְּתֵיבָה,
תִּשְׁכַּח לָהּ. וּבְגִין דָּא מַאן דְּאָכִיל חָמֵץ בַּפֶּסַח, אִיהוּ אַקְדִּימַת לֵיהּ מוֹתָא,
וְלִיְדַע דְּמִית הוּא בְּעָלְמָא דֵין, וּבְעָלְמָא דְאָתֵי, כְּתִיב וְנִכְרְתָה הַנֶּפֶשׁ הַהִיא.

731. He said to him: "But father, it is also written: **'You shall eat
no leavened bread (*chametz*) with it...'** (Deuteronomy 16:3), namely
we see that a warning is also used for *chametz*, which is the Male of the
Klipah." **He replied:'** In honor of the sacrifice, scripture used many
extra words,** and therefore says: 'You shall eat no leavened bread with
it....' (Ibid.) **But initially,** about leavened bread (*chametz*) it was said, **'...
no leavened bread shall be eaten'** (Exodus 13:3) which **is the language
of request. But afterwards,** about leavened (*machmetzet*), **a warning** is
used: **'You shall eat nothing...'** (Exodus 12:20) for the Female of the
Klipot **is the harshest of the two of them,** of the Male and Female of
the Klipah." [He asks:] **"What is the reason for leavened (*machmetzet*)**
being so called?" [He answers:] **"It is because there is a smell of death
there. Leavened bread (*Chametz*)** alludes to **the Male** and has therefore
no allusion to death, **but leavened (*machmetzet*) is Female,** and it is
written: **'Her feet go down to death....'** (Proverbs 5:5) Thus **the first
and last letters of the word** *machmetzet* (מחמצת) are Mem and Tav

that **spell** dead (*met;* מת). **Thus she,** the Female, **greets anyone who eats leavened bread (Chametz) on Pesach with death, and it should be known that he dies in this world and in the World to Come, as it is written: '…that soul shall be cut off.' (Exodus 12:19)"**

Matzah fights and subdues evil.

732. מַצָּה אֲמַאי אִתְקְרִיאַת מַצָּה. אֶלָּא הָכִי תָּנֵינָן, שַׁדַּי: בְּגִין דְּאָמַר לְעוֹלָמוֹ דַּי, דְּיֵאמַר לְצָרוֹתֵינוּ דַּי. אוֹף הָכִי מַצָּה, בְּגִין דְּקָא מְעַדֵּד דְּמַבְרַחַת לְכָל סִטְרִין בִּישִׁין, וְעָבֵיד קְטָטָה בַּהוּ, כְּגַוְונָא דְּשַׁדַּי דִּמְזוּזָה, דְּמַבְרִיחַ לְשֵׁדִים וּמַזִּיקִים דְּתַרְעָא, אוֹף הָכִי אִיהִי מַבְרַחַת לוֹן מִכָּל מִשְׁכְּנֵי קְדוּשָׁה, וְעָבֵיד מְרִיבָה וּקְטָטָה בַּהוּ. כד"א, מַסָּה וּמְרִיבָה. ע"ד כְּתִיב מַצָּה. וְהָא מַסָּה בְּסָמֶךְ אִיהוּ. אֶלָּא תַּרְגּוּמוֹ דְּמַסָּה, אִיהוּ מַצּוּתָא.

732. [He asks:] **"Why is unleavened bread called Matzah?"** [He answers:] **"Rather, we have thus learned: Shadai,** meaning, **May He Who said to His world 'Enough (*dai*),' say to our troubles 'Enough,'** namely may He chase away from us Judgments and troubles. **Matzah is likewise, for it subdues and subjugates; namely it chases away the evil ones of all sides and makes a quarrel with them, just as the Name Shadai of the Mezuzah chases away the evil spirits and demons that are at the gate.** So too, Matzah **chases them away from all the dwellings of Holiness, and makes a quarrel (*merivah*) and a fight with them, as it is written: '…Masah and Merivah…' (Exodus 17:7) and therefore the name is written as Matzah."** He asks: **"But *masah* (מסה) is spelled with a Samech (ס),** and not with a Tzadi (צ)?" He answers: **"The Aramaic translation of Masah (מסה) is *matzuta* (מצותא),** and therefore Matzah (מצה) is spelled with a Tzadi (צ).

A Synopsis
The Faithful Shepherd talks about the Ten Plagues and about God's intention to punish all the rulers of Egypt because they misled mankind and made themselves Divine. He examines the

reason why unleavened bread (Matzah) was to be eaten for seven days, and he brings in the factors of the Seven Sefirot and the Seven Planets and the Seven Blessings.

The Egyptians were smitten with 250 Plagues at the sea.

רעיא מהימנא

733. אָמַר רַעְיָא מְהֵימָנָא, כְּגוֹן לִישָׁנָא דְּאִיהוּ מַקֵּל לְכָל אַנְשֵׁי בֵּיתֵיהּ, וְאִיהוּ לִישָׁנָא דְּאָת ו', וְאִיהוּ מַטֶּה דְּבֵיהּ עֲשַׂר אוֹתְיוֹת, וּבֵיהּ מָחָא קוּדְשָׁא בְּרִיךְ הוּא עַל יְדוֹי י' מָחָאן. וּבְגִין דְּכָל מָחָאן הֲווֹ מִסִּטְרָא דְּה' ה', ר' עֲקִיבָא אוֹמֵר, מִנַּיִן שֶׁכָּל מַכָּה וּמַכָּה שֶׁהֵבִיא הַקָּדוֹשׁ בָּרוּךְ הוּא עַל הַמִּצְרִים בְּמִצְרַיִם הָיְתָה שֶׁל חָמֵשׁ מַכּוֹת וְכוּ', אָמוּר מֵעַתָּה וְכוּ'. וְאָת ה' סַלְקָא בְּאָת י' לְחַמְשִׁין מָחָאן, חָמֵשׁ זִמְנִין חַמְשִׁין, אִינּוּן ר"ן. וּבג"ד, וְעַל הַיָּם לָקוּ ר"ן מַכּוֹת.

Ra'aya Meheimna (Faithful Shepherd)

733. The Faithful Shepherd said: **"Just as the tongue is a rod over all members of the household,** [which he bases on what he said in verse 724: 'and smite it with the rod'] for he reprimands them with his tongue, which is the same for them as though he has reprimanded them with a rod. **And the tongue is the secret of the letter Vav (ו),** which is Zeir Anpin that is called Yud-Hei-Vav-Hei (יהוה), **and is a rod in which are ten letters,** for Yud-Hei-Vav-Hei spelled out with Alefs (א) has ten letters: Yud-Vav-Dalet, Hei-Alef, Vav-Alef-Vav, Hei-Alef (יוד הא ואו הא), **and the Holy One, blessed be He, smote them with Ten Plagues through it. And since all the Plagues were from the side of the two Hei's (ה)** of the Yud-Hei-Vav-Hei, therefore, **Rav Akiva says:** 'How do we know that each plague the Holy One, blessed be He, brought down on the Egyptians in Egypt consisted of five plagues? We should deduce from this that...' (the Haggadah). And the letter Hei (ה; 5) times the letter Yud (י; 10) gives fifty plagues, and Hei (5) times fifty is 250, which is why at the sea they were smitten with 250 Plagues."

Joseph wanted to place his brothers in control over the deities of Egypt.

734. אָמַר יוֹסֵף, כָּל מֵיטַב אֶרֶץ מִצְרַיִם רַעְמְסֵס הִיא, וְהַהִיא אַרְעָא אַפְרִישׁוּ לְדַחֲלָן דִּלְהוֹן, לְרַעְיָא וּלְמֵיהַךְ בְּכָל עִנּוּגִין דְּעָלְמָא. וְכָל מִצְרָאֵי חֲשִׁיבוּ לְאִינּוּן דְּרָעָן לְדַחֲלֵיהוֹן, כְּדַחֲלֵיהוֹן. וְדָא שָׁאִיל יוֹסֵף מִפַּרְעֹה, לְשַׁלְטָאָה אֲחוֹי עַל דַּחֲלָן דְּמִצְרָאֵי, דְּאִתְכַּפְיָין תְּחוֹת יְדֵיהוֹן, כַּעֲבָדִים בָּתַר מַלְכֵּיהוֹן, לְמֶהֱוֵי כֻּלְּהוּ מִתְכַּפְיָין תְּחוֹת שֵׁם יְיָ' מִסִּטְרַיְיהוֹן, וְלָא שַׁלִּיט בְּעָלְמָא אֶלָּא שֵׁם יְדֹוָד. וְאִתְכַּפְיָין כָּל מְמָנָן תְּחוֹת יְדֵיה.

734. Joseph said: "The best of the land of Egypt is Rameses, and this is the land that they set aside for their deity to pasture in all the delights of the world. And all the Egyptians considered those who tend their idols as their deities." And this is why Joseph requested from Pharaoh the land of Rameses to tend their flocks, **so as to place his brothers in control over the deities of Egypt so that they should be subjugated under them as slaves under their king, so they will all be subjugated under the Name of Yud-Hei-Vav-Hei on their side, and that none should rule in the world except the Name of Yud-Hei-Vav-Hei, and that all the appointed ministers should also be subjugated to Him.**

Tending Egypt's flocks was a foreshadow for the future Redemption.

735. וּלְאַחֲזָאָה לוֹן, דְּאִיהוּ עָתִיד לְאִיתְפָּרְעָא מִנְּהוֹן, הֲדָא הוּא דִּכְתִיב, וּבְכָל אֱלֹהֵי מִצְרַיִם אֶעֱשֶׂה שְׁפָטִים אֲנִי יְדֹוָד. כַּד מַטְעָיִין לְבִרְיָין וְעָבְדִין גַּרְמַיְיהוּ אֱלֹהוּת. וּבְגִין דְּטָלֶה מְמָנָא דִּילֵיה, אִיהוּ רַב עַל כָּל מְמָנָן דֶּאֱלֹהִים אֲחֵרִים, מָנֵי קוּדְשָׁא בְּרִיךְ הוּא לְיִשְׂרָאֵל, וְיִקְחוּ לָהֶם אִישׁ שֶׂה לְבֵית אָבוֹת שֶׂה לַבָּיִת, וְאַשְׁלִיט לוֹן עֲלֵיה, וְתַפְסֵי לֵיה תָּפִיס בְּתִפְיִשָׁה דִּלְהוֹן יוֹמָא וּתְרֵין וּתְלַת. וּלְבָתַר דָּא אַפִּיקוּ לֵיה לְדִינָא לְעֵינֵי כָּל מִצְרָאֵי, לְאַחֲזָאָה דֶּאֱלָהָא דִּלְהוֹן בִּרְשׁוּ דְּיִשְׂרָאֵל לְמֶעְבַּד בֵּיה דִּינָא.

735. And to show them that He will in the future punish them, as it is written: "...and against all the gods of Egypt I will execute

Judgments: I am the Lord" (Exodus 12:12) because they mislead mankind and make themselves divine; and since the appointee of the ram is greater than the appointees of the other gods, the Holy One, blessed be He, commanded Israel: "...they shall take to them every man a lamb, according to the house of their fathers, a lamb for a house" (Exodus 12:3); and He gave them control over it, and they took hold of it as they did for one day, and for two and three days, and afterwards, they brought it out before the eyes of all Egypt for Judgments, to demonstrate that their deity is at Israel's disposal to punish it.

The Pascal sacrifice was more difficult for Egypt than all ten plagues.

736. בג"ה, אַל תֹּאכְלוּ מִמֶּנּוּ נָא וּבָשֵׁל מְבוּשָׁל בַּמָּיִם כִּי אִם צְלִי אֵשׁ רֹאשׁוֹ עַל כְּרָעָיו וְעַל קִרְבּוֹ, לְמֶהֱוֵי דָן בְּאֵשׁ צָלִי, וּמְנֵי לְזָרְקָא לְגַרְמֵיהּ דִּילֵיהּ בְּשׁוּקָא בְּבִזוּי. וּבג"ה, וְעֶצֶם לֹא תִשְׁבְּרוּ בוֹ. וּמְנֵי לְיוֹמָא ד', בָּתַר דַּהֲוָה תָּפִיסׁ ג' יוֹמִין קָשׁוֹר, לְמֶעְבַּד בֵּיהּ דִּינָא. וְדָא קַשְׁיָא לוֹן מִכָּל מַכְתְּשִׁין דְּמָחָא לוֹן קוּדְשָׁא בְּרִיךְ הוּא, עַל יְדָא דְּרַעְיָא מְהֵימְנָא. וְלֹא עוֹד, אֶלָּא דְּמְנֵי דְּלָא לְמֵיכַל לֵיהּ בְּתִיאוּבְתָּא. וּמִיַּד דְּוַזְמָאן גַּרְמוֹי בְּשׁוּקָא, וְלֹא יַכְלִין לְשֵׁזָבָא לֵיהּ, דָּא קַשְׁיָא לוֹן מִכֹּלָּא. וְלֹא עוֹד, אֶלָּא דְּאִתְּמַר בְּהוֹ, וּמַקֶּלְכֶם בְּיֶדְכֶם, לְאִתְכַּפְיָא כָּל דַּחֲלָן דְּמִצְרָאֵי, תְּחוֹת יְדַיְיהוּ. וּבְגִין דְּאִינוּן בְּכוֹרוֹת מִמָּנָן, כְּתִיב וַיְיָ' הִכָּה כָל בְּכוֹר.

736. Therefore it is written: "Eat not of it raw, nor boiled at all in water, but roast with fire; its head with its legs, and with its entrails..." (Exodus 12:9) so that it should be punished in the roasting fire. And He commanded that its bones be cast with contempt into the marketplace, and therefore: "...nor shall you break a bone of it." (Exodus 12:46) And He commanded that on the fourth day, after it had been bound for three days, Judgment be enacted upon it. And this was harder for them than all the Plagues with which the Holy One, blessed be He, smote them through the Faithful Shepherd. Furthermore, He commanded that it not be

eaten with appetite, but with a full stomach. And immediately on their seeing its bones in the marketplace and being unable to rescue it, this was the most difficult thing for them. Furthermore, about them it is said: "...and your staff in your hand..." (Exodus 12:11) to subdue all the idols of Egypt under their hands. And since their gods are the firstborn of the chieftains, it is written: "...the Lord smote all the firstborn...." (Exodus 12:29)

The seven orbiting planets are from the side of Good and Evil,
where Matzah is on the inside and Chametz on the outside.

737. בָּתַר כָּל דָּא כְּתִיב, לֹא יֵאָכֵל וָזֶמֶץ שִׁבְעַת יָמִים תֹּאכַל עָלָיו מַצּוֹת לֶחֶם עֹנִי. וּכְתִיב כָּל מַוְזֶמֶצֶת לֹא תֹאכֵלוּ. אָמְרוּ רַעְיָא מְהֵימָנָא, אֲמַאי בְּנֵי דְּלָא לְמֵיכַל וָזֶמֶץ שִׁבְעַת יוֹמִין, וּלְמֵיכַל בְּהוֹן מַצָּה. וַאֲמַאי לֹא יֵאָכֵל, וַאֲמַאי לֹא תֹאכֵלוּ. אֶלָּא ז' כֹּכְבֵי לֶכֶת וְאִינּוּן: שצ"ם חנכ"ל. וְאִינּוּן מִסִּטְרָא דְּטוֹב וָרָע, נְהוֹרָא דְּלְגוֹ מַצָּה. קְלִיפָה דִּלְבַר חָמֵץ. וְאִינּוּן זָמֵן וְאִינּוּן דְּכַר מַוְזֶמֶצֶת נוּקְבָּא.

737. And after all this, it is written: "...no leavened bread (*chametz*) shall be eaten..." (Exodus 13:3) [and] "...seven days you shall eat unleavened bread (*Matzot*) with it, the bread of affliction...." (Deuteronomy 16:3) And it is written: "You shall eat nothing leavened (*machmetzet*)...." (Exodus 12:20) The Faithful Shepherd said: "Why did He command not to eat leavened bread for seven days, but to eat unleavened bread (*matzah*) on them? And why in one case is it written: 'no... shall be eaten...' (Exodus 13:3) while in the other case it is written: 'You shall eat nothing...' (Exodus 12:20)?" He answers: "Rather, there are seven orbiting planets, and they are: Saturn (*Shabtai*), Jupiter (*Tzedek*), Mars (*Ma'adim*), Sun (*Shemesh*), Venus (*Nogah*), Mercury (*Kochav*), and Moon (*Yare'ach*), which are the seven Sefirot: Chesed, Gevurah, Tiferet, Netzach, Hod, Yesod, and Malchut that are in the Vessels of the Achorayim of Malchut. And they are from the side of Good and Evil, for the Light that is within is Matzah, while the Klipah that is on the outside is Chametz. And

the Chametz is masculine, while *machmetzet* is feminine, and they are Male and Female of that same Klipah that is on the outside. And about the Male of the Klipah, which is not that grave, it is said: "No… shall be eaten," (Exodus 13:3) but about the Female of the Klipah, which is a serious matter, it is said: "You shall eat nothing…." (Exodus 12:20)

Matzah is guarded from the Klipot, for Zeir Anpin.

738. מַצָּה דְּלֹגוֹ שְׁמוּרָה. וְאִינּוּן, שֶׁבַע הַנְּעָרוֹת הָרְאוּיוֹת לָתֶת לָהּ מִבֵּית הַמֶּלֶךְ. וְאִתְּמַר עָלַיְיהוּ, וּשְׁמַרְתֶּם אֶת הַמַּצּוֹת. מַצָּה אִיהִי שְׁמוּרָה לְבַעְלָהּ, דְּאִיהוּ ו'. וּבֵיהּ אִתְעָבֵיד מִצְוָה.

738. **The Matzah that is within** the seven aforementioned planets **is guarded** from the Klipot, **which are "…the seven maidens who were chosen to be given her, out of the king's house…" (Esther 2:9)** namely the Achorayim Vessels of the Malchut of Atzilut, within which the Chochmah is clothed during the Gadlut [Maturity] of Malchut. **And about them it is said: "And you shall watch over the unleavened bread…." (Exodus 12:17) Matzah is guarded** from the Klipot, **for her Husband, who is Vav (ו),** namely Zeir Anpin, which is the secret of the Vav of Yud-Hei-Vav-Hei (יהוה). **And with it,** the Vav, Matzah (מצה) **becomes *mitzvah* (precept; מצוה).**

Removing Chametz from Malchut, and blessing Her with seven blessings.

739. וּמַאן דְּנָטִיר לָהּ לְגַבֵּי יָהּ, דְּגְּנִיזִין בְּמ"ץ מִן מַצָּה, וְאִינּוּן. י"ם ה"ץ. וּמְנֵי קוּדְשָׁא בְּרִיךְ הוּא לְבָרֵךְ לָהּ שֶׁבַע בְּרָכוֹת לֵיל פֶּסַח, דְּאִינּוּן שֶׁבַע הַנְּעָרוֹת דִּילָהּ, שעצ"ם חזכ"ל. וּמְנֵי לְאַעְבְּרָא מִנְּהוֹן חָמֵץ וּמַחְמֶצֶת, דְּאִינּוּן עֲנָנִים וַחֲשׁוּכִין דִּמְכַסְיָין עַל נְהוֹרִין, דְּשׁוֹבָעָה כֹּכְבֵי לֶכֶת, דְּאִתְּמַר בְּהוֹן וַתְּבֹאנָה אֶל קַרְבֶּנָה וְלֹא נוֹדַע כִּי בָאוּ אֶל קַרְבֶּנָה וּמַרְאֵיהֶן רַע, וָשׁוֹךְ כַּאֲשֶׁר בַּתְּחִלָּה. דְּכֹל כַּךְ וַחֲשׁוּכָא דַּעֲנָנֵי דִּלְהוֹן, דְּלָא יַכְלִין נְהוֹרִין לְאַנְהָרָא לְהוֹן, וּבְגִין דָּא וְלֹא נוֹדַע כִּי בָאוּ אֶל קַרְבֶּנָה.

ע"כ רַעְיָא מְהֵימְנָא

739. He who guards it for Yud-Hei (יה), that are hidden in the Mem-Tzadi (מצ) of Matzah (מצה), since according to the Atbash cipher, **Yud (י) is Mem (מ), Hei (ה) is Tzadi (צ),** as the Mem of Matzah is replaced by Yud, and the Tzadi of Matzah is replaced by Hei, which is the secret of Yud-Hei being hidden in the Mem-Tzadi of Matzah. **And the Holy One, blessed be He, commanded to bless Malchut with seven blessings on the Eve of Pesach, which are her seven maidens,** namely the seven vessels, Chesed, Gevurah, Tiferet, Netzach, Hod, Yesod, and Malchut of Malchut of Atzilut from the aspect of Achorayim, as mentioned, which are called: **Saturn (*Shabtai*), Jupiter (*Tzedek*), Mars (*Ma'adim*), Sun (*Shemesh*), Venus (*Nogah*), Mercury (*Kochav*), and Moon (*Yare'ach*). And He commanded that** the Klipot, which are **Chametz (leavened bread) and *machmetzet* (leavened) be removed from them, for they are dark clouds that cover the Lights of the seven orbiting planets, about which it is said: "And they came into their midst, but it could not be known that they had come into their midst, for their appearance was bad," darkness, "as at the beginning." (Genesis 41:21) For the darkness of their clouds is so** strong **that the Lights** that are in the seven planets **are unable to shine to them, and for this reason: "...it could not be known that they had come into their midst...." (Ibid.)**
End of Ra'aya Meheimna (Faithful Shepherd)

106. "Shout down the beast of the reeds"

A Synopsis

Rav Shimon explains the meaning of the wild beast and the reed grass. He says that the reed is the head over all the Kingdoms and in the future God will break it like a reed.

The Male of the Klipah has some attachment to Malchut.

740. רִבִּי שִׁמְעוֹן פָּתַח וְאָמַר, גְּעַר חַיַּת קָנֶה עֲדַת אַבִּירִים בְּעֶגְלֵי עַמִּים. גְּעַר
חַיַּת, דָּא חַיָּה דְּאִתְאֲחָד בָּהּ עֵשָׂו. קָנֶה: תָּנֵינָן, דִּבְיוֹמָא דְּנָסַב שְׁלֹמֹה מַלְכָּא
בַּת פַּרְעֹה, בָּא גַּבְרִיאֵל, נָעַץ קָנֶה בְּיַמָּא רַבָּא, וְעָלֵיהּ אִתְבְּנֵי קַרְתָּא דְרוֹמִי.
מַאי קָנֶה. דָּא דְּכוּרָא דְּהַאי חַיָּה בִּישָׁא, דְּאִית לֵיהּ סְטְרָא זְעֵירָא בְּאַחֲדוּתָא
דִקְדוּשָׁה. וְדָא אִיהוּ קָנֶה, דְּנָעִיץ בְּיַמָּא רַבָּא. וּבג"כ אִיהִי שַׁלְטָא עַל עָלְמָא,
וְעַל שׁוּלְטָנוּ דָּא כְּתִיב, קָנֶה וָסוּף קָמֵלוּ. קָנֶה, שׁוּלְטָנוּתָא וְרֵאשׁ לְכָל מַלְכָוָון.
תּוּ קָנֶה, דְּזַמִּין קוּדְשָׁא בְּרִיךְ הוּא לְתַבְּרָא לֵיהּ כְּקָנֶה דָּא.

**740. Rav Shimon opened with, "'Shout down the beast of the reeds,
the congregation of mighty bulls among the calves of the peoples ….'
(Psalms 68:31) 'Shout down the beast' refers to that beast that Esau
held on to. 'Reeds' is as we have learned, for on the day that Solomon
married the daughter of Pharaoh, Gabriel came and stuck a reed
in the sea, and the city of Rome was built on it.** He asks: **"What is
'reed'?"** He answers: **"It is the male of that wicked animal** onto which
Esau held, **which has a small part in the unity of Holiness, and this
is the reed that** Gabriel **stuck into the great sea. And for this reason
it rules the world, and about this rule it is written: '…the reeds and
rushes shall wither.' (Isaiah 19:6) 'Reed' is the regime and head over
all Kingdoms, and furthermore** it is for this reason called **'reed,'** since
**in the future the Holy One, blessed be He, is going to break it as
a reed.**

Explanation: Lili"t and Sama"el are called the beast of the reeds, as they
are the Male and Female aspect of the Klipah, and Esau is attached to
them. This is: **"'Shout down the beast' refers to that beast that Esau
held on to."** The Male of the Klipah is like an intermediary between
the Holiness and the Klipah, since the Male called "reed" holds on to
the Malchut of Holiness, and attached to him is the impure Female that
is called "beast," which is the Chochmah of the Klipah. This is: **"Reed
is the male of that wicked animal that has a small part in the unity**

of Holiness," as the Male is attached to the Malchut of Holiness, "and this is the reed that Gabriel stuck into the great sea." The great sea is Malchut, to which the reed, the male of the Klipah, is attached.

When the Chet of Chametz is broken it becomes Matzah.

741. ת"ח, בְּמִצְרַיִם אִיהִי שַׁלְטָא, וּמִנָּהּ נַפְקוּ כַּמָּה שָׁלְטָנִין לְזַנְיָיהוּ, וְכֻלָּא בְּרָזָא דְּחָמֵץ, כֵּיוָן דְּתָבַר לָהּ קוּדְשָׁא בְּרִיךְ הוּא, אַפִּיק חָמֵץ וְאָעִיל מַצָּה. בְּמָה בְּחוּטָא זְעֵירָא מִכֹּלָּא, תָּבַר חו' דְחָמֵץ, וְאִתְעֲבֵיד מַצָּה. אִינּוּן אַתְווֹן. אֶלָּא דְּתָבַר חו' דְּהַאי חַיָּה, דְּאִקְרֵי חָמֵץ. וע"ד אִקְרֵי חַיַּת קָנֶה, דְּנוֹחַ לְאִתְבְּרָא כְּקָנֶה דָּא. בְּמָה אִתְבַּר. בְּחוּטָא זְעֵירָא כְּנִימָא, תָּבַר חו' וְאִתְעֲבָר מֵאַיתָנָהּ, וַהֲוָה מַצָּה. וע"ד כְּתִיב, גְּעַר חַיַּת קָנֶה, גָּעַר בָּהּ קוּדְשָׁא בְּרִיךְ הוּא, וְאִתְבַּר חו' חָמֵץ, וְאִתְעֲבֵיד ה'.

741. "Come and see, in Egypt that '…beast of the reeds…' (Psalms 68:31) rules, and from it emerge all types of regimes, and they all are in the secret of Chametz. Since the Holy One, blessed be He, broke it, He removed the Chametz (חָמֵץ) and introduced Matzah (מַצָּה)." He asks: "What did He use to break it?" He answers: "With the smallest and thinnest thread, He broke the letter Chet (ח) of Chametz (חָמֵץ), and it became the letters of Matzah (מַצָּה); He broke the letter Chet of this beast (chayah; חַיָּה) called Chametz. Thus it is called '…the beast of the reeds…' (Ibid.) because it is as easy to break as this reed." He asks: "With what was it broken?" He answers: "It was with a thread as small as a strand of hair that He broke the Chet and removed it from its former state and it became Matzah (מַצָּה). Therefore it is written: 'Shout down the beast of the reeds…' (Ibid.) for the Holy One, blessed be He, rebuked it, and the Chet (ח) of Chametz was broken and became a Hei (ה).

From kaneh (reed) to hineh (behold).

742. וְזַמִּין קוּדְשָׁא בְּרִיךְ הוּא לְתַבְּרָא לֵיהּ לְהַהוּא קָנֶה, כְּגַוְונָא דָא, יַתְבַּר רַגְלֵיהּ דְּק' מִקָנֶה, וְיִשְׁתְּאַר הִנֵּה. הִנֵּה יְיָ' אֱלֹהִים בְּחָזָק יָבֹא וּזְרוֹעוֹ מוֹשְׁלָה לוֹ הִנֵּה שְׂכָרוֹ אִתּוֹ וּפְעוּלָתוֹ לְפָנָיו. מַאי וּפְעוּלָתוֹ. דָּא פָּעַל דְּהַהִיא ק' דְּיִתְבַּר לָהּ, וְאִיהִי פְּעוּלָה לְפָנָיו, אִיהוּ יַעֲבַר רַגְלֵיהּ, וִיהֵא הִנֵּה רִאשׁוֹן לְצִיּוֹן הִנֵּה הִנָּם וְגוֹ'.

742. "And in the future the Holy One, blessed be He, will break that reed as follows: He will break off the foot of the Kof (קְ) of *kaneh* (reed; קָנֶה) so *hineh* (behold; הִנֵּה) will remain. It is written, 'Behold (*hineh*), the Lord God will come with might, and His arm shall rule for Him: behold (*hineh*), His reward is with Him, and His hire before Him.' (Isaiah 40:10)" He asks: "What is the meaning of 'and His hire (lit. His action)' (Ibid)?" He answers: "This is the action to break the leg of that letter Kof, and it is an action before Him, for He will remove the foot of the Kof (קְ) of *kaneh* (קָנֶה), making it into *hineh* (הִנֵּה). 'A harbinger to Zion will I give: "Behold (*hineh*), behold them…."' (Isaiah 41:27)"

Explanation: The "beast of the reed" is the secret of the Male and Female of the Klipah that cleave to the Left without the Right. They draw Chochmah of the Left from above downward, and through this, the channels of Malchut clog up. The "reed," the Male of the Klipah, is attached to Malchut in the secret of **"the reed that is stuck into the great sea,"** as mentioned earlier, and Chametz is the secret of the "beast," namely the Female of the Klipah. In order to unclog the channels of abundance in Malchut it is necessary to break the reed and the beast of the Klipah, who cover the Lights of Malchut. This is done by diminishing the Upper Three of the Left so that the "beast of the reed" can no longer nourish from there, and thus they will separate from Malchut. Then the channels of abundance in Malchut open up.

This is considered as breaking the leg of the Chet of Chametz, which is the beast of the Klipah, since the breaking of the Netzach, Hod, and Yesod of the Vessels cause the Upper Three of the Lights to disappear. Thus, Chametz transforms to a Matzah reserved for Her husband, namely that the flow of Chochmah will not shine in Her except in the aspect of the Lower Six of Chochmah, meaning from below upward. This prevents the beast of the reed from having access, and She is protected and reserved for Zeir Anpin, Her husband. This is also considered as breaking the leg of the Kof of *kaneh* (reed; קָנֶה), which is the Male of the Klipah that is wedged in Malchut. Then *kaneh* becomes *hineh*, which is the secret of the verse "...behold (*hineh*; הִנֵּה), His reward is with Him..." (Isaiah 40:10) because once the leg of the Kof breaks, the reward of the Righteous is revealed.

This is: **"He broke the letter Chet of this beast (chayah; חַיָּה) called Chametz,"** namely He diminished the Upper Three of the Left, by which the leg of the Chet of Chametz breaks. However, this diminishment can happen either by revealing the Man'ula (Lock), which is the Malchut of the attribute of Judgment, which is a powerful force that diminishes even the Lower Six of Chochmah, meaning even from drawing Chochmah from below upward. Or it can be diminished by revealing the Maftecha (Key), where only the Upper Three of Chochmah are diminished but the Lower Six remain. This is: **"With the smallest and thinnest thread, He broke the letter Chet of Chametz (וֹבֹמֵץ),"** namely with the Maftecha, which is a small diminishment, did He break the Chet of Chametz. Thus **"it became the letters of Matzah (מַצָּה),"** meaning that the Lower Six of Chochmah called Matzah remained, due to the fact that its diminishment was not severe from the aspect of Man'ula.

Together with the breaking of the leg of the Chet of Chametz, which is the Female of the Klipah, also the leg of the Kof of *kaneh* is broken, which is the Male of the Klipah. This is: **"He will break off the foot of the Kof (קָ) of *kaneh* (reed; קָנֶה) so *hineh* (behold; הִנֵּה) will remain."**

This means that the reed will detach from Malchut and Malchut will remain reserved and protected alone, since Malchut is called "behold" (*hineh*). This is: **"Behold (*hineh*), the Lord God will come with might… behold (*hineh*), His reward is with Him, and His hire before Him." (Isaiah 40:10)** After the reed (*kaneh*) broke and detached from Malchut, then the channels of abundance in Malchut opened up and the reward of the Righteous is revealed. This is the secret of **"behold (*hineh*), His reward is with Him, and His hire before Him." (Ibid.)** He asks: **"What is the meaning of 'and His hire (lit. His action)' (Ibid)?"** He answers: **"This is the action to break** the leg **that letter Kof,"** since the breaking of the leg of the Kof is the secret of "and His action before Him," for the reward and the action of reducing the Upper Three come at the same time. **"…and it is an action before Him (lit. to His face),"** namely since the Upper Three are called Face, and the act of reducing that occurs to the Upper Three is considerd an action to His face, and therefore "it is an action to His face." Then the following will be fulfilled: **"A harbinger to Zion…." (Isaiah 41:27)**

A Synopsis

Rav Shimon says that Esau is Rome that is attached to the reed that Gabriel stuck in the great sea; the reed is also called "leavened bread." When the Redemption comes, God will break that reed and the Temple will be revealed in the world. The Faithful Shepherd compares the two Temples to the pupils of the eye that are clouded. He talks about the two Messiahs and looks forward to the day when the rule of Rome will be broken.

The kingdom of Esau will be broken at the time of the Redemption.

רעיא מהימנא

743. רִבִּי שִׁמְעוֹן פָּתַח וְאָמַר, גְּעַר חַיַּת קָנֶה עֲדַת אַבִּירִים בְּעֶגְלֵי עַמִּים. גְּעַר חַיַּת קָנֶה, דָּא קָנֶה דְּאִתְאֲחִיד בֵּיה עֵשָׂו, דְּאִיהִי קַרְתָּא דְרוֹמִי רַבְּתָא, דְּנָעַץ גַּבְרִיאֵל קָנֶה בְּיַמָּא רַבָּא, וּבָנוּ עֲלֵיהּ כְּרָךְ גָּדוֹל דְּרוֹמִי. קָנֶה דְּזַמִּין. וְכַד יֵיתֵי

פּוּרְקָנָא לְיִשְׂרָאֵל, יִתְבַּר לֵיהּ. הה"ד גְּעַר חַיַּת קָנֶה עֲדַת. וּמִתְעַבָּר מִיַּד חָמֵץ
מֵעָלְמָא. מַחְמֶצֶת דִּילֵיהּ רוֹמִי. וְיִתְגַּלְיָא מַצָּה בְּעָלְמָא, דְּאִיהִי בֵּי מַקְדְּשָׁא
דְּבַיִת רִאשׁוֹן וּבַיִת שֵׁנִי.

Ra'aya Meheimna (Faithful Shepherd)

743. Rav Shimon opened with the verse: '"Shout down the beast of the reeds, the congregation of mighty bulls among the calves of the peoples.' (Psalms 68:31) 'Shout down the beast of the reeds…' (Ibid.) refers to a reed to which Esau is attached, which is the great city of Rome, which Gabriel stuck as a reed in the great sea, which is a secret of the reed being attached to Malchut called 'the great sea', **and on it a large city Rome was built,** which is the secret of the kingdom of Esau. And it is **a reed that is** called **Chametz (leavened bread). When the Redemption comes to Israel, He will break** that reed, **as it is written: 'Shout down the beast, the congregation…' (Ibid.)** and the Chametz that is drawn from the reed **is immediately removed from the world,** with **its** *machmetzet* (מַחְמֶצֶת), namely its Female, **which is** the city **Rome, and Matzah (unleavened bread) will be revealed in the world, which is the Holy Temple of the First and Second Temple,** which are Binah and Malchut."

Se'or and Chametz cover the two eyes from seeing the Two Temples.

744. אָמַר ר"מ, דְּאִינּוּן לָקֳבֵל בַּת עַיִן יָמִין, וּבַת עַיִן שְׂמֹאל. וְאִינּוּן לָקֳבֵל רוֹמִי
רַבְּתָא, רוֹמִי זְעֵירָא. לָקֳבֵל תְּרֵין עֲנָנִין, דִּמְכַסְּיָין עַל בַּת עֵינָא יְמִינָא וּשְׂמָאלָא.
וְאִינּוּן לָקֳבֵל שְׂאוֹר וְחָמֵץ. וְעַד דְּאִלֵּין יִתְבַּעֲרוּן מֵעָלְמָא כֹּל יֵרָאֶה וּבַל יִמָּצֵא
חַד מִנַּיְיהוּ, בַּיִת רִאשׁוֹן וְשֵׁנִי לָא יִתְגַּלְיָין בְּעָלְמָא.

744. The Faithful Shepherd said, "They, the First and Second Temple, **correspond to the pupil of the right eye and the pupil of the left eye, and they correspond to the large and small Rome, corresponding to the two clouds that cover the pupils of the right** eye **and of the left** eye. **They,** in turn, **correspond to leaven (se'or) and leavened bread**

(*chametz*). And as long as these are not removed from the world, not to be seen or not to be found, the First and Second Temple are unable to be revealed in the world."

The two Messiahs will remove the two Klipot.

745. וְאַסְוָותָא דַּעֲנָנָא עֵינָא, דְּאַחֲשִׁיךְ לְבַת עֵינָא יָמִין וּשְׂמֹאל, מַה יְהֵא אַסְוָותָא דִּלְהוֹן. מָרָה דְּעֶגְלָא. וְהַיְינוּ שָׁם יִרְעֶה עֵגֶל וְשָׁם יִרְבָּץ. שָׁם יִרְעֶה עֵגֶל, דָּא מָשִׁיחַ בֶּן יוֹסֵף, דְּאִתְּמַר בֵּיהּ בְּכוֹר שׁוֹרוֹ הָדָר לוֹ. וְשָׁם יִרְבָּץ, דָּא מָשִׁיחַ בֶּן דָּוִד. חַד אַעְבָּר רוֹמִי רַבָּתִי. וְחַד אַעְבָּר רוֹמִי זְעֵירְתָּא. דְּמִיכָאֵל וְגַבְרִיאֵ"ל לָקֳבְלַיְיהוּ אִינּוּן.

745. He asks: "And what healing will there be for the clouds that darken the pupils of the right and left eyes? What will be their remedy?" He answers: "It is the gall of a calf, as in: '…there shall the calf feed, and there shall he lie down….' (Isaiah 27:10) '…there shall the calf feed…' refers to Messiah son of Joseph, about whom it is said: 'His firstborn ox, glory to him…' (Deuteronomy 33:17), which is the secret of the face of the ox from the left side. '…and there shall he lie down…' refers to Messiah son of David. One removes the large Rome, namely Messiah son of David, and the other removes the small Rome, namely Messiah son of Joseph; and corresponding to them are Michael and Gabriel, where Michael corresponds to Messiah son of David and Gabriel to Messiah son of Joseph.

Explanation: the large Rome and the small Rome are two Klipot that correspond to Binah and Malchut of Holiness. They are two clouds, Right and Left, Male and Female, which darken the Light of Chochmah that is drawn from the pupil of the eye. They are the secret of the "beast of the reeds" that was mentioned in verse 741, as they draw Chochmah from above downward, thus covering the Lights of Malchut. The remedy for this is to reduce the Upper Three of the Left, as explained there. This is: "What will be their remedy? It is the gall of a calf," because the gall is the secret of the Female Judgments that diminish the Upper Three of the Left.

The leg of the Kof goes down to death, and eventually it will be broken.

746. וּבְגִין דָּא ו', דְּאִיהוּ חוּטָא זְעֵירָא, תָּבַר לָהּ, וְיֵיעוֹל ה' בְּאַתְרָהָא. דִּבְקַדְמֵיתָא קָנֶה וָסוּף קָמֵלוּ. קָנֶה שָׁלְטָנוּתָא דְּרוֹמִי, וָסוּף לְכָל מַלְכִין, דְּעָתִיד קוּדְשָׁא בְּרִיךְ הוּא לְתַּבְּרָא לֵיהּ. גְּעַר חַיַּת קָנֶה, גְּעַר חַיָּה בִּישָׁא, ו' מִן חָמֵץ, וְאַתְּבַּר רַגְלֵיהּ מִן מַחְמֶצֶת, דְּאִתְּמַר בָּהּ רַגְלֶיהָ יוֹרְדוֹת מָוֶת. וְעוֹד גְּעַר חַיַּת קָנֶה, יַתְבַּר רֶגֶל קוֹף מִן קָנֶה, וְיִשְׁתְּאַר הִנֵּה. מִיָּד הִנֵּה יְיָ' אֱלֹהִים בְּחָזָק יָבֹא, רִאשׁוֹן לְצִיּוֹן הִנֵּה הִנָּם וְלִירוּשָׁלַם מְבַשֵּׂר אֶתֵּן. הִנֵּה: ס' בָּתַר אֶלֶף וּמָאתָן.

746. "And hence the Chet (ח), which is a thin thread, is broken, and is replaced with a Hei (ה), turning the Chametz (חומץ) into Matzah (מצה). For initially, '...the reeds and rushes (*suf*) shall wither' (Isaiah 19:6) 'Reeds' refers to the rule of Rome, which is the last (*sof*) of all the kings, and which in the future the Holy One, blessed be He, will break. 'Shout down the beast of the reeds...' (Psalms 68:31) means rebuking the wicked beast, which is the Chet of Chametz, and the foot of the Chet of *machmetzet* (מחמצת) is broken, of which it is said: 'Her feet go down to death....' (Proverbs 5:5) Moreover, 'Shout down the beast of the reeds' (Ibid.) means that He will break the foot of the Kof (ק) of *kaneh* (קנה), and *hineh* (behold; הנה) remains. Immediately, 'Behold (*hineh*), the Lord God will come with might...' (Isaiah 40:10) and 'A harbinger to Zion will I give: "Behold, behold them (*hineh hinam*); and to Jerusalem a messenger of good tidings."' (Isaiah 41:27) The numerical value of *hineh* is sixty, namely sixty years after the year 1200 all these verses will be fulfilled.

Vayetze

22. His thought was with Rachel

A Synopsis

Jacob thought of Rachel while making love with Leah. This act cost Reuben his patrimony. This is a very important and insightful passage that illuminates the relation of thought to action. Wisdom can be seen on a man's face and in his eyes. On the other hand, whoever indulges in evil contemplation lives in lies or false consciousness. Such a person is not able to see good when it comes. Accordingly, bad acts follow bad contemplation.

The Relevance of this Passage

Consciousness creates reality. For this reason, the Other Side attempts to raise doubts, create uncertainties, and induce immoral and negative thinking. The great gift of contemplation and consciousness even has the power to determine the grade of soul that is drawn to an unborn child at the moment of conception. The spiritual influences of this passage help us abolish doubts and negative thoughts, particularly during moments of intimacy and times of adversity. It is then that we are most vulnerable, and it is then that the Other Side unleashes a mind storm of negativity.

The Creator brought Israel closer through the bread of poverty.

219. פָּתַח רַבִּי חִיָּיא וַאֲמַר, בָּרִאשׁוֹן בְּאַרְבָּעָה עָשָׂר יוֹם לַחֹדֶשׁ בָּעֶרֶב תֹּאכְלוּ מַצֹּת, וּכְתִיב שִׁבְעַת יָמִים תֹּאכַל עָלָיו מַצּוֹת לֶחֶם עֹנִי, לֶחֶם עֹנִי כְּתִיב, הַאי מִלָּה אִתְעָרוּ בָּהּ חַבְרַיָּיא. אֲבָל תָּא חֲזֵי, כַּד הֲווֹ יִשְׂרָאֵל בְּמִצְרַיִם, הֲווֹ בִּרְשׁוּתָא אָחֳרָא, כַּד בָּעָא קוּדְשָׁא בְּרִיךְ הוּא לְקָרְבָא לוֹן לְגַבֵּיהּ, יָהַב לוֹן אֲתַר דְּלֶחֶם עֹנִי. לֶחֶם עֹנִי, מַאן עֹנִי, דָּא דָּוִד מַלְכָּא, דִּכְתִיב בֵּיהּ כִּי עָנִי וְאֶבְיוֹן אָנִי.

219. Rav Chiya began the discussion with the verses, "'In the first month, on the fourteenth day of the month at evening, shall you eat

unleavened bread…' (Exodus 12:18) and '…seven days shall you eat
upon it unleavened bread, the bread of affliction (lit. 'of poverty')….'
(Deuteronomy 16:3) Note that 'bread of poverty (oni; עֹנִי)' is spelled
without the letter Vav (ו). **The friends were already engaged on this
account. But come and behold, when Israel were in Egypt, they
were under a foreign domain. When the Holy One, blessed be He,
wanted to bring them near to Him, He gave them the grade of the
bread of poverty."** He asks: **"Who is the poor referred to in, 'bread
of poverty' (Ibid.)?"** He answers: **"He is King David, of whom it is
written, '…for I am poor and needy.' (Psalms 86:1)**

Explanation: King David is the secret of the Nukva when She receives
the Illumination of the Left from Binah, as then She is in equal stature to
Zeir Anpin in the secret of the Fourth Leg of the Throne—Binah. Then
the Nukva is cleaved to Binah and does not unite with Her husband
Zeir Anpin. Thus She is poor without Light and is called "bread of
poverty" (Deuteronomy 16:3) since Chochmah does not shine without
Chasadim, and then She says "…for I am poor and needy." (Psalms 86:1)
This grade of the Nukva is Her first grade. This is: **"When the Holy
One, blessed be He, wanted to bring them near to Him, He gave
them the grade of the bread of poverty."** When He took them out of
Egypt, from the domain of the Other Side, and wanted to bring them
close to Holiness, He gave them the "bread of poverty" grade of Nukva,
for it is the first grade of Nukva as explained.

First Matzah, then Mitzvah.

220. וְהַאי לֶחֶם עֹנִי אִקְרֵי מַצָּה, נוּקְבָא בְּלָא דְכוּרָא, מִסְכְּנוּתָא הֲוֵי, אִתְקְרִיבוּ
לְגַבֵּי מַצָּה בְּקַדְמֵיתָא, כֵּיוָן דְּקָרִיבוּ לוֹן יַתִּיר, עַיֵּיל לוֹן קוּדְשָׁא בְּרִיךְ הוּא,
בְּדַרְגִּין אָחֳרָנִין, וְאִתְחַבַּר דְּכוּרָא בְּנוּקְבָא. וּכְדֵין, מַצָּה כַּד אִתְחַבְּרַת
בְּדְכוּרָא, אִקְרֵי מִצְוָה, בְּתוֹסֶפֶת וא"ו, הה"ד כִּי הַמִּצְוָה הַזֹּאת, בְּגִינֵי כָּךְ,
מַצָּה בְּקַדְמֵיתָא, וּלְבָתַר מִצְוָה.

220. "This bread of poverty is called Matzah (מצה), without the letter Vav, Zeir Anpin, **because the Female without the Male is poor**, for She lacks Chasadim, as explained in the previous paragraph. **First,** Israel **approached the** aspect of **Matzah,** being the first grade. **After He brought them a bit closer, the Holy One, blessed be He, brought them to other grades, and the Male joined the Female,** that is, She was united with Zeir Anpin and received Chasadim from Him. **Then, when Matzah was united with the Male, it was called Precept (***Mitzvah;* **מצוה) with the letter Vav,** for it alludes to Zeir Anpin. **This is the meaning of the verse, 'For this commandment....'** (Deuteronomy 30:11) **Therefore, in Her first** grade **She is called Matzah, and afterwards** in other grades, **She is called Precept (Mitzvah)."**

Matzah from the land of the living, and Manna from Heaven.

224. אָמַר רִבִּי וְיָיא, וַדַּאי עַל הַאי קְרָא דַּאֲמַרְתְּ, דָּכִירְנָא דְּאוֹלִיפְנָא מִסָּבָאי, חַד מִלָּה עִלָּאָה, בְּפֶסַח, דְּיָהַב לוֹן קוּדְשָׁא בְּרִיךְ הוּא לְיִשְׂרָאֵל לֶחֶם דָּא, בְּאַרְעָא דְּחַיֵּי, וּלְבָתַר לֶחֶם מִן הַשָּׁמַיִם, לֶחֶם דָּא, וְהָא אוּקִימְנָא מִלָּה.

224. Rav Chiya said, "Assuredly, regarding this verse you quoted I remember learning about a Supernal matter concerning Pesach from my grandfather. The Holy One, blessed be He, gave Israel this bread, the secret of Mochin, **from the land of the living,** namely the Nukva called Matzah. **Later, this bread became bread from the Heaven,** namely from Zeir Anpin called Heaven. **This has already been explained."**

Vayechi

33. The world is judged four times a year

A Synopsis

Rav Yehuda discusses the four times of the year that the world is judged. During these four times of the year, Chesed, Gevurah, Tiferet, and Malchut are present to judge the world. We learn of the significance of corn to the Judgment on Pesach (Passover), the significance of the fruits of the tree to the Judgment on Shavuot, and the significance of water to the Judgment on Sukkot. We are also told that Rosh Hashanah is the head of God's year, and it is the time when all the inhabitants of the world pass before God. Finally, Rav Yosi reminds us that man's deeds are recorded every day. Each morning his soul entreats him to repent and to follow the righteous path. Those who ignore this warning will have their deeds recorded. Only the righteous have nothing to fear in this world and in the World to Come.

The Relevance of this Passage

The awesome power of the major holidays and their particular rituals is released into our world, helping us atone for our sins, lessen judgments decreed against us, and transform our inner character. Relative to the degree of atonement in our heart, this passage helps us alter our destiny in positive ways by controlling the seed and "head of God's year." Awareness of the importance of atonement and spiritual growth is deepened in our consciousness, inspiring us to pursue self-transformation for the purpose of achieving closeness to the Light of the Creator

Matzah is the starting point for Israel to enter the Holy Portion.

353. תָּאנָא, אָמַר ר' יְהוּדָה, בְּמַתְנִיתָא דִּילָן אוּקִימְנָא, הָא דְּתָנִינָן בְּאַרְבָּעָה פְּרָקִים בַּשָּׁנָה הָעוֹלָם נְדוֹן, בַּפֶּסַח עַל הַתְּבוּאָה, בַּעֲצֶרֶת עַל פֵּירוֹת הָאִילָן, בְּרֹאשׁ הַשָּׁנָה כָּל בָּאֵי הָעוֹלָם עוֹבְרִים לְפָנָיו כִּבְנֵי מָרוֹן, וּבֶחַג נְדוֹנִין עַל הַמַּיִם,

הָא אוֹקִימְנָא מִלֵּי, וְרָזָא דְּמַתְנִיתָא אוֹקִימְנָא, בְּפֶסַח עַל הַתְּבוּאָה וכו', לְקָבֵיל רְתִיכָא עִלָּאָה, רָזָא דַּאֲבָהָן, וְדָוִד מַלְכָּא. בְּפֶסַח עַל הַתְּבוּאָה, דְּהָכֵי הוּא מַמָּשׁ, וְהָא אוֹקִימְנָא מִלָּה דָּא, עַל מָה אַתְיָא מַצָּה בְּפֶסַח, וְהָא דִּינָא הוּא, דִּינָא דְּמַלְכוּתָא דִּינָא, וְדָא שֵׁירוּתָא, דְּשֵׁירָאן יִשְׂרָאֵל לְמֵיעַל בְּחוּלָקָא קַדִּישָׁא דְּקוּדְשָׁא בְּרִיךְ הוּא, וּלְבַעֲרָא מִנַּיְיהוּ חָמֵץ, דְּאִיהוּ טַעֲוָן אָחֳרָנִין, דִּי מְמַנָּן עַל עַמִּין עעכו"ם, דְּאִקְרוּן אֱלֹהִים אֲחֵרִים, אֱלֹהֵי נֵכָר, וְאִקְרוּן חָמֵץ, יֵצֶר הָרָע, וּלְמֵיעַל בְּמַצָּה, חוּלָקָא קַדִּישָׁא דְּקוּדְשָׁא בְּרִיךְ הוּא. בְּגִין כָּךְ, בְּפֶסַח נְדוֹנִין עַל הַתְּבוּאָה, וְאוֹקִימְנָא דְּעָלְמָא אִתְּדָן עַל דִּינָא דְה"א.

353. We have learned, Rav Yehuda said, "We have explained in the Baraita that the world is judged four times a year: on Pesach concerning grain; on Atzeret concerning the fruits of the tree; on Rosh Hashanah all the inhabitants of the world pass before Him like a flock of sheep; and on the festival of Sukkot they are judged concerning water. We have explained the secret of the Baraita, that grain on Pesach, corresponds to the **Supernal Chariot, the secret of the Patriarchs,** Chesed, Gevurah, and Tiferet, and King David, Malchut." In other words, these four times mentioned in the Baraita are the secret of the Patriarchs and King David. He explains, **"On Pesach concerning grain, for it is literally so. We have already explained regarding this matter: Why does Matzah come on Pesach? It is because Matzah is Judgment, and the law of the Kingdom (Malchut) is the prevailing law.** Thus, the Matzah is a law or Judgment. **This is the starting point for Israel to enter the Holy Portion of the Holy One, blessed be He, and remove the leavened bread, which is a foreign deity appointed over the idolatrous nations called other gods, foreign gods, also called leavened bread and the Evil Inclination. To enter the Matzah,** Malchut, **is to enter the Holy Portion of the Holy One, blessed be He. This is why on Pesach they are judged concerning grain,** as we explained that the world is sentenced based on the **Judgment of Hei,** Malchut, and grain (Tevuah; תבואה) is the letters of *Tavo*-Hei (תבוא ה; lit. 'Hei shall come')."

Mishpatim

18. Two Messiahs

The Left rejects and the Right brings close.

477. דְּרוֹעָא שְׂמָאלָא, אִתְּמַר בֵּיהּ, שְׂמָאל דּוֹחָה, וְיָמִין מְקָרֶבֶת. דְּאַף עַל
גַּב דְּאַקְדִּים בְּתִשְׁרֵי, דְּאוּקְמוּהָ בֵּיהּ מָארֵי מַתְנִיתִין, בְּתִשְׁרֵי עֲתִידִין לְהִגָּאֵל.
תְּהֵא דּוֹחָה, בְּגִין דְּלָא יָמוּת מָשִׁיחַ בֶּן אֶפְרַיִם, דּוֹחָה מִתִּשְׁרֵי דְּאִיהִי שְׂמָאל.
עַד דְּיִקְרַב יָמִין, פֶּסַח דְּרוֹעָא יְמִינָא. לְקַיֵּים בָּהּ, כִּימֵי צֵאתְךָ מֵאֶרֶץ מִצְרַיִם
אַרְאֶנּוּ נִפְלָאוֹת וְהַאי אִיהוּ בְּנִיסָן נִגְאֲלוּ וּבְנִיסָן עֲתִידִין לְהִגָּאֵל. לְקַיֵּים בְּהוֹן
וּבְחֶסֶד עֶלְיוֹן רִחַמְתִּיךְ אָמַר גּוֹאֲלֵךְ יְיָ'.

477. Of the left arm, Gevurah, it is said, "The left pushes aside, the right brings near." (Tractate Sotah 47a) Even though he sped **up** the time for Redemption **to the month of Tishrei, as the masters of Mishnah have established "in Tishrei they are destined to be redeemed"** (Tractate Rosh Hashanah 11a), nevertheless since Tishrei is the Left of the months **it will push aside** the Redemption **so that the Messiah son of Ephraim will not die** by the Judgments of the Left. For the Messiah son of Ephraim is the reincarnation of Yaravam who has Accusers upon him for sinning and causing others to sin. **Therefore, it is pushed aside from Tishrei, which is Left, until the Right brings new,** namely **Pesach, the Right Arm,** Chesed. Then they will be redeemed **to fulfill the verse, "As in the days of your coming out of the land of Egypt, I will show him marvelous things." (Micah 7:15) Hence, "they were redeemed in Nissan, and in Nissan will they again be redeemed," (Tractate Rosh Hashanah 11b) to fulfill the prophecy, "'...but with everlasting Love will I have Mercy on you,' says the Lord, your Redeemer." (Isaiah 54:8)**

Messiah son of Josef is destined to obliterate the wicked.

479. אֲבָל בְּדַרְגָּא דְּמָשִׁיחַ בֶּן יוֹסֵף, אִיהוּ דְּקָא רָמִיז, עַתָּה יְלַחֲכוּ הַקָּהָל אֶת
כָּל סְבִיבֹתֵינוּ כִּלְחוֹךְ הַשּׁוֹר אֵת יֶרֶק הַשָּׂדֶה. דְּעָלַיְיהוּ אִתְּמַר, בִּפְרֹחַ רְשָׁעִים
כְּמוֹ עֵשֶׂב וְגוֹ'. מִפֶּסַח וְעַד תִּשְׁרֵי, יְהֵא פּוּרְקָנָא דְּאִיהוּ עַד. וּמִתַּמָּן וְאֵילָךְ
יְהֵא הַשְׁמָדָה דִּלְהוֹן, לְהִשָּׁמְדָם עֲדֵי עַד. כַּד מָטוּ לְתִשְׁרֵי דְּאִיהוּ שׁוֹר, בֵּיהּ
כִּלְחוֹךְ הַשּׁוֹר.

479. But about the level of Messiah son of Joseph the verse alludes
to, "…Now this congregation will lick up everything around us, as
the ox licks up the grass of the field…" (Numbers 22:4) referring to
Messiah son of Joseph, who is called "Ox." **About them, it is written:
"When wicked spring like grass…." (Psalms 92:8) From Pesach
until Tishrei will be the Redemption** called "forever" (*ad*; עַד) **from
then on will come their destruction, as it is written: "…that they shall
be destroyed forever (*adei ad*; עֲדֵי עַד)" (Ibid.) until Tishrei arrives,
which is an Ox, and then "…as the ox licks…" (Numbers 22:4) will
be fulfilled.**

Tetzaveh

5. Giving a portion to the Other Side

A Synopsis

We read that if Job had given a portion to everyone then the Accuser or negative force would not have been able to approach him later. Rav Shimon says that when the Other Side is given a proper portion, it removes itself from the Sanctuary; therefore the side of Holiness rises higher and higher. God aroused the Accuser against Job because of his incorrect offering. We are told that God united with Israel in Egypt at Pascal while the Other Side was occupied with Job. Regarding the unleavened bread, Rav Shimon says that the Evil Inclination in a person is like yeast in a dough; it enters the belly of a person slowly and then multiples there until the whole body is mixed with it. This is idolatry.

Eating Chametz on Pesach is akin to idol worshipping.

49. כְּתִיב אֱלֹהֵי מַסֵּכָה לֹא תַעֲשֶׂה לָךְ, וּכְתִיב בַּתְרֵיהּ אֶת חַג הַמַּצּוֹת תִּשְׁמֹר. מַאי הַאי לְגַבֵּי הַאי. אֶלָּא הָכִי אוּקְמוּהָ, מַאן דְּאָכִיל חָמֵץ בְּפֶסַח כְּמַאן דְּפָלַח לכו"ם אִיהוּ.

49. It is written: "You shall make you no molten gods" (Exodus 34:17), followed by, "The feast of unleavened bread (Matzot) shall you keep...." (Ibid. 18) He asks: "Why is one adjacent to the other?" He answers: "This is what has been explained, that whoever eats leaven (Chametz) on Pesach, it is as if he worships idols.

The Evil Inclination is like yeast that slowly expands.

50. ת"ח, כַּד נָפְקוּ יִשְׂרָאֵל מִמִּצְרַיִם נָפְקוּ מֵרְשׁוּ דִּלְהוֹן, מֵרְשׁוּ אַחֲרָא, מֵהַהוּא רְשׁוּ דְּאִקְרֵי חָמֵץ, נַהֲמָא בִּישָׁא. וְעַ"ד אִקְרֵי כו"ם הָכִי, וְדָא אִיהוּ רָזָא דְיֵצֶר הָרָע, פּוּלְחָנָא נוּכְרָאָה, דְּאִקְרֵי אוּף הָכִי שְׂאוֹר. וְדָא אִיהוּ יֵצֶר הָרָע, דְּהָכִי

אִיהוּ יֵצֶר הָרָע בְּבַר נָשׁ, כִּחֲמִיר בְּעִיסָה, עָאל בִּמְעוֹי דְּבַר נָשׁ זְעֵיר זְעֵיר,
וּלְבָתַר אַסְגֵּי בֵּיה, עַד דְּכָל גּוּפָא אִתְעֲרַב בַּהֲדֵיה. וְדָא אִיהוּ כּו"ם. וְעַל דָּא
כְּתִיב, לֹא יִהְיֶה בְךָ אֵל זָר. אֵל זָר וַדַּאי.

50. "Come and behold, when Israel left Egypt, they left their
jurisdiction, namely the rule of the other Side, the rule that is called
'leaven,' evil bread. Therefore, idol worship is called by that name,
Chametz (Leaven). This is the secret of the Evil Inclination that is idol
worship, which is also called yeast (se'or). This is the Evil Inclination
because the Evil Inclination in the person is like yeast in a dough.
It enters the belly of the person slowly and then multiplies there
until the whole body is mixed with it. This is idolatry. Therefore,
it is written: 'There shall be no strange god (El) among you...'
(Psalms 81:10), assuredly a strange god (El).

SEVENTH DAY
OF PESACH

BESHALACH

11. "And the Angel of God... moved"

A Synopsis

This passage contains an obscure but beautiful description of the energy flow on the Supernal levels, the sea with its waves of Judgments rising and falling, the angels who are the fish of that sea, and the four directions of the world. It ends by saying: Let those who have wings stand firm. Let those who have faces cover their faces until He departs on His journeys. Then, "And the Angel of God... moved...." (Exodus 14:19)

With the seventy-two letters, the stones returned to their place.

תּוֹסֶפְתָּא

134. וַיִּסַּע מַלְאַךְ הָאֱלֹהִים וְגוֹ'. (מַתְנִיתִין) עַד לָא אִשְׁתְּכַח אֲוֵירָא דַּכְיָא, וְלָא נְהִירִין, אֲבָנִין נְקִיבָן הֲווֹ סְתִימָאן. תְּלַת רוּחִין דְּכְלִילָן בִּתְלַת, הֲווֹ שְׁקִיעָן. וּמַיִין סְתִימָן תְּחוֹת נוּקְבֵי. בְּשַׁבְעִין וּתְרֵין אַתְוָון אִתְהַדָּרוּ לְאַתְרַיְיהוּ אִינּוּן אֲבָנִין.

Tosefta (Addendum)

134. "And the Angel of God... moved...." (Exodus 14:19) Mishnah: Before there was pure air and before it shone, the punctured stones were clogged. Three winds that are included in three were submerged, and water was concealed under the holes. With the seventy-two letters, these stones returned to their place.

The three times seventy-two letters became one group.

135. בָּתַר שַׁבְעִין וּתְרֵין דַּרְגִּין, וְכֵן תְּלַת זִמְנִין, אִתְבָּקְעוּ וְאִתְנְקִיבוּ אֲבְנֵי, תְּחוֹת צְרוֹרָא דַּהֲוָה זָקִיק, וְאִתְכְּנָפוּ דַּרְגִּין, וְאִתְעֲבִידוּ כְּנוּפְיָא חֲדָא.

135. After the seventy-two levels, which are three times seventy-two letters, **the stones were split and punctured under an engraved bundle. And the levels gathered together and became one group.**

The division into two levels, where part when up and part went down.

136. לְבָתַר אִתְפְּלְגוּ, וְאִתְעָבִידוּ תְּרֵין דַּרְגִּין, פַּלְגוּתָא מַיָּא אַגְלִידוּ, וּפַלְגוּתָא אִשְׁתְּקָעוּ. אִלֵּין סְלִיקוּ, וְאִלֵּין נַחֲתוּ, מֵהָכָא שָׁרָא עָלְמָא לְאִתְפַּלְגָא.

136. **Afterwards, they divided and became two levels** of water. **Half of the water congealed and half of it sank. Part went up and part went down. From here, the world started to divide.**

The four directions: Chesed, Gevurah, Tiferet, and Malchut.

137. צְרוֹרָא אַחֲרָא אִית לְעֵילָּא, וְהוּא גְּלִיפָא בְּעַ"ב וְחָתִימָן דְּגוּשְׁפַּנְקָא תַּקִּיפָא, וּבְהוּ שִׁקְיעָן גַּלְגַּלּוֹי דְּיַמָּא. כַּד נַטְלִין, אִתְפְּלְגוּ לְאַרְבַּע זַוְיָין. פַּלְגוּ וְחַד סָלִיק, וּפַלְגוּ וְחַד נָחִית, פַּלְגוּ וְחַד לְסִטַר צָפוֹן, וּפַלְגוּ וְחַד לְסִטַר דָּרוֹם. כַּד מִתְחַבְּרָן כַּחֲדָא, גּוּמְרִין דְּלַהֲטִין קַיָּימִין, בְּלַהֲט שִׁנָּנָא דְּחַרְבָּא דְּמִתְהַפְּכָא.

137. **There is another bundle Above that is engraved with seventy-two Seals of the strong Seal Ring, and in these the waves of the sea are submerged. When they travel, they divide to four corners. One part rises,** for it illuminates from below upward, namely the Nukva, which is the secret of west. **One part descends,** for it illuminates from above downward with the Light of Chasadim, namely Zeir Anpin, which is the secret of east. **One part toward the north,** which is the Left Column, Gevurah, **and one part toward the south,** which is the Right Column, Chesed. **When they unite together, there are flaming coals in the blade of the Revolving Sword.**

The wind blows on the Judgments of the waves.

138. חַד קַיְימָא נָעִיץ בְּגוֹ יַמָּא, דַּרְגָּא שְׁלִיחָא דְּאַפַּרְכָא עִלָּאָה, סָלִיק בְּהַהוּא קַיְימָא לְעֵילָּא לְעֵילָּא, אִסְתַּכַּל לְמֵרָחֲוִיק, קְטוּרָא דְּאַרְבִּין דְּשָׁאטִין בְּיַמָּא. מַאן חָמֵי גַּלְגַּלִּין דְּסַלְקִין וְנַחְתִּין וְרוּחָא דְּנָשְׁיב בְּהוּ, וְנוּנֵי יַמָּא נַגְדִין כָּל אִינּוּן אַרְבִּין לְכָל סִטְרֵי עָלְמָא.

138. One pillar is thrust into the sea. The level, which is a messenger of the Supernal state, which is Malchut that is from the chest and higher, **rises in this pillar higher and higher, and looks at a distance** to see **a band of ships floating in the sea. Who observes the waves rising and falling** because of the Judgments that they contain, **and the wind,** which is the Central Column, **blows on them** and quiets them, **and the fish of the sea,** who are the angels, **pull all these ships in all directions of the world.** In this manner is Chochmah revealed.

Metatro"n draws Chochmah and then sits like a king on his throne.

139. הַהוּא דַּרְגָּא, כַּד נָחִית מֵהַהוּא, קַיְימֵי אֶלֶף בִּימִינֵיהּ, וְאֶלֶף בִּשְׂמָאלֵיהּ, הֲוָה תָב וְיָתִיב בְּאַתְרֵיהּ, כְּמַלְכָּא בְּכוּרְסְיֵהּ, הַהוּא דַּרְגָּא דְּכַד שָׁאטֵי יַמָּא לְאַרְבַּע סִטְרֵי עָלְמָא, עִמֵּיהּ נַפְקַת, בֵּיהּ תֵּבַת, הוּא תָב בְּקִיּוּמָא דְּמַלְכָּא.

139. When that level, namely Metatro"n, **descended** from above the chest, **a thousand stand at his right and a thousand stand at his left,** meaning that he draws Chochmah, alluded to in the number 1,000, both on his right and on his left. **And he returns** from the chest and below, **and sits in his place like a king on his throne. When the sea,** which is Malchut, **swims to the four directions of the world, that level goes out with it and returns with it, and it returns with the establishing of the king.**

An announcement is made.

140. כְּדֵין כָּרוֹזִין נָפְקִין, מַאן מָארֵי דְעַיְינִין, יְזַדְקְפָאן לוֹן לְעֵילָא לְעֵילָא. מָארֵיהוֹן דְּגַדְפִין יְקוּמוּן בְּקִיּוּמַיְיהוּ. מָארֵי דְאַנְפִּין, יַחְפְּיָין לוֹן, עַד דְּנָטִיל בְּמַטְלָנוֹי. כְּדֵין וַיִּסַּע מַלְאַךְ הָאֱלֹהִים.
(עַד כָּאן)

140. Then announcements are made. Let him, who is of those who have eyes, raise them higher and higher. Let those who have wings stand firm. Let those who have faces cover their faces until He departs on His journeys. Then, "And the Angel of God... moved...." (Exodus 14:19)
(End of Tosefta)

Beshalach

14. "And moved... And it came... And stretched out..."

A Synopsis

Rav Aba tells us that at the moment of the Splitting of the sea the moon, Malchut, became attired on one side with the Crowns of Supernal Chesed, on the Left Side by the spears of Gevurah and on the Third Side by a purple garment called Tiferet. The number seventy-two is used repeatedly for emphasis and to draw together the various concepts. The seventy-two Crowns in each of the Three Columns are combined in Malchut, and the Holy Name ascends from them, which is the secret of the Chariot. Rav Aba explains how the seventy-two letters are written and arranged. We learn that the Holy One, blessed be He, is perfect because He encompasses the Left Side and the Right Side and we must never forget that Judgment is part of His concealed nature, so we must be careful not to incur it.

Rav Yitzchak returns to the time when Israel were trapped on the seashore with the enemy behind and the sea in front, and says that their prayers and cries to God awakened the collective Light of Above, and the sea executed the Supernal Laws. Rav Shimon adds that when the world needs Mercy, the Holy One, blessed be He, takes pity and listens.

The Right Column of the Seventy-Two Names.

160. תָּא חֲזֵי, בְּהַהִיא שַׁעֲתָא אִשְׁתְּלִים סִיהֲרָא מִכֹּלָּא, וְיָרְתָא שַׁבְעִין וּתְרֵין שְׁמָהָן קַדִּישִׁין, בִּתְלַת סִטְרִין. חֲדָא אִתְלַבְּשָׁא בְּעַטְרוֹי דְּחֶסֶד עִלָּאָה, בְּשַׁבְעִין גְּלִיפִין דִּנְהִירוּ דְּאַבָּא עִלָּאָה, דְּאַנְהִיר לָהּ.

160. Come and see, at that moment the moon, Malchut, **became full in all** aspects **and inherited Seventy-Two Holy Names on three**

sides, namely Three Columns. **On one side,** Malchut **was attired with the Crowns of the Supernal Chesed, with seventy engravings of the Light of Supernal Aba illuminating Her,** which is the secret of "And moved (*vayisa*)...." (Exodus 14:19)

The Left Column of the Seventy-Two Names.

161. סְטְרָא תִּנְיָינָא, אִתְלַבְּשַׁת בְּרוּמְחֵי דִּגְבוּר"ה, בְּשִׁתִּין פּוּלְסֵי דְּנוּרָא, וַעֲשָׂרָה דִּילָהּ דְּנָחֲתוּ מִסְּטְרָא דְּאִמָּא עִלָּאָה בְּנִימוּסֵי גְּלִיפִין.

161. On the Second Side, Malchut **was attired with the spears of Gevurah,** meaning the Judgments in Her, **by sixty lashes of fire and ten** lashes **of Her own that descended from the side of Supernal Ima in engraved Judgments.** And this is the secret of the Left Column and the verse: "And it came (*vayavo*)...." (Exodus 14:20)

The Central Column of the Seventy-Two Names.

162. סְטְרָא תְּלִיתָאֵי, אִתְלַבְּשַׁת בִּלְבוּשֵׁי אַרְגְּוָנָא, דְּלָבִישׁ מַלְכָּא עִלָּאָה קַדִּישָׁא, דְּאִקְרוּן תִּפְאֶר"ת, דְּיָרִית בְּרָא קַדִּישָׁא, בְּשַׁבְעִין עִטְרִין עִלָּאִין, מִסְּטְרָא דְּאַבָּא וְאִמָּא, וְהוּא כָּלִיל לְהַאי סְטְרָא וּלְהַאי סְטְרָא.

162. On the third side, Malchut **was attired in a purple garment that the Supernal King, called Tiferet, wore and which the Holy Son,** who is Tiferet, **inherited with the 70 Supernal Crowns from the side of Aba and Ima. He includes this side and that side,** namely the Right, which is Chesed, and the Left, which is Gevurah, which is the secret of "And stretched out (*vayet*)...." (Exodus 14:21)

Explanation of the matter: The root of the Columns are in Binah. The Right column in Her is called Supernal Aba, the Left Column in Her is called Supernal Ima, and the Central Column in Her is Tiferet that mediates between them. This is the secret of "Three come out of one..."

(Zohar, Beresheet A 363), and all the greatness that the Lower causes the Upper is acquired by the Lower as well, so "...one is found with three" (Ibid.) and Tiferet also merits the two Lights, Right and Left, of Aba and Ima. Afterwards, when Tiferet achieves the Three Columns, two from Aba and Ima and one from His own, He gives them to Malchut. In verse 160, this is: **"the moon became full in all, and inherited Seventy-Two Holy Names"** because these Three Columns are the secret of the three verses: *Vayisa...*, *Vayavo...*, *Vayet...* (Exodus 14:19-21), within each of which are seventy-two letters, and the combination of them together creates Seventy-Two Holy Names, which is one letter from each of the three verses. This is: **"On one side... the Light of Supernal Aba,"** which is the Right Column of Binah that shines to Chesed of Tiferet. Malchut was attired with the Crowns of this Supernal Chesed of Tiferet, and it is the secret of the verse: *Vayisa....* (Exodus 14:19)

From Gevurah of Tiferet She also receives the Illumination of the Left Column from Supernal Ima, which is called **"sixty lashes of fire,"** in the secret of the verse "...sixty mighty men surround it...." (Song of Songs 3:7) Thus "Malchut **was attired with the spears of Gevurah,"** namely the Gevurah within Tiferet, **"by sixty lashes...from the side of supernal Ima,"** as Tiferet receives them from the Left Column of Supernal Ima, and is the secret of the verse: *Vayavo....* (Exodus 14:20) She also receives from Tiferet of Tiferet, meaning the actual aspect of the Central Column. Thus **"On the third side,** Malchut **was attired in a purple garment"** because since it is the Central Column, it includes two colors, white and red, whose combination is the secret of the color purple, **"which the Holy Son inherited... from the side of Aba and Ima,"** which are the two Columns of Binah, which He inherited in the secret of "three come out of one, one is found with three," (Zohar, Beresheet A 363), as mentioned earlier.

Know that in reality the two Columns, Right and Left, in Binah are called Chochmah and Binah but their Names were changed to Aba and

Ima. We need to understand why their Names were changed to Aba and Ima, and we also need to understand why Tiferet, the Central Column, is called their Son. Usually, the Lights develop as a chain one from the other, in the secret of cause and effect in gradual order. But here the Lights emerged not in gradual order, since one correction was made where Malchut ascended to Binah, and Binah received the form of the limited Malchut. Thus [Binah's] Binah-Tiferet-Malchut descended to the grade of Zeir Anpin. Therefore during Gadlut, when Binah elevates Her Binah-Tiferet-Malchut from the grade of Zeir Anpin, Zeir Anpin too elevates with them to the place of Binah. Through this, a Central Column is created there, which receives the Lights of Binah, even though according to the gradual order Zeir Anpin is not worthy at all to receive and shine like Binah. Since this Light reached Zeir Anpin outside the gradual order, but only due to the descension of the Binah-Tiferet-Malchut of Binah and them elevating Zeir Anpin to the place of Binah, and also due to the matter of "three are found in one..." (Zohar, Beresheet A 363), therefore this Light is called Newborn Light and not by way of the gradual development of cause and effect. Thus Zeir Anpin is called Son, namely Newborn Light, and Chochmah and Binah are called Aba and Ima (Father and Mother) because they birthed this Light called Zeir Anpin.

Two witnesses, two scribes, and two colors.

163. וּתְרֵין עֲטָרִין מִסִּטְרָא דְּאַבָּא וְאִימָא, וְאִינוּן שַׁבְעִין וּתְרֵין שְׁמָהָן. וְתָגֵינָן בְּסִטְרָא דְּחֶסֶ"ד שַׁבְעִין, וּתְרֵין סָהֲדִין. בְּסִטְרָא דִגְבוּרָא שַׁבְעִין, וּתְרֵין סוֹפְרִין. בְּסִטְרָא דְת"ת שַׁבְעִין, וּתְרֵין גַּוְונִין לְאִתְפָּאֲרָא.

163. There are two Crowns from the side of Aba and Ima, which are Seventy-Two Names. We learned that there are seventy from the side of Chesed plus two witnesses. From the side of Gevurah, there are seventy plus two scribes. From the side of Tiferet, there are seventy plus two colors for glorification.

Explanation: The previous paragraph explains that Tiferet, Zeir Anpin, bestows 70 Crowns from each Column to Malchut. The reason is that even though Zeir Anpin receives the Three Columns of Binah, He nevertheless does not receive from the essence of the Upper Three of the two Columns that are in Binah, which are called Aba and Ima, but only from their Lower Seven, each of which include 10, thus three times 70 Crowns. However, according to this, why is it called Seventy-Two Names when it should be called 70 Names? This is: **"two Crowns from the side of Aba and Ima, which are Seventy-Two Names,"** because besides the 70 Crowns He receives from the two Columns in Binah that are called Aba and Ima, which are the secret of the Lower Seven Sefirot, he further receives two Crowns from the aspect of the Upper Three of Aba and Ima in the secret of "...one is found with three," (Zohar, Beresheet A 363) Because of this, Tiferet, which is the aspect of the Lower Seven, ascended and became Da'at, which is the aspect of the Upper Three. Thus because of the addition of the two Crowns of these Upper Three, it is called Seventy-Two Names.

This addition exists in each of His Three Columns, where in Chesed they are called **"two witnesses,"** in Gevurah **"two scribes"** and in Tiferet **"two colors."** The reason they are called this is like the analogy of a gift-document that has the scribe's writing and the signature of the witnesses. The main power of the gift-document is surely the writing of the scribe, who writes and specifies all the valuables the giver provides to the receiver. Nevertheless, without the signature of the witnesses the document would be worthless. Not to mention if the signature of the witnesses was there without the writing of the scribe, assuredly this would be worthless.

The Seventy-Two Names here is mainly to draw Chochmah to the Nukva, in the secret of "And traveled... And came... And stretched...." (Exodus 14:19-21) You already know that Chochmah is only drawn from the Left Column, yet it cannot shine without being clothed in Chasadim of the Right Column. Therefore the Zohar likens the two Crowns of the Left Column to **"two scribes,"** as the scribe's writing is the main power of the document. And it likens the two Crowns of the Right Column to **"two witnesses,"** since even though they add nothing to the writing of the scribe they nevertheless sustain the entire document, because without them the document is worthless. So too here, without the Chasadim the Illumination of Chochmah is worthless, as it cannot shine without Chasadim, and therefore they are called **"two witnesses."** [The Zohar] likens the two Crowns of the Central Column to **"two colors,"** the reason being that colors indicate Judgments, and the Central Column produces Judgments in the secret of the Masach of Chirik, as is known. But if they are Judgments, what relation do they have to the Upper Three to be called two Crowns? This is: **"seventy plus two colors for glorification,"** because not only do these Judgments not damage any of the Lights but the opposite—they glorify them because without them there would be no unification between the two Columns, as is known.

Seventy-two Crowns from each Column come together to form Seventy-Two Names.

164. וּבְהַאי אֲתָר, אִתְגְּלִיף חַד בְּחַד, וְאִסְתְּלִיק שְׁמָא קַדִּישָׁא, רָזָא דִּרְתִיכָא, וְהָכָא אִתְגְּלִיפוּ אֲבָהָתָא, לְאִתְחַבְּרָא בְּחַד, וְהוּא שְׁמָא קַדִּישָׁא גְּלִיפָא בְּאַתְווֹי.

164. In this place, namely Malchut, **they are engraved one in the other,** so that the seventy-two Crowns in every Column are composed of each other. **And the Holy Name emerges from them, which is the secret of the Chariot,** for they become seventy-two Names, each one consisting of three letters. **Here the Patriarchs are engraved,** which are Chesed-Gevurah-Tiferet, the Three Columns, **to be joined together. Thus is the Holy Name engraved with its** seventy-two **letters.**

The first sequence —Chesed.

165. צֵרוּפָא דְּאַתְוָון אִלֵּין, אַתְוָון קַדְמָאֵי, רְשִׁימִין כְּסִדְרָן בְּאֹרַח מֵישָׁר, בְּגִין דְּכֻלְּהוּ אַתְוָון קַדְמָאֵי אִשְׁתְּכָחוּ בְּחֶסֶ"ד, לְמֶהַךְ בְּאֹרַח מֵישָׁר, בְּסִדּוּרָא מִתַּתְקָן.

165. The combination of these letters are as follows: **the first letters,** namely the seventy-two letters in the verse, "And moved (*vayisa*)…" (Exodus 14:19) **are written in their order in a straightforward manner** since straight is an indication of Chesed **because all the first letters are in Chesed,** namely in the Right Column, **to follow a straightforward manner, in a proper order.**

8	7	6	5	4	3	2	1
מ	מ	ע	א	שׁ	ל	א	ו
ד	פ	ע	ח	ר	פ	ל	י
מ	ג	מ	ר	א	ג	ה	ס
א	י	ו	י	ל	י	י	ע
ח	ה	ד	ה	ו	מ	ם	מ
ר	ם	ה	מ	י	ח	ה	ל
י	ו	ע	ו	ל	ג	ה	א
ה	י	ג	י	ר	ה	ל	ר
מ	ע	ז	ס	מ	י	ר	ה

Scanning (right side)

Scanning (bottom)

The second sequence—Gevurah.

166. אַתְוָון תִּנְיָינֵי, רְשִׁימִין בְּגִלְגּוּלָא לְמַפְרֵעַ, בְּגִין דְּכֻלְּהוּ אַתְוָון תִּנְיָינֵי, מִשְׁתַּכְחוּ בִּגְבוּרָה, לְנַלָּאָה דִינִין וְזִינִין דְּאַתְיָין מִסִּטְרָא דִשְׂמָאלָא.

166. The second letters, namely the seventy-two letters in the verse, "And came (*vayavo*)..." (Exodus 14:20) **are written backwards,** meaning they are written from below upward, **for all the second seventy-two letters pertain to Gevurah so as to reveal Judgments and weapons that come from the Left Column.** And when they are in reverse order, they allude to Judgment.

9	ה	כ	ל	ה	ל	י	ל	ה
8	ק	ר	ב	ז	ה	א	ל	ז
7	ה	ל	י	ל	ה	ו	ל	א
6	שׁ	ר	ו	י	א	ר	א	ת
5	י	ה	ע	ג	ז	ו	ה	ח
4	י	שׁ	ר	א	ל	ו	י	ה
3	ו	ב	י	ז	מ	ח	ג	ה
2	ח	ג	ה	מ	צ	ר	י	ס
1	ו	י	ב	א	ב	י	ז	מ

Scanning

Scanning

The third sequence—Tiferet.

167. אַתְוָון תְּלִיתָאֵי, אִינּוּ אַתְוָון רְשִׁימָן, לְאַחֲזָאָה גַּוְונִין, לְאִתְעַטְּרָא בְּמַלְכָּא קַדִּישָׁא. וְכֹלָּא בֵּיהּ מִתְחַוְברָן וּמִתְקַשְׁרָן, וְהוּא אִתְעַטָּר בְּעִטְרוֹי בְּאֹרַח מֵישָׁר, וְרָשִׁים לְהַאי סְטָרָא וּלְהַאי סְטָרָא, כְּמַלְכָּא דְּאִתְעַטָּר בְּכֹלָּא.

167. The third letters, namely the seventy-two letters in the verse, "And stretched out (*vayet*)..." (Exodus 14:21) **are letters that are written to show the colors** that are the Judgments, **with which to adorn the Holy King,** which is the secret of the seventy-two colors of glorification. **They all join and are bound to Him** because He is the Central Column. **And He is adorned with His Crowns in a straightforward manner and**

makes an imprint on this side and the other side, namely to the Right Column and to the Left Column since He enables the Illumination of both, **as a King who is adorned with everything.**

8	7	6	5	4	3	2	1
י	ה	י	י	ה	ו	ד	ו
ב	י	ל	ם	י	ל	ו	י
ק	ם	ה	ע	ם	ר	ע	ט
ע	ל	ו	י	ב	י	ל	מ
ו	ח	י	ה	ר	ה	ה	שׁ
ה	ר	עׁ	כ	ו	ו	י	ה
מ	ב	ם	ל	ח	ה	ם	א
י	ה	א	ה	קׁ	א	ו	ת
ם	ו	ת	ל	ד	ת	י	י

Scanning (right side, vertical)

← Scanning

Why the third sequence is not written half straightforward and half in reverse.

168. הָכָא אִתְרְשִׁים שְׁמָא קַדִּישָׁא גְּלִיפָא בְּע"ב תֵּיבִין, דְּמִתְעַטְּרֵי בַּאֲבָהָתָא, רְתִיכָא קַדִּישָׁא עִלָּאָה. וְאִי תֵּימָא, הָנֵי אַתְוָון תְּלִיתָאֵי, מ"ט לָאו אִינּוּן כְּתִיבִין, מִנְהוֹן בְּאָרַח מֵישָׁר כְּסִדּוּרָן, וּמִנְהוֹן לְמַפְרֵעַ, לְיַשְׁרָא לְהַאי סִטְרָא, וּלְהַאי סִטְרָא, דְּהָא תָּנֵינָן, אַתָּה כּוֹנֵנְתָּ מֵישָׁרִים, קוּדְשָׁא בְּרִיךְ הוּא עָבֵד מֵישָׁרִים לִתְרֵי סִטְרֵי, וּכְתִיב וְהַבְּרִיוֹ הַתִּיכוֹן בְּתוֹךְ הַקְּרָשִׁים וְגוֹ', דָּא קוּדְשָׁא בְּרִיךְ הוּא. רִבִּי יִצְחָק אָמַר, דָּא יַעֲקֹב, וְכֹלָּא חַד.

168. Here the Holy Name is marked, engraved with seventy-two words, namely that the three times seventy-two letters in each of the Three Columns combine and join together, and they form seventy-two words, and each word contains three letters from the Three Columns, which are adorned by the Patriarchs, namely Chesed-Gevurah-Tiferet, which are the Supernal Holy Chariot. He asks: "Why are the third letters not written in two ways, part of them straightforward and part of them in reverse, to be equal to both sides? Meaning to the Right Column and to the Left Column, since it sustains the Illumination of both. Because we learned that, '...You have established equity...' (Psalms 99:4), means that the Holy One, blessed be He, establishes equity and sustains on both sides. It is written, 'And the middle bar in the midst of the boards...' (Exodus 26:28), which is the Holy One, blessed be He, namely the Central Column that sustains the two Sides. If so, it should have been written 'half straightforward,' like the Right Column, and 'half in reverse order,' like the Left Column." Rav Yitzchak said: "This is Jacob, and it is all one," because Jacob also indicates the Central Column.

Scanning ←

כהת	אכא	ללה	מהש	עלם	סיט	ילי	והו	1
הקם	הרי	מבה	יזל	ההע	לאו	אלד	הזי	2
וזהו	מלה	יייי	נלך	פהל	לוו	כלי	לאו	3
ועור	לכב	אום	ריי	שאה	ירת	האא	נתה	4
ייז	רהע	וזלם	אני	מנד	כוק	להוז	יוזו	5
מיה	עשל	ערי	סאל	ילה	וול	מיכ	ההה	6
פוי	מבה	נית	נגא	עמם	הועש	דני	והו	7
מחי	עלו	יהה	ומב	מצר	הרח	ייל	נמם	8
מום	היי	יבמ	ראה	וזבו	איע	מנק	דמב	9

The wise person guards himself from the King, even when the King is happy.

169. אֶלָּא לְמַלְכָּא דְּאִיהוּ שְׁלִים מִכֹּלָא, דַּעְתֵּיהּ שְׁלִים מִכֹּלָא, מָה אָרְחֵיהּ
דְּהַהוּא מַלְכָּא. אַנְפּוֹי נְהִירִין כְּשִׁמְשָׁא תָּדִיר, בְּגִין דְּאִיהוּ שְׁלִים. וְכַד דָּאִין,

דְּאִין לְטָב וְדָאִין לְבִישׁ. וְעַל דָּא בָּעֵי לְאִסְתַּמְּרָא מִינֵּיהּ. מַאן דְּאִיהוּ טִפְּשָׁא,
וְחָמֵי אַנְפּוֹי דְּמַלְכָּא נְהִירִין וְחַיְיכָן, וְלָא אִסְתְּמַר מִינֵּיהּ. וּמַאן דְּאִיהוּ חַכִּימָא, אַף
עַל גַּב דְּחָמֵי אַנְפּוֹי דְּמַלְכָּא נְהִירִין, אָמַר מַלְכָּא וַדַּאי שְׁלִים הוּא, שְׁלִים הוּא
מִכֹּלָּא, דַּעְתֵּיהּ שְׁלִים, אֲנָא חָמֵי דְּבַהֲהוּא נְהִירוּ, דִּינָא יָתִיב וְאִתְכַּסְיָא, אע"ג
דְּלָא אִתְחֲזֵי, דְּאִי לָאו הָכִי, לָא יְהֵא מַלְכָּא שְׁלִים, וְעַל דָּא בָּעֵי לְאִסְתַּמְּרָא.

169. He answers: "This is similar to a king who is the most complete
of all, and his mind is the most complete of all. What is the custom of
that king? His face always shines like the sun because he is complete.
And when he judges, he judges for good and for bad. Therefore
it is necessary to be guarded from him. He who is stupid sees the
shining, laughing face of the king and does not guard himself from
him. But even though he sees the face of the king shining, the wise
man says: 'The king is surely perfect and complete in everything, his
mind is whole. Yet I see that in that shine there sits Judgment but it is
concealed, [and] even though it is not visible, because otherwise the
king would not be perfect, it is therefore necessary to be cautious.'

There is always a balanced amount of Judgment, even when all looks happy.

170. כַּךְ קוּדְשָׁא בְּרִיךְ הוּא, שְׁלִים תָּדִיר בְּהַאי גַּוְונָא וּבְהַאי גַּוְונָא, אֲבָל לָא
אִתְחֲזֵי, אֶלָּא בִּנְהִירוּ דְּאַנְפִּין. וּבְגִין כַּךְ, אִינּוּן טִפְּשִׁין חַיָּיבִין לָא אִסְתַּמְּרָן מִינֵּיהּ.
אִינּוּן חַכִּימִין זַכָּאִין, אַמְרִין, מַלְכָּא שְׁלִים הוּא, אַף עַל גַּב דְּאַנְפּוֹי אִתְחֲזְיָין
נְהִירִין, דִּינָא אִתְכַּסְיָא בְּגַוֵּיהּ, בְּגִין כַּךְ בָּעֵי לְאִסְתַּמְּרָא מִינֵּיהּ.

170. "So it is with the Holy One, blessed be He. He is always perfect
in this manner and that manner, meaning in the Right Side and in the
Left Side, but He only appears with a shining face. Therefore, these
wicked fools are not cautious with Him. But the righteous wise men
say: 'The King is perfect, and even though His Face appears shining,
Judgment is concealed in it. Therefore, it is necessary to be cautious
with Him.'"

Explanation: With this he answers the question, **"Why were the seventy-two letters of the Central Column not written half straightforward and half reversed so that it can include as well the Judgments of the Left?"** The answer is that the Judgments of the Left are concealed in it, and its face is always shining and happy, like the Lights of the Right. Therefore, its letters are written only in a straightforward way, like the Right.

Judgments are only visible in Malchut.

171. אָמַר רִבִּי יְהוּדָה, מֵהָכָא, אֲנִי יְיָ' לֹא שָׁנִיתִי. לָא דָלִיגְנָא לַאֲתָר אַחֲרָא, בְּ אִתְכְּלִיל כֹּלָּא. הָנֵי תְּרֵי גַּוְונֵי בִּי אִתְכְּלִילָן, בְּגִין כָּךְ כֹּלָּא בְּאַרְחוֹ מֵישָׁר מֵישָׁר אִתְחֲזֵיָא, וְאַף עַל גַּב דְּאַתְוָון אֲחִידָן לְהַאי סְטְרָא וּלְהַאי סְטְרָא, כְּסִדְרָן כְּתִיבִין.

171. Rav Yehuda said: "From here, we can answer the question of why the seventy-two letters of the Central Column were not written half straightforward and half in reverse, since it is written, **'For I am the Lord, I do not change...'** (Malachi 3:6), meaning, **'I did not skip to a different place.** Even though the two Columns are included in Me, still in all I did not change Myself because of this to jump to the Left aspect. Rather, I remained in the Right aspect **because everything is included in Me, and these two colors,** white and red, **are included in Me,** namely in My Chasadim. The Illumination of the Left is not visible in Me but only in Malchut.' Therefore **all** the letters that are in the Central Column **appear in a straightforward way. Even though the letters are attached to both sides,** namely to the Right and Left, nevertheless **they are written in their order in a straightforward way.**

Atika Kadisha shines Chasadim to Zeir Anpin,
thus adorning the Patriarchs.

172. וַיִּסַּע מַלְאַךְ הָאֱלֹהִים הַהוֹלֵךְ לִפְנֵי מַחֲנֵה יִשְׂרָאֵל וַיֵּלֶךְ מֵאַחֲרֵיהֶם וַיִּסַּע עַמּוּד הֶעָנָן מִפְּנֵיהֶם וַיַּעֲמֹד מֵאַחֲרֵיהֶם. עַד כָּאן סְטְרָא חַד, וְחֶסֶד לְאַבְרָהָם.

אָמַר רִבִּי שִׁמְעוֹן, אֶלְעָזָר בְּרִי, תָּא וַחֲזֵי רָזָא דָא. כַּד עַתִּיקָא קַדִּישָׁא אַנְהִיר
לְמַלְכָּא, אַנְהִיר לֵיהּ, וְעַטְרִין לֵיהּ, בְּכִתְרִין קַדִּישִׁין עִלָּאִין, כַּד מָטָאן לְגַבֵּיהּ
מִתְעַטְּרֵי אֲבָהָתָא, בְּשַׁעֲתָא דְּמִתְעַטְּרֵי אֲבָהָתָא, כְּדֵין הוּא שְׁלִימוּ דְכֹלָּא.
כְּדֵין מַטְרוֹנִיתָא, נַטְלָא בְּמַטְלָנָיהָא, בְּהַהוּא שְׁלִימוּ דַּאֲבָהָתָא. וְכַד מִתְעַטְּרָא
מִכֻּלְּהוֹן, כְּדֵין אִתְחַבְּרָא, וּרְשׁוּתָא דְכֹלָּא בִּידָהָא.

172. "And the Angel of God, who went before the camp of Israel, moved and went behind them; and the pillar of the cloud went from before their faces, and stood behind them." (Exodus 14:19) Until this point is one side, Chesed to Abraham, the Right Column. Rav Shimon said: "Elazar, my son, come and see this secret. When Atika Kadisha shone upon the King, who is Zeir Anpin, He illuminated on Him and crowned Him with the Supernal Holy Crowns, which are the Light of Chasadim of Supernal Aba and Ima, the Upper Three [Sefirot]. When Chasadim reached Him, the Patriarchs, who were the Three Columns, Chesed-Gevurah-Tiferet, were adorned. Then there was complete perfection. Then the Queen went on Her journeys with that perfection of the Patriarchs. And when She becomes adorned by all, through all three Patriarchs that are the Three Columns, She is then joined and has authority over everything.

The Names are the adornment of the Patriarchs.

173. כְּגַוְונָא דָא שְׁמָא קַדִּישָׁא גְּלִיפָא בְּאַתְווֹי רְשִׁימִין בִּרְתִיכָא עִלָּאָה קַדִּישָׁא
עִטּוּרָא דַּאֲבָהָן.

173. "Similarly, the Holy Name is engraved with the letters that are imprinted on the Supernal Chariot, for they are the adornment of the Patriarchs."

Three times Uvchen in the Prayers of Rosh Hashanah and Yom Kippur.

174. אָמַר רְבִּי יֵיסָא, אַשְׁכַּחְנָא בְּרָזָא דָּא בִּתְקִיעוֹתָא דְּרַב הַמְנוּנָא סָבָא, תְּלָת וּבְכֵן וּבְכֵן, לָקֳבְלֵי הֲנֵי תְּלָת. וְכָךְ הוּא סִדּוּרָא. א"ר יוֹסֵי, כֹּלָּא אִתְכְּלִיל בְּהַאי שְׁמָא קַדִּישָׁא, וְאִסְתַּיֵּים בֵּיהּ, אִשְׁתְּכַח דִּשְׁלִימוּ דִּרְתִיכָא קַדִּישָׁא אִית בֵּיהּ.

174. Rav Yesa said: "We found this secret in the Blowing of the Shofar of Rav Hamnuna Saba three times, 'And so... And so... And so (**Uvchen... Ucvhen... Uvchen...**),' namely in, 'And so, may Your Name be sanctified...' 'And so, instill your awe...' and 'And so, give glory....' But it does not count, 'And so, shall the righteous.....' **They correspond to these three** verses, 'And moved..." "And it came..." "And stretched out....." (Exodus 14:19-21) **This is the order,** three and no more. *B'chen* (בכן; so) equals seventy-two in numerical value, so the three times *Uvchen* allude to the three Columns of the Name of seventy-two." **Rav Yosi said: "Everything is included and concealed in this Holy Name,** meaning that all Three Columns of the seventy-two Names are included in Malchut, **so we find that the perfection of the Holy Chariot is in it,** in Malchut." Therefore there are four times seventy-two: the Three Columns, Chesed-Gevurah-Tiferet, and Malchut. And also four times "And so (*Uvchen*)..." including "And so, shall the righteous...."

The Seventy-Two Names are split into three thirds.

175. אָמַר רְבִּי שִׁמְעוֹן, הַאי הוּא שְׁמָא קַדִּישָׁא, עֲטוּרָא דַּאֲבָהָן, דְּמִתְעַטְּרָא בְּגִלוּפַיְיהוּ, בְּחוֹבּוּרָא כַּחֲדָא. שְׁלִימוּ דִּרְתִיכָא קַדִּישָׁא. וְאִתְכְּלִיל בְּאַרְבְּעִין וּתְמַנְיָא תֵּיבוּתָא, דְּאִיהוּ שְׁלִימוּ דְּכֹלָּא, וְעָקָרָא דְּשָׁרְשִׁין.

175. Rav Shimon said: "This is the Holy Name, the adornment of the Patriarchs, who are Chesed-Gevurah-Tiferet. **For they become adorned in their engraving when they join together. They are the**

**perfection of the Holy Chariot, which is included in 48 words and is
the perfection of everything and the mainstay of the roots.**

Explanation: The Seventy-Two Names, which are seventy-two
combinations of three letters each, are split into thirds, since it has
Three Columns. The first-third is Chesed, Right Column; the second-
third is Gevurah, Left Column; and the third-third is Tiferet, Central
Column. It is known that the main Columns are Right and Left, which
are the aspect of the Upper Three, and the Central Column is only a
sustainer of their Illumination, and it is the aspect of the Six Corners. In
the first two-thirds, which are Chesed and Gevurah, there are 48 words.
Thus **"which is included in 48 words,"** as all the Lights of this Name
is included in the first two thirds, which are the 48 words, **"and is the
perfection of everything and the mainstay of the roots,"** since the two
Columns, Right and Left, are the completion of the entire Name and
the main aspect of the roots, as all the roots are found in them. The
lower third, which includes the 24 letters of the third Column, are only
branches of the Upper ones, as it receives from them in the secret of "one
is found with three, three are established by one." (Zohar, Beresheet
A 363)

Three sets of twenty-four, which total seventy-two.

176. תָּא חֲזֵי, גּוּפָא דְּאִילָנָא, אֲנָ"י אָלֶ"ף נוּ"ן יוֹ"ד. רֵישָׁא דְּכָל עַנְפֵי אִילָנָא,
וָה"ו. וְהָא אִתְּעֲרוּ חַבְרַיָּא, כְּלָלָא דַּעֲנָפִין וְגוּפָא וְשָׁרָשָׁא, בְּאַרְבְּעִין וּתְמַנְיָא
תֵּיבִין. וְהָא אִתְרְשִׁים בִּתְלַת עָלְמִין עָלָּאִין, וּבג' עָלְמִין תַּתָּאִין.

**176. "Come and see, the trunk of the tree is the Name Alef-Nun-
Yud,** which is found in the middle of the Seventy-Two Names, namely
the 37th Name. **The top of all the branches of the tree** is the Name
Vav-Hei-Vav, which is the first Name of the Seventy-Two Names.
**The friends have already mentioned that the whole of the branches
and the trunk and the root are found in 48 words,** meaning in the

first two-thirds of the seventy-two words. **So it is etched in the Three Upper Worlds,** Chochmah-Binah-Da'at that are included in the first 24 words, which are Chesed and Right Column, **and in the Three Lower Worlds,** Chesed-Gevurah-Tiferet that are included in the second 24 words, which are Gevurah and Left Column.

Explanation: The Three Columns—Chesed, Gevurah, and Tiferet—are composed of each other, and each one has three. So the Right Column is considered Chochmah-Binah-Da'at, the Left Column Chesed-Gevurah-Tiferet, and the Central Column Netzach-Hod-Yesod. Therefore the first two-thirds of the Seventy-Two Names are considered Chochmah-Binah-Da'at and Chesed-Gevurah-Tiferet.

The three sets of twenty-four correspond to Holy, Holy, Holy.

177. לְקֶבְלֵיהּ, קָדוֹשׁ קָדוֹשׁ קָדוֹשׁ ה' צְבָאוֹת. קָדוֹשׁ לְעֵילָּא. קָדוֹשׁ בְּאֶמְצָעִיתָא. קָדוֹשׁ לְתַתָּא. קָדוֹשׁ חֶסֶד. קָדוֹשׁ גְּבוּרָה. קָדוֹשׁ תִּפְאֶרֶת. וְכֻלְּהוּ בְּשַׁבְעִין וּתְרֵין אִתְגְּלִיפוּ, כְּמָה דְּאִתְּמַר. בְּרִיךְ הוּא, בְּרִיךְ שְׁמֵיהּ לְעָלַם וּלְעָלְמֵי עָלְמִין אָמֵן.

177. "**Corresponding to it,** to the Chesed-Gevurah-Tiferet of the Three Columns of the Name of seventy-two, **is '…Holy, Holy, Holy, is the Lord of Hosts (*Tzva'ot*)….'** (Isaiah 6:3) **'Holy' Above,** in Chochmah-Binah-Da'at, **'Holy' in the Middle,** in Chesed-Gevurah-Tiferet, **and 'Holy' Below,** in Netzach-Hod-Yesod. Also the first **'Holy' is Chesed,** the second **'Holy' is Gevurah, and** the third **'Holy' is Tiferet,** namely as was written before, that Chesed-Gevurah-Tiferet are the secret of Chochmah-Binah-Da'at, Chesed-Gevurah-Tiferet, and Netzach-Hod-Yesod. **They are all engraved in seventy-two, as explained. Blessed is He blessed is His Name forever and ever. Amen.**

The Israelites started to pray when they saw soldiers ready to attack.

178. אָמַר רִבִּי יִצְחָק, בְּשַׁעֲתָא דְּשָׁרוּ יִשְׂרָאֵל עַל יַמָּא, וְזָמוּ לְכַמָּה אֻכְלוֹסִין, לְכַמָּה חַיָּילִין, לְכַמָּה מַשִׁירְיָין, מֵעֵילָא וְתַתָּא, וְכֻלְּהוּ בְּכְנוּפְיָא עֲלַיְיהוּ דְּיִשְׂרָאֵל, שָׁרִיאוּ בְּצְלוֹ מִגּוֹ עָאקוּ דִּלְהוֹן.

178. Rav Yitzchak said: "At the time that Israel camped by the sea, they saw many multitudes, many soldiers, and many camps Above and Below. They all came and gathered against Israel, who started to pray from their anguish.

The Israelites saw trouble on all sides.

179. בֵּיהּ שַׁעֲתָא, וְזָמוּ יִשְׂרָאֵל עָאקוּ מִכָּל סִטְרִין, יַמָּא בְּגַלּוֹהִי דְּזַקְפָן קָמַיְיהוּ. בַּתְרַיְיהוּ, כָּל אִינּוּן אֻכְלוֹסִין, כָּל אִינּוּן מַשִׁירְיָין דְּמִצְרַיִם, לְעֵילָא עֲלַיְיהוּ כַּמָּה קַטֵיגוֹרִין. שָׁרִיאוּ צַוְוחִין לְקוּדְשָׁא בְּרִיךְ הוּא.

179. "At that moment, Israel saw trouble on all sides. The sea with its towering waves was in front of them, all these multitudes and all the camps of Egypt were behind them, and Above there were many Prosecutors against them. They started to cry to the Holy One, blessed be He.

The matter depended upon Atika Kadisha, not Zeir Anpin.

180. כְּדֵין כְּתִיב, וַיֹּאמֶר יְיָ' אֶל מֹשֶׁה מַה תִּצְעַק אֵלָי. וְתָאנָא בְּסִפְרָא דִּצְנִיעוּתָא, אֵלַי, דַּיְיקָא, בְּעַתִּיקָא תַּלְיָא כֹּלָּא. בֵּיהּ שַׁעֲתָא אִתְגְּלֵי עַתִּיקָא קַדִּישָׁא, וְאִשְׁתְּכַח רַעֲוָא בְּכֻלְּהוּ עָלְמִין עִלָּאִין, כְּדֵין נְהִירוּ דְּכֹלָּא, אִתְנְהִיר.

180. "Then it is written, 'And the Lord said to Moses, "Why do you cry out to Me?...."'" (Exodus 14:15) We learned in the Hidden Book (*Sifra Ditzniuta*) that 'to Me' is exact, for it is the attribute of Zeir Anpin, because it all depends upon Atika. At that moment,

Atika Kadisha was revealed, goodwill was present in all the Worlds Above, and then the Light of all shone."

Explanation: It is known that the wisdom of Egypt was from the Left Side, in the secret of "...the great crocodile, who lies in your river...." (Ezekiel 29:3) This wisdom has a root in the Binah of Arich Anpin that went out of its head. To split the Red Sea and drown the Egyptians it was first necessary to nullify their lofty root in Holiness, which is in Arich Anpin. This was not possible except through the great Light of Atika Kadisha, which is the root of all. This is the meaning of Zeir Anpin asking, **"Why do you cry out to Me? ..." (Exodus 14:15)** since **"it all depends upon Atika,"** whose great Light can cancel out the root of the Egyptians in the Binah of Arich Anpin, as a candle in front of a torch. This is: **"then the Light of all shone,"** because the Light of Atika Kadish is the Light of all, and all are canceled out compared to its Light. Through this, the lofty root of Egypt was temporarily nullified.

Children, life, and sustenance all depend upon Atika.

181. אָמַר רַבִּי יִצְחָק, כְּדֵין, כַּד אִתְנְהִיר כֹּלָּא כַּחֲדָא, וְעָבֵד יַמָּא נִימוּסִין עִלָּאִין, וְאִתְמְסָרוּ בִּידוֹי עִלָּאִין וְתַתָּאִין. וּבְגִינֵי כַּךְ, קַשְׁיָא קַמֵּי קוּדְשָׁא בְּרִיךְ הוּא כֹּלָּא, כִּקְרִיעַת יַם סוּף, וְכֹלָּא הָכִי אוּקְמוּהָ. מַאי טַעֲמָא. בְּגִין דִּקְרִיעַת יַם סוּף בְּעַתִּיקָא תַּלְיָיא.

181. Rav Yitzchak said: "Then, when everything shone together, as even though the Light of Atika [Kadisha] is concealed Chasadim it nevertheless includes Chochmah as well, since the Chochmah in Arich Anpin is definitely received by [Atika], and therefore the Chasadim in Atik [Yomin] are more valuable than the Chochmah in Arich Anpin, and it is considered that [Atik] includes [Chochmah] so the Chochmah and Chasadim shine together in it. Therefore **the sea executed the Supernal Decrees,** namely the commandment to drown the Egyptians and save Israel, **because those Above and those Below were given**

over to it. **Therefore** we say that children, life, and sustenance **all are as difficult before the Holy One, blessed be He, as the Splitting of the Red Sea. And everybody says this."** [He asks:] **"What is the reason?"** [He answers:] **"Because splitting the sea depends on Atika,"** as written in the previous paragraph.

The Holy One, blessed be He, listens to the distress of the deer.

182. אָמַר רִבִּי שִׁמְעוֹן, וַד אַיַּילְתָּא אִית בְּאַרְעָא, וְקוּדְשָׁא בְּרִיךְ הוּא עָבֵיד סַגִּיא בְּגִינָהּ, בְּשַׁעֲתָא דְהִיא צֹווַחַת, קוּדְשָׁא בְּרִיךְ הוּא שָׁמַע עָאקוּ דִילָהּ, וְקָבִיל קָלָהּ. וְכַד אִצְטְרִיךְ עָלְמָא לְרַחֲמֵי לְמַיָּיא, הִיא יָהֲבַת קָלִין, וְקוּדְשָׁא בְּרִיךְ הוּא שָׁמַע קָלָהּ, וּכְדֵין חַיִּיס עַל עָלְמָא, הה"ד כְּאַיָּל תַּעֲרוֹג עַל אֲפִיקֵי מָיִם.

182. **Rav Shimon said: "There is one deer on Earth and the Holy One, blessed be He, does much for her. When she cries, the Holy One, blessed be He, hearkens to her distress and listens to her voice. And when the world needs Mercy on water, she expresses her voice and the Holy One, blessed be He, hearkens to her voice. Then** the Holy One, blessed be He, **has Mercy on the world, as it is written, 'As the hind pants for water….'** (Psalms 42:2)

The Holy One, blessed be He, sends a snake to open the womb of the deer.

183. וְכַד בַּעְיָא לְאוֹלָדָא, הִיא סְתִימָא מִכָּל סִטְרִין, כְּדֵין אַתְיָיא וְשַׁוִּיאַת רֵישָׁא בֵּין בִּרְכָּהָא, וְצֹווַחַת וְרָמַת קָלִין, וְקוּדְשָׁא בְּרִיךְ הוּא חַיִּיס עָלָהּ, וְזַמִּין לְקָבְלָהּ וַד נָחָשׁ, וְנָשִׁיךְ בְּעַרְיָיתָא דִילָהּ, וּפַתְחוֹ לָהּ, וְקָרַע לָהּ הַהוּא אֲתָר, וְאוֹלִידַת בְּיָד. אר"ע בְּהַאי מִכָּה, לָא תִשְׁאַל וְלָא תְנַסֶּה אֶת יְיָ', וְהָכִי דַּווְקָא.

183. **"When she needs to give birth, she is stopped from all sides. She places her head between her knees, cries and screams, and the Holy One, blessed be He, has pity on her. He sends a snake that bites her genitals, opens her and tears that place for her, and she**

gives birth immediately." Rav Shimon said: "In this matter do not question and do not test the Lord. For it is exactly so."

The Israelites saw the minister of Egypt removed from his dominion.

184. וַיּוֹשַׁע יְיָ' בַּיוֹם הַהוּא אֶת יִשְׂרָאֵל וְגוֹ', וַיַּרְא יִשְׂרָאֵל אֶת מִצְרַיִם מֵת, הַהוּא שֻׁלְטָנָא מְמַנָּא דְּמִצְרָאֵי, אַחֲמֵי לוֹן קוּדְשָׁא בְּרִיךְ הוּא, דְּאַעֲבַר לֵיהּ, בִּנְהַר דִּינוּר, דַּהֲוָה בְּשִׂפְתָּא דְּיַמָּא רַבָּא. מֵת, מַאי טַעֲמָא מֵת. כְּמָה דְּאוּקְמוּהָ, דְּאַעְבְּרוּ לֵיהּ, מֵהַהוּא שֻׁלְטָנוּתָא דִּילֵיהּ.

184. "Thus the Lord saved Israel that day... Israel saw Egypt dead...." (Exodus 14:30) The Holy One, blessed be He, showed them the minister appointed over Egypt who He, had passed through the River of Fire that was on the shore of the Upper Sea, which is Malchut. [He asks:] **"Dead. What is the reason that he died,** as there is no death among the angels?" [He answers:] **"It is, as we have established, that he was removed from his dominion,** and it was considered for him as death."

Beshalach

16. "Then sang Moses"

A Synopsis

Rav Yehuda opens with "Before I found you in the belly I knew you." He says that the Holy One, blessed be He, sent down a true prophet and a Faithful Shepherd for the children of Israel, who was Moses. He put a great and Holy Spirit into him, and appointed him over all that was His. When Moses emerged into the world, the Shechinah illuminated him, and the Holy One, blessed be He, read over him, "Before I found you in the belly I knew you; and before you did come out of the womb I sanctified you, and I ordained you a prophet to the nations." (Jeremiah 1:5) We read various interpretations of "Then sang Moses, and the children of Israel..." (Exodus 15:1) Rav Shimon says that it is the song of the Queen to the Holy One, blessed be He. It contains the world that has passed, and the World to Come, and the bonds of Faith, and the Days of King Messiah, and all the other praises of those Above and Below are dependent on it. Rav Yosi submits that "This song to the Lord" (Ibid.) is the river that is Binah that emerges from Eden. And lastly, Rav Yehuda speaks about the time that "the Lord caused the sea to go back by a strong east wind all the night," (Exodus 14:21) saying that all the Egyptians Below and the Princes Above were given over into the hands of the Queen, for Her to do vengeance on them.

The Creator granted the Holy Spirit to Moses.

207. אָז יָשִׁיר מֹשֶׁה. ר' יְהוּדָה פָּתַח, בְּטֶרֶם אֶצָּרְךָ בַבֶּטֶן יְדַעְתִּיךָ וְגוֹ'. זַכָּאָה וְחוּלָקֵהוֹן דְּיִשְׂרָאֵל, דְּקוּדְשָׁא בְּרִיךְ הוּא אִתְרָעֵי בְּהוֹ יַתִּיר מִכָּל שְׁאָר עַמִּין. וּמִסַּגִּיאוּת רְחִימוּתָא דְּרָחִים לְהוֹ, אוֹקִים עָלַיְיהוּ נְבִיאָה דִקְשׁוֹט, וְרַעְיָא מְהֵימָנָא. וְאִתְּעַר עֲלֵיהּ רוּוָחָא קַדִּישָׁא, יַתִּיר מִכָּל שְׁאָר נְבִיאֵי מְהֵימְנֵי, וְאַפִּיק לֵיהּ מֵחוּלָקֵיהּ מַמָּשׁ, מִמַּה דְּאַפְרִיעַ יַעֲקֹב מִבְּנוֹי לְקוּדְשָׁא בְּרִיךְ הוּא, שִׁבְטָא דְּלֵוִי, וְכֵיוָן דַּהֲוָה לֵוִי דִּילֵיהּ, נָטַל לֵיהּ קוּדְשָׁא בְּרִיךְ הוּא, וְאַעְטַר לֵיהּ בְּכַמָּה

עָטְרִין, וּמָשַׁח לֵיהּ בְּמִשְׁחָא רְבוּת קַדִּישָׁא דִלְעֵילָּא, וּכְדֵין אַפִּיק מִבְּנוֹי, רוּחָא
קַדִּישָׁא לְעָלְמָא, וְזָרִיז לֵיהּ בְּהֵימְנוּיֵי קַדִּישֵׁי, מְהֵימָנוּתָא רַבָּא.

207. "Then sang Moses...." (Exodus 15:1) Rav Yehuda opened: "'Before I formed you in the belly I knew you...' (Jeremiah 1:5). Blessed is the portion of Israel, as the Holy One, blessed be He, desired them more than all the other nations. And for the great love that He had for them, He set up for them a true prophet and a Faithful Shepherd, and aroused over him a Holy Spirit, more than the other faithful prophets. He took him out of His own portion, meaning from what Jacob had separated as a tithe of his sons to the Holy One, blessed be He, namely the tribe Levi. Since Levi was His, the Holy One, blessed be He, received him and adorned him with many Crowns, and anointed him with the Holy Anointing Oil of Above. And then he produced from his children a Holy Spirit into the world and girded him with his Holy girdles of the great Faith, which is Binah.

When the soul of Moses descended to the world.

208. תָּנָא, בְּהַהִיא שַׁעֲתָא דְּמָטָא זִמְנֵיהּ דְּמֹשֶׁה נְבִיאָה מְהֵימְנָא לְאַוְחָתָא
לְעָלְמָא, אַפִּיק קוּדְשָׁא בְּרִיךְ הוּא רוּחָא קַדִּישָׁא מִגּוֹ אֶבֶן דְּסַפִּירוּ דְּאֶבֶן טָבָא,
דַּהֲוָה גְּנֵיז בְּמָאתַן וְאַרְבְּעִין וּתְמַנְיָא נְהוֹרִין, וְאִתְנְהִיר עָלֵיהּ. וְאַעְטְרֵיהּ בְּעֵ"ה
עָטְרִין, קָיְימֵי קָמֵיהּ, וְאַפְקִיד לֵיהּ בְּכֹל דִּילֵיהּ. וְיָהַב לֵיהּ מֵאָה וְשִׁתִּין וּתְלַת
מַפְתְּחָן. וְאַעְטַר לֵיהּ בְּחַמֵשׁ עָטְרִין, וְכָל עָטְרָא וְעָטְרָא סַלִּיק וְאַנְהִיר בְּאֶלֶף
עָלְמִין דְּנַהֲרִין, וּבוּצִינִין דְּנָגְנִין בְּגִנְוַיָּיא דְמַלְכָּא קַדִּישָׁא עִלָּאָה.

208. We learned, at that moment when the time had come for Moses, the Faithful Prophet, to descend to the world, the Holy One, blessed be He, brought forth a Holy Spirit from a hewn block of Sapphire, the precious stone, which is Malchut, which was concealed within 248 Lights, and shone on him. And He crowned him with 365 Crowns and they stood before Him, and He appointed him

over all that was His. He gave him 173 Keys, and crowned him with five Crowns. Every single Crown ascends and shines in a thousand Worlds that illuminate, and candles that are concealed in the treasures of the Supernal Holy King.

Explanation of the matter: The Zohar goes on to explain the Mochin that Moses merited before he came down to Earth. It is known that, in general, the order of Mochin is that first one receives Six Corners with no head, which is the secret of the Chasadim that lack the Upper Three, and then one receives the Upper Three in the aspect of Neshamah, then in the aspect of Chayah, and finally in the aspect of Yechidah. It is also known that 248 is the aspect of Six Corners, and 365 is the aspect of the Upper Three. This is: "the Holy One, blessed be He, brought forth a Holy Spirit... which was concealed within 248 Lights," by which Moses achieved the Mochin of Six Corners, "He crowned him with 365 Crowns," namely the Mochin of the Upper Three, and "He gave him 173 Keys," namely the Lights of the Central Column, which are termed "Keys" because the Right and Left Columns cannot shine until the Central Column comes and opens them.

Then the Central Column receives the entire measurement of Lights he caused to come out in the two Upper Columns. From the Right Column he receives 100 Lights, namely all its Ten Sefirot, since they are Light of Chasadim. From the Left Column, which is Light of Chochmah, he only receives 70 Crowns, and not the Upper Three of Chochmah, which is why 30 is missing. However, he has the collective aspect of the Upper Three, and they are considered to only amount to three. Therefore "173 keys." It then explains the Mochin of Chayah, and this is: "and crowned him with five Crowns," which are Chesed, Gevurah, Tiferet, Netzach, and Hod. "Every single Crown ascends and shines in a thousand Worlds," which are the Sefirot of Aba and Ima, whose Sefirot each amount to 1,000 in number. It then explains the Mochin of Yechidah, and this is: "and candles that are concealed in the treasures of the

Supernal Holy King," namely that they are concealed and clothed in Supernal Aba, who is called the Supernal Holy King, and they are the Lights of Arich Anpin, which is the secret of Yechidah.

Moses was destined to rule and provoke the worlds.

209. כְּדֵין אַעְבְּרֵיה בְּכָל בּוּצִינִין דִּבְגִנְתָּא דְעֵדֶן, וְאַעֲלֵיה בְּהֵיכָלֵיה, וְאַעְבְּרֵיה בְּכָל חַיָּלִין וְחֵיִיסִין דִּילֵיה. כְּדֵין אִזְדַעְזָעוּ כֻּלְהוּ, פָּתְחוּ וְאָמְרוּ, אִסְתַּלָּקוּ מִסְּחֲרָנֵיה, דְּהָא קוּדְשָׁא בְּרִיךְ הוּא אִתְּעַר רוּחָא לְשַׁלְטָאָה לְמִרְגַּז עָלְמִין. קָלָא נָפַק וְאָמַר, מַאן הוּא דֵין, דְּכָל מַפְתְּחָן אִלֵּין בִּידֵיהּ. פָּתַח קָלָא אַחֲרָא וְאָמַר, קַבִּילוּ לֵיה בְּגַוַוייכוּ, דָּא הוּא דְּזַמִּין לְנַחְתָּא בֵּין בְּנֵי נָשָׁא, וְזַמִּינָא אוֹרַיְיתָא, גְּנִיזָא דְגִנְזַיָּא, לְאִתְמַסְּרָא בִּידֵיהּ, וּלְאַרְעֲשָׁא עָלְמִין דִּלְעֵילָּא וְתַתָּא עַל יְדָא דְּדֵין. בֵּיהּ שַׁעֲתָא אִתְרְגִישׁוּ כֻּלְהוּ, וְנַטְלִין אֲבַתְרֵיה, פָּתְחוּ וְאָמְרוּ, הִרְכַּבְתָּ אֱנוֹשׁ לְרֹאשֵׁנוּ בָּאנוּ בָאֵשׁ וּבַמַּיִם.

209. Then He passed him through all the Lights in the Garden of Eden and brought him into His Palace, and passed him by His hosts and camps. Then they all trembled, opened and said: "Remove yourselves from his vicinity, for the Holy One, blessed be He, has aroused a spirit to rule and provoke the worlds." A voice emitted and said: "Who is this with all these keys in his hands?" Another voice opened and said: "Accept him among you, he is the one who will descend among the people. And the Torah, which is the most concealed of everything that is concealed, is going to be given into his hands, to shake the worlds that are Above and Below through him." At that moment, they all became excited and traveled after him. They opened and said: "You have caused a man to ride over our heads; we went through fire and through water...." (Psalms 66:12)

The letters of Moshe—Mem, Shin, and Hei.

210. כְּדֵין סַלְקָא הַהוּא רוּחָא, וְקַיְימָא קָמֵי מַלְכָּא. מ' פָּתִיחָא, סָלִיק וְאִתְעַטָּר בְּעִטְרוֹי, וְאַעְטְרֵיה בִּתְלַת מֵאָה וְעֶשְׂרִין וְחָמֵשׁ עִטְרִין, וְאַפְקִיד מַפְתְּחָוֹי בִּידֵיהּ.

ע' דַּאֲבָהָתָא, אַעְטְרוּ לֵיהּ בְּתְלַת עִטְרִין קַדִּישִׁין, וְאַפְקִידוּ כָּל מַפְתְּחָן דְּמַלְכָּא בִּידֵיהּ, וְאַפְקִידוּ לֵיהּ בְּהֵימְנוּתָא, מְהֵימָנָא דְּבֵיתָא. ה' סַלְקָא וְאִתְעַטְרָא בְּעִטְרוֹי, וְקַבִּילַת לֵיהּ מִן מַלְכָּא.

210. Then that spirit of Moses **rose and stood before the King. The open Mem (מ) rose and put on its Crowns,** while He crowned the spirit **with 325 Crowns and deposited His Keys into his hands. The Shin (ש)** alludes **to the** three **Patriarchs, who crowned him with three Holy Crowns, deposited all the Keys of the King in his hands, and appointed him faithfully** to be **the trustee of the House. The Hei (ה) rose and crowned itself with its Crowns, and received him from the King.**

Explanation: Concerning the secret of the Supernal Throne above the chest of Zeir Anpin, it is known that Chesed-Gevurah-Tiferet of Zeir Anpin are the three Legs of the Throne, and the Malchut that is there is the secret of the fourth Leg. And the Throne itself is the secret of Binah. This is the secret of the three letters Mem, Shin, and Hei. Mem is the secret of the Throne itself, Shin is the secret of the three Legs of the Throne—Chesed-Gevurah-Tiferet, and Hei is the secret of Malchut, the fourth leg. Moses was the Chariot of the Central Column, the secret of Zeir Anpin. This is the secret of Moses achieving Binah, since he was the chariot of the Central Column that mediates between the Right and Left of Binah.

This is: **"Then that spirit rose and stood before the King,"** meaning that he was a Chariot to the King, Zeir Anpin, and then they bestowed to him three letters: Mem, Shin, and Hei. **"The open Mem rose and put on its crowns,"** meaning that the Throne rose and was crowned with its Mochin that emerged and were revealed by the Central Column in the secret of "three come out of one." Then: **"while He crowned it with 325 crowns,"** in the secret of "…one is found with three." (Zohar, Beresheet A 363) The reason it is called 325 (שכה) Crowns is because

it comes from "and the wrath of the King subsided (*shachacha*; שׁכּה)"
(Esther 7:10) since before the Central Column mediated between the
two Columns of Binah there was dissension between the Right and Left,
and through his mediation the dispute subsided (*shacha*; שׁכה) and was
quieted. Since the subsiding (*shacha*; שׁכה) was the entire cause of the
Mochin of Zeir Anpin he receives from Binah, [the Zohar] therefore
terms them the 325 (שׁכה) crowns. **"And deposited His keys into
his hands,"** as we explained that the Lights of the Central Column are
called Keys.

**"The Shin of the three Patriarchs, who crowned him with three Holy
Crowns,"** are the Three Columns, Chesed-Gevurah-Tiferet, of Zeir
Anpin above the chest, which are termed the three Legs of the Throne.
"And deposited all the Keys of the King in his hands," namely all the
Mochin of Zeir Anpin, which from the aspect of the Central Column
are called Keys, as mentioned. **"And appointed him faithfully the
trustee of the House."** The Nukva included in Zeir Anpin is called
"House," and since he [Moses] receives all the Mochin of Zeir Anpin he
becomes trusted to bestow to the House, Nukva. Thus **"The Hei rose,"**
which is Malchut that rose above the chest, **"and crowned itself with its
Crowns,"** meaning that She receives Three Columns, Chesed-Gevurah-
Tiferet of Zeir Anpin, and becomes the fourth Leg of the Throne, **"and
received him from the King,"** meaning that She receives the soul of
Moses from the King.

*Malchut received the soul of Moses and
gave him weapons with which to smite Pharoah and Egypt.*

211. כְּדֵין, נָחַת הַהוּא רוּחָא בְּאַרְבִּין דְּשָׁאטָן, בְּהַהוּא יַמָּא רַבָּא, וְקַבִּילַת לֵיהּ
לְגַדְלָא לֵיהּ לְמַלְכָּא, וְהִיא יָהֲבַת לֵיהּ מִתַּמָּן זְיִינִין, לְאַלְקָאָה לְפַרְעֹה וּלְכָל
אַרְעֵיהּ. וּבְשַׁבְתָּא וּבְרֵישֵׁי יַרְחֵי, סַלְקַת לֵיהּ לְמַלְכָּא, כְּדֵין אִקְרֵי שְׁמֵיהּ, בְּאִלֵּין
אַתְוָון רְשִׁימִין.

211. Then when Malchut received him, **that spirit** of Moses **descended on the ships that sail in that great Sea,** which is Malchut, and Malchut **accepted him in order to raise him to the King,** so he can clothe Zeir Anpin, which happens by him receiving the Illumination of Malchut and the Gadlut [Maturity] from Her. **She gave him weapons from there,** from the aspect of the great Sea in Her, which is the secret of the Illumination of the Left, **with which to smite Pharaoh and his whole land. And on Shabbat and Rosh Chodesh, She elevates him to the King,** who is Zeir Anpin. **Then his name is expressed in these letters that are imprinted,** which are Mem, Shin, and Hei, as written above.

The 425 Engravings helped the soul of Moses to materialize in this world.

212. וּבְהַהִיא שַׁעֲתָא, דְּנָפַק לְנַחְתָּא לְאַרְעָא, בְּזַרְעָא דְּלֵוִי, אִתְתָּקָנוּ אַרְבַּע מְאָה וְעֶשְׂרִין וְחָמֵשׁ בּוּצִינִין לְמַלְכָּא, וְאַרְבַּע מְאָה וְעֶשְׂרִין וְחָמֵשׁ גְּלִיפִין מְמַנָּן, אוֹזִיפוּהָ לְהַהוּא רוּחָא לְאַתְרֵיהּ, כַּד נָפַק לְעָלְמָא, אִתְנַהֲרָא ה בְּאַנְפּוֹי, וּבֵיתָא אִתְמַלְיָיא מִזִּיוְתֵיהּ. בֵּיהּ שַׁעֲתָא, קָרָא עָלֵיהּ קוּדְשָׁא בְּרִיךְ הוּא, בְּטֶרֶם אֶצָּרְךָ בַבֶּטֶן יְדַעְתִּיךָ וּבְטֶרֶם תֵּצֵא מֵרֶחֶם הִקְדַּשְׁתִּיךָ נָבִיא לַגּוֹיִם נְתַתִּיךָ.

212. At the moment that he emerged to descend to the Earth to become clothed in a body in the seed of Levi, 425 Candles were prepared for the King, who is Zeir Anpin, **and 425 appointed Engravings escorted the spirit** of Moses **to his place. When he emerged in the world, the Hei,** which is the Shechinah, **illuminated on him and the House became full with its splendor. At that moment, the Holy One, blessed be He, read over him, "Before I formed you in the belly I knew you; and before you did come out of the womb I sanctified you, and I ordained you a prophet to the nations."** (Jeremiah 1:5)

Explanation: The name Tav-Caf-Hei (תכ"ה; 425) emerges by a Unification (Zivug) on the Curtain (Masach) that diminishes the Supernal Spirit to allow it to materialize and be clothed in a body, in the womb of its mother. There is a stature of Light that emerges by this Zivug, which is the secret of the 425 Candles that are prepared for the King. The powers of diminishment that come from this Masach are called 425 Engravings, and they become appointed to bring this spirit down to the womb of its mother—thus **"escorted the spirit to its place."** After it is fixed in the sevent months of pregnancy, the Shechinah shone on him, and therefore **"the Hei illuminated on him."**

Moses and the Israelites saw the minister of Egypt dead.

213. רִבִּי יִצְחָק אָמַר, בֵּיהּ שַׁעֲתָא קָטַל קוּדְשָׁא בְּרִיךְ הוּא לְרַבְרְבָא מְמָנָא דְּמִצְרָאֵי, וְחָזְמוּ לֵיהּ מֹשֶׁה וּבְנֵי יִשְׂרָאֵל, כְּדֵין אָמְרוּ שִׁירָה. הה"ד, וַיַּרְא יִשְׂרָאֵל אֶת מִצְרַיִם מֵת, אָז יָשִׁיר מֹשֶׁה וּבְנֵי יִשְׂרָאֵל.

213. Rav Yitzchak said: "At that time, the Holy One, blessed be He, slew the minister appointed over Egypt. Moses and Israel saw him, then recited the song. This is what is written: 'And Israel saw Egypt dead...' (Exodus 14:30) 'Then sang Moses and the children of the children of Israel....' (Exodus 15:1)"

What is the secret of az (then)?

214. אָז יָשִׁיר מֹשֶׁה וּבְנֵי יִשְׂרָאֵל וְגוֹ'. רִבִּי אַבָּא פָּתַח וְאָמַר, אִסְתַּכַּלְנָא בְּכָל תּוּשְׁבְּחָן דְּשַׁבְּחוּ לְקוּדְשָׁא בְּרִיךְ הוּא, וְכוּלָּם פָּתְחוּ בְּאָז. אָז אָמַר שְׁלֹמֹה. אָז יְדַבֵּר יְהוֹשֻׁעַ, אָז יָשִׁיר יִשְׂרָאֵל. מ"ט.

214. "Then sang Moses and the children of Israel...." (Exodus 15:1) Rav Aba opened the discussion and said: "I examined all the praises with which they praised the Holy One, blessed be He, and they all started with 'Then (az)': 'Then spoke Solomon...' (I Kings 8:12); 'Then spoke Joshua...' (Joshua 10:12); 'Then sang Israel....' (Numbers 21:17) What is the reason for this?"

Alef is Atika and Zayin is Malchut, which make up the word az.

215. אֶלָּא הָכִי תָּאנָא, כָּל נִסִּין וְכָל גְּבוּרָן דְּאִתְעֲבִידוּ לְהוּ לְיִשְׂרָאֵל, כַּד אִתְנְהִיר נְהִירוּ דְּעַתִּיקָא קַדִּישָׁא בְּעִטְּרוֹי, גְּלִיפִין רְשִׁימִין בָּא', בָּא' אַנְקִיב בַּחֲשׁוֹכִי, וְנָהִיר לְכָל עִיבָר. וְכַד אִתְחַבָּר נְהִירוּ דְּאָלֶ"ף וּמָטֵי לְזַיִּ"ן, מַאן זַיִּ"ן, דָּא חֶרֶב לַיְיָ' מָלְאָה דָם. כְּדֵין עָבֵיד נִסִּין וּגְבוּרָאן, בְּגִין דְּאִתְחַבָּר א' עִם זֹ'. וְדָא הוּא שִׁירָתָא. שִׁירָתָא הִיא דְּכָל סִטְרִין, וְדָא הוּא אָז יָשִׁיר.

215. He answers: "This is what we learned. All the miracles and all the mighty deeds that were performed for Israel happened **when the Light of Atika Kadisha,** which is Arich Anpin, **shone with its Crowns,** namely the Illumination of the Upper Three [Sefirot], when it returns Binah-Tiferet-Malchut to its head. **They are engraved and imprinted by Alef (א),** as the top Yud of the Alef is the Right Column, the lower Yud of the Alef is the Left Column, and the line between them is the Central Column that mediates. **א The Alef penetrates the darkness,** alluding to the Central Column of the Alef that penetrates and diminishes the Left Column, which is darkness, into the aspect of the Six Corners of the Upper Three. Then it **shines to every side,** meaning with both Chochmah and Chasadim. **And when the Light of the Alef joins and reaches the Zayin, that Zayin (lit. weapon) is, 'The sword of the Lord is filled with blood...' (Isaiah 34:6),** namely Malchut when it is stretched toward the Left. **Then it performs miracles and mighty deeds because the Alef (א) and Zayin (ז) have joined. And this is a song, a song that illuminates to all sides,** both Chochmah and Chasadim. **And hence 'Then (az; אז) sang....' (Exodus 15:1)"**

The righteous are destined to resurrect and sing Az yashir (Then sang).

216. יָשִׁיר, שָׁר מִבָּעֵי לֵיהּ. אֶלָּא מִלָּה דָּא תַלְיָא, וְאַשְׁלִים לְהַהוּא זִמְנָא, וְאַשְׁלִים לְזִמְנָא דְּאָתֵי, דְּזְמִינִין יִשְׂרָאֵל לְשַׁבְּחָא שִׁירָתָא דָּא. מֹשֶׁה וּבְנֵי יִשְׂרָאֵל, מִכָּאן אוֹלִיפְנָא, דְּצַדִּיקַיָּיא קַדְמָאֵי, אע"ג דְּאִסְתָּלָקוּ בְּדַרְגִּין עִלָּאִין דִּלְעֵילָּא, וְאִתְקַשָּׁרוּ בִּקְשׁוּרָא דִּצְרוֹרָא דְּחַיֵּי, זְמִינִין כֻּלְּהוּ לְאַחֲיָיא בְּגוּפָא,

וּלְמֶחֱמֵי אַתְוָן וּגְבוּרָן דְּקָא עָבֵיד קוּדְשָׁא בְּרִיךְ הוּא לְיִשְׂרָאֵל. וּלְמֵימַר שִׁירָתָא
דָא, הה"ד אָז יָשִׁיר מֹשֶׁה וּבְנֵי יִשְׂרָאֵל.

216. He asks: "'Then sang (lit. will sing) Moses....' (Exodus 15:1)
Should it have been written, 'sang Moses'?" He answers: "This matter
is suspended until the time to come **because he perfected it for that
time and perfected it for the future to come since Israel will praise
this song** in the time to come. '...Moses and the children of Israel....'
(Ibid.) From here we learned that even though the early righteous
men ascended to the highest levels that are Above and have been
bound in the Bond of Life, they will all stand up to be resurrected in
a body and recite this song. This is what is written, 'Then will sing
Moses and the children of Israel....' (Ibid.)"

*The world exists only for the sake of those
who make themselves into leftovers.*

217. ר' שִׁמְעוֹן אָמַר מֵהָכָא, יוֹסִיף יְיָ' שֵׁנִית יָדוֹ לִקְנוֹת אֶת שְׁאָר עַמּוֹ. לִקְנוֹת:
כד"א, יְיָ' קָנָנִי רֵאשִׁית דַּרְכּוֹ. אֶת שְׁאָר עַמּוֹ: אִלֵּין אִינּוּן צַדִּיקַיָּיא דִּבְהוֹן,
דְּאִקְרוּן שְׁאָר, כד"א וַיִּשָּׁאֲרוּ שְׁנֵי אֲנָשִׁים בַּמַּחֲנֶה. וְתָנֵינָן, לֵית עָלְמָא מִתְקַיְּימָא
אֶלָּא עַל אִינּוּן דְּעַבְדֵי גַּרְמַיְיהוּ שִׁירַיִים.

217. Rav Shimon said: "Hence, 'The Lord shall again, a second time
stretch forth His hand to recover the remnant of His people....'
(Isaiah 11:11) 'To recover (*liknot*)' as in, 'The Lord acquired me
(*kanani*) as the beginning of His way....' (Proverbs 8:22) 'The
remnant of His people' refers to the Righteous among them, who
are called 'remnants (*she'ar*)' as it is written, 'And there remained
two men in the camp....' (Numbers 11:26) We learned they are called
remnants because **the world exists only for the sake of those who
make themselves into leftovers (*shirayim*).** Therefore the righteous are
called "remnants (*she'ar*)," derived from leftovers (*shirayim*)."

At the Resurrection, the Creator will lower
the souls of the Righteous to this world.

218. וְאִי תֵימָא, הוֹאִיל וְאִתְקַשָּׁרוּ בִּצְרוֹרָא דְחַיֵּי, וּמִתְעַנְּגֵי בְּעִנּוּגָא עִלָּאָה, אֲמַאי יָחִית לוֹן קוּדְשָׁא בְּרִיךְ הוּא לְאַרְעָא. פּוּק וְאוֹלִיף מִזִּמְנָא קַדְמָאָה, דְּכָל אִינּוּן רוּחִין וְנִשְׁמָתִין, דַּהֲווֹ בְּדַרְגָּא עִלָּאָה דִלְעֵילָא וְקוּדְשָׁא בְּרִיךְ הוּא אָחִית לְהוּ לְאַרְעָא לְתַתָּא. כָּל שֶׁכֵּן הַשְׁתָּא, דְּבָעֵי קוּדְשָׁא בְּרִיךְ הוּא לְיַשְׁרָא לַעֲקִימָא, כד"א כִּי אָדָם אֵין צַדִּיק בָּאָרֶץ אֲשֶׁר יַעֲשֶׂה טוֹב וְלֹא יֶחֱטָא. וְאִי תֵימָא, אִינּוּן דְּמִיתוּ בְּעֵטְיוֹ דְנָחָשׁ. אֲפִילוּ אִינּוּן יְקוּמוּן, וִיהוֹן מָארֵי דְעֵיטָא, לְמַלְכָּא מְשִׁיחָא.

218. "You may ask, since they are tied in the Bond of Life and delight in the Supernal delight, why does the Holy One, blessed be He, lower them to the Earth? Go and learn, even from the first time, the time they were born and emerged into the world, **when all the spirits and souls were in the highest level Above, the Holy One, blessed be He, lowered them to the Earth Below. All the more so now, since the Holy One, blessed be He, wants to straighten out that which is crooked** by showing them the miracles and marvels that He will perform for the children of Israel. Even though they are righteous, nevertheless, **it is written, 'For there is no righteous man upon the earth who does good and does not sin.' (Ecclesiastes 7:20) And you may ask, what of those who died because of the advice of the serpent,** who did no sin, why should they arise? **Even they will arise and will be advisers to the Messiah.**

Moses is destined to sing again at the time of the Redemption.

219. וְעַל דָּא תָּנֵינָן, מֹשֶׁה זַמִּין לְמֵימַר שִׁירָתָא לְזִמְנָא דְאָתֵי. מ"ט. בְּגִין דִּכְתִיב, כִּימֵי צֵאתְךָ מֵאֶרֶץ מִצְרַיִם אַרְאֶנּוּ נִפְלָאוֹת. אַרְאֶנּוּ, אַרְאֶה מִבָּעֵי לֵיהּ. אֶלָּא אַרְאֶנּוּ מַמָּשׁ, לְמַאן דְּוָזְבַּא בְּקַדְמֵיתָא, יֶחֱמֵי לֵיהּ תִּנְיָינוּת, וְדָא הוּא אַרְאֶנּוּ, וּכְתִיב אַרְאֶנּוּ בְּיֵשַׁע אֱלֹהִים, וְאַרְאֵהוּ בִּישׁוּעָתִי. וּכְדֵין אָז יָשִׁיר מֹשֶׁה וּבְנֵי יִשְׂרָאֵל אֶת הַשִּׁירָה הַזֹּאת לַיְיָ'.

219. "Therefore, we learned Moses will sing the song in the future to come." [He asks:] "What is the reason?" [He answers:] "Because it is written, 'As in the days of your coming out the land of Egypt, I will show him marvelous things….' (Micah 7:15)" He asks: "'I will show him'? It should have been said 'I will show you.'" He answers: "Rather, I will show the very one who saw originally, namely Moses, for he will see a second time, and this is the meaning of 'I will show him.' (Ibid.) It is written, '…I will show him the salvation of God' (Psalms 50:23) and, '…show him My salvation.' (Psalms 91:16) And 'Then shall sing Moses and the children of Israel to the Lord….' (Exodus 15:1)

Saying Az yashir every day with intention.

220. שִׁירָתָא דְּמַטְרוֹנִיתָא לְקוּדְשָׁא בְּרִיךְ הוּא. תָּנֵינָן, כָּל בַּר נָשׁ דְּאָמַר שִׁירָתָא דָּא בְּכָל יוֹמָא, וּמְכַוֵּין בָּהּ, זָכֵי לְמֵימְרָא לְזִמְנָא דְּאָתֵי. דְּהָא אִית בָּהּ עָלְמָא דַּעֲבַר, וְאִית בָּהּ עָלְמָא דְּאָתֵי, וְאִית בָּהּ קִשְׁרֵי מְהֵימְנוּתָא, וְאִית בָּהּ יוֹמֵי דְּמַלְכָּא מְשִׁיחָא. וְתָלֵי עֲלָהּ, כָּל אִינּוּן תּוּשְׁבְּחָאן אַחֲרָנִין, דְּקָאמְרֵי עֵלָּאֵי וְתַתָּאֵי.

220. "It is the song of the Queen, which is Malchut, to the Holy One, blessed be He. We have learned that every person who says this song daily and has the proper intention merits to say it in the time to come. It contains the world that has passed, and it contains the World to Come, and it contains the Bonds of Faith, and it contains the Days of King Messiah. And all the other praises from those Above and those Below stir from it."

The song is feminine since it is the Queen praising the King.

221. הַשִּׁירָה שִׁיר זֶה מִבָּעֵי לֵיהּ. אֶלָּא שִׁירָתָא, דְּקָא מְשַׁבְּחַת מַטְרוֹנִיתָא לְמַלְכָּא. וּמֹשֶׁה מִתַּתָּא לְעֵילָּא קָאָמַר, וְהָא אוּקְמוּהָ. לַיְיָ': בְּגִין דְּאַנְהִיר לָהּ

מַלְכָּא אַנְפָּהָא, ר' יוֹסֵי אָמַר, דְּכָל אִינּוּן מְשִׁיחָן, דַּהֲווֹ נַגְדִּין, מָשִׁיךְ מַלְכָּא
קַדִּישָׁא לְקַבְּלָהּ, בְּגִינֵי כַּךְ מְשַׁבְּחָא לֵיהּ מַטְרוֹנִיתָא.

221. He asks: "It is written, *Hashirah* (this song), which is feminine but should it not have said *shir zeh* (this song) in the masculine form?" He answers: "But this is the song with which the Queen praises the King, Zeir Anpin, and that Moses said from Below to Above, from Malchut to Zeir Anpin. Therefore it is said *shirah* (feminine), and it has already been explained. '...to the Lord.' (Exodus 15:1) She sings to the Lord because the King has welcomed Her." Rav Yosi said: "All these ointments, meaning the Lights that flowed, the Holy King poured to Her. Therefore, the Queen praised Him."

Moses and the Israelites sang on the Queen's behalf.

222. אָמַר רִבִּי יְהוּדָה, אִי הָכִי, אֲמַאי כְּתִיב מֹשֶׁה וּבְנֵי יִשְׂרָאֵל, וְהָא
מַטְרוֹנִיתָא בַּעְיָא לְשַׁבְּחָא. אֶלָּא, זַכָּאָה חוּלָקֵהוֹן דְּמֹשֶׁה וְיִשְׂרָאֵל, דְּאִינּוּן הֲווֹ
יַדְעִין לְשַׁבְּחָא לְמַלְכָּא, בְּגִין מַטְרוֹנִיתָא כַּדְקָא יֵאוֹת, בְּגִין דְּכָל הַהוּא חֵילָא
וּגְבוּרָה דִּילָהּ, יַרְתָא מִן מַלְכָּא.

222. Rav Yehuda said: "If so, that it is the song of the Queen to the King, why is it written, 'Moses and the children of Israel...' (Exodus 15:1) seeing that it is for the Queen to praise?" He answers: "Blessed is the portion of Moses and Israel that they knew how to praise the King for the Queen's sake in the proper manner because She inherited all Her strength and might from the King."

The Shechinah in exile cries out to Yesod for blessings.

223. ר' חִיָּיא פָּתַח וְאָמַר, קוּמִי רֹנִּי בַלַּיְלָה לְרֹאשׁ אַשְׁמוּרוֹת. קוּמִי רֹנִּי: דָּא
כְּנֶסֶת יִשְׂרָאֵל. בַּלַּיְלָה. בַּגָּלוּתָא: בְּגָלוּתָא. ר' יוֹסֵי אָמַר, בַּלַּיְלָה: בְּזִמְנָא דְּהִיא שַׁלְטָא
וּמִתְעָרָא, לְרֹאשׁ אַשְׁמוּרוֹת, בְּרֹאשׁ מִבָּעֵי לֵיהּ. אֶלָּא לְרֹאשׁ, כְּמָה דִּכְתִיב, עַל

רֹאשׁ הַמִּטָּה. וְאוֹקִימְנָא, רֹאשׁ הַמִּטָּה, דָּא יְסוֹד. אוּף הָכָא לְרֹאשׁ, דָּא יְסוֹד,
דְּמַטְרוֹנִיתָא מִתְבָּרְכָא בֵּיהּ. רֹאשׁ אַשְׁמוּרוֹת: דָּא הוּא רֵישָׁא, דְּנֶצַח וְהוֹד.

223. Rav Chiya opened and said: "'Arise, cry out in the night: for
the beginning of the watches....' (Lamentations 2:19) 'Arise, cry
out' refers to the Congregation of Israel, which is Malchut; 'in the
night,' means the Exile." Rav Yosi says: "'In the night' refers to the
time when She awakens and rules because Malchut rules at night.
'For the beginning of the watches' should have been written, 'In the
beginning.'?" He answers: "'For the beginning (lit. head),' (Ibid.) is
as it is written, '...upon the head of the bed.' (Genesis 47.31) We
have established that the head of the bed is Yesod. Also, here 'for
the beginning (head)' is Yesod, by which the Queen is blessed.
'...beginning of the watches...' (Lamentations 2:19) is the head of
Netzach and Hod, which is Yesod."

Yesod is the head of Returning Light.

224. ר' יוֹסֵי אָמַר, דָּא הוּא רֵישָׁא דְּכִתְרֵי מַלְכָּא וְסִיּוּמָא. רִבִּי אַבָּא אָמַר,
לְרֹאשׁ אַשְׁמוּרוֹת כְּתִיב חָסֵר, וְדָא הוּא רֵישָׁא, רֹאשׁ הַמִּטָּה. וְכֹלָּא בְּמַלְכָּא
קַדִּישָׁא עִלָּאָה אִתְּמַר, וְדָא הוּא לַיְיָ'.

224. Rav Yosi said: "This is the beginning of the Crowns of the King
and the end." For from the aspect of the nine Sefirot of Direct Light of
Zeir Anpin, it is the bottom one that ends. From the aspect of the nine
Sefirot of Returning Light of Zeir Anpin that illuminate from below
upward, Yesod is considered the Keter of Returning Light. Since it is
the beginning of the Sefirot of Returning Light, the Torah therefore
calls it '...the beginning of the watches....' (Lamentations 2:19) Rav Aba
said: "For the head of the watches (אשמרות) is spelled without a Vav
(ו), which alludes to Malchut, and this Yesod is a head to Her, and is
thus called ...'the head of the bed....' (Genesis 47.31) It is all said in
reference to the Supernal Holy King, that is Zeir Anpin, meaning

Yesod of Zeir Anpin, **and this is** the meaning of, '...this song **to the Lord...'** (Exodus 15:1) meaning to Yesod of Zeir Anpin."

The song is sung to Binah.

225. רִבִּי יֵיסָא אָמַר, הַשִּׁירָה הַזֹּאת לַיְיָ', דָּא הוּא נַהֲרָא דְּנָפִיק מֵעֵדֶן, דְּכָל מִשְׁחָא וּרְבוּ נָפִיק מִנֵּיהּ, לְאַדְלְקָא בּוּצִינִין. וּמַשְׁמַע לְבָתַר דִּכְתִיב אָשִׁירָה לַיְיָ', דָּא הוּא מַלְכָּא קַדִּישָׁא עִלָּאָה, וְעַל דָּא לָא כְּתִיב אָשִׁירָה לוֹ.

225. Rav Yesa said: "'...this song to the Lord...' (Exodus 15:1) is the **River,** which is Binah **that emerges from Eden,** which is Chochmah, meaning Binah that emerged from the head of Arich Anpin. **For all the oil and greatness,** meaning all the Mochin of Zeir Anpin and Nukva, and Briyah, Yetzirah, and Asiyah, **emerge from it. This is understood from the following** verse, **which says: '...'I will sing to the Lord...'"** (Ibid.) which refers to the **Supernal Holy King,** Zeir Anpin. **Therefore it is not written, 'I will sing to Him'** because the previous 'to the Lord' in 'this song to the Lord,' (Exodus 15:1) is Binah and not Zeir Anpin.

Meriting to sing the Song of the sea.

226. וַיֹּאמְרוּ לֵאמֹר, לְדָרֵי דָּרִין, בְּגִין דְּלָא יִתְנְשֵׁי מִנַּיְיהוּ לְעָלְמִין. דְּכָל מַאן דְּזָכֵי לְהַאי שִׁירָתָא בְּהַאי עָלְמָא, זָכֵי לָהּ בְּעָלְמָא דְּאָתֵי, וְזָכֵי לְשַׁבְּחָא בָּהּ בְּיוֹמוֹי דְּמַלְכָּא מְשִׁיחָא, בְּחֶדְוָותָא דִּכְ"י בְּקוּדְשָׁא בְּרִיךְ הוּא. דִּכְתִיב לֵאמֹר, לֵאמֹר בְּהַהוּא זִמְנָא. לֵאמֹר בְּאַרְעָא קַדִּישָׁא, בְּזִמְנָא דְּשָׁרוּ יִשְׂרָאֵל בְּאַרְעָא. לֵאמֹר בְּגָלוּתָא. לֵאמֹר בְּפוּרְקָנָא דִּלְהוֹן דְּיִשְׂרָאֵל. לֵאמֹר לְעָלְמָא דְּאָתֵי.

226. "'...and spoke, saying...' (Exodus 15:1) meaning to say **to the following generations so that this will never be forgotten from them. Anyone who is worthy of this song in this world merits it in the World to Come, and will be worthy of praising with it in the Days of King Messiah in the rejoining of the Congregation of Israel**

with the Holy One, blessed be He. It is written, 'saying,' meaning 'saying it at that time,' 'saying it in the Holy Land' in the time when Israel will be settled in the land, 'saying it during exile,' 'saying it at the redemption of Israel,' 'saying it in the World to Come.'

Zeir Anpin was crowned with His Crowns
to bring forth blessings and mighty deeds.

227. אָשִׁירָה לַיְיָ' נָשִׁיר מִבָּעֵי לֵיהּ, מַאי אָשִׁירָה. אֶלָּא בְּגִין דַּהֲווֹ מְשַׁבְּחָן תּוּשְׁבְּחָתָא דְּמַטְרוֹנִיתָא. לַיְיָ': דָּא מַלְכָּא קַדִּישָׁא. כִּי גָאֹה גָּאָה: דְּסָלִיק וְאִתְעַטָּר בְּעִטְרוֹי, לְאַפָּקָא בִּרְכָאן וְחֵילִין וּגְבוּרָאן, לְאַסָּקָא בְּכֹלָּא. כִּי גָאֹה גָּאָה: גָּאֹה בְּהַאי עָלְמָא, גָּאָה בְּעָלְמָא דְּאָתֵי. כִּי גָאֹה בְּהַהוּא זִמְנָא, גָּאָה, בְּגִין דְּיִתְעַטָּר בְּעִטְרוֹי בְּחֶדְוָותָא שְׁלֵימוּתָא.

227. "'I will sing to the Lord....' (Exodus 15:1)" He asks: "It should have said: 'We will sing.' Why does it say, 'I will sing'?" He answers: "It is because they were reciting the praises of the Queen, as mentioned earlier, and it is therefore written, 'I will sing' in the singular. '...to the Lord...' (Ibid.) refers to the Holy King, who is Zeir Anpin '...for He has triumphed gloriously...'(Ibid.) meaning that He ascended and was crowned with His Crowns to bring forth blessings and strength and mighty deeds, with all of which to be elevated. '...for He has triumphed...' in this world, 'gloriously' in the World to Come. 'He triumphed gloriously' (Ibid.) at that time in order to be crowned afterwards, with His Crowns in complete joy.

The Creator first executes Judgment Above
and then executes Judgment Below.

228. סוּס וְרוֹכְבוֹ רָמָה בַיָּם, שׁוּלְטָנוּתָא דִלְתַתָּא, וְשׁוּלְטָנוּתָא דִלְעֵילָּא דַּאֲחִידָן בְּהוּ, אִתְמְסָרוּ בְּהַהוּא יַמָּא רַבָּא, וְשָׁלְטָנוּתָא רַבָּא לְמֶעְבַּד בְּהוּ נוּקְמִין. וְתָגֵינָן, לָא עָבֵיד קוּדְשָׁא בְּרִיךְ הוּא דִּינָא לְתַתָּא, עַד דְּיַעֲבֵיד בְּשׁוּלְטָנֵיהוֹן לְעֵילָּא, הַהַ"ד, יִפְקוֹד יְיָ' עַל צְבָא הַמָּרוֹם בַּמָּרוֹם וְעַל מַלְכֵי הָאֲדָמָה עַל הָאֲדָמָה.

228. "'...the horse and his rider He cast into the sea' (Exodus 15:1), namely **the dominion of Below,** which is the 'horse,' **and the dominion of Above they grasp onto,** which is 'his rider.' **Both of them were given over to that Great Sea and the great dominion, to take revenge on them. And we learned, the Holy One, blessed be He, does not execute Judgment Below until He does so with their government Above. This is the meaning of:** 'The Lord will punish the host of the high ones on high, and the kings of the earth upon the earth.' (Isaiah 24:21)"

All the multitudes of Egypt Above and Below were given over to Malchut.

229. רָמָה בַיָּם, אָמַר ר' יְהוּדָה, בֵּיה בְּלֵילְיָא, אִתְּעַר גְּבוּרָא תַּקִּיפָא, דִּכְתִיב בֵּיהּ וַיּוֹלֶךְ יְיָ' אֶת הַיָּם בְּרוּחַ קָדִים עַזָּה כָּל הַלַּיְלָה. בְּהַהוּא זִמְנָא, בָּעָאת מַטְרוֹנִיתָא מִן מַלְכָּא, כָּל אִינּוּן אֹכְלוֹסִין דִּלְתַתָּא, וְכָל אִינּוּן שׁוּלְטָנִין דִּלְעֵילָא, דְּיִתְמַסְרוּן בִּידָהָא. וְכֻלְּהוּ אִתְמְסָרוּ בִּידָהָא, לְמֶעְבַּד בְּהוּ נוּקְמִין, הה"ד סוּס וְרֹכְבוֹ רָמָה בַיָּם. בַּיָּם סְתָם, לְעֵילָּא וְתַתָּא.

229. "'He cast into the sea' (Exodus 15:1)," Rav Yehuda said: "**That night, a mighty power was awakened, as it is written,** '...and the Lord caused the sea to go back by a strong east wind all that night....' (Exodus 14:21) At that time, the Queen requested of the King that all the multitudes of the Egyptians **Below** and all the ministers **Above** be given over into Her hands. They were all given over into Her power to do vengeance with them. As it is written, '...the horse and its rider He cast into the sea.' (Exodus 15:1) Here, 'into the sea' is written **without adjectives,** alluding both to the sea **Above and** the sea **Below.**

COUNTING OF
THE OMER

Tetzaveh

7. Matzot and the Counting of the Omer

A Synopsis

We read that in order to raise Malchut to be connected with the supernal days above, men must stand on their feet to count the Omer. The Counting of the Omer is the secret of the Male, being connected to the Holy Covenant, so women are exempted from this counting. Rav Shimon says that throughout the Seven Supernal Days of Zeir Anpin, one of the Lower Days of Malchut becomes Holy, and this Lower Day is called "a week." When the Seven Sefirot of Malchut are sanctified through the Forty-Nine Supernal Sefirot, the House is prepared so that Malchut can unite with Zeir Anpin; then it is called Shavuot. Then the fiftieth day, Binah, rules over the forty-nine days and, by way of awakening the Lower Beings, produces the Torah.

Guarding ourselves from anger, like Matzah is guarded from Chametz.

61. ת"ח, הַאי אִיהוּ רוּגְזָא דְּאִיהוּ כו"ם, סִטְרָא אַחֲרָא, כְּמָה דְּאַמָרָן, דְּבָעֵי בַּר
נָשׁ לְאִסְתַּמְּרָא מִנֵּיהּ וּלְאִתְפָּרָשָׁא מֵעֲלוֹי, וְעַ"ד כְּתִיב אֱלֹהֵי מַסֵּכָה לֹא תַעֲשֶׂה
לָךְ. לָךְ: בְּגִין לְאַבְאָשָׁא גַּרְמֵךְ. וּכְתִיב בַּתְרֵיהּ אֶת חַג הַמַּצּוֹת תִּשְׁמֹר. תִּשְׁמֹר:
דָּא סִטְרָא דִּקְדוּשָׁה, דְּבָעֵי בַּר נָשׁ לְנַטְרָא לֵיהּ, וְלָא יָחֲלַף לֵיהּ בְּגִין סִטְרָא
אַחֲרָא. וְאִי יָחֲלַף לֵיהּ הָא אִיהוּ מַסְאִיב, וְסָאִיב לְכָל מַאן דְּקָרִיב בַּהֲדֵיהּ.

61. Come and see, this anger is idolatry, the Other Side, as we have said. Thus, a person must guard himself against it and separate from it. Therefore it is written: "You shall make no molten gods for yourself," (Exodus 34:17) "for yourself" means to not harm yourself. And immediately following, it is written: "The Feast of Unleavened Bread shall you keep...." (Ibid. 18) "Keep" refers to the side of Holiness that a person should keep and not exchange it for the

Other Side. If he exchanges it for the Other Side, he becomes defiled and defiles whoever comes near him.

The days of Sukkot are Supernal, and the days of Pesach are of Below.

62. אֶת חַג הַמַּצּוֹת תִּשְׁמֹר, הַאי אִיהוּ אֲתָר דְּאִקְרֵי שָׁמוֹר. וּבג"כ כְּתִיב, אֶת חַג הַמַּצּוֹת תִּשְׁמֹר שִׁבְעַת יָמִים תֹּאכַל מַצּוֹת כַּאֲשֶׁר צִוִּיתִיךָ. שִׁבְעַת יָמִים אִלֵּין, לָאו אִינּוּן כְּשִׁבְעַת הַיָּמִים דְּסֻכּוֹת, דְּאִינּוּן עִלָּאִין וְאִלֵּין תַּתָּאִין. וְעַל דָּא, בְּאִינּוּן הַלֵּל גָּמוּר, וּבְהָנֵי לָאו הַלֵּל גָּמוּר, וְעַל דְּאִינּוּן לְתַתָּא, שִׁבְעַת יָמִים תֹּאכַל מַצּוֹת. מַצֹּת כְּתִיב חָסֵר בְּלָא ו', דְּעַד לָא שָׁרְאן אִינּוּן יוֹמִין עִלָּאִין, רָזָא דְּו'.

62. "The Feast of Unleavened Bread (Matzot) shall you keep…." (Exodus 34:18) This is a place called "Keep" (Shamor), namely Malchut that is called *shamor,* and therefore it is written: "The Feast of Unleavened Bread (Matzot) shall you keep, seven days shall you eat Matzot as I have commanded you…." (Exodus 34:18) These seven days of the Festival of Matzot, are not like the seven days of Sukkot because those of Sukkot are Supernal, namely the Seven Sefirot: Chesed, Gevurah, Tiferet, Netzach, Hod, Yesod, and Malchut of Binah, which Zeir Anpin and Nukva ascended to and clothed. But those of the Festival of Matzot are of Below, namely the Seven Sefirot: Chesed, Gevurah, Tiferet, Netzach, Hod, Yesod, and Malchut of Malchut. Therefore during those of Sukkot we say a complete Halel, and during those of the Festival of Matzot we do not say a complete Halel. And because they are seven days of Below, of Malchut, it is written "… seven days shall you eat Matzot…." (Ibid.) The word Matzot (מצת) is written without a Vav (ו), to show that it was before the Supernal Days, the secret of Vav, Zeir Anpin, rested on them.

Why Malchut goes down after the first day of Pesach.

63. וְאִי תֵימָא, כֵּיוָן דְּהַאי רָזָא דְּחַג הַמַּצּוֹת אִתְקַדָּשׁ, אֲמַאי נַחְתָּא, דְּהָא תְּנֵינָן מַעֲלִין בַּקֹדֶשׁ וְלָא מוֹרִידִין, אֲמַאי נַחְתָּא לְתַתָּא בְּאִינּוּן יוֹמִין תַּתָּאִין.

63. If you ask: "As the secret of the Feast of Unleavened Bread (Matzot) has been sanctified, since on the first night of Pesach, Zeir Anpin and Nukva were sanctified and received the Mochin of Supernal Aba and Ima, meaning that they ascended and clothed them, **why did** Malchut again **go down from Her place? Have we not learned that 'One elevates in sanctity and does not downgrade'** (Tractate **Menachot 99b)? Why did She go** from Aba and Ima **down to the Lower seven days?"**

Malchut elevates on the first night and
then descends to elevate Her household.

64. ת"ח, כְּתִיב וְכִפֶּר בַּעֲדוֹ וּבְעַד בֵּיתוֹ וְגוֹ', מַאן דִּיכַפֶּר, אִצְטְרִיךְ לְכַפֶּרָא
עֲלֵיה בְּקַדְמֵיתָא, וּבָתַר עַל בֵּיתֵיה. כְּגַוְונָא דָא, הַאי דַּרְגָּא, שָׁאֲרֵי לְאִתְקַדְּשָׁא
וּלְנַפְקָא בִּקְדוּשָׁה, לְכַפֶּרָא עֲלֵיה, וְכֵינָן דְּאִיהוּ אִתְקַדְּשׁ, בָּעֵי לְכַפֶּרָא עַל
בֵּיתֵיה, וּלְקַדְּשָׁא לוֹן, וְעַל דָּא נַחְתָּא לְתַתָּא לְקַדְּשָׁא לְבֵיתֵיה. וּבְמָה מְקַדְּשׁ לוֹן,
בְּיִשְׂרָאֵל דִּלְתַתָּא. וְכֵינָן דְּאַלֵּין מִתְקַדְּשָׁאן, בָּעֵינָן לְסַלְּקָא לָה לְעֵילָא, דְּהָא
כַּד בֵּיתָא דְּמַטְרוֹנִיתָא אִתְקַדְּשַׁת, כְּדֵין סַלְקָת לְעֵילָא, לְאִתְקַשְּׁרָא בְּאִינּוּן
יוֹמִין עִלָּאִין לְעֵילָא.

64. Come and see, it is written: "…and make atonement for himself, and for his house" (Leviticus 16:6), **to teach that one who atones has to atone for himself first, and afterwards, for his household. Similarly this grade,** namely Malchut, **started to be sanctified and to emerge into Holiness** during the first night of Pesach, **to atone for Herself. As soon as She was sanctified, She had to atone for Her household and sanctify them. Therefore She came down to sanctify Her house. How are they sanctified? It is through Israel below. Once they were sanctified, they need to raise Her up because when the house of the Queen,** which is Malchut, **is sanctified, She then rises to be connected with the Supernal Days Above.**

Explanation: It is known that there is no disappearance in spirituality, and any change in place does not mean that it has left and disappeared from the original place and gone to a second place but rather it is only an additional space, where it completely remains in the original place and it also comes to the second place. According to this, on the first night of Pesach, when Zeir Anpin and Nukva ascended to Aba and Ima and Nukva was set with the Mochin of Aba and Ima, Nukva remains in Her place Below as well. This is the secret of Chesed, Gevurah, Tiferet, Netzach, Hod, Yesod, and Malchut of Nukva that remain Below in Her place are called the House of Nukva because it is likened to Nukva ascending Above and not taking Her house with Her. It is found that the great correction Nukva received on the first night of Pesach did not reach her House that remained Below at all.

Thus **"one who atones… started to be sanctified and to emerge into Holiness to atone for Herself,"** for on the first night of Pesach She began to be sanctified in the aspect of "…make atonement for himself…" (Leviticus 16:6) as She Herself receives the correction due to her ascension. **"As soon as She was sanctified, She had to atone for Her household"** because Her house—her seven Sefirot: Chesed, Gevurah, Tiferet, Netzach, Hod, Yesod, and Malchut that remained below and did not ascend with Her; did not yet receive atonement in the secret of the Day of Atonement (Yom Kippur), which is Ima. **"Therefore She came down to sanctify Her house."** Thus after the first night of Pesach, Malchut descended from Aba and Ima to Her place to sanctify Her seven Sefirot that remained Below. **"How are they sanctified? It is through Israel below,"** meaning through Israel observing "The Feast of Unleavened Bread (Matzot) shall you keep seven days…" (Exodus 34:18) the seven days are corrected, which are her seven Sefirot—Chesed, Gevurah, Tiferet, Netzach, Hod, Yesod, and Malchut—that remained Below and are called Her House, in the secret of "…and for his house…" (Leviticus 16:6) as mentioned earlier. **"Once they were sanctified, they need to raise Her up…."** meaning after these seven days received correction in their place, they need to again raise Malchut to Aba and Ima, which is done through the Counting of the Omer, as he goes on to explain.

When a prayer or praise relates to Zeir Anpin
it must be recited standing up.

65. וְעַל דָּא אֲנָן עַבְדִּין חוּשְׁבָּנָא, בְּקָיוּמָא עַל קַיְיִמִין, בְּגִין דְּאִינּוּן יוֹמִין יוֹמִין עִלָּאִין אִינּוּן, וְכֵן בְּכָל זִמְנָא דְּעָאל בַּר נָשׁ לְאִינּוּן יוֹמִין עִלָּאִין, בֵּין בִּצְלוֹתָא, בֵּין בְּשִׁבְחָא, אִצְטְרִיךְ לְקָיְימָא עַל רַגְלוֹי, יַרְכִין וְגוּפָא כַּחֲדָא תַּמָּן. יַרְכִין וְגוּפָא לְקָיְימָא, כִּדְכוּרָא דְּקָיְימָא בְּחֵילֵיהּ, וְלָא כְּנוּקְבָא דְּאָרְחָהָא לְמֵיתַב. וְעוֹד בְּגִין שִׁבְחָא דְּעָלְמָא עִלָּאָה.

65. For this purpose, we make a reckoning, meaning that we count the Omer **standing on our feet because the days that we count are Supernal Days,** namely the Sefirot of Zeir Anpin, which is Male. **Likewise, every time a person enters the Supernal Days** of Zeir Anpin, **both in prayer and in praise, that person must stand on his legs so that the legs and body** serve **there** in Zeir Anpin equally **together. The legs and body** must **stand like a man who stands with power, and not like a woman who customarily sits. Also, for the praise of the Upper World,** one should stand.

Explanation: Male Light shines from above downward, which is the aspect of the Upper Three. Therefore his entire Head, Middle and End, which are Chochmah-Binah-Da'at, Chesed-Gevurah-Tiferet, Netzach-Hod-Yesod need to be used to clothe the Light. Therefore, one who is in prayer or in praise of Zeir Anpin, who is Male, must also be standing on his legs so that his Netzach-Hod-Yesod called legs also be in use. But Female Light shines from below upward, which is the aspect of Six Corners [Sefirot] that lack the Upper Three, and therefore they only need the Head and the Middle, which are Chochmah-Binah-Da'at and Chesed-Gevurah-Tiferet of the Vessels to clothe the Lights of Ruach and

Nefesh. And the Netzach-Hod-Yesod, the secret of the legs, are found vacant with no Light, and they are not in use at all, like one who sits on a chair, where his legs are not in use. Therefore, when a person is in prayer or praise to Malchut, which is Female, he needs to be sitting as well and not using his legs, since there is an opposite value between Vessels and Lights, where if Netzach-Hod-Yesod of Vessels are lacking there is a lack of Chochmah-Binah-Da'at of Lights.

Women are exempt from Counting the Omer.

66. וּבְגִין דְּאִיהוּ רָזָא דִּדְכוּרָא, נָשִׁים פְּטוּרוֹת מֵחוּשְׁבְּנָא דָא, וְלָא מִתְוַזְּיָן לְמִימְנֵי בַּר דְּכוּרִין, לְאִתְקַשְּׁרָא כָּל חַד כַּדְקָא יֵאוֹת. כְּגַוְונָא דָא, יֵרָאֶה כָּל זְכוּרְךָ, דְּכוּרִין, וְלָא נָשִׁין. בְּגִין דְּרָזָא דִבְרִית בִּדְכוּרָא אִיהוּ, וְלָא בְּנוּקְבָּא, וּבְגִין דְּקַיְימָא רָזָא לְעֵילָּא, נָשִׁין לָא מִתְחַיְּיבָן.

66. Since the Counting of the Omer **is the secret of the Male,** as we draw the Supernal Sefirot of Zeir Anpin, **women are exempted from this counting. Only the men are obligated to count, to bind each one properly. Thus "...all you males shall appear..."** (Exodus 23:17), **for the males are obligated to appear but not the women. This is because the secret of the Covenant is in the Male but not in the Female. Since the secret is Above in the Male, in Zeir Anpin, women are not obligated.**

The Seven Lower days of Malchut, which are each a week long,
receive Holinesss from Zeir Anpin.

67. וְרָזָא אוֹלִיפְנָא הָכָא, דִּבְכָל שִׁבְעַת יוֹמִין מֵאִלֵּין יוֹמִין עִלָּאִין, נַטְלָא קְדוּשָׁא יוֹמָא חַד דְּאִלֵּין תַּתָּאֵי, וְהַאי תַּתָּאָה אִקְרֵי שָׁבוּעַ, דְּאִתְקַדָּשׁ בְּשִׁבְעָה יוֹמִין עִלָּאִין. וְכֵן בְּכָל שִׁבְעָה וְשִׁבְעָה מֵאִינּוּן חַמְשִׁין יוֹמִין, עַד וְלָא עַד בִּכְלָל, וְכַד אִשְׁתְּכָחוּ אַרְבְּעִין וּתְשַׁע יוֹמִין עִלָּאִין, אִשְׁתְּכָחוּ לְתַתָּא שֶׁבַע יוֹמִין, דְּאִתְקַדָּשׁוּ בְּהוֹ וְכָל חַד אִקְרֵי שָׁבוּעַ, דְּעָאל בְּאִינּוּן שֶׁבַע. וְעַל דָּא כְּתִיב, שֶׁבַע שַׁבָּתוֹת תְּמִימוֹת תִּהְיֶינָה. בְּגִין דְּאִינּוּן נוּקְבִין, נָקַט קְרָא לִישָׁנָא דְנוּקְבִין.

67. Here we have learned a secret: From each of the Seven Supernal Days of Zeir Anpin, **one of the Lower Days** of Malchut **receives Holiness. This Lower Day** of Malchut **is called a week because it is sanctified from the Seven Supernal Days. Similarly, it is so for each and every seven of these Fifty Supernal Days, until but not including** the Fiftieth Day, meaning that the Fiftieth Day is not included among those that correct the Lower Days. **When there are Forty-Nine Supernal Days present, then Below,** in Malchut, Her **Seven Days are sanctified,** because each day is corrected by Seven Supernal Days, for through Chesed, Gevurah, Tiferet, Netzach, Hod, Yesod, and Malchut of Chesed of Zeir Anpin, Chesed of Malchut is corrected. And through Chesed, Gevurah, Tiferet, Netzach, Hod, Yesod, and Malchut of Gevurah of Zeir Anpin, Gevurah of Malchut is corrected, and so on in this manner. **Each one** that is corrected in Malchut **is called a week because it enters into those Seven** Supernal Days. **Therefore it is written: "…seven complete Shabbatot shall there be" (Leviticus 23:15),** which indicates the Seven Lower Days, which are Chesed, Gevurah, Tiferet, Netzach, Hod, Yesod, and Malchut of Malchut, as each one is called a "week." **Because they are Female,** being that they are the seven Sefirot of Malchut, **the Torah uses the feminine suffix** for them, as it is written: "…seven complete Shabbatot shall there be; שבתות תמימות תהיינה." (Ibid.)

Israel Below depend upon the sanctification of Malchut.

68. וְכַד אִתְקַדָּשׁוּ בְּהוּ, וּבֵיתָא, מִתַּתְקְנָא לְאִתְחַבְּרָא אִתְּתָא בְּבַעְלָהּ, כְּדֵין אִקְרֵי חַג שָׁבוּעוֹת, מֵאִינּוּן נוּקְבֵי דְּשָׁארוּ עֲלַיְיהוּ אִינּוּן יוֹמִין עִלָּאִין, דְּאִתְקַדָּשׁוּ בְּהוּ. ובג"כ כְּתִיב בְּשָׁבוּעוֹתֵיכֶם, אִינּוּן דִּלְכוֹן, וְלָא כְּתִיב בְּשָׁבוּעוֹת, בְּגִין דְּהָכִי נָמֵי מִתְקַדְּשִׁין יִשְׂרָאֵל לְתַתָּא עִמְּהוֹן.

68. When the seven Sefirot of Malchut **are sanctified through them,** through the Forty-Nine Supernal Sefirot, **and the House,** which is the seven Sefirot of Malchut that were not corrected during the first night of

Pesach, **is prepared so a wife would unite with her husband,** namely so Malchut would unite with Zeir Anpin, **it is then called Shavuot, named after the Females,** meaning the seven Sefirot of Malchut that are called "Seven Weeks," as mentioned earlier, **upon Whom the Supernal Days dwell,** which are the Forty-Nine Days of Zeir Anpin, **through which they are sanctified. Therefore it is written "…in your Weeks…" (Numbers 28:26),** which means **that they are yours. It is not written "in the Feast of Weeks,"** because just as the seven Sefirot of Malchut were sanctified, which are called "Weeks," **Israel Below were also sanctified with them** because Israel below depend upon the sanctification of Malchut, from Whom they receive; therefore, it says: "…in your weeks…." (Ibid.)

The Fiftieth Day is Binah, which rules over
the forty-nine Sefirot of Zeir Anpin.

69. וְעַל דָּא כַּד מָטוֹן לְתֵשַׁע וְאַרְבְּעִין יוֹמִין, הַהוּא יוֹמָא עִלָּאָה דְּעָלַיְיהוּ, דְּאִיהוּ יוֹמָא דְּחַמְשִׁין, דְּשַׁלִּיט עַל תִּשְׁעָה וְאַרְבְּעִין יוֹמִין, רָזָא דִּכְלָלָא דְּאוֹרַיְיתָא, בְּתִשְׁעָה וְאַרְבְּעִין אַנְפִּין, וּכְדֵין הַהוּא יוֹמָא עִלָּאָה, יוֹמָא דְּחַמְשִׁין, בְּאִתְעָרוּתָא דִּלְתַתָּא, אַפִּיק אוֹרַיְיתָא כְּלָלָא בְּתִשְׁעָה וְאַרְבְּעִין אַנְפִּין.

69. When we reach Forty-Nine Days, that Supernal Day which is Above them, the Fiftieth Day, which is Binah, **rules over the Forty-Nine Days,** namely the Forty-Ninth Sefirot of Zeir Anpin, **which are the secret of the entirety of the Torah,** meaning Zeir Anpin that is called "Torah," **which has Forty-Nine aspects. Then through the awakening of the Lower Beings that Supernal Day, the Fiftieth Day,** Binah, **produces the Torah,** which is Zeir Anpin, meaning the Mochin of His Upper Three Sefirot, **which is the entirety of the Forty-Nine aspects,** which are established through the Counting of the Forty-Nine Days.

EMOR

29. The Counting of the Omer

A Synopsis

Rav Aba says that when Israel were in Egypt they were attached to impurity until they were circumcised and attained the Covenant. He says that seven Shabbatot need to be counted in order to merit Zeir Anpin on the Holiday of Shavuot.

Once Israel were attached to the Holy Portion, their impurity stopped.

162. רִבִּי אַבָּא וְרִבִּי חִיָּיא הֲווֹ אָזְלֵי בְּאוֹרְחָא, אָמַר ר' חִיָּיא, כְּתִיב, וּסְפַרְתֶּם לָכֶם מִמָּחֳרַת הַשַּׁבָּת מִיּוֹם הֲבִיאֲכֶם אֶת עֹמֶר הַתְּנוּפָה. מַאי קָא מַיְירֵי. אָ"ל, הָא אוּקְמוּהָ חַבְרַיָּיא. אֲבָל ת"ח, יִשְׂרָאֵל כַּד הֲווֹ בְּמִצְרַיִם, הֲווֹ בִּרְשׁוּתָא אָחֳרָא, וַהֲווֹ אֲחִידָן בִּמְסָאֲבוּתָא, כְּאִתְּתָא דָּא, כַּד הִיא יָתְבָא בְּיוֹמֵי דִּמְסָאֲבוּתָא. בָּתַר דְּאִתְגְּזָרוּ, עָאלוּ בְּחוּלָקָא קַדִּישָׁא, דְּאִקְרֵי בְּרִית. כֵּיוָן דְּאִתְאֲחִידוּ בֵּיהּ, פָּסַק מְסָאֲבוּתָא מִנַּיְיהוּ, כְּדָא אִתְּתָא כַּד פָּסְקוּ מִנָּה דְּמֵי מְסָאֲבוּתָא. בָּתַר דְּאִתְפְּסָקוּ מִנָּה, מַה כְּתִיב. וְסָפְרָה לָהּ שִׁבְעַת יָמִים. אוּף הָכָא, כֵּיוָן דְּעָאלוּ בְּחוּלָקָא קַדִּישָׁא, פָּסְקָא מְסָאֲבוּ מִנַּיְיהוּ, וְאָמַר קוּדְשָׁא בְּרִיךְ הוּא, מִכָּאן וּלְהָלְאָה חוּשְׁבָּנָא לְדַכְיוּתָא.

162. Rav Aba and Rav Chiya were walking along the way. Rav Chiya said: "It is written, 'And you shall count for yourselves from the morrow after the Shabbat, from the day that you brought the Omer of the wave offering....' (Leviticus 23:15) What does this mean?" He **said to him, "Come and see, when Israel were in Egypt, they were under another power, and were attached to impurity as a woman sitting in her days of uncleanness. After they were circumcised, they entered the Holy portion called Covenant (Brit),** which is the secret of Malchut. **Once they were attached to it, impurity stopped from among them, as a woman whose blood of uncleanness stopped from her. After** the blood of uncleanness **stopped from her, it is written,**

'...then she shall number to herself seven days....' (Leviticus 15:28)
Here too, once they came in the Holy portion, the Covenant, their
impurity stopped and the Holy One, blessed be He, said: 'From now
on it is a reckoning for purity.'

The Counting was a means of purification.

163. וּסְפַרְתֶּם לָכֶם, לָכֶם דַּיְיקָא, כד"א וְסָפְרָה לָהּ שִׁבְעַת יָמִים, לָהּ: לְעַצְמָהּ.
אוּף הָכָא לָכֶם: לְעַצְמְכֶם. וְלָמָּה. בְּגִין לְאִתְדַּכְּאָה בְּמַיִּין עִלָּאִין קַדִּישִׁין, וּלְבָתַר
לְמֵיתֵי לְאִתְחַבְּרָא בֵּיהּ בְּמַלְכָּא, וּלְקַבְּלָא אוֹרַיְיתֵיהּ.

163. "In '...and you shall count for yourselves...'" (Leviticus 23:15)
[the word] 'yourselves' is specific, as it is written, '...then she shall
number to herself seven days...' (Leviticus 15:28) where 'to herself'
means for her sake. Here too, 'for yourselves,' means for your own
sake." [He asks:] "Why is that?" [He answers:] "It is to be purified in
Supernal Holy Waters, which is the Illumination of Binah, through
the Counting of the Omer. After that, in Shavuot, they shall come and
join the King, Zeir Anpin, and receive His Torah."

Seven weeks instead of seven days to be purified by Binah.

164. הָתָם וְסָפְרָה לָהּ שִׁבְעַת יָמִים, הָכָא שֶׁבַע שַׁבָּתוֹת, אֲמַאי שֶׁבַע שַׁבָּתוֹת.
בְּגִין לְמִזְכֵּי לְאִתְדַּכְּאָה בְּמַיִּין, דְּהַהוּא נָהָר דְּנָגֵיד וְנָפֵיק. וְאִקְרֵי מַיִם חַיִּים.
וְהַהוּא נָהָר, שֶׁבַע שַׁבָּתוֹת נָפְקוּ מִנֵּיהּ. וְעַ"ד שֶׁבַע שַׁבָּתוֹת וַדַּאי, בְּגִין לְמִזְכֵּי
בֵּיהּ, כְּמָה דְּאִתְּתָא, דַּכְיוּ דִּילָהּ בְּלֵילְיָא, לְאִשְׁתַּמְּשָׁא בְּבַעְלָהּ.

164. He asks: "There, in relation to the menstruating woman,
it is written, '...then she shall number to herself seven days...'
(Leviticus 15:28) while here it says, '...seven complete Shabbatot....'
(Leviticus 23:15) Why are seven Shabbatot needed here?" He answers:
"This is to be worthy of being purified by the water from the flowing
and emerging river, which is Binah, the Lights of which are called

Living Waters. From that river, seven Shabbatot emerge, which are the seven Sefirot, Chesed, Gevurah, Tiferet, Netzach, Hod, Yesod, and Malchut, in each of which are seven Sefirot, Chesed, Gevurah, Tiferet, Netzach, Hod, Yesod, and Malchut. They are Forty-Nine Sefirot, in the secret of the Forty-Nine Gates of Binah. **Therefore seven Shabbatot are surely** needed to be counted **to merit** Zeir Anpin on the Holiday of Shavuot and receive the Torah **like a wife on her night of cleanness, to unite with her husband."**

At Mount Sinai, the dew fell on the Israelites and purified them.

165. כַּךְ כְּתִיב וּבְרֶדֶת הַטַּל עַל הַמַּחֲנֶה לָיְלָה. עַל הַמַּחֲנֶה כְּתִיב, וְלָא כְּתִיב וּבְרֶדֶת הַטַּל לָיְלָה. אֶלָּא עַל הַמַּחֲנֶה, בְּגִין דְּיוֹרַד מֵהַהוּא נְקוּדָה, עַל אִינוּן יוֹמִין דְּאִתְקְרִיאוּ מַחֲנֶה. וּמִתְוַתֶּרֶת בְּמַלְכָּא קַדִּישָׁא, וְאֵימָתַי נָחַת הַאי טַלָּא. כַּד קְרִיבוּ יִשְׂרָאֵל לְטוּרָא דְּסִינַי, כְּדֵין נָחַת הַהוּא טַלָּא בִּשְׁלִימוּ, וְאַדְכֵּי, וְאִתְפַּסְקַת זוּהֲמָתָן מִנַּיְיהוּ, וְאִתְחַבָּרוּ בֵּיה בְּמַלְכָּא וּכְנֶסֶת יִשְׂרָאֵל, וְקַבִּילוּ אוֹרַיְיתָא, וְהָא אוֹקִימְנָא. וּבְהַהוּא זִמְנָא, וַדַּאי כָּל הַנְּחָלִים הוֹלְכִים אֶל הַיָּם, לְאִתְדַּכְּאָה וּלְאִסְתַּחֲאָה, וְכֹלָּא אִתְקְשָׁרוּ וְאִתְחַבָּרוּ בֵּיה בְּמַלְכָּא קַדִּישָׁא.

165. It is written this way, "And when the dew fell upon the camp at night...." (Numbers 11:9) It is written: "upon the camp" and not "when the dew fell in the night," but "upon the camp." (Ibid.) **The reason is that** the dew, namely abundance, **falls down from that point,** Chochmah, **upon these Forty-Nine days** in Binah **called "camp,"** and Binah **joined** them **through the Holy King,** Zeir Anpin. [He asks:] **"When did the dew fall?"** [He answers:] **"When Israel approached Mount Sinai** on Shavuot, **the dew then descended completely and purified** Israel, **and the filth was stopped from them,** namely the filth of the Serpent that he injected into Eve through the sin of the Tree of Knowledge of Good and Evil. **They joined the King and the Congregation of Israel, and received the Torah. We have already explained this. At that time, surely 'All the rivers run into the sea...'** (Ecclesiastes 1:7) **to be purified and to wash,** meaning that all the

abundance of the Sefirot of Zeir Anpin go to Malchut called "Sea,"
and Malchut achieves an equal stature to Zeir Anpin face-to-face, **and
everything is attached and united with the Holy King,** Zeir Anpin,
the Central Column, as the Holiday of Shavuot is His aspect.

Those who count the Omer merit the Torah on Shavuot.

166. ת"ח, כָּל בַּ"נ דְּלָא מָנֵי וחוּשְׁבָּנָא דָא, אִינּוּן שֶׁבַע שַׁבָּתוֹת תְּמִימוֹת, לְמִזְכֵּי
לְדַכְיוּתָא דָא. לָא אִקְרֵי טָהוֹר, וְלָאו בְּכְלָלָא דְּטָהוֹר הוּא. וְלָאו הוּא כְּדַאי
לְמֶהֱוֵי לֵיהּ חוּלָקָא בְּאוֹרַיְיתָא, וּמַאן דִּמָטֵי דְּכֵי לְהַאי יוֹמָא, וְחוּשְׁבָּנָא לָא
אִתְאֲבִיד מִנֵּיה, כַּד מָטֵי לְהַאי לֵילְיָא, לִבְעֵי לֵיהּ לְמִלְעֵי בְּאוֹרַיְיתָא, וּלְאִתְחַבְּרָא
בָּה, וּלְנַטְרָא דַּכְיוּ עִלָּאָה, דִּמָטֵי עָלֵיהּ בְּהַהוּא לֵילְיָא, וְאִתְדְּכֵי.

**166. "Come and see, whoever did not count this reckoning, these
seven complete Shabbatot, to earn this purity is not considered pure
and is not among the pure, nor is he worthy of having a portion in
the Torah. And whoever arrives pure on that day,** Shavuot, **and did
not lose the count,** upon reaching that night of Shavuot, **he needs
to be occupied in the Torah and unite with it, and keep Supernal
purity that comes to him on that night, so he is purified."**

EMOR

31. The Counting of the Omer and the Holiday of Shavuot

A Synopsis

We are told that Israel do not recite the Halel in full as in the days of Pesach since they are not yet properly whole and pure. We are told about the Fifty Days of Purification, the purpose of which is to enter the secret of the World to Come to receive the Torah, and to draw Malchut near Zeir Anpin. Forty-Nine of those days are all the aspects of the Torah, while the Fiftieth Day is the secret of the Torah itself. On the Fiftieth Day, Shavuot, the hidden is revealed. The two loaves of the offering are the secret of the two Shechinahs, the Upper and the Lower, that unite together. Zeir Anpin receives from Above and from Below, from Binah and Malchut, because Shabbat is a secret Above and Below.

The Precept to Count the Omer.

רעיא מהימנא

174. וּסְפַרְתֶּם לָכֶם מִמָּחֳרַת הַשַּׁבָּת וְגוֹ'. פָּקוּדָא דָּא, לְסְפּוֹר סְפִירַת הָעֹמֶר, הָא אוֹקִימְנָא, וְרָזָא דָּא, יִשְׂרָאֵל, אַף עַל גַּב דְּאִתְדַּכּוּ לְמֶעְבַּד פִּסְחָא, וְנָפְקוּ מִמְסָאֲבוּ, לָא הֲווֹ שְׁלֵמִין וְדַכְיָין כַּדְקָא חֲזֵי. וְעַ"ד, לָא הַלֵּל גָּמוּר בְּיוֹמֵי דְּפִסְחָא, דְּעַד כְּעַן לָא אִשְׁתְּלִימוּ כַּדְקָא יָאוּת.

Ra'aya Meheimna (Faithful Shepherd)
174. "…and you shall count for yourselves from the morrow after the Shabbat…." (Leviticus 23:15) This Precept is to count the Counting of the Omer, which we already explained. This is a secret, for Israel, even though they were purified so as to perform the Paschal sacrifice and came out of their defilement, were not yet properly whole and pure. Hence the Halel is not recited in full on the days of Pesach, since they are not yet properly complete.

Fifty Days of purification.

175. כְּאִתְּתָא דְּנָפְקָא מִמְּסָאֲבוּ, וְכֵיוָן דְּנָפְקָא, מִתַּמָּן וּלְהָלְאָה, וְסָפְרָה לָהּ. אוּף הָכָא יִשְׂרָאֵל, כַּד נָפְקוּ מִמִּצְרַיִם, נָפְקוּ מִמְּסָאֲבוּ, וְעָבְדוּ פֶּסַח, לְמֵיכַל בְּפָתוֹרָא דַּאֲבוּהוֹן, וּמִתַּמָּן וּלְהָלְאָה יַעַבְדוּן חוּשְׁבָּנָא, לְמִקְרַב אִתְּתָא לְבַעְלָהּ, לְאִתְחַבְּרָא בַּהֲדֵיהּ, וְאִינּוּן חַמְשִׁין יוֹמִין דְּדַכְיוּ, לְאַעֲלָא לְרָזָא דְּעָלְמָא דְּאָתֵי. וּלְקַבְּלָא אוֹרַיְיתָא, וּלְמִקְרַב אִתְּתָא לְבַעְלָהּ.

175. This is like **a woman who comes out of her uncleanness. From the time she comes out, "...then she shall number to herself** seven days...." (Leviticus 15:28) **Here too, when Israel came out of Egypt, they came out of impurity, and performed the Pesach, eating at their Father's Table,** namely Malchut called "Table." **From that time on, let them do the reckoning to draw a woman to her husband so she would join him. These are the Fifty Days of purification, the purpose of which is to enter the secret of the World to Come,** which is Binah that has Fifty Gates, **to receive the Torah and to draw a woman near her husband,** namely to unite Malchut with Zeir Anpin.

Only men Count the Omer, and it is done standing up.

176. וּבְגִין דְּאִלֵּין יוֹמִין, יוֹמִין דְּעָלְמָא דִּדְכוּרָא, לָא אִתְמְסַר חוּשְׁבָּנָא דָּא אֶלָּא לְגַבְרֵי בִּלְחוֹדַיְיהוּ. וְעַ"ד חוּשְׁבָּנָא דָּא, בַּעֲמִידָה אִיהוּ, וּמִלִּין דְּעָלְמָא תַּתָּאָה, בִּישִׁיבָה, וְלָא בַּעֲמִידָה. וְרָזָא דָּא, צְלוֹתָא דַּעֲמִידָה, וּצְלוֹתָא מְיוּשָׁב.

176. **Since these days are the days of the Male world** of Zeir Anpin, **only men are obligated to count. Hence the counting is done standing up.** But **that which pertains to the Lower World,** which is Malchut, **is done sitting, not standing. This is the secret of the prayer recited standing up,** the Amidah Prayer, **and the prayer recited sitting down,** from "Who forms the light" until the Amidah Prayer.

Forty-Nine is the aspect of the Torah and Fifty is the Torah itself.

177. וְאִלֵּין חַמְשִׁין, מ"ט אִינּוּן, כְּלַל אַנְפֵּי אוֹרַיְיתָא, דְּהָא בְּיוֹמָא דְּחַמְשִׁין, אִיהוּ רָזָא דְּאוֹרַיְיתָא מַמָּשׁ. וְאִלֵּין אִינּוּן חַמְשִׁין יוֹמִין, דְּבֵיהּ שְׁמִטָה וְיוֹבְלָא. וְאִי תֵימָא, חַמְשִׁין, מ"ט אִינּוּן. חַד טְמִירָא אִיהוּ, וְעָלְמָא אִסְתְּמִיךְ עֲלֵיהּ. וּבַהַהוּא יוֹמָא דְּחַמְשִׁין, אִתְגַּלְיָא טְמִירָא, וְאִתְכַּסְיָא בֵּיהּ. כְּמַלְכָּא דְּאָתֵי לְבֵי עוֹעִיבְיֵהּ, וְאִשְׁתְּכַח תַּמָּן, אוּף הָכָא יוֹמָא דְּחַמְשִׁין, וְהָא אוֹקִימְנָא רָזָא דָא.

177. As for those Fifty Days, **Forty-Nine** Days **are all the aspects of the Torah,** since there are Forty-Nine aspects of purity in the Torah, **while the Fiftieth Day is the secret of the Torah itself. And these are Fifty Days, within which is a Sabbatical year (Shmita) and Jubilee (Yovel),** seven Sabbatical years and one Jubilee. **You may ask how there are fifty,** if there are only **forty-nine,** as we do not count the Fiftieth. He answers: **"One is hidden, and the world is supported by it. On the Fiftieth Day,** Shavuot, **the hidden is revealed and concealed in it, as a king coming to his friend's house to stay there. Here too, such is the Fiftieth Day, whose secret we have already explained."**

Mar'ot HaSulam – Visions of the Ladder
Extra Explanation from Rav Ashlag

Explanation of the matter: Zeir Anpin is called Torah, and its root is from the Upper Three—Chochmah, Binah and Da'at—of Yisrael-Saba and Tevunah that are the secret of Binah. [Zeir Anpin] ascended there in the secret of the Central Column called Da'at, and He mediated between the two Columns—Chochmah and Binah of Yisrael-Saba and Tevunah—and He remained there. Afterwards, in the secret of "…three come out of one, one is found with three…" (Zohar, Beresheet A 363) these Three Columns from the Upper Three of Yisrael-Saba and Tevunah are drawn to Zeir Anpin that is Below. The Tiferet that is below the Chest, plus the Netzach-Hod-Yesod of Yisrael-Saba and Tevunah, which are considered the Lower Seven Sefirot of Yisrael-Saba and Tevunah, are clothed within Zeir Anpin and bring forth within him

Ten Sefirot. From the Netzach-Hod-Yesod of Yisrael-Saba and Tevunah come nine Sefirot—Chochmah-Binah-Da'at, Chesed-Gevurah-Tiferet, Netzach-Hod-Yesod—of Zeir Anpin, and from the Half of Tiferet that is from the chest of Yisrael-Saba and Tevunah and below comes the Keter of Zeir Anpin.

So even though the essence of the root of Zeir Anpin is in the Upper Three of Yisrael-Saba and Tevunah, in the secret of their Da'at, He nevertheless has no part in the half of the Partzuf that is from the chest of Yisrael-Saba and Tevunah and above. This is because the Curtain (Parsa) that is at the place of the chest of Yisrael-Saba and Tevunah interrupts between them. The reason for this is that the Judgments are in the secret of the Curtain (Parsa) in the secret of Malchut elevating there, and they act from the Curtain and below, but not at all from the curtain and above because Judgments and coarseness cannot rise beyond the place they are at.

This leaves a great difference between above the curtain of Yisrael-Saba and Tevunah, where no Judgments grasp at all, and below the curtain of Yisrael-Saba and Tevunah, where the Judgments already have a grasp. It is found that since Zeir Anpin is below the Curtain of Yisrael-Saba and Tevunah the Judgments have access to Him, He cannot receive the abundance that is above the Curtain that is pure of all Judgment. Thus the Curtain at the Chest of Yisrael-Saba and Tevunah limits Zeir Anpin so He cannot receive from the upper half of the Partzuf of Yisrael-Saba and Tevunah.

Know that this Curtain of Yisrael-Saba and Tevunah is the secret of the Fiftieth Gate of Binah, which even Moses did not achieve, since Moses is the secret of Zeir Anpin and Zeir Anpin also does not achieve it, as explained. For this reason we can say that the Fiftieth Gate is one Sefirah, which is Tiferet of Yisrael-Saba and Tevunah that becomes the Keter of Zeir Anpin, which is the place of the Curtain in the chest. And we can say that the half until the chest, which is the secret of Yud-Hei of Yisrael-Saba and Tevunah that is above the Curtain, is a complete Partzuf—Chochmah, Binah, Da'at, Chesed, Gevurah, and half of Tiferet—because when the Judgments of the Curtain will be nullified and the Fiftieth Gate will be revealed, Zeir Anpin will have access to the entire upper half of the Partzuf of Yisrael-Saba and Tevunah. Therefore the entire upper half of the Partzuf of Yisrael-Saba and Tevunah is considered to be the Fiftieth Gate.

Thus **"As for those Fifty, Forty-Nine are all the aspects of the Torah, while the Fiftieth Day is the secret of the Torah itself."** From the chest of Yisrael-Saba and Tevunah and above is considered their Upper Three and their Yud-Hei, and from their chest and below is considered the Lower Seven of Yisrael-Saba and Tevunah and Vav-Hei. And since Zeir Anpin only clothes the chest of Yisrael-Saba and Tevunah and below, He only has the aspect of the Lower Seven—Chesed-Gevurah-Tiferet, Netzach-Hod-Yesod-Malchut—of Yisrael-Saba and Tevunah, lacking their Upper Three. Therefore He has place for the Klipot to hold in the secret of "…one opposite the other…" (Ecclesiastes 7:14), from the force of Curtain of Yisrael-Saba and Tevunah that is on Him, as mentioned earlier. This is the secret of the Torah, Zeir Anpin, having Forty-Nine Ways of Purity and Forty-Nine Ways of Impurity, [meaning, you can see every law in Forty-Nine Ways to rule it as pure, or Forty-Nine Ways to rule it as impure], namely "one opposite the other" (Ibid.), which is **"Forty-Nine are all the aspects of the Torah,"** meaning that opposite them are forty-nine aspects of the Klipot.

But in the Fiftieth Gate, which is the secret of the entire Tiferet of Yisrael-Saba and Tevunah or the entire upper half of the Partzuf from the chest up, lies the essence of the Torah, which has no counterpart in the Klipah. Thus **"while the Fiftieth Day is the secret of the Torah itself,"** since it has no place for the Judgments and Klipot to hold to, and there lies the essence of the root of Zeir Anpin called Torah, for he is there in the secret of the Da'at of Yisrael-Saba and Tevunah, as mentioned. **"…and these are Fifty Days, within which are a Sabbatical year (Shmita) and Jubilee (Yovel),"** as the Lower Seven of Yisrael-Saba and Tevunah from the Chest down are the secret of *Shmita*, due to Malchut elevating to the place of the Curtain of Yisrael-Saba and Tevunah from the chest down, and therefore Binah itself (called *Yovel*) is not considered there. Therefore it is the secret of the Seven Sabbatical Years, which are [considered] Forty-Nine Days. And only the Fifteith Gate that is above the Curtain there is the secret of *Yovel*, which is the Fiftieth Year.

"You may ask how there are Fifty, if **there are** only **Forty-Nine,"** for if so we should have counted Fifty days and not only Forty-Nine. He answers: **"One is hidden,"** namely the Fiftieth Gate is hidden and unachievable because of the Malchut that ascended to the Curtain, so Zeir Anpin cannot receive from the Tiferet of Yisrael-Saba and Tevunah that is above the Chest, as mentioned. **"And the world is supported by it."** In other words, it cannot be revealed completely because the world, the secret of Malchut, is supported there by the Curtain because with Her elevating there She receives the sweetening of Binah, which is the attribute of Mercy, because Tiferet is the Binah of the Body, and without this the world cannot exist.

"On the Fiftieth Day, the hidden is revealed and concealed in it." In other words, the hidden, which is the Fiftieth Gate, on one hand is revealed, and on the other hand it is considered as if it is still hidden there, for it cannot be revealed completely until the Final Correction, when the Malchut of Tzimtzum Alef (First Constriction) will be corrected and will be able to receive the Supernal Light. At that point there will be no more need for Malchut to be sweetened by Binah in the secret of the Curtain, and the Curtain covering the Fiftieth Gate will be completely void. Then there will be a total achievement of the Fiftieth Gate for each person. But before this, it is only open through the elevation of the levels. And even so there are two aspects: One is in the days of Solomon, when

Zeir Anpin and Nukva were constantly set in the place of Supernal Aba and Ima, and one is in the rest of the generations when Zeir Anpin and Nukva are only from the chest of Yisrael-Saba and Tevunah and below, from the aspect of what is constant.

You need to know here that even though there are elevations of levels on Shabbats and Holidays and during prayer, nevertheless where the Partzufim stand does not change at all in terms of its constant setting. I will bring now a brief explanation that relates to our discussion. From the aspect of its constant setting, Zeir Anpin clothes Yisrael-Saba and Tevunah from the chest down, as mentioned. Therefore from the aspect of its constant setting, Zeir Anpin only has Six Corners [Sefirot] with no Head, meaning without Upper Three. Only from the aspect of the elevation of levels can Zeir Anpin elevate up to the Head of Arich Anpin, meaning three levels above Him. Nevertheless, even so He remains clothing Yisrael-Saba and Tevunah from the chest down like from the aspect of its constant setting. This is because the Partzufim above Him also ascended three levels like Him, namely when Zeir Anpin ascended to the place of Yisrael-Saba and Tevunah from the chest up, first Yisrael-Saba and Tevunah ascended to Aba and Ima, and Aba and Ima to Arich Anpin, and so on in this manner.

It turns out that even though Zeir Anpin ascended to Yisrael-Saba and Tevunah, he enclothes only from their chest down because from their chest up ascended to Aba and Ima. The same for the second level, where Zeir Anpin ascends to Supernal Aba and Ima, it must be that before then Yisrael-Saba and Tevunah also ascended to the next level, meaning to Arich Anpin, and Aba and Ima to Atik [Yomin]. So even though Zeir Anpin ascended to the space of Aba and Ima, he only enclothes Yisrael-Saba and Tevunah from the Chest down, since from the chest up of Yisrael-Saba and Tevunah is already in the space of Arich Anpin. And the same for the third level, where Zeir Anpin ascends to Arich Anpin, He only clothes Yisrael-Saba and Tevunah from the Chest down, because it must be that Yisrael-Saba and Tevunah from the Chest up already ascended to the space of Atik [Yomin], and Aba and Ima to the space of the Te'amim of SaG of Adam Kadmon. You find that even though Zeir Anpin ascended to the Head of Arich Anpin, He still clothes Yisrael-Saba and Tevunah from the Chest down like in the aspect of the constant setting.

On Shavuot, Zeir Anpin ascends to the space of the Head of Arich Anpin, where first Yisrael-Saba and Tevunah ascend to the space of Atik, and Aba and Ima to the space of the Te'amim of SaG of Adam Kadmon because the Nekudot of SaG are clothed in Atik. Then two aspects are considered in Yisrael-Saba and Tevunah. The first is that they too, ascended to the SaG of Adam Kadmon together with Aba and Ima because during the Unification [Zivug,] Aba and Ima and Yisrael-Saba and Tevunah are found on the same level. The second aspect is that they are only in the space of Atik because that is their third level, as mentioned earlier. The difference between them is massive because from the first aspect, where Yisrael-Saba and Tevunah are included in Aba and Ima, Yisrael-Saba and Tevunah are also found in the Te'amim of SaG of Adam Kadmon where there is no Curtain at all, since the Curtain begins at the Nekudot of SaG of Adam Kadmon. Because this is so, Yisrael-Saba and Tevunah already exist without a Curtain, which is the secret of the revelation of the Fiftieth Gate, like in the Final Correction, because the Lower that ascends to the Upper becomes like it. And from the second aspect, where Yisrael-Saba and Tevunah are found to be only in the space of Atik, the Curtain still rules and the Fiftieth Gate is still concealed, and Zeir Anpin cannot receive from above the chest of Yisrael-Saba and Tevunah.

This is: **"On the Fiftieth Day the hidden is revealed and concealed in it,"** for on one hand the Fiftieth Gate, which is the Fiftieth Day, is revealed because then on Shavuot, Zeir Anpin ascends to Arich Anpin, and Aba and Ima that include within them Yisrael-Saba and Tevunah ascended to the Te'amim of SaG of Adam Kadmon where there is no Curtain, which is the same as the voiding of the Curtain at the Final Correction. Thus, Zeir Anpin is able to receive from above the chest of Yisrael-Saba and Tevunah, which is the secret of its Yud-Hei, because there is no difference there between below the Curtain and above the Curtain since there is no dividing Curtain. Thus on the Fiftieth Day, which is Shavuot, the Fiftieth Gate is revealed.

However, on the other hand, according to the order of elevation, it is considered that Yisrael-Saba and Tevunah are only in the space of Atik, since this is their third level, where the Curtain rules, and the Fiftieth Gate is not revealed at all and is still covered. Therefore this Illumination of the collective of Aba and Ima and Yisrael-Saba and Tevunah that reveals the Fiftieth Gate is considered as if it only reaches the Keter of Zeir Anpin alone, meaning the half of Tiferet of Yisael-Saba and Tevunah from the chest down, which is the Keter of Zeir Anpin. And since it is part of the Sefirot of Yisrael-Saba and Tevunah it receives from the general Yisrael-Saba and Tevunah within Aba and Ima. But the Netzach-Hod-Yesod of Yisrael-Saba and Tevunah that are clothed within Zeir Anpin and are comingled with the Vessels of Zeir Anpin cannot receive from the Illumination of the revelation of the Fiftieth Gate, since the particular Yisrael-Saba and Tevunah is considered as if it is in the space of Atik, as mentioned earlier.

This is: **"as a king coming to his friend's house to stay there"** because this elevation of Yisrael-Saba and Tevunah in the space of SaG of Adam Kadmon is not a complete elevation, rather it is like a king that comes for a short time to his friend's house and is found there. So too, Yisrael-Saba and Tevunah come during the Unification (Zivug) to be included in Aba and Ima but eventually they return to the space of Atik. Therefore, the revelation of the Fiftieth Gate does not reveal the entire Partzuf of the half of Yisrael-Saba and Tevunah from the Chest up but only its Tiferet alone, which is Keter of Zeir Anpin that receives this revelation, and not the Lower Seven Sefirot called Netzach-Hod-Yesod of Yisrael-Saba and Tevunah, since they are comingled and clothed in the Vessels of Zeir Anpin, as mentioned earlier.

This applies in every generation, except for the generation of Solomon, for then Malchut was in her full completeness in the aspect of the constant setting because Zeir Anpin and Malchut were set then to clothe Aba and Ima from the chest down in a constant way, due to Yisrael-Saba and Tevunah and Aba and Ima becoming one Partzuf in a constant way. So when Zeir Anpin ascended to Arich Anpin, Yisrael-Saba and Tevunah and Aba and Ima ascended to the Te'amim of SaG of Adam Kadmon, and then there was no differentiation between Yisrael-Saba and Tevunah and Aba and Ima. This is why the Fiftieth Gate was revealed in an even more complete way. Also the Yud-Hei that is from the Chest up of Yisrael-Saba and Tevunah were revealed to their Lower Seven that are clothed within Zeir Anpin.

In verse 180, it later says: **"Once Solomon came, he individualized them, as it is written, '…seven days, and seven days…' (I Kings 8:65)"** meaning that the Fiftieth Gate shone completely in the two times "seven days," which are the seven aspects of Yud-Hei, as mentioned in Zohar, Emor 68, and the seven aspects of Vav-Hei, which are below the chest. In verse 181, this is: **"no one else needed to individualize them except Solomon. For the seven days below did not shine wholly until Solomon arrived,"** because the seven aspects of Yud-Hei do not shine below the chest of Yisrael-Saba and Tevunah in the place of Vav-Hei, and therefore there are only seven days alone here. And even so, in the days of Solomon it was still not considered fully complete, since elevation of levels are still needed, and the real revelation of the Fiftieth Gate will be at the Final Correction, as mentioned earlier.

The Precept to celebrate Shavuot.

178. פִּקּוּדָא בָּתַר דָּא, לְמֶעְבַּד חַג שָׁבוּעוֹת, דִּכְתִיב וְעָשִׂיתָ חַג שָׁבוּעוֹת לַיְיָ אֱלֹהֶיךָ. שָׁבוּעוֹת: עַל דְּעָאלוּ יִשְׂרָאֵל לְרָזָא דַּחֲמִשִּׁין יוֹמִין, דְּאִינּוּן שִׁבְעָה שָׁבוּעוֹת, וּבְקָרְבָּנָא דְּעֹמֶר, אִתְבְּטַל יֵצֶר הָרָע, דְּעָרְקַת מֵאֵשֶׁת חַיִל. וְכַד תַּפַּן לָא אִתְקְרִיב, מִתְדַּבְּקִין יִשְׂרָאֵל בְּקוּדְשָׁא בְּרִיךְ הוּא, וְאִתְבְּטַל מֵעֵילָּא וּמִתַּתָּא.

178. The following Precept is to celebrate the Holiday of Shavuot, as written: "And you shall keep the Feast of Weeks to the Lord your God…." (Deuteronomy 16:10) It is called **Shavuot (weeks), since Israel have entered the secret of the Fiftieth Day, which are seven weeks.** In other words, the Fiftieth day alone is comprised of seven weeks, as the Fiftieth Day is the secret of the Fiftieth Gate, which is the secret of Yud-Hei of Yisrael-Saba and Tevunah, which has Seven Sefirot: Chochmah, Binah, Right of Da'at, Left of Da'at, Chesed, Gevurah, and a third of Tiferet until the chest that is together with Malchut in the place of the chest (as mentioned in Zohar, Emor 68). **Through the offering of the Omer,** the Barley Offering, **the Evil Inclination,** which is the Wife of Harlotry, **is voided, fleeing the Woman of Valor.** And when the Wife of Harlotry **does not approach** the Woman of Valor, **Israel cleave to the Holy One, blessed be He,** in the secret of the seven weeks, **and the Evil Inclination is voided from Above and from Below,** not having a grasp on Zeir Anpin and Malchut.

On Atzeret the Evil Inclination is voided.

179. וּבְגִין כַּךְ אִקְרֵי בְּגַוְונָא דָּא עֲצֶרֶת, דְּאִית בֵּיהּ בִּטּוּל יֵצֶר הָרָע. וְעַל דָּא לָא כְּתִיב בֵּיהּ חַטָּאת, כִּשְׁאָר זִמְנִין, דִּכְתִיב בְּהוּ חַטָּאת לַיְיָ'. וּכְדֵין כָּל נְהוֹרִין אִתְכְּנָשׁוּ לְאֵשֶׁת חַיִל, וּבְגִין כַּךְ עֲצֶרֶת.

179. This is why it is named **Atzeret (Assembly or stopping), for in it is the voiding of the Evil Inclination. For that reason, no Sin-Offering is mentioned in relation to it, as during other festivals,**

where Sin-Offering is mentioned. Here it does not say "one he-goat as a sin-offering," and it is because in a Sin-Offering there is a portion for the Externals, and here they are already voided, so we do not need to give them a portion. **All the Lights** of the seven weeks **then gather to the Woman of Valor,** Malchut. **For that reason it is called an Assembly (***Atzeret***).**

The seven weeks Above and the seven weeks Below
are included in the Fiftieth Day.

180. שְׁבוּעוֹת, וְלָא כְּתִיב כַּמָּה אִינּוּן. אֶלָּא בְּכָל אֲתַר דְּאִתְּמַר סְתָם, שְׁמָא גְּרִים דְּאִינּוּן מִן שֶׁבַע. וּכְתִיב שִׁבְעָה שָׁבוּעוֹת תִּסְפָּר לָךְ, אֲמַאי כְּתִיב שָׁבוּעוֹת בִּלְחוֹדוֹי. אֶלָּא הָכִי אִצְטְרִיךְ שָׁבוּעוֹת סְתָם, לְאַכְלְלָא עֵילָּא וְתַתָּא, דְּהָא בְּכָל אֲתַר דְּאִלֵּין מִתְעָרֵי, אִלֵּין אוּף הָכִי מִתְעָרֵי עִמְּהוֹן. עַד לָא הֲוָה שְׁלֹמֹה, לָא הֲווֹ אִתְגַּלְיָין, כֵּיוָן דְּאָתָא שְׁלֹמֹה, עָבֵד בְּנַיְיהוּ פְּרָט. דִּכְתִיב, שִׁבְעַת יָמִים וְשִׁבְעַת יָמִים, דָּא אִיהוּ פְּרָט.

180. He asks: "It is written: **'***shavuot* **(weeks),' but not how many weeks there are."** And he answers: **"Wherever it plainly says** weeks, **the name implies there are seven** weeks, **as written: 'Seven weeks shall you number to you.' (Deuteronomy 16:9)"** He asks: **"Why does it say only 'weeks' when there are seven?"** He answers: **"So it should be** written **plainly 'weeks,'** for the purpose of **including** the seven weeks **above and** the seven weeks **below,** which are all included in the fiftieth day. **For whenever these,** the seven weeks above **stir, these** the seven weeks below **stir as well. Until Solomon came** and attained the Fiftieth Gate, and the moon was full, **they were not revealed. Once Solomon came, he individualized them, as written: 'seven days, and seven days.' (I Kings 8:65) This is individualization,** that is, the fourteen days revealed by the fiftieth gate were detailed.

In the days of Solomon, the Fiftieth Gate was revealed.

181. בְּזִמְנָא אָחֳרָא בִּכְלַל, שָׁבוּעוֹת סְתָם. וְלָא אִצְטְרִיךְ לְבַר נָשׁ אָחֳרָא לְמֶעְבַּד מִנְּהוֹן פְּרָט, בַּר שְׁלֹמֹה. בְּגִין דְּאִינּוּן שִׁבְעַת יָמִים דִּלְתַתָּא, לָא נְהִירוּ בִּשְׁלִימוּ, עַד דְּאָתָא שְׁלֹמֹה, וּכְדֵין קַיְּימָא סִיהֲרָא בְּאַשְׁלָמוּתָא, בְּאִינּוּן שִׁבְעַת יוֹמִין. וְהָכָא חַג שָׁבוּעוֹת סְתָם, בְּגִין דְּאִתְכְּלִלוּ תַתָּאֵי בְּעִלָּאֵי, וְלָא אַנְהִירוּ כְּיוֹמָא דִּשְׁלֹמֹה.

181. **"During other times,** besides the days of Solomon, there are no individual fourteen days, but **only included in weeks in general, for no one else may individualize them except Solomon. For the seven days below did not shine wholly** from the seven days above, **until Solomon arrived and the moon remained full during these seven days. But here, it is plainly 'feast of weeks,'** not mentioned in detail, **because the lower** seven days **were included in the upper** seven days **and do not shine** there **as during the days of Solomon."**

LAG B'OMER

PROLOGUE

10. The vision of Rav Chiya

Rav Chiya is worthy of elevation to the highest Spiritual Worlds, and to meet with the Holy Kabbalist Rav Shimon bar Yochai and his son Rav Elazar. Rav Chiya spends time studying with his great Master in the Supernal Academy, where Rav Shimon teaches the greatest of souls. The Messiah himself comes to spend time with Rav Shimon. These spiritual words of wisdom instill in us the ability to connect ourselves to the Supernal Worlds Above.

Rav Chiya contemplates how Rav Shimon
could be taken by dust of the earth.

49. אִשְׁתַּטַּח רַבִּי חִיָּיא בְּאַרְעָא וּנְשַׁק לְעַפְרָא, וּבְכָה וַאֲמַר, עַפְרָא עַפְרָא, כַּמָּה אַתְּ קְשֵׁי קְדָל, כַּמָּה אַתְּ בַּחֲצִיפוּ, דְּכָל מַחֲמַדֵּי עֵינָא יִתְבְּלוֹן בָּךְ, כָּל עַמּוּדֵי נְהוֹרִין דְּעָלְמָא תֵּיכוֹל וְתֵידוֹק. כַּמָּה אַתְּ וַחֲצִיפָא, בּוֹצִינָא קַדִּישָׁא דַּהֲוָה נָהִיר עָלְמָא שַׁלִּיטָא רַבְרְבָא מְמַנָּא דִּזְכוּתֵיהּ מְקַיֵּים עָלְמָא, אִתְבְּלֵי בָּךְ. רַבִּי שִׁמְעוֹן נְהִירוּ דְּבוֹצִינָא, נְהִירוּ דְּעָלְמִין, אַנְתְּ בָּלֵי בְּעַפְרָא וְאַנְתְּ קַיָּים וּנְהַג עָלְמָא. אִשְׁתּוֹמֵם רִגְעָא וְדָא, וַאֲמַר עַפְרָא עַפְרָא לָא תִתְגָּאֵי, דְּלָא יִתְמַסְרוּן בָּךְ עַמּוּדִין דְּעָלְמָא, דְּהָא רַבִּי שִׁמְעוֹן לָא אִתְבְּלֵי בָּךְ.

49. Rav Chiya prostrated himself on the earth, kissed the dust and cried out: "Dust, dust how stiff-necked (stubborn) you are; how shameless you are that all the delights of the eye perish within you. You consume all the beacons of Light in the world and grind them. How impertinent you are. The Holy Luminary that illuminated the world; the great leader who governs the entire world and whose merit sustains the world is consumed by you. Rav Shimon, the Light of the Illumination, the Light of the Worlds. You perish in the dust while you sustain and govern the world." He then fell into a reverie for a moment and said: "Dust, dust, be not proud because the pillars of the world will not be delivered into your hands; and Rav Shimon shall not be consumed by you."

Rav Chiya fasted for eighty days and saw a vision.

50. קָם רַבִּי חִיָּיא וַהֲוָה בָּכֵי. אֲזַל, וְרַבִּי יוֹסֵי עִמֵּיהּ. מֵהַהוּא יוֹמָא אִתְעַנֵּי אַרְבְּעִין יוֹמִין לְמֶחֱמֵי לְרַבִּי שִׁמְעוֹן. אָמְרוּ לֵיהּ לֵית אַנְתְּ רַשַּׁאי לְמֶחֱמֵי לֵיהּ. בָּכָה וְאִתְעַנֵּי אַרְבְּעִין יוֹמִין אַחֲרָנִין, אַחֲזִיאוּ לֵיהּ בְּחֵיזְוָא לְרַבִּי שִׁמְעוֹן וְרַבִּי אֶלְעָזָר בְּרֵיהּ, דַּהֲווֹ לָעָאן בְּמִלָּה דָּא דַּאֲמַר רַבִּי יוֹסֵי, וַהֲווֹ כַּמָּה אַלְפִין צַיְיתִין לְמִלּוּלֵיהּ.

50. Rav Chiya stood up and walked along weeping, accompanied by Rav Yosi. He fasted from that day on for forty days so that he might meet with Rav Shimon. They told him: "You are not fit to see him." He then wept and fasted for another forty days. They showed him Rav Shimon and Rav Elazar his son, in a vision. They were discussing the interpretation of that word, which Rav Yosi mentioned in the name of Rav Shimon. **And many thousands were listening to his words.**

Rav Shimon and Rav Elazar flew to the Heavenly Yeshivah
and shone more than the sun.

51. אַדְהָכֵי, וְחָמָא כַּמָּה גַּדְפִין רַבְרְבִין עִלָּאִין, וּסְלִיקוּ עֲלַייהוּ רַבִּי שִׁמְעוֹן וְרַבִּי אֶלְעָזָר בְּרֵיהּ וּסְלִיקוּ לִמְתִיבְתָּא דִּרְקִיעָא, וְכָל אִלֵּין גַּדְפִין הֲווֹ מְחַכָּאן לְהוּ. וְחָמָא דְּמִתְהַדְּרָן וּמִתְחַדְּשָׁן בְּזִיווֹ וּנְהִירוּ יַתִּיר מִנְּהוֹרָא דְּזִיוָא דְּשִׁמְשָׁא.

51. Meanwhile, he saw many great Celestial Wings. Rav Shimon and his son Rav Elazar mounted on them and were borne aloft to the Heavenly Yeshivah. And all those Wings were waiting for them. **He then saw** that Rav Shimon and Rav Elazar **were renewed constantly by their own splendor and shone more than the sun.**

Rav Chiya saw the pillars of the world and was in awe.

‎52. פָּתַח רָבִּי שִׁמְעוֹן וַאֲמַר, יֵיעוֹל רַבִּי חִיָּיא וְלֶיחֱמֵי, בְּכַמָּה דְזַמִּין קָדוֹשׁ בָּרוּךְ הוּא לְאַחֲדָתָא אַנְפֵּי צַדִּיקַיָּיא לְזִמְנָא דְאָתֵי. זַכָּאָה אִיהוּ מַאן דְעָאל הָכָא בְּלָא כִסּוּפָא וְזַכָּאָה מַאן דְקָאִים בְּהַהוּא עָלְמָא, כְּעַמּוּדָא תַקִּיף בְּכֹלָּא, וַחֲמָא דַהֲוָה עָאל וַהֲוָה קָם רַבִּי אֶלְעָזָר וּשְׁאָר עַמּוּדִין דִלְתַּבִין תַּמָּן. וְהוּא הֲוָה כָּסִיף, וְאִשְׁתְּמִיט גַּרְמֵיהּ, וְעָאל וְיָתֵיב לְרַגְלוֹי דְרַבִּי שִׁמְעוֹן.

52. Rav Shimon opened the discussion and said: "Let Rav Chiya enter and see how much the Holy One, blessed be He, shall restore the faces of the righteous in the World to Come. How happy is he who comes here without shame, and how happy is he who stands erect in that world as a strong Pillar that bears all." Rav Chiya saw himself **entering, and Rav Elazar stood up. So did all of the other Pillars** of the world, **which had previously been sitting there.** They all stood up before Rav Chiya. **And he,** Rav Chiya, **was embarrassed. As he entered, he detached himself and sat at the feet of Rav Shimon.**

A voice called out to those hidden ones whose eyes are open.

‎53. קָלָא נָפַק וַאֲמַר, מָאִיךְ עֵינָךְ לָא תִזְקוֹף רֵישָׁךְ, וְלָא תִסְתַּכַּל. מָאִיךְ עֵינוֹי, וַחֲמָא נְהוֹרָא דַהֲוָה נָהִיר לְמֵרָחוֹק. קָלָא אַהֲדַר כְּמִלְקַדְמִין, וַאֲמַר עִלָּאִין סְתִימִין פְּקִיחֵי עֵינָא, אִינּוּן דִמְשַׁטְטֵי בְּכָל עָלְמָא, אִסְתְּכָלוּ וַחֲמוּ. תַּתָּאִין דְמִיכִין סְתִימִין בְּחוֹרֵיכוֹן, אִתְעָרוּ.

53. A voice came forth, saying: "Lower your eyes, do not raise your head up, and do not look." He lowered his eyes and saw a Light that shone from afar. **The voice returned and said: "You hidden and unseen Celestials on high, you whose eyes are open and wander throughout the world, behold and see. Earthly beings that are in slumber,** with the Light of your eyes **concealed in Your** eye sockets, **wake up.**

Only those who have transformed bitterness to sweetness can enter.

54. מָאן מִנְּכוֹן, דִּי וַחֲשׁוֹכָא מְהַפְּכָן לִנְהוֹרָא, וְטַעֲמִין מְרִירָא לְמִתְקָא, עַד לָא יֵיתוּן הָכָא. מָאן מִנְּכוֹן, דִּמְחַכָּאן בְּכָל יוֹמָא לִנְהוֹרָא דְּנָהִיר בְּשַׁעֲתָא דְּמַלְכָּא פָּקִיד לְאַיַּלְתָּא, וְאִתְיַיקַּר, וְאִתְקְרֵי מַלְכָּא מִכָּל מַלְכִין דְּעָלְמָא. מָאן דְּלָא מְצַפֶּה דָא בְּכָל יוֹמָא בְּהַהוּא עָלְמָא, לֵית לֵיהּ חוּלָקָא הָכָא.

54. "Who among you has during his lifetime in this world **transformed darkness into Light and the taste of bitter into sweet before he came here? Who among you has awaited eagerly every day the Light that shines when the King calls upon the Gazelle? As then, the glory** of the King increases, **and He is called the King of all the other kings of the world. Because he who does not await eagerly for this every day,** as he lives **in that world,** meaning this world **has no part here."**

The Winged One was above all the Pillars.

55. אַדְּהָכֵי וְחָמָא כַּמָּה מִן חַבְרַיָּיא, סַחֲרָנֵיהּ כָּל אִינּוּן עַמּוּדִין דְּקַיָּימִין. וַחֲמָא דְּסָלִיקוּ לוֹן לִמְתִיבְתָּא דִּרְקִיעָא, אִלֵּין סָלְקִין, וְאִלֵּין נָחֲתִין, וְעֵילָּא דְּכֻלְּהוּ וַחֲמָא בָּארֵי דְּגַדְפֵּי דַּהֲוָה אָתֵי.

55. Meanwhile, he saw many of his friends gathering around the standing Pillars, and he saw how they elevated them to the Heavenly Yeshivah. Some were ascending while others were descending. And high above them all, he saw the Winged One, who is Metatro"n, **approach.**

The King sheds tears every day about the pain of the Shechinah.

56. וְהוּא אוֹמֵי אוֹמָאָה, דְּשָׁמַע מֵאֲחוֹרֵי פַּרְגּוֹדָא, דְּמַלְכָּא מְפַקֵּד בְּכָל יוֹמָא וְדָכִיר לְאַיַּלְתָּא דִּי שְׁכִיבַת לְעַפְרָא, וּבָעַט בְּעִיטִין בְּהַהוּא שַׁעֲתָא בִּתְלַת מְאָה וְתִשְׁעִין רְקִיעִין, וְכֻלְּהוּ מְרַתְּתִין וְזָעִין קַמֵּיהּ. וְאוֹרִיד דִּמְעִין עַל דָּא, וְנָפְלֵי אִינּוּן דִּמְעִין רְתִיחִין כְּאֶשָּׁא לְגוֹ יַמָּא רַבָּא, וּמֵאִינּוּן דִּמְעִין קָאֵים הַהוּא מְמַנָּא

דְיַמָּא, וְאִתְקַיַּים, וְקָדִישׁ שְׁמֵיהּ דְּמַלְכָּא קַדִּישָׁא, וְקָבֵּיל עֲלֵיהּ לְמִבְלַע כָּל מֵימוֹי דִּבְרֵאשִׁית, וְיִכְנוֹשׁ לְהוֹ לְגַוֵּיהּ, בְּשַׁעְתָא דְּיִתְכַּנְּשׁוּן כָּל עַמְמַיָּא עַל עַמָּא קַדִּישָׁא, וִיגֻבוּן מַיָּא, וְיַעַבְרוּן בְּנֶגְבּוּ.

56. The angel Metatro"n **swears that he heard from behind the curtain how the King attends the Gazelle every day and remembers how She lies in the dust. At that time, He kicks 390 Heavens, which all quake and tremble with fear because of Him. And He,** the King, **sheds tears because of this**—that the Shechinah lies in the dust. **And the tears, that are hot as fire, fall down into the Great Sea. By the power of these tears, the Minister who rules the Sea,** and is called Rahav, **is sustained and stays alive. And He sanctifies the Name of the Holy King by taking it upon Himself to swallow all the waters of the days of Creation. He gathers them all within Himself so that on that day when all the nations assemble against the Holy Nation, the waters may dry up while they cross over on dry land.**

King Messiah comes to each Academy to sign and seal their teachings.

57. אַדְהָכֵי, שְׁמַע קָלָא דַּאֲמַר, פַּנּוּ אֲתַר פַּנּוּ אֲתַר, דְּהָא מַלְכָּא מְשִׁיחָא אָתֵי לִמְתִיבְתָּא דְּרַבִּי שִׁמְעוֹן, בְּגִין דְּכָל צַדִּיקַיָּא דְּתַמָּן רֵישֵׁי מְתִיבְתָּא. וְאִינּוּן מְתִיבְתֵּי דְּתַמָּן רְשִׁימִין אִינּוּן. וְכָל אִינּוּן חַבְרִין דִּי בְּכָל מְתִיבְתָּא, סַלְקֵי מִמְּתִיבְתָּא דְּהָכָא לִמְתִיבְתָּא דִּרְקִיעָא. וּמְשִׁיחַ אָתֵי בְּכָל אִינּוּן מְתִיבְתֵּי, וְחָתִים אוֹרַיְיתָא מִפּוּמַיְיהוּ דְּרַבָּנָן. וּבְהַהִיא שַׁעֲתָא אָתֵי מְשִׁיחַ מִתְעַטַּר מִן רֵישֵׁי מְתִיבְתֵּי בְּעִטְרִין עִלָּאִין.

57. Meanwhile, he heard a voice call out: "Move aside, make room. King Messiah is coming to the Academy of Rav Shimon" because all the Righteous People that are there are the Heads of the Academies, **which are known up there. And all the disciples of each Academy ascend from this Academy here to the Heavenly Academy. And Messiah visits all these Academies and signs the Torah with the seal of the teachings that come from the mouths of the learned Ravs.**

At that time, King Messiah came to the Academy of Rav Shimon crowned by Heavenly Crowns that He had received from the Heads of the Academies.

Messiah praises Rav Shimon's teachings.

58. בְּהַהוּא שַׁעְתָא, קָמוּ כָּל אִינוּן חַבְרַיָּיא, וְקָם ר' שִׁמְעוֹן, וַהֲוָה סָלֵיק נְהוֹרֵיהּ עַד רוּם רָקִיעַ, אָמַר לֵיהּ רַבִּי זַכָּאָה אַנְתְּ, דְּאוֹרַיְיתָךְ סָלְקָא בִּתְלַת מְאָה וְשַׁבְעִין נְהוֹרִין וְכָל נְהוֹרָא וּנְהוֹרָא אִתְפָּרְשַׁת לְשִׁית מְאָה וּתְלֵיסַר טַעֲמִין סָלְקִין וְאַסְתַּחְזִין בְּנַהֲרֵי אֲפַרְסְמוֹנָא דַּכְיָא. וְקוּדְשָׁא בְּרִיךְ הוּא אִיהוּ חָתִים אוֹרַיְיתָא מִמְּתִיבְתָּךְ, וּמִמְתִיבְתָּא דְּחִזְקִיָּה מֶלֶךְ יְהוּדָה, וּמִגּוֹ מְתִיבְתָּא דַּאֲחִיָּה הַשִּׁילוֹנִי.

58. At the same time, all the friends and Rav Shimon as well, stood up. Rav Shimon's Light reached up to the highest Firmament. Messiah **said to him:** "Rav, how blessed you are, that your Torah (teachings) has been elevated by the Illumination of 370 Lights. And every single Light has been explained in 613 ways. Then they rise up and bathe themselves in the rivers of pure balsam. And the Holy One, blessed be He, approves the Torah study of your Academy, of the Academy of Hezekiah King of Judah, and of the Academy of Achiya HaShiloni.

The Winged One noticed Rav Chiya.

59. וַאֲנָא לָא אָתֵינָא לְמוֹזְחַם לִמְתִיבְתָּךְ, אֶלָּא מָאֲרֵי דְּגַדְפִין אָתֵי הָכָא, דְּהָא יָדַעְנָא דְּלָא יֵיעוֹל גּוֹ מְתִיבְתֵּי אַחֲרִיתֵי, אֶלָּא בִּמְתִיבְתָּךְ. בְּהַהִיא שַׁעְתָא סָח לֵיהּ ר' שִׁמְעוֹן, הַהוּא אוּמָאָה דְּאוֹמֵי מָאֲרֵי דְּגַדְפִין. כַּדְּ אִזְדַּעֲזַע מְשִׁיחַ וְאָרֵים קָלֵיהּ, וְאִזְדַּעֲזָעוּ רְקִיעִין, וְאִזְדַּעֲזַע יַמָּא רַבָּא, וְאִזְדַּעֲזַע לִוְיָתָן, וְחָשִׁיב עָלְמָא לְאִתְהַדְבְּכָא, אַדְהָכֵי חָמָא לְר' חִיָּיא לְרַגְלוֹי דְּרַבִּי שִׁמְעוֹן. אָמַר, מַאן יָהֵיב הָכָא בַּר נָשׁ לָבִישׁ מַדָּא דְּהַהוּא עָלְמָא. אָמַר רַבִּי שִׁמְעוֹן דָּא אִיהוּ רַבִּי חִיָּיא, נְהִירוּ דְּבוֹצִינָא דְּאוֹרַיְיתָא. אָמַר לֵיהּ, יִתְכַּנֵּשׁ הוּא וּבְנוֹי, וְלֶיהֱווֹן מִמְּתִיבְתָּא דִּילָךְ. אָמַר רַבִּי שִׁמְעוֹן זִמְנָא יִתְיְהֵב לֵיהּ. יָהֲבוּ לֵיהּ זִמְנָא.

59. "I have come to approve the Torah of your Academy only because the Winged One is on his way here, and I know that he shall not enter any other Academy, only yours." Meanwhile, he told Rav Shimon about the oath taken by the Winged One. Then Messiah trembled and raised up his voice. The Heavens also trembled, as did the Great Sea and the Whale. The world was about to collapse. Also at this time, he noticed Rav Chiya sitting at the feet of Rav Shimon. He said: "Who allowed a human being, wearing the cloaks of that world, namely the physical body of this world, here?" Rav Shimon answered: "This is Rav Chiya the shining Light of the Torah." He said: "Let he and his sons be gathered, meaning, let them pass away from this world, and join your Academy." Rav Shimon said: "Let him be given time." And time was given to him.

Rav Chiya praises the Righteous, and Rav Shimon specifically.

60. וְנָפַק מִתַּמָּן מְזַדַעֲזָע, וְזָלְגָן עֵינוֹי דְמִעִין. אוֹזְדַעֲזָע רִבִּי חִיָּיא, וּבְכָה וַאֲמַר, זַכָּאָה חוּלְקֵהוֹן דְּצַדִיקַיָּיא בְּהַהוּא עָלְמָא, וְזַכָּאָה חוּלְקֵיהּ דְּבַר יוֹחָאי דְּזֶכָה לְכָךְ. עֲלֵיהּ כְּתִיב לְהַנְחִיל אוֹהֲבַי יֵשׁ וְאוֹצְרוֹתֵיהֶם אֲמַלֵּא.

60. He, Messiah, left there trembling all over, his eyes brimming with tears. Rav Chiya was deeply shaken and wept. Then he said: "How happy are the righteous with their portion in the World to Come, and how happy is the son of Yochai, who has this distinction. He is described by the verse, 'I may cause those who love me to inherit substance; and I will fill their treasures.' (Proverbs 8:21)"

PROLOGUE

20. Rav Shimon's departure from the cave

The Zohar recounts the final day Rav Shimon and his son Rav Elazar spent in the cave where Rav Shimon had buried himself neck deep in the ground for thirteen years, during his learning of the Zohar. Rav Shimon at last emerges from the cave, battered and decomposed. He credits his total disregard for the comforts and desires of his body as the secret behind the revelation of the wisdom of the Zohar. By relating this passage to our own lives, we too, can arouse the will and self-control for overcoming destructive tendencies, which are rooted in the Desire to Receive for the Self Alone.

The soul of Rav Shimon shines like the radiance of the sun.

185. רַבִּי פִּינְחָס הֲוָה שְׁכִיחַ קַמֵּי דְּרַבִּי רְחוּמָאי בְּכֵיף יַמָּא דְּגִנּוֹסָר. וּב"נ רַב וּקְשִׁישָׁא דְּיוֹמִין הֲוָה, וְעֵינוֹי אִסְתַּלָּקוּ מִלְּמֶחֱמֵי. אָמַר לְרַבִּי פִּינְחָס, וַדַּאי שְׁמַעְנָא דְּיוֹחָאי חַבְרָנָא אִית לֵיהּ מַרְגָּלִית אֶבֶן טָבָא, וְאִסְתַּכַּלִית בִּנְהוֹרָא דְּהַהִיא מַרְגָּלִית, נָפְקָא כִּנְהִירוּ דְּשִׁמְשָׁא מִנַּרְתְּקָהּ, וְנָהֲרָא כָּל עָלְמָא.

185. Rav Pinchas frequently visited Rav Rechumai at the shore of the Sea of Galilee. He was a great man who was full of years and had lost his eyesight. He said to Rav Pinchas: "I have heard that our friend Yochai has a jewel, a precious stone, namely a son. And I **have observed the Light of that jewel,** and it **shines like the radiance of the sun as it emerges out from its sheath and illuminates the whole world."**

Explanation: Malchut with all Her corrections is called a precious stone and is called a jewel. He says that **"our friend Yochai has a jewel, a precious stone,"** meaning that he already achieved Malchut in all Her corrections and adornments. He saw with Divine Inspiration that the Light of the jewel shines like the light of the sun when it emerges from its sheath, which is the secret of the future correction of Malchut when the light of the moon will be like the light of the sun, as then She illuminates the entire world. After the Light of Malchut became the light of the sun and ascended to the Heaven, She shone from the Heaven to the Earth as one pillar of Light to the entire world. It went on to shine until Rav Shimon bar Yochai managed to fix the Throne of Atik as is needed. The allusion is that he already merited the two revelations of the Final Correction, which are the **"six verses and the six mentions of the Name."** (Zohar, Prologue 145) **"Light extends from the Heavens down to the Earth"** is the secret of the six verses, and **"until the Atik Yomin appears and is properly seated upon the Throne"** is the secret of the six mentions of the Name, study there well.

Rav Pinchas is urged to go after Rav Shimon and Rav Elazar.

186. וְהַהוּא נְהוֹרָא קָאֵים מִשְּׁמַיָּא לְאַרְעָא, וְנָהִיר כָּל עָלְמָא, עַד דְּיָיְתֵיב עַתִּיק יוֹמִין, וְיָתִיב עַל כָּרְסַיָּיא כִּדְקָא יָאוֹת. וְהַהוּא נְהוֹרָא כָּלִיל כֹּלָּא בְּבֵיתָךְ, וּמֵהַהוֹרָא דְּאִתְכְּלִיל בְּבֵיתָךְ, נָפִיק נְהִירוּ דַּקִּיק וְזָעֵיר, וְנָפִיק לְבַר וְנָהִיר כָּל עָלְמָא, זַכָּאָה חוּלָקָךְ. פּוּק בְּרִי פּוּק, זִיל אַבַּתְרֵיהּ דְּהַהִיא מַרְגָּלִית דְּנָהִיר עָלְמָא, דְּהָא שַׁעֲתָא קָיְימָא לָךְ.

186. "And that Light extends from the Heavens down to the Earth, and shines to the whole world until the Atik Yomin, who is Keter, **appears and is properly seated upon the Throne,** namely until the End of the Correction. **And this Light is contained entirely in your household,** namely in your daughter, because the daughter of Rav Pinchas was the wife of Rav Shimon bar Yochai. **And from the Light that is contained in your household, a small and thin Light emerges,** namely the son of his daughter, who is Rav Elazar, **and brightens up the whole world. How happy is your lot. Go my son, go. Go after that jewel that shines and lights up all the world, as the hour is propitious for you."**

Explanation: The daughter of Rav Pinchas ben Yair was the wife of Rav Shimon, thus it is found that Rav Shimon being contained in the house of Rav Pinchas ben Yair refers to Rav Elazar who emerged from the Light contained in the house of Rav Pinchas ben Yair, who is Rav Shimon and his wife, and brightened up the whole world.

Rav Pinchas sent birds to find Rav Shimon's whereabouts.

187. נָפַק מִקַּמֵּיהּ וְקָאִים לְמֵיעַל בְּהַהִיא אַרְבָּא, וּתְרֵין גּוּבְרִין בַּהֲדֵיהּ וְזָבְא תְּרֵין צִפֳּרִין דַּהֲווֹ אַתְיָין וְטָסִין עַל יַמָּא, רָמָא לוֹן קָלָא וַאֲמַר, צִפֳּרִין צִפֳּרִין דְּאַתּוּן טָאסִין עַל יַמָּא וַחֲמֵיתוּן דּוּךְ דְּבַר יוֹחָאי תַּמָּן, אִשְׁתָּהֵי פּוּרְתָּא אֲמַר צִפֳּרִין צִפֳּרִין זִילוּ וַאֲתִיבוּ לִי. פְּרְחוּ וַאֲזְלוּ, עָאלוּ בְּיַמָּא וְאָזְלֵי לְהוֹן.

187. He went out from before him and was about to enter a boat, accompanied by two people. He saw two birds flying toward him over the sea. He raised up his voice and said: "Birds, birds, you who fly over the waters, have you seen the place where the son of Yochai is?" He waited awhile and then said: "Birds, birds, go and bring me back an answer." They flew away; they flew into the sea and disappeared.

Explanation: Rav Shimon ran away because of the government who decreed that he be killed, and he and his son hid in a cave (as brought in Tractate Shabbat 33b), and they did not know where he was. Therefore Rav Pinchas ben Yair went out to find him in the islands of the sea.

Rav Pinchas finds and meets Rav Shimon.

188. עַד דְּנָפַק, הָא אִינּוּן צִפֳּרִין אַתְיָין, וּבְפוּמָא דְּוַזְדָא מִנַּיְיהוּ פִּתְקָא וְדָא, וּכְתִיב בְּגַוֵּיהּ, דְּהָא בַּר יוֹחָאי נָפַק מִן מְעַרְתָּא, וְרַבִּי אֶלְעָזָר בְּרֵיהּ אָזַל לְגַבֵּיהּ, וְאַשְׁכַּח לֵיהּ מְשַׁנֵּא, וְגוּפֵיהּ מַלְיָא וְחֲלוּדִין. בָּכָה בַּהֲדֵיהּ, וַאֲמַר, וַוי דַּחֲמֵיתָךְ בְּכָךְ. אֲמַר, זַכָּאָה חוּלְקִי דַּחֲמֵית לִי בְּכָךְ, דְּאִלְמָלֵא לָא חֲמֵיתָא לִי בְּכָךְ לָא

הַוֵינָא בְּכָךְ. פָּתַח רַבִּי שִׁמְעוֹן בְּפִקּוּדֵי אוֹרַיְיתָא וַאֲמַר, פִּקּוּדֵי אוֹרַיְיתָא דִּיהַב
קָדוֹשׁ בָּרוּךְ הוּא לְיִשְׂרָאֵל כֻּלְּהוּ בְּאוֹרַיְיתָא בְּאֹרַח כְּלַל כְּתִיבֵי.

188. Before he went on board the ship, **the two birds appeared again. In the mouth of one of them was a letter informing him that** Rav Shimon, **the son of Yochai, had left the cave together with his son, Rav Elazar.** Rav Pinchas **went to meet him.** He saw that he had **completely changed, and his body was full of scars and sores** from staying so long in the cave. **He wept together** with him **and said: "Woe, that I have seen you so."** Rav Shimon replied: **"How happy is my lot, that you have seen me so. Because had you not seen me thus I would not have been so."** Rav Shimon opened the discussion on the **Precepts of the Torah and said: "The precepts of the Torah that were given to Israel by the Holy One, blessed be He, are all written in the Torah in general."**

Explanation: Due to the many years Rav Shimon was in the cave, where he was forced to sit there inside the earth so that he can be covered and deal with the Torah, because of this, his body was filled with holes. [Rav Pinchas ben Yair] cried over him and said: **"Woe that I have seen you thus."** Rav Shimon replied: **"How happy is my lot, that you have seen me so. Because had you not seen me thus I would not have been so."** In other words, he would not have merited the revelation of the secrets of the Torah because the entire exaltedness of his great wisdom he received in those thirteen years he hid in the cave.

VAYECHI

19. Rav Yitzchak sat sadly

A Synopsis

Rav Yitzchak asks Rav Yehuda for three things that were troubling him. Rav Yehuda then asks him why he thinks he is going to die. Rav Yitzchak explains that he no longer sees his shadow. They go to see Rav Shimon, who protects them from the Angel of Death. Rav Shimon asks Rav Yitzchak if he has seen his father today, for if so, that means he will die. Rav Shimon summons God to prepare to take Rav Yehuda away. Rav Yitzchak then sleeps and sees his father in his dream, who tells him that they are preparing his chamber in Heaven. Next, Rav Shimon asks God that Rav Yitzchak will not die, and the wish is granted. Not only that, Rav Yitzchak is given seventy places with doors to seventy worlds. Rav Yitzchak is then told that he will discover the secrets with Rav Shimon upon his death.

The Revelence of this Passage

The profound greatness of Rav Shimon is made evident here through his influence and connection to the Creator Who allows him to turn aside the Angel of Death on behalf of a fellow Rav, reversing a decree of death. Moreover, great Spiritual Worlds and treasures await Rav Yitzchak in the World to Come, by virtue of his association to Rav Shimon. In effect, this ancient passage is telling us that anyone who truthfully embraces the path of Rav Shimon and connects deeply to the Zohar and its wisdom will have the power to stop the Angel of Death in its tracks and secure a place high in the Heavens in the World to Come. The Light emitted here helps to facilitate our connection to the path of the Zohar and deepens our relationship with the giant of all kabbalists, the Master Rav Shimon bar Yochai.

Rav Yitzchak sat sadly.

144. ר' יִצְחָק, הֲוָה יָתֵיב יוֹמָא חַד, אַפִּתְחָא דְּר' יְהוּדָה, וַהֲוָה עָצֵיב, נָפֵיק ר' יְהוּדָה, אַשְׁכְּחֵיהּ לְתַרְעֵיהּ, דַּהֲוָה יָתֵיב וְעָצֵיב, א"ל מַאן יוֹמָא דֵין מִשְׁאָר יוֹמִין.

144. Rav Yitzchak sat sadly one day by the door of Rav Yehuda. Rav Yehuda came out and found him sitting in sadness at his door. He said to him: "Why is today different than other days?"

Three requests from Rav Yitzchak.

145. א"ל, אָתֵינָא לְגַבָּךְ, לְמִבְעֵי מִינָךְ תְּלַת מִלִּין: חַד, דְּכַד תֵּימָא מִלֵּי דְאוֹרַיְיתָא, וְתִדְכַּר מֵאִינוּן מִלִּין דַּאֲנָא אֲמֵינָא, דְּתֵימָא לוֹן מִשְׁמִי, בְּגִין לְאַדְכָּרָא שְׁמִי. וְחַד דְּתִזְכֵּי לְיוֹסֵף בְּרִי בְּאוֹרַיְיתָא. וְחַד, דְּתֵיזֵיל לְקִבְרִי כָּל ז' יוֹמִין, וְתִבְעֵי בָּעוּתִיךְ עָלַי.

145. He said to him: "I come to you to request from you three things. The first is that when you say words of the Torah, and you shall say the things that I said, say them in my name so as to mention my name. Also, that you shall teach Torah to my son, Joseph, and that you shall go to my grave all the seven days of mourning and pray for me."

Rav Yitzchak did not see his shadow and felt it was his time to depart.

146. א"ל מִנַּיִן לָךְ. א"ל, הָא נִשְׁמָתִי אִסְתַּלְּקַת מִינִּי בְּכָל לֵילְיָא, וְלָא אַנְהֵיר לִי בְּחֶלְמָא, כְּמָה דַּהֲוָה בְּקַדְמֵיתָא, וְעוֹד דְּכַד אֲנָא מַצְלֵינָא, וּמַטֵינָא לְשׁוֹמֵעַ תְּפִלָּה, אַשְׁגַּחְנָא בְּצוּלְמֵי דִּילִי בְּכוּתְלָא, וְלָא חָמֵינָא לֵיהּ, וַאֲמֵינָא דְּהוֹאִיל וְצוּלְמָא אִתְעֲבַר וְלָא אִתְחֲזֵי, דְּהָא כָּרוֹזָא נָפֵיק וְכָרֵיז, דִּכְתִיב אַךְ בְּצֶלֶם יִתְהַלֶּךְ אִישׁ, כָּל זִמְנָא דְּצוּלְמָא דְּבַר נָשׁ לָא יִתְעֲבַר מִנֵּיהּ, יִתְהַלֶּךְ אִישׁ, וְרוּחֵיהּ אִתְקַיְּימָא בְּגַוֵּיהּ, אִתְעֲבַר צוּלְמָא דְּבַר נָשׁ וְלָא אִתְחֲזֵי, אִתְעֲבַר מֵהַאי עָלְמָא.

146. He said to him: "How do you know you are going to die?" Rav Yitzchak said to him: "My soul departs from me every night but it does not enlighten me with dreams as before. Moreover, when I pray and reach the part of 'who hears prayer,' I look at my shadow upon the wall but do not see it. I think I shall die since the shadow is gone from me and cannot be seen. For a herald comes forth and proclaims, as it is written, 'Surely every man walks in a shadow....' (Psalms 39:7) As long as his shadow has not gone from him, 'every man walks' and his spirit is within him. Once a man's shadow is no longer seen, he passes away from this world."

Rav Yehuda asks that Rav Yitzchak reserve
a place for him in the Upper Worlds.

147. א"ל וּמֵהָכָא, דִּכְתִיב כִּי צֵל יָמֵינוּ עֲלֵי אָרֶץ. א"ל, כָּל אִלֵּין מִלִּין דְּאַתְּ בָּעֵי עֲבִידְנָא, אֲבָל בָּעֵינָא מִינָךְ דִּבְהַהוּא עָלְמָא, תְּבָרֵיר דּוּכְתָּאי גַּבָּךְ, כְּמָה דַּהֲוֵינָא בְּהַאי עָלְמָא. בָּכָה רִבִּי יִצְחָק וַאֲמַר, בִּמְטוּ מִינָךְ, דְּלָא תִתְפָּרֵשׁ מִנָּאִי כָּל אִלֵּין יוֹמִין.

147. Rav Yehuda said to him: "It is also derived from the verse, '... because our days upon Earth are a shadow.' (Job 8:9)" Rav Yehuda said to him: "I shall carry out your requests. But I also ask that you shall reserve a place for me by you in the other world, as I was by your side in this world." Rav Yitzchak wept and said: "Please do not go away from me all these days."

Rav Shimon saw the Angel of Death dancing around Rav Yitzchak.

148. אֲזָלוּ לְגַבֵּיהּ דְּרִבִּי שִׁמְעוֹן, אַשְׁכְּחוּהוּ דַּהֲוָה לָעֵי בְּאוֹרַיְיתָא, זָקִיף עֵינוֹי ר"ש, וְחָמָא לְרִבִּי יִצְחָק, וְחָמָא לְמַלְאָךְ הַמָּוֶת דְּרָהִיט קַמֵּיהּ, וְרָקִיד קַמֵּיהּ. קָם רִבִּי שִׁמְעוֹן, אָחִיד בִּידֵיהּ דְּרִבִּי יִצְחָק, אֲמַר, גּוֹזַרְנָא, מַאן דְּרָגִיל לְמֵיעַל, יֵיעוֹל. וּמַאן דְּלָא רָגִיל לְמֵיעַאל, לָא יֵיעוֹל. עָאלוּ רִבִּי יִצְחָק וְרִבִּי יְהוּדָה, קָטֵיר מַלְאַךְ הַמָּוֶת לְבַר.

148. They went to Rav Shimon and found him occupied with the Torah. Rav Shimon lifted up his eyes and saw the Angel of Death running and dancing before Rav Yitzchak. Rav Shimon stood up, held Rav Yitzchak by the hand and said: "I decree that whoever is accustomed to come to me shall enter, and he who is not accustomed shall not come." Rav Yitzchak and Rav Yehuda came in. He thus tied the Angel of Death outside, unable to come in.

Rav Elazar guarded the entrance so no entity may enter.

149. אַשְׁגָּח ר"ש, וְחָזְמָא, דְּעַד כְּעַן לָא מָטָא עִדָּנָא, דְּהָא עַד תְּמַנְיָא שַׁעֲתֵי דְיוֹמָא הֲוָה זִמְנָא, אוֹתְבֵיהּ קַמֵּי ר"ש, וַהֲוָה לָעֵי לֵיהּ בְּאוֹרַיְיתָא. אר"ש לְרַבִּי אֶלְעָזָר בְּרֵיהּ, תִּיב אַפִּתְחָא וּמַה דְּתֶחֱמֵי, לָא תִשְׁתָּעֵי בַּהֲדֵיהּ, וְאִי יִבְעֵי לְמֵיעָאל הָכָא, אוֹמֵי אוֹמָאָה דְּלָא לֵיעוֹל.

149. Rav Shimon looked and saw that his time had not yet come to die, until the eighth hour of the day. Rav Shimon placed him before him and studied the Torah with him. Rav Shimon said to his son Rav Elazar: "Sit at the door, and whoever you see do not speak with him; if he shall want to enter, swear he may not enter."

Before one leaves this world they see their departed relatives.

150. אָמַר ר"ש לְרַבִּי יִצְחָק, וְחָמִית דְּיוֹקְנָא דַּאֲבוּךְ יוֹמָא דָא, אוֹ לָא. דְּהָא, תָּנֵינָן, בְּשַׁעְתָּא דְּבַר נָשׁ אִסְתַּלָּק מֵעַלְמָא, אֲבוֹי וְקָרִיבוֹי מִשְׁתַּכְּחִין תַּמָּן עִמֵּיהּ, וְחָמֵי לוֹן וְאִשְׁתְּמוֹדַע לוֹן, וְכָל אִינוּן דַּהֲוָה מְדוֹרֵיהּ גַּבַּיְיהוּ בְּהַהוּא עַלְמָא בְּדַרְגָּא חַד, כֻּלְּהוּ מִתְכַּנְּשֵׁי וּמִשְׁתַּכְּחֵי עִמֵּיהּ, וְאָזְלִין עִם נִשְׁמָתֵיהּ, עַד אֲתַר דְּתִשְׁרֵי בְּאַתְרֵיהּ. אָמַר, עַד כְּעַן לָא חֲמֵינָא.

150. Rav Shimon said to Rav Yitzchak: "Have you seen your father's image today or have you not? For we have learned that when a man departs from the world, his father and relatives are there with him, and he sees and recognizes them. And all those with whom he will dwell in the other world in the same grade, all gather to be with him, and accompany his soul to its dwelling place." Rav Yitzchak said: "Until now I have not seen the image of my father."

Rav Shimon becomes the guarantor for Rav Yitzchak.

151. אַדְהָכֵי קָם ר' שִׁמְעוֹן וַאֲמַר, מָארֵי דְעָלְמָא, אִשְׁתְּמוֹדַע רִבִּי יִצְחָק לְגַבָּן, וּמֵאִנּוּן שִׁבְעָה עַיְינִין דְּהָכָא הוּא, הָא אֲחִידְנָא בֵּיה, וְהַב לִי. נָפַק קָלָא וַאֲמַר, כּוּרְסְיָיא דְמָארֵיה קְרִיבָא בְּגַדְפוֹי דְר' שִׁמְעוֹן, הָא דִידָךְ הוּא, וְעִמָּךְ תַּיְיתֵיה, בְּזִמְנָא דְּתֵיעוֹל לְמֵיתָב בְּכוּרְסְיָךְ. אָמַר ר"ע וַדַּאי.

151. **Among this, Rav Shimon stood up and said: "Master of the universe, Rav Yitzchak is known by us, and he is one of the seven eyes here,** namely one of the seven students who remained alive when they went out of the Holy Great Assembly [Idra Raba]. **Behold, I hold him, give him to me." A voice resounded saying: "The throne of His Master,** namely the Nukva, **has approached** for unification **through the wings of Rav Shimon,** namely through his work and elevating Mayin Nukvin. **Behold, Rav Yitzchak is yours, and you shall come with him when you shall sit in your throne,"** namely when Rav Shimon will depart from the world. **Rav Shimon said: "Certainly,** I shall do so and bring him with me when I will depart from the world."

No decree of judgment can exist in the place of Rav Shimon.

152. אַדְהָכֵי, חָמָא רִבִּי אֶלְעָזָר, דַּהֲוָה אִסְתַּלִּיק מַלְאַךְ הַמָּוֶת, וַאֲמַר, לֵית קוּסְטָרָא דְּטִיפְסָא, בַּאֲתַר דְּרִבִּי שִׁמְעוֹן בֶּן יוֹחָאי שְׁכִיחַ. אָמַר רִבִּי שִׁמְעוֹן לְרִבִּי אֶלְעָזָר בְּרֵיה, עוּל הָכָא, וְאָחֵיד בֵּיה בְּרִבִּי יִצְחָק, דְּהָא וָמֵינָא בֵּיה דְּמִסְתָּפֵי, עָאל רִבִּי אֶלְעָזָר, וְאָחֵיד בֵּיה. וְרִבִּי שִׁמְעוֹן אַהֲדַר אַנְפֵּיה וְלָעֵי בְּאוֹרַיְיתָא.

152. **Among this, Rav Elazar saw the Angel of Death departing. He said: "No decree of judgment can exist in the place of Rav Shimon." Rav Shimon said to his son Rav Elazar: "Come here and hold Rav**

Yitzchak, for I see he is afraid." Rav Elazar entered and held him, and Rav Shimon turned to study the Torah.

Rav Yitzchak fell asleep and saw his departed father.

153. נָיֵים רִבִּי יִצְחָק, וְחָזֵי לַאֲבוֹי, א"ל בְּרִי, זַכָּאָה חוּלָקָךְ, בְּעָלְמָא דֵין, וּבְעָלְמָא דְאָתֵי, דְּהָא בֵּין טַרְפֵּי אִילָנָא דְחַיֵּי דְּגִנְתָּא דְעֵדֶן, אִתְיְהֵיב אִילָנָא רַבָּא וְתַקִּיף בִּתְרֵין עָלְמִין, ר"ש בֶּן יוֹחָאי הוּא, דְּהָא הוּא אָחִיד לָךְ בְּעַנְפּוֹי, זַכָּאָה חוּלָקָךְ בְּרִי.

153. Rav Yitzchak slept and saw his father. His father **said to him:** "Son, happy is your portion in this world and in the World to Come, for you sit among the leaves of the Tree of Life in the Garden of Eden. A great and strong tree in both worlds is Rav Shimon, who holds you in his boughs. Happy is your portion, my son."

The portion of Rav Yitzchak in the world of Truth.

154. אָמַר לֵיהּ אַבָּא, וּמָה אֲנָא הָתָם, אָמַר לֵיהּ תְּלַת יוֹמִין הֲווֹ דְּוָחֲפוֹ אַדְרָא דְּמִשְׁכָּבָךְ, וְתַקִּינוּ לָךְ כַּמָּה פְתִיחָן, לְאַנְהָרָא לָךְ מֵאַרְבַּע סִטְרִין דְּעָלְמָא, וַאֲנָא חֲמֵינָא דּוּכְתֵּיךְ וְחָדֵינָא, דַּאֲמֵינָא זַכָּאָה חוּלָקָךְ בְּרִי. בַּר דְּעַד כְּעָן, בְּרָךְ לָא זָכֵי בְּאוֹרַיְיתָא.

154. He said to him: "Father, what am I there?" in the world of Truth. He said to him: "For three days they have been hastily preparing your chamber with open windows to shine upon you from the four directions of the world. I have seen your place and rejoiced, and I said: 'Happy is your portion, son.' [They answered:] 'Except that until now your son did not merit Torah,' and I was distressed over this."

Rav Shimon requested, and it was granted.

155. וְהָא הַשְׁתָּא הֲוֵי זְמִינִין לְמֵיתֵי גַּבָּךְ, תְּרֵיסַר צַדִּיקַיָּא דְּחַבְרַיָּא, וְעַד דַּהֲוֵינָא נָפְקֵי, אִתְּעַר קָלָא בְּכֻלְּהוּ עַלְמִין, מַאן חַבְרִין דְּקָיְימִין הָכָא, אִתְעַטָּרוּ, בְּגִינֵיהּ דְּרִבִּי שִׁמְעוֹן, שְׁאֶלְתָּא שָׁאִיל, וְאִתְיְיהֵיב לֵיהּ.

155. "And now, twelve righteous men from among the friends were preparing to come to you. As they were going, a sound went forth in all the worlds, 'Friends who stand here, bedeck yourself for Rav Shimon who has asked a request of the Holy One, blessed be He, that Rav Yitzchak shall not die, **and it was granted him.'**

Rav Shimon grasps the Lower Seven Sefirot of every Partzuf of Atzilut.

156. וְלָא דָא בִּלְחוֹדוֹי, דְּהָא שַׁבְעִין דּוּכְתֵּי מִתְעַטְּרָן הָכָא דִּילֵיהּ. וְכָל דּוּכְתָּא וְדוּכְתָּא, פָּתְחִין פְּתִיחָן לְשַׁבְעִין עָלְמִין, וְכָל עָלְמָא וְעָלְמָא, אִתְפַּתַּח לְע' רְהִיטִין, וְכָל רְהִיטָא וּרְהִיטָא, אִתְפַּתַּח לְשַׁבְעִין כִּתְרִין עִלָּאִין, וּמִתַּמָּן אִתְפַּתָּחוּ אָרְחִין לְעַתִּיקָא, סְתִימָאָה דְּכֹלָּא, לְמֶחֱמֵי בְּהַהוּא נְעִימוּתָא עִלָּאָה דְּנָהֲרָא, וּמְהַנְיָא לְכֹלָּא, כְּמָה דְּאַתְּ אָמֵר, לַחֲזוֹת בְּנוֹעַם ה' וּלְבַקֵּר בְּהֵיכָלוֹ, מַהוּ וּלְבַקֵּר בְּהֵיכָלוֹ, הַיְינוּ דִּכְתִיב בְּכָל בֵּיתִי נֶאֱמָן הוּא.

156. "Not only this but seventy places are adorned for him here. Each place has doors opening to seventy Worlds, each World opening to seventy Running Channels, and each Running Channel opened to seventy Supernal Crowns, and from there ways are open to Atika, the Most Concealed of All, to see the highest pleasantness that delights and shines upon all, as it is said: '...to behold the pleasantness of the Lord, and to inquire in His temple.' (Psalms 27:4) What is 'To inquire in His temple'? It is as it is written, '...for he is the trusted one in all My house.' (Numbers 12:7)"

Explanation of the matter: We have no attainment in the Upper Three, only in the Lower Seven Sefirot alone. Indeed the meaning is that regarding the Upper Three we do not even have attainment in the Upper Three of the Ten Sefirot of the World of Asiyah, and in the Lower Seven Sefirot it is possible for rare individuals to achieve, even the Lower Seven Sefirot of the Upper Three of the World of Atzilut. The father of Rav Yitzchak is informing that Rav Shimon grasps the Lower Seven Sefirot of every Partzuf of Atzilut, and even the Lower Seven of the Upper Three of Atzilut. A **"place"** is the Nukva of Zeir Anpin, in the secret of the verse: "...Behold, there is a place with Me...." (Exodus 33:21) Thus **"seventy places are adorned for him here,"** namely the Lower Seven of Nukva, each of which are composed of ten, thus seventy. Zeir Anpin is named **"World,"** in the secret of the verse: "...the world is built on kindness..." (Psalms 89:3), which is: **"Each place has doors opening to seventy Worlds,"** which are the Lower Seven of Zeir Anpin, each of which are composed of ten.

The Lights of Binah are called **"Running Channels,"** in the secret of the verse: "...for in haste did you leave the land of Egypt..." (Deuteronomy 16:3) which is the secret of Binah. Thus **"each World opening to seventy Running Channels,"** which are the Seven Sefirot of Yisrael-Saba and Tevunah, each of which are composed of ten. The Sefirot of Chochmah, which are the Partzuf of Supernal Aba and Ima, are called Supernal Crowns. Thus **"each Running Channel opened to seventy Supernal Crowns,"** and from them to the Lower Seven of Atik, which is, **"and from there ways are open to Atika, the most concealed of all."** When it says that they open one from the other, the meaning is as follows: These five Partzufim are clothed one on top of the other, and the beginning is from Nukva. So it is considered that openings are opened to Zeir Anpin from Her, as She clothes Him, and so too, from Zeir Anpin to Yisrael-Saba and Tevunah, and from Yisrael-Saba and Tevunah to Supernal Aba and Ima, and from Supernal Aba and Ima to the Lower Seven of Arich Anpin, which is called Atika , since each one clothes the other, as is known.

Partaking in the feast of Rav Shimon.

157. אֲמַר לֵיהּ אַבָּא, כַּמָּה זִמְנָא יְהִיבוּ לִי בְּהַאי עַלְמָא, א"ל לֵית לִי רְשׁוּתָא,
וְלָא מוֹדְעֵי לֵיהּ לְבַר נָשׁ, אֲבָל בְּהִלּוּלָא רַבָּא דְּר' שִׁמְעוֹן, תְּהֵא מִתַקֵּן פָּתוֹרֵיהּ,
כד"א צְאֶינָה וּרְאֶינָה בְּנוֹת צִיּוֹן בַּמֶּלֶךְ שְׁלֹמֹה בָּעֲטָרָה שֶׁעִטְּרָה לּוֹ אִמּוֹ בְּיוֹם
חֲתֻנָּתוֹ וּבְיוֹם שִׂמְחַת לִבּוֹ.

157. He said to him: "Father, how long am I given to live in this world?" He said to him: "I was not given permission to tell you this, and man is not made to know. But at the feast for Rav Shimon, namely on his day of departure, when there will be great joy in all the worlds for all the secrets he reveals, as mentioned in the Small Assembly (Idra Zuta), **you shall be there to set his table,** meaning to partake in revealing secrets with him. **As it is said, 'Go forth, daughters of Zion, and behold King Solomon with the crown with which his mother crowned him on the day of his wedding, and on the day of the gladness of his heart.' (Song of Songs 3:11)"**

Rav Yitzchak awoke and prostrated himself before Rav Shimon.

158. אַדְהָכִי אִתְעַר רִבִּי יִצְחָק, וַחֲדֵי וְחָיֵיהּ, וְאַנְפּוֹי נְהִירִין, חָמָא רִבִּי שִׁמְעוֹן,
וְאִסְתַּכַּל בְּאַנְפּוֹי, א"ל מִלָּה חַדְתָּא שְׁמַעְתָּא, אֲמַר לֵיהּ וַדַּאי, סָח לֵיהּ,
אִשְׁתַּטַּח קַמֵּיהּ דְּרִבִּי שִׁמְעוֹן.

158. Rav Yitzchak then awoke, laughed, and his face shone. Rav Shimon looked at his face and said to him: "You have heard something new." Rav Yitzchak said to him: "Surely I have heard." **He told him** what he saw in his dream. Rav Yitzchak **prostrated himself** on the ground **before Rav Shimon.**

Rav Yitzchak commited to study Torah with his son.

159. תָּאנָא, מֵהַהוּא יוֹמָא, הֲוָה רִבִּי יִצְחָק אָחֵיד לִבְרֵיה בִּידֵיה, וְלָעֵי לֵיה בְּאוֹרַיְיתָא, וְלָא הֲוָה שַׁבְקֵיה. כַּד הֲוָה עָאל קַמֵּיה דְּרִבִּי שִׁמְעוֹן, אוֹתְבֵיה לִבְרֵיה לְבַר, וְיָתֵיב קַמֵּיה דְּרִבִּי שִׁמְעוֹן, וַהֲוָה קָרֵי קַמֵּיה ה' עָשְׁקָה לִי עָרְבֵנִי.

159. We have learned that from that day onward Rav Yitzchak would hold his son in his hand, study the Torah with him, and never left him. When he came before Rav Shimon, he made his son sit outside. He used to come in and sit before Rav Shimon and call before him, "... 'Lord, I am oppressed, be You my security.'" (Isaiah 38:14)

Naso

5. A wife suspected of adultery (Sota)

A Synopsis

Elijah says that when Israel desecrates the Torah God sends them into exile, through which experience they become cleansed and purified and refined. At the Final Redemption Israel will be tested like they were at the waters of Marah. Elijah says that in the future the children of Israel will leave the exile with mercy because they will taste from the Tree of Life that is the book of the Zohar.

Israel in the future will taste from the Zohar and leave the exile with Mercy.

90. וְהַמַּשְׂכִּלִים יָבִינוּ, מִסִּטְרָא דְּבִינָה, דְּאִיהוּ אִילָנָא דְּחַיֵּי, בְּגִינַיְיהוּ אִתְּמַר, וְהַמַּשְׂכִּלִים יַזְהִירוּ כְּזוֹהַר הָרָקִיעַ דִּילָךְ דְּאִיהוּ סֵפֶר הַזֹּהַר, מִן זוֹהֲרָא דְּאִימָא עִלָּאָה תְּשׁוּבָה. בְּאִלֵּין לָא צְרִיךְ נִסָּיוֹן, וּבְגִין דַּעֲתִידִין יִשְׂרָאֵל לְמִטְעַם מֵאִילָנָא דְּחַיֵּי, דְּאִיהוּ הַאי סֵפֶר הַזֹּהַר, יִפְּקוּן בֵּיהּ מִן גָּלוּתָא בְּרַחֲמֵי. וְיִתְקַיֵּים בְּהוֹן, יְיָ' בָּדָד יַנְחֶנּוּ וְאֵין עִמּוֹ אֵל נֵכָר.

90. **"…but the wise shall understand" (Daniel 12:10),** since they are from the side of Binah, which is the Tree of Life. For them, it was said, **"And the wise shall shine like the brightness (zohar) of the Firmament" (Daniel 12:3) with your composition,** of Rav Shimon bar Yochai, **which is the Book of the Zohar, from the Light of the Supernal Ima** called **repentance. They do not require a test, and because Israel in the future will taste from the Tree of Life, which is this Book of the Zohar, they will leave the exile with mercy. About them, this verse will be fulfilled: "The Lord alone guided them, and there was no strange god with him." (Deuteronomy 32:12)**

Naso (Idra Rabba)

1. The Foreword to the Holy Idra Raba

A Synopsis

Rav Shimon tells the friends what he wishes to reveal to them and invites them to a new understanding. He is anguished over the question of whether to reveal secrets, until Rav Aba reassures him that the friends all fear God. Rav Shimon tells the friends that this is a time to act for God because people have forsaken His Torah. He talks about the talebearer who is not settled in his mind and is not trustworthy to receive secrets, and he contrasts this to a faithful spirit who is stable and conceals matters. When Rav Shimon begins to reveal secrets, the place shakes and the friends tremble.

Rav Shimon tells the friends that it is a time to act.

1. תָּנֵא, אָמַר ר"ע לְחַבְרַיָּיא, עַד אֵימַת גֵיתִיב בְּקָיְימָא דְּחַד סַמְכָא. כְּתִיב עֵת לַעֲשׂוֹת כַּיְיָ' הֵפֵרוּ תּוֹרָתֶךָ. יוֹמִין זְעִירִין, וּמָארֵי דְחוֹבָא דָּחִיק. כְּרוֹזָא קָארֵי כָּל יוֹמָא, וּמְחַצְּדֵי חַקְלָא זְעִירִין אִינּוּן. וְאִינְהוּ בְּשׁוּלֵי כַרְמָא. לָא אַשְׁגָּחָן, וְלָא יַדְעִין, לְאָן אֲתַר אָזְלִין כְּמָה דְיָאוּת.

1. We have learned that Rav Shimon said to the friends: "Until when will we sit in the reality of one pillar, namely in the aspect of the World of Tohu (Formless), where the Lower Seven Sefirot were in one line, one above the other. Rav Shimon wanted to reveal to them here the matter of the grades of the World of Correction, which are with three Pillars, the secret of the Three Columns: Right, Left, and Central. **It is written: 'It is time to act for the Lord: they have made void your Torah.' (Psalms 119:126) The days are few and the sin-master,** meaning the prosecutor, **applies pressure. Every day the proclamation resounds** for repentance **and the reapers of the field are few,** meaning those who merited the crop of the Supernal Field, Malchut, which are the understandings of the secrets of Torah. **They,** even those who acheived,

are found **at the end of the Vineyard,** which is Malchut. **Even they do
not pay attention and do not properly know where they are going.**

The weapons of the friends.

2. אִתְכְּנָשׁוּ חַבְרַיָּיא לְבֵי אִדְרָא, בְּלוֹבָשִׁין שַׁרְיָן סַיְיפֵי וְרוּמְחֵי בִּידֵיכוֹן,
אֲזְדְּרָזוּ בְּתִקּוּנַיְכוּן. בְּעֵיטָא, בְּחָכְמְתָא, בְּסוּכְלְתָנוּ. בְּדַעְתָּא. בְּחֵיזוּ. בִּידִין.
בְּרַגְלִין. אַמְלִכוּ עֲלֵיכוֹן לְמַאן דְּבִרְשׁוּתֵיהּ חַיֵּי וּמוֹתָא. לְמִגְזַר מִלִּין דִּקְשׁוֹט.
מִלִּין דְּקַדִּישֵׁי עֶלְיוֹנִין צַיְיתֵי לְהוּ, וַחֲדָאן לְמִשְׁמַע לְהוּ, וּלְמִנְדַּע לְהוּ.

**2. "Gather, friends, to the chamber, dressed in shields with swords
and spears in your hands,** which represent unifications to destroy the
Klipot. **Hurry with your Corrections,** meaning hurry to make the
corrections of the Three Columns: Chochmah-Binah-Da'at, Chesed-
Gevurah-Tiferet, Netzach-Hod-Yesod, **with counsel, with wisdom,
with understanding, with knowledge, with appearance, with hands,**
Chesed-Gevurah-Tiferet, **and with legs,** Netzach-Hod-Yesod. **Appoint
as king over you, he who has the authority of life and death to decree
truthful words, words to which the Supernal Holy Beings will listen,
and will be glad to hear and to know them."**

Revealing the secrets to those who are worthy.

3. יָתִיב ר"ש וּבְכָה, וְאָמַר וַוי אִי גָּלֵינָא, וַוי אִי לָא גָּלֵינָא. חַבְרַיָּיא דַּהֲוָה תַּמָּן
אִשְׁתִּיקוּ. קָם ר' אַבָּא וא"ל, אִי נִיחָא קַמֵּיהּ דְּמֹר לְגַלָּאָה, הָא כְּתִיב סוֹד
יְיָ' לִירֵאָיו, וְהָא חַבְרַיָּיא אִלֵּין דַּחֲלִין דְּקוּדְשָׁא בְּרִיךְ הוּא אִינּוּן, וּכְבָר עָאלוּ
בְּאִדְרָא דְּבֵי מַשְׁכְּנָא, מִנְּהוֹן עָאלוּ, מִנְּהוֹן נַפְקוּ.

**3. Rav Shimon sat down and wept. He said: "Woe if I do reveal and
woe if I do not reveal."** If he does not reveal, the new Torah revelations
will get lost, and if he does reveal, perhaps someone unworthy will hear
the secrets of the Torah. **The friends that were there kept silent.
Rav Aba stood up and said to him: "If my lord is graceful enough to**

reveal, behold it says, 'The secret of the Lord is with them that fear Him....' (Psalms 25:14) These friends fear the Holy One, blessed be He. They have already gained entry to the Assembly of the Tabernacle (Idra devei Mashkena, Mishpatim 520). We have learned that **some of them entered** this Great Assembly (Idra Raba) **and some of them exited,** but not all, since three friends passed away.

The counting of the friends.

4. תָּאנָא, אִתְמְנוּ חַבְרַיָּיא קַמֵּיהּ דר"ש, וְאִשְׁתְּכָחוּ, רִבִּי אֶלְעָזָר בְּרֵיהּ. וְר' אַבָּא. וְר' יְהוּדָה. וְרִבִּי יוֹסֵי בַּר יַעֲקֹב. וְר' יִצְחָק. וְר' חִזְקִיָּה בַּר רַב. וְר' חִיָּיא. וְר' יוֹסֵי. וְר' יֵיסָא. יְדִין יָהֲבוּ לר"ש, וְאֶצְבְּעָן זַקְפוּ לְעֵילָא. וְעָאלוּ בְּחַקְלָא בֵּינֵי אִילָנֵי וְיָתְבוּ. קָם ר"ש וְצַלֵּי צְלוֹתֵיהּ, יָתִיב בְּגַוַויְיהוּ וְאָמַר, כָּל חַד יְשַׁוֵּי יְדוֹי בְּתוּקְפֵּיהּ. שָׁווּ יְדַיְיהוּ, וְנָסִיב לוֹן . פָּתַח וְאָמַר אָרוּר הָאִישׁ אֲשֶׁר יַעֲשֶׂה פֶסֶל וּמַסֵּכָה מַעֲשֵׂה יְדֵי חָרָשׁ וְשָׂם בַּסָּתֶר וְעָנוּ כָל הָעָם וְאָמְרוּ אָמֵן.

4. We have learned, the friends were counted before Rav Shimon. The following were present: Rav Elazar, his son, Rav Aba, Rav Yehuda, Rav Yosi ben Yaakov, Rav Yitzchak, Rav Chizkiyah bar Rav, Rav Chiya, Rav Yosi, and Rav Yesa. They gave their hands to Rav Shimon with the fingers straightened upward. They entered the field among the trees and sat down. Rav Shimon stood up and prayed his prayer, sat down among them and said: "Let everyone place his hands in his bosom." Each one placed his hands in his own bosom, and Rav Shimon **accepted them.** He opened and said: "... 'Cursed be the man that makes any carved or molten idol, abhorred by the Lord, the work of the hands of a craftsman, and sets it up in secret. And all the people,** all the friends, **shall answer and say, "Amen."'** (Deuteronomy 27:15)"

Explanation: Right after the friends were counted before him, they fulfilled what he cautioned them in verse 2, **"Hurry with your corrections,"** and they immediately performed the unification of the

Three Columns—Right, Left, and Central, to draw them to Malchut. They performed an action Below to awaken its corresponding level Above, therefore: **"They gave their hands to Rav Shimon,"** as Rav Shimon is the secret of Da'at, the root of the Central Column, so they gave him their hands, Right and Left, and their Right and Left included and united together through Rav Shimon, the Central Column. Through this, the unification of the Three Columns was awakened Above. Then, **"with the fingers,"** which allude to the Illumination of Chochmah that is in the fingers, **"straightened upward,"** so that they will only shine from below upward, since after the Right and Left are included together through the Central Column the Chochmah of the Left only shines from below upward.

After this, they needed to draw the entire Illumination of the Three Columns to Malchut. Thus **"They entered the field among the trees and sat down,"** namely the secret of the Field of Holy Apples, which is Malchut. And they sat to draw to Her the Chochmah in the aspect of sitting, which is the secret of the Six Corners [Sefirot] of Chochmah. This is: **"Let everyone place his hands in his bosom,"** as the bosom indicates the concealment of the Upper Three, since putting the hand in the bosom is an act of concealment. However, there are two aspects of putting the hand in the bosom. One aspect is in the secret of placing the Yud (י) in Ohr (אור), where Ohr becomes Avir (אויר), which applies in the Right Column in the secret of the Vowel of Cholam, which produces Six Corners [Sefirot] without a head. And there is a putting of the hand in the bosom that applies in the Central Column, which causes a diminishment of the Upper Three of Chochmah so that only the Six Corners of Chochmah remain there. The Central Column diminishes the Left Column so that it only shines from below upward, which is the aspect of the Six Corners of Chochmah.

To explain this, I will expound the secret of the verse: "And the Lord said to him again: Put your hand into your bosom. And he put his hand into his bosom" (Exodus 4:6), which is the secret of placing the Yud (י) into *Ohr* (אור), which diminishes it to be *Avir* (אויר), which is the secret of Six Corners with no head that applies in the Right Column in the Vowel of Cholam. Afterwards, "and he took it out," (Ibid.) meaning he returned to take out the Yud from *Avir*, and *Avir* went back to being *Ohr*, thus revealing the Light of Chochmah from above downward, which applies in the Left Column in the Vowel of Shuruk before the correction of the Central Column, when it has Harsh Judgments that conceal and block all the Lights, since the Chochmah is without Chasadim. Therefore, "... and, behold, it was leprous as snow." (Ibid.) since the blocking and closing of the Lights is the secret of leprosy (*tzara'at*), which is why *tzara'at* in Aramaic is *segiru* (lit. closing). Afterwards, the correction of the Central Column is revealed, and this is the secret of: "And He said: 'Return your hand to your bosom'..." (Exodus 4:7) the secret of the first action of the Central column, which is that it awakens the Masach of Chirik from the aspect of Man'ula (Lock) that diminishes it to become Six Corners [Sefirot]. Then, "And he took it from his bosom" (Ibid.) in the secret of the second action, as the word "from his bosom" is exact, since the meaning of him taking it out is that he returned to reveal the Chochmah but the revelation was clothed by the bosom, meaning that he only drew the Six Corners of Chochmah. Then all the Columns united one with the other, and the Chochmah was clothed with Chasadim. This is the secret of: "...and, behold, it had resumed its fleshy appearance" (Ibid.) since it returned in the aspect of the Upper Three, but with the Six Corners of Chochmah, as mentioned.

This is the meaning of: **"Let everyone place his hands in his bosom,"** meaning in the bosom of the Central Column, so that when they bring them out of the bosom the Left hand will shine only from below upward, namely with the clothing of the bosom, as this is the main purpose of the entire correction of the Central Column, which is the secret of Chirik. Therefore Rav Shimon, who is the aspect of the Central Column, cautioned them about this. Thus **"Each one placed his hands,** and he accepted them," they placed their hands in their bosom, and Rav Shimon took them from their bosom, meaning that he took their hands from the bosom with the clothing of the bosom, as is the way of the Central Column, and **"He opened and said, 'Cursed be the man that makes any carved or molten idol...'"** since the drawing of Chochmah from above downward is a carved and molten ox idol, the work of the hands of a craftsman, who places it in the hidden of the world, meaning who reveals what is needed to be concealed and covered. Therefore in the end he made them swear on this.

The Torah becomes void when it is not observed with its corrections.

5.ה. פָּתַח ר"ע וְאָמַר, עֵת לַעֲשׂוֹת לַיְיָ', אֲמַאי עֵת לַעֲשׂוֹת לַיְיָ'. מִשׁוּם דְּהֵפֵרוּ תּוֹרָתֶךָ. מַאי הֵפֵרוּ תּוֹרָתֶךָ, תּוֹרָה דִלְעֵילָּא. דְּאִיהִי מִתְבַּטְּלָא אִי לָא יִתְעֲבֵיד בְּתִקּוּנוֹי דָא. וּלְעַתִּיק יוֹמִין אִתְּמַר. כְּתִיב אַשְׁרֶיךָ יִשְׂרָאֵל מִי כָמוֹךָ. וּכְתִיב, מִי כָמוֹךָ בָּאֵלִים יְיָ'.

5. Rav Shimon opened and said: "'It is time to act for the Lord, for they have made void your Torah' (Psalms 119:126), meaning: **why is this a time to act for the Lord? Because 'they have made void your Torah.'** What does 'they have made void your Torah' mean? It means **they have made void the Torah Above,** which is the secret of Zeir Anpin **because it becomes void if it is not observed with its corrections,** as it will explain shortly. This verse **was said to Atik Yomin,** which is the beginning of the root of all the corrections, as it will explain shortly. **It says, 'Happy are you, Israel: who is like you...'** (Deuteronomy 33:29) because they adhere to the Central Column, **and 'Who is like you, the Lord, among the Elim....' (Exodus 15:11)"** This applies to Zeir Anpin, who is the Central Column.

Rav Shimon, Rav Elazar, and Rav Aba were the collective of all.

6. קָרָא לְרִבִּי אֶלְעָזָר בְּרֵיהּ, אוֹתְבֵיהּ קַמֵּיהּ, וּלְרִבִּי אַבָּא מִסִּטְרָא אַחֲרָא, וְאָמַר אֲנָן כְּלָלָא דְּכוֹלָא. עַד הַשְׁתָּא אִתְתְּקָנוּ קַיָּימִין. אִשְׁתִּיקוּ, שַׁמְעֵי קָלָא, וְאַרְכּוּבְתָן דָּא לְדָא נַקְשָׁן. מַאי קָלָא. קָלָא דִּכְנוּפְיָיא עִלָּאָה דְּמִתְכַּנְּפֵי.

**6. He called his son Rav Elazar and sat him in front of him, and
he** sat **Rav Aba on the other side and said: "We are the collective of
all,"** since the soul of Rav Elazar was of Chochmah and that of Rav Aba
was Binah, and Rav Shimon himself was Da'at that unifies Chochmah
and Binah to each other. That is why he said that they include all, since
Chochmah, Binah, and Da'at include all the grades. **"Until now the
pillars were constructed,"** meaning that until this point they were
involved in correcting the Three Columns, which are called Three
Pillars. **They were silent. They heard a sound and their knees were
knocking together** out of fear. **What was the sound? That was the
sound of the friends above who were gathering,** meaning the Chariots
of the Holy One, blessed be He, as mentioned in the Idra [Zuta] of
Zohar, Ha'azinu verse 29.

The matter depends on love.

7. ז. חַדֵּי ר"ש וְאָמַר, יְיָ' שָׁמַעְתִּי שִׁמְעֲךָ יָרֵאתִי הָתָם יֵאוֹת הֲוָה לְמֶהֱוֵי דָחִיל. אֲנָן בְּחַבִּיבוּתָא תַּלְיָיא מִלְּתָא, דִּכְתִיב וְאָהַבְתָּ אֵת יְיָ' אֱלֹהֶיךָ, וּכְתִיב מֵאַהֲבַת יְיָ' אֶתְכֶם, וּכְתִיב אָהַבְתִּי אֶתְכֶם וְגוֹ'.

**7. Rav Shimon rejoiced and said, "The Lord, I have heard Your
renown, and I am afraid..."** (Habakkuk 3:2). **It was true there that
he feared,** since his root was from the Left Column, but **as for us** who
are united with the Central Column, **the matter depends on love,**
meaning Chasadim, which are the aspect of love, **as it is written: 'And
you shall love the Lord your God...'** (Deuteronomy 6:5) and **'...**

because the Lord loved you… (Deuteronomy 7:8) and also 'I have loved you….' (Malachi 1:2)"

Only those with a settled spirit can be trusted to keep a secret.

8. ר"ש פָּתַח וְאָמַר, הוֹלֵךְ רָכִיל מְגַלֶּה סּוֹד וְנֶאֱמַן רוּחַ מְכַסֶּה דָבָר. הוֹלֵךְ רָכִיל, הַאי קְרָא קַשְׁיָא, אִישׁ רָכִיל מִבָּעֵי לֵיהּ לְמֵימַר, מַאן הוֹלֵךְ. אֶלָּא מַאן דְּלָא אִתְיַישָׁב בְּרוּחֵיהּ, וְלָא הֲוֵי מְהֵימָנָא, הַהוּא מִלָּה דְּשָׁמַע, אָזִיל בְּגַוְּוֵיהּ כְּחֵיזְרָא בְּמַיָּא, עַד דְּרָמֵי לֵיהּ לְבַר. מ"ט. מִשּׁוּם דְּלֵית רוּחֵיהּ רוּוְחָא דְקִיּוּמָא. אֲבָל מַאן דְּרוּחֵיהּ רוּוְחָא דְקִיּוּמָא, בֵּיהּ כְּתִיב, וְנֶאֱמַן רוּחַ מְכַסֶּה דָבָר. וְנֶאֱמַן רוּחַ, קִיּוּמָא דְרוּוְחָא. בְּרוּוְחָא תַּלְיָיא מִלְתָא. וּכְתִיב, אַל תִּתֵּן אֶת פִּיךָ לַחֲטִיא אֶת בְּשָׂרֶךָ.

8. Rav Shimon opened and said: "'He who reveals a secret goes as a talebearer, and the faithful of spirit conceals a matter.' (Proverbs 11:13). This verse is difficult, as it should have said 'is a talebearer.'" [He asks:] **"What is, 'goes as a talebearer'?"** He replies: **"It refers to someone who is not settled in mind and not trustworthy. Whatever he has heard goes within him like a board in the water** that does not sink **until it is expelled outside,** meaning to say he has no rest until he reveals whatever he heard to someone else." [He asks:] **"What is the reason?"** [He answers:] **It is because his spirit is not stable** and settled. **Of him who has a** stable and **lasting spirit, it says '…and the faithful of spirit conceals a matter.' (Ibid.) A faithful spirit means a stable spirit. It all depends on the spirit. It is also written: 'Do not let your mouth cause your flesh to sin….' (Ecclesiastes 5:5)**

Rav Shimon begins to reveal the secrets of secrets.

9. וְלֵית עָלְמָא מִתְקַיְּימָא אֶלָּא בְּרָזָא. וְכִי אִי בְּמִלֵּי עָלְמָא אִצְטְרִיךְ רָזָא. בְּמִלִּין רָזִין דְּרָזַיָּיא דְּעַתִּיק יוֹמִין, דְּלָא אִתְמְסָרָאן אֲפִילוּ לְמַלְאָכִין עִלָּאִין עאכ"ו. אר"ש, לִשְׁמַיָּא לָא אֵימָא דְּיֵיצִיתוּן, לְאַרְעָא לָא אֵימָא דְּתִשְׁמַע, דְּהָא אֲנָן

קְיוּמֵי עָלְמִין. תָּנָא רָזִין דְּרָזִין, כַּד פָּתַח ר"ש בְּרָזֵי דְרָזִין, אוֹדַעְנָע אַתְרָא, וְחַבְרִין אִתְחַלְחָלוּ.

9. "The world is preserved only through secrecy and if, in worldly things, secrecy is a prerequisite, it is so much more certain that the mysteries of mysteries of Atik Yomin are not even passed on to the Angels Above." Rav Shimon said: "To the Heavens, I do not say to listen. To the earth I don't say to hear, since we maintain the worlds." That is to say, Moses and Isaiah made the Heavens and Earth witnesses to punish the children of Israel if they do not maintain the Worlds, that the Heavens will not give its rain nor the Earth its crops. But Rav Shimon was speaking to the righteous, who maintain the world and have no need for witnesses. **We have learned of the mysteries of mysteries. When Rav Shimon began with the secrets of secrets, the place shook and the friends trembled.**

Naso

51. The passing of the three friends

A Synopsis

We learn that before they could leave the chamber, Rav Yosi, Rav Chizkiyah, and Rav Yesa died, and the other friends saw Holy Angels carrying them away. Rav Shimon is beside himself with fear that his revelations have caused this event, until a voice tells him that he deserves praise. The voice says that the souls of the friends passed away through perfection and that they joined with great passionate will and valor at the time of their deaths. The uppermost Angels took their souls and raised them Above. All the faces of the friends were shining brightly. Rav Aba was sad for some days until he and Rav Shimon saw the Angels showing their dead friends the treasures and chambers prepared for their honor, and then he was comforted. From that day on, the friends did not leave Rav Shimon's house, and no one else was ever present when he revealed secrets to them. He called them 'the seven eyes of the Lord,' and Rav Yehuda referred to him as "Shabbat," from which all six days get their blessing.

The passing of three friends.

353. תָּנָא, עַד לָא נַפְקוּ חַבְרַיָּיא מֵהַהוּא אִדְרָא, מִיתוּ ר' יוֹסֵי בַּר' יַעֲקֹב, וְר' חִזְקִיָּה, וְר' יֵיסָא. וְחָמוּ חַבְרַיָּיא, דַּהֲווֹ נַטְלִין לוֹן מַלְאָכִין קַדִּישִׁין בְּהַהוּא פַּרְסָא. וְאר"ש מִלָּה, וְאִשְׁתְּכָכוּ. צָוֵוח וְאָמַר, שְׁמָּא וֹ"ו גְּזֵרָה אִתְגְּזַר עֲלָנָא לְאִתְעַנְּשָׁא, דְּאִתְגְּלֵי עַל יְדָנָא, מַה דְּלָא אִתְגְּלֵי מִיּוֹמָא דְּקָאִים מֹשֶׁה עַל טוּרָא דְסִינַי, דִּכְתִיב וַיְהִי שָׁם עִם יְ' אַרְבָּעִים יוֹם וְאַרְבָּעִים לַיְלָה וְגוֹ'. מַה אֲנָא הָכָא. אִי בְּגִין דָּא אִתְעַנְּשׁוּ.

353. We have learned that before these friends came out from that chamber, Rav Yosi ben Rav Yaakov, Rav Chizkiyah, and Rav Yesa died. The friends saw that Holy Angels carried them in that veil.

Rav Shimon said something and the friends calmed down. He cried out and said: "Perhaps, Heaven forbid, a sentence was decreed for us to be punished, since it was revealed through us what has not been revealed since the day Moses stood on Mount Sinai, as it is written: 'And he was there with the Lord forty days and forty nights....' (Exodus 34:28) Why am I here if this is the reason for their punishment?"

Rav Shimon is consoled by a Heavenly voice.

354. שָׁמַע קָלָא, זַכָּאָה אַנְתְּ ר"ש, זַכָּאָה חוּלָקָךְ וְחוּלָקָא דְּחַבְרַיָּיא וְחַבְרַיָּיא, אִלֵּין דְּקַיְימִין בַּהֲדָרְ, דְּהָא אִתְגְּלֵי לְכוֹן מַה דְּלָא אִתְגְּלֵי לְכָל חֵילָא דִּלְעֵילָּא, אֲבָל ת"ח, דְּהָא כְּתִיב, בִּבְכוֹרוֹ יְיַסְּדֶנָּה וּבִצְעִירוֹ יַצִּיב דְּלָתֶיהָ. וכ"ש דְּבִרְעוּ סַגִּי וְתַקִּיף, אִתְדַּבָּקוּ נַפְשָׁתְהוֹן בְּשַׁעֲתָא דָּא דְּאִתְנְסִיבוּ. זַכָּאָה חוּלָקֵהוֹן, דְּהָא בִּשְׁלֵימוּתָא אִסְתָּלָקוּ.

354. He heard a voice say: "Happy are you Rav Shimon, and happy is your lot and the lot of the friends that are with you, since it was revealed to you what has not been revealed to all the legions Above. However, come and see that it is written: '...he shall lay its foundation with his firstborn, and with his youngest son shall he set up the gates of it.' (Joshua 6:26) Certainly, the souls of the friends are ever devoted with great, strong will and valor at the time they were taken by the angels. Praised is their lot, for out of completion they passed away."

Explanation: Jericho is the Achorayim (Exterior) of Malchut, where curses lie. Joshua cursed that whoever builds Her Achorayim will have all his children die, which is "it is written: '...he shall lay its foundation with his firstborn...' (Joshua 6:26)" and if the builder completes the Achorayim of Malchut, he needs to give up all of his children for it. "Certainly, the souls of the friends ever devoted with great, strong will and valor," since they completed the building of the Panim (Interior) of Malchut, where blessings lie, surely their reward is very great. And if they passed away, then all the completion reached them with them passing away. **"Praised is their lot, for out of completion they passed away."**

The reason they passed away was already explained (Zohar, Acharei Mot 398) that at the end of the Idra [Raba] they had reached the level of the Final Correction, when the Curtain is removed and the entire difference between the Chest up and the Chest down is voided. Therefore these three friends whose souls were from the aspect of the Chest down were voided, and they ascended to a higher level—they became like the level of the Chest up. And since from the collective aspect it was not yet time for this correction, therefore they needed to depart from this world and ascend Above. Thus **"The friends saw that Holy Angels carried them in that veil,"** meaning that they departed due to the voiding of the Curtain, so it is considered that the Angels took them in that veil that went away. This is why it says: **"Praised is their lot, for out of completion they passed away,"** since the completion they merited, which is the removal of the curtain that others will not achieve until the Final Correction, was what caused them to depart.

The three friends ascended with the veil.

355. תָּאנָא, בְּעוֹד דְּאִתְגַּלְיָין מִלִּין, אִתְרְגִישׁוּ עִלָּאִין וְתַתָּאִין, וְקָלָא אִתְּעַר בְּמָאתָן וְחַמְשִׁין עָלְמִין דְּהָא מִלִּין עַתִּיקִין לְתַתָּא אִתְגַּלְיָין, וְעַד דְּאִלֵּין מִתְבַּסְּמָן נִשְׁמָתַיְיהוּ בְּאִינּוּן מִלִּין, נַפְקָא נִשְׁמָתַיְיהוּ בִּנְשִׁיקָה, וְאִתְקְשַׁר בְּהַהוּא פַּרְסָא, וְנַטְלִין לְהוּ מַלְאֲכֵי עִלָּאֵי, וְסַלְּקִין לוֹן לְעֵילָא. וַאֲמַאי אִלֵּין. מִשּׁוּם דְּעָאלָן וְלָא נַפְקוּ וְמִנָּא אַחֲרָא מִן קַדְמַת דְּנָא, וְכֻלְּהוּ אַחֲרָנֵי עָאלוּ וְנַפְקוּ.

355. We have learned that while these matters were revealed, Higher and Lower Beings trembled and a sound was roused and declared in **250 Worlds that ancient matters were revealed Below. While they were still soothing their souls with these matters, their soul left**

with a kiss and was tied to that veil, and the uppermost Angels took them and raised them Above.

Explanation: The part of Zeir Anpin from the Chest down is considered 250 Worlds. Netzach and Hod are 200, and half of Tiferet is 50. We already explained that the reason of their passing was because the part of the Chest down received all its corrections at the conclusion of the Idra, and the Curtain was void, as mentioned earlier. Thus **"Higher and Lower Beings trembled,"** since the revelation of the secrets corrected the entire Partzuf, both from the Chest up and from the Chest down. **"and a sound was roused in 250 Worlds,"** meaning from the chest down, **"that ancient matters were revealed Below,"** and all the corrections relating to the Chest down were revealed, and since these three friends were from the aspect of the Chest down, therefore **"while they were still soothing their souls with these matters,"** meaning as the corrections of their souls go on to be completed, **"their soul left with a kiss and was tied to that veil."** Since their souls were from the aspect of the Curtain, once the 250 Worlds finished to be completed and the Curtain was voided, their souls ascended up together with the Curtain, as explained in the previous paragraph.

The world was blessed because of the friends.

356. אר"ע, כַּמָה זַכָּאָה חוּלָקְהוֹן דְּהָנֵי תְּלָתֵי תְּלָתָא, וְזַכָּאָה חוּלָקָנָא לְעָלְמָא דְּאָתֵי, בְּגִין דָּא. נָפַק קָלָא תִּנְיָנוּת וְאָמַר, וְאַתֶּם הַדְּבֵקִים בַּיְיָ' אֱלֹהֵיכֶם חַיִּים כֻּלְּכֶם הַיּוֹם. קָמוּ וְאַזְלוּ. בְּכָל אֲתָר דַּהֲווֹ מִסְתַּכְּלֵי סָלִיק רֵיחִין. אר"ע שָׁמַע מִיצָה, דְּלְעָמָא מִתְבָּרֵךְ בְּגִינָן. וַהֲווֹ נַהֲרִין אַנְפּוֹי דְּכֻלְּהוּ, וְלָא הֲווֹ יַכְלִין בְּנֵי עָלְמָא לְאִסְתַּכְּלָא בְּהוּ.

356. Rav Shimon said: "How happy is the lot of these three, and praised is our lot in the World to Come for this." A second voice sounded and said: "And you who cleaved to the Lord your God are all alive this day." (Deuteronomy 4:4) They got up and left.

Everywhere they looked, fragrances ascended. Rav Shimon said: "It seems from this that the world is being blessed because of us." All their faces were shining bright and people could not look at them.

Rav Aba saw the souls of the three friends with the Angels and was settled.

357. תָּאנָא, עֲשָׂרָה עָאלוּ, וְשֶׁבַע נַפְקוּ, וַהֲוָה חַדֵי ר"ע. וְרִבִּי אַבָּא עָצִיב. יוֹמָא חַד הֲוָה יָתִיב ר"ע וְרִבִּי אַבָּא עִמֵּיה, אר"ע מִכָּה, וְוָזְמוּ לְאִלֵּין תְּלָתָא דַּהֲווֹ בְּיַיְתִין לְהוֹן מַלְאֲכִין עִלָּאִין, וּמְחַוְזָין לְהוּ גְּנִיּזִין וְאִדְּרִין דִּלְעֵילָּא, בְּגִין יְקָרָא דִּלְהוֹן. וַהֲווֹ עַיְּלֵי לוֹן בְּטוּרֵי דְּאַפַּרְסְמוֹנָא דַּכְיָא. נָח דַּעְתֵּיה דְּרִבִּי אַבָּא.

357. We have learned that ten entered the gathering and seven left it. Rav Shimon was rejoicing but Rav Aba was sad. One day, Rav Shimon was sitting with Rav Aba. Rav Shimon said something. They saw the three friends, whom Celestial Angels were bringing and showing them the Supernal treasures and chambers for their honor, and they brought them to the mountains of pure balsam. Rav Aba's mind settled.

The remaining seven were called the "seven eyes of the Lord."

358. תָּאנָא, מֵהַהוּא יוֹמָא לָא אַעְדּוּ חַבְרַיָּיא מִבֵּי ר"ע. וְכַד הֲוָה ר"ע מְגַלֶּה רָזִין, לָא מִשְׁתַּכְחִין תַּמָּן אֶלָּא אִינוּן. וַהֲוָה קָארֵי לְהוּ רִבִּי שִׁמְעוֹן, שִׁבְעָה אֲנָן עֵינֵי יְיָ'. דִּכְתִיב, שִׁבְעָה אֵלֶּה עֵינֵי יְיָ' וְעָלָן אִתְּמַר. א"ר אַבָּא, אֲנָן שִׁיתָא בּוֹצִינֵי, דְּנַהֲרָאן מִשְּׁבִיעָאָה. אַנְתְּ הוּא שְׁבִיעָאָה דְּכֹלָּא. דְּהָא לֵית קִיּוּמָא לְשִׁיתָא, בַּר מִשְּׁבִיעָאָה. דְּכֹלָּא תָּלֵי בִּשְׁבִיעָאָה. רִבִּי יְהוּדָה קָארֵי לֵיה עַבָּת, דְּכֻלְּהוּ שִׁיתָא מִגַּוֵּיה מִתְבָּרְכִין, דִּכְתִיב שַׁבָּת לַיְיָ', קֹדֶשׁ לַיְיָ', מַה שַׁבָּת לַיְיָ' קֹדֶשׁ, אוֹף ר"ע עַבָּת לַיְיָ' קֹדֶשׁ.

358. We have learned that from that day on, the friends did not leave the residence of Rav Shimon. When Rav Shimon was revealing secrets, nobody was present except for them. Rav Shimon referred to them as "We are the seven eyes of the Lord, as it is written:

'Those seven [are] the eyes of the Lord...' (Zechariah 4:10), which is applicable to us." Rav Aba said: "We are six candles who are lit from the seventh, which is the secret of Binah. You are the seventh of all because the six cannot exist, which are Chesed, Gevurah, Tiferet, Netzach, Hod, and Yesod, except through the seventh, which is Binah, since everything is dependent on the seventh." Rav Yehuda would call him "Shabbat," from which all six days get their blessing, as it is written: "...Shabbat to the Lord..." (Exodus 20:10) "... 'Holy to the Lord.'" (Exodus 28:36) Just as Shabbat is Holy to the Lord, so is Rav Shimon a Holy Shabbat to the Lord."

HA'AZINU

The Holy Idra Zuta (Smaller Assembly)

6. The day when Rav Shimon wanted to depart from the world

A Synopsis

This section begins to tell about the events surrounding Rav Shimon's voluntary departure from the world. Many of the friends are with him, although they come and go as Rav Shimon requests them to. A fire encircles the whole house as he prepares to reveal things that he has never before had permission to reveal, and Rav Aba is charged with writing down his revelations. Rav Shimon begins by saying that the living are the righteous, and anyone who is wicked is considered to be dead. He says that God delights in the honor of the righteous even more than His own honor. Next Rav Shimon tells the other friends that he can see two friends who died some time earlier together with seventy righteous people all shining with the radiance of the most hidden Atika Kadisha; at this statement the other friends tremble. Rav Shimon says that during his whole life he was attached to God, and now at the end God and all His holy followers have come joyfully to listen to hidden secrets and to the praise of Atika Kadisha.

Rav Shimon's house was full, and the fire around the house ceased.

23. תָּאנָא בְּהַהוּא יוֹמָא דר"ש בָּעָא לְאִסְתַּלְּקָא מִן עָלְמָא, וַהֲוָה מְסַדֵּר מִלּוֹי, אִתְכְּנָשׁוּ חַבְרַיָּיא לְבֵי ר"ש, וַהֲווֹ קַמֵּיהּ ר' אֶלְעָזָר בְּרֵיהּ, וְר' אַבָּא, וּשְׁאָר חַבְרַיָּיא, וַהֲוָה מַלְיָא בֵּיתָא. זָקִיף עֵינוֹי ר"ש, וְחָמָא דְּאִתְמְלֵי בֵּיתָא. בָּכָה ר"ש וְאָמַר, בְּזִמְנָא אַחֲרָא כַּד הֲוֵינָא בְּבֵי מַרְעֵי, הֲוָה רַבִּי פִּנְחָס בֶּן יָאִיר קַמַּאי, וְעַד דְּבָרִירְנָא דּוּכְתָּאי אוֹרִיכוּ לִי עַד הַשְׁתָּא. וְכַד תַּבְנָא, אַסְחַר אֶשָּׁא מִקַּמַּאי, וּמֵעָלְמִין לָא אִתְפְּסַק, וְלָא הֲוָה עָאל בַּר נָשׁ, אֶלָּא בִּרְשׁוּתָא. וְהַשְׁתָּא וְחָמֵינָא דְּאִתְפְּסַק, וְהָא אִתְמְלֵי בֵּיתָא.

23. We learned that on the day Rav Shimon wanted to depart from the world and was putting his affairs in order, the friends gathered in the house of Rav Shimon. Before him were his son Rav Elazar, Rav Aba, and rest of the friends, and the house was full. Rav Shimon lifted up his eyes and saw that the house became full. Rav Shimon wept and said: "Another time when I was ill Rav Pinchas ben Yair was before me, and until I figured out my place in the Garden of Eden they waited for me until now. When I returned, a fire encircled me, which never stopped. No one entered my house except by permission. Now I see the fire [has] stopped, and behold the house is full."

The fire returned, and only Rav Elazar and Rav Aba remained inside.

‎24. עַד דַּהֲווֹ יַתְבֵי, פָּתַח עֵינוֹי ר"ע, וְחָמָא מַה דְּחָמָא, וְאַסְחַר אֶשָׁא אֶשָׁא בְּבֵיתָא, נַפְקוּ כּוּלְהוּ, וְאִשְׁתָּאֲרוּ רִבִּי אֶלְעָזָר בְּרֵיהּ, וְרִבִּי אַבָּא. וּשְׁאַר חַבְרַיָּיא יָתְבוּ אַבְרַאי. אר"ע לְרִבִּי אֶלְעָזָר בְּרֵיהּ, פּוּק חֲזֵי, אִי הָכָא רִבִּי יִצְחָק, דַּאֲנָא מִעָרְבָנָא לֵיהּ, אֵימָא לֵיהּ דִּיסַדֵּר מִלּוֹי, וְיֵתִיב לְגַבָּאי, זַכָּאָה חוּלְקֵיהּ.

24. While they were sitting, Rav Shimon opened his eyes and saw what he saw, and fire encircled the house. Everybody left, and only his son Rav Elazar and Rav Aba remained, while the rest of the friends stayed outside. Rav Shimon said to his son Rav Elazar: "Go out and see if Rav Yitzchak is here because I was a guarantor for him (Zohar, Vayechi 159). Tell him to settle his affairs and sit by me. Happy is his portion."

The reunion of the Great Assembly.

‎25. קָם ר"ע, וְיָתִיב, וְחַיֵּיךְ, וְחַדֵּי. אָמַר, אָן אִינּוּן חַבְרַיָּיא. קָם רִבִּי אֶלְעָזָר, וְאָעִיל לוֹן. יָתְבוּ קַמֵּיהּ. זָקִיף יְדוֹי ר"ע, וּמְצַלֵּי צְלוֹתָא, וַהֲוֵי חַדֵּי, וְאָמַר, אִינּוּן חַבְרַיָּיא דְּאִשְׁתְּכָחוּ בְּבֵי אִדְרָא, יְזְדַּמְנוּן הָכָא. נַפְקוּ כֻּלְּהוּ, וְאִשְׁתָּאֲרוּ רִבִּי אֶלְעָזָר בְּרֵיהּ, וְרִבִּי אַבָּא, וְרִבִּי יְהוּדָה, וְרִבִּי יוֹסֵי, וְרִבִּי חִיָּיא. אַדְהָכִי, עָאל

רִבִּי יִצְחָק, א"ל ר"ע, כַּמָּה יָאוּת וֹוּלָקָךָ, כַּמָּה חֵידוּ בָּעֵי לְאִתּוֹסְפָא לָךָ בְּהַאי יוֹמָא, יָתִיב רִבִּי אַבָּא בָּתַר כַּתְפוֹי, וְרִבִּי אֶלְעָזָר קַמֵּיה.

25. Rav Shimon rose and sat down, laughed and rejoiced. He said: "Where are the friends?" Rav Elazar arose and let them in, and they sat before him. Rav Shimon raised his hands, recited a prayer and was glad. He said: "Let the friends that were present at the Assembly, namely the Idra Raba, **come here."** They all left, and Rav Elazar his son, Rav Aba, Rav Yehuda, Rav Yosi, and Rav Chiya stayed. In the meanwhile Rav Yitzchak entered. Rav Shimon said to him: "How beautiful is your portion. How much joy should be added to you on this day." Rav Aba sat behind him and Rav Elazar before him.

Rav Shimon wished to reveal all the secrets he has not revealed until now.

26. אר"ע, הָא הַשְׁתָּא שַׁעֲתָא דִרְעוּתָא הוּא, וַאֲנָא בָּעֵינָא לְמֵיעַל בְּלָא כִּסוּפָא לְעָלְמָא דְאָתֵי. וְהָא מִלִּין קַדִּישִׁין דְּלָא גְּלֵיאָן עַד הַשְׁתָּא, בָּעֵינָא לְגַלָּאָה קַמֵּי שְׁכִינְתָּא, דְּלָא יֵימְרוּן דְּהָא בִּגְרִיעוּתָא אִסְתַּלַּקְנָא מֵעָלְמָא. וְעַד כְּעַן כְּסֵן טְמִירִן הֲווֹ בְּלִבָּאִי, לְמֵיעַל בְּהוּ לְעָלְמָא דְאָתֵי.

26. Rav Shimon said: "Now it is a time of goodwill, and I want to come without shame into the World to Come. Here are Holy matters that I have not revealed until now. I wish to reveal them before the Shechinah so it shall not be said that I have gone from this world in want; until now they have been hidden in my heart, so I can enter through them into the World to Come.

Rav Aba wrote down and Rav Elazar recited.

27. וְכַךְ אַסְדַּרְנָא לְכוּ, רִבִּי אַבָּא יִכְתּוֹב, וְרִבִּי אֶלְעָזָר בְּרִי יִלְעֵי, וּשְׁאָר חַבְרַיָּיא יְרַחֲשׁוּן בְּלִבַּיְיהוּ. קָם רִבִּי אַבָּא מִבָּתַר כַּתְפוֹי. וְיָתִיב רִבִּי אֶלְעָזָר בְּרֵיה קַמֵּיה, א"ל קוּם בְּרִי, דְּהָא אַוְחֲרָא יָתִיב בְּהַהוּא אֲתָר, קָם רִבִּי אֶלְעָזָר.

27. "This is how I am going to arrange you: Rav Aba shall write, Rav Elazar my son shall recite orally, and the other friends shall speak in their hearts." Rav Aba rose from behind his back. Rav Elazar was sitting in front of him. Rav Shimon said to him: "Rise my son, for another shall sit in this place." Rav Elazar arose.

The righteous are called living; the wicked are called dead.

28. אִתְעֲטָף ר״ע, וְיָתִיב. פָּתַח וְאָמַר, לֹא הַמֵּתִים יְהַלְלוּ יָהּ וְלֹא כָּל יוֹרְדֵי דוּמָה. לֹא הַמֵּתִים יְהַלְלוּ יָהּ, הָכִי הוּא וַדַּאי, אִינּוּן דְּאִקְרוּן מֵתִים, דְּהָא קוּדְשָׁא בְּרִיךְ הוּא וַי אִקְרֵי, וְהוּא שָׁארֵי בֵּין אִינּוּן דְּאִקְרוּן חַיִּים, וְלָא עִם אִינּוּן דְּאִקְרוּן מֵתִים. וְסוֹפֵיהּ דִּקְרָא כְּתִיב, וְלֹא כָּל יוֹרְדֵי דוּמָה, וְכָל אִינּוּן דְּנַחְתִין לְדוּמָה, בַּגֵּיהִנָּם יִשְׁתַּאֲרוּן. שָׁאנֵי אִינּוּן דְּאִקְרוּן חַיִּים, דְּהָא קוּדְשָׁא בְּרִיךְ הוּא בָּעֵי בִּיקָרֵיהוֹן.

28. Rav Shimon wrapped himself in his garment and sat down. He opened and said: "'The dead cannot praise Yah, nor can any who go down into silence (dumah).' (Psalms 115:17) Surely 'The dead cannot praise Yah...' namely those who are considered dead because the Holy One, blessed be He, is called living and dwells among those who are called living, namely the righteous, and not with those that are considered dead, namely the wicked. The end of the verse proves it, as it is written, '...nor can any who go down into silence (dumah),' (Ibid.) namely all those who go down to the angel Dumah, and remain in Gehenom. But it is not so with those who are called living, the righteous, which the Holy One, blessed be He, delights to honor."

The Holy One, blessed be He, desires the honor of the righteous.

29. אר״ע, כַּמָּה עַנְיָא שַׁעְתָּא דָא מֵאַדְרָא. דִּבְאַדְרָא אוֹדְמַן קוּדְשָׁא בְּרִיךְ הוּא וּרְתִיכוֹי. וְהַשְׁתָּא, הָא קוּדְשָׁא בְּרִיךְ הוּא הָכָא, וְאָתֵי עִם אִינּוּן צַדִּיקַיָּיא דִּבְגִנְתָא דְעֵדֶן, מַה דְּלָא אִעְרְעוּ בְּאַדְרָא. וְקוּדְשָׁא בְּרִיךְ הוּא בָּעֵי בִּיקָרֵיהוֹן

דְּצַדִּיקַיָּא יַתִּיר מִיקָרָא דִּילֵיהּ, כְּמָה דִּכְתִיב בִּירָבְעָם, דַּהֲוָה מְקַטֵּר וּמַפְלַח
לַע"ז, וְקוּדְשָׁא בְּרִיךְ הוּא אוֹרִיךְ לֵיהּ. וְכֵיוָן דְּאוֹשִׁיט יְדֵיהּ לָקֶבְלֵי דְּעִדּוֹ נְבִיאָה,
אִתְיְבַּשׁ יְדֵיהּ, דִּכְתִיב וַתִּיבַשׁ יָדוֹ וְגוֹ'. וְעַל דְּפָלַח לַע"ז לָא כְּתִיב, אֶלָּא עַל
דְּאוֹשִׁיט יְדֵיהּ לְעִדּוֹ נְבִיאָה. וְהַשְׁתָּא קוּדְשָׁא בְּרִיךְ הוּא בָּעֵי בִּיקָרָא דִּילָן,
וְכֻלְּהוּ אָתָאן עִמֵּיהּ.

29. Rav Shimon said: "How different is this time from the Idra Raba
in the portion of Naso, **since in the Idra the Holy One, blessed be He,
came with His Chariots. Now the Holy One, blessed be He, is here,
coming with the righteous who are in the Garden of Eden, which
has not happened at the Idra. And the Holy One, blessed be He,
considers the honor of the righteous more than His own honor, as
written about Jeroboam that he used to make offerings and worship
idols, yet the Holy One, blessed be He, waited for him** and did not
punish him. **But once he stretched his hands against Ido the prophet,
his hand dried up, as it is written, 'And his hand… dried up….'** (I
Kings 13:4) **It is not mentioned because he worshipped idols but
because he put out his hand against Ido the prophet. Now the Holy
One, blessed be He, desires our honor** since **all** the righteous in the
Garden of Eden **came with Him."**

*Rav Hamnuna and seventy righteous souls
descend to listen to Rav Shimon.*

30. אָמַר, הָא רַב הַמְנוּנָא סָבָא הָכָא, וְסַחֲרָנֵיהּ ע' צַדִּיקֵי גְּלִיפָן בְּעִיטְרִין,
מְנַהֲרִין כָּל חַד וְחַד מִזִּיהֲרָא דְּזִיוָא דְּעַתִּיקָא קַדִּישָׁא, סְתִימָא דְּכָל סְתִימִין.
וְהוּא אָתֵי לְמִשְׁמַע בְּחֶדְוָותָא, אִלֵּין מִלִּין דַּאֲנָא אֵימָא. עַד דַּהֲוָה יָתִיב, אָמַר,
הָא רַבִּי פִּנְחָס בֶּן יָאִיר הָכָא, אַתְקִינוּ דּוּכְתֵּיהּ, אִזְדַּעֲזָעוּ חַבְרַיָּא דַּהֲווֹ תַּמָּן,
וְקָמוּ וְיָתְבוּ בְּשִׁיפּוּלֵי בֵּיתָא. וְרַבִּי אֶלְעָזָר וְרַבִּי אַבָּא, אִשְׁתָּאֲרוּ קַמֵּיהּ דְּר"ש.
אר"ש, בְּאִדְרָא אִשְׁתְּכַחְנָא דְּכָל חַבְרַיָּא הֲווֹ אַמְרֵי, וַאֲנָא עִמְּהוֹן. הַשְׁתָּא
אֵימָא אֲנָא בִּלְחוֹדַאי, וְכֻלְּהוּ צַיְיתִין לְמִלּוּלֵי עִלָּאִין וְתַתָּאִין. זַכָּאָה חוּלָקִי
יוֹמָא דֵּין.

30. Rav Shimon said: "Here is Rav Hamnuna Saba, and around him seventy righteous people engraved with Crowns, each one shining from the splendor of the radiance of the most concealed Atika Kadisha. He comes gladly to listen to the things I am saying." As he was sitting he said: "Since Rav Pinchas ben Yair is here, prepare his seat." The friends that were there trembled, rose and sat at the corners of the house, and Rav Elazar and Rav Aba remained before Rav Shimon. Rav Shimon said: "In the Idra Raba the state was that all the friends were talking and I among them. Now I shall alone speak and everyone will listen to my words, Higher and Lower Beings. Happy is my portion on this day."

Rav Shimon cleaved to Creator all his life.

31. פָּתַח ר"ש וְאָמַר, אֲנִי לְדוֹדִי וְעָלַי תְּשׁוּקָתוֹ. כָּל יוֹמִין דְּאִתְקְטַּרְנָא בְּהַאי עָלְמָא, בְּחַד קְטִירָא אִתְקְטַרְנָא בֵּיהּ בְּקוּדְשָׁא בְּרִיךְ הוּא, וּבג"כ הַשְׁתָּא וְעָלַי תְּשׁוּקָתוֹ. דְּהוּא וְכָל סִיעֲתָא קַדִּישָׁא דִּילֵיהּ, אָתוּ לְמִשְׁמַע בְּחֶדְוָה, מִלִּין סְתִימִין, וּשְׁבָחָא דְּעַתִּיקָא קַדִּישָׁא, סְתִימָא דְּכָל סְתִימִין, פָּרִישׁ וְאִתְפְּרַשׁ מִכֹּלָּא, וְלָא פָּרִישׁ, דְּהָא כֹּלָּא בֵּיהּ מִתְדַּבַּק, וְהוּא מִתְדַּבַּק בְּכֹלָּא הוּא כֹּלָּא.

31. Rav Shimon opened and said: "'I am my beloved's, and his desire is toward me.' (Song of Songs 7:11) All the days I was connected to this world, I was attached with one connection to the Holy One, blessed be He, and therefore now, '…His desire is toward me.' (Ibid.) For He and all His Holy Camp have come with joy to listen to hidden words and the praise of the most hidden Atika Kadisha, which is separated and divided, yet is not divided, since everything cleaves to Him and He cleaves to everything; He is everything."

HA'AZINU

48. The passing away of Rav Shimon ben Yochai

A Synopsis

Rav Aba recounts that after Rav Shimon uttered the word "life," all his words ceased. The light in the room was so great that Rav Aba could not look, and two voices were heard saying "For length of days, and long life", and then, "He asked life of You." We are told of the miraculous events that happened during the rest of that day.

Rav Shimon left the world with the word "life."

196. א"ר אַבָּא, לָא סְיֵּים בּוּצִינָא קַדִּישָׁא לְמֵימַר וַיִּים, עַד דְּאִשְׁתְּכָכוּ מִלּוֹי, וַאֲנָא כָּתַבְנָא, סָבַרְנָא לְמִכְתַּב טְפֵי, וְלָא שְׁמַעְנָא. וְלָא זָקִיפְנָא רֵישָׁא, דִּנְהוֹרָא הֲוָה סַגִּי, וְלָא הֲוָה יָכִילְנָא לְאִסְתַּכְּלָא. אַדְהָכִי אִזְדַּעֲזַעְנָא, שְׁמַעְנָא קָלָא דְּקָאֲרֵי וְאָמַר אֹרֶךְ יָמִים וּשְׁנוֹת וַיִּים וְגוֹ'. שְׁמַעְנָא קָלָא אַחֲרָא, וַיִּים שָׁאַל מִמְּךָ וְגוֹ'.

196. Rav Aba said: "The Holy Luminary barely finished uttering 'life,' when his words ceased. I was writing and was about to write more, yet heard nothing. I did not raise my head because the light was great and I could not look. I then trembled and heard a voice calling and saying, 'For... length of days, and long life...' (Proverbs 3:2), and then I heard another voice, 'He asked life of You....' (Psalms 21:5)

The Holy Luminary departed the world with a smiling face.

197. כָּל הַהוּא יוֹמָא, לָא אַפְסִיק אֶשָּׁא מִן בֵּיתָא, וְלָא הֲוָה מַאן דְּמָטֵי לְגַבֵּיהּ, דְּלָא יָכִילוּ דִּנְהוֹרָא וְאֶשָּׁא הֲוָה בְּסוּחֲרָנֵיהּ. כָּל הַהוּא יוֹמָא נָפִילְנָא עַל אַרְעָא, וְגָעֵינָא. בָּתַר דְּאָזִיל אֶשָּׁא, חֲמֵינָא לְבוּצִינָא קַדִּישָׁא קֹדֶשׁ הַקֳּדָשִׁים, דְּאִסְתַּלַּק מִן עָלְמָא, אִתְעַטָּף שָׁכִיב עַל יְמִינֵיהּ, וְאַנְפּוֹי חַיְיכִין.

197. "All that day the fire did not cease from the house, and no one reached him for they could not because of the light and fire that encircled him. All that day, I was prostrated on the ground, crying loudly. After the fire was gone, I saw that the Holy Luminary, the Holy of Holies, was gone from the world, wrapped around and lying on his right side with a smiling face.

The great loss of the friends of Rav Shimon.

198. קָם רַבִּי אֶלְעָזָר בְּרֵיהּ, וְנָטִיל יְדוֹי וְנָשִׁיק לוֹן, וַאֲנָא לָחִיכְנָא עַפְרָא דִּתְחוֹת רַגְלוֹי. בָּעוּ חַבְרַיָּיא לְמִבְכֵּי, וְלָא יָכִילוּ לְמַלְּלָא. שָׁארוּ חַבְרַיָּיא בִּבְכִיָּה, וְרַבִּי אֶלְעָזָר בְּרֵיהּ נָפִיל תְּלַת זִמְנִין, וְלָא יָכִיל לְמִפְתַּח פּוּמֵיהּ. לְבָתַר פָּתַח וְאָמַר, אַבָּא אַבָּא. תְּלַת הֲווֹ, חַד אִתְחַזָרוּ. הַשְׁתָּא תְּנוּד חֵיוָתָא, צִפֳּרָאן טָאסִין, מִשְׁתַּקְעָן בְּנוּקְבָּאן דְּיַמָּא רַבָּא, וְחַבְרַיָּיא כֻּלְּהוּ שַׁתְיִין דָּמָא.

198. "Rav Elazar his son rose, took his hands and kissed them, while I licked the dirt under his feet. The friends wanted to cry and could not speak. Rav Elazar his son prostrated three times and could not open his mouth. He then started saying: 'Father, father, there were **three that** became **one again.** Namely there were three great men in the land, Rav Elazar, his father Rav Shimon bar Yochai, and his father-in-law Rav Pinchas ben Yair. Now Rav Elazar is orphaned of his father-in-law and his father Rav Shimon and only one remains in the world. After this Great Tree is gone, under which the beasts of the field used to walk and in whose boughs dwelt the birds of the sky and that had food for everyone, **now the beasts will wander and the birds** that used to dwell in its boughs **will sink into the chasm in the Great Sea, and the friends,** instead of the food they received from it **will drink blood.'"**

Rav Elazar and Rav Aba dealt with the body of Rav Shimon.

199. קָם רַבִּי חִיָּיא עַל רַגְלוֹי וְאָמַר, עַד הַשְׁתָּא בּוּצִינָא קַדִּישָׁא מִסְתַּכַּל עֲלָן. הַשְׁתָּא לָאו הוּא עִדָן, אֶלָּא לְאִשְׁתַּדְּלָא בִּיקָרֵיהּ. קָם רַבִּי אֶלְעָזָר וְרִבִּי אַבָּא,

נָטְלוּ לֵיהּ בְּטִיקְרָא דְּסִיקְלָא, מַאן חֲמָא עִרְבּוּבְיָא דַּחֲבְרַיָּיא, וְכָל בֵּיתָא הֲוָה
סָלִיק רֵיחִין. סְלִיקוּ בֵּיהּ בְּפוּרְיֵיהּ, וְלָא אִשְׁתְּמֵשׁ בֵּיהּ, אֶלָּא ר' אֶלְעָזָר וְר' אַבָּא.

199. Rav Chiya stood on his feet and said: "Up until now the Holy
Luminary used to protect us. Now it is not the time to do anything
except to deal with his honor." Rav Elazar and Rav Aba rose and
took him from his place **to a bed made like a ladder** to raise him on
his bed. **Who has ever seen such confusion of the friends. The whole
house emitted good fragrances. They raised him on his bed, and
none dealt with him but Rav Elazar and Rav Aba.**

A quarrel broke out about where Rav Shimon was to be buried.

200. אָתוּ טְרִיקִין, וּמָארֵי תְּרִיסִין דִּכְפַר צִפֳּרִי וְטַרְדָא בְּהוּ בְּנֵי מְרוֹנְיָא, צַוְוחִין
בְּקָטִירִין, דְּוְזְעֵיבוּ דְּלָא יִתְקְבַר תַּמָּן. בָּתַר דְּנָפַק פּוּרְיָיא, הֲוָה סָלִיק בַּאֲוִירָא.
וְאֶשָּׁא הֲוָה לָהִיט קַמֵּיהּ, שָׁמְעוּ קָלָא, עוּלוּ וְאָתוּ, וְאִתְכְּנָשׁוּ לְהִילוּלָא דְּרִבִּי
שִׁמְעוֹן, יָבֹא שָׁלוֹם יָנוּחוּ עַל מִשְׁכְּבוֹתָם.

200. Bullies and armed people came from the village of Tzipori,
who wanted him to be buried there and came to take him by force. **The
inhabitants of Meron drove them away and shouted at them in their
multitudes, because they did not want him to be buried there** but
where they themselves lived. **After the bed left the house, it rose in the
air and fire burned before it. They heard a voice: "Come and gather
to the feast of Rav Shimon. 'He shall come in peace, they shall rest
in their beds….'"** (Isaiah 57:2)

Rav Shimon was an Earth trembler and a provoker of Kingdoms.

201. כַּד עָאל לִמְעַרְתָּא שָׁמְעוּ קָלָא בִּמְעַרְתָּא, זֶה הָאִישׁ מַרְעִישׁ הָאָרֶץ מַרְגִּיז
מַמְלָכוֹת, כַּמָּה פִּטְרִין בִּרְקִיעָא מִשְׁתַּכְּכִין בְּיוֹמָא דֵּין בְּגִינָהּ, דְּנָא רשב"י,
דְּמָארֵיהּ מִשְׁתַּבַּח בֵּיהּ בְּכָל יוֹמָא. זַכָּאָה חוּלָקֵיהּ לְעֵילָּא וְתַתָּא. כַּמָּה גְּנִיזִין

עִלָּאִין מִסְתַּמְּרָן לֵיהּ, עָלֵיהּ אִתְּמַר וְאַתָּה לֵךְ לַקֵּץ וְתָנוּחַ וְתַעֲמוֹד לְגוֹרָלְךָ לְקֵץ הַיָּמִין.

עַד כָּאן הָאִדְרָא קַדִּישָׁא זוּטָא

201. When he entered the cave, they heard a voice inside the cave: "This is the man who caused the Earth to tremble, who provoked Kingdoms. How many prosecutors in the Firmament are quieted today for your sake? This is Rav Shimon bar Yochai, whose Master is praised by him every day. Blessed is his portion Above and Below. How many Supernal treasures await him. Of him it says, "And you, go to the end; and you shall rest and arise to your lot at the end of days." (Daniel 12:13)

End of the Idra Kadisa Zuta (Holy Smaller Assembly)

ZOHAR CHADASH: BERESHEET

55. When Rav Shimon became ill

A Synopsis

When Rav Shimon became ill he explained to the other friends that his case is not being judged by the Higher Court but by God Himself. We hear that when a man is lying down ill, the Upper Court studies his case, but one who is judged instead by God is blessed because God is entirely of Mercy. Rav Shimon speaks to Supernal Beings who cannot be heard or seen by the others, but they smell fragrant scents. During a mystical journey Rav Shimon has picked his place in the Upper World to Come, and has spoken with Adam; Rav Shimon agrees not to reveal Adam's sin to the whole world but only to the other friends.

Rav Shimon was not judged by an angel or a judge.

794. ת"ר, כְּשֶׁחֲלָה רַבִּי שִׁמְעוֹן בֶּן יוֹחָאי. עָאלוּ קַמֵּיהּ ר' פִּנְחָס, וְר' חִיָּיא, וְר' אַבָּהוּ. אָמְרוּ לוֹ, מַאן דְּהוּא קַיָּימָא דְּעָלְמָא, שָׁכִיב. אֲמַר לוֹן, לָא בֵּי דִינָא דִלְעֵילָּא מְעַיְּינִין בְּדִינָאי, דְּהָא אֲנָא חֲזָאי דְּלֵית אֲנָא מִתְיְיהֵב לְמַלְאָכָא וּלְדַיָּינָא דִלְעֵילָּא. דַּאֲנָא לָאו כִּשְׁאָר בְּנֵי נָשָׁא.

794. The sages taught us that when Rav Shimon bar Yochai fell ill, Rav Pinchas, Rav Chiya, and Rav Abahu came before him. They said to him, "Why is the pillar of the world lying ill?" He said to them, "The Upper Court does not examine my case, for I see I am not handed over to an angel, nor to a judge Above, for I am not as other men.

Only the Creator judged Rav Shimon's case.

795. אֶלָּא הַאי דִּינָא דִּילִי, קֻבְּ"ה דַּיְנֵיהּ, וְלָא בֵּי דִינֵיהּ. וְהַיְינוּ דַּאֲמַר דָּוִד, בִּבְעוּתֵיהּ קַמֵּיהּ שָׁפְטֵנִי אֱלֹהִים וְרִיבָה רִיבִי. וְכֵן שְׁלֹמֹה אֲמַר, לַעֲשׂוֹת מִשְׁפַּט עַבְדּוֹ, הוּא בִּלְחוֹדוֹי, וְלָא אַחֲרָן.

795. "But my case is judged by the Holy One, blessed be He, not by His Court. This is what David meant in his prayer before Him, 'Judge me, God, and plead my cause...' (Psalms 43:1) and Solomon similarly said, '...to do justice to His servant...' (I Kings 8:59)—He alone and no other.

The Upper Court studies the merit and guilt of man.

796. דְּהָא תָּנֵינָן, כְּשֶׁהָאָדָם הוּא שׁוֹכֵב, בֵּי דִינָא דִּלְעֵילָא מִסְתַּכְּלִין בְּדִינוֹי, אִית מִנְּהוֹן דְּנָטָאן לְכַף זְכוּת, דְּאַחֲזְיָין זְכוּתָא דְּבַר נָשׁ, וְאִית מִנְּהוֹן דְּנָטָאן לְכַף חוֹבָה, דְּאַחֲזְיָין חוֹבָה דְּבַר נָשׁ. וּנְפִיק אִינִישׁ מִן דִּינָא, כְּמָה דְּהוּא בָּעֵי.

796. "For we have learned that when a man lies down ill, the Upper Court studies his case. Some tend toward acquittal, and present the merit of man; some tend to guilty sentencing and present the man's sins. The man leaves the court as he deserves.

The Creator always tends toward merit.

797. אֲבָל מַאן דְּדָאִין לֵיהּ מַלְכָּא עִילָאָה, דְּשַׁלִּיט עַל כּוֹלָא, הוּא טַב, וְלָא יָכִיל אִינִישׁ לְמֶהֱוֵי בְּהַהוּא דִינָא, בַּר טַב. מ"ט, דְּהָא תָּנֵינָן, דְּכִילוֹי דְּמַלְכָּא עִילָאָה, נָטֵי לִזְכוּתָא תָּדִיר, וְהוּא כּוֹלֵיהּ צַד רַחֲמָנוּתָא, וּבִידוֹי לְשָׁבְקָא לְחֶטָאִין וְחוֹבִין, הה"ד כִּי עִמְּךָ הַסְּלִיחָה וְגו', וְלֹא עִם אַחֵר.

797. "But he who is judged by the Supernal King who rules over all, is good, and a man can only be good when facing that Judgment. The reason is that we learned that the character of the Supernal

King always tends to merit, and He is all of the side of Mercy, able to forgive sins and transgressions. Hence it says: 'But there is forgiveness with You...' (Psalms 130:4) and with no one else.

No one could stop Rav Shimon.

798. וּבְג"כ בָּעֵינָא קַמֵּיהּ דְּהוּא יָדִין דִּינָאי, וַאֲנָא אָעֵיל תְּלֵיסַר אַבָּבֵי לְעָלְמָא דְּאָתֵי, דְּלָא אֲעַבְרוּ לוֹן בַּר אֲבָהָתָא, וְלָא יְהָא מַאן דִּימְחֵי בִּידִי, וְעוֹד דְּלָא אֶתְבַּע רְשׁוּתָא מִנַּיְהוּ.

798. "I have therefore asked before Him that He will judge me. And I caused the Thirteen Attributes of Mercy to enter into the openings of the World to Come, which no one crossed over and placed there except the Patriarchs. There was no one to stop me and moreover, I did not even ask permission."

Rav Shimon disappeared for a moment and returned.

799. אר"שׁ מִלָּה, וְחָמוּן בֵּי מַרְעֵיהּ, דְּלָא הֲוָה הוּא תַּמָּן. תְּוָוהוּ, וְלָא הֲוָה יָכִיל חַד מִנַּיְהוּ לְמַלְלָא בְּפוּמֵיהּ, מִדְּוְחִילוּ רַבָּה דַּהֲוֵי עֲלֵיהוֹן. עַד דַּהֲווֹ יַתְבֵי, סָלֵיק לוֹן רֵיחִין דְּבוּסְמֵי סַגִּיאִין, וְכָל חַד וְחַד מִנַּיְהוּ אִתְיַישַּׁר וְחֵילֵיהּ, עַד דַּחֲמוּ לְרַבִּי שִׁמְעוֹן, וַהֲוָה מְמַלֵּל מִלִּין, וְלָא הֲוָה חָמָאן אַחֲרָן בַּר בִּינֵיהּ.

799. Rav Shimon said something, and they observed his bed, but Rav Shimon was not there. They were amazed, and no one was able to open his mouth, for the great fear that was upon them. While they sat, fragrant scents arose of many spices, and they were each strengthened until they saw Rav Shimon. He was talking to someone but they saw no one else there except him.

The friends heard Rav Shimon talking to someone.

800. לְבָתַר עִידָן, אֲמַר לוֹן ר"ע, וְחַמֵּיתוּן מִידֵי. א"ל ר' פִּנְחָס, לָא, אֶלָּא כּוּלָנָא תְּוָוהִין עַל דְּלָא חָמֵינָא לָךְ בְּבֵי מַרְעָךְ, זְמַן רַב, וְכַד חָמֵינָא לָךְ סָלֵיק לָךְ רֵיחִין דְּבוּסְמִין דְּגִנְתָּא דְּעֵדֶן, וְשָׁמַעְנָא קָלָךְ מְמַלֵּל, וְלָא יַדְעָנָא מָאן מְמַלֵּל עִמָּךְ.

800. After a while, Rav Shimon said to them, "Have you seen anything?" Rav Pinchas said to him, "No, but we were all amazed at not seeing you in your bed for a long time, and when we saw you, fragrant scents of the spices of the Garden of Eden rose to you. We heard your voice talking but did not know who talked with you."

The friends did not merit to hear who Rav Shimon was talking to.

801. אֲמַר לוֹן, וְלָא שְׁמַעְתּוּן מִלָּה אוֹחֲרָנָא בַּר מִדִּידִי. אֲמָרוּ לָאו. אֲמַר לוֹן, לֵית אַתּוּן חַזְיָין לְמֶחֱמֵי סְבַר עַתִּיק יוֹמִין.

801. He said to him, "Have you not heard any other words but my own?" They said, "No." He said to them, "You are not worthy of beholding the sight of Atik Yomin (Ancient One)."

The place of Rav Pinchas was below Rav Elazar.

802. אֲמַר לוֹן, אֵימָא לְכוּ מִלָּה, תְּוָוהְנָא עַל ר' פִּנְחָס, דְּלָא חָמָא. דַּאֲנָא וְחָמֵית לֵיהּ כְּעַן בְּהַהוּא עָלְמָא, לְתַתָּא מֵרַבִּי אֶלְעָזָר בְּרִי.

802. He said to them, "Let me now say something to you. I am surprised that Rav Pinchas did not see, for I see him now in that World beneath the place of **Rav Elazar my son.**

Rav Shimon's place was next to Achiyah the Shilonite.

803. וּכְעַן שָׁדָרוּ בְּדִילִי מִלְעֵילָא, וְאַחְזִיאָן לִי אַתְרָא דְּצַדִּיקַיָּא לְעָלְמָא דְאָתֵי,
וְלָא אִתְיִישַׁר בְּלִבָּאי דּוּכְתָּאי, בַּר עִם אֲחִיָּה הַשִּׁילוֹנִי. וּבְרִירְנָא דּוּכְתָּאי,
וְאָתֵינָא, וַאֲתוֹ עִמִּי תְּלַת מְאָה גִּשְׁמָתִין דְּצַדִּיקַיָּא, וְעֵילָא מִנְּהוֹן אָדָם הָרִאשׁוֹן,
דַּהֲוָה יָתִיב גַּבָּאי, וְהוּא הֲוָה מְמַלֵּל עִמִּי. וּבָעֵי, דְּלָא יִתְגְּלֵי חוֹבֵיהּ לְכָל עָלְמָא.
בַּר הַהוּא דְּאָמְרָה אוֹרַיְיתָא בְּגִינֵיהּ, וְאִתְכַּסֵּי בְּהַהוּא אִילָנָא דְּגִנְתָּא דְּעֵדֶן.

803. "Now they have sent for me from Above, and showed me
the dwelling place of the righteous in the World to Come, but my
heart was not settled about my place unless it was with Achiyah
the Shilonite. I picked my place and came, and with me came three
hundred souls of the righteous with Adam above them, who sat by
me and talked with me. He asked of me that his sin not be revealed
to the whole world, except what the Torah said of him, and it [the
sin] **hid in the Tree in the Garden of Eden** so that the world does not
know what it is.

The Creator does not wish to make Adam's sin known.

804. וַאֲמֵינָא לֵיהּ אֲנָא דְּהָא אֲנָא וַחַבְרַיָּיא גְּלוֹ. אָמַר הַהוּא דְּגִלּוּ וַחַבְרַיָּא בֵּינַיְיהוּ טַב
וְשַׁפִּיר, אֲבָל לִשְׁאָר בְּנֵי עָלְמָא לָא. מַאי טַעְמָא, דְּחָס קָבָּ"ה עַל יְקָרֵיהּ, וְלָא
בָּעֵא לְפַרְסוּמֵי חוֹבֵיהּ, אֶלָּא בְּהַהוּא אִילָנָא דַּאֲמַר דַּאֲכַל מִנֵּיהּ.

804. "I said to him that the friends have discovered and revealed
his sin. He said that it is well that the friends have related it among
themselves, but not to the other inhabitants of the world. Why?
Because the Holy One, blessed be He, has mercy upon his honor,
and does not wish to make known his sin to all, except that Tree, as
He said, of which he ate.

Most people do not understand the sin of Adam.

805. וְקָכ"ה גָּלֵי לִי בְּרוּחַ הַקְּדֶשׁ, וּלְחַבְרַיָּא, דְּלִישְׁתָּעוּ אִינּוּן בֵּינַיְיהוּ, וְלָא לְדַרְדְּקֵי דְּחַבְרַיָּא, וּלְאִינּוּן דְּיֵיתוּן לְעָלְמָא. דְּהוּא מִלָּה דְּלָא יָדְעֵי כָּל אִינָשֵׁי, וְטָעַיִן בֵּיהּ. לָאו מִשּׁוּם חוֹבְתָא דְּחָב, אֶלָּא מִשּׁוּם יְקָרָא דִּשְׁמָא עִילָאָה, דִּבְנֵי נָשָׁא לָא זְהִירִין בֵּיהּ, וּכְתִיב זֶה שְׁמִי לְעוֹלָם. וְיֵיתוּן לְמִשְׁאַל מַה דְּלָא צְרִיכֵי לוֹן.

805. "The Holy One, blessed be He, revealed this to me through the Holy Spirit, and to the friends, that they may speak among themselves but not reveal it to the lesser friends and to those who will come into the world. For this matter not all people understand and they mistake it. Therefore his sin is not to be revealed, **not because of** how great **the sin he committed** was, **but for the sake of the glory of the most High Name, which people are not careful of. And it is written, '...this is My Name forever** (le'olam)**...'** (Exodus 3:15), which means to conceal it (leha'alimo). **Otherwise they might ask what they should not.**

A teacher needs to be careful not to reveal the Name to all.

806. וְהַיְינוּ דִּכְתִיב, פֶּן יֶהֶרְסוּ אֶל ה' לִרְאוֹת וְנָפַל מִמֶּנּוּ רָב, מַאי וְנָפַל מִמֶּנּוּ רָב. הָכֵי גְּזַרְנָא, הַאי חַבְרָא דְּאוֹרֵי שְׁמָא קַדִּישָׁא לְכוֹלָא, הוּא נָפִיל וְנִתְפַּס בְּהַהוּא חוֹבָא, יַתִּיר מִנַּיְיהוּ, דִּכְתִיב וְנָפַל מִמֶּנּוּ רָב, הָרַב נוֹפֵל וְנִתְפַּס בְּאוֹתוֹ עָוֹן.

806. "This is the meaning of, 'lest they break through to the Lord to gaze, and many (rav) **of them may perish (lit. 'and a Rav will fall').' (Exodus 19:21)"** He asks: **"What is the meaning of 'and a Rav will fall'?** He answers: **"I have so decreed that a friend who teaches the Holy Name to all falls and is punished in that sin more than they, as it is written 'and a Rav will fall,' meaning the Rav who falls and is punished for in that sin."**

Rav Elazar's portion in the World to Come.

807. קָרִיב לְגַבֵּיהּ רַבִּי אֶלְעָזָר בְּרֵיהּ, א"ל אַבָּא, מָה אֲנָא הָתָם. א"ל זַכָּאָה
וֹזַלְקָךְ בְּרִי, זְמַן סַגִּי יְהֵא דְלָא תִּתְקַבֵּר גַּבָּאי, אֲבָל בְּהַהוּא עָלְמָא, דּוּכְתָּא
דִידִי וְדִידָךְ בְּרִירְנָא. זַכָּאִין אִינוּן צַדִּיקַיָּא, דְּזַמִּינִין אִינוּן לְמִשַׁבְּחֵי לְמָארֵי
עָלְמָא, כְּאִינוּן מַלְאָכִין עַמְּשִׁין דְּקַמֵּיהּ, הה"ד, אַךְ צַדִּיקִים יוֹדוּ לִשְׁמֶךָ יֵשְׁבוּ
יְשָׁרִים אֶת פָּנֶיךָ.

807. Rav Elazar his son came near him. He said to him, "Father, what am I there?" He said to him, "Happy is your portion, son. For a long time you will not be buried by me, but in that World I have selected my place and yours. Happy are the righteous, who will praise the Master of the universe in the future, like the angels and the servants before him. Hence it is said, 'Surely the righteous shall give thanks to Your Name; the upright shall dwell in Your presence.' (Psalms 140:14)"

SHAVUOT

PROLOGUE

14. The night of the Bride

The Zohar examines the Holiday of Shavout (Holiday of Weeks), when the presence of the Creator unites completely to our physical world. Shavout connects us to the original revelation of Light that occurred on Mount Sinai. The union between the presence of God [the Light or Shechinah] and the physical world produced total perfection. The Light on Mount Sinai radiated with such intensity that it banished the dark forces of death and decay, and the Israelites experienced true immortality. Likewise, the forces transmitted through the Aramaic text of the Zohar arouse the spiritual energy of immortality and remove the power of death from our lives. The kabbalists reveal a secret concerning the force called Death: It not only strikes and affects the physical body, but it is also the unseen motivating force responsible for the demise of relationships, prosperity, and happiness in any form.

Engagnig with the Torah the entire night of Shavuot.

125. רַבִּי שִׁמְעוֹן הֲוָה יָתֵיב וְלָעֵי בְּאוֹרַיְיתָא, בְּלֵילְיָא דְּכַלָּה אִתְחַבְּרַת בְּבַעְלָהּ, דְּתָנִינָן כָּל אִינוּן חַבְרַיָּא דִּבְנֵי הֵיכָלָא דְּכַלָּה, אִצְטְרִיכוּ בְּהַהִיא לֵילְיָא, דְּכַלָּה אוֹזְדַּמְנַת לְמֶהֱוֵי לְיוֹמָא אַחֲרָא גּוֹ חוּפָּה בְּבַעְלָהּ, לְמֶהֱוֵי עִמָּהּ כָּל הַהוּא לֵילְיָא, וּלְמֶחֱדֵי עִמָּהּ בְּתִקּוּנָהָא דְּאִיהִי אִתְתַּקְּנַת, לְמִלְעֵי בְּאוֹרַיְיתָא, מִתּוֹרָה לִנְבִיאִים, וּמִנְּבִיאִים לִכְתוּבִים, וּבְמִדְרְשׁוֹת דִּקְרָאֵי, וּבְרָזֵי דְּחָכְמְתָא. בְּגִין דְּאִלֵּין אִינוּן תִּיקּוּנִין דִּילָהּ וְתַכְשִׁיטָהָא. וְאִיהִי וְעוּלֵמְתָהָא עָאלַת וְקָיְימַת עַל רֵישַׁיְיהוֹן, וְאִתְתַּקְּנַת בְּהוּ וְחָדֵת בְּהוּ כָּל הַהוּא לֵילְיָא. וּלְיוֹמָא אָחֳרָא לָא עָאלַת לַחוּפָּה אֶלָּא בַּהֲדַיְיהוּ, וְאִלֵּין אִקְרוּן בְּנֵי חוּפָּתָא. וְכֵיוָן דְּעָאלַת לְחוּפָּתָא, קָדוֹשׁ בָּרוּךְ הוּא שָׁאֵיל עֲלַיְיהוּ וּמְבָרֵךְ לוֹן, וּמְעַטֵּר לוֹן בְּעִטְרָהָא דְּכַלָּה, זַכָּאָה חוּלְקֵהוֹן.

125. Rav Shimon was sitting and dealing with the Torah on the night when the Bride, who is Malchut, **unites with Her Husband. For we have learned that all the friends who are the Members of the**

Bride's Chamber should remain with the Bride all that night, on the morrow of which is the day of Shavuot, **the Bride-to-be is prepared to go in the Chupah (Marriage Canopy) with Her Husband, and to be with Her all that night and rejoice with Her as with her correction She is adorned,** namely **to deal with the Torah, and from the Torah to the Prophets, and from the Prophets to the Writings, and then to the Expositions of the Scriptures and to the Inner Secrets of Wisdom because these are Her corrections and Her ornaments. And She,** the Bride, **approaches Her bridesmaids and sets Herself over their heads. She is prepared by them and rejoices with them all night. The day after,** on the Day of Shavuot, **She does not enter under the Chupah (Marriage Canopy) without them. These,** the friends who dealt with the Torah all night long, **are called the Members of the Canopy. Once She comes to the Canopy, the Holy One, blessed be He, inquires after them, blesses them, and crowns them with the Crowns of the Bride. Happy is their portion.**

Explanation of these words: There are two explanations for this and both go hand-in-hand. The first [explanation] is that the days of exile are called "Night" because it is a time of the concealment of His Face from the children of Israel. Then all the forces of separation have power over those who serve the Creator. Despite all that, it is specifically at that time that the Bride unites with Her Husband through the Torah and the Precepts performed by the righteous who at that time are called the Supporters of the Torah. All the exalted levels, called secrets of the Torah, are revealed by them, and for that reason they are called their Makers. They are, so to speak, the Makers of the Torah (Zohar, Prologue, 124). And we find that the days of exile are called **"the night in which the bride unites with her husband."** And all the friends, members of the bride's chamber, they are **"the Supporters of the Torah."**

After the End of the Correction and the Complete Redemption, which is the secret of the verse: "but it shall be one particular day which shall be known to the Lord, neither day nor night; and it shall come to pass that at evening time there will be light." (Zechariah 14:7) is what is meant in: **"on the morrow of which, the Bride-to-be is prepared to go in the canopy with Her husband."** Then the BaN will return to be SaG, and the MaH will be AV. Therefore, it is considered as "the morrow" and a new canopy. The righteous at that time are called the Members of the Canopy, which is the secret of those who study the Torah that have no aspect of Asiyah (Action), for then it is said: "...the earth shall be full of the knowledge of the Lord...." (Isaiah 11:9) And since these righteous people raise the BaN to be SaG by means of their good deeds, through the power of them drawing upon the awe [that they had] in the past, they are considered to be the making of this new Marriage Canopy. And for this, they are called Members of the Canopy.

The second interpretation is that the night of Shavuot is called **"the night when the Bride unites with Her Husband... on the morrow of which, the Bride-to-be is prepared to go in the Chupah (Marriage Canopy) with Her Husband"** meaning on the day of Shavuot, the day of the Receiving of the Torah. In fact it has the same notions as the first explanation mentioned earlier because on the day of the Receiving of the Torah there was already the aspect of the End of the Correction, in the secret of "He shall swallow up death forever; and the Lord God will wipe away the tears from off all faces...." (Isaiah 25:8) Similarly the sages taught about the verse: "...engraved (*charut*) upon the Tablets." (Exodus 32:16) [They said]: "Do not pronounce it *charut* (engraved) but rather *cherut* (freedom) because they achieved freedom from the angel of death." (Shemot Rabba 41:7) Yet, because of the Sin of the Golden Calf, they again corrupted that which was rectified. Thus, the concept of the day of the Receiving of the Torah has the same notion as the End of the Correction.

We find that on the night before the Receiving of the Torah all the unifications that took place during the Days of Concealment were completed. That night was therefore considered as the **"the night when the Bride unites with Her husband... on the morrow of which, the Bride-to-be is prepared to go in the Chupah (Marriage Canopy) with Her Husband,"** which is the Holiday of Shavuot, when the correction is finished with freedom from the Angel of Death. It is the time when the righteous, through their good deeds, make a new Canopy for the Bride.

I am more at ease with continuing the interpretation according to the first explanation, and the reader by himself can transpose these words to [the explanation of] the Day of Shavuot because it is one matter.

This is: **"all the friends who are the Members of the Bride's Chamber should remain with the Bride all that night"** meaning all those who support the Torah, who are called Members of the Bride's Chamber (as mentioned in the previous section), need to cleave to the Holy Shechinah, who is called the bride, throughout all that night of the exile. Then during the days of the exile, She is corrected through the supporters of the Torah by means of their good deeds, Torah study, and the Precepts that they perform until they purify Her from the aspect of good and evil. Then She would be ready for those who study the Torah, who have nothing of the aspect of Asiyah (Action), as She is wholly good without bad (Zohar, Prologue, 123). Therefore, the supporters of the Torah, who are the Members of the Bride's Chamber, need to rejoice with Her for this great correction done to the Bride by them. Thus **"and rejoice with Her as with her correction She is adorned, to deal with the Torah,"** namely through the following corrections, **"from the Torah to the Prophets..."** and they need to perform them with joy.

It has been explained that all the levels and revelation of the secrets of the Torah, which build the Shechinah to Her complete correction, are all done only by those who support the Torah during the days of exile. All these levels and statures, therefore, which emerge during the time of exile, are called the corrections of the bride and her ornaments, as it goes on to detail: **"from the Torah to the Prophets…"** since Chesed, Gevurah, and Tiferet are the Secret of Torah; Netzach and Hod are the Secret of Prophets; and the Malchut itself is the Secret of the Writings. The Mochin of the Six Corners [Sefirot] that they draw to Her are the Expositions of the Scriptures, and the Mochin of the Upper Three that they draw to Her are the Secrets of the Wisdom. All these corrections need to be drawn to the bride on that night, since by them the Bride is finished for the End of the Correction, which is the secret of the day of the canopy.

Concerning **"She approaches Her bridesmaids…."** the angels who envelop the vessels of the Achorayim (Exterior) of Malchut of the first state are called the maids that attend the Shechinah. And [the Zohar] says that the Shechinah **"sets Herself over the heads"** of those who support the Torah, in the secret of the verse "and over my head the Shechinah of El" (from the Bedtime Shema Reading). And together with Her are the maids that serve Her, and She rejoices with them as She goes on to be corrected by them. This is: **"and rejoices with them all night,"** meaning throughout the time of corrections called "Night" (see also in Zohar Chadash, Song of Songs 159). **"The day after"** meaning that on the day of the End of the Correction, which is the day of the Canopy, She can only enter under the Canopy with those who support the Torah, who built and corrected her sufficiently, **"from the Torah to the Prophets…"** as mentioned earlier. They are therefore called the members of the Canopy.

Concerning **"Once She comes to the canopy,"** you already know that the End of the Correction will bring nothing new with it. Rather, through the Supernal Light of Atik Yomin, all the Mayin Nukvin, Mayin Duchrin, Unifications, and levels that emerged during the six thousand years, one after the other, will gather into one unification and one great and precious stature. Through this, everything will be corrected. (Zohar, Prologue, 91); then the Bride will enter the Canopy. Thus **"the Holy**

One, blessed be He, inquires after them," that is, after each and every
one who ever raised Mayin Nukvin for a Supernal Unification. He sits,
so to speak, and waits until they will all gather, so it is as if He inquires
after and waits for each and every one. After they gather, the union of "...
of Kabze'el, who had done mighty deeds (rav pe'alim mikavtze'el)..." (II
Samuel 23:20) takes place. **"He blesses them and crowns them"** they
are all blessed and crowned simultaneously. And then the correction that
is called **"the Crowns of the Bride"** is finished.

Those who prepare the adornments of the Bride
are written in the Book of Remembrance.

126. וַהֲוָה רַבִּי שִׁמְעוֹן וְכָלְהוֹ חַבְרַיָּיא מְרַנְּנִין בְּרִנָּה דְאוֹרַיְיתָא, וּמְחַדְּשָׁן מִלִּין
דְאוֹרַיְיתָא כָּל חַד וְחַד מִנַּיְיהוּ, וַהֲוָה חָדֵי רַבִּי שִׁמְעוֹן וְכָל שְׁאָר חַבְרַיָּא. אֲמַר
לוֹן רַבִּי שִׁמְעוֹן: בְּנַי, זַכָּאָה חוּלָקֵכוֹן, בְּגִין דִּלְמָחָר לָא תֵעוֹל כַּלָּה לַחוּפָּה אֶלָּא
בַּהֲדַיְיכוּ, בְּגִין דְכָלְהוֹ דִמְתַקְּנִין תִּקּוּנָהָא בְּהַאי לֵילְיָא וְחָדָאן בָּהּ, כָּלְהוֹ יְהוֹן
רְשִׁימִין וּכְתִיבִין בְּסִפְרָא דְּדִכְרָנַיָּא, וְקֻדְשָׁא בָּרִיךְ הוּא מְבָרֵךְ לוֹן בְּשַׁבְעִין
בִּרְכָאן וְעִטְרִין דְּעָלְמָא עִלָּאָה.

**126. And Rav Shimon and all the friends were chanting the songs
of the Torah. Every one of them taught new interpretations of the
Torah, and Rav Shimon was rejoicing together with all the friends.
Rav Shimon said to them: "My sons, how happy is your lot because
tomorrow the Bride shall not approach the Bridal Canopy without
you. Because all those who prepare the adornments of the Bride
during this night and rejoice with Her shall all be written and
registered in the Book of Remembrance. And the Holy One, blessed
be He, blesses them with seventy Blessings and Crowns from the
Upper World."**

Explanation of the words: The **Book of Remembrance** is mentioned
in: "You have said, 'It is vain to serve God... they have indeed done evil
and endured; they have indeed dared God and escaped.' Then they

who feared the Lord spoke to one another: and the Lord hearkened, and heard it, and a Book of Remembrance was written before Him for those who feared the Lord, and took heed of His Name... And they shall be Mine, said the Lord of Hosts, on that day which I appoint as my particular day...." (Malachi 3:14-17) We have to understand these matters. When they said to one another and conversed these vile things such as: "It is vain to serve God; and what profit is it that we have kept His charge" (Ibid.), why would the prophet say about them: "Then they who feared the Lord spoke to one another" (Ibid.)? Not only that, but they are written in "a Book of Remembrance before him for those who feared the Lord, and took heed of His Name" (Ibid.)?

The idea is that at the time of the End [of Correction], when the great union of Atik Yomin will be revealed, is in the secret of "rav pe'alim mikavtze'el (lit. many actions gathering to one)" (II Samuel 23:20), a great Light will be revealed throughout all the Worlds, by which all flesh will return with true repentance out of love. And it is known that the sages said: "the one who merits repenting out of love, his malicious actions become merits." (Tractate Yoma 86b) Therefore the prophet said about those wicked when they talked and spoke to one another these vile and despicable things, saying: "...It is vain to serve God, and what profit is it that we have kept his charge..." For on the great day of the End of the Correction, when the Light of Repentance out of love will be revealed, even these malicious sins, and there is nothing worse than them, will turn into merits as well; and those who speak [these vile things] will be considered as those who fear God. That is, at the End of Correction, as the prophet concludes: "'...they shall be Mine,' said the Lord of Hosts, on that day which I appoint as My particular day..." (Malachi 3:17) which is the day of the End of the Correction.

Therefore there must be a Book of Remembrance before Him containing all the malicious actions and crimes done in the world. He requires them for the day that He appoints as the particular day, for then they will transform into merits and gather and complete the stature of Light of the End of the Correction. As it says: "...and a Book of Remembrance was written before Him for those who fear the Lord and take heed of His Name. 'And they shall be Mine, said the Lord of Hosts, on that day which I appoint as My particular day.' (Malachi 3:16-17) For then I require them to complete the stature. Thus the prophet concludes: "...and I will have compassion for them, as a man feels compassion for his own son who serves him." (Ibid.) Because then will they be precious to Me and beloved to Me as if they were among those who serve Me. This is why the Zohar says: **"shall all be written and registered in the Book of Remembrance,"** for it comes to include that even the malicious actions they committed will then be written and registered in the Book of Remembrance. And the Creator will write them down as if they were merits, and as if they had served Him with [the iniquities], as the prophet said.

The number seventy indicates the Mochin of Chochmah and Upper Three, which are called Crowns. The secret of blessing indicates the Light of Chasadim, as the world was created with [the letter] Bet, which signifies blessing, which is: "The world shall be built by kindness..." (Psalms 89:3) and it is the aspect of the Six Corners [Sefirot]. He says that at the End of the Correction, the Light of Chasadim will also be in the aspect of seventy Crowns just like the Chochmah, for the MaH and BaN will ascend to AV and SaG. Thus **"the Holy One, blessed be He, blesses them with seventy Blessings and Crowns from the Upper World"** of AV and SaG. Therefore even blessings are described at that time by the number seventy.

The Bride rejoices with the friends who supported Her in the night.

127. פָּתַח רַבִּי שִׁמְעוֹן וַאֲמַר הַשָּׁמַיִם מְסַפְּרִים כְּבוֹד אֵל וְגוֹ', קְרָא דָּא הָא אוֹקִימְנָא לֵיהּ. אֲבָל בְּזִמְנָא דָּא, דְּכַלָּה אִתְעָרָא לְמֵיעַל לַחוּפָּה בְּיוֹמָא דְּמָחָר,

אִתְתַּקְנַת וְאִתְנְהִירַת בְּקִשׁוּטָהָא, בַּהֲדֵי חַבְרַיָּיא דְּחָדָאן עִמָּהּ כָּל הַהִיא לֵילְיָא, וְאִיהִי חָדָאת עִמְּהוֹן.

127. Rav Shimon opened and said: "'The Heavens declare the glory of God…. (Psalms 19:2) I have already established this verse. But when the Bride awakens on the morning of the following day to enter under the Bridal Canopy, She is fixed and shines with Her ornaments with the friends who rejoiced with Her that entire night, and She rejoices with them.

The Shechinah and Her hosts wait for all those
who prepared Her in the night.

128. וּבְיוֹמָא דְּמָחָר כַּמָּה אוּכְלוּסִין חַיָּילִין וּמַשְׁרְיָין מִתְכַּנְּשִׁין בַּהֲדָהּ, וְאִיהִי וְכֻלְּהוֹ, מְחַכָּאן לְכָל חַד וְחַד דְּתִקְּינוּ לָהּ בְּהַאי לֵילְיָא, כֵּיוָן דְּמִתְחַבְּרָן כַּחֲדָא וְאִיהִי חָמָאת לְבַעְלָהּ, מַה כְּתִיב, הַשָּׁמַיִם מְסַפְּרִים כְּבוֹד אֵל. הַשָּׁמַיִם, דָּא חָתָן דְּעָאל לַחוּפָּה. מְסַפְּרִים, מְנַהֲרִין כְּזוֹהֲרָא דְּסַפִּיר, דְּנָהִיר וְזָהִיר מִסְּיֵיפֵי עָלְמָא וְעַד סְיֵיפֵי עָלְמָא.

128. "On the following day, how many legions, hosts, and camps gather around Her. She and all the others, all these hosts and camps, wait for each and every one of those who prepared her by studying the Torah on this night. Once they, Zeir Anpin and Malchut, join together, and She, Malchut, sees Her Husband, Zeir Anpin, it is written: 'The Heavens declare the glory of God….' 'The Heavens' refers to the Groom, Zeir Anpin called the "Heavens" who enters under the Bridal Canopy; 'declare' (*mesap'rim*; מְסַפְּרִים) means that they shine like the radiance of the Sapphire (*Sapir*; סַפִּיר), which shines and radiates from one end of the world to the other."

Explanation of the words: The day of the End of the Correction is called **"the following day"** as the sages said: "today to do them, and tomorrow to receive reward for them." (Tractate Eruvin 22a) The **"legions"** are people of the land, who do not serve the Creator. The **"hosts"** are the servants of the Creator, and **"camps"** indicate the Upper Camps, which are angels that accompany the souls, in the secret of the verse: "For He shall give His angels charge over you, to protect you in all your paths." (Psalms 91:11) **"She and all the others wait for each and every one"** was explained in verse 125, where just as the Creator inquires after each and every one, so does the Shechinah wait for each and every one. Thus **"Once they join together, and She sees Her Husband..."** since She cannot see Her Husband before they all gather, as mentioned earlier, and they are mutually dependent.

[Concerning] **"'The Heavens' refers to the Groom who enters under the Bridal Canopy."** [The Zohar] explains the verse as referring to the End of the Correction, about which it is said, "And the light of the moon shall be as the light of the sun...." (Isaiah 30:26) And he says that Heaven is the Groom that enters under the Canopy because the Holy One, blessed be He, is called "Heaven." And at the time of the End of the Correction, He is called a Groom, in the secret of the verse, "...and as the groom rejoices with the bride, so shall your God rejoice with you...." (Isaiah 62:5) The meaning is that wherever it is written: "And the Lord came down..." it is a matter of Judgment (Gevurah), since it indicates a descent from His grade and loftiness, where "...strength and gladness are in His place." (I Chronicles 16:27) Yet at the End of the Correction— when all the blemishes and iniquities will turn into merits because then it shall be clear that all the descents were actually ascents—the Holy One, blessed be He, is called a Groom and the Holy Shechinah is called a Bride.

Bride (*kalah*; כלה) denotes the End of the Correction, as in: "And it was on the day that Moses finished (*kalot*; כלות) setting up the Tabernacle...." (Numbers 7:1) That means that he concluded all the work on the Tabernacle and setting it up. And the word Groom (*chatan*; חתן) also indicates a descent, as we translate the Hebrew word *red* (go down; רד) as *chot* (חות) in Aramaic, and as the sages said: "descend (*nechet*; נחת) a level to marry a woman," (Tractate Yevamot 63b) Yet, this descent is greater than all other previous ascents since it is toward the Bride, namely the Shechinah during the End of the Correction, who is then called *kalah* (bride or finished; כלה).

The Canopy (*chupah*; חופה;) is the gathering and assembly of all the Returning Light that emerged by means of the Mayin Nukvin that the righteous raised through all the Unifications of the Holy One, blessed be He, and His Shechinah, which manifested one after the other throughout the days and times of the six thousand years [of the Tikkun (Correction) process]. Now they become one Great Light of Returning Light that ascends and hovers (*chofef*; חופף) above the Holy One, blessed be He, and His Shechinah, which are now called Groom and Bride. The Returning Light hovers over them like a Canopy. Therefore, at that time the righteous are called the Members of the Canopy because each and every one takes part in this Canopy to the extent of the Mayin Nukvin he raised to the Masach in Malchut to raise Returning Light. This is: **"'The Heavens' refers to the Groom who enters under the bridal canopy,"** referring to the time of the End of the Correction when the Holy One, blessed be He, is called a Groom, and He enters then under His Wedding Canopy.

Regarding, **"'declare' (*mesap'rim*) means that they shine"** "declare" is the secret of the Great Unification that will be in the future, which is the same wording as: "...a wife *mesaperet* (converses) with her husband." (Tractate Berachot 3a) And Sapphire (*Sapir*) is the Name of the Holy Shechinah, coming from: "...and under His feet, as the work of a sapphire brick...." (Exodus 24:10) "The radiance of the Sapphire" is the Returning Light She raises from Below Upward. **"Shines"** refers to Direct Light, and **"radiates"** refers to Returning Light. He says that through this Great Unification that takes place at the End of the Correction, which is the gathering of all the unifications, the Direct Light and Returning

Light of this particular Unification **"shines and radiates from one end of the world to the other,"** which is the secret of: **"The Heavens declare...."** (Psalms 19:2)

On Shavuot the Shechinah has splendor upon splendor,
dominion upon dominion.

129. כְּבוֹד אֵל, דָּא כְּבוֹד כַּלָּה דְּאִקְרֵי אֵל, דִּכְתִיב אֵל זוֹעֵם בְּכָל יוֹם. בְּכָל יוֹמֵי שַׁתָּא אִקְרֵי אֵל, וְהַשְׁתָּא, דְּהָא עָאלַת לַחוּפָּה, אִקְרֵי כָּבוֹד, וְאִקְרֵי אֵל, יְקָר עַל יְקָר. נְהִירוּ עַל נְהִירוּ, וְשָׁלְטָנוּ עַל שָׁלְטָנוּ.

129. **"'...the glory of God (El)...' (Psalms 19:2) is the glory of the Bride,** Malchut, **which is called El. As it is written, 'and God (El) who has indignation every day.' (Psalms 7:12) During all the days of the year She is called El, but now,** in the Holiday of Shavuot, **after entering under the Bridal Canopy, She is called 'Glory' and 'El,'** which means **preciousness upon preciousness, splendor upon splendor, and dominion upon dominion."**

Explanation: The Name El is the Great Name of Kindness (Chesed). Yet the verse says, "...God (El) has indignation every day" (Psalms 7:12) and seemingly it is the opposite of kindness. The idea is that it is the secret of the verse: "...and there was evening and there was morning, day one." (Genesis 1:5) The Holy Shechinah is the secret of "...the small luminary to rule the night" (Genesis 1:16) and She is called the Awe of Heaven because the righteous need to raise Mayin Nukvin through their awakenings from Below and to set Her in the secret of the Masach that raises Returning Light. Then the abundance is drawn from Above downward, and in no other way, as it is known. This is the secret of: "... and God (Elohim) created it so that men should fear from before Him." (Ecclesiastes 3:14) because the awakening from Below and the elevation of Mayin Nukvin is impossible without awe.

This is the secret of Her ruling by night because through the lack of Light, which is the aspect of night that includes all Judgments and suffering that are the opposite of the attribute of day that is kindness, there is awe before Him. Were it not for awe, the attribute of day and morning would not be revealed. This is the secret of: "...and there was evening and there was morning, day one" (Genesis 1:5) because the night also comes into the morning, for were it not for the night there would be no morning, and it is not possible any other way. This is the secret of: **"...and God (El) has indignation every day"** (Psalms 7:12) because the attribute of Kindness called El is revealed solely through the night, which is the aspect of indignation. Therefore the wrath is also considered kindness, for it is impossible for kindness to be revealed in any other way. From this perspective the Holy Shechinah is also called El.

"'The glory of God (El)' is the glory of the Bride, which is called El," meaning that from the aspect of what is written: "God (El) has indignation every day" which means that there cannot be day without the night's indignation. **"During all the days of the year She is called El."** This is the case with the six working days. It is said of each of them, "...and there was evening and there was morning, day one," or "day two" etc. (Genesis 1) Thus we find that the night enters under the category of the day. Therefore throughout the six working days, and also during the six thousand years, She is called El, which is the Name of Kindness (Chesed).

This is: **"but now, after entering..."** because with the great unification of the End of the Correction, the light of the moon will be as the light of the sun in the secret of: "...but it shall come to pass that at evening time there will be light." (Zechariah 14:7) We find that Her levels are twofold because even in the six thousand years, as the aspect of the light of the moon, she was in the secret of: "...and there was evening and there was morning..." (Genesis 1:5) And when She is as big as the sun, which is Zeir Anpin called Glory, She therefore has glory upon glory; for now

She becomes the essence of Glory since she has grown as Zeir Anpin. And "glory" (*kavod*) is translated in Aramaic as "precious" (*yekar*), and therefore: **"preciousness upon preciousness."**

Also **"splendor upon splendor"** for even during the six thousand years, She was included in the light of morning, in the secret of: "...and there was evening and there was morning, day one." (Genesis 1:5) But now, when She is as big as the sun, She becomes the essence of Light. Thus She has her own Light upon the Light that She had when She was included [in the Light of the morning] beforehand. And also **"dominion upon dominion"** because during the six thousand years She had dominion, which is governance, only in the aspect of: "the small luminary to rule the night." (Genesis 1:16) And now also the governance of the day was added to Her since She has grown as the light of the sun, which governs the day. And it informs us that we must not be mistaken in saying that while She has grown to be as the light of the sun, Her own levels that She had from the six thousand years are annulled, Heaven forbid. This is not so. Rather, there is only an addition here to Her own levels, in a way that She has **"preciousness upon preciousness."**

The friends that prepared the Bride are known by name.

130. כְּדֵין בְּהַהִיא שַׁעֲתָא, דִּשְׁמַיָּא עָאל לַחוּפָּה וְאָתֵי וְנָהִיר לָהּ, כָּל אִינּוּן חַבְרַיָּיא דְּאַתְקִינוּ לָהּ, כֻּלְּהוּ אִתְפָּרְשֵׁי בִּשְׁמָהָן תַּמָּן, הה"ד וּמַעֲשֵׂה יָדָיו מַגִּיד הָרָקִיעַ. מַעֲשֵׂה יָדָיו, אִלֵּין אִינּוּן מָארֵי קְיָימָא דִּבְרִית, אִקְרוּן מַעֲשֵׂה יָדָיו, כד"א וּמַעֲשֵׂה יָדֵינוּ כּוֹנְנֵהוּ, דָּא בְּרִית קְיָימָא דְּוַחְתִים בְּבִשְׂרָא דְּבַר נָשׁ.

130. Then, when the Heavens, Zeir Anpin, **enter under the Bridal Canopy and come to shine upon Her, all those friends who prepared Her,** by studying the Torah all night, **are recognized and known by their names. As it is written: "...and the Firmament proclaims His handiwork." (Psalms 19:2) "His handiwork" refers to those who own the Sign of the Covenant, who are called His handiwork. As it**

is written: "...and the work of our hands establish it" (Psalms 90:17) which is the Sign of the Covenant (the Circumcision) marked on man's flesh.

Explanation: The friends are the supporters of the Torah, which contains in it Asiyah, which is good and evil. He says that even those parts whose evil is not yet corrected are also recognized by their names of Holiness. This is: "As it is written: '...and the Firmament proclaims His handiwork'" (Psalms 19:2) since the Firmament is the secret of the Book of Remembrance, as will be explained below, which is the secret of the Light of the Great Unification that leads to repentance out of love, where "the malicious actions turn into merits." (Tractate Yoma 86b) And even those who allowed their mouth to speak evil, it will be said of them: "...then they who feared the Lord spoke to one another...." (Malachi 3:16) (As mentioned above in verse 126; study there).

So we find that this Asiyah, which is the "supporters of the Torah" that contains good and evil—where for he who merits it is good and for he who does not merit it is bad—now elevates to become Holy and becomes the handiwork of the Holy One, blessed be He. Thus even for those who did not merit, the Firmament proclaims on them: "...then they who feared the Lord spoke to one another..." (Malachi 3:16) as mentioned earlier. So it is found that all the friends perfomed only the work of Holiness because they prepared Her for the Canopy, and they are all recognized by their names.

Regarding, "...and the work of our hands establish it." (Psalms 90:17) Seemingly, the proof [he brings] acts as a contradiction, since the verse says: "the work of our hands" rather than His handwork. However he only offers proof from the verse that the Sign of the Covenant is called "the work of our hands" because "establish it" is Yesod that establishes and founds the whole building. And the correction of the Yesod is with the Circumcision. From this [we take that] the Sign of the Covenant is called "the work of our hands" (Ibid.) because we remove the foreskin from the Yesod and this is the work of our hands. And this is so only before the End of the Correction. At the End of the Correction, it will be revealed that everything is the handiwork of the Holy One, blessed be He, and He Himself will be removing the foreskin. Therefore **"those who own the Sign of the Covenant are called His handiwork"** because at that time, the Holy One, blessed be He, Himself will remove the foreskin, which is the secret of: **"...the Firmament proclaims His handiwork."** (Psalms 19:2) And he brings proof that the correction of the Covenant is now called "the work of our hands" from the verse, **"...the work of our hands establish it."** (Psalms 90:17)

Keeping the Holy Covenant.

131. רַב הַמְנוּנָא סָבָא אֲמַר הָכֵי, אַל תִּתֵּן אֶת פִּיךְ לַחֲטִיא אֶת בְּשָׂרֶךָ, דְּלָא יְהֵיב בַּר נָשׁ פּוּמֵיהּ, לְמֵיתֵי לְהִרְהוּרָא בִּישָׁא, וְיֵהֵא גָרִים לְמֶחֱטֵי לְהַהִיא בְּשַׂר קֹדֶשׁ דַּחֲתִים בֵּיהּ בְּרִית קַדִּישָׁא. דְּאִלּוּ עָבִיד כֵּן מָשְׁכִין לֵיהּ לַגֵּיהִנֹּם, וְהַהוּא דִּמְמוּנֶה עַל גֵּיהִנֹּם דּוּמָ"ה שְׁמֵיהּ, וְכַמָּה רִבּוֹא דִּמְלְאֲכֵי חַבָּלָה בַּהֲדֵיהּ, וְקָאִים עַל פִּתְחָא דְּגֵיהִנֹּם, וְכָל אִינוּן דְּנָטְרוּ בְּרִית קַדִּישָׁא, בְּהַאי עָלְמָא, לֵית לֵיהּ רְשׁוּ לְמִקְרַב בְּהוֹ.

131. Rav Hamnuna Saba said the following. "'Do not let your mouth cause your flesh to sin....' (Ecclesiastes 5:5) This means that a person should not allow his mouth to be the cause of bringing upon himself evil thoughts, thereby bringing sin to the sacred flesh where the Holy Covenant is marked. Because if he does so he shall be dragged into Gehenom. He who is in charge of Gehenom is called Dumah. And together with many tens of thousands of destructive angels, they all stand at the opening of Gehenom. But he has no permission to touch all those who have kept the Holy Covenant in this world."

When it says **"bringing upon himself evil thoughts"** it means a warning that every person should guard his mouth, which is the matter of raising Mayin Nukvin by means of Torah [study] and prayer so that it is in a state of utmost purity. If the Other Side has any hold on it, then the Other Side would receive his Mayin Nukvin; and with that force he would cause him to have second thoughts about the Creator; namely to have strange thoughts, Heaven forbid, **"thereby bringing sin to the sacred flesh where the Holy Covenant is marked"** because by these thoughts he is actually "pulling the foreskin" over the Holy Covenant, and the Holy Soul falls captive to the hands of the Other Side. And then the Other Side pulls his soul to Gehenom. This is according to what Rav Elazar said (Zohar, Prologue 68) where from that word a false firmament, which is called *Tohu* (Chaos), is created and it falls into the hands of Lili"th; study there. Though, here he speaks specifically of the blemish of the Holy Covenant.

Regarding, **"thereby bringing sin to the sacred flesh where the Holy Covenant is marked"** this refers to the Holy Soul that is connected and protected by the Holy Covenant, as said in the Zohar: "and from my flesh I would see God (Eloha)...." (Job 19:26) What is meant by "and from my flesh"? It should have been "and from myself." Rather [it says] "from my flesh" specifically. We learned that as long as a man is sealed with the Holy Sign of this Covenant, he literally sees the Holy One, blessed be He, from it. And the Holy Soul is unified in him [through the Sign of the Covenant]. And if the person does not merit, since he did not keep that Sign, it is written "From the soul of God (Eloha) they shall be banished...." (Job 4:9) (Zohar, Lech Lecha 410-411), study there. And it says here [in the Zohar] **"thereby bringing sin to the sacred flesh, where the Holy Covenant is marked,"** meaning that by the force of these [negative] thoughts, the foreskin, which is the Other Side, comes back to touch the Holy Covenant, and thus "the soul of God (Eloha)" immediately departs from him. This is the secret of when the Zohar said that the Tree cried out: "Evil one, do not touch me." (Zohar Hashmatot, Beresheet 305) Because the Tree is Yesod, and the crown of Yesod is the secret of the Tree of Knowledge of Good and Evil.

Regarding, **"He who is in charge of Gehenom is called Dumah"** He is called Dumah from the word *demamah* (silence) because he takes away the breath of life, leaving him in silence, which is death. We can further explain that He is the angel that brings the [negative] thoughts to the sinner and makes [him think that] the thoughts of the Holy One, blessed be He, are *domeh* (similar) to the thoughts of a mere human. As long as the person understands that His thoughts are not like our thoughts, nor His ways to our ways, meaning that no mind can grasp Him at all, neither His thoughts nor His conduct, then it would be unimaginable to him to have any [negative] thought against Him, Heaven forbid. Rather, due to the sin, the angel Dumah longs for him and brings spirit of nonsense to make him say that a mere human resembles the Creator in knowledge and mind. Then [that person] is susceptible to all kinds of thoughts and [the angel] pulls him to Gehenom.

We see that his entire strength lies in the name Dumah. This is the secret of: "Who performs mighty acts like You, and who is similar (*domeh*) to You, a King who causes death and brings back to life" (from the Amidah Prayer). In thinking that [we are] similar (*domeh*) to You, Heaven forbid, there is death; and in understanding that none are similar (*domeh*) to Him there is life. This is: **"many tens of thousands of destructive angels, they all stand at the opening of Gehenom"** since the [negative] thoughts [Dumah] brings upon people are many tens of thousands to no-end. And all these [thoughts] are at the opening of Gehenom, meaning that it is an opening through which the person is pulled to Gehenom, and not Gehenom in itself. Thus **"But he has no permission to touch all those who have kept the Holy Covenant in this world."** Meaning, that even though they are not completely clean and still have the aspect of Asiyah, good and evil, nevertheless if they keep the Holy Covenant in such a way that they will never come to an [evil] thought, the angel Dumah has no permission to pull them to Gehenom.

The situation of King David with Batsheba.

132. דָּוִד מַלְכָּא בְּשַׁעְתָּא דְּאֵירַע לֵיהּ הַהוּא עוֹבָדָא, דָּחִיל, בְּהַהִיא שַׁעְתָּא סָלֵיק דוּמָ"ה קַמֵּי ה' קַדוֹשׁ בָּרוּךְ הוּא. וְאָמַר לֵיהּ, מָארֵי דְּעָלְמָא כְּתִיב בְּאוֹרַיְתָא, וְאִישׁ אֲשֶׁר יִנְאַף אֶת אֵשֶׁת אִישׁ, וּכְתִיב וְאֶל אֵשֶׁת עֲמִיתְךָ וְגוֹ', דָּוִד דְּקִלְקֵל בְּרִית בְּעֶרְוָה מַהוּ. אָמַר לֵיהּ קַדוֹשׁ בָּרוּךְ הוּא, דָּוִד זַכָּאָה הוּא, וּבְרִית קַדִּישָׁא עַל תִּקוּנֵיהּ קַיְּימָא, דְּהָא גְּלֵי קָדָמַי דְּאִזְדַּמְּנַת לֵיהּ בַּת שֶׁבַע מִיּוֹמָא דְּאִתְבְּרֵי עָלְמָא.

**132. "When that situation occurred, King David was very fearful.
At that time, Dumah ascended to the Holy One, blessed be He,
stood before Him, and said: 'Master of the universe, in the Torah
it says of "...the man that commits adultery with another man's
wife... the adulterer and the adulteress shall surely be put to death."
(Leviticus 20:10) Furthermore, it is written, 'Moreover, you shall
not lie carnally with your neighbor's wife, to defile yourself with
her.' (Leviticus 18:20) So what is to become of David, who profaned
his Covenant with an *ervah* (prohibited sexual act)?" The Holy
One, blessed be He, said to him, "David is righteous. And the Holy
Covenant remains intact because it is known to Me that Batsheba
was assigned to him since the day the world was created."**

Explanation: Even though he did not sin, as the sages said: "Whoever
said that David sinned is mistaken" (Tractate Shabbat 56:1) fear still
came upon him as if he were indeed an actual sinner. And he explains
that this was because of Dumah's accusations, as shall be explained
soon. **"It is written in the Torah: '...and the man that commits
adultery...' (Leviticus 20:10) and also 'you shall not lie carnally with
your neighbor's wife,' (Leviticus 18:20)"** [The Zohar] brings two
verses, one as punishment and one as a warning. When it says **"the Holy
Covenant remains intact,"** the Creator replied to him that David had
no sinful thoughts because Batsheva was his mate since the creation of
the world (Tractate Sanhedrin 107a). Therefore he did not blemish his

Covenant, Heaven forbid, **"and the Holy Covenant remains intact."**
And when he desired [her], he desired what was his.

The reason Uriah married her before David is explained in the Zohar:
"Uriah married her with mercy even though she was not his" (Zohar,
Acharei Mot 395), study there. We need to understand this because
male and female are two halves of the body, so if she is a half of King
David's body, how did Uriah take her, as he has no relation to her?

The answer is that Batsheva is truly David's female counterpart from
the day of the creation of the world, since David is the male within
Malchut and Batsheva is the female within Malchut. But just as during
the correction of Malchut for the emanation of the worlds there was the
aspect of Malchut ascending to Binah to sweeten Her by the attribute of
Mercy, so too, Bat-Sheva needed this sweetening by the Upper Three,
without which she would not be fit to birth the soul of King Solomon.

Uriah (אוריה) the Hittite was a very high soul, as he was completely
from the aspect of the Upper Three, and His name proves it: *Ohr Yah*
(Light of Yud-Hei; אור יה) because he had nothing of the aspect of the
Six Corners, which are Vav-Hei (וה). Thus, to sweeten Batsheva with
the attribute of Mercy, Uriah, who is the aspect of the Upper Three,
married her and she was sweetened through him. And after that she was
worthy for kingship over Israel. Thus **"Uriah took her with mercy,"**
meaning to sweeten her with Mercy, through the Name Yud-Hei in
Uriah (אוריה). Therefore he married her even though she was not his.
This will be explained further.

King David was legally with Batsheba.

‏133. אָמַר לֵיהּ אִי הָכֵי צַּלֵי, קַמֵּיהּ לָא צַלֵי. אָמַר לֵיהּ, וְתוּ בְּהָיאֵתְרָא הֲוָה מַה
דַּהֲוָה, דְּהָא כָּל אִינוּן דְּעָאלוּ לִקְרָבָא, לָא עָאל חַד מְנַיְיהוּ עַד דְּאַפְטַר בְּגֵט
לְאִנְתְּתֵיהּ. אָמַר לֵיהּ אִי הָכֵי, הֲוָה לֵיהּ לְאוֹרְכָא תְּלַת יַרְחֵי וְלָא אוֹרִיךְ. אָמַר

לֵיהּ, בְּמַאי אוֹקִים מִלָּה, בָּאֲתַר דְּוֹוַיְיִשִׁינָן דְּהִיא מְעוּבֶּרֶת, וְגָלֵי קֳדָמַי דְּאוֹרִיָּה
לָא קָרִיב בָּהּ לְעָלְמִין, דְּהָא שְׁמִי חָתִים בְּגַוֵּיהּ לְסַהֲדוּתָא, כְּתִיב אוֹרִיָּה, וּכְתִיב
אוֹרִיָּהוּ, שְׁמִי חָתוּם בַּהֲדֵיהּ, דְּלָא שִׁמֵּשׁ בָּהּ לְעָלְמִין.

133. Dumah said to Him: "If this is known to you, it is not known
to him." He, the Holy One, blessed be He, said to him: "Not only
that, but all that happened was permitted and done lawfully because
every man that went to war did not leave before he had given a bill
of divorce to his wife." He said to Him: "If this is so, he should then
have waited for three months, which he did not." He replied: "When
is this applied? Only in cases where we suspect that she might be
pregnant. And it is known to Me for certain that Uriah never
touched her because My Name is sealed in him as a testimony. For
it is written Uriah (אוריה), which consists of the letters *Ohr Yah* (Light
of Yud-Hei). And it can also be written Uriyahu (אוריהו), which is
formed by the letters Ohr Yud-Hei-Vav, for My Name is sealed in him
as a testimony that he never had intercourse with her."

Explanation of these words: We need to understand how the Name Yud-
Hei in Uriah testifies about him that he never touched Batsheva. This is
explained by a verse in the Prophet Nathan's allegory (II Samuel 12:3).
[Nathan] likens David to a wealthy man, and Uriah to a poor man, and
Batsheva to the poor man's lamb, and the Other Side to a wanderer. And
he says that the poor man has nothing but one little lamb, and so on. The
secret of these matters is that Uriah was from the aspect of the Upper
Three lacking the Six Corners [Sefirot]. As the Zohar specifies, "it is
written Uriah (אוריה) and it is written Uriyahu (אוריהו)" because
[in Jeremiah 26:21] Uriyahu is spelled with Yud-Hei-Vav; Yud-Hei are
the Upper Three and the Vav (6) is the Six Corners . Yet here Uriah is
spelled without a Vav (ו) to indicate he had nothing of the Six Corners
but only Chochmah without Chasadim.

Therefore he was considered "a poor man without everything," since the Light of Chasadim is alluded to in "everything." This is: "The poor man had nothing except one little ewe lamb, which he had bought and nourished it…" (II Samuel 12:3), which is Batsheva who he bought. This indicates that she is not part of his soul but he bought her in order to nurture her and correct her with Mercy, which is "…he had bought and nourished it…." (Ibid.) It further says, "and it grew up together with him, and with his children." (Ibid.) This indicates that he imparted to her his Gadlut [Maturity] as he did for his children, meaning in a way that "it ate of his own bread and drank of his own cup and lay in his bosom." (Ibid.)

However, we should not mistakenly think that he approached her [sexually], therefore the verse concludes, "…and she was like a daughter to him" (Ibid.), and not a wife. Thus the verse testifies that Uriah never approached her, and the Zohar explains the reason he did not approach her. Therefore, it says: **"it is written Uriah and it is written Uriyahu, for My Name is sealed in him that he never had intercourse with her,"** namely the Name Yud-Hei without Vav, which indicates that he lacks the aspect of Chasadim, which is Vav. Thus he could not approach her because there can be no union without the Light of Chasadim. We find that [the letters] Yud-Hei that are sealed in his name testifies about him that he was not fit to have intercourse with her.

The matter was known to the Creator but not to David.

134. אֲמַר לֵיהּ מָארֵי דְעָלְמָא, הָא מָה דַאֲמָרִית, אִי קַמָּךְ גָּלֵי דְלָא שְׁכִיב בַּהֲדָהּ אוּרִיָּה, קַמֵּיהּ מִי גָלֵי, הֲוָה לֵיהּ לְאוֹרְכָא לָהּ תְּלַת יַרְחֵי, וְתוּ אִי יָדַע דְּלָא שְׁכִיב בַּהֲדָהּ לְעָלְמִין, אַמַּאי שָׁדַר לָהּ דָּוִד וּפָקֵיד עֲלֵיהּ לְשַׁמָּשָׁא בְּאִנְתְּתֵיהּ, דִּכְתִיב רֵד לְבֵיתְךָ וּרְחַץ רַגְלֶיךָ.

134. [Dumah] said to Him: "Master of the universe, this is exactly what I have said. If it is known to You that Uriah never slept with

her, it is not known to him. Therefore he should have waited for three months. And furthermore if You say that David **knew that he had never slept with her,** then why did he send Uriah home and command him to have intercourse with his wife? Since it is written: 'Go down to your house and wash your feet....' (II Samuel 11:8)"

King David was forgiven on Yom Kippur.

135. אֲמַר לֵיהּ, וַדַּאי לָא יָדַע, אֲבָל יַתִּיר מִתְּלַת יַרְחֵי אוֹרִיךְ, דְּהָא אַרְבַּע יַרְחֵי הֲוֹו, דְּהָכֵי תָּנֵינָן בְּחַמְשָׁה וְעֶשְׂרִים דְּנִיסָן אַעֲבַר דָּוִד כָּרוֹזָא בְּכָל יִשְׂרָאֵל, וַהֲווֹ עִם יוֹאָב בְּשַׁבְעָה יוֹמִין דְּסִיוָן, וְאָזְלוּ וְחַבָּלוּ אַרְעָא דִּבְנֵי עַמּוֹן, וְתַמּוּ, וְאָב, וֶאֱלוּל, אִשְׁתָּהוּ שָׁם. וּבְאַרְבָּעָה וְעֶשְׂרִים בֶּאֱלוּל הֲוָה מַה דַּהֲוָה מִבַּת שֶׁבַע, וּבְיוֹמָא דְּכִפּוּרֵי מָחַל לֵיהּ קָדוֹשׁ בָּרוּךְ הוּא הַהוּא חוֹבָא. וְאִית דְּאָמְרֵי בּוֹ' בַּאֲדָר אַעֲבַר כָּרוֹזָא, וְאִתְכַּנָּשׁוּ בַּחֲמֵיסַר דְּאִיָּיר, וּבַחֲמֵיסַר בֶּאֱלוּל הֲוָה מַה דַּהֲוָה מִבַּת שֶׁבַע, וּבְיוֹמָא דְּכִפּוּרֵי אִתְבְּשַׂר גַּם יי' הֶעֱבִיר חַטָּאתְךָ לֹא תָמוּת. מַאי לֹא תָמוּת, לֹא תָמוּת בִּידָא דְּדוּמָה.

135. He said to Dumah: "He certainly did not know. So he waited more than three months, as four months had passed." Because we have learned that on the twenty-fifth day of Nissan, David sent an announcement to go out to war. And they were with Joab on the seventh day of Sivan, as they went and destroyed the land of the children of Amon. There they remained during the months of Sivan, Tammuz, Av, and Elul. And on the twenty-fourth day of Elul, the event with Batsheva occurred. Then on Yom Kippur, the Holy One, blessed be He, forgave him for that sin. And there are those who claim that on the seventh day of Adar the announcement was sent, and all arms were gathered on the fifteenth day of Iyar. So what happened with Batsheva occurred on the fifteenth day of Elul. While on Yom Kipur, he received the message "…The Lord also has put away your sin; you shall not die." (II Samuel 12:13) What is the meaning of "you shall not die"? It means that he shall not die at the hand of Dumah.

Explanation: Dumah is the one in charge over prohibited relations, and this sin was forgiven for him on Yom Kippur. Thus he was not to die at the hand of Dumah. Nevertheless, his death was caused by the sin of Uriah, as he was [sent to be] killed by the sword of Amon, as the scriptures testified, "Because David did that which was right in the eyes of the Lord, and turned not aside from anything that He commanded him all the days of his life, save only in the matter of Uriah the Hittite." (I Kings 15:5) This is: **"he shall not die at the hand of Dumah"** who is in charge over prohibited relations but only for the matter of Uriah the Hittite.

The Negative Angel could not harm David
since David had already accepted responsibility for his actions.

‎136. אָמַר דּוּמָה: מָארֵי דְעָלְמָא, הָא מִלָּה חֲדָא אִית לִי גַּבֵּיה, דְּאִיהוּ אַפְתַּח פּוּמֵיה וַאֲמַר חַי ה' כִּי בֶן מָוֶת הָאִישׁ הָעוֹשֶׂה זֹאת, וְאִיהוּ דָן לְנַפְשֵׁיה. טְרוֹנְיָיא אִית לִי עֲלֵיה. אָמַר לֵיה, לֵית לָךְ רְשׁוּ, דְּהָא אוֹדֵי לְקַבָּאי וַאֲמַר חָטָאתִי לַה', וְאַף עַל גַּב דְּלָא חָב. אֲבָל בַּמֶּה דְחָטָא בְּאוּרִיָּה, עוֹנְשָׁא כְּתָבִית עֲלֵיה, וְקִבֵּל. מִיָּד אַהֲדַר דּוּמָ"ה לְאַתְרֵיה בְּפַחֵי נֶפֶשׁ.

136. Dumah said: "Master of the universe, I have one thing against him. He opened his mouth and said: 'As the Lord lives, the man that has done this deserves to die.' (II Samuel 12:5) So he has condemned himself to death, and therefore I have the power over him" to bring death upon him. **He said to him,** to Dumah: **"You have no permission** to bring death upon him **because he has already confessed in front of Me saying, 'I have sinned against the Lord' (II Samuel 12:13) even though he did not sin. Although his sin against Uriah was in killing him, I have written his punishment and he has accepted it." Immediately Dumah returned to his place, disappointed.**

Explanation of these words: It was explained earlier regarding Circumcision that the Name Eloha (אלוה) is connected to the Sign of

the Covenant (Verse 131). In the Hei (ה) of the Name Eloha, which
is Malchut, there are two points: Judgment and Mercy. The entire
correction of the Circumcision is for the force of Judgment to be hidden
and concealed while the [force of] Mercy is revealed, and then the Name
Eloha (אלוה) rests upon him. Although the Malchut upon which occurred
the first Tzimtzum also exists there, which is the aspect of Judgment,
from where all the Externals are nourished, yet since it is hidden and
concealed and only the attribute of Mercy from Binah is revealed, the
Externals have no power to grasp it. As it is said earlier, **"But he has
no permission to touch all those who have kept the Holy Covenant
in this world."** (Verse 131) But he who blemishes the Covenant finds
himself exposing the Judgment aspect of Malchut, namely the letter Hei
of Eloha. Immediately, all the Externals come near to nourish from Her,
for She is their portion and entire vitality. Therefore the Holy Soul,
which is the Name Eloha, immediately departs, in the secret of the verse,
"From the soul of God (Eloha) they shall be banished…." (Job 4:9)

David was from the aspect of Malchut that is sweetened by the attribute
of Mercy. He therefore required extra protection so that the aspect of
Judgment in Malchut will not be revealed in him. Therefore by saying,
"as the Lord lives, the man that has done this deserves to die" (II
Samuel 12:5)—where he made a judgment that whoever blemishes the
Covenant by giving the poor man's lamb to the wanderer, who is the
Other Side, his sentence is death—the aspect of Judgment was actually
revealed in him before the Other Side that is the angel Dumah, who
therefore wanted to hold onto David's soul. With these words the force
of Judgment that was concealed and hidden within him was exposed.
This is what the angel Dumah said, **"I have one thing against him.
He opened his mouth and said: 'as the Lord lives, the man that has
done this deserves to die.' (II Samuel 12:5) So he has condemned
himself,"** meaning that by the words of judging one who blemishes the
Covenant to death, he sentenced himself to death because the Judgment

concealed and hidden in his soul was exposed. Therefore: **"I have the power over him,"** I have control over him to suck [the life] from his soul.

"He said to him: 'You have no permission because he has already confessed in front of Me saying, "I have sinned against the Lord" (II Samuel 12:13), even though he did not sin." It was already explained that through his words he judged himself to death, as he exposed the aspect of Judgment before the Other Side, which is the same as a person who blemished his Covenant. And the angel Dumah wanted to hold onto his soul and pull it to hell, as mentioned earlier. Yet the Holy One, blessed be He, said that he has already confessed and repented for the prohibited relation even though he did not sin at all in this regard, as mentioned earlier. Therefore this penitence helped him with what he condemned himself of, and thus: **"You have no permission." "Although his sin against Uriah was** in killing him, **I have written his punishment and he has accepted it."** In other words, he had already received his punishment from Me for the sin of killing Uriah with the sword of Bnei-Amon, and you do not have a say in it because you are in charge only over prohibited relations. **"Immediately Dumah returned to his place, disappointed,"** meaning to the entrance of Hell (Gehenom), which is his place, as mentioned earlier.

The Creator guarded King David from the Negative Angel.

137. וְעַל דָּא אָמַר דָּוִד, לוּלֵי יי' עֶזְרָתָה לִי כִּמְעַט שָׁכְנָה דוּמָה נַפְשִׁי. לוּלֵי ה' עֶזְרָתָה לִי, דַּהֲוָה אַפּוֹטְרוֹפָּא דִילִי. כִּמְעַט שָׁכְנָה וְגוֹ', מַהוּ כִּמְעַט, כְּחוּטָא דַּקִּיק. כְּשִׁעוּרָא דְּאִית בֵּינִי וּבֵין סִטְרָא אָחֳרָא, כְּהַהוּא שִׁיעוּרָא הֲוַת דְּלָא שָׁכְנָה דוּמָה נַפְשִׁי.

137. Concerning this David said: "Unless the Lord had been my help, my soul had almost dwelt in silence (dumah)." (Psalms 94:17) "Unless the Lord had been my help" means that had He **not become David's keeper and guarded him** from the angel Dumah, **David's**

"soul had almost dwelt with Dumah." [He asks:] **"What is 'had almost dwelt'?"** [He answers:] **"That is to say like the distance of a thin thread that is between me and the Other Side was the distance that 'my soul had almost dwelt in silence (dumah),'** namely with the angel Dumah in Gehenom."

Explanation of these words: David is the secret of Malchut of which it is said, "Her feet go down to death…" (Proverbs 5:5) because She is the aspect of the ending of Holiness from which the Other Side and the Klipot are sustained, in the secret of the verse, "…and His kingdom rules over all." (Psalms 103:19) However, when the Malchut is corrected with the attribute of Mercy, in the manner that Rav Hiya said (in verse 122), She is then considered as two points, which are the point of Judgment from Herself and the point of Mercy that She received from Binah. The Judgment within Her is concealed and hidden, and only the Mercy in Her exists ostensibly, study there. Through this correction the Other Side does not have from the Light of Malchut anything but a thin Illumination, which is just a root aspect that is enough to sustain the Klipot. But they have no power of extending. This root is also called a **"thin thread,"** which means a thin root for sins, as the sages said: "At first it resembles the strands of a spider web, and then it becomes like cart ropes." (Tractate Sukkah 52a) It is called thin because Judgment is concealed and hidden in the point of Mercy, as mentioned earlier.

But a person who blemishes his Circumcision causes the point of Judgment in Malchut to be revealed, and then the Klipot get close to Her and extract from there much abundance, thus receiving the power to greatly expand. The man who does so loses his soul by his own hands, in the secret of the verse: "From the soul of God (Eloha) they shall be perished…." (Job 4:9) When he merits and does Teshuvah, he returns and corrects the Malchut with the correction of the attribute of Mercy. For this reason it is called Teshuvah, which are the letters of *Tashuv* Hei (Return the Hei), meaning that he restores Her to Her place, to the attribute of Mercy, while the force of Judgment is again concealed in Her, in the secret of just a thin Illumination.

This is: **"'Unless the Lord had been my help...' (Psalms 94:17)** and **was my keeper,"** namely accepted David's repentance and pushed back the angel Dumah to his place, as mentioned earlier, since he returned and restored Malchut to Her place, to the attribute of Mercy, and only left a thin Illumination for the attribute of Judgment, **"had almost,"**[meaning] **like the distance of a thin thread that is between me and the Other Side,** namely the minimum distance that must remain between Malchut and the Other Side in order to give it sustenance for its existence with a thin Illumination, which is called a **"thin thread." "...was the distance that 'my soul had almost dwelt in silence (dumah). (Ibid.)'"** This distance saved David from falling into the hands of the angel Dumah. In other words, had the force of Judgment in Malchut not been restored to be a thin thread, David would have dwelt in the hands of Dumah.

One should be careful not to condem themselves to Judgment.

וּבְגִין כָּךְ בָּעֵי לְאִסְתַּמְּרָא בַּר נָשׁ דְּלָא יֵימָא מִלָּה כְּדָוִד, בְּגִין דְּלָא יָכִיל .138
לְמֵימַר לְדוּמָה, כִּי שְׁגָגָה הִיא, כְּמָה דַּהֲוָה לְדָוִד, וְנָצַח לֵיהּ קָדוֹשׁ בָּרוּךְ הוּא
בְּדִינָא. לָמָּה יִקְצֹף הָאֱלֹהִים עַל קוֹלֶךָ, עַל הַהוּא קוֹל דְּאִיהוּ אָמַר. וְחִבֵּל
אֶת מַעֲשֵׂה יָדֶיךָ, דָּא בְּשַׂר קֹדֶשׁ בְּרִית קַדִּישָׁא דְּפָגִים וְאִתְמְשַׁךְ בְּגַוַּיְהוּ עַל
יְדָא דְדוּמָה.

138. Therefore every person should be careful not to say a word like David because he will not be able to say to the angel Dumah, "...it was an error..." (Ecclesiastes 5:5), as it was with David, where the Holy One, blessed be He, defeated [Dumah] in Judgment. "...why should God be angry at your voice..." (Ibid.), namely that voice [of David] who spoke. "...and destroy the work of your hands" (Ibid.), namely the sacred flesh, which is **the Holy Covenant that he damaged,**

and because of which he is to be dragged down to Gehenom by the angel Dumah.

Explanation of the matter: There are two aspects of Teshuvah. "One is Teshuvah out of fear, wherein malicious actions turn into unintentional errors, and the second is Teshuvah out of love, wherein malicious actions turn into merits." (Tractate Yoma 86b) The explanation is that before the End of the Correction, as long as the force of Judgment is needed in the world, in the secret of the verse, "…and God has brought to pass that men revere Him." (Ecclesiastes 3:14) No matter what, Malchut is found to forcibly be sustaining the other side in the amount of a thin Illumination so that the Klipot and the Other Side would not be annulled. Therefore, the entire correction of Malchut is in the secret of two points, Mercy and Judgment, where the Judgment is hidden and concealed while the Mercy is revealed. Therefore She has within Her [the aspect of] fear, in the secret of the Tree of [Knowledge of] Good and Evil—where if he merits it is good; if he does not merit it is evil.

It is found that the Teshuvah we do during the six thousand years is merely Teshuvah out of fear, wherein malicious actions turn into unintentional errors. Through Teshuvah we restore the Malchut to the attribute of Mercy, and the Judgment within it is concealed to the amount of a thin Illumination and a **"thin thread"** because Malchut must remain in the attribute of fear, which is why it is called Teshuvah out of fear. That **"thin thread"** that must remain is called unintentional errors because the unintentional error in itself is not a sin; rather, unintentional errors lead the person to commit malicious transgressions, because one does not sin intentionally before stumbling first with an unintentional transgression. So it is with that **"thin thread"** that remains in Malchut, since even though it remains there it is not considered a sin. Yet due to this concealed Judgment we come to commit intentional transgressions.

This is the secret of what the sages said that at first [the Evil Inclination] is as a hairbreadth, namely as that **"thin thread,"** and afterwards, if the circumcision is not properly protected it becomes as thick as a cart rope because the attribute of Judgment in Malchut is revealed. This is the secret of Dumah sitting at the opening of Gehenom, which is the force of the thin thread that is merely an opening, in the secret of "at first it is as a hairbreadth." Therefore this Teshuvah we do is considered as if our transgressions were atoned for and turned into unintentional errors, for the **"thin thread"** remains, which is capable of bringing us to commit intentional transgressions. As for the second form of Teshuvah that is out of love, and within which intentional transgressions turn into merit, see verse 126.

"Therefore every person should be careful not to say a word like David," meaning that he must not say a word that would cause the attribute of Judgment in Malchut to be revealed, as David did, **"because he will not be able to say to Dumah, '…it was an error…'"** (Ecclesiastes 5:5) because he is not certain that he would be able to return and repent immediately so that his transgression would be atoned and turn into an unintentional error, **"as it was with David, where the Holy One, blessed be He, defeated [Dumah] in judgment."** [Since] David who did what was right in the eyes of the Creator all the days of his life and never had any sin in his life except in the case of Uriah, the Holy One, Blessed be He, became his guardian and helped him to immediately repent so his transgression became an unintentional one, as it says: **"Unless the Lord had been my help, my soul had almost dwelt in silence (Dumah)"** (Psalms 94:17) But everyone else should be afraid that they would not be able to say before the angel **"…it was an error…"** (Ecclesiastes 5:5), and that they would fall into the hands of Dumah to hell.

"…and destroy the work of your hands" (Ibid.), namely the sacred flesh, which is **the Holy Covenant that he damaged, and because of**

which he is to be dragged down to Gehenom by the angel Dumah, since the correction of the **Holy Covenant** is called **the work of our hands** as said **"...and may the work of our hands establish it...."** **(Psalms 90:17)** And the secret of the Holy Soul is called the Holy Flesh, in the secret of the verse, "...and through my flesh, I shall see God (Eloha)..." (Job 19:26) (as mentioned earlier in the explanation of verse 131) where through the revelation of Judgment that is in Malchut, the Tikkun (Correction) of the Covenant is damaged and the soul is pulled to hell by the hand of Dumah, as mentioned earlier.

In verse 139 it says: **"Therefore '...the Firmament proclaims His handiwork.' (Psalms 19:2)"** The word "therefore" refers to the entire article of Rav Hamnuna that was brought earlier, where after it explained the concept of the Correction of Circumcision, both its reward and punishment, and that therefore it is called "the work of our hands," he goes back to the original topic relating to the Final Correction as that day in which Heaven, which is the Groom, enters his Wedding Canopy with the bride. He says: **"Therefore"** the verse says regarding the Final Correction, **"...the Firmament proclaims His handiwork," (Ibid.)** for then it will be revealed that all those corrections are not "the work of our hands" but "His handiwork." which is "the Firmament" on which the Great Unification takes place in the secret of *rav pe'alim mikavtze'el* (lit. many actions gathering to one), and "proclaims" is the idea of the revelation of the drawing of abundance.

Know that this is the entire difference between this world before the Correction and at the End of the Correction because before the End of the Correction, Malchut is called the Tree of [Knowledge of] Good and Evil, as mentioned earlier. The meaning of this is that Malchut is the secret of the Creator's Providence in this world, and as long as the recipients have not reached perfection so as to be able to fully receive His complete goodness that He conceived for us in the Thought of Creation, the Providence must be in the way of good and evil, reward and punishment. This is because our Vessels of Receiving are still filthy with selfish receiving that is very limited in its capacity and also separates us from the Creator. And the complete bestowal of goodness, in the great measure that He conceived for us, is only in the aspect of sharing, which is a pleasure that has no bounds or limits. This is not so with selfish receiving, which is very limited and restricted, because satiation immediately extinguishes the pleasure.

This is the secret of the verse, "The Creator has made everything for His own sake..." (Proverbs 16:4), meaning that all the actions that occur in the world were originally created only to bestow pleasure to Him. Thus people are found attending to the dealings of the world in the exact opposite of what they were originally created for. The Holy One, blessed be He, says "the whole world was created for My sake," namely "The Creator has made everything for His own sake..." (Proverbs 16:4) as well as, "Every one that is called by My Name... and whom I have created for My glory." (Isaiah 43:7) And we say the exact opposite, for we say that the world was created just for us, and we wish to swallow in our belly all the goodness of the world for our pleasure and for our glory. No wonder, therefore, we are still unworthy of receiving His complete goodness.

Thus we experience His Providence as good and evil, namely in the form of reward and punishment, for they are interdependent, since reward and punishment is based on good and evil. And once we use the Vessels of Receiving for the opposite reason they were created for, we necessarily feel that the actions of [the Creator's] Providence are like evil toward us. For it is a law that the Created Being cannot receive evil from the Creator openly because it is a flaw in His glory, Heaven forbid, that the Created Being would conceive Him as a doer of evil. This is not appropriate to the Perfect Doer. Therefore when a person feels bad, to that same extent the denial of the Creator's Providence is upon him, Heaven forbid, and the Supernal Doer, blessed be He, is hidden from him, which is the greatest punishment in the world. Thus sensing the good and evil in His Providence causes the sense of reward and punishment.

He who strives to not separate from his certainty in the Creator, even when he tastes evil in Providence, is rewarded; and if, Heaven forbid, he does not make the effort, he is punished because he is separated from the certainty in the Creator. We find that even though He [the Creator] alone has done, does, and will do all actions in their entirety, it nevertheless remains hidden from those who experience good and evil because in the time of evil, the Other Side is given power to conceal His providence and faithfulness, and they come to the great punishment of separation and become full of thoughts of denial. Correspondingly when they repent with Teshuvah, they receive a reward and can again cleave to the Creator.

Yet through the governance of reward and punishment itself, the Creator prepared that eventually through it we merit the End of the Correction. Meaning that all people will attain the Vessels of Receiving that are corrected to be for the sake of bestowing pleasure to their maker, in accordance with the verse, "The Creator has made everything for His own sake..." (Proverbs 16:4) like they were first created, as mentioned earlier. Then the Great Unification of Atik Yomin will be revealed, and thus we reach the state of Teshuvah out of love, turning all malicious misdeeds into merits and all pains into great benefits, and then His detailed Providence will be revealed throughout the entire world. Meaning that everyone will see that He alone has done, does, and will do all these prior deeds and actions because now that evil and punishment has already turned into goodness and merits it is possible to conceive their Doer, since they are now worthy of being His handiwork, since now they will praise and bless him for all the conceived evils and punishments in the moment.

This is the principal essence of the article since up to now the corrections were also considered **"the work of our hands"** (Psalms 90:17) and therefore we received reward and punishment for them. However with the Great Unification of the End of the Correction it will be revealed that both the corrections [we did] and the punishments were all merely **"His handiwork,"** as mentioned earlier. This is the meaning of what it says: **"...the Firmament proclaims His handiwork..."** (Psalms 19:2) because the Great Unification above the Firmament will proclaim that everything is **"His handiwork"** and that He alone has done, does, and will do all the actions.

The Firmament inscribes each of the supporters
of the Bride and fulfills their desires.

139. וּבְגִין כָּךְ וּמַעֲשֵׂה יָדָיו מַגִּיד הָרָקִיעַ, אִלֵּין אִינּוּן חַבְרַיָּיא דְּאִתְחַבָּרוּ בְּכַלָּה דָּא. וּמָארֵי קַיָּימָא דִּילָהּ. מַגִּיד וְרָשִׁים כָּל חַד וְחַד. מַאן הָרָקִיעַ. דָּא אִיהוּ הָרָקִיעַ דְּבֵיהּ חַמָּה וּלְבָנָה וְכֹכְבַיָּא וּמַזָּלֵי, וְדָא אִיהוּ סֵפֶר זִכְרוֹן, אִיהוּ מַגִּיד וְרָשִׁים לְהוֹ וּכְתִיב לְהוֹ, לְמֶהֱוֵי בְּנֵי הֵיכָלָא וּלְמֶעְבַּד רְעוּתְהוֹן תָּדִיר.

139. Therefore "...the Firmament proclaims His handiwork." (Psalms 19:2) These are the friends who have joined this Bride, Malchut, by studying the Torah during the night of Shavuot, **and Her Members of the Covenant** who are called "His handiwork" **proclaim and inscribe each one.** [He asks:] **"What is the Firmament?"** [He answers:] **"It is where the sun, moon, stars, and constellations are located, and it is called the Book of Remembrance. It announces, registers, and inscribes them so that they can be members of its palace, and it can always fulfill their desires."**

Explanation of these words: Yesod of Zeir Anpin—where the unification for the manifestation of all statures and Upper Levels takes place, which are **"the sun, moon, stars, and constellations"**—is called **"Firmament,"** as it says in the Zohar: **"And God set them in the Firmament of**

Heaven.' (Genesis 1:17) When they all exist in it they rejoice with each other. The moon then diminishes its light before the sun. From then onward, all the light that the sun receives is for the purpose of shining on Her, as it is written: '...to give light upon the Earth.' (Ibid.)" (Zohar Beresheet A 402)

Explanation: All the Upper Luminaries were placed in the Firmament of Heaven, which is Yesod of Zeir Anpin, and "they all exist in it." It joyfully unites with the Nukva that is called Earth, and gives her all those great lights, which is the secret of, "...to give light upon the Earth." (Genesis 1:17) Then it is considered that the Malchut (moon) is smaller than the sun, which is Zeir Anpin.

But at the End of the Correction, "Rav Yitzchak said, it is written, 'the light of the moon shall be as the light of the sun, and the light of the sun shall be sevenfold, as the light of the seven days, and so on.' (Isaiah 30:26)" (Zohar, Beresheet A 403) Meaning that then Malchut will not be smaller than Zeir Anpin but grow as large as Zeir Anpin during the Six Days of Creation, and Zeir Anpin itself will rise sevenfold as the Six Days of Creation. "Rav Yehudah asks there: 'When will that take place?' [He answers:] 'This shall be in the time about which it is written: "He will swallow death forever..."'" (Isaiah 25:8), then, it is written, '...on that day the Lord (Yud-Hei-Vav-Hei) shall be One, and His Name One' (Zechariah 14:9)," study there. Meaning the Firmament, which is Zeir Anpin, is Yud-Hei-Vav-Hei and is called "sun," and "His Name" is the Nukva that receives from Him and is called "moon." During the six thousand years that receive from the Six Days of Creation, it was not revealed to them that "He and His Name are One," (Ibid.) because the moon is smaller than the sun that is Zeir Anpin, which is called Yud-Hei-Vav-Hei.

The matter of the Malchut being small is that it is set in the secret of Asiyah that has good and evil, reward and punishment (as said at length above in the previous paragraph, study there carefully). And there is a great difference between "He" and "His Name," because in "His Name," which is Malchut, the unifications come one after the other—at times unified and at times separated. But at the End of the Correction, meaning **"in the time that it is written 'He will swallow death forever...' (Isaiah 25:8)"** then **"...the Lord shall be One, and His Name One."** (Zechariah 14:9) for His Name, which is the Nukva, will return to being the actual Light of Zeir Anpin, which is all good without any evil. And detailed Providence will be revealed in Her, as mentioned earlier, which is the secret of: **"...the light of the moon shall be as the light of the sun."** (Isaiah 30:26)

Therefore at that time the Nukva will be called a **Book of Remembrance,** since Malchut is called a Book, as all the actions of people are recorded in Her. And Yesod of Zeir Anpin is called Remembrance because it remembers the actions in the world and examines [the conduct of] all the Creatures of yore, and through it everyone receives abundance, as mentioned earlier in the secret of the verse, **"...to give light upon the earth."** (Genesis 1:17) During the six thousand years before the End of the Correction, we find that Book is on its own and Remembrance is on its own; meaning at times joined and at times separated. But at the End of the Correction these two levels become one, in the secret of, "The Lord (Yud-Hei-Vav-Hei) shall be One, and His Name One." (Zechariah 14:9) Then the Malchut itself is called a Book of Remembrance because they are actually one now since the light of the moon becomes as the light of the sun.

This is: **"What is the Firmament? It is where the sun, moon, stars and constellations are located."** Namely Yesod of Zeir Anpin wherein all the luminaries in the world emerge and where they exist. And He bestows them onto the Malchut when She is smaller than Him and not yet in the state of, "The Lord shall be One, and His Name One." (Ibid.) **"And it is the Book of Remembrance,"** and He Himself will also be the aspect of the Malchut of the End of the Correction, for which reason she will be called a Book of Remembrance because then the Malchut will receive the entire aspect of Zeir Anpin. This Firmament that is called Remembrance will then be called a Book of Remembrance, which is the aspect of the Malchut Herself called Book; and the Remembrance, which is the Firmament, will be actually one with Her, as said, "...on that day the Lord shall be One, and His Name One." (Zechariah 14:9)

The Sefirot of Zeir Anpin praise those who engaged
in the Torah on the night of Shavuot.

140. יוֹם לְיוֹם יַבִּיעַ אוֹמֶר, יוֹמָא קַדִּישָׁא מֵאִינּוּן יוֹמִין עִלָּאִין דְּמַלְכָּא מִשַׁבְּחִין לוֹן לְחַבְרַיָּיא, וְאָמְרִין, הַהִיא מִלָּה דַּאֲמַר כָּל חַד לְחַבְרֵיהּ. יוֹמָא לְיוֹמָא יַבִּיעַ הַהוּא אוֹמֶר וּמְשַׁבַּח לֵיהּ. וְלַיְלָה לְלַיְלָה, כָּל דַּרְגָּא דְּאַשְׁלִים בְּלֵילְיָא, מִשַׁבְּחָן דָּא לְדָא, הַהוּא דַּעַת דְּכָל חַד מֵחַבְרֵיהּ, וּבִשְׁלִימוּ סַגִּי אִתְעֲבִידוּ לוֹן חַבְרִין וּרְחִימִין.

140. "Day to day utters speech" (Psalms 19:3) refers to a Holy Day of those Supernal Days of the King, namely the Sefirot of Zeir Anpin that are called Days, that praise the friends, who dealt with the Torah during the night of Shavuot, and say that word that each one said to the other. This is: "Day to day utters" that same "speech," thereby praising Him. "...and night to night," (Ibid.) namely each level that governs the night, which are the Sefirot of Malchut, who governs at night, praise one another with the knowledge that each receives from the other. And from perfect completion they each become friends and beloved ones.

Explanation: After [the Zohar] explained that "...the Firmament proclaims His handiwork" (Psalms 19:2), the Book of Remembrance is mentioned in [the Book of] Malachi, where he continues to explain the following verses in the same manner the prophet detailed there concerning what is written in the Book of Remembrance. He says there:

"You have said, 'It is vain to serve God; and what profit is it that we have kept His charge, and that we have walked mournfully because of the Lord of Hosts....' (Malachi 3:14) Then they who feared the Lord spoke to one another: and the Lord hearkened, and heard it, and a Book of Remembrance was written before Him for those who feared the Lord, and took heed of His Name. 'And they shall be Mine,' said the Lord of Hosts, 'on that day which I appoint as My particular day; and I will spare them, as a man spares his own son who serves him.'" (Malachi 3:14-17)

So you find that **"that word that each one said to the other,"** namely "It is vain to serve God (Elohim); and what profit is it that we have kept His charge..." (Ibid.) are recorded in the Book of Remembrance "for those who feared the Lord and took heed of His Name."(Ibid.) For the Creator will spare them "as a man spares his own son who serves him," (Ibid.) namely only "for that day which I appoint as My particular day," (Ibid.) which is the day of the End of the Correction.

The explanation is that before the End of the Correction—namely before we have prepared our Vessels of Receiving to Receive only for the Sake of Bestowing pleasure to our Creator and not for our selfish benefit— Malchut is called the Tree of Good and Evil because the Malchut is the way the world is governed according to humanity's actions. And since we are not prepared to receive all the fulfillment and the goodness that the Creator conceived for us in the Thought of Creation, for the said reason above in the previous paragraph, therefore we must accept the governance of good and evil from Malchut. This governance prepares us to eventually correct our Vessels of Receiving for the Sake of Sharing and to merit the fulfillment and the goodness He has thought for us. We have already spoken of this at length in the previous paragraph, study there well. There we explained that our experience of good and evil is also a cause for the matter of reward and punishment, for the experience of pain causes separation from the certainty in the Creator; study there.

We find that if the person, when experiencing pain, strives to not damage his faith due to that, but is able to observe the Torah and its Precepts in completeness, he thereby receives a reward. And if, Heaven forbid, he does not pass the test but obtains separation, he is filled with negative thoughts, as explained there. About these negative thoughts, we know that the sages said in Tractate Kidushin 40a said that the Holy One, Blessed Be He, punishes for them as if they were actions. Concerning this, it is written: "That I may take the House of Israel in their own heart...." (Ezekiel 14:5) We also know that "...the righteousness of the righteous shall not deliver him in the day of his transgression...." (Ezekiel 33:12) Although this refers to only "he who regrets his former [good] acts" (Tractate Kidushin 40b), indeed sometimes negative thoughts overcome the person until he regrets, Heaven forbid, the many good deeds that he performed, and says, "'...What profit is it that we have kept His charge, and that we have walked mournfully because of the Lord of Hosts?'" (Malachi 3:14) as then he becomes completely wicked. By regretting his former [good] acts, with that evil thought, he loses all the good deeds he performed. As it is written: "...the righteousness of the righteous shall not deliver him in the day of his transgression." (Ezekiel 33:12) Nevertheless Teshuvah is beneficial. However then he is considered as starting to serve the Creator anew, and he is like a newborn baby, since all his righteousness from prior days passed and vanished.

Thus the governance of good and evil causes us many ascents and descents—each person according to where he is, as mentioned earlier. And know that because of this, every ascent is considered as a day on its own because due to the great descent he experienced in the meantime as he was regretting his former [good] actions, he is found to be like a newborn baby at the time of the ascent, as mentioned earlier. Thus at every ascent, he is like a beginner who starts serving the Creator anew, and therefore every ascent is considered a day on its own. In the same way, every descent is considered as a night on its own.

This is: "'Day to day utters speech' (Psalms 19:3) a Holy Day of those Supernal Days of the King," meaning that with every ascent of a person who then cleaves to the Supernal Days of the Holy One, Blessed be He, they "praise the friends and say that word that each one said to the other" for through the Great Unification at the time of the End of the Correction, they will merit Teshuvah out of love, since they will complete the correction of the Vessels of Receiving so that they would be only for the Sake of Bestowing pleasure to the Creator, Blessed be He. With that unification, all the great pleasure and goodness of the Thought of Creation will be revealed to us. Then we will undoubtedly see that all those punishments [we suffered] during the days of descent, to the point where we started having negative thoughts of regret about former good actions, actually purified us and were a direct cause for all the happiness and goodness that has reached us at the time of the End of the Correction. Were it not for those terrible punishments, we would never have come to this fulfillment and goodness. Then these malicious actions turn into actual merits.

This is: "Day to day utters speech" (Psalms 19:3) as each and every ascent before the End of the Correction is one day "of those Supernal Days of the King that praise the friends," and we find now that it comes back and is revealed in all its glorified perfection that pertains to that day, and it praises the friends, the supporters of the Torah, with "that word that each one said to the other," which is, "...It is vain to serve God (Elohim); and what profit is it that we have kept His charge,..." (Malachi 3:14) which then brought them great punishments. But now they have turned into merits, since the perfection and happiness of that day could not have manifested now with the same glory and majesty, were it not for those punishments. For that reason those who uttered those words were considered as "those who feared the Creator and took heed of His Name" just like the true good deeds. It is therefore said about them as well, "...and I will spare them, as a man spares his own son who serves him." (Malachi 3:17)

Thus "'Day to day utters' that same 'speech,' thereby praising Him" because all those nights are the descents, the sufferings, and the punishments that interrupted the cleaving to the Creator, until they became many days, one after the other. But now that even the nights and the darkness in between have become merits and good deeds as well, and "…the night shines like the day…" (Psalms 139:12), and darkness as light, there are no more interruptions between them. So all six thousand years are found to be joined into one great day alone. And all the unifications that emerged one after the other, each one revealing ascents and grades distinct from each other, as mentioned earlier, now are found assembled into a single stature of unification that is high and elevated, and shines from one end of the world to the other. This is the secret of, "Day to day utters speech" (Psalms 19:3) because that aforementioned word that separated between day to day now becomes a great praise, "thereby praising Him" because it became a merit. Therefore they all become one day to the Creator.

This is what was said, "'…and night to night,' (Ibid.) each level that governs the night praise one another with the knowledge that each receives from the other." All of these words and sufferings called "nights," which caused the levels to become interrupted one after the other, now even they shine like day because they have all gathered and became one receptacle for the great knowledge that fills the whole land with the "knowing" of the Creator. We find that each night by itself would have remained in darkness had it not come now to one gathering with all the nights; for each night receives its portion in the knowledge only by joining the other nights. Therefore it is considered that each night "expresses knowledge" (Ibid.) to its companion because it would not be prepared for the knowledge without uniting with its friend.

This is: "each level that was made complete during the night," namely each night that has now become perfected as a receptacle for the knowledge of the Creator, "praise one another." We find that each one praises the other because of that knowledge of the other, since the piece of knowledge that each one received was from the other by becoming united with its companion night, for it would not have received it without joining its friend because only all of them gathered together became worthy of receiving that great knowledge. **"And from perfect completion they each become friends and beloved ones,"** meaning with the great perfection that they received together, all the nights became beloved friends to each other.

In the End of the Correction all the pain that existed in history
will transform into great Light.

141. אֵין אוֹמֶר וְאֵין דְּבָרִים בִּשְׁאָר מִילִין דְּעָלְמָא. דְּלָא אִשְׁתַּמְעוּ קַמֵּי מַלְכָּא קַדִּישָׁא וְלָא בָּעֵי לְמִשְׁמַע לוֹן. אֲבָל הָנֵי מִילֵי, בְּכָל הָאָרֶץ יָצָא קַוָּם. עַבְדֵי מְשִׁיחָא אִינּוּן מִלִּין, בְּדוֹרֵי עָלָּאֵי וּמְדוֹרֵי תַּתָּאֵי. מֵאִלֵּין אִתְעֲבִידוּ רְקִיעִין, וּמֵאִלֵּין אֶרֶץ מֵהַהִיא תּוּשְׁבַּחְתָּא. וְאִי תֵימָא, דְּאִינּוּן מִלִּין בַּאֲתַר חָד. מִשַּׁטְטָא בְּעָלְמָא, בִּקְצֵה תֵבֵל מִלֵּיהֶם.

141. "There is no speech nor are there words..." (Psalms 19:4) **of the rest of the words of the world that are not heard before the Holy King and that He is not interested in hearing them. But these words, "Their voice carries out through all the Earth..."** (Psalms 19:5), **as these words draw a line between the inhabitants of Above and the inhabitants of Below. From these words, Firmaments are made, and from these words and from that praise, the earth is molded. And if you should say that these words wander around the world in one place,** the verse states, **"...and their words to the end of the world...."** (Ibid.)

Explanation of these words: Up to this point we have spoken about the most terrible punishments and sufferings, namely the separation from the certainty in the Creator. Now he says that even the punishments and sufferings from **"the rest of the words of the world,"**—namely the individual transgressions, the sufferings of hell, the bodily pains and the like, which fill this entire world—they too, gather to be included in this Great Unification in the secret of the verse, "And it shall come to pass that as the Creator rejoiced over you to do you good and to multiply you; so the Creator will rejoice over you to destroy you and to annihilate you...." (Deuteronomy 28:63) For they all gather and become one Great Light, and they turn into joy and great rejoicing. Thus **"'There is no speech nor are there words...' (Psalms 19:4) of the rest of the words of the world,"** which are all the pains of this world, **"that are not heard before the Holy King,"** when they turn into joy and rejoicing, **"and that He is not interested in hearing them"** because due to them turning into joy and rejoicing, the Holy King would come back after them and desire to hear them. In other words, the memory of any sorrow and pain from prior days will cause now, at the End of the Correction, great joy and pleasure. This is the secret of the verse, "and in that time, says the Lord, the iniquity of Israel shall be sought for and there shall be none..." (Jeremiah 50:20) because at the time they turn into merits they will cause so much satisfaction that the iniquities from bygone days would be sought after in order to joke about it; but they would not be found. In other words, it would seem to us that they no longer exist in their true form as they were in bygone days. Thus **"and that He is not interested in hearing them,"** meaning that there is neither saying nor words that he would not repeat willingly and with great desire to hear them because now they are all Sacred and steadfast Lights.

This great stature that rises through the Great Unification, made from all the souls and all deeds both good and evil together, at the End of the Correction, [that Stature] is considered as a line and a Pillar of Light that shines from one end of the world to the other, which is the secret of the Great Unification in the secret of the verse, **"...the Lord shall be One and His Name One." (Zechariah 14:9)** "...these words," namely the [common] words of the world mentioned earlier in the previous section, **"their voice carries out through all the Earth..." (Psalms 19:5)** because the stature that emerges through these words, which are all the types of sufferings and punishments, shine from one end of the world to the other, namely **"through all the Earth." (Ibid.)**

Concerning **"the inhabitants of Above and the inhabitants of Below,"** this is a very exalted matter and I shall strive to explain it as [much as] possible. We should know that the order of sequence of time in the Eternal is not as it is in this world. We find that when the Creator thought of creating the world, for Him all the souls were already created with all their behaviors, until their complete perfection that is required for them so that they can receive all the bliss and goodness that He planned to delight [in] them with, since with the Creator, the upcoming serves as the present, and future and past do not apply to Him. From this you will understand what the sages said, "The Holy One, Blessed Be He, showed Adam every generation and its preachers..." (Tractate Sanhedrin 38b) and similarly [it was shown] to Moses (as said in the Zohar, Lech Lecha 331 and Zohar, Vayechi 369), which is seemingly puzzling. How could He have shown them if they had not yet been created? Rather, it is like we said that all the souls with all their behaviors until the End of the Correction already emerged before Him in existence. They are all present in the secret of the Upper Garden of Eden, and from there they descend and come vested in bodies in this world, each one in its own time. From there the Holy One, Blessed Be He, showed them to Adam and to Moses and to all those worthy of it. This is a lengthy subject that not every mind can grasp.

This is the secret of what is written in the Zohar, Terumah 163: **"Just as they are united Above in the secret of one, so She is united Below in the secret of one"** because the stature of the Great Unification at the End of the Correction, in the secret of the verse, "...the Lord shall be One and His Name One," (Zechariah 14:9) has already emerged Above, [made] of all the souls and all the deeds in the world that will be created until the End of the Correction, that is, from the aspect of the Eternity of the Creator for whom the whole future serves as present. It is found that this Pillar of Light that shines from one end of the world to the other and will shine at the End of the Correction is already established in the Upper Garden of Eden and shines before Him in the same way it will be revealed to us at the End of the Correction. This is the meaning of what he says there [Terumah 163]: **"one alongside with the other; the Holy One Blessed Be He is one,"** as at the time of the End of the Correction, the two statures will shine one alongside with the other, and then "...the Lord shall be One and His Name One." (Zechariah 14:9) This is the meaning of: **"these words draw a line between the inhabitants of Above and the inhabitants of Below,"** one alongside with the other. That stature shines to the inhabitants of Above, who are all the souls that are in the Upper Garden of Eden, and it shines to the inhabitants of Below, who are all the souls after they actually are vested in a body in this world and have reached the End of the Correction. In other words, these two statures shine together at the End of the Correction, and then the Creator's unity will be revealed in the secret of "...the Lord shall be One and His Name One." (Zechariah 14:9)

The Zohar informs us not to make the mistake of thinking that this Pillar of Light that shines in the Upper Garden of Eden extends and shines at the End of the Correction in this world. Therefore, he says that this is not so. Rather, **"from these words, Firmaments are made,"** since that stature emerges over the Yesod of Zeir Anpin that is called Firmament (as mentioned earlier in verse 138). Therefore, there is still this distinction that is in all the Unifications, since the stature emerges first from the Firmament upward, and after that it shines to the recipients from the Firmament downward. The stature that emerges from the Firmament and upward is called "Heaven," and the stature that is received from the Firmament downward is called "Earth." This is the meaning of when the Zohar says that when the Line of Light unites the inhabitants of Above and the inhabitants of Below, there is still the distinction between that of the Upper Garden of Eden to the inhabitants of this world because the stature of Unification that emerges from the Firmament upward is received by the inhabitants of the Upper Garden of Eden. **"From them, Firmaments are made,"** meaning a New Heaven for the inhabitants of Above. And only the splendor that extends from the Firmament downward is received by the inhabitants of Below, and is called a "New Earth." Therefore, he concludes: **"from that praise,"** meaning that the inhabitants of Below attain only the aspect of "praise" and "splendor" that extends from Heaven to Earth.

This is: **"And if you should say that these words... in one place,"** since it was explained that the Unification is done in the same way as all the Unifications, where [the stature] from the Firmament and Above extends to the Firmament and Below, therefore it is possible to mistakenly say that it is just the aspect of a **"thin line"** that rises in the secret of one place, as mentioned in the Workings of Creation, "...'Let the waters... be gathered together (lit. be lined) to one place...'" (Genesis 1:9); that is, only to the interior of the worlds that reaches Israel alone and not to the exterior of the worlds (see Zohar, Beresheet A 218). He says that it is not so, but rather they **"wander around in the world,"** as the Light wanders around and fills the world from one end of the world to the other, namely: **"and their words to the end of the world,"** that is, even to the exterior of the worlds. It reaches the nations of the world as well, in the secret of the verse, "...for the earth shall be full of the knowledge of the Lord...." (Isaiah 11:9)

Zeir Anpin is adorned from the Pillar of Light.

‏142. וְכֵיוָן דְּאִתְעֲבִידָא רְקִיעִין מִנְהוֹן, מָאן שַׁרְיָא בְּהוֹן, הָדַר וַאֲמַר לַשֶּׁמֶשׁ שָׂם אֹהֶל בָּהֶם, הַהוּא שִׁמְשָׁא קַדִּישָׁא שָׁוֵי מְדוֹרֵיהּ וּמִשְׁכָּנֵיהּ בְּהוֹ, וְאִתְעַטַּר בְּהוֹ.

142. "Since Firmaments are made from them, who resides there? He repeats and says: '...In them He set a tent for the sun.' (Psalms 19:5)

That Holy Sun, which is Zeir Anpin, **has made His abode and dwelling place in them and crowned Himself with them."**

Explanation: He asks: "Since he says that the Pillar of Light emerges from the Firmament upward, and that only 'praise' is extended from the Firmament downward, therefore we need to ask who serves in that Pillar of Light? Meaning **'Who dwells in them?'"** He answers: "Zeir Anpin Who is called Sun is adorned and puts His abode in that Pillar of Light because he is adorned with that Pillar as if it was under the [Wedding] Canopy, since [the word] "tent" means a "canopy covering" over the person." Thus **"...In them He set a tent for the sun."** (Psalms 19:5)

Zeir Anpin emerges like the sun to the place of Malchut.

143. כֵּיוָן דְּשָׁרֵי בְּאִינוּן רְקִיעִין וְאִתְעֲטַר בְּהוּ, כְּדֵין, וְהוּא כְּחָתָן יוֹצֵא מֵחֻפָּתוֹ, חָדֵי וְרָהִיט בְּאִינוּן רְקִיעִין, נָפַק מִנַּיְיהוּ, וְעָאל וְרָהִיט גּוֹ מִגְדְּלָא וְזֹדָא אָחֲרָא, בְּאֲתַר אָחֲרָא. מִקְצֵה הַשָּׁמַיִם מוֹצָאוֹ, וַדַּאי מֵעָלְמָא עִלָּאָה, נָפִיק וְאַתְיָא, דְּאִיהוּ קְצֵה הַשָּׁמַיִם לְעֵילָּא. וּתְקוּפָתוֹ, מַאן תְּקוּפָתוֹ, דָּא קְצֵה הַשָּׁמַיִם לְתַתָּא דְּאִיהִי תְּקוּפַת הַשָּׁנָה דְּאַסְחַר לְכֹל סְיִיפִין. וְאִתְקַשְׁרַת מִן הַשָּׁמַיִם עַד רְקִיעָא דָּא.

143. Because Zeir Anpin **resides among those Firmaments and crowns Himself with them, He "...is as a bridegroom coming out of his chamber...."** (Psalms 19:6) **He is happy and runs along these Firmaments. Then, he leaves them and enters into another tower in a different place; this tower comes "...from the end of the heaven...."** (Psalms 19:7) **It certainly comes from the Supernal World, which is the Upper "end of the heaven"** (Ibid.), namely Binah. [He asks:] **"...and his circuit...'** (Psalms 19:7), **what is his circuit?"** [He answers:] **"It is the lower 'end of the heaven'** (Ibid.), namely Malchut. This **is the circuit of the year that revolves around all the 'ends.' It is attached from the Heavens to this Firmament."**

Explanation: The Zohar here alludes to a great and awesome secret, which is the sun emerging from its sheath, namely from its canopy. After the Great Unification has taken place **in those Firmaments,** in the secret of the Canopy, it emerges from those Firmaments into **one other tower in a different place,** namely the place of Malchut, which is called "A tower of strength is the Name of the Lord…" (Proverbs 18:10) because then Malchut rises up and unites with Him in the secret of "One."

The end of Malchut is called **the circuit of the year,** since before the Correction, the Klipot called the "End of Days" would grasp there (as said in Zohar, Bo 31). Now after the End of the Correction we need to further correct that aspect particularly, and this is done by the sun emerging from its sheath, in the secret of the verse, **"He is like a Bridegroom coming out of his Wedding Canopy…"** (Psalms 19:7) shining and coming **into one tower** that is Malchut, as mentioned earlier. And then "he rejoices like a valiant man to run his course" (Psalms 19:6), because he runs in that tower, **"…and his circuit to their ends…"** (Psalms 19:7) because he shines **from the Upper End of the Heaven** to all the ends that are in Malchut, so as to correct **that circuit of the year of the Lower End of the Heaven.** Thus **it revolves around all the "ends"** because this correction finishes to correct all the aspects of End that are in Malchut, and with that She is **attached from the Heavens to this Firmament,** meaning that Malchut receives the Illumination of the Upper End of the Heaven to this Firmament of Zeir Anpin.

At the End of the Correction there will be no concealment, only revelation.

144. וְאִין נִסְתָּר מֵחַמָּתוֹ דְּהַהִיא תְּקוּפָה דָא, וּתְקוּפָה דְּשִׁמְשָׁא דְּאַסְחַר בְּכָל סִטְרָא, וְאִין נִסְתָּר, לֵית דְּאִתְכַּסֵּי מִנֵּיה מִכָּל דַּרְגִּין עִלָּאִין, דַּהֲוֹוּ כֻּלְּהוּ מִסְחֲרָן וְאַתְיָין לְגַבֵּיה, וְכָל חַד וְחַד לֵית מַאן דְּיִתְכַּסֵּי מִינֵּיה. מֵחַמָּתוֹ, בְּשַׁעְתָּא דְּאִתְחַמֵּם, וְתָב לְגַבַּיְיהוּ בְּתִיוּבְתָּא שְׁלִים. כָּל שִׁבְחָא דָא וְכָל עִלּוּיָא דָא, בְּגִין אוֹרַיְיתָא הוּא, דִּכְתִיב תּוֹרַת ה' תְּמִימָה.

144. "...and none are hidden from his heat" (Psalms 19:7) of that circuit, which is the circuit of the year or from the circuit of the sun that revolves in all directions. "...and none are hidden," namely **there is none from all the Supernal levels who can hide from Him, as everything revolves and comes to Him. Each and every one cannot be hidden from Him. "From His heat,"** as He heats up and **returns** to the friends **the instant they have reached full repentance. All this praise and all this glorification is the result of their** study of the **Torah, as it is written: "The Torah of the Lord is perfect...."** (Psalms 19:8)

Explanation: After this Great Unification a covering and a concealment is made for all these Upper Lights (as mentioned in Zohar, Prologue 94), and therefore this new Unification of that one tower is required, in the secret of **"and his circuit to their ends,"** where He comes back and reveals all the Upper Lights that were concealed because of the nullification of the BaN before it ascended to SaG, as mentioned earlier; study there (in verse 94). This is: **"And none are hidden from his heat' of that circuit, or from the circuit of the sun that revolves in all directions."** This unification of the sun's seasons with the season of the year, as mentioned earlier, corrects the endings of Malchut from every side, that is, from every aspect, until it is enough for the complete correction, where BaN ascends and returns to be SaG, which is a complete correction from every aspect. After this, **"'And none are hidden,' there is none from all the Supernal Levels who can hide from Him,"** since all Upper Levels and Lights return and become revealed to the utmost revelation, **"as everything revolves and comes to Him. Each and every one cannot be hidden from Him,"** because all Levels and Lights return and come back to Him slowly until there is nothing hidden from Him.

This is: **"'From His heat,' as He heats up and returns the instant they have reached full repentance."** In other words, this revelation does not occur in an instant because the season of the sun gradually shines until it

is warmed enough for complete repentance in accordance with the words
of the sages, where the wicked are judged by it while the righteous are
healed by it. And then they merit the said great revelation.

Six Tetragrammatons mentioned corresponding
to the six letters of the word beresheet.

145. שִׁית זִמְנִין כְּתִיב הָכָא ה', וְשִׁית קְרָאֵי מִן הַשָּׁמַיִם מִסַּפְּרִים עַד תּוֹרַת
יי' תְּמִימָה, וְעַל רָזָא דָא כְּתִיב בְּרֵאשִׁית, הָא שִׁית אַתְוָן. בָּרָא אֱלֹהִים אֶת
הַשָּׁמַיִם וְאֶת הָאָרֶץ, הָא שִׁית תֵּיבִין. קְרָאֵי אוֹחֲרָנִין לָקֳבֵל שִׁית זִמְנִין ה', שִׁית
קְרָאֵי בְּגִין שִׁית אַתְוָן דְּהָכָא, שִׁית שְׁמָהָן בְּגִין שִׁית תֵּיבִין דְּהָכָא.

**145. "the Lord (Yud-Hei-Vav-Hei)" is mentioned six times here,
and there are six verses from "The Heavens declare…" until "The
Torah of the Lord is perfect…." (Psalms 19:2-8) And based on the
same secret it is written: "In the beginning (*beresheet;* בראשית)…"
(Genesis 1:1), which includes six letters. "…God created the Heaven
and the Earth (bara Elohim et hashamayim ve'et ha'aretz)" (Ibid.)
contains six words. The other verses (Psalms 19:8-11)** beginning
with "The Torah of the Lord is perfect…" and ending with "They are
more desirable than gold…" only **correspond to the six times "the
Lord"** appears in them; however the six verses themselves are not
expounded upon. **The six verses (Psalms 19:2-8)** from "The Heavens
declare…" to "The Torah of the Lord is perfect…" **are for the six letters
here** in the word *beresheet*, **while the six Names are for the six words
here,** which are "God created the Heaven and the Earth." (Genesis 1:1)

Explanation of the words: It is known that every level that is revealed in
the worlds first appears in the aspect of letters, as then it is still unknown.
After that it comes as a combination of words, and then what is in the
level is known, as has been explained earlier in the secret of the 216 letters
and seventy-two words (Zohar, Prologue 116). This is the secret of the
six letters in the word *beresheet*, which already contain the entire existence

of Heaven and Earth in the secret of their six letters. Yet they are still unknown, as they are only implied in letters and not combined into words. Afterwards, there are six words: **"God created the heaven and the earth (bara Elohim et hashamayim ve'et ha'aretz)…" (Genesis 1:1)** and here what is contained in the word *beresheet* (בראשית) becomes revealed; this being the Heaven and the Earth and their entirety. In the same way we understand the six verses from "The Heavens declare…" to "The Torah of the Lord is perfect…" (Psalms 19:2-8), to still be the beginning of the revelation of the End of the Correction, that is, still in the aspect of letters, so are the six letters of the word *beresheet*. The complete revelation of the End of the Correction begins from [the verse], "The Torah of the Lord is perfect…" (Psalms 19:8-11) and onward, for there are six times [the Name] Yud-Hei-Vav-Hei [is mentioned] there, and each Name indicates an attainment. This indicates that only after complete repentance, in the secret of the verse, "…none are hidden from his heat," (Psalms 19:7) are all the combinations of words that were present at the Great Unification at the End of the Correction revealed—namely the six names.

This is: **"And based on the same secret it is written, 'In the beginning (Beresheet)' (Genesis 1:1), which includes six letters. 'Elohim created the heaven and the earth (bara Elohim et hashamayim ve'et ha'aretz)' (Ibid.) contains six words."** According to the secret of the six verses and six Names mentioned earlier, six letters in [the word] Beresheet are written in the Torah where the Heaven and the Earth are concealed, and with the [following] six words they become revealed, namely *"bara Elohim et hashamayim ve'et ha'aretz."* Similarly, [in] the six verses from "The Heavens declare…" to "The Torah of the Lord is perfect…" (Psalms 19:2-8) the Great Unification of the End of the Correction has not yet been completely revealed in its essence, only afterwards, after the verse "…and none are hidden from his heat," (Psalms 19:7) were the six Names revealed. With these six Names, the entire Great Revelation of the End of the Correction reaches its perfection and essence.

Thus **"The other verses correspond to the six times 'the Lord'"**
because the verses written after [the verse] "and none are hidden from
his heat" (Psalms 19:7) to the end of the Psalm allude to the six Names
written in them. We find that **"the six verses are for the six letters
here, and the six Names are for the six words that are here,"** meaning
as explained, that the six verses from "The Heavens declare..." to "The
Torah of the Lord is perfect..." (Psalms 19:2-8) are like the six letters
in the word *beresheet* (בראשית) that are not completely revealed. And
the six Names in the verses from "The Torah of the Lord is perfect..."
to the end [of the Psalm] are like [for] the six words "...God (Elohim),
created, the, Heaven and the Earth." (Genesis 1:1) that have now reached
their perfection here. And it comes to teach us that in the six verses [of
Psalms 19:2-8] their level was still unknown, and they are like the six
letters of *beresheet* (בראשית); but after, in the other verses that contain
the six Names [Psalms 19:8-11], they reached the desired revelation.

The soul of Benayahu ben Yehoyada.

146. עַד דַּהֲווֹ יַתְבֵי, עָאלוּ רַבִּי אֶלְעָזָר וְרַבִּי אַבָּא, אָמַר לוֹן: וַדַּאי אַנְפֵּי
שְׁכִינְתָּא אַתְיָין, וְעַל דָּא פְּנִי"אֵל קָרֵינָא לְכוֹ, דְּהָא חֲמֵיתוּן אַנְפֵּי שְׁכִינְתָּא אַפִּין
בְּאַפִּין, וְהַשְׁתָּא דְּקָא יְדַעְתּוּן וְגַלֵּי לְכוֹ קְרָא דּוּבְנָיָהוּ בֶּן יְהוֹיָדָע, וַדַּאי דְּמִלָּה
דַּעַתִּיקָא קַדִּישָׁא אִיהוּ, וּקְרָא דְּאֲבַתְרֵיהּ, וְהַהוּא דִּסְתִּים מִכֹּלָּא אָמְרוּ.

146. As they were sitting, his son, Rav Elazar, and Rav Aba entered.
He said to them: "Certainly the face of the Shechinah has come, and
this is why I have called you Peniel (Face of El), for You have seen
the face of the Shechinah face-to-face. Now, because you received
the knowledge that was revealed to you with the scripture about
Benayahu ben Yehoyada, it is certainly a matter that belongs to
Atika Kadisha, which is the secret of Keter and also the following
verse, which reads, "And he slew an Egyptian...." (I Chronicles 11:23)
And the one who is most concealed, Atika Kadisha, said it."

Explanation: It is related to the subject of the donkey driver, who revealed to Rav Elazar and Rav Abba the soul of Benayahu ben Yehoyada, for which reason Rav Shimon called them Peniel (Zohar, Prologue 119). The soul of Benayahu ben Yehoyada is actually the stature that will be revealed at the End of the Correction, as mentioned there. This is why the matter of the covering and concealment of all the Upper Lights happened to them as well (as mentioned in Zohar, Prologue 113), as explained here concerning the unification of the circuit of the sun and the circuit of the year. This lasted until they went to Rav Shimon ben Lekunya and saw Rav Shimon [bar Yochai] there. Then they again merited all those Lights, as explained there.

This is the meaning of what Rav Shimon is saying here: **"Now, because you received the knowledge that was revealed to you by the scripture about Benayahu ben Yehoyada."** He hinted to them that they have already attained the [level of the] six verses of "The Heavens declare..." (Psalms 19:2-7) and they are already at the [level of the] six Names in the last verses [of that Psalm] because the [level of the] soul of Benayahu ben Yehoyada has already been openly revealed to them. At the time they attained [the level of] the soul of Benayahu ben Yehoyada through that donkey driver, their attainment was not yet known because they were then at the level of the six verses, and therefore they experienced that path of miracles and signs. But now the [level of the] soul of Benayahu was openly known to them.

"Now, because you received the knowledge that was revealed to you by the scripture about Benayahu ben Yehoyada, it is certainly a matter that belongs to Atika Kadisha, and the following verse," because the soul of Benayahu ben Yehoyada is the secret of the matter of Atika, namely the Great Unification of Atik Yomin, [of] which **"you received the knowledge"** even then. But now it became known to you that even **the following verse**, which is **"...he slew the two lion-hearted men of Moab..."** (I Chronicles 11:22), **"and he slew the Egyptian**

man…" (Ibid. 23)—that all these verses are also the matters of Atika, **"and the One who is most concealed said it,"** namely Atik Yomin who is the most concealed.

Two verses that both allude to Moses.

147. וְהַאי קְרָא אִיהוּ בְּאֲתָר אָחֳרָא כְּגַוְונָא דָא. פָּתַח וַאֲמַר וְהוּא הִכָּה אֶת הָאִישׁ הַמִּצְרִי אִישׁ מִדָּה חָמֵשׁ בָּאַמָּה, וְכֹלָּא רָזָא וְדָא אִיהוּ, הַאי מִצְרִי הַהוּא דְּאִשְׁתְּמוֹדָע, גָּדוֹל מְאֹד בְּאֶרֶץ מִצְרַיִם בְּעֵינֵי עַבְדֵי וְגוֹ', רַב וְיַקִּירָא, כְּמָה דְּגָלֵי הַהוּא סָבָא.

147. This verse, "And he slew an Egyptian…" (II Samuel 23:21) **is explained in another place,** at a different level, **in this way. He opened and said, "'And he slew an Egyptian man, a man of great stature, five cubits high…' (I Chronicles 11:23), and all are related to the same secret. This Egyptian is that one who is known** and described by the verse, **'…very great in the land of Egypt in the eyes of the servants'** (Exodus 11:3), **for he is great and honored, as that old man revealed.** (Zohar, Prologue 99)"

Explanation: The verse that was explained by Rav Hamnuna Saba, namely **"And he slew the Egyptian man, a fine looking man…"** (II Samuel 23:21) is explained on another level, in another manner according to the words in the Book of Chronicles as it explains further. **"And he slew the Egyptian man…."** (I Chronicles 11:23) **And all is one secret.** The two verses are one secret because in II Samuel 23:21 it is written: **"And he slew an Egyptian man, a fine looking man…"** and here in Chronicles it is written: **"And he slew an Egyptian man, a man of great stature, five cubits high…."** Both are one secret, and they relate to Moses, and the difference in words will be explained before us.

Moses is called a man of great stature and a fine looking man.

148. וְהַאי קְרָא בִּמְתִיבְתָּא עִלָּאָה אִתְּמָר, אִישׁ מִדָּה כֹּלָּא חַד, אִישׁ מַרְאֶה
וְאִישׁ מִדָּה כֹּלָּא חַד, בְּגִין דְּאִיהוּ שַׁבָּת וּתְחוּמָא. דִּכְתִיב וּמַדּוֹתֶם מִחוּץ לָעִיר,
וּכְתִיב לֹא תַעֲשׂוּ עָוֶל בַּמִּשְׁפָּט בַּמִּדָּה, וְעַל דָּא אִישׁ מִדָּה אִיהוּ. וְאִיהוּ בַּמְּשׁ
אִישׁ מִדָּה, אִיהוּ אָרְכֵיהּ מִסְיָיפֵי עָלְמָא וְעַד סְיָיפֵי עָלְמָא. אָדָם הָרִאשׁוֹן הָכֵי
הֲוָה. וְאִי תֵימָא, הָא כְּתִיב חָמֵשׁ בָּאַמָּה. אִינּוּן חָמֵשׁ בָּאַמָּה מִסְיָיפֵי עָלְמָא עַד
סְיָיפֵי עָלְמָא הֲוָה.

148. This scripture was studied in the Celestial Academy. "...a man of great stature..." (I Chronicles 11:23), all is one as "...a fine looking man (*ish mar'eh*)..." (II Samuel 23:21) and "...a man of great stature (*ish midah*)" (I Chronicles 11:23) are both the same because they represent the Shabbat and the Shabbat Boundaries. As it is written: "And you shall measure from outside the city..." (Numbers 35:5) and "You shall do no wrong in judgment, in land-measure (*midah*)...." (Leviticus 19:35) Therefore this is a man of great stature (*midah*). He is literally a man of measure (*midah*), who stretches out from one end of the world to the other. And so was Adam. And if you say, "But it is written, 'five cubits?'" (I Chronicles 11:23), remember that these five cubits extended from one end of the world to the other."

Explanation: This is the Academy of the Holy One, blessed be He. Concerning the members of that Academy, Rav Shimon said: "I have seen distinguished people; and they are few." (Tractate Sukkah 45b) And there is a Terrestrial Academy, and it is the Academy of Metatro"n. [Rav Shimon] informs us that this verse the old sage [Rav Hamnuna Saba] has explained was expounded in the Celestial Academy.

[The term] **"...a fine looking man (*ish mar'eh*)..."** (II Samuel 23:21) is the level of Moses, about whom it was said: "Never again did there arise in Israel a prophet like Moses..." (Deuteronomy 34:10), which is the secret of: "...in vision (*mar'eh*) and not in riddles...." (Numbers 12:8) "...a man of great stature (*ish midah*)…" (I Chronicles 11:23) refers also to the secret of vision (*mar'eh*), but in the secret of the measure (*midah*) of that vision. The secret of the measure of that vision is from one end of the world to the other. Vision (*mar'eh*) and measure (*midah*) are similar to Shabbat and the Boundary [Eruv] of Shabbat, as the Boundary of Shabbat is the edge of the measure of Shabbat. However in the 6,000 years, the measure of the Boundary of Shabbat is limited to only 2,000 *amot*, and after the end of the Correction the Boundary of Shabbat will be from one end of the world to the other, which is the secret of "And the Lord shall be king over all the land…" (Zechariah 14:9)

This is: "**…a fine looking man (*ish mar'eh*)…" (II Samuel 23:21) and "…a man of great stature (*ish midah*)" (I Chronicles 11:23) are both the same, because they represent the Shabbat and the Shabbat Boundaries. As it is written: "And you shall measure from outside the city…" (Numbers 35:5), and, "You shall do no wrong in judgment, in land-measure (*middah*)…." (Leviticus 19:35)** We see that just as measure (*midah*) is the edge of a boundary, so does "…a man of great stature (*ish midah*)…" (I Chronicles 11:23) refer to the edge of the Boundary of Shabbat after the End of the Correction, which is from one end of the world to the other. This is: **"He is literally a man of measure (*midah*)."** Man of measure means the owner of that measure, literally. In other words, the measure does not rule over him but he is the ruler of the measure and determines it based on his own will and desire.

Thus **"And so was Adam,"** namely before he sinned with the Tree of Knowledge, when his length was from one end of the world to the other (Tractate Chagigah 12a) and he shone from one end of the world to the other, as is the measure of the Shabbat Boundary after the End of the Correction. [Concerning] **"these five cubits extended from one end of the world to the other,"** "these five cubits" are the secret of the Ten Sefirot that are primarily Keter, Chochmah, Binah, Tiferet, and

Malchut, which after the End of the Correction will spread from one
end of the world to the other.

The staff of Moses had the Yud-Hei-Vav-Hei inscribed on it.

149. וּבְיַד הַמִּצְרִי חֲנִית, כד"א כִּמְנוֹר אוֹרְגִים, דָּא מַטֵּה הָאֱלֹהִים דַּהֲוָה
בִּידֵיה, וְזָקִיק בְּשְׁמָא גְּלִיפָא מְפָרַשׁ, בִּנְהִירוּ דְּצֵרוּפֵי אַתְוָן, דַּהֲוָה גָּלִיף בְּצַלְאֵל
וּמְתִיבְתָּא דִּילֵיה, דְּאִקְרֵי אוֹרֵג, דִּכְתִיב מִלֵּא אוֹתָם וגו', וְחָרָשׁ וְחֹשֵׁב וְרוֹקֵם
וגו'. וְהַהוּא מַטֵּה הֲוָה נָהִיר שְׁמָא גְּלִיפָא בְּכָל סִטְרִין בִּנְהִירוּ דְּחַכִּימִין דַּהֲווֹ
מְגַלְּפִין שְׁמָא מְפָרַשׁ בְּאַרְבְּעִין וּתְרֵין גַּוְונֵי. וּקְרָא מִכָּאן וּלְהָלְאָה, כְּמָה דַּאֲמַר,
זַכָּאָה חוּלָקֵיה.

149. "…and in the Egyptian's hand was a spear…" (II Samuel 23:21)
as you say "…like a weaver's beam…" (I Samuel 17:7), which is
the Staff of God (Elohim) that was in his hand and upon which
the Explicit Name was engraved, with the radiance of the letter
combinations, which Betzalel and his Academy engraved. This is
called "weaving," as is written: "…them He has filled with wisdom
of heart… of the craftsman and of the embroiderer… and of the
weaver…." (Exodus 35:35) The engraved Name shone from within
this Staff in all directions through the Illumination of the wise men
that engraved the Explicit Name in forty-two ways. The remaining
verses from here onward is similar to what he, the old man, has
already explained. Happy is his lot.

Explanation: The secret of the permutations of the letters into Holy
Names are called the "crafts of a weaver (*ma'aseh oreg*)" Just like a
weaver who weaves threads into clothes, so do the letters join and
unite into words of the Holy Names, which mean Holy Attainments.
The Zohar says that in the Staff of God in Moses' hand was engraved
those combinations of letters of the Holy Name that Betzalel and his
Academy engraved during the work of the Tabernacle. This is why the
staff of God (Elohim) was called a "weaver's beam" (*manor orgim*), so

named after Betzalel that was called a weaver (*oreg*), and beam (*manor*) is like luminary (*ma'or*), and the weaver (*oreg*) is Betzalel. To imply that the Light of the permutations of letters of the Explicit Name was in the aspect of the Light of the Explicit Name that Betzalel engraved, thus **"with the radiance of the letter combinations, which Betzalel and his Academy engraved."**

Before the End of the Correction, the staff was not shining from all directions, since there was a difference between the Staff of God (Elohim) and the staff of Moses. Concerning the staff of Moses it is said: "Put out your hand and grasp it by its tail... and it became a staff in his hand." (Exodus 4:4) Consequently it evidently did not shine from all directions. Yet after the End of the Correction it shines from all directions. This is: **"The engraved Name shone from within this Staff in all directions by the Illumination of the wise men that engraved the Explicit Name in forty-two ways."** The Explicit Name that was engraved on the Staff was shining in every direction, namely in the aspect of "He shall swallow up death forever..." (Isaiah 25:8), as mentioned earlier. It therefore was shining from all sides equally. And the Light of the Name that was engraved on the Staff was in the secret of the Illumination of wisdom of the 42-Lettered Name.

Whoever prepares the Bride on Shavuot will be protected all year.

150. תִּיבוּ יַקִּירִין תִּיבוּ, וּנְחַדֵּשׁ תִּקּוּן דְּכַלָּה בְּהַאי לֵילְיָא. דְּכָל מַאן דְּאִשְׁתַּתַּף בַּהֲדָהּ בְּהַאי לֵילְיָא, יְהֵא נָטִיר עֵילָא וְתַתָּא כָּל הַהִיא שַׁתָּא, וְיַפִּיק שַׁתָּא בִּשְׁלָם. עֲלַיְיהוּ כְּתִיב וְחוֹנֶה מַלְאַךְ ה' סָבִיב לִירֵאָיו וַיְחַלְּצֵם טַעֲמוּ וּרְאוּ כִּי טוֹב יְיָ'.

150. "Be seated, honored ones. Be seated and let us renew the preparations of the Bride for this night. Because whoever joins Her, on this night, shall be protected all that year Above and Below and will complete his year in peace. About them it is written, 'The angel of

the Lord encamps round about them that fear Him, and He delivers them. Taste and see that the Lord is good...."' (Psalms 34:8-9)

There are two explanations in this, which both together are true (study above, verse 125), and so is the explanation for, **"and will complete his year in peace."** According to the first explanation that is presented there it follows the literal sense that because the day of the Giving of the Torah [Shavuot] is the aspect of the Light of the End of the Correction, the aspect of "He shall swallow up death forever..." (Isaiah 25:8) and freedom from the Angel of Death, it is therefore appropriate to strive to draw this Light in its time on Shavuot—for it is the nature of the luminaries to be renewed in their time. Thus one can be assured now as well that he shall complete his year in peace and will have freedom from the Angel of Death.

According to the second explanation, which is that it refers to the actual time of the End of the Correction, the explanation for completing the year in peace is as follows: Malchut is called "year," and due to the renewal of the luminaries of the supporters of the Torah it will be guaranteed after the End of the Correction that he completely corrects the year—Malchut—because the aspect of the renewal of the luminaries of the supporters of the Torah is called the Correction of the Night of the Bride, which is Malchut called "year," as said there. Through this, he shall complete the year in peace in all perfection, as explained.

YITRO

13. "In the third month"

A Synopsis

This section tells us of the two lights of the right and the left called Gemini, which is the constellation that rules over the third month, Sivan. Uriel rules over this month, and we are told of his camps, each of which has Keys of Light issuing from the Inner Supernal Electrum (*Chasmal*). Rav Shimon explains the significance of twins in terms of the birth of Jacob and Esau, and then says that the Torah itself is twins—the Written Torah and the Oral Torah—given in the third month to the triple nation of the Three Fathers. And finally he tells us that the Torah was given in three parts—the Torah, the Prophets, and the Writings. But the important conclusion is that all is one.

The third month is Tiferet, ruled by the Angel Uriel.

235. בַּחֹדֶשׁ הַשְּׁלִישִׁי לְצֵאת בְּנֵי יִשְׂרָאֵל וְגוֹ', דְּשָׁלִיט בֵּיהּ אוריא"ל, רַב מְמָנָא, וּתְלַת מְאָה וְשִׁתִּין וְחָמֵשׁ רִבּוֹא מַשְׁרְיָין עִמֵּיהּ, כְּחוּשְׁבָּן יוֹמֵי שַׁתָּא. וְכֻלְּהוּ אִית לוֹן תְּלַת מְאָה וְשִׁתִּין וְחָמֵשׁ מַפְתְּחָן נְהוֹרִין, מֵהַהוּא נְהוֹרָא דְּנָפְקָא מִגּוֹ חַשְׁמַל עִלָּאָה פְּנִימָאָה גְּנִיז וְסָתִים, דִּי רָזִין דְּאַתְוָון קַדִּישִׁין עִלָּאִין דִּשְׁמָא קַדִּישָׁא, תַּלְיָין בֵּיהּ.

235. "In the third month, after the children of Israel went out of the land of Egypt...." (Exodus 19:1) **The Great Minister, Uriel, rules over this month,** for Nissan, Iyar, and Sivan correspond to Chesed-Gevurah-Tiferet, where in Chesed Michael rules, in Gevurah Gabriel, and in Tiferet Uriel. **He is accompanied by 365 [units of] ten thousand camps, corresponding to the number of days of the year,** which are 365 days of the solar year. **And all of them have 365 Keys of Light issuing from the Inner Supernal Electrum (*Chashmal*) that**

is stored away and concealed, and in which the secrets of the Holy Supernal Letters of the Holy Name are suspended.

The camps of Uriel hold the Keys of the Light that comes from the chashmal.

236. וְאִיהוּ רָזָא דְּאִישׁ תָּם, מָארֵיהּ דְּבֵיתָא, אִישׁ הָאֱלֹהִים. תָּם: דְּתַמָּן סִיוּמָא וְקִשְׁרָא דִּתְפִילִין, וְיַעֲקֹב אִישׁ תָּם הֲוָה. וּבְדִיּוּקְנֵיהּ, קַיְימָא רָזָא דְּחַשְׁמַל פְּנִימָאָה עִלָּאָה טָמִיר וְגָנִיז. וְכָל נְהוֹרִין סְתִימִין עִלָּאִין נָקִיט אִיהוּ, וְנַפְקֵי מִנֵּיהּ, וְכֻלְּהוּ מַשְׁרְיָין נַקְטֵי אִינּוּן מַפְתְּחָן דְּהַהוּא נְהוֹרָא דְּנָפִיק מִגּוֹ חַשְׁמַל.

236. This is the secret of "…a plain man (*ish tam*)"… (Genesis 25:27), who is Jacob, the secret of Tiferet, meaning that **he is the master of the house, a man of God (Elohim).** The Malchut from above the chest is called *tam* (plain or complete), and Jacob (Yaakov) is the husband of Malchut, so therefore he is called *ish tam* (lit. man of *tam*), as he is Her man and husband. [The word] *tam* can also mean "complete" **for there is the ending of the knot of the Tefilin,** which is the secret of the Malchut that is called "Leah." **Jacob was the man of tam,** meaning her husband. **And in his shape stands the secret of the Inner Supernal Chashmal that is concealed and stored, and he holds all the Hidden Supernal Lights, and they issue forth from him. And all the camps** of the mentioned Angel Uriel **hold the Keys of that Light that issues from the Electrum (Chashmal).**

The mentioned Light includes two Lights; white and red.

237. וְהַהוּא נְהוֹרָא, כָּלִיל בִּתְרֵין נְהוֹרִין, וְאִינּוּן חַד. נְהוֹרָא קַדְמָאָה, אִיהוּ נְהוֹרָא חִוְּורָא, דְּלָא שַׁלְטָא בֵּיהּ עֵינָא, וְדָא אִיהוּ נְהוֹרָא דְּגָנֵיז לְצַדִּיקַיָּיא. כד"א אוֹר זָרוּעַ לַצַּדִּיק וְגוֹ'. נְהוֹרָא תִּנְיָינָא, אִיהוּ נְהוֹרָא מְנַצְצָא מִכָּל הַטָּא, כְּגַוֶון סוּמָק. וְאִתְכְּלִילוּ תְּרֵין נְהוֹרִין כַּחֲד, וַהֲווֹ חַד.

237. And that Light includes the two Lights of the Right and the Left, **and yet in it they are one** Light. **The first Light is a white Light,**

which no eye has access to, and this is the Light stored away for the righteous, as it is written: "Light is sown for the righteous...." (Psalms 97:11) And the second Light is a Light that gleams and sparkles red, which is the secret of the Left Light. And both of them are included as one in it, and they became one.

The two Lights are represented by the constellation Gemini.

238. וְהַאי אוּרִיאֵ"ל רַב מִמְנָא, וְכָל אִינּוּן מַשִׁירְיָין, נַטְלֵי הַהוּא נְהוֹרָא, וּבְגִין דְּכָלִיל בְּתְרֵין, אִקְרֵי תְּאוֹמֵי"ם. וְעַל דָּא שַׁלְטָא בֵּיהּ, הַהוּא מַזָּלָא דְּאִקְרֵי בְּרָזָא דִּילֵיהּ תְּאוֹמִים, וּבֵיהּ אִתְיְהִיבַת אוֹרַיְיתָא. וּמִכָּאן אִתְמַשְׁכָאן דַּרְגִּין לְתַתָּא, עַד דְּסַלְקִין בִּשְׁמָהָן, לְאַנְהָרָא עָלְמָא.

238. And this Uriel, the Great Minister, and all those camps with him take that Light, and because it is composed of both, it is called Gemini (Twins; *Te'omim*; תאומים). Therefore that constellation rules over this month, which is called Gemini [Twins] after its secret, in which the Torah was given. And from here all the grades are drawn down until they ascend by name to illuminate the world.

Only the sign of Gemini has a mouth, to allude to the constant study of Torah.

239. כָּל שְׁאַר מַזָּלֵי, לֵית לוֹן פֶּה וְלָשׁוֹן, וְהַאי אִית לֵיהּ פֶּה וְלָשׁוֹן כְּלִילָן כַּחֲדָא. וְעַל דָּא בְּאוֹרַיְיתָא, וְהָגִיתָ בּוֹ יוֹמָם וְלַיְלָה כְּתִיב. יוֹמָם, לְקָבֵל לָשׁוֹן. לַיְלָה, לְקָבֵל פֶּה. וְכֹלָּא כְּלִיל כַּחֲדָא. וּבְכֹלָּא סָלִיק תְּאוֹמִים.

239. None of the other signs that rule in other months have a mouth or tongue; nonetheless this one, Gemini, has a mouth and tongue included as one. Therefore in the Torah it is written: "...and you shall meditate therein day and night...." (Joshua 1:8) "Day" corresponds to the tongue, which is Zeir Anpin, and "night" corresponds to the

mouth, which is Malchut, **and all is included in** the secret of **the Gemini (Te'omim; תאומים).**

Jacob alone represented twins since he was the Central Column.

240. תּוֹמִים כְּתִיב, וְעַל דָּא כְּתִיב תּוֹמִים, וְהִנֵּה תוֹמִים בְּבִטְנָהּ. אִי תֵימָא דִּבְגִין תַּרְוַוְיְיהוּ קָאָמַר. לָאו הָכִי, דְּהָא עֵשָׂו לָא סָלִיק בְּרָזָא דָא. אֶלָּא בְּגִין יַעֲקֹב קָאָמַר, וּשְׁבָחָא דָא, דַּהֲוָה בִּמְעָהָא דְּהַהִיא צַדֶּקֶת, קָא מְשַׁבַּח קְרָא. וּבְגִין דַּהֲוָה תַּמָּן הַהוּא רָשָׁע, אִסְתַּלָּק מִתַּמָּן אָלֶף.

240. It is written: "...twins (tomim; תומים)..." (Genesis 25:24) **without the letter Alef (א), and in relation to this secret it is written:** *Tomim in,* **"...behold, there were twins (tomim) in her womb."** (Genesis 25:24). **If you say that it says** *tomim* **about them both,** Esau and Jacob, **it is not so, as Esau is not included in this secret. Rather about Jacob** alone **does it say** *tomim* **of Jacob,** for Jacob is the secret of the Central Column that includes two Lights, the Right and the Left, and he is called *tomim* after those two Lights. When the scripture says: "behold there were twins (*tomim*)," it indicates that he, Jacob, was in her womb. **And the scripture praises Jacob for being in the womb of that righteous woman, yet because the wicked** Esau **was there too, the letter Alef (א) departed,** and it is written *tomim* without Alef.

Jacob took Nissan, Iyar, and Sivan, and Esau took Tammuz and part of Av.

241. וְכֹלָּא רָזָא וְחַדָא. יַעֲקֹב נָטִיל בְּרָזָא דִּילֵיהּ, תְּרֵין יַרְחִין נִיס"ן וְאיי"ר, וְאִתְכְּלִיל אִיהוּ בְּרָזָא דְּסִיוָן, דְּאִיהוּ תְּאוֹמִים. עֵשָׂו, נָטִיל בְּרָזָא דִּילֵיהּ, תְּרֵין יַרְחִין תַּמּוּ"ז אָ"ב, וְאִיהוּ לָא אִשְׁתְּכַח, וְאִתְאֲבִיד, דְּהָא אֱלוּ"ל לָאו דִּילֵיהּ הוּא, וַאֲפִילוּ אָ"ב, ט' יוֹם אִינּוּן דִּילֵיהּ, וְלָא יַתִּיר, וְאִתְאֲבִיד, וְלָא אִשְׁתְּכַח, וְלָאו אִיהוּ בְּרָזָא דִּתְאוֹמִים, אֶלָּא אִתְפְּרַשׁ לְחוֹדֵיהּ, וְסָטָא לְסִטְרָא אַחֲרָא בַּאֲפִיסָה וּשְׁמָמוּ, כַּד"א, הָאוֹיֵב תַּמּוּ וְחֳרָבוֹת לָנֶצַח.

241. All is one secret, for Jacob receives through his secret, Tiferet, the Central Column, **the two months Nissan and Iyar, and he is included in the secret of** the month **Sivan, which is** the sign of **Gemini.** In other words, by being included in the month of Sivan—which includes two months, Nissan and Iyar, which are Right and Left, and is why it is called the sign of Gemini—Jacob, who is included in it, also takes these two months. **Esau, in his own secret, receives the two months of Tammuz and Av, and he is not found** in the Central Column, which is Elul, **and he is lost, since Elul is not his. Even** in the month of **Av, only nine days are his, and no more.** Therefore, **he is lost and is not found, and he is not in the secret of Twins,** which is the Central Column. **Rather, he separated himself and turned toward the Other Side in naught and desolation, as it is written: "The enemies are come to an end in perpetual ruins...." (Psalms 9:7)**

The Torah is in the secret of twins—the Written Torah and the Oral Torah.

242. וּבְגִין דְּיַעֲקֹב אִיהוּ תְּאוֹמִים, אִתְיְהִיבַת אוֹרַיְיתָא לִבְנוֹי בַּחֹדֶשׁ תְּאוֹמִים, וְאוֹרַיְיתָא בְּרָזָא דִתְאוֹמִים, תּוֹרָה שֶׁבִּכְתָב, וְתוֹרָה שֶׁבְּע"פ. בַּחֹדֶשׁ תְּלִיתָאֵי, לְעַם תְּלִיתָאֵי, בְּדַרְגִּין תְּלִיתָאִין, תּוֹרָה תְּלִיתָאֵי: תּוֹרָה, נְבִיאִים, וּכְתוּבִים. וְכֹלָּא חַד.

242. Because Jacob is Twins, the Torah was given to his children in the month of the Twins. The Torah is in the secret of Twins, which is **the Written Torah and the Oral Torah.** It was given **in the third month to the Triple Nation,** as it is composed of **three grades,** namely the three Patriarchs, **a tripled Torah—the Torah, the Prophets, and the Writings, and all is one.**

The Creator examined all the nations before giving the Torah to Israel.

243. בַּחֹדֶשׁ הַשְּׁלִישִׁי וְגוֹ'. פָּרְשָׁתָא דָא בְּהַאי קְרָא אוּקְמוּהָ לֵיהּ לְעֵילָא. תָּאנֵי רַבִּי חִיָּיא, בְּהַהוּא זִמְנָא דִּבְמָטוּ יִשְׂרָאֵל לְטוּרָא דְסִינַי, כָּנִישׁ לְהוּ קוּדְשָׁא בְּרִיךְ

הוּא לְזַרְעֵיּן דְּיִשְׂרָאֵל, וְאַשְׁגַּח לֵיהּ בְּכָלְּהוּ, וְלָא אַשְׁכַּח בְּכָלְּהוּ זַרְעָא דְּיִשְׂרָאֵל
פְּסִילוּ, אֶלָּא כָּלְּהוּ זַרְעָא קַדִּישָׁא, כָּלְּהוּ בְּנֵי קְשׁוֹט.

243. "In the third month..." (Exodus 19:1) We have already explained this verse earlier in this portion. Rav Chiya said that at the time Israel approached Mount Sinai, the Holy One, blessed be He, gathered the seeds of the nation of Israel and examined them all. And He found no blemish in all the seeds of Israel but saw they were all a Holy Seed and children of Truth.

Moses was the messenger of the Creator
to draw the Israelites closer with love.

244. בְּהַהוּא זִמְנָא אָמַר קוּדְשָׁא בְּרִיךְ הוּא לְמֹשֶׁה, הַשְׁתָּא אֲנָא בָּעֵי לְמֵיהָב
אוֹרַיְיתָא לְיִשְׂרָאֵל, מָשִׁיךְ לְהוּ בִּרְחִימוּתָא דַּאֲבָהָן, בִּרְחִימוּתָא דְּרָחִימְנָא לְהוּ,
וּבְאַתְוָון דַּעֲבָדִית לְהוּ. וְאַתְּ הֱוֵי לִי שְׁלוּחָא, וְאָתֵיב מִלִּין אִלֵּין. אָמַר ר' יוֹסֵי
אָמַר ר' יְהוּדָה, כַּךְ אָמַר קוּדְשָׁא בְּרִיךְ הוּא לְמֹשֶׁה, בְּמִלָּה דָּא הֱוֵי לִי שְׁלִיחָא
מְהֵימְנָא, לְאַמְשָׁכָא יִשְׂרָאֵל אֲבַתְרַאי.

244. At that time, the Holy One, blessed be He, said to Moses, "Now do I wish to give Israel the Torah. Draw them with the love of the Patriarchs, with the love that I love them, and by the signs that I have performed for them. And you shall be My messenger. Go and tell them these words." Rav Yosi said in the Name of Rav Yehuda: "This is what the Holy One, blessed be He, said to Moses, 'With this these words you shall be My faithful messenger to draw Israel toward Me.'"

Emor

25. Why there are not seven days to Shavuot?

A Synopsis

We learn why the day of Shavuot is the bond of Faith that bonds everything together, and why that day is not extended to seven days.

Why Shavuot does not contain seven days.

140. אָ"ל ר' יְהוּדָה, שַׁפִּיר הוּא, וְהָכִי הוּא וַדַּאי. וְהַאי זִמְנָא אָחֱרָא שְׁמַעֲנָא לֵיהּ בְּהַאי גַּוְונָא, וְאַנְשֵׁינָא מִכֵּי. הַשְׁתָּא בִּמִלָּה אָחֳרָא בָּעֵינָא לְמִנְדַּע, הָא חֲזֵינָא בְּפֶסַח ז', וּבְסֻכּוֹת ז', וּשְׁלִימוּ דְּחֶדְוְותָא בְּיוֹמָא אָחֳרָא. בִּשְׁבוּעוֹת, אֲמַאי לָא אִשְׁתְּכָחוּ בֵּיהּ ז' יָמִים, וְהָא הָכָא אִתְחֲזֵי יַתִּיר מִכֹּלָּא.

140. Rav Yehuda said: "This is well and assuredly it is so. I have already heard this another time this way, but I forgot. Now I wish to know something else. We see that on Pesach there are seven days, and on Sukkot there are seven days, and the completeness of joy of Sukkot is on another day, Shmini Atzeret. But why are there not seven days to Shavuot? Is it not appropriate here to have seven days more than all others?"

Explanation: Shavuot is the time of the Giving of the Torah, which is more important than all. Furthermore, Pesach is the secret of Right Column, Sukkot is Left Column, and Shavuot is the Central Column that includes within it the two Columns. So it should have in it seven days more than the others.

The praise of Israel is that they are one.

141. פָּתַח וְאָמַר, וּמִי כְעַמְּךָ כְּיִשְׂרָאֵל גּוֹי אֶחָד בָּאָרֶץ. וְכִי בַּאי שְׁנָא הָכָא דְּאִקְרוּן יִשְׂרָאֵל אֶחָד, יַתִּיר בְּאֲתַר אָחֳרָא. אֶלָּא, כֵּיוָן דְּשִׁבְטָא דְיִשְׂרָאֵל,

אַתְיָיא לְפָרְשָׁא, קָרָא כֹן אֶחָד, דְּהָא בְּכָל אֲתַר שְׁבָחָא דְיִשְׂרָאֵל אֶחָד הוּא.
מ"ט. בְּגִין דְּכָל קְשִׁירוּ דְּעֶלְאֵי וְתַתָּאֵי, בְּהַאי אֲתַר דְּאִקְרֵי יִשְׂרָאֵל אִשְׁתְּכַח.
דְּאִתְקְשַׁר בְּמָה דִלְעֵילָא, וְאִתְקְשַׁר בְּמָה דִלְתַתָּא, וְאִתְקְשַׁר בכ"י. וְעַ"ד
אִקְרֵי כֹלָּא אֶחָד. וּבַאֲתַר דָּא אִשְׁתְּמוֹדְעָא מְהֵימְנוּתָא, וְקִשּׁוּרָא שְׁלֵימָא,
וְיִחוּדָא עִלָּאָה קַדִּישָׁא.

141. He opened and said: "'And who is like Your nation, like Israel, who are one nation in the land….'" (II Samuel 7:23) He asks: "What is different here that Israel are called 'one' more than in other places?" He answers: "Since its purpose here is to specify Israel's praise, he called them 'one.' For in every place the praise of Israel is 'one.'" [He asks:] "What is the reason?" [He answers:] "It is that the whole bond of the Upper and Lower Beings is in the place called Israel, namely Zeir Anpin that is called Israel, since it is connected with that which is Above, namely above its chest, which is Chasadim, and is connected to that which is Below, namely Netzach-Hod-Yesod that are below His chest, whence the abundance of Chochmah comes. And it is connected with the Congregation of Israel, Malchut, where Chochmah is revealed. Therefore, since it connects the three places, all is called 'one.' In that place people can know Faith, Malchut, the Complete Bond, Netzach-Hod-Yesod, and the Supernal Holy Union that is in the Upper Three [Sefirot].

Shavuot is the bond of Faith.

142. וְעַ"ד, יוֹמָא דָא, קִשּׁוּרָא דִּמְהֵימְנוּתָא הוּא, קִשּׁוּרָא דְּכֹלָּא. וּכְתִיב עֵץ
חַיִּים הִיא לַמַּחֲזִיקִים בָּהּ אִילָנָא הוּא דְּאִקְרֵי אֶחָד. וְעַ"ד בְּגִין דְּאִינּוּן מִתְקַשְּׁרֵי
בַּאֲתַר דָּא, אִקְרֵי הָכִי. וְעֵץ חַיִּים אֶחָד הוּא וַדַּאי אִקְרֵי, בְּגִין דְּכֹלָּא בֵּיהּ
אִתְקְשַׁר, וְיוֹמָא דִילֵיהּ, אֶחָד וַדַּאי, קִשּׁוּרָא דְּכֹלָּא, וְאֶמְצָעִיתָא דְּכֹלָּא.

142. "This is why this day of Shavuot, which is the Central Column that corresponds to Zeir Anpin that is called Israel, is the bond of Faith that bonds everything. Also, it is written, 'She is a Tree of Life to those who grasp her...' (Proverbs 3:18) since the Tree of Life, Zeir Anpin, **is a Tree that is called 'one.' Therefore, since** Israel Below **are attached** and hold **to this place,** the Tree of Life, Zeir Anpin, **they are so called** 'one.' **The Tree of Life is called 'one,' since everything is attached to it, and its day,** Shavuot, **is assuredly 'one,' bonding everything and being the center of everything,** since it is the Central Column.

The Tree of Life is in the middle, attached to all sides.

143. הה"ד וְעֵץ הַחַיִּים בְּתוֹךְ הַגָּן, בְּתוֹךְ מַמָּשׁ, בְּמִצִיעוּת, וְאָחִיד בְּכָל סִטְרִין, וְאִתְקְשַׁר בֵּיהּ. וְעַ"ד פֶּסַח וְסֻכּוֹת, וְהוּא בְּאֶמְצָעִיתָא. בְּגִין דְּאִיהוּ אֶמְצָעִיתָא דְּכֹלָּא, וְדָא הוּא שְׁבָחָא דְּאוֹרַיְיתָא בְּהַאי יוֹמָא, וְלָא יַתִּיר, שְׁבָחָא דִּמְהֵימְנוּתָא, וְקִשּׁוּרָא דְּכֹלָּא. א"ר יְהוּדָה, בְּרִיךְ רַחֲמָנָא דְּשָׁאִילְנָא, וְזַכֵינָא לְהַנֵּי מִילֵי.

143. "This is the meaning of, '...and the Tree of Life in the midst of the Garden..." (Genesis 2:9) as Zeir Anpin called the Tree of Life **is actually inside, in the center, and includes all directions,** namely the Right and Left Columns, **and is attached to them. Therefore there is Pesach and Sukkot, and it,** Shavuot, **is between them,** since Pesach is the Right Column, Sukkot the Left Column, and Shavuot the Central Column **since it is central to everything. This is why this day is the praise of the Torah,** namely the time of the Giving of our Torah, **and no more,** for the Torah is the secret of Zeir Anpin, the Central Column, **and it is the praise of Faith,** Malchut, **and the bonding of everything,** namely the Upper Three [Sefirot], for all those are tied to the Central Column." **Rav Yehuda said: "Blessed is the Merciful One that I have asked and attained these matters."**

Israel are destined to praise the Creator like their praise on Pesach.

144. א"ר יִצְחָק, חֶדְוָוֹתָא וְשִׁירָתָא, זְמִינִין יִשְׂרָאֵל לְשַׁבָּחָא לְקוּדְשָׁא בְּרִיךְ הוּא, כְּהַאי שְׁבָחָא דִּמְשַׁבְּחֵי יִשְׂרָאֵל בְּלֵילְיָא דְּפִסְחָא, דכ"י אִתְגַּדְּשַׁת

בְּקְדוּשָׁה דְּמַלְכָּא. הה"ד הַשִּׁיר יִהְיֶה לָכֶם כְּלֵיל הִתְקַדֶּשׁ חָג. כְּלֵיל הִתְקַדֶּשׁ
חָג דַּיְיקָא. בָּרוּךְ יְיָ'. לְעוֹלָם אָמֵן וְאָמֵן.

144. Rav Yitzchak said: "Israel are destined to praise the Holy One, blessed be He, with joy and song, as that praise Israel recite on the night of Pesach, when the Congregation of Israel, which is the secret of night, is sanctified with the sanctification of the King, by the Great Unification (Zivug) in the place of Aba and Ima (as mentioned in Zohar, Emor 134). This is the meaning of, 'You shall have a song, as in the night when a holy solemnity is kept....' (Isaiah 30:29) 'The night when a holy solemnity is kept' (Ibid.) is precise, such as that Unification on the night of Pesach. Blessed is the Lord forever and ever. Amen and Amen."

EMOR

27. The Festival of Shavuot

A Synopsis

We hear about the rejoicing of all the trees when Malchut is perfected. The entire bond of Faith comes from the Tree, Zeir Anpin. We are told that the Congregation of Israel, like a Bride, is given portions from each of the grades. Rav Shimon tells about the union of Zeir Anpin and Malchut. We hear about the Tree that is the torso and about all the limbs that are the Sefirot that are attached to it. The feast days of the branches of the Tree were throughout the days of Sukkot, and after that on Shmini Atzeret is the joy of the Tree itself. The Tree atones for the Evil Inclination in man when the leavened bread is brought. The Torah is called "a Tree of Life" because its roots are in the deep river of Binah.

The King comes to unite with the Congregation of Israel on Shavuot.

149. וְדָא שֶׁבַע שַׁבָּתוֹת תְּמִימוֹת, לְבָתַר דְּסַלְּקִין שֶׁבַע שַׁבָּתוֹת אִלֵּין, אָתָא מַלְכָּא קַדִּישָׁא לְאִזְדַּוְּוגָא בָּהּ בכ"י, וְאוֹרַיְיתָא אִתְיְיהִיבַת. וּכְדֵין אִתְעַטָּר מַלְכָּא בְּיִחוּדָא שְׁלִים, וְאִשְׁתְּכַח אֶחָד לְעֵילָא וְתַתָּא. וְכַד אַתְּעַר מַלְכָּא קַדִּישָׁא, וּמָטָא זִמְנָא דְּאוֹרַיְיתָא. כָּל אִינּוּן אִילָנִין דִּמְבַכְּרֵי אִבַּיְיהוּ, סַלְּקִין שִׁירָתָא. וּמַאי אַמְרֵי בְּשַׁעֲתָא דִּמְלַכְטֵי לְהוֹן, פַּתְחֵי וְאַמְרֵי, יְיָ' בַּשָּׁמַיִם הֵכִין כִּסְאוֹ וּמַלְכוּתוֹ בַּכֹּל מָשָׁלָה. יְיָ' בַּהֲשָׁמַיִם חַסְדֶּךָ. וּכְתִיב, וְכָל עֲצֵי הַשָּׂדֶה יִמְחֲאוּ כָף.

149. This is the meaning of, "...seven complete Shabbats..." (Leviticus 23:15), which means that **after seven Shabbats have passed, the Holy King comes to unite with the Congregation of Israel,** since through these Forty-Nine Sefirot of Zeir Anpin Her [Malchut's] entire stature is built, **and the Torah is given. Then the King,** Zeir Anpin, **is adorned by the complete union, and He is found one Above and Below. When the Holy King is awakened and the time of the Torah comes, all the trees that produce the First Fruits start**

singing, because through the Illumination of the union they produce their First Fruits. [He asks:] **"What do they sing when** the fruits **are gathered?"** [He answers:] **"They open and say: 'The Lord has established His throne in the Heavens; and His kingdom rules over all' (Psalms 103:19),** as the throne, Malchut, is built and established in the Heavens, Zeir Anpin, by His Forty-Nine Sefirot. Then Malchut reigns over all. **And it is written, 'Your steadfast love, the Lord, is in the Heavens...' (Psalms 36:6),** which means that Chasadim flow from Zeir Anpin to Malchut. **And it is also written, '...and all the trees of the field shall clap their hands' (Isaiah 55:12),"** namely the Illumination of Malchut called "Field" will clap hands. In relation to this union, Rav Shimon opened the article with the verse, "Then shall the trees of the wood sing for joy...." (I Chronicles 16:33)

The renewal of the Bride.

150. תּוּ פָּתַח וְאָמַר, בְּמִזְמוֹר שִׁירוּ לַיְיָ' שִׁיר חָדָשׁ כִּי נִפְלָאוֹת עָשָׂה. שִׁיר חָדָשׁ אִקְרֵי. בְּגִין כַּךְ בְּהַקְרִיבְכֶם מִנְחָה חֲדָשָׁה. הָתָם מִנְחַת קְנָאוֹת, הָכָא מִנְחָה חֲדָשָׁה. וַחֲדָשָׁה דְּוּוֹדָשָׁא דְּכַלָּה הָכָא. קְשׁוּרָא דְּכַלָּה דְּעֵילָּא וְתַתָּא, קְשׁוּרָא דִּמְהֵימְנוּתָא. וְעַ"ד יַעֲקֹב שְׁלֵימָא אִתְעַטָּר בְּעִטְרוֹי, וְאוֹרַיְיתָא אִתְיְהִיבַת.

150. He further opened and said: "'A Psalm. Sing to the Lord a new song; for He has done marvelous things....' (Psalms 98:1) The song that the trees recite when the fruits are gathered **is called a new song. For that reason** it is written, **'...when you bring a new meal offering....' (Numbers 28:26) There,** in relation to the Omer, **it is a meal offering of jealousies,** namely a barley meal offering, **while here it is a new offering.** It is considered **new because the Bride is renewed here,** for Malchut is built anew by the Sefirot of Zeir Anpin, **which is the bond of the Bride Above and Below,** above the chest and below the chest of Zeir Anpin, **the bond of Faith. Therefore Jacob the complete one,** Zeir Anpin, **is adorned with his Crowns and the Torah is given.**

What the individual says when giving the First Fruits to the priest.

151. וְכַד מָטוּן בִּכּוּרִים לְגַבֵּי כַּהֲנָא, הֲוָה בָּעֵי בַּר נָשׁ לְמֵימַר וּלְפָרָשָׁא מִלִּין, עַל הַהוּא אִילָנָא דְּאַרְעָא, דְּאִשְׁתְּכָלִים כְּגַוְונָא דִּלְעֵילָא, בִּתְרֵיסַר תְּחוּמִין, בְּשַׁבְעִין עֲנְפִין, וּבָעָא לְאוֹבָדָא לֵיהּ לָבָן אֲרַמָּאָה, דְּאִתְפְּגִים עָלְמָא בְּגִינֵיהּ. וְקוּדְשָׁא בְּרִיךְ הוּא שֵׁזִיב לֵיהּ, וְאִתְעַטָּר בִּבְנוֹי כְּמָה דְּאוֹקִימְנָא. בְּגִין הַהוּא אִילָנָא, דְּכָל קִשּׁוּרָא דִּמְהֵימְנוּתָא, בֵּיהּ תַּלְיָא. וְעַל דָּא מִנְחָה חֲדָשָׁה אִתְקְרֵי. מַ"ט. בְּגִין דְּחֶדְוָותָא דְעֵלָּאֵי וְתַתָּאֵי הוּא, וְחֶדְוָותָא דְסִיהֲרָא. וּבְכָל זִמְנָא וַדְתּוּתֵי דְסִיהֲרָא, קִשּׁוּרָא דִּמְהֵימְנוּתָא הוּא, וְחֶדְוָותָא דִּילָהּ.

151. "When the First Fruits came to the priest, the individual needed to say and explain the matters about that tree in the land that is perfected in the likeness of Above, which is Zeir Anpin, **with twelve regions,** which are the twelve diagonal borders that are Chesed, Gevurah, Tiferet, and Malchut, each composed of three columns, **and seventy branches** of the Seventy-Two Names, which are 70 Sanhedrin and two witnesses. **And that Laban the Aramaean wished to destroy him, causing the world to be damaged, and that the Holy One, blessed be He, saved the world and was adorned by His children,** namely the souls of Israel, **as we explained. For the entire bond of Faith,** which is Malchut, **comes from that Tree,** Zeir Anpin. **This is why** Malchut **is then called a new meal offering."** [He asks:] **"What is the reason?"** [He answers:] **"It is because it is the rejoicing of the Upper and Lower Beings as well as the moon,** Malchut. **Every time the moon,** Malchut, **is renewed, it is the bond of Faith** with Zeir Anpin **and Her joy.**

The Bride receives a portion from all.

152. לְמַלְכָּא דַּהֲווֹ לֵיהּ בְּנִין, וּבְרַתָּא חֲדָא, אַתְקִין סְעוּדָתָא לְכָלְהוּ בְּנִין, לָא אִשְׁתְּכַחַת הַהִיא בְּרַתָּא עַל פָּתוֹרָא. כַּד אָתָאת, אֲמֶרֶת לְמַלְכָּא, מָארִי, לְכָל אֲנָךְ זְמִינַת וְיָהֲבַת לְכָל חַד מָאנִין יְדִיעָן, וְלִי לָא יָהֲבַת חוּלָקָא בֵּינַיְיהוּ. אֲ"ל, חַיָּיִךְ בְּרַתִּי, מָנָא דִילָךְ יִשְׁתְּכַח עַל חַד תְּרֵין. הָא כֹּלָּא יִתְּנוּן לָךְ מֵחוּלָקֵיהוֹן.

אִשְׁתְּכָחוּ לְבָתַר בִּידָהָא וְחוּלָקִין, עַל חַד תְּרֵין מַלְכָּא. כַּךְ כְּנֶסֶת יִשְׂרָאֵל,
מִכֻּלָּא נַטְלָא וְחוּלָקִין, וְעַל דָּא אִתְקְרֵי כַּלָּה, כְּלוּלָּא. כְּכַלָּה דְּכֹלְּהוּ מְזַבְּנִין לָהּ
מָאנִין וְחוּלָקִין וְתַכְשִׁיטִין, כַּךְ הִיא כ"י, וַדְּתוּתֵי דִילָהּ בְּכֹלָּא, וְכֹלָּא יָהֲבִין לָהּ
חוּלָקִין וּמָאנִין.

152. "This is likened **to a king who had sons and one daughter. He prepared a meal for all his sons, but the daughter did not sit at the table. When she came, she said to the king: 'My Master, you have invited all my brothers and have given each one certain portions but you have not given me a portion among them.' He said to her: 'Upon your life, daughter, you shall have a double portion, for each will give you of their share.' Thus she later had a double portion,** more than anyone. So the Congregation of Israel took portions from each of the grades, both from Chochmah and Chasadim, **and therefore She is called a Bride (**Kalah**),** since she is **composed (**kelulah**) of everything, as a bride, to whom everyone gives garments, portions, and jewels. Such is the Congregation of Israel. She is renewed in all** the grades, **and everyone gives Her portions and garments,** namely Mochin and the garments of Mochin.

The joy of the Congregation of Israel is when the King is crowned.

153. תָּא וְחֲזֵי, בְּשַׁעֲתָא דְּמַלְכָּא קַדִּישָׁא אִשְׁתְּכַחוּ בְּעֶטְרוֹי, וֶחֶדְוָותָא דִּכְנֶסֶת
יִשְׂרָאֵל הוּא. וְכַד אוֹרַיְיתָא אִתְיְהִיבַת, אִתְעַטְּרַת כְּנֶסֶת יִשְׂרָאֵל בְּעֶטְרִין
עִלָּאִין, וּבְגִין דְּכָל קְשָׁרָא דִּמְהֵימְנוּתָא, אִתְקְשַׁר בְּהַאי אִילָנָא, אִקְרֵי יוֹם
אֶחָד. דִּכְתִיב, וְהָיָה יוֹם אֶחָד הוּא יִוָּדַע לַיְיָ'. יוֹם אֶחָד וַדַּאי, דְּכ"י יוֹם אֶחָד,
בְּקִשּׁוּרָא דִּלְעֵילָּא.

153. "Come and see, when the Holy King, Zeir Anpin, is adorned with the Mochin of the Upper Three [Sefirot], **it is the joy of the Congregation of Israel** because she too, is with those Mochin. **When the Torah was given, the Congregation of Israel was adorned with Celestial Crowns, and since the entire bond of Faith,** Malchut, **was**

attached to this Tree, to Zeir Anpin, it is considered one day, as it is written, 'but it shall be one particular day which shall be known as the Lord's....' (Zechariah 14:7) Assuredly it is one day, since the Congregation of Israel is one day with the Supernal Bond, namely united with Zeir Anpin, for Zeir Anpin is not called "One" unless He is united with Malchut.

The various bonds of Zeir Anpin unite as one and unite with Malchut.

154. קְשׁוּרָא דִּלְעֵילָּא, רֵישָׁא וְגוּלְגַּלְתָּא וּמוֹחֵי. קְשׁוּרָא אָחֳרָא, תְּרֵין דְּרוֹעִין וְגוּפָא. דַּאֲחִידָן, בְּחֵילָא דְּרֵישָׁא. וְאוֹקְמָא רַב הַמְנוּנָא, בִּתְלַת קְשִׁירִין דַּאֲבָהָתָא. תְּרֵין קָיְימִין דִּלְתַתָּא דְּאִתְמְשָׁכוּ בְּמִשְׁחָא רְבוּת, בִּתְרֵין דַּרְגִּין, תְּרֵין נַחֲלִין, לְאַכְנָשָׁא זַרְעָא, לְאַפָּקָא בְּדַרְגָּא אָחֳרָא, בְּפוּם אַמָּה. אִילָנָא דָא, הוּא גוּפָא דְּאֶמְצָעִיתָא, דְּאָחִיד לְכָל הָנֵי, וְכֹלָּא מִתְקַשְּׁרָן בֵּיהּ, וְהוּא בְּהוֹן, וְעַל דָּא כֹּלָּא חַד. וְכַד אִזְדַּוְּוגַת בֵּיהּ מַטְרוֹנִיתָא, כְּדֵין הוּא אֶחָד, וְהָא אוֹקִימְנָא מִלֵּי.

154. "The Supernal Bond, in Zeir Anpin, is the Head, which is the Skull and the Brains (Mochin). The Skull is Keter and the Brains are Chochmah-Binah-Da'at. Another bond is the two arms, Chesed and Gevurah, and the torso, which is Tiferet. These Chesed-Gevurah-Tiferet are attached by means of the Head, namely they come from Chochmah-Binah-Da'at that are in the Head. Rav Hamnuna explained it as the three Knots of the Patriarchs, namely Chesed-Gevurah-Tiferet, the two Pillars, Netzach and Hod that flow with the Anointing Oil in two grades, Right and Left, in two rivers, the secret of skies, to gather the seed in them, namely the abundance of Chesed-Gevurah-Tiferet and Chochmah-Binah-Da'at, to bring them out in another grade, the Central Column, at the opening of the cubit, which is Yesod. The Tree is the Torso in the middle, Tiferet that is attached to all those, Chochmah-Binah-Da'at, Chesed-Gevurah-Tiferet, Netzach-Hod-Yesod, and they are all attached to it so that everything is one. And when the Matron, Malchut, is united with

it, then it is one completely. **We already explained these matters.**
(Zohar, Emor 96)"

Malchut is called Assembly since all the Sefirot gather toward Her.

155. תָּא חֲזֵי, כְּתִיב בַּיּוֹם הַשְּׁמִינִי עֲצֶרֶת. מַאן עֲצֶרֶת. אֶלָּא בְּהַהוּא אֲתַר,
דְּכֹלָּא מִתְקַשְּׁרָן כַּחֲדָא, אִקְרֵי עֲצֶרֶת, מַאי עֲצֶרֶת, כְּנִישׁוּ. וְאִי תֵּימָא הָכָא
דְּאִקְרֵי עֲצֶרֶת, מַאי טַעֲמָא. אֶלָּא בְּכָל אִינּוּן יוֹמִין, יוֹמֵי סְעוּדָתֵי דְּעַנְפֵי אִילָנָא
הֲוֹו. וְעַל דָּא, שִׁבְעִין פָּרִים אִינּוּן. לְבָתַר, חֶדְוָתָא דְּאִילָנָא מַמָּשׁ, וְחֶדְוָותָא
דְּאוֹרַיְיתָא. וּבְגִינֵיהּ הוּא יוֹמָא חַד עֲצֶרֶת. וְחֶדְוָתָא דְּאוֹרַיְיתָא, וְחֶדְוָותָא
דְּאִילָנָא, דְּהוּא גּוּפָא.

155. [He asks:] **"Come and see, it is written, 'On the eighth day you
shall have a solemn Assembly (Shmini Atzeret)….' (Numbers 29:35)
What is the assembly?"** He answers: **"The place in which everything
is connected together is called an 'assembly,'** which is Malchut Who
receives from all the Sefirot." [He asks:] **"Because what does 'assembly'
mean? A gathering. You may ask: 'What is the reason that it is called
an assembly here?'"** He answers: **"Throughout the days** of Sukkot
were the feast days of the branches of the Tree, namely the seventy
ministers that come from the outer part of Zeir Anpin, **hence there are
seventy bullocks** sacrificed on the seven days of Sukkot. **After that,** on
Shmini Atzeret, **it is the joy of the Tree itself,** Zeir Anpin Himself,
**and for Him there is one assembly day, which is the joy of the Torah,
the joy of the Tree, which is the Torso,** namely Zeir Anpin.

When the King is present, everything is there in Him.

156. וְעַל דָּא לֵית חוּלָקָא בְּהַאי יוֹמָא, אֶלָּא לְקוּדְשָׁא בְּרִיךְ הוּא וכו"י. בְּג"כ,
עֲצֶרֶת תִּהְיֶה לָכֶם, לָכֶם, וְלָא לְאַחֲרָא. דְּהָא בְּעַעֲתָא דְּמַלְכָּא אִשְׁתְּכַח, כֹּלָּא
אִשְׁתְּכַח בֵּיהּ. וְעַ"ד תָּנֵינָן, בַּעֲצֶרֶת עַל פֵּירוֹת הָאִילָן, וְהָא אוּקְמוּהָ בְּג"כ אֶחָד
אִקְרֵי, אֶחָד וַדַּאי, כְּמָה דְּאַמְרָן.

156. "Therefore only the Holy One, blessed be He, and the Congregation of Israel take part in this day, Shmini Atzeret. For that reason, '...you shall have a solemn assembly...' (Numbers 29:35) you and no other, because when the King is present, everything is there in Him. Therefore we have learned: 'On Atzeret concerning the fruits of the Tree,' (Tractate Rosh Hashanah 16a) which alludes to Zeir Anpin that is called Tree, whose day it is. This was already explained. For that reason He is called One, being united with Malchut. Surely one, as we said.

We bring Chametz on Shavuot because the Tree includes all.

157. ת"ח, מַה כְּתִיב, מִמּוֹשְׁבוֹתֵיכֶם תָּבִיאוּ לֶחֶם תְּנוּפָה וְגוֹ', סֹלֶת תִּהְיֶינָה חָמֵץ תֵּאָפֶינָה. מַאי שְׁנָא הָכָא חָמֵץ, אֶלָּא בְּגִין דְּכֹלָּא אֲחִידָן בֵּיה בְּאִילָנָא, דְּהָא בְּאִילָנָא אֲחִידָן עַנְפִין, בְּאִילָנָא אֲחִידָן עָלִין, קְלִיפִין, דִּינִין סַגִּיאִין בְּכָל סִטְרִין, כֹּלָּא אִשְׁתְּכַח בֵּיה. וּבְגִין דְּהַאי אִילָנָא, מְכַפֵּר עַל יֵצֶר הָרָע, דְּהוּא בְּבֵי מוֹתְבֵיה דְּבַר נָשׁ.

157. "Come and see, it is written, 'You shall bring out of your habitations two wave loaves... they shall be of fine flour; they shall be baked with leaven (*chametz*)....' (Leviticus 23:17) Why is it different here that we bring leaven?" He answers: "It is because all are attached to the Tree, Zeir Anpin, when it is in completeness on Shavuot, since the branches are attached to the Tree, leaves are attached to the Tree, which are Klipot and many Judgments on every side, and it sweetens them. Everything is in it, for that Tree atones for the Evil Inclination in its dwelling place in man." For this reason leaven is brought that day, which is an indication that though Klipot are attached to it, they are nevertheless sweetened and there is no fear of their attachment.

The Torah is called the Tree of Life that stems from Binah.

158. אָמַר רְבִּי אֶלְעָזָר, מֵהַאי אִילָנָא אִתְזָנוּ כָּל שְׁאָר אִילָנִין לְתַתָּא. וְהוּא
אִשְׁתָּרְשָׁא עַל חַד נַהֲרָא עֲמֵיקָא, דְּנָגִיד וְנָפִיק וְלָא פַּסְקִין מֵימוֹי לְעָלְמִין.
עֲלֵיהּ כְּתִיב וְהָיָה כְּעֵץ שָׁתוּל עַל מַיִם וְעַל יוּבַל יְשַׁלַּח שָׁרָשָׁיו, וְעַל דָּא אִקְרֵי
אוֹרַיְיתָא, עֵץ חַיִּים הִיא וְגוֹ'. וּמַאי וְתוֹמְכֶיהָ מְאוּשָּׁר. הָא אוּקְמוּהָ, אֲבָל
וְתוֹמְכֶיהָ מְאוּשָּׁר, כד"א בְּאָשְׁרִי כִּי אִשְׁרוּנִי בָּנוֹת.

158. Rav Elazar said: "From this Tree, Zeir Anpin, **the other trees Below are nourished,** which are the grades in Malchut and Briyah, Yetzirah, and Asiyah. **It has its roots in a deep river that flows, and whose waters never stop flowing,** namely Binah. **It is written of it, 'For he shall be like a tree planted by the waters, and that spreads out its roots by the river...' (Jeremiah 17:8),** the river being Binah. **Hence the Torah,** Zeir Anpin, **is called "She is a Tree of Life..." (Proverbs 3:18),** since life is drawn from Binah." [He asks:] **"What is meant by, 'and happy are those who hold her fast' (Ibid.)?"** [He answers:] **"We explained it, yet 'happy are those who hold her fast' is similar to, 'Happy am I (***Oshri***), for the daughters will call me blessed...' (Genesis 30:13),** which alludes to Binah called Asher."

Emor

30. Shavuot Night

A Synopsis

We learn that one should study the Oral Torah on the night of Shavuot so that everything will be purified, and one should study the Written Torah on the day of Shavuot so that everything will be united. We read of the preparations for that Unification.

The night is the Oral Torah, and the day is the Written Torah.

167. וְאוֹלִיפְנָא, דְּאוֹרַיְיתָא דְּבָעֵי לֵיהּ לְמִלְעֵי בְּהַאי לֵילְיָא, אוֹרַיְיתָא דבע"פ, בְּגִין דְּיִתְדְּכוּן כַּחֲדָא, מִמַּבּוּעָא דְּנַחֲלָא עֲמִיקָא. לְבָתַר, בְּהַאי יוֹמָא, לֵיתֵי תוֹרָה שֶׁבִּכְתָב, וְיִתְחַבֵּר בָּהּ, וְיִשְׁתַּכְּחוּן כַּחֲדָא בְּזִוּוּגָא חַד לְעֵילָּא. כְּדֵין מַכְרִיזֵי עָלֵיהּ וְאָמְרֵי, וַאֲנִי זֹאת בְּרִיתִי אוֹתָם אָמַר יְיָ' רוּחִי אֲשֶׁר עָלֶיךָ וּדְבָרַי אֲשֶׁר שַׂמְתִּי בְּפִיךָ וְגוֹ'.

167. **We learned that the Torah that one needs to study this night** of Shavuot **is the Oral Torah,** which is Malchut **so that** Malchut and Israel, Her children, **will be purified together by the flowing of the deep river,** namely from Binah. **After that, during the day** on Shavuot **the Written Torah,** which is Zeir Anpin, **will come and join it,** Malchut, **so they will be together, united as one Above.** A proclamation then resounds concerning him, saying, "As for Me, this is My Covenant with them, says the Lord; My spirit that is upon you, and My words which I have put in your mouth…." (Isaiah 59:21)

Staying up all night on Shavuot to receive the Holy inheritance.

168. וְעַל דָּא, וַחֲסִידֵי קַדְמָאֵי לָא הֲווֹ נָיְימֵי בְּהַאי לֵילְיָא, וַהֲווֹ לָעָאן בְּאוֹרַיְיתָא, וְאָמְרֵי, נֵיתֵי לְאַחֲסָנָא יְרוּתָא קַדִּישָׁא, לָן, וְלִבְנָן, בִּתְרֵין עָלְמִין. וְהַהוּא לֵילְיָא

כְּנֶסֶת יִשְׂרָאֵל אִתְעַטְּרָא עָלַיְיהוּ, וְאַתְיָא לְאִזְדַּוּוְגָא בֵּיהּ בְּמַלְכָּא, וְתַרְוַיְיהוּ מִתְעַטְּרֵי עַל רֵישַׁיְיהוּ, דְּאִינּוּן דְּזַכָּאן לְהָכִי.

168. Therefore the pious in ancient times did not sleep that night but were studying the Torah, saying, "Let us come and receive this Holy inheritance for us and our children in both worlds." That night, the Congregation of Israel is an adornment over them, and she comes to unite with the King. Both crown the heads of those who merit this.

Preparing the jewels of the Bride.

169. ר״ע הָכִי אָמַר, בְּשַׁעֲתָא דְּמִתְכַּנְּשֵׁי חַבְרַיָּיא בְּהַאי לֵילְיָא לְגַבֵּיהּ, נֵיתֵי לְתַקְּנָא תַכְשִׁיטֵי כַּלָּה, בְּגִין דְּתִשְׁתְּכַח לִמְחָר בְּתַכְשִׁיטָהָא, וְתִקּוּנָהָא, לְגַבֵּי מַלְכָּא כַּדְקָא יָאוּת. זַכָּאָה חוּלָקֵיהוֹן דְּחַבְרַיָּיא, כַּד יִתְבַּע מַלְכָּא לְמַטְרוֹנִיתָא, מַאן תַּקִּין תַּכְשִׁיטָהָא, וְאַנְהִיר עִטְרָהָא, וְשַׁוֵּי תִקּוּנָהָא. וְלֵית לָהּ בְּעָלְמָא, מַאן דְּיָדַע לְתַקְּנָא תַכְשִׁיטֵי כַּלָּה, אֶלָּא חַבְרַיָּיא, זַכָּאָה חוּלָקֵיהוֹן בְּעָלְמָא דֵּין וּבְעָלְמָא דְּאָתֵי.

169. Rav Shimon said the following when the friends gathered with him that night: "Let us come and prepare the jewels of the Bride, namely draw Mochin upon Malchut, **so that tomorrow She will be bejeweled** with Mochin **and properly ready for the King.** Happy is the portion of the friends, when the King will ask the Queen who prepared her jewels, illuminated her Crowns and put on her adornments. No one in the world knows how to fix the adornments of the Bride except for the friends. Happy is their portion in this world and in the World to Come."

Binah readies the King, and the friends ready the Matron.

170. ת״ח, וְחַבְרַיָּיא מִתַקְּנֵי בְּהַאי לֵילְיָא תַכְשִׁיטָהָא לְכַלָּה, וּמְעַטְּרֵי לָהּ בְּעִטְרָהָא, לְגַבֵּי מַלְכָּא. וּמַאן מַתְקִין לֵיהּ לְמַלְכָּא, בְּהַאי לֵילְיָא, לְאִשְׁתַּכְּחָא בָּהּ בְּכַלָּה, לְאִזְדַּוּוְגָא בָּהּ בְּמַטְרוֹנִיתָא. נַהֲרָא קַדִּישָׁא עֲמִיקָא דְּכָל נַהֲרִין,

אִימָּא עִלָּאָה. הה"ד, צְאֶינָה וּרְאֶינָה בְּנוֹת צִיּוֹן בַּמֶּלֶךְ שְׁלֹמֹה וְגוֹ'. לְבָתַר
דְּאַתְקִינַת לֵיהּ לְמַלְכָּא, וְאַעְטָּרַת לֵיהּ, אַתְיָת לְדַכְּאָה לָהּ לְמַטְרוֹנִיתָא,
וּלְאִינּוּן דְּמִשְׁתַּכְּחֵי גַּבָּהּ.

170. Come and see, the friends prepare that night jewels for the
Bride, who is Malchut, and decorate her with Crowns to the King.
And who attends to the King, Zeir Anpin, that night so that He will
be with the Bride, and unite with the Matron, Malchut? It is the deep
stream, the deepest among the rivers, which is Supernal Ima, which
is Binah Who readies Zeir Anpin. This is the secret of, 'Go forth,
daughters of Zion, and behold King Solomon with the crown with
which his mother crowned him.' (Song of Songs 3:11) After Binah
readied the King and crowned him, she comes to purify the Matron
and those who stand by her, namely the friends that busy themselves
with preparing her.

Binah is like a mother who readies her son before the wedding.

171. לְמַלְכָּא דַּהֲוָה לֵיהּ בַּר יְחִידָאי, אָתָא כְּזִוּוּגָא לֵיהּ בְּמַטְרוֹנִיתָא עִלָּאָה, כָּאי
עֲבָדַת, אִמֵּיהּ כָּל הַהוּא לֵילְיָא, עָאלַת לְבֵי גְּנִיזָהָא, אַפִּיקַת עִטְרָא עִלָּאָה,
בְּשַׁבְעִין אַבְנֵי יְקָר סַחֲרָנָא, וְאַעְטָּרַת לֵיהּ. אַפִּיקַת לְבוּשִׁין דְּמֵילַת וְאַלְבִּישַׁת
לֵיהּ, וְאַתְקָנַת לֵיהּ בְּתִקּוּנֵי דְּמַלְכִין.

171. This is likened to a King who had an only son whom he was
about to marry to a lofty Matron. All that night, his mother
came to the treasure chambers and brought out a superior crown
surrounded by seventy precious stones, and crowned him. She
took out silken garments and put them on him, and fixed him with
royal embellishments.

The Matron and Her maidens purify themselves in the ritual bath.

172. לְבָתַר עָאלַת לְבֵי כַלָּה, וְחָמַאת עוּלֵימְתָאָ, דְּקָא מִתַּקְּנֵי עֲטָרָהָא, וּלְבוּשָׁהָא, וְתַכְשִׁיטָהָא, לְתַתְּקְנָא לָהּ. אָמְרָה לוֹן, הָא אֲתַתְקֵינַת בֵּי טְבִילָה, אֲתַר דְּמַיִּין נַבְעִין, וְכָל רֵיחִין וּבוּסְמִין סוּחֲרָנֵי אִינּוּן בַּיִּין, לְדַכְאָה לְכַלָּתִי, לֵיתֵי כַלָּתִי, מַטְרוֹנִיתָא דִּבְרִי, וְעוּלֵימְתָאָ, וְיִתְדְּכוּן בְּהַהוּא אֲתַר דְּאַתַתְקֵינַת בֵּי טְבִילָה, דְּמַיִּין נַבְעִין דְּעַמִי. לְבָתַר תַקִּינוּ לָהּ בְּתַכְשִׁיטָהָא, אַלְבִּישׁוּ לָהּ לְבוּשָׁהָא, אַעֲטָרוּ לָהּ בְּעֲטָרָהָא. לִמְחָר כַּד יֵיתֵי בְּרִי לְאִזְדַּוְּוגָא בְּמַטְרוֹנִיתָא, יַתְקִין הֵיכְלָא לְכֻלְּהוּ, וְיִשְׁתְּכַח מָדוֹרֵיהּ בְּכוּ כַּחֲדָא.

172. His mother **then entered the bride's home and saw maidens preparing crowns, garments and jewelry to adorn her. She said to them, "Behold, I prepared a house for a ritual bath, a place of fresh water with all scents and spices around it to purify my bride. Let the bride, my son's Matron, come together with her maidens, and let them purify themselves where I prepared a ritual bath that I have of fresh water. Afterwards, adorn her with her jewels, dress her with her garments, and put on her crowns. Tomorrow, when my son shall come to unite with the Matron, he shall prepare a palace for all, and he shall place his abode amongst you together."**

The King, the Matron, and the friends abide in one place.

173. כַּךְ מַלְכָּא קַדִּישָׁא וּמַטְרוֹנִיתָא, וְחַבְרַיָּיא, כְּהַאי גַּוְונָא. וְאִימָּא עִלָּאָה דִּמְתַּקְּנַת כֹּלָּא. אִשְׁתְּכַחוּ דְּמַלְכָּא עִלָּאָה, וּמַטְרוֹנִיתָא, וְחַבְרַיָּיא, מָדוֹרֵיהוֹן כַּחֲדָא, וְלָא מִתְפָּרְשִׁין לְעָלְמִין. הה"ד, יְיָ' בִּי מִי יָגוּר בְּאָהֳלֶךָ וְגוֹ', הוֹלֵךְ תָּמִים וּפֹעֵל צֶדֶק. מַאן הוּא פּוֹעֵל צֶדֶק. אֶלָּא, אִלֵּין אִינּוּן דִּמְתַּקְּנֵי לְמַטְרוֹנִיתָא בְּתַכְשִׁיטָהָא, בִּלְבוּשָׁהָא, בְּעֲטָרָהָא. וְכָל חַד, פּוֹעֵל צֶדֶק אִקְרֵי. א"ר חִיָּיא, אַלְמָלֵא לָא זָכֵינָא בְּעָלְמָא, אֶלָּא לְמִשְׁמַע מִלִּין אִלֵּין דַּי. זַכָּאָה חוּלָקֵיהוֹן דְּאִינּוּן דְּמִשְׁתַּדְּלֵי בְּאוֹרַיְיתָא, וְיַדְעִין אוֹרְחוֹי דְּמַלְכָּא קַדִּישָׁא, דְּרָעוּתָא דִּלְהוֹן בְּאוֹרַיְיתָא, עֲלַיְיהוּ כְּתִיב כִּי בִי חָשַׁק וַאֲפַלְּטֵהוּ. וּכְתִיב אֲשַׂגְּבֵהוּ וְאֲכַבְּדֵהוּ.

173. So it is with the Holy King, the Matron, Malchut, and the friends, and also Supernal Ima, Binah, Who prepares everything. It is found that the Supernal King, Zeir Anpin, the Matron, Malchut, and the friends live together and never separate. This is the meaning behind, "...who shall abide in Your tent... He that walks uprightly, and acts justly...." (Psalms 15:1-2) Who acts justly? Those who prepare the Matron with her adornments, garments, and Crowns. Each one is considered one who acts righteously, since Malchut is called righteousness. Rav Chiya said: "If I achieved nothing in this world except to hear these words, it would suffice me. Happy is the portion of those who study the Torah and know the ways of the Holy King, Whose desire is for the Torah. Of them it is written, 'Because he has set his delight upon Me, therefore I will set him on high... I will deliver him, and honor him.' (Psalms 91:14-15)

EMOR

31. The Counting of the Omer and the Holiday of Shavuot

A Synopsis

We are told that Israel do not recite the Halel in full as in the days of Pesach since they are not yet properly whole and pure. We are told about the fifty days of purification, the purpose of which is to enter the secret of the World to Come, to receive the Torah, and to draw Malchut near Zeir Anpin. Forty-Nine of those days are all the aspects of the Torah, while the Fiftieth day is the secret of the Torah itself. On the Fiftieth day, Shavuot, the hidden is revealed. The two loaves of the offering are the secret of the two Shechinahs, the Upper and the Lower, Who join together. Zeir Anpin receives from Above and from Below, from Binah and Malchut because Shabbat is a secret Above and Below.

The seven weeks Above and Below are included in the Fiftieth Day.

180. שְׁבוּעוֹת, וְלָא כְּתִיב כַּמָּה אִינּוּן. אֶלָּא בְּכָל אֲתַר דְּאִתְּמַר סְתָם, שְׁמָא גָּרִים דְּאִינּוּן מִן שֶׁבַע. וּכְתִיב שִׁבְעָה שָׁבוּעוֹת תִּסְפָּר לָךְ, אֲמַאי כְּתִיב שְׁבוּעוֹת בְּלְחוֹדוֹי. אֶלָּא הָכִי אִצְטְרִיךְ שָׁבוּעוֹת סְתָם, לְאַכְלְלָא עֵילָא וְתַתָּא, דְּהָא בְּכָל אֲתַר דְּאָלֵין מִתְעָרֵי, אִלֵּין אוּף הָכִי מִתְעָרֵי עִמְּהוֹן. עַד לָא הֲוָה שְׁלִמוּ, לָא הֲווֹ אִתְגַּלְיָין, כֵּיוָן דְּאָתָא שְׁלִמוּ, עָבֵד מִנַּיְיהוּ פְּרָט. דִּכְתִיב, שִׁבְעַת יָמִים וְשִׁבְעַת יָמִים, דָּא אִיהוּ פְּרָט.

180. [He says:] "It is written **Shavuot (weeks)** but not how many weeks there are." He answers: "**Wherever it plainly says** weeks, **the name implies there are seven** weeks, **as it is written, 'Seven weeks shall you number to you....'** (Deuteronomy 16:9) **And why does it only say 'weeks'** when there are seven? **It actually should be** written **plainly 'weeks,'** for it comes **to include the** seven weeks **Above and the** seven weeks **Below,** as all are included in the Fiftieth day. **For whenever these,** the seven weeks Above, **stir, these,** the seven weeks Below, **stir as well.**

Until Solomon came and attained the Fiftieth Gate, and the moon was full, **they were not revealed. Once Solomon came, he individualized them, as it is written, '…seven days, and seven days….'** (I Kings 8:65) **This is individualization,** namely the fourteen days revealed by the Fiftieth Gate were detailed."

Only in the generation of King Solomon was the Fiftieth Gate revealed.

181. בְּזִמְנָא אָחֳרָא בִּכְלַל, שָׁבוּעוֹת סְתָם. וְלָא אִצְטְרִיךְ לְבַר נָשׁ אָחֳרָא לְמֶעְבַּד מִנְּהוֹן פְּרָט, בַּר שְׁלֹמֹה. בְּגִין דְּאִינּוּן שִׁבְעַת יָמִים דִּלְתַתָּא, לָא נְהִירוּ בִּשְׁלִימוּ, עַד דְּאָתָא שְׁלֹמֹה, וּכְדֵין קַיְּימָא סִיהֲרָא בְּאַשְׁלְמוּתָא, בְּאִינּוּן שִׁבְעַת יוֹמִין. וְהָכָא חַג שָׁבוּעוֹת סְתָם, בְּגִין דְּאִתְכְּלָלוּ תַּתָּאֵי בְּעִלָּאֵי, וְלָא אַנְהִירוּ כְּיוֹמָא דִשְׁלֹמֹה.

181. During other times, besides the days of Solomon, there are no individual fourteen days, but **only included in weeks in general, for no one else may individualize them except Solomon. For the seven days Below did not shine wholly** from the seven days Above, **until Solomon arrived and the moon remained full during these seven days. But here, it is plainly "Feast of Weeks,"** not mentioned in detail, **because the Lower** Seven Days **were included in the Upper** Seven Days **and do not shine** there as during the days of Solomon.

The two loaves of Shavuot represent Binah and Malchut that join together.

182. פִּקּוּדָא בָּתַר דָּא, לְקָרְבָא שְׁתֵּי הַלֶּחֶם. הָא אוּקִימְנָא, שְׁתֵּי הַלֶּחֶם: תַּרְתֵּי שְׁכִינְתֵּי, עֵילָּא וְתַתָּא, וְאִתְחַבְּרָן כַּחֲדָא. לְגַבֵּיהוֹן, תְּרֵין נַהֲמֵי בְּשַׁבָּת, מְזוֹנָא חַד תְּרֵין, דְּעֵילָּא וְתַתָּא. וְעַל דָּא כְּתִיב, שְׁנֵי הָעֹמֶר לָאֶחָד. לָאֶחָד וַדַּאי, לְאִתְיַחֲדָא בְּאֲתַר חַד. לְהַהוּא דְּאִקְרֵי אֶחָד. וּמַאן אִיהוּ. הַקּוֹל קוֹל יַעֲקֹב, דְּאִיהוּ יָרִית עֵילָּא וְתַתָּא, תְּרֵין נַהֲמֵי כַּחֲדָא. וּבְגִין דְּשַׁבָּת אִיהוּ רָזָא דְעֵילָּא וְתַתָּא, וְכֹלָּא אִיהוּ שַׁבָּת, תְּרֵין נַהֲמֵי.

182. The following Precept is to offer the two loaves, as we explained that the two loaves are the secret of the two Shechinahs, the Upper, Binah, **and the Lower,** Malchut, **that join together,** and the Lower Beings who receive from Malchut are as if they receive from Binah, since they are joined. **There are two corresponding loaves of bread on Shabbat,** the double bread, **which is a double provision, from Above and from Below,** from Binah and from Malchut. **Therefore it is written: "…two Omers for one man…"** (Exodus 16:22), which also alludes to Binah and Malchut. **Surely they are "for one" because they come together in one place,** namely **in that which is called "One."** **What is it? It is, "…the voice is Jacob's voice…"** (Genesis 27:22), namely Zeir Anpin, **Who receives from Above and from Below,** from Binah and Malchut, namely **two loaves together. This is because Shabbat is the secret of Above and Below** together; because Malchut ascends then and clothes Binah, they are joined together, **and everything** together **is called Shabbat,** namely **the two loaves.**

In each Holiday, we sacrifice an additional offering.

‫183. פְּקוּדָא בָּתַר דָּא לְהַסְדִּיר לֶחֶם וּלְבוֹנָה, לְהַקְרִיב עֹמֶר. דִּכְתִיב וַעֲשִׂיתֶם בְּיוֹם הֲנִיפְכֶם אֶת הָעֹמֶר כֶּבֶשׂ תָּמִים לְעוֹלָה. וְכֵן בְּשָׁבוּעוֹת לְהַקְרִיב שְׁתֵּי הַלֶּחֶם, וְהָכִי בְּכָל יוֹמִין טָבִין, לְהַקְרִיב קָרְבָּן דְּמוּסָפִין. אֶלָּא וַדַּאי בְּכָל יוֹמָא דְּמוֹעֲדַיָּיא צָרִיךְ לְקָרְבָּא קָרְבְּנָא דִּילֵיהּ. צָרִיךְ לְקָרְבָא עֲלֵיהּ תּוֹסֶפֶת דְּאִית לֵיהּ, כְּגוֹן תּוֹסֶפֶת כְּתוּבָּתָא וּמַתְּנָתָא, דְּאוֹסִיף וְיָהַן לְכַלָּה. וְשַׁבָּת מַלְכְּתָא, דְּאִיהִי כַּלָּה, בְּשַׁבָּתוֹת וּבְכָל יוֹמִין טָבִין, צְרִיכָה תּוֹסֶפֶת, דְּאִינּוּן מוּסָפִין דְּקָרְבְּנִין, וּמַתְּנָתָא, דְּאִינּוּן מַתְּנוֹת כְּהוּנָה.‬

183. The following Precept is to arrange the bread and the Frankincense for the Omer offering, as it is written: **"And you shall offer that day when you wave the Omer a lamb without blemish of the first year for a burnt offering** to the Lord… And the meal offering thereof shall be two tenth measures of fine flour mingled…." (Leviticus 23:12-13) **Similarly, to sacrifice the two loaves on**

Shavuot. And so too, to sacrifice an additional (Musaf) sacrifice on all holidays. Assuredly on every day during the festivals, its sacrifice should be offered, namely the sacrifice of the day, just like during weekdays, and also on it sacrifice the addition it has, namely the secret of the additional Light on that holiday. This is like an addition on the Ketubah and gifts the groom gives the bride. Also the Shabbat Queen, Malchut, is a bride during Shabbats and all holidays, and is in need of an addition, which are the additional (Musaf) sacrifices, and the offerings, which are the offering from the priesthood.

The two loaves represent the Two Tablets.

184. וּבְשָׁבוּעוֹת דְּאִיהוּ מַתַּן תּוֹרָה, דְּאִתְיְיהִיבוּ תְּרֵין לוּחִין דְּאוֹרַיְיתָא, מִסִּטְרָא דְּאִילָנָא דְּחַיֵּי, צָרִיךְ לְקָרְבָא לְגַבַּיְיהוּ, שְׁתֵּי הַלֶּחֶם דְּאִינּוּן ה"ה דְּהָא אִיהוּ נַהֲמָא דְּאוֹרַיְיתָא, דְּאִתְּמַר בֵּיהּ לְכוּ לַחֲמוּ בְּלַחְמִי, ה"ה, מִן הַמּוֹצִיא לֶחֶם מִן הָאָרֶץ.

184. On Shavuot, which is the Giving of the Torah, when the two Tablets of the Torah, Binah and Malchut, were given from the aspect of the Tree of Life, which is Zeir Anpin, we need to sacrifice to them the two loaves of bread, the secret of Hei and Hei (ה"ה), namely Binah and Malchut, the two Hei's of the Yud-Hei-Vav-Hei. For they are the bread of the Torah, Zeir Anpin, of which it is said, "Come, eat of my bread...." (Proverbs 9:5) They are Hei and Hei of 'Hamotzi (who brings forth; הַמּוֹצִיא)... Ha'aretz (the earth; הָאָרֶץ).' The Earth is the Lower Hei, Malchut, and the Hei of Hamotzi is the first Hei, Binah.

The bread of wheat is human food, and the Omer of barley is animal food.

185. וְהַאי אִיהוּ מַאֲכַל אָדָם, דְּאִיהוּ יוֹ"ד ה"א וָא"ו ה"א. זֹאת הַתּוֹרָה אָדָם. אָדָם כִּי יַקְרִיב מִכֶּם קָרְבָּן לַיָי. עוֹמֶר שְׂעוֹרִין, מַאֲכָל בְּעִירָן, דְּאִינּוּן חֵיוָות הַקֹּדֶשׁ, דְּמִנְּהוֹן צָרִיךְ לְקָרְבָא, הה"ד מִן הַבְּהֵמָה. אֵלִים: מְנַגְּחִים בְּמַתְנִיתִין, בְּאִלֵּין פַּשְׁטִין. מִן הַבָּקָר: פָּרִים מְנַגְּחִים בְּמַתְנִיתִין, בְּתוּקְפָּא יַתִּיר. וּמִן הַצֹּאן:

שְׁאָר עַמָּא, קָרְבְּנָא דִּלְהוֹן צְלוֹתִין, וְעָלַיְיהוּ אִתְּמַר, וְאַתֵּן צֹאנִי צֹאנֵי צֹאן מַרְעִיתִי אָדָם אַתֶּם.

185. This, the two loaves, **is food for man, who is Yud-Vav-Dalet, Hei -Alef, Vav-Alef-Vav, Hei-Alef (הֹא ואו הֹא יוֹד),** which has the same numerical value as *adam* (man; 45), namely Zeir Anpin that includes the two Hei's. This is the meaning of, **"This is the Torah: (when) a man...."** (Numbers 19:14) It indicates that the Torah, which is the secret of Zeir Anpin, is the secret of the Yud-Hei-Vav-Hei of MaH (מ"ה; 45), the numerical value of *adam* (man; 45). **"If any man of you bring an offering [of the cattle] to the Lord. [You shall choose your offering from the herd and from the flock.]"** (Leviticus 1:2) is the secret of food for man. But **the Omer of barley is food for animals, which are the Holy Living Creatures, of which one should offer. This is the secret of: "of the cattle" (Ibid.),** which is the secret of **the rams that lock horns** against each other **in the Mishnah regarding the literal explanation of the Torah.** These are the sages that fight each other when explaining the Mishnah. **"...of the herd..." (Ibid.)** refers to **bullocks that gore each other more forcefully in the Mishnah. "... and of the flock..." (Ibid.) refers to the rest of the people, whose sacrifice is prayer, of whom it is said, "But you My flock, the flock of My pasture, you are men...."** (Ezekiel 34:31) "...the flock of My pasture..." (Ibid.) are those who study the literal meaning of the Torah only. "...you are men..." (Ibid.) are the sages who study Kabbalah, who cleave to Zeir Anpin, the secret of Yud-Hei-Vav-Hei of the spelling out of MaH (הֹא ואו הֹא יוֹד; 45), which is the numerical value of *adam* (man; 45).

A Synopsis

We are given more details about the sacrifices and the offerings. We are told that the masters of Kabbalah derive from the aspect of the Tree of Life; the rest of the people are from the side of the Tree of Knowledge of Good and Evil that are the permissible and the forbidden. Those from the Tree of Life are men whose Torah is the Bread of God.

Kabbalah is the Tree of Life, and the Mishnah is
the Tree of Knowledge of Good and Evil.

186. דְּמָארֵי קַבָּלָה, וּמָארֵי מִדּוֹת, אִינּוּן מִסִּטְרָא דְּאִילָנָא דְּחַיֵּי. שְׁאַר עַמָּא מִסִּטְרָא דְּאִילָנָא דְּטוֹב וָרָע, אָסוּר וְהֶתֵּר. וּבְגִין דָּא, מִן הַבְּהֵמָה, מַאֲכָל דִּלְהוֹן, עֹמֶר לֶחֶם שְׂעוֹרִים, וַיָּמָד שֵׁשׁ שְׂעוֹרִים. וַיָּשֶׁת עָלֶיהָ, אוֹרַיְיתָא דִּבְעַל פֶּה, דְּשִׁיתא סִדְרֵי מִשְׁנָה. אֲבָל אִלֵּין דְּאִילָנָא דְּחַיֵּי, דְּאִינּוּן אָדָם אוֹרַיְיתָא דִּלְהוֹן, נַהֲמָא דְּקוּדְשָׁא בְּרִיךְ הוּא. הה"ד, לְכוּ לַחֲמוּ בְלַחְמִי וְהַיְינוּ שְׁתֵּי הַלֶּחֶם. וְדָא כֻלְּהוּ תָּנָאִין וַאֲמוֹרָאִין, וְאָמְרוּ מַאן קָאֵים קַמֵּי סִינַי.
ע"כ רעיא מהימנא

186. **The masters of Kabbalah and masters of qualities,** who are cleaved to the qualities of Zeir Anpin, **are from the side of the Tree of Life,** which is Zeir Anpin, called "man." **The rest of the people are from the side of the Tree of Knowledge of Good and Evil, which are the permissible and the forbidden.** This is the Angel Metatro"n, who is so called. He is a Chariot to Malchut called Mishnah, and he includes the Four Holy Living Creatures. **Therefore those "...of the cattle..."** (Leviticus 1:2) **eat an Omer of barley bread,** as written: "...he **measured six measures of barley, and laid it on her....."** (Ruth 3:15) This is the secret of **the Oral Torah of the Six Orders of the Mishnah. But those from the Tree of Life,** the masters of Kabbalah, **are men whose Torah is the bread of the Holy One, blessed be He,** namely the food of Zeir Anpin that is called "man." **This is the meaning of, "Come, eat of my bread,"** namely the two loaves of bread. All the

Tannaim and Amoraim rejoiced and said: "Who can stand before Sinai, namely before the Faithful Shepherd, who is called Sinai."
End of Ra'aya Meheimna (Faithful Shepherd)

PINCHAS

113. Shavuot

A Synopsis

We learn that the Torah depends on the River issuing forth from Eden.

The "day" of the First Fruits refers to Zeir Anpin.

766. וּבְיוֹם הַבִּכּוּרִים בְּהַקְרִיבְכֶם מִנְחָה חֲדָשָׁה וְגוֹ'. אָמַר רְבִּי אַבָּא, יוֹם הַבִּכּוּרִים, מַאן יוֹם. דָּא נָהָר הַיּוֹצֵא מֵעֵדֶן, דְּאִיהוּ יוֹמָא מֵאִינּוּן בְּכוּרִין עִלָּאִין. וְדָא אִיהוּ דְּאוֹרַיְיתָא תַּלְיָא בֵּיהּ, וְאִיהוּ אַפִּיק כָּל רָזִין דְּאוֹרַיְיתָא. וּבְגִין דְּאִיהוּ אִילָנָא דְחַיֵּי, פְּרִי אִילָנָין אִצְטְרִיכוּ לְאַיְיתָאָה.

766. **"And on the day of the First Fruits, when you bring a new meal offering to the Lord..."** (Numbers 28:26) Rav Aba said, "It is written 'the day of the first fruits,' (Ibid.) but what does 'day' refer to?" He answers that **this is a river issuing forth from Eden,** namely Zeir Anpin, **which is a day of those Upper First Fruits,** namely Yud-Hei, Aba and Ima, who are called First Fruits. **And upon it the Torah depends,** namely Zeir Anpin, **and He brings forth all the secrets of the Torah, and because He is the Tree of Life, the Fruit of the Tree has to be brought.**

A Synopsis

Moses says that Israel is the First Fruits for God of all the nations in the world. He tells us that Vav (ו) is the River that comes out of Eden, and that when the River comes out then all the secrets of the Torah also come out. Moses talks about the six Sefirot that are called the primordial years of the creation of the world. As the six Sefirot preceded the world and all the creatures, they are called First Fruits. Man is called the firstborn son after the Name of the sign of

the covenant that is Yud (י). Lastly the Faithful Shepherd tells us
that the Torah is called "Glory," and anyone who studies Torah is
called a king.

Israel is considered the firstborn of the Creator.

רעיא מהימנא

767. וּבְיוֹם הַבִּכּוּרִים בְּהַקְרִיבְכֶם מִנְחָה חֲדָשָׁה וְגוֹ'. רַבִּי אַבָּא אָמַר, יוֹם
הַבִּכּוּרִים אִינּוּן בִּכּוּרִים עִלָּאִין דְּאוֹרַיְיתָא. הֲ"ד, רֵאשִׁית בִּכּוּרֵי אַדְמָתְךָ
תָּבִיא וְגוֹ'. אָמַר ר"מ, כְּגַוְונָא דְּבִכּוֹרִים לְאִמְּהוֹן, אוֹף הָכִי אִתְקְרִיאוּ פֵּירוֹת
בִּכּוּרִים, דְּפֵירוֹת דְּאִילָנִין, כְּבִכּוּרָה בַּתְאֵנָה, הָכִי יִשְׂרָאֵל קַדְמוֹנִים וּבִכּוּרִים
לְקוּדְשָׁא בְּרִיךְ הוּא, מִכָּל אוּמִּין דְּעָלְמָא, הֲ"ד קֹדֶשׁ יִשְׂרָאֵל לַיְדֹוָ"ד וְגוֹ'.
וּבְגִ"ד אִתְּמַר בְּהוֹן, תָּבִיא בֵּית יְהֹוָה אֱלֹהֶיךָ. וּבְגִין דָּא אוּמִין עכו"ם, דְּאִתְּמַר
בְּהוֹן וַיֹּאכְלוּ אֶת יִשְׂרָאֵל בְּכָל פֶּה. יֶאְשָׁמוּ רָעָה תָּבֹא אֲלֵיהֶם.

Ra'aya Meheimna (Faithful Shepherd)

767. "And on the day of the first fruits, when you bring a new meal
offering to the Lord." (Numbers 28:26) Rav Aba said, "'The day of
the first fruits' (Ibid.) refers to the Upper First Fruits of the Torah,
namely Aba and Ima, as it is written: 'The first of the first fruits of
your land you shall bring….' (Exodus 23:19)" The Faithful Shepherd
said, "Just as the firstborn to their mother, so are the first fruits of
the tree called, '…the first ripe fruit in the fig…' (Hosea 9:10) so too,
are Israel the first fruits for the Holy One, blessed be He, of all the
nations of the world, as it is written: 'Israel is holy to the Lord, the
first fruits of His harvest….' (Jeremiah 2:3) For this reason, about
them it is said, about the first fruits that allude to Israel, '…you shall
bring to the house of the Lord your God…' (Exodus 23:19), namely
that they should merit complete redemption. And because of what is
said about the idolatrous nations, '…and they devour Israel with
open mouth…' (Isaiah 9:11) about them is also said, '…all that devour
him shall be held guilty; evil shall come upon them.' (Jeremiah 2:3)

Zeir Anpin is called Firstborn, and all that branches
from Him are called First Fruits.

768. אוֹף הָכִי ו' דְּכָלִיל שִׁית סְפִירָאָן, וְאִיהוּ בֵּן י"ה, אִתְקְרֵי בַּכ"ר. וְכָל עַנְפִין דְּנַפְקִין מִנֵּיהּ דִּבְהוֹן רָאשִׁין, אִתְקְרִיאוּ בְּכוּרִים. ו' אִיהוּ נָהָר, מֵאִינוּן בְּכוּרִים עִלָּאִין, וְהַהוּא נָהָר נָפִיק מֵעֵדֶן. וְדָא אִיהוּ דְּאוֹרַיְיתָא תַּלְיָא בֵּיהּ. וְכַד נָפִיק נַפְקֵי כָּל רָזִין דְּאוֹרַיְיתָא, וּבְגִין דְּאִיהוּ אִילָנָא דְּחַיֵּי אוֹרַיְיתָא, הֲדָא הוּא דִּכְתִּיב, עֵץ חַיִּים הִיא לַמַּחֲזִיקִים בָּהּ. וּפִקּוּדִין דִּילָהּ דַּמְיָין לְאִיבָּא פְּרִי דְּאִילָנִין, אִצְטְרִיכוּ לְאַיְיתָאָה.

768. "And so too, Vav (ו), which is Zeir Anpin, **that includes six Sefirot, and is the son of Yud-Hei,** Aba and Ima that are called First Fruits, **is called a Firstborn. And all the branches that come out from it and in which there are heads,** the levels that contain the Upper Three Sefirot that are termed 'head,' **are called First Fruits. Vav is a river of those Upper First Fruits,** being Zeir Anpin, **and this is the River that comes out of Eden,** which is Yud-Hei, **and it is on this that the Torah is dependent. And when it comes out** and is revealed, **then all secrets of the Torah come out because it is both the Tree of Life and the Torah, as it is written, 'She is a Tree of Life to those who lay hold on Her....' (Proverbs 3:18) And the Precepts** of Zeir Anpin, who is the Torah, **are like the buds of the fruit of the Tree that have to be brought** to the house of the Lord."

Why it takes six months for fruits to ripen,
and why the Sefirot are called Living Creatures.

769. אָמַר רַעְיָא מְהֵימְנָא וְאִי תֵּימְרוּן אֲמַאי בְּכוּרִים, דִּלְהוֹן אִתְקְרִיאוּ בִּמְנֶזה וַדָשָׁה, בְּשִׁית יַרְחִין לְשִׁיּת יַרְחִין. וּמִבַּר נָשׁ דְּאִתָּמַר בֵּיהּ כִּי הָאָדָם עֵץ הַשָּׂדֶה לְתִשְׁעָה יַרְחִין, אוֹ לְשִׁבְעָה. וּבְעֵירָא אוֹף הָכִי, שִׁבְעַת יָמִים יִהְיֶה תַּחַת אִמּוֹ וּמִיּוֹם הַשְּׁמִינִי וָהָלְאָה יֵרָצֶה לְקָרְבַּן אִשֶּׁה לַיהֹוָה, לְקָרְבָּא קָרְבְּנָא קֳדָם יְיָ'. וְעוֹד סְפִירָאָן, בְּהוֹן שֵׁם יְהֹוָה, וְכָל כִּנּוּיִין דִּילֵיהּ, אֲמַאי אִתְקְרִיאוּ בְּשֵׁם חַיּוֹן.

769. The Faithful Shepherd said, "You might ask why are the first fruits that are called '…a new meal offering…' (Numbers 28:26) to be found on the tree **for periods of six months?** That is, during the six months of the winter and autumn they are on the tree as a fetus in its mother's womb, and from when they start growing until they are fully ripe another six months pass. **What is the reason for this taking six months? And again, about man it is said, '…For is the tree of the field a man….' (Deuteronomy 20:19)** What is the reason for his having **a nine- or seven-month** gestation period? **And about cattle it is also** said, **'then it shall be seven days with his mother; and from the eighth day and thenceforth it shall be accepted for an offering made by fire to the Lord' (Leviticus 22:27), namely to be offered as a sacrifice before the Lord.** And what is the reason for the seven days being required? **Furthermore, why are the Sefirot, in which are the Name of Yud-Hei-Vav-Hei and all His appellations, called by the Names of the Living Creatures,** namely Lion, Ox, Eagle, and Man?"

The six months allude to the six Sefirot that preceded the world.

770. אֶלָּא מִנְחָה וַחֲדָשָׁה בְּאֹרַח רָזָא, דָּא שְׁכִינְתָּא. מִשִּׁית יַרְחִין לְשִׁית יַרְחִין, אִינּוּן שִׁית סְפִירָאן, דְּאִתְקְרִיאוּ שָׁנִים קַדְמוֹנִיּוֹת לִבְרִיאַת עָלְמָא, דְּאִינּוּן שִׁיתָא אַלְפֵי שְׁנִין הֲוֵי עָלְמָא, מִסִּטְרָא דְּאִימָּא עִלָּאָה. וּמִסִּטְרָא דְּאִימָּא תַּתָּאָה, אִתְקְרִיאוּ יַרְחִין. וּבְגִין דְּקַדְמוּ לְעָלְמָא, וְכָל בִּרְיָין, אִתְקְרִיאוּ בִּכּוּרִים.

770. He answers: **"However, '…a new meal offering…' (Numbers 28:26) in the way of secret means the Shechinah. From six months to six months** that the fruits are gestating on the Tree **refers to the six** Sefirot Chesed, Gevurah, Tiferet, Netzach, Hod, and Yesod **that are called the primordial years of the creation of the world, which are the secret of the six thousand years that the world has been in existence,** and they are called 'years' **from the aspect of Supernal Ima,** which is Binah, **while from the aspect of Lower Ima,** which is Malchut, **they are called 'months.' And because these** six

Sefirot **preceded the world and all the creatures, they are called First Fruits,** and this is the secret why the fruit of the Tree are First Fruits of six months, from the time they start growing until they are fully ripe, namely corresponding to Chesed, Gevurah, Tiferet, Netzach, Hod, and Yesod from the aspect of Malchut.

Nine months of pregnancy plus man equals ten.

771. וּשְׁכִינְתָּא מִנְוָה וַחֲדָשָׁה, מִסִּטְרָא דְּחֵיָּיה, דְּאִתְּמַר בָּה וּדְמוּת פְּנֵיהֶם פְּנֵי אָדָם. וְאִיהוּ תֵּשַׁע לְחֶשְׁבּוֹן זְעֵיר דַּחֲנוֹךְ. אִיהוּ בַּר נָשׁ דְּאִתְיְלִיד לְתִשְׁעַ יַרְחִין דְּעוֹבְרָא, דְּאִיהִי עֲשִׂירָאָה. וּבְדָא כָּלִיל מִכֻּלְּהוּ, וְאִתְקְרֵי בֵּן בּוּכְרָא, עַל שֵׁם אוֹת בְּרִית, דְּאִיהוּ י', טִפָּה קַדְמָאָה דְּאִתְמְשַׁךְ מִנֵּיהּ זֶרַע יוֹרֶה כְּחֵץ. דְּאִיהוּ ו', וְאִיהוּ י', סָלִיק עַל ו', כְּאִיבָא דְּסָלִיק עַל עַנְפָא דְּאִילָנָא.

771. **"And the Shechinah is '...a new meal offering...' (Numbers 28:26) from the aspect of the Living Creature about Whom is said, 'As for the likeness of their faces, they had the face of a man....' (Ezekiel 1:10)** That is the nine months of gestation, for the numerical value of 'man' (adam; 45) **is nine in the small numerical value of Enoch.** The value of the letters is considered only as a number of units in the secret of the small numerical value that pertains to Metatro"n, who is called Enoch—such that the letter Mem (40) will be only four and so too, Tav (400) will be only four, and so on—so that the numerical value of Adam (45) is nine, as four plus five equals nine. **And this is** the secret of **man, who is born after nine months of gestation,** and the born man **is the tenth** to them **and is thereby included in all Ten Sefirot. And** man **is named the 'firstborn son'** after the Sign of the Covenant, which is Yesod, **which is Yud (10 י),** named after **the first drop drawn out of him, a seed shot as an arrow,** from which man is born. And every drop is called Yud because it includes Ten Sefirot. **And** Yesod is Vav (6 ו) and the drop is **as Yud that rises over Vav,** which is Yesod, **just as the fruit rises over the branch of the tree. And**

because there are the Upper Three in the Ten Sefirot, which are the secret of First Fruits, man is therefore called a 'firstborn son.'

The First Fruits ripen first because they contain the Upper Three Sefirot.

772. וְאע"ג דְּכַמָּה עַנְפִין אִית בְּאִילָנָא, וְכַמָּה תְּאֵנִים עֲלַיְיהוּ, אִינּוּן דְּאַקְדִּימוּ בְּקַדְמֵיתָא, אִתְקְרִיאוּ בִּכּוּרִים. אִלֵּין אִינּוּן רֵישִׁין דְּכֻלְּהוּ. כְּגַוְונָא דְּלְהוֹן אִתְּמַר שְׂאוּ שְׁעָרִים רָאשֵׁיכֶם. שְׂאוּ מָרוֹם עֵינֵיכֶם וּרְאוּ מִי בָרָא אֵלֶּה. שְׂאוּ אֶת רֹאשׁ כָּל עֲדַת בְּנֵי יִשְׂרָאֵל.

772. "And although there are many branches on the tree, on which are a number of figs, those that ripen **first at the beginning are called First Fruits. And these are the 'heads' of all of them, and on a par with them it is said: 'Lift up your heads, you gates...'** (Psalms 24:7), meaning, **'Lift up your eyes on high, and behold who has created these?'** (Isaiah 40:26) and also **'Take the sum (lit. 'Lift the head') of all the congregation of the children of Israel....'** (Numbers 1:2)

Explanation: The Zohar says that the reason why man is called Firstborn is that he comes from the drop of Yesod, which is the secret of Yud that includes Ten Sefirot, within which are the Upper Three—Keter, Chochmah, Binah—which are called First Fruits. According to this, all humankind should be the first fruits, so why is only the first son called Firstborn? To answer this the Zohar says: **"And although there are many...those** that ripen **first at the beginning are called First Fruits."** The revelation of the Upper Three, which are called First Fruits, is only on the first fruit and on the first born son. The Upper Three are not revealed on the remaining children even though they come from the Yud. This is: **"And these are the 'heads' of all of them,"** as the first son is the head of all the others. This means that the Upper Three called "head" are revealed in him, and from him the head shines to the remaining children. The Zohar brings evidence that "head" refers to the Upper Three from the verse: **"Lift up your heads, you gates...,"**

(Psalms 24:7) as the lifting up here refers to the Upper Three, like in the verse **"Lift up your eyes on high…"** (Isaiah 40:26), which refers to the Upper Three, since eyes refer to Chochmah. Similarly, "Lift the head of all the congregation of the children of Israel…" (Numbers 1:2) also refers to the Upper Three. So too, the First Fruits are called "head" due to the Upper Three.

The Gates are the Celestial Academy and
the doors are the Terrestrial Academy.

773. שְׂאוּ שְׁעָרִים רָאשֵׁיכֶם. שְׁעָרִים אִלֵּין, אִינוּן חַמְשִׁין תַּרְעִין דְּבִינָה. דְּאִיהִי מְתִיבְתָּא דִלְעֵילָא. וּשְׂאוּ פִּתְחֵי עוֹלָם, דְּמְתִיבְתָּא תַּתָּאָה, דְּכָל מַאן דְּאִשְׁתָּדַּל בְּאוֹרַיְיתָא לְסוֹף מִתְנַשֵּׂא. הֲהַ"ד, אִם נָבַלְתָּ בְהִתְנַשֵּׂא. וְאוֹקְמוּהָ מָארֵי מַתְנִיתִין, כָּל הַמְנַבֵּל עַצְמוֹ עַל דִּבְרֵי תוֹרָה, לְסוֹף מִתְנַשֵּׂא, וְיָבֹא מֶלֶךְ הַכָּבוֹד, וְלֵית כָּבוֹד אֶלָּא תּוֹרָה.

73. "'Lift up your heads, you gates….' (Psalms 24:7) 'Gates' here are the Fifty Gates of Binah, which are the Celestial Academy. '…and be lifted up, you everlasting doors…' (Ibid.) refers to the doors of the Terrestrial Academy,** which is Malchut, **for everyone who engages in the Torah is, at the end, lifted, as it is written: 'If you have done foolishly in lifting yourself up….' (Proverbs 30:32) And the sages of the Mishnah taught, 'Whoever abases himself (acts foolishly) for words of the Torah will, in the end, be exalted.' (Tractate Berachot 63b) And this is the meaning of '…and the King of glory shall come in' (Psalms 24:7), since there is no glory except the Torah.**

One who studies Torah is a king in both Worlds.

774. מֵהָכָא, מַאן דְּיָלִיף אוֹרַיְיתָא דְּאִתְקְרִיאַת כָּבוֹד, אִקְרֵי מֶלֶךְ. וְלָא הֵימָא בְּהַהוּא עָלְמָא דְּאָתֵי וְלָא יַתִּיר, אֶלָּא מֶלֶךְ בִּתְרֵין עָלְמִין, בְּדִיוּקְנָא דְּמָארֵיה. וּבְגִין דָּא כָּפוּל פָּסוּקָא תְּרֵין זִמְנִין, חַד מִי זֶה מֶלֶךְ הַכָּבוֹד. תִּנְיָינָא מִי הוּא זֶה

מֶלֶךְ הַכָּבוֹד. שְׂאוּ שְׁעָרִים רָאשֵׁיכֶם, מַאי רָאשֵׁיכֶם תְּרֵין זִמְנִין. אִינּוּן חֵיוָן דִּמֶרְכַּבְתָּא עִלָּאָה, וְחֵיוָן דִּמֶרְכַּבְתָּא תַּתָּאָה.
ע"כ רעיא מהימנא

774. "From here we learn **that whoever learns Torah, which is called 'Glory,' is himself called 'a king,'** for it is written '...and the King of glory shall come in.' (Psalms 24:7) **And it should not be said that he is a king in the World to Come and no more than that, for he is a king in both worlds in the image of his Master. And this is why the line appears twice: 'Who is this king of glory?' (Ibid. 8) and 'Who is this king of glory?' (Ibid. 10),** which indicates both worlds: this world and the World to Come. **The verse 'Lift up your heads, you gates...'** (Psalms 24:7) appears twice." He asks: "**What is the meaning of 'your heads' twice?**" He answers: "**These are the Living Creatures of the Upper Chariot,** which is above the chest of Zeir Anpin, **and the Living Creatures of the Lower Chariot** that are in Malchut."
End of Ra'aya Meheimna (Faithful Shepherd)

A Synopsis
Rav Shimon explains the meaning of "lift up your heads, you gates." We learn that God sanctifies all the festivals and makes sure that all the Hosts of Heaven become sanctified along with the children of Israel, in one unity.

Each of the Fifty Gates of Binah have a head.

775. רִבִּי שִׁמְעוֹן פָּתַח קְרָא וְאָמַר, שְׂאוּ שְׁעָרִים רָאשֵׁיכֶם וְגוֹ'. הַאי קְרָא אוּקְמוּהָ וְאִתְּמַר. אֲבָל שְׂאוּ שְׁעָרִים רָאשֵׁיכֶם, אִלֵּין אִינּוּן תַּרְעִין עִלָּאִין, תַּרְעִין דִּסְכְלְתָנוּ עִלָּאָה. וְאִינּוּן חַמְשִׁין תַּרְעִין. רָאשֵׁיכֶם, אִינּוּן רָאשִׁים מַאן אִינּוּן. אֶלָּא, כָּל חַד וְחַד, אִית לֵיהּ רֵישָׁא לְאִתְפַּשְּׁטָא וּלְמֵיעַל דָּא בְּדָא, וּלְאַכְלְלָא דָּא בְּדָא.

775. Rav Shimon opened with a verse, saying: "'Lift up your heads, you gates...' (Psalms 24:7) This verse has been taught and we have learned it. But 'Lift up your heads, you gates...' (Ibid.) these are the Upper Gates, the Gates of upper understanding, and they are fifty in number. '...your heads...' (Ibid.) He asks: "What heads does this refer to?" He answers that **each one,** namely each gate, **has a head to be unclothed and enter into one another and to be incorporated within each other.**

The heads are the Patriarchs.

776. אַשְׁכַּחְנָא בְּסִפְרָא דַּחֲנוֹךְ, שְׂאוּ שְׁעָרִים, אִלֵּין אִינּוּן תַּרְעִין דִּלְתַתָּא מֵאֲבָהָן, וְאִינּוּן תְּלָתָא בַּתְרָאִין. רָאשֵׁיכֶם: אִלֵּין אִינּוּן רָאשֵׁי אַלְפֵי יִשְׂרָאֵל, וְאִינּוּן אֲבָהָן עִלָּאֵי, וְאִינּוּן רָאשִׁין דְּאִינּוּן תַּרְעִין. וּבְגִין אִלֵּין דְּאִינּוּן אוֹפַנִּים, דְּסָחֲרָן וְנַטְלִין לוֹן עַל כַּתְפַּיְיהוּ, אַמְרֵי שְׂאוּ שְׁעָרִים רָאשֵׁיכֶם, שְׂאוּ לְמַאן. לְרָאשֵׁיכֶם. דְּאִינּוּן רָאשִׁין עָלַיְיכוּ, וְשַׁלְטָנִין עָלַיְיכוּ. וְהִנָּשְׂאוּ פִּתְחֵי עוֹלָם. אִלֵּין אִמָּהָן וְאַרְבַּע אִינּוּן דִּלְתַתָּא.

776. "I found in the Book of Enoch: 'Lift up your heads, you gates...' (Psalms 24:7) these are the Gates that are below the patriarchs, namely below Chesed, Gevurah, and Tiferet, which are called 'patriarchs,' **and they are the last three** Sefirot, namely Netzach, Hod, and Yesod. '...your heads...' (Ibid.) **are the heads of the thousands of Israel, and they are the Upper Patriarchs,** namely Chesed, Gevurah, and Tiferet, which, during Gadlut, become Chochmah, Binah, and Da'at, **and they are the heads of those Gates. And for the sake of these,** Netzach, Hod, and Yesod, **which are the Ofanim that encompass and bear them on their shoulders, we say: 'Lift up your heads, you gates...'** (Ibid) He asks: "Lift up whom?" He answers: "**Your heads, for they,** Chesed, Gevurah, and Tiferet, **are heads over you and have control over you. '...and be lifted up, you everlasting doors....'** (Psalms 24:7), these **are the Matriarchs, and they are four who are below,** namely Chesed,

Gevurah, Tiferet, and Malchut that are in Malchut, where Sarah is Chesed, Rivkah is Gevurah, Leah is Tiferet, and Rachel is Malchut.

Explanation: Above the Chest of Zeir Anpin, which is the secret of Chesed, Gevurah, and Tiferet, it is Chasadim with concealed Chochmah. And below the Chest of Zeir Anpin is the place of the revelation of Chochmah, yet it is lacking Chasadim, and Chochmah cannot shine without Chasadim. For Zeir Anpin to have unification with Malchut it is first necessary for the Netzach, Hod, and Yesod, and the Chesed, Gevurah, and Tiferet, to be incorporated one with the other. Then Netzach, Hod, and Yesod will have both Chochmah and Chasadim, and can thus shine and bestow to Malchut. So too, will Chesed, Gevurah, and Tiferet, which are Chasadim, be completed by the revelation of Chochmah that is in the Netzach, Hod, and Yesod.

It is then considered that Netzach, Hod, and Yesod are gates for Chesed, Gevurah, and Tiferet, as the complete Illumination of Chasadim from Chesed, Gevurah, and Tiferet of Zeir Anpin cannot be received before Chochmah is revealed in the Netzach, Hod, and Yesod of Zeir Anpin, because without them the Chasadim in Chesed, Gevurah, and Tiferet are in the aspect of the Lower Six without a head. But after Chochmah is revealed in Netzach, Hod, and Yesod, and Chesed, Gevurah, Tiferet, Netzach, Hod, and Yesod are all incorporated with each other, the Chesed, Gevurah, and Tiferet are considered heads, for due to them, they are in the aspect of the Upper Three called heads. So Netzach, Hod, and Yesod are the gates through which Chesed, Gevurah, and Tiferent ascend to become the aspect of heads.

This is: "**And for the sake of these,** Netzach, Hod, and Yesod, **which are the Ofanim that encompass and bear them on their shoulders."** Netzach, Hod, and Yesod of Zeir Anpin are called Ofanim, and they bear on their shoulders the Chesed, Gevurah, and Tiferet of Zeir Anpin, since they lift them up to the level of "heads." And it says "on their shoulders" because just like man's shoulders carry man's head, so do the Netzach, Hod, and Yesod carry the Chesed, Gevurah, and Tiferet to the level of head. This is: **"we say: 'Lift up your heads, you gates...' (Ibid) for they are heads over you and have control over you."** Meaning, we tell Netzach, Hod, and Yesod to lift their heads, namely that they should lift the Chesed, Gevurah, and Tiferet to be heads. And **"over you"** really means "for your sake," so **"for they are heads over you and have control over you"** means that it is for your sake that they are heads and have control. In other words, the Upper Three, which are termed head and ruler, are revealed in them due to you. Then **"...and be lifted up, you everlasting doors..." (Psalms 24:7)**, namely to bestow to and lift up Malchut as well.

The Torah in the ark is Zeir Anpin united with Malchut.

777. וְיָבֹא מֶלֶךְ הַכָּבוֹד, דָּא מַלְכָּא עִלָּאָה דְּכֹלָּא, דְּאִיהוּ מֶלֶךְ מֵהַהוּא כָּבוֹד, דְּנָהִיר לְסִיהֲרָא, וּמַאן אִיהוּ. יְיָ' צְבָאוֹת. וְיָבֹא, לְאָן אֲתַר. לְמֵיעַל אוֹרַיְיתָא בַּאֲרוֹנָא, בְּחִבּוּרָא חֲדָא, כְּדְקָא יָאוּת. וְכֵיוָן דְּהַאי עָאל לְאַתְרֵיה, כְּדֵין אוֹרַיְיתָא עָאל בַּאֲרוֹנָא. וְאִתְחַבַּר וְחִבּוּרָא חֲדָא, אוֹרַיְיתָא עִלָּאָה, בְּאוֹרַיְיתָא דִּבְעַל פֶּה, מִתְחַבְּרוּ לְפָרְשָׁא מִילִין סְתִימִין.

777. "'...and the king of glory shall come in...' (Psalms 24:7) this is the Supernal King over all, namely Zeir Anpin, which includes these Chesed, Gevurah, Tiferet, Netzach, Hod, and Yesod, **for He is King of that same glory because He gives light to the moon,** which is Malchut called 'Glory.'" He asks: **"And who is this?"** He answers: **"It is 'Adonai Tzva'ot...' (Ibid. 10),** namely Zeir Anpin, who is so called, **'shall come' (Ibid. 7)."** He asks: **"To what place** shall he come?" He answers: **"To bring the Torah,** which is Zeir Anpin, **into the Ark,** which is Malchut, **in one union as is fitting. For after the former has entered His place,** namely after Zeir Anpin has united with Malchut, which is His place, it is then considered that **the Torah,** which is the aspect of Zeir Anpin, **has entered the Ark,** which is the aspect of Malchut. **And they have**

become joined together in one union, the Upper Torah, which is the aspect of Zeir Anpin, with the Oral Torah, which is the aspect of Malchut, for they join together in order to interpret hidden matters, namely to reveal the secrets of the Torah to the righteous."

When Israel sanctify the months Below, it is announced Above.

778. אֵימָתַי. בְּשָׁבוּעוֹתֵיכֶם. לְמִנְיָנָא דְּאַתּוּן מוֹנִין. דְּבְכָל שַׁעֲתָא דְּיִשְׂרָאֵל עָבְדִין חוּשְׁבָּנִין לְיַרְחִין וְזִמְנִין, קוּדְשָׁא בְּרִיךְ הוּא אַתְקִין תֵּיבָה גּוֹ אִינּוּן רְקִיעִין, וְאַעְבַּר כָּרוֹזָא, הָא בְּנֵי לְתַתָּא, קַדְּשׁוּ יַרְחָא, קַדְּשׁוּ זִמְנָא, אִתְקַדְּשׁוּ כֻּלְּכוּ לְעֵילָּא. וְעָבֵד לְכָל חֵילֵי דִּבְשָׁמַיָּא, דְּמִתְקַדְּשִׁין כַּחֲדָא בְּעַמָּא קַדִּישָׁא, וְכֻלְּהוּ נַטְרֵי כַּחֲדָא, נְטִירָא חֲדָא, וְעַל דָּא בְּשָׁבוּעוֹתֵיכֶם, לְמִנְיָנָא דְּאַתּוּן מוֹנִין אִינּוּן שֶׁבַע שַׁבָּתוֹת.

778. He asks: "When is this unity made?" He answers: "About this it is written: 'And on the day of the first fruits, when you bring a new meal offering to the Lord in your feast of weeks…' (Numbers 28:26), meaning it is according to your reckoning. For whenever Israel make calculations regarding the new moons and festivals, the Holy One, blessed be He, sets an Ark within the Heavens, namely one that is like the lectern ark of the cantor, and passes a proclamation: 'My sons on earth have sanctified the month, sanctified the festival. Sanctify yourselves, all of you in Heaven.' And He sees to it that all the Hosts of the Heavens become sanctified as one with the Holy people and they all keep one observance on the day that Israel determined Below. Therefore it is written: 'in your… weeks…' (Numbers 28:26), namely according to your reckoning of these seven weeks.

114. "But you shall surely let the mother go"

A Synopsis

Rav Shimon uses the analogy of the mother bird brooding over her chicks to show how Israel must count seven weeks and thereby draw down seven Sefirot.

Seven Shabbats include Malchut.

779. וּכְדֵין מָשִׁיךְ קוּדְשָׁא בְּרִיךְ הוּא, מְשִׁיכוּ דְּשֶׁבַע דַּרְגִּין לְתַתָּא, בְּהַהוּא דַּרְגָּא דְּאִתְאֲחַד בְּהוּ, בְּאִינּוּן שֶׁבַע שַׁבָּתוֹת. וְאִי תֵּימָא, וְהָא שִׁיתָּא אִינּוּן וְלָא יַתִּיר. אֶלָּא כְּדֵין אִימָא יָתְבָא עַל אֶפְרוֹחִין, וְאִשְׁתְּכָחַת רְבִיעָא עָלַיְיהוּ. וַאֲנַן מְפַרְחִין לָהּ, וְנַטְלִין אִינּוּן שִׁית בְּנִין. בְּהַאי דַּרְגָּא דִּלְתַתָּא, לְקַיְּימָא דִּכְתִיב, שַׁלֵּחַ תְּשַׁלַּח אֶת הָאֵם וְאֶת הַבָּנִים וְגוֹ'.

779. "And then the Holy One, blessed be He, draws down seven grades to that grade, namely Malchut, which unites with them, with those seven Shabbats, which are the secret of Chesed, Gevurah, Tiferet, Netzach, Hod, Yesod, and Malchut. If you ask: 'Aren't there six grades, and no more?' namely Chesed, Gevurah, Tiferet, Netzach, Hod, and Yesod, for Malchut is the one that receives from them and is not part of the reckoning. The answer is: Then mother, namely Binah, sits upon the young, which are Chesed, Gevurah, Tiferet, Netzach, Hod, Yesod, and Malchut, and is found brooding over them. Binah is sent to fly away from them, and we take those six young ones, namely Chesed, Gevurah, Tiferet, Netzach, Hod, and Yesod, with the grade that is below them, namely Malchut, to fulfill the verse: 'But you shall surely let the mother go, and take the young to you...' (Deuteronomy 22:7), where the mother is Binah and the young are Chesed, Gevurah, Tiferet, Netzach, Hod, Yesod, and Malchut. And we therefore draw down seven Shabbats, namely Malchut as well. And having drawn down Malchut as well, we draw down Chesed, Gevurah, Tiferet Netzach, Hod, and Yesod to incorporate them in Malchut."

115. Israel know how to hunt good game

A Synopsis

Rav Hamnuna Saba continues the analogy and tells how Malchut, as though a chick, is coaxed out from under the Mother, Binah, with soft little prayers. Then Malchut stays with Israel, and the other Sefirot, like more small birds, fly out to Israel as well. We learn that one cannot pursue the Mother, Binah, for she is inconceivable.

There are five main Sefirot, and Yesod and Malchut are the two sums.

780. רַב הַמְנוּנָא סָבָא אָמַר, בְּהַאי יוֹמָא, לָא נַטְלִין יִשְׂרָאֵל אֶלָּא חָמֵשׁ בְּנִין, וְאִינּוּן חֲמִשָּׁה וְחוּמְשֵׁי תוֹרָה. וְאִי תֵּימָא שִׁיתּ אִינּוּן. אֶלָּא שֶׁבַע אִינּוּן, בְּחַד צִפֵּר דְּאִשְׁתְּכַח בֵּין גַּדְפָהָא דְּאִימָא. וְיִשְׂרָאֵל, יַדְעֵי לְמֵיצָד צֵידָא טָבָא, רַבָּא וְיַקִּירָא. מַה עָבְדֵי. מַפְּקֵי מִתְּחוֹת גַּדְפָהָא דְּאִימָּהָא, הַהוּא צִפּוֹרָא, בִּלְחִישׁוּ דְּפוּמָא מִכְּלַחֲשׁוּ לְגַבָּהּ, לְחִישׁוּ בָּתַר לְחִישׁוּ.

780. Rav Hamnuna Saba said: "On that day Israel takes only five sons, which are the five books of the Torah, namely Chesed, Gevurah, Tiferet, Netzach, and Hod of Zeir Anpin, which are the five parts of Zeir Anpin, who is called 'Torah.' **And should you object, saying that the Sefirot are six in number,** for there is also Yesod, the truth **really** is that **there are seven, together with a certain bird,** which is Malchut, **that is found between the wings of the mother,** which is Binah. The reason why he calculated only five grades, Chesed, Gevurah, Tiferet, Netzach, and Hod, is that there are in essence only five grades, and Yesod and Malchut are two sums of those five, and they contain nothing new. **And Israel know how to hunt for good and valuable game. What do they do? They draw out that bird,** which is Malchut, **from under the wings of the mother with whispers they utter with their mouths, whisper after whisper,** namely with many prayers.

119. "Also on the day of the First Fruits"

A Synopsis

Rav Shimon tells Moses that it is through Moses' deeds that the Shechinah is renewed in the prayers of the Patriarchs. He goes on to speak about the renewal that takes place during the prayers of the Feast of Weeks. His exposition includes a discussion of the numerical value of "all" (kol), the sea of the Torah, and Malchut that is the end of all the seas. The numbers seven and fifty are emphasized.

Moses and the Patriarchs are the First Fruits of the Shechinah.

803. אָמַר בּוּצִינָא קַדִּישָׁא, קוּם רַעְיָא מְהֵימָנָא מִשְׁנָתָךְ, דְּאַנְתְּ וַאֲבָהָן יְשֵׁנֵי עָפָר אִתְקְרוּן, דְּעַד כְּעַן הֲוֵיתוּן מִשְׁתַּדְּלִין בְּאוֹרַיְיתָא, בְּאִינּוּן יְשֵׁנִים בַּמִּשְׁנָה, דְּאִתְּמַר בְּהוֹן עַל הָאָרֶץ תִּישָׁן. וּבְיוֹם הַבִּכּוּרִים בְּהַקְרִיבְכֶם מִנְחָה וְדַעְשָׂה לַיהוָ"ה. אַתּוּן אִינּוּן בִּכּוּרִים דִּשְׁכִינְתָּא, וּבְעוֹבָדִין דִּלְכוֹן, אִיהִי אִתְחַדְּשַׁת בִּצְלוֹתִין דַּאֲבָהָן בְּכָל יוֹמָא. דְּאוֹקְמוּהָ מָארֵי מַתְנִיתִין, תְּפִלּוֹת כְּנֶגֶד אָבוֹת תִּקְנוּם. וּבק"ש דְּאָמַר רַעְיָא מְהֵימָנָא שְׁמַע יִשְׂרָאֵל, וְאוֹקְמוּהָ כָּל הַקּוֹרֵא ק"ש בְּכָל יוֹם, כְּאִלּוּ הוּא מְקַיֵּים וְהָגִיתָ בּוֹ יוֹמָם וְלָיְלָה.

803. Said the Holy Luminary, namely Rav Shimon: **"Arise, Faithful Shepherd, from your sleep, for you and the Patriarchs are called 'those that sleep in the dust,' for until now you have engaged in the Torah with the sleepers of the Mishnah, about whom it is said, 'and on the ground shall you sleep.' (Pirkei Avot 6:4) And it is said: 'And on the day of the First Fruits, when you bring a new meal offering to the Lord....' (Numbers 28:26) You are the First Fruits of the Shechinah, and through your deeds** the Shechinah is **renewed by the prayers of the Patriarchs each day, as the masters of the Mishnah taught: The prayers were established corresponding to the Patriarchs, and through the Shema Reading which the Faithful Shepherd,** Moses, **said, 'Hear Israel...' (Deuteronomy 6:4); and it has been taught that anyone who recites the Shema every day, it**

is as if they fulfilled, '...but you shall contemplate therein day and night....' (Joshua 1:8)

The Shechinah is renewed by prayer.

804. וַדַּאי בִּצְלוֹתִין דִּלְכוֹן, בִּקְרִיאַת שְׁמַע דִּלְכוֹן, שְׁכִינְתָּא אִיהִי אִתְחַדְּשַׁת קַמֵּיה דְקוּדְשָׁא בְּרִיךְ הוּא. ובג"ד, וְהִקְרַבְתֶּם מִנְחָה חֲדָשָׁה לַיהֹוָה. בִּצְלוֹתִין דְּאִינּוּן בַּאֲתָר דְּקָרְבְּנִין. בְּאָן קָרְבְּנִין דִּצְלוֹתִין אִיהִי מִתְחַדֶּשֶׁת. בְּשָׁבוּעוֹתֵיכֶם. דְּהַיְינוּ שָׁבוּעוֹת, דְּבֵיה מַתַּן תּוֹרָה, וְאִתְקְרֵי וַחֲמִשִּׁים יוֹם לָעוֹמֶר. וּבֵיה שִׁבְעָה שָׁבוּעוֹת, מִסִּטְרָא דְּהַהוּא דְּאִתְּמַר בֵּיה, שֶׁבַע בַּיּוֹם הִלַּלְתִּיךְ, וְאִיהִי מַלְכוּת כַּלָּה. כְּלִילָא מִשֶּׁבַע סְפִירָן, כְּלִילָא בַּבִּינָה, דְּאִיהִי אִתְפַּשְּׁטַת בָּה' סְפִירָאן לְחַמְשִׁין.

804. "Certainly, through your prayer and through your Shema Reading, the Shechinah is renewed before the Holy One, blessed be He, and this is why it is said: '...and you shall present a new meal offering to the Lord...' (Leviticus 23:16), namely through the prayers that are instead of sacrifices." He asks: "But through which sacrifices, namely prayers, is She renewed?" He answers: "Through '...your (Feast of) Weeks....' (Numbers 28:26); namely Shavuot, which is when the Torah was given, and that is called Fifty Days of the Counting of the Omer, and comprises seven weeks, from the side of the one about whom it is said, 'Seven times a day I praise You...' (Psalms 119:164), which is Malchut, called a 'bride,' and is composed of the Seven Sefirot—Chesed, Gevurah, Tiferet, Netzach, Hod, Yesod, and Malchut—and is a part of Binah that spreads out in five Sefirot—Chesed, Gevurah, Tiferet, Netzach, and Hod—into fifty.

The sea of Torah is Binah that issues forth Zeir Anpin.

805. יְסוֹד כָּל, כָּלוּל מֵאִלֵּין וַחֲמִשִּׁין. כַּ"ל ה': כָּ"ל ה'. כְּלִילָא מֵחֲמִשִּׁים, כֻּלְּהוּ נְבִלְעִים בְּגוֹ וַחֲמִשִּׁים, וְחָכְמָה דְּאִיהִי, י' עִלָּאָה, מוּבְלַעַת בְּגוֹ וַחֲמִשִּׁין. ה' זִמְנִין עֶשֶׂר. ה' בִּינָה. ה'. י' חָכְמָה. י' עֲשַׂר זִמְנִין ה' הַיְינוּ וַחֲמִשִּׁין וּבְחוּשְׁבָּן כָּ"ל. וּבְחוּשְׁבָּן

יְ"ם. וְאִיהוּ יַם הַתּוֹרָה. מִקּוֹרָא דִּילֵיהּ כֶּתֶר, דְּלֵית לֵיהּ סוֹף. שְׁאַר סְפִירָאן,
אִתְקְרִיאוּ עַל שְׁמָהּ שִׁבְעַת יָמִים. וּמַלְכוּת יַם סוֹף, סוֹף דְּכָל יָמִים.

805. "**Yesod, which is called 'all'** (*kol*; כל)**, whose numerical value is
fifty, is also composed of these fifty,** namely Chesed, Gevurah, Tiferet,
Netzach, and Hod, each of which is composed of ten. Malchut is called
'bride' (*kalah*; כלה)**,** and whose letters can be read as, *kol* Hei (כל ה; all
five), namely **five Sefirot composed of fifty. Each of them are absorbed
in the fifty. Chochmah, which is Upper Yud, is absorbed within the
fifty,** as Hei (ה; 5) times Yud (י; 10) equals fifty, where **Hei is Binah
and Yud is Chochmah,** and there are Yud-Hei in Chochmah, which
when multiplied by each other make fifty, and there are Yud-Hei in
Binah; and when **Yud is** multiplied **by Hei, the result is fifty, and this
is the numerical value of the word 'all'** (*kol*)**,** as mentioned, **and the
numerical value of the word 'sea'** (*yam*; 50)**,** since Binah is called 'sea,'
whose numerical value amounts to fifty. **And the reference is to the Sea
of the Torah,** where from Binah, called 'sea,' emerges the Torah, which
is Zeir Anpin. **Its origin is Keter, which is infinite. The remaining
Sefirot,** namely Chesed, Gevurah, Tiferet, Netzach, Hod, Yesod, and
Malchut, **are named 'Seven Seas' after it,** and since the numerical value
of the word 'sea' is fifty, it follows that in each of them there is fifty. **And
Malchut** is called **the 'reed'** (*suf*) **sea because it is the end** (*sof*) **of all
the seas.**

The meal offering was five times a tenth measure, which is fifty.

806. ובג"ד דְּאִינּוּן חַמְשִׁין שֶׁבַע שָׁבוּעוֹת, מִנְחָתָם שְׁלֹשָׁה עֶשְׂרוֹנִים, וּשְׁנֵי
עֶשְׂרוֹנִים. וְחֶמֶשׁ, דְּאִינּוּן חֲמֵשׁ וּמִנְיַין עָשָׂר. הה"ד, וּמִנְחָתָם סֹלֶת בְּלוּלָה בַּשֶּׁמֶן
שְׁלֹשָׁה עֶשְׂרוֹנִים לַפָּר הָאֶחָד וּשְׁנֵי עֶשְׂרוֹנִים לָאַיִל הָאֶחָד עִשָּׂרוֹן עִשָּׂרוֹן לַכֶּבֶשׂ
הָאֶחָד לְשִׁבְעַת הַכְּבָשִׂים. וְשִׁבְעַת הַכְּבָשִׂים, לָקֳבֵל שֶׁבַע שַׁבָּתוֹת תְּמִימוֹת
תִּהְיֶינָה. כָּל חַד עִם שִׁית יוֹמִין דִּילֵיהּ.

806. "And because each one of the seven weeks is fifty, as mentioned earlier, 'And their meal offering... three tenth measures for one bullock, two tenth measures for one ram' (Numbers 28:28), making altogether five tenth measures, which are five times ten, for each tenth measure is ten, and five tenth measures are fifty. This is the meaning of the verse, 'And their meal offering of fine flour mingled with oil, three tenth measures for one bullock, two tenth measures for one ram, a tenth measure for one lamb, for the seven lambs.' (Numbers 28:28-29) The 'seven lambs' correspond to '... seven complete Shabbats shall there be' (Leviticus 23:15), and these are seven Malchuts, for Malchut is called 'Shabbat,' and each one has six days with it, namely Chesed, Gevurah, Tiferet, Netzach, Hod, and Yesod, which amount to fifty with the day of Shavuot."

127. Shavuot

A Synopsis

Rav Shimon says that burnt offerings are not required during Shavuot because Israel have already observed the days of purity and the Other Side now has no hold over them. Shavuot belongs to the Tree of Life and not to the Tree of Knowledge of Good and Evil.

Fire is not mentioned since on Shavuot,
Malchut has no attachment to Judgment.

879. וְהִקְרַבְתֶּם עוֹלָה לְרֵיחַ נִיחוֹחַ לַיְיָ'. ת"ח, בְּפֶסַח כְּתִיב, וְהִקְרַבְתֶּם אִשֶּׁה עוֹלָה לַיְיָ'. וְהָכָא לָא כְּתִיב אִשֶּׁה, אֶלָּא וְהִקְרַבְתֶּם עוֹלָה. מ"ט. יוֹמָא דָא, יוֹמָא דְעָיֵילַת כַּלָּה לְחוּפָּה אִיהוּ. וְיִשְׂרָאֵל בָּנוּ יוֹמִין דְּדַכְיוּ. יוֹמִין וְשָׁבוּעִין, וְאִתְכְּלִילוּ וְעָאלוּ בְּיוֹמִין דְּדַכְיוּ. וְהִיא נַפְקַת מִכָּל סִטְרָא בִּישָׁא, וְעַטְרֵת יוֹמֵי דַכְיוּ כַּדְקָא חֲזֵי. וְרָזָא דָא, מַלְכָּא טַעַם בְּתוּלָה טָעִים. בג"כ לָא כְּתִיב בֵּיהּ אִשֶּׁה, דְּהָא אַחֲרָא לָא קָרִיב לְמַשְׁכְּנָא, וְהָא אִתְרַחַק מִתַּמָּן. וע"ד אֵשִׁים לָאו הָכָא, וְלָאו אִצְטְרִיכוּ לְהָכָא, וְיִשְׂרָאֵל מְרַחֲקָן אִינוּן מִן סִטְרָא בִּישָׁא. א"ר אַבָּא, עֲדַיִין צְרִיכִין אֲנָן לְפִתְחָא דָא לְמִפְתַּח.

879. "And you shall offer a burnt offering for a sweet savor to the Lord." (Numbers 28:27) "Come and see, about Pesach it is written: 'You shall offer a sacrifice made by fire for a burnt offering to the Lord....' (Numbers 28:19) Yet here it is not written 'a sacrifice made by fire' but 'And you shall offer the burnt offering....' (Numbers 28:7)" He asks: "What is the reason for this?" He answers: "The reason is that this day of Shavuot is a day when the bride enters the wedding canopy, namely Malchut enters the wedding canopy with Zeir Anpin, and Israel emerge from the counting of the days and weeks of purity, and are taken in and enter into these days of purity, namely the secret of the seven days Chesed, Gevurah, Tiferet, Netzach, Hod, Yesod, and Malchut—that in each one are Chesed, Gevurah, Tiferet, Netzach, Hod, Yesod, and Malchut, making a total of forty-nine days. And She, Malchut, has emerged from the aspect of everything bad, namely they no longer have any hold over her, and has observed the days of purity as fitting, namely the forty-nine days of the Counting. And this is the secret of the king who savored the taste of a virgin. In other words, it is the secret of the verse, '...a virgin, and no man had known her...' (Genesis 24:16), which is the secret that it is evident that no man from the Other Side had any hold on her. And this is why it is not written, 'a sacrifice made by fire' since no other came close to the Sanctuary, which is Malchut, and the other side has already been removed from there. Thus there are not, nor is there any need for, offerings made by fire in this case, since Israel have removed themselves from the Evil Side." Rav Aba said, "We still have to further open this opening."

Explanation: The fire offerings are Judgment, and since Malchut here already left all Her judgments it therefore does not say "a sacrifice made by fire" but only "And you shall offer a burnt offering..." (Numbers 28:27) without mentioning fire.

Shavuot is the day of the Tree of Life.

880. אר"ע, אֲרִימִית יְדַי בְּצַלּוֹ לְמַאן דִּבְרָא עָלְמָא, וְרָזָא דָא, אַשְׁכַּחְנָא בְּסִפְרֵי קַדְמָאֵי, אִשִּׁים אִינּוּן בְּאֶמְצָעִיתָא, וְאַתְיָין בְּסִטְרָא דָא וּבְסִטְרָא דָא, אֲדַבְּקוּ בְּאִילָנָא דְּדַעַת טוֹב וָרָע, אֲדַבְּקָן בְּרַע, וְאֲדַבְּקָן בְּטוֹב. ובג"כ, בִּשְׁאָר יוֹמִין כְּתִיב בְּהוּ אִשֶּׁה עוֹלָה. אֲבָל בְּהָנֵי יוֹמָא, דְּאִילָנָא דְּחַיֵּי קַיְּימָא, וְלָא אַחֲרָא, לֵית אֲנָן צְרִיכִין לְאִשֶּׁה, וְלָא אִצְטְרִיךְ לְמֶהֱוֵי תַּמָּן. וְיוֹמָא דָא, יוֹמָא דְּאִילָנָא דְּחַיֵּי אִיהוּ, וְלָא דְּדַעַת טוֹב וָרַע. ובג"ד, וְהִקְרַבְתֶּם עוֹלָה לְרֵיחַ נִיחֹחַ לַיְיָ', וְלָא אִשֶּׁה לַיְיָ' עוֹלָה. וְעוֹלָה, לָשׁוֹן עוֹלָה, כְּמָה דְּאִתְּמַר, וְהָא אִתְעֲרְנָא מִלֵּי דְּפָרִים בְּנֵי בָקָר, וְכָל הַהוּא קָרְבָּן.

880. Rav Shimon said, "I lift up my hands in prayer to He who created the world. This secret I have found in the books of the early masters: Offerings made by fire are in between good and evil, **and they come on this side and on that side, for they are attached to the Tree of Knowledge of Good and Evil** and are, therefore **attached to both the bad and to the good. For this reason, on the other days, it is written: '…a sacrifice made by fire for a burnt offering…'** (Numbers 28:19) for they contain Judgments and have a hold on the Tree of Knowledge of Good and Evil. **But on these days,** namely on Shavuot, **when the Tree of Life and no other is to be found, we do not need an offering made by fire, and it does not have to be there, as this day** of Shavuot **belongs to the Tree of Life and not the Tree of Knowledge of Good and Evil. This is why** Scripture says, **'And you shall offer the burnt offering for a sweet savor to the Lord'** (Numbers 28:27) and not 'a sacrifice made by fire to the Lord for a burnt offering.' And the meaning of **'burnt offering'** (olah) is derived from **'ascent'** (olah), for it ascends to the Most High One, **as we have learned. And we have already clarified these matters** in the commentary **about one-year old bullocks and that entire offering."**

Yitro

17. "And it came to pass, on the third day"

A Synopsis

The theme of Mercy and Judgment is continued in this section. The "third day" of the title verse refers to Tiferet that is Mercy. Good deeds are necessary to deserve Mercy, and this idea is explored through looking at the verse, "We have a little sister and she has no breasts; what shall we do for our sister in the day when she shall be spoken for."

When the Israelites came to Mount Sinai, they had no deeds or merits.

283. וַיְהִי בַיּוֹם הַשְּׁלִישִׁי וְגוֹ'. ר' אַבָּא פָּתַח, אָחוֹת לָנוּ קְטַנָּה וְשָׁדַיִם אֵין לָהּ מַה נַעֲשֶׂה לַאֲחוֹתֵנוּ בַּיּוֹם שֶׁיְדוּבַּר בָּהּ. אָחוֹת לָנוּ קְטַנָּה, דָּא כְּנֶסֶת יִשְׂרָאֵל, דְּאִקְרֵי אָחוֹת לְקוּדְשָׁא בְּרִיךְ הוּא. וְשָׁדַיִם אֵין לָהּ, הַיְינוּ דִּתְנֵינָן, בְּשַׁעֲתָא דְּקָרִיבוּ יִשְׂרָאֵל לְטוּרָא דְּסִינַי, לָא הֲוָה בְּהוֹן זַכְוָון, וְעוֹבָדִין טָבִין, לְאַגָּנָא עָלַייהוּ, דִּכְתִיב וְשָׁדַיִם אֵין לָהּ. דְּהָא אִינּוּן תִּקּוּנָא וְשַׁפִּירוּ דְּאִתְּתָא, וְלֵית שַׁפִּירוּ דְּאִתְּתָא אֶלָּא אִינּוּן. מַה נַעֲשֶׂה לַאֲחוֹתֵנוּ. מַה יִתְעֲבִיד מִינָּהּ, בְּשַׁעֲתָא דְּקוּדְשָׁא בְּרִיךְ הוּא, יִתְגְּלֵי בְּטוּרָא דְּסִינַי, לְמַלְּלָא בְּפִתְגָּמֵי אוֹרַיְיתָא, וְיִפָרוּז נִשְׁמָתְהוֹן מִנַּייהוּ.

283. "And it came to pass, on the third day..." (Exodus 19:16) Rav Aba opened the discussion with the verse, 'We have a little sister and she has no breasts; what shall we do for our sister on the day she is spoken against?' (Song of Songs 8:8) 'A little sister...' (Ibid.) is the Congregation of Israel that is called 'the sister of the Holy One, blessed be He.' '...she has no breasts...' (Ibid.) is as we have learned, that when Israel approached Mount Sinai, they had in them no merits or good deeds to protect them, therefore it is written, '...she has no breasts...' (Ibid.) since they are the beauty of a woman, and a woman's beauty comes from them alone. '...What shall we do for our sister...' (Ibid.); that is, what will be done with them when the Holy

One, blessed be He, reveals Himself on Mount Sinai to proclaim the words of the Torah, for their souls will fly away from them."

The Angels sanctify the Name Above, and Israel sanctify the Name Below.

.284 אָמַר ר' יוֹסֵי. בְּהַהוּא שַׁעֲתָא דְּקָרִיבוּ יִשְׂרָאֵל לְטוּרָא דְסִינַי, בְּהַהוּא לֵילְיָא וְנָגְהֵי, תְּלָתָא יוֹמִין דְּלָא אִזְדַּוְּוגוּ לְאַנְתְּתַיְיהוּ, אָתוּ מַלְאָכִין עִלָּאִין, וְקַבִּילוּ לְיִשְׂרָאֵל בַּאֲחַוְותָא. אִינּוּן מַלְאָכִין לְעֵילָּא, וְיִשְׂרָאֵל מַלְאָכִין לְתַתָּא. אִינּוּן מְקַדְּשִׁין שְׁמָא עִלָּאָה לְעֵילָּא, וְיִשְׂרָאֵל מְקַדְּשִׁין שְׁמָא עִלָּאָה לְתַתָּא.

284. Rav Yosi said, "At the time Israel approached Mount Sinai, together with that night and the following morning; it was three days altogether during which the people abstained from marital intercourse with their wives. The Holy Angels came and received them with brotherhood, for they are angels Above and Israel are angels Below; they sanctify the Supernal Name Above, while Israel sanctify the Supernal Name Below.

The Angels asked what they could do to honor Israel.

.285 וְאִתְעַטָּרוּ יִשְׂרָאֵל בְּשַׁבְעִין כִּתְרִין בְּהַהוּא לֵילְיָא. וּמַלְאֲכֵי עִלָּאֵי הֲווֹ אַמְרֵי אָחוֹת לָנוּ קְטַנָּה וְשָׁדַיִם אֵין לָהּ, דְּלֵית בְּהוּ זַכְוָון וְעוֹבָדִין טָבִין. מַה נַּעֲשֶׂה לַאֲחוֹתֵנוּ, כְּלוֹמַר מַה נַיְקָר וְרַבּוּ נַעֲבִיד לַאֲחַתָנָא דָּא בְּיוֹמָא דְּקוּדְשָׁא בְּרִיךְ הוּא יִתְגְּלֵי בְּטוּרָא דְסִינַי לְמֵיהַב לְהוּ אוֹרַיְיתָא.

285. "And Israel were crowned with seventy crowns on that night. Then the Supernal Angels said, 'We have a little sister and she has no breasts,' for they have no merits and good deeds, so 'what shall we do for our sister?' That is, how shall we honor her on the day when the Holy One, blessed be He, reveals Himself on Mount Sinai to give them the Torah?'

The Creator was revealed with Mercy.

286. וַיְהִי בַיּוֹם הַשְּׁלִישִׁי, כְּתִיב הֱיוּ נְכוֹנִים לִשְׁלֹשֶׁת יָמִים אַל תִּגְּשׁוּ אֶל אִשָּׁה
וַיְהִיוּ בַיּוֹם הַשְּׁלִישִׁי. ר' שִׁמְעוֹן אָמַר, בְּשַׁעֲתָא דְּקוּדְשָׁא בְּרִיךְ הוּא בָּעָא
לְאִתְגַּלָּאָה בְּטוּרָא דְּסִינַי, קָרָא קוּדְשָׁא בְּרִיךְ הוּא לְכָל פָּמַלְיָא דִּילֵיהּ, אָמַר
לוֹן, הַשְׁתָּא יִשְׂרָאֵל רַבְיָין, דְּלָא יַדְעִין נִימוּסֵי, וַאֲנָא בָּעֵי לְאִתְגְּלֵי עָלַיְיהוּ, אִי
אִתְגְּלֵי עָלַיְיהוּ בְּחֵילָא דִּגְבוּרָה, לָא יַכְלִין לְמִסְבַּל. אֲבָל אִתְגְּלֵי עָלַיְיהוּ בְּרַחֲמֵי,
וִיקַבְּלוּן נִימוּסֵי, הה"ד, וַיְהִי בַיּוֹם הַשְּׁלִישִׁי. בַּיּוֹם הַשְּׁלִישִׁי וַדַּאי דְּאִיהוּ רַחֲמֵי
מְנָלָן, דִּכְתִיב, וַיֵּט שָׁמַיִם וַיֵּרַד.

286. "It is written, 'Be ready by the third day, come not near a woman,' (Exodus 19:15) and this is 'And it came to pass, on the third day....' (Exodus 19:16)" Rav Shimon said, "At the time the Holy One, blessed be He, desired to be revealed on Mount Sinai, He gathered all His retinue and told them, 'Now Israel are like children who do not know My commandments, and I desire to be revealed before them with Mercy, and they will accept My Law.' Therefore it is written, 'And it came to pass on the third day...' (Exodus 19:16) On the third day specifically, for it is Tiferet, which is Mercy." He asks: "And how do we know all that?" He answers: "For it is written, 'He bowed the Heavens also, and came down...' (II Samuel 22:10)," and 'Heavens' are Tiferet, which is Mercy, as is explained earlier.

The Creator first extended Mercy and then Gevurah.

287. וּבְהַאי אִתְגְּלֵי קוּדְשָׁא בְּרִיךְ הוּא לְיִשְׂרָאֵל, אַקְדִּים לְהוּ רַחֲמֵי בְּקַדְמֵיתָא.
וּלְבָתַר אָתְיְיהִיב לְהוּ אוֹרַיְיתָא, מִסִּטְרָא דִּגְבוּרָה. בַּיּוֹם הַשְּׁלִישִׁי, דְּהָכִי אִתְחֲזֵי
לְהוּ, דִּבְגִינֵי כָךְ יִשְׂרָאֵל אִקְרוּן.

287. "This is how the Holy One, blessed be He, revealed Himself before Israel. He extended Mercy at first, and afterwards He gave them the Torah from the side of Gevurah on the third day. Thus, both Mercy and Judgment were included, as is appropriate for them.

Hence, they are called Israel, for the name Israel constitutes mercy and Judgment."

Kindness extends in the morning.

288. בִּהְיוֹת הַבֹּקֶר, דִּכְתִּיב, בֹּקֶר לֹא עָבוֹת. הָא אִי הֲוָה עָבוֹת קַדְרוּתָא אִשְׁתְּכַח, וְלָא אִתְגַּלְיָיא חֶסֶ"ד. וְאֵימָתַי אִתְגַּלְיָיא חֶסֶ"ד. בַּבֹּקֶר. כְּד"א, הַבֹּקֶר אוֹר. דְּכַד נָהִיר צַפְרָא, חֶסֶ"ד אִשְׁתְּכַח בְּעָלְמָא, וְדִינִין מִתְעַבְּרָן. וּבְזִמְנָא דְּלָא נָהִיר בֹּקֶר, דִּינִין עַד כְּעַן לָא מִתְעַבְּרָן. דִּכְתִּיב, בְּרָן יַחַד כֹּכְבֵי בֹקֶר וַיָּרִיעוּ כָּל בְּנֵי אֱלֹהִים. כֵּיוָן דְּאִתְעַבְּרָן אִינּוּן כֹּכְבַיָּא וְנָהִיר שִׁמְשָׁא, בֵּיהּ שַׁעֲתָא כְּתִיב, בֹּקֶר לֹא עָבוֹת. וְחֶסֶ"ד אִתְּעַר בְּעָלְמָא תַּתָּאָה, בְּהַהִיא שַׁעֲתָא כְּתִיב, בִּהְיוֹת הַבֹּקֶר. וְכֵיוָן דְּמִתְעַבְּרָן כֹּכְבַיָּא בֹקֶר אִשְׁתְּכַח.

288. "...when it was morning...." (Exodus 19:16) It is written: "In a morning without clouds..." (II Samuel 23:4) for if it were a cloudy morning, there would have been darkness in it and kindness (Chesed) would not have been revealed. And when does kindness reveal itself? In the morning, as it is written: "the morning is light...." (Genesis 44:3) Thus, as soon as the day breaks, Mercy is present in the world and Judgments are removed. But when the morning does not shine, Judgments are not removed, as it is written: "When the morning stars sang together and all the sons of God shouted for joy." (Job 38:7) As soon as the stars fade away and the sun shines at that time, as it is written: "A morning without clouds..." (II Samuel 23:4) and Mercy is awakened in the Lower World. At that time it is written "...when it was morning..." (Exodus 19:16) for once the stars faded morning appeared.

Abraham's merit is awakened in the morning.

289. אָמַר ר' יוֹסֵי, בִּהְיוֹת הַבֹּקֶר שָׁארִי קוּדְשָׁא בְּרִיךְ הוּא לְאִתְגַּלָּאָה בְּטוּרָא דְּסִינַי. תָּאנָא, בִּהְיוֹת הַבֹּקֶר, כַּד אִתְּעַר כּוּתֵיהּ דְּאַבְרָהָם, דִּכְתִּיב בֵּיהּ וַיַּשְׁכֵּם אַבְרָהָם בַּבֹּקֶר.

289. Rav Yosi said, "'...when it was morning...' (Exodus 19:16) the Holy One, blessed be He, started to reveal Himself on Mount Sinai. We learned that, '...when it was morning...,' (Ibid.) means when the merit of Abraham is awakened, of whom it is written, 'And Abraham went early in the morning....'" (Genesis 19:27)

18. "There were thundering and lightning"

A Synopsis

The sages offer various ideas about "voices." Rav Aba says that it means two voices—water and wind—which became one. Rav Yosi says that it is one voice that never ceases. Rav Yosi says that it comes from three—wind, water, and fire. The discussion moves to lightning and then to the "fiery law" that is the Torah. We also learn that the sound of the Shofar came forth to break the heavy dark cloud.

Two Voices, which were one.

290. וַיְהִי קֹלֹת וּבְרָקִים, אָמַר רַבִּי אַבָּא, קֹלֹת כְּתִיב חָסֵר. תְּרֵין קָלִין דְּאִתְהַדְּרוּ לְחַד, דָּא נָפְקָא מִן דָּא, רוּחָא מִמַּיָּא. וּמַיָּא מֵרוּחָא. תְּרֵין דְּאִינוּן חַד, וְחַד דְּאִיהוּ תְּרֵי.

290. "...there were thundering (*kolot*) and lightning...." (Exodus 19:16) Rav Aba said, "*Kolot* (קֹלֹת) is spelled without Vav (ו), the indication of the plural form, **signifying that there were two thunders (lit. voices) that became one again, one emanating from the other—wind from water and water from wind; two that are one, and one that is two.**" Therefore the word *kolot* is written without Vav.

Explanation: Just like a physical voice is composed of wind and water, so too, is a spiritual voice composed of water, the Right Column, and wind, the Central Column. In the wind and water there are two aspects: the first is in the Three Columns of Binah, where the Central Column that is wind is a result of the Right Column that is water, and thus **"wind from water."** The second is in the Three Columns of Zeir Anpin because afterwards, when the Central Column extends down from Binah to Zeir Anpin in the secret of 'one is sustained by three' (Zohar, Beresheet A 363), it is found that the Central Column is a root and cause of the Right and Left Columns. Thus water, the Right Column, is considered a result of the wind, the Central Column. This is: **"water from wind."** Yet on one hand we can say that these two aspects are one, since nothing is drawn to Zeir Anpin except what there is in Binah, and this is: **"two voices that became one again, one emanating from the other."** And on the other hand we can say that they are two, as one voice is in Binah and the other voice is in Zeir Anpin. This is: **"two that are one, and one that is two,"** for it can be said either way. Therefore, Kolot (Voices) is written without a Vav, which would have indicated plurality.

One Voice that includes all Voices and never ceases.

291. אָמַר רַבִּי יוֹסֵי, קֹלֹת חַד, וְאִיהוּ קָלָא רַבְרְבָא תַּקִּיפָא, דְּלָא פַּסְקַת לְעָלְמִין, הַהוּא דִּכְתִיב בֵּיהּ קוֹל גָּדוֹל וְלֹא יָסָף דְּהָא שְׁאַר קָלִין אִתְפַּסְקָן, דְּתַנְיָא, בְּאַרְבְּעָה תְּקוּפִין בַּשַּׁתָּא, קָלָא אִתְפַּסְקַת, וּכְדֵין דִּינִין מִתְעָרִין בְּעָלְמָא. וְהַאי קָלָא דְּכָלִיל שְׁאַר קָלִין בֵּיהּ, לָא אִתְפָּסַק לְעָלְמִין, וְלָא אִתְעֲבַר מִקִּיוּמָא שְׁלִים וְתוּקְפָּא דִּילֵיהּ. תָּאנָא, הַאי קָלָא, קָלָא דְּקָלִין, קָלָא דְּכָלִיל כָּל שְׁאַר קָלִין.

291. Rav Yosi said, "Kolot means one; this voice is a mighty and strong one that never ceases, as it is written, '…a great voice, and it did not cease…' (Deuteronomy 5:19), which is the secret of the Ruach in Supernal Aba and Ima, where the Yud never leaves their air (avir), and their Ruach stature always stays intact without changing, and this Ruach also shines in the great Zeir Anpin and Nukva. This **is because all the other voices do cease. As we learned, four times a year the Voice ceases, and then Judgments are awakened in the world. But this Voice, which includes the other Voices, never ceases and never**

abates of its full existence and force. We have learned that this Voice is the Voice of Voices, the Voice which contains all other Voices."

Explanation: Four times a year, the dominion of the Left Column is awakened, and the Voice ceases, which is the secret of the stature of Chasadim, and Judgments rule the world. But this only refers to the Voice of Yisrael Saba and Tevunah and the Voice of Zeir Anpin. The Left has no influence on the Voice of Aba and Ima to stop it, and Chasadim never cease from them. This Voice includes all the Voices below it.

Lightning in the rain indicates a union of atypical love.

292. אָמַר ר' יְהוּדָה, לֵית קָלָא, אֶלָּא מִסִּטְרָא דְרוּחָא וּמַיָּא וְאֶשָּׁא. וְכֹלָּא עָבֵיד קָלָא, וְאִתְכְּלִיל דָּא בְּדָא, וְעַ"ד כְּתִיב קֹלֹת. וּבְרָקִים, א"ר יוֹסֵי, הַיְינוּ דִכְתִיב, בְּרָקִים לַמָּטָר עָשָׂה שַׁלְהוֹבָא בְּעוֹטְרֵי, קְטִירָא דְרַחֲמֵי בְּחֵיבָתָא, דְלָא שְׁכִיחוּ.

292. Rav Yehuda said, "There is no voice except from the side of wind, water, and fire, which are the Three Columns, **and the Voice,** which is the Central Column, **does it all,** and through it the Columns **are included in each other** and become one. **Therefore the word** *kolot* **is spelled** without Vav, which would indicate the plural form." **"...and lightning..."** (Exodus 19:16) Rav Yosi cited this verse and explained, **"'...He makes lightning for the rain...'** (Psalms 135:7), meaning that "lightning" is the combination of fire and water, as lightning in the rain, **since the flame** of the lightning **in the rain** indicates that it is **a union of Mercy with atypical love.**

The Torah was given with Left and Right.

293. תָּנָא, ר' יְהוּדָה אוֹמֵר, בְּסִטְרָא דְּבוּרָה, אוֹרַיְיתָא אִתְיְיהִיבַת. אָמַר רַבִּי יוֹסֵי, אִי הָכִי בְּסִטְרָא שְׂמָאלָא הֲוֵי. אָמַר לֵיהּ, אִתְהַדָּר לִימִינָא. דִּכְתִיב בִּימִינוֹ

אֶשׁ דָת לָמוֹ. וּכְתִיב יְמִינְךָ יְיָ' נֶאְדָרִי בַּכֹחַ וְגוֹ'. אַשְׁכְּחָן שְׂמָאלָא דְּאִתְחֲזַר לִימִינָא, וִימִינָא לִשְׂמָאלָא, הָא גְּבוּרָה לִימִינָא.

293. Rav Yehuda said, "We have learned that the Torah was given from the side of Gevurah." Rav Yosi said, "In that case the Torah must be of the Left side." He said, "It returned to the Right, as it is written, '…from His right hand went a fiery law for them' (Deuteronomy 33:2) and 'Your right hand, Lord, is glorious in power….' (Exodus 15:6) **So we see that the Left is included within the Right,** since it is written, 'From His right hand a fiery law for them' (Deuteronomy 33:2), **and the Right is included within the Left** as it is written, 'Your right hand, Lord, is glorious in power.' (Exodus 15:6) **Thus Gevurah,** which is the Left, **is included within the Right.**

A loud Shofar sound issued from the heavy cloud.

294. וְעָנָן כָּבֵד עַל הָהָר וְגוֹ', עֲנָנָא תַּקִּיף, דְּעָקִיעַ בְּאַתְרֵיהּ, דְּלָא נָטִיל. וְקֹל שׁוֹפָר חָזָק מְאֹד, מִגּוֹ דַּעֲנָנָא תַּקִּיף הֲוָה, נָפִיק הַהוּא קָלָא, כד"א וַיְהִי כְּשָׁמְעֲכֶם אֶת הַקּוֹל מִתּוֹךְ הַחֹשֶׁךְ.

294. "'…and a heavy cloud upon the mountain…' (Exodus 19:16), meaning, a very mighty cloud **stuck in one place** because of its heaviness **that does not move** from place to place as do other clouds. '…and the sound of a Shofar exceedingly loud…' (Ibid.), meaning that sound was very strong, for it issued from the midst of the heavy cloud in order to break it, **as it is written, 'When you heard the voice out of the midst of the darkness….' (Deuteronomy 5:20)"**

Three kinds of darkness.

295. אָמַר רַבִּי יְהוּדָה, תְּלַת חֲשׁוֹכֵי הֲווֹ, דִּכְתִיב עָנָן וְחֹשֶׁךְ וַעֲרָפֶל. וְהַהוּא קָלָא הֲוָה נָפִיק פְּנִימָאָה מִכֻּלְּהוּ. אָמַר רַבִּי יוֹסֵי, פְּנִימָאָה דְּכֹלָּא הֲוָה, דְּבֵיהּ כְּתִיב, קוֹל גָּדוֹל וְלֹא יָסָף.

295. Rav Yehuda said, "There were three kinds of darkness, for it is written, '...darkness, clouds, and thick fog.' (Deuteronomy 4:11) And that voice, namely the voice of the Shofar, came forth from the innermost depths." Rav Yosi said, "The innermost of all of them was the Voice of which it is written, '...a great voice, and it did not cease....'" (Deuteronomy 5:19)

19. "And all the people saw the voices"

A Synopsis

Here the experience where Moses talked face-to-face with God on Mount Sinai is compared to Ezekiel's visions. It is pointed out that Ezekiel saw the Shechinah and the hand of God, but Moses was greater because he saw the head and body of Zeir Anpin. All the people who were on the mountain literally "saw the voice" as it was carved out of darkness, cloud, and fog—and figuratively they saw what no one in succeeding generations would ever again see until the time of Messiah, and that was the supernal Illumination that showed them all hidden and veiled knowledge.

The Voices were engraved on the darkness.

296. אָמַר ר' אַבָּא כְּתִיב וְכָל הָעָם רֹאִים אֶת הַקּוֹלוֹת. רֹאִים, שׁוֹמְעִים מִבָּעֵי לֵיהּ. אֶלָּא הָכִי תָּנֵינָן, אִינּוּן קָלִין, הֲוּוֹ מִתְגַּלְּפֵי בְּהַהוּא חֲשׁוֹכָא וַעֲנָנָא וְקַבְלָא, וּמִתְחַזְיָין בְּהוּ, כְּמָה דְּאִתְחֲזֵי גּוּפָא, וְחָמָאן מַה דְּחָמָאן, וְשַׁמְעִין מַה דְּשַׁמְעִין, מִגּוֹ הַהוּא חֲשׁוֹכָא וְקַבְלָא וַעֲנָנָא, וּמִגּוֹ הַהוּא חֵיזוּ דַּהֲוּוֹ חָמָאן, הֲוּוֹ נְהִירִין בִּנְהִירוּ עִלָּאָה, וְיַדְעִין, מַה דְּלָא יָדְעֵי דָרִין אוֹחֲרָנִין, דְּאָתוּ בַּתְרַיְיהוּ.

296. Rav Aba said, "It is written, 'And all the people saw the thundering (lit. 'the voices')....' (Exodus 20:15)" He asks: "Why is it written 'saw,' rather than 'heard'?" He answers that we have already learned that those voices were carved out upon the darkness, cloud, and the fog—visible as a body is. And they saw what they saw, and heard what they heard from within the darkness, cloud, and fog. And because they saw that sight they were illuminated with a Supernal Illumination and knew things beyond the understanding of all other generations to come.

The Israelites saw all hidden things face-to-face.

297. וְכָלְהוּ, הֲווֹ חָמָאן אַפִּין בְּאַפִּין, הה"ד, פָּנִים בְּפָנִים דִּבֶּר יְיָ' עִמָּכֶם. וּמַאן הֲווֹ חָמָאן. תָּאנֵי רַבִּי יוֹסֵי, מִנְּהִירוּ דְּאִינּוּן קַלָן, דְּלָא הֲוָה קוֹל, דְּלָא הֲוָה נָהִיר בִּנְהִירוּ, דְּמִסְתַּכְּלֵי בֵּיה כָּל גְּנִיזִין, וְכָל טְמִירִין, וְכָל דָּרִין דִּיֵיתוּן עַד מַלְכָּא מְשִׁיחָא. וּבְגִינֵי כַּךְ כְּתִיב וְכָל הָעָם רֹאִים אֶת הַקּוֹלֹת, רֹאִים רְאִיָּה מַמָּשׁ.

297. "All of them saw face-to-face, as it is written, 'The Lord spoke with you face-to-face....' (Deuteronomy 5:4)" He asks: "And what did they see?" Rav Yosi explains, "As there was not a Voice that did not shine, from the Illumination of those Voices, they could see all things hidden and concealed that will never be revealed to succeeding generations until the days of King Messiah. Therefore it is written, 'And all the people saw the voices...' (Exodus 20:15) saw, literally."

The Israelites saw the Shechinah.

298. אָמַר רַבִּי אֶלְעָזָר, וְכָל הָעָם רֹאִים. רֹאִים: כְּמָה דַּאֲמֵינָא, דְּחָמוּ מִנְּהִירוּ דְּאִינּוּן קַלָן, מַה דְּלָא חָמוּ דָּרִין בַּתְרָאִין אַחֲרָנִין. אֶת הַקּוֹלֹת: כד"א, וָאֶרְאֶה אֶת יי'. וָאֶרְאֶה יְיָ', לָא כְּתִיב, אֶלָּא אֶת יְיָ'. אוּף הָכָא, וְכָל הָעָם רֹאִים הַקּוֹלֹת לֹא נֶאֱמַר, אֶלָּא אֶת הַקּוֹלֹת.

298. Rav Elazar said, "'And all the people saw...' means, as we have said, that they saw all those wonderful things that no generation after will ever see, by means of the Illumination of those Voices. '...the voices...' (Exodus 20:15) has the same meaning as in the verse, '...I saw the Lord (*et adonai*)....' (Isaiah 6:1) It is written, 'the Lord' preceded by the particle *Et* (את), which means that he saw the Shechinah that is called *Et*. **In this verse it is also written, 'And all the people saw the voices (*et hakolot*)...' (Exodus 20:15) with the particle *Et* (lit. 'the'),** to indicate that they saw the Shechinah.

Every word Et in the Torah comes to include something additional.

299. כְּגַוְונָא דָא, אֶת הַשָּׁמַיִם וְאֶת הָאָרֶץ, דְּהָא אָתִין דְּבָאוֹרַיְיתָא, לְאַסְתַּכְּלָא בְּחָכְמְתָא אִתְיְיהִיבוּ. כַּבֵּד אֶת אָבִיךָ וְאֶת אִמֶּךָ כַּבֵּד אֶת יְיָ' מֵהוֹנֶךָ. וְכֻלְּהוּ לְאִתְכַּלְלָא בְּהוּ מִלָּה אוּחֲרָא. אוּף הָכָא, אֶת הַקּוֹלֹת, לְאַסְגָּאָה הַהוּא קָלָא אוּחֲרָא לְתַתָּא, דְּכָנִישׁ לוֹן לְגַבֵּיהּ, מַה דְּנָפִיק מִנַּיְיהוּ, דְּבֵיהּ חָמָאן וּמִסְתַּכְּלָן בְּחָכְמְתָא עִלָּאָה כָּל גִּנְזִין עִלָּאִין, וְכָל רָזִין טְמִירִין וּסְתִימִין, מַה דְּלָא אִתְגַּלְיָיא לְדָרִין בַּתְרָאִין, דְּאָתוּ בַּתְרֵיהוֹן, וְלָא לְדָרִין דְּיֵיתוּן לְעָלְמִין, עַד זִמְנָא דְּיֵיתֵי מַלְכָּא מְשִׁיחָא. דִּכְתִיב, כִּי עַיִן בְּעַיִן יִרְאוּ בְּשׁוּב יְיָ' צִיּוֹן. וְאֶת הַלַּפִּידִים, בְּקַדְמֵיתָא בְּרָקִים, וְהַשְׁתָּא לַפִּידִים. כֹּלָּא חַד. אֲבָל מִדְּאִתְתַּקָּנוּ בְּתִקּוּנוֹי לְאִתְחֲזָאָה, אִתְקְרוּן הָכִי.

299. "In the same manner we can explain the verse, '…the Heaven (*et hashamayim*) and the Earth (*ve'et ha'aretz*)' (Genesis 1:1), since every *Et* (lit. 'the') in the Torah was given to look into wisdom, as in the verse, 'Honor (*kaved et*) your father and (*ve'et*) your mother…' (Exodus 20:12) and 'Honor (*kaved et*) the Lord with your substance….' (Proverbs 3:9) They are all interpreted as including another matter. Here too, 'the Voices (*et hakolot*)' include that other Voice below, Malchut, which gathers into Itself the other Voices and that which emerges from Them. In it, Malchut, the people saw and beheld, through sublime Wisdom, all the Celestial treasures and all the hidden mysteries that were never revealed to succeeding generations or to any far away generations, and will not be revealed until the days of King Messiah. As it is written, '…for they shall see eye-to-eye the Lord returning to Zion.' (Isaiah 52:8)" He asks: "Why is the word 'lightning' first called '…*berakim* (ברקים)…' (Exodus 19:16) and afterwards '…*lapidim* (לפידים)…' (Exodus 20:15)?" He answers that both of them have one meaning, for when the *berakim* are quite formed and ready to appear, they are called *lapidim*.

The first two Utterances were said at the same time.

300. וְאֵת קוֹל הַשּׁוֹפָר. תָּאנֵי רַבִּי יִצְחָק, כְּתִיב אַחַת דִּבֶּר אֱלֹהִים שְׁתַּיִם זוּ שָׁמַעְתִּי, כד"א, אָנֹכִי, וְלֹא יִהְיֶה לְךָ.

300. "...and the sound of the Shofar...." (Exodus 20:15) Rav Yitzchak says, "It is written, 'God has spoken once, twice have I heard this....' (Psalms 62:12) as is written 'I am the Lord, your God...' (Exodus 20:2) and 'You shall not make for yourself....' (Exodus 20:3) 'I am...' (Exodus 20:2) signifies the secret of Binah and 'You shall not make for yourself...' (Exodus 20:3) signifies the secret of Zeir Anpin, and both of them were heard at once. Also in this verse, the sound is Zeir Anpin and the Shofar is Binah, and both were heard at the same time."

The sound from Binah is called "Shofar."

301. א"ר יְהוּדָה, קֹל בַּשׁוֹפָר מִבָּעֵי לֵיהּ. הַשּׁוֹפָר לָמָּה. אֶלָּא, הַהוּא קוֹל דְּאִקְרֵי שׁוֹפָר. דִּכְתִיב, וְהַעֲבַרְתָּ שׁוֹפָר תְּרוּעָה בַּחֹדֶשׁ הַשְּׁבִיעִי בְּעָשׂוֹר לַחֹדֶשׁ בְּיוֹם הַכִּפּוּרִים, בְּדָא אִתְקְרֵי שׁוֹפָר.

301. Rav Yehuda said, "It should have said 'the sound in the Shofar' so why does it say **'...of the Shofar....' (Exodus 20:15)?"** He answers, **"That Voice was called 'Shofar,' as in the verse, 'Then shall you cause the Shofar to sound on the tenth day of the seventh month, on the Day of Atonement....' (Leviticus 25:9) On** Yom Kippur **it is called 'Shofar,'** meaning that when the sound issues from Binah, the sound is called 'Shofar.'"

Fire, wind, and water are included in the sound of the Shofar.

302. א"ר יוֹסֵי, מַה שׁוֹפָר, אַפִּיק קָלָא, אֶשָּׁא וְרוּחָא וּמַיָּא, אוּף הָכָא, כֹּלָּא אִתְכְּלִיל בְּהַאי, וּמְדָּא נָפְקִין קָלִין אַחֲרָנִין.

302. Rav Yosi said, "As the physical **Shofar makes a sound** that includes **fire, air, and water, here too everything is included in it,** for here in the sound that comes out from the Shofar, fire, wind, and water are included—which are Chesed, Gevurah, and Tiferet, the secret of the Three Columns. **And from this sound other sounds emerge.**"

The Shofar is Binah, and the sound is Zeir Anpin.

303. א״ר אֶלְעָזָר, קוֹל דְּנָפִיק מְשׁוֹפָר, דְּמַשְׁמַע דְּשׁוֹפָר חַד, וְקוֹל נָפִיק מִנֵּיה, וְשׁוֹפָר בְּקִיּוּמֵיה שְׁכִיחַ, וּבְגִינֵי כָּךְ כְּתִיב, קוֹל הַשּׁוֹפָר.

303. Rav Elazar said, "'…the sound of the shofar…' (Exodus 20:15) means **the sound that comes out from a Shofar, which means that the Shofar is one and the sound that comes from it is one,** as the sound is the secret of Zeir Anpin and the Shofar is the secret of Binah. **The Shofar stands by itself** separate from the sound that comes out of it, **and therefore it is written, '…the sound of the Shofar…' (Ibid.)** and not, 'the sound in the shofar.'"

The etymology of Shofar indicates glory and beauty.

304. רַבִּי יְהוּדָה אָמַר הָכִי, קוֹל הַשּׁפָר, הַשּׁפָר כְּתִיב וָחָסֵר, כד״א, שְׁפַר קֳדָם דָּרְיָוֶשׁ. מִלְכִי יִשְׁפַּר עֲלָךְ. שְׁפַר קֳדָמַי לְהַחֲוָיָא.

304. Rav Yehuda said, "In '…the sound of the Shofar…' (Exodus 20:15) the word 'Shofar' (שׁפָר) is spelled without the letter Vav (ו) since it has the same meaning **as in the verse, 'It pleased (shafar; שְׁפַר) Dariush….' (Daniel 6:2) '…King, let my counsel be acceptable (yishpar; יִשְׁפַּר) to you…' (Daniel 4:24) and, 'I thought it good (shefar; שְׁפַר) to report the signs and wonders' (Daniel 3:32),** meaning that these are expressions that speak of glory and beauty, which alludes to Zeir Anpin, the secret of Tiferet."

Everything depends on the sound of the Shofar.

305. רַבִּי שִׁמְעוֹן אָמַר, קוֹל הַשּׁוֹפָר, אַתְרָא דְּקָלָא נָפִיק מִנֵּיהּ, אִקְרֵי שׁוֹפָר. תּוּ אָמַר רַבִּי שִׁמְעוֹן, תָּא חֲזֵי, קוֹל הַשּׁוֹפָר: אַתְרָא דְּקָלָא, הַיְינוּ דִּכְתִיב, כִּי עַל כָּל מוֹצָא פִי יְיָ' יִחְיֶה הָאָדָם. מַאי מוֹצָא פִּי יְיָ'. דָּא קוֹל הַשּׁוֹפָר, הוּא רַב מִכָּל שְׁאַר קָלֵי תַּתָּאֵי, וְתַקִּיפָא מִכֻּלְּהוּ, דִּכְתִיב וְקוֹל שֹׁפָר חָזָק מְאֹד, וְעַל כָּל שְׁאַר קָלִין לָא אִתְּמַר חָזָק מְאֹד. בְּהַאי קוֹל הַשּׁוֹפָר תַּלְיָא כֹּלָּא, וְדָא הוּא דְּאִקְרֵי קוֹל גָּדוֹל, דִּכְתִיב קוֹל גָּדוֹל וְלֹא יָסָף. וְאִקְרֵי קוֹל דְּמָמָה דַקָּה, נְהִירוּ דְּבוּצִינֵי, דְּהוּא זַךְ וְדַקִּיק, וְזָכִיךְ וְנָהִיר לְכֹלָּא.

305. **Rav Shimon said, "'...the sound of the Shofar...' (Exodus 20:15) means that the place from which the sound comes out is called 'Shofar,'** for the sound is Zeir Anpin and the Shofar is Binah, and Zeir Anpin issues from Binah, as is known." **Rav Shimon continued and said, "Come and behold, '...the sound of the Shofar...' (Ibid.) refers to the place of the Voice, for it is written, '...by all that issues from the mouth of the Lord shall a man live.' (Deuteronomy 8:3)** He asks: **"What is 'all that issues from the mouth of the Lord...'?"** He answers: **"this is the sound of the Shofar, which is greater than any other lower voices, and stronger than them all, as it is written, '...the sound of a Shofar exceedingly loud....' (Exodus 19:16)** Of other voices it is not said 'exceedingly loud' (lit. 'very strong'). **Everything depends on this sound of the Shofar, and it is called 'a great voice,' as it is written, '...a great voice, and it did not cease...' (Deuteronomy 5:19), and is called '...a still small voice' (I Kings 19:12), which is the Light of the luminaries that is pure and subtle, and purifies and illuminates all things.**

The Shofar sound causes silence and awe.

306. דְּמָמָה, מַהוּ דְּמָמָה. אָמַר ר"ע, דְּבָעֵי ב"נ לְמִשְׁתּוֹקָא מִנֵּיהּ, וּלְמֶחֱסַם פּוּמֵיהּ. כד"א, אָמַרְתִּי אֶשְׁמְרָה דְּרָכַי מֵחֲטוֹא בִלְשׁוֹנִי אֶשְׁמְרָה לְפִי מַחְסוֹם.

דְּבְמָה אִיהִי שְׁתוּקָא דְּלָא אִשְׁתְּמַע לְבַר. וַיַּרְא הָעָם וַיָּנֻעוּ וַיַּעַמְדוּ מֵרָחוֹק, דְּחָזוּ מַה דְּחָזוּ. וַיָּנֻעוּ כד"א וַיָּנֻעוּ אַמּוֹת הַסִּפִּים מִקּוֹל הַקּוֹרֵא.

306. "It is written, 'Still.'" He asks: "**What does 'still' mean?**" Rav Shimon said, "**One must be silent** with awe **and shut his mouth, as it is written, 'I said, "I will take heed of my ways that I sin not with my tongue, I will keep a muzzle on my mouth...."'** (Psalms 39:2) The word 'still' means silence in which no voice is heard outside. '...**when the people saw it, they were shaken and stood afar off,'** (Exodus 20:15) because they saw what they saw and were frightened. The word 'shaken' (also 'moved') has the same meaning as in, '**And the posts of the door moved at the voice of him....'** (Isaiah 6:4)"

20. "And God (Elohim) spoke"

A Synopsis

We are told here of God's admonitions to his chosen people so that they will merit the World to Come and be worthy of the Heaven Above, Zeir Anpin, and the Earth Above, Malchut. Rav Shimon explains that the heritage of Jacob bestowed through Isaac's blessing means that Jacob and all his descendants will be revived by the dew of Heaven, that is, raised from the dead in the Time to Come. When God spoke, each word rose and descended, was watered with the Heavenly Dew, encircled Israel, and brought back their souls. Then it was engraved upon the Tablets of Stone, and each word was like a treasure house full of precious secrets and laws. He who occupies himself with the study of the Torah's secrets and laws is saved from the fire of Gehenom, and this is due to the merit of Abraham, who pled for the children of Israel. Lastly we are told that the smoke that came out of Sinai was the Shechinah who manifested Herself there to the people.

The fire of Torah saves from the fire of Gehenom.

351. אָמַר ר' יִצְחָק, אֲמַאי אִתְיְהִיבַת אוֹרַיְיתָא בְּאֶשָּׁא וַחֲשׁוֹכָא, דִּכְתִיב וְהָהָר
בֹּעֵר בָּאֵשׁ עַד לֵב הַשָּׁמַיִם חֹשֶׁךְ עָנָן וַעֲרָפֶל. דְּכָל מַאן דְּיִשְׁתָּדַל בְּאוֹרַיְיתָא,
אִשְׁתֵּזִיב מֵאֶשָּׁא אוֹחֲרָא דְּגֵיהִנָּם, וּמֵחֲשׁוֹכָא דִּמְחַשְׁכִין כָּל שְׁאַר עַמִּין לְיִשְׂרָאֵל,
דִּבְזְכוּתֵיהּ דְּאַבְרָהָם אִשְׁתֵּזִיבוּ יִשְׂרָאֵל מֵאֶשָּׁא דְּגֵיהִנָּם.

351. Rav Yitzchak asked, "Why was the Torah given in fire and
darkness, as it is written, 'And the mountain burned with fire
to the Heart of Heaven, with darkness, clouds and thick fog.'
(Deuteronomy 4:11)" He answered, "The reason is **that he who is
occupied with the study of the Torah will be saved from the other
fire of Gehenom, and from the darkness that the other nations
bring upon Israel. It was in the merit of Abraham that Israel were
saved from the fire of Gehenom.**

Avraham pleaded for the Israelites to escape the fire of Gehenom.

352. דְּתָנֵינָא אָמַר לֵיהּ קוּדְשָׁא בְּרִיךְ הוּא לְאַבְרָהָם, כָּל זִמְנָא דְּבְנֶיךָ יִשְׁתַּדְּלוּן
בְּאוֹרַיְיתָא, יִשְׁתֵּזְבוּן מֵאִלֵּין. וְאִי לָא, הָא נוּרָא דְּגֵיהִנָּם דְּשַׁלְטָא בְּהוּ,
וְיִשְׁתַּעְבְּדוּן בֵּינֵי עֲמַמְיָא. א"כ, בִּתְרֵי קְטוּרֵי לָא מִזְדַּקְפָן מִלִּין, אֶלָּא אִי נִיחָא
קַמָּךְ, יִשְׁתֵּזְבוּן מִנּוּרָא דְּגֵיהִנָּם, וְיִשְׁתַּעְבְּדוּן בֵּינֵי עֲמַמְיָא, עַד דְּיֵתוּבוּן גַּבָּהּ.
אָמַר לֵיהּ יֵאוֹת הוּא וַדַּאי, הה"ד אִם לֹא כִי צוּרָם מְכָרָם. מַאן הוּא צוּרָם. דָּא
הוּא אַבְרָהָם. דִּכְתִיב הַבִּיטוּ אֶל צוּר וְאֹצַבְתֶּם. וַיְיָ' הִסְגִּירָם, דָּא קוּדְשָׁא בְּרִיךְ
הוּא, דְּאַסְתָּכַּם עַל יְדוֹי.

352. "For we have learned, the Holy One, blessed be He, said to
Abraham, '**As long as your children shall study the Torah they will
be saved** from fire and darkness, but if not, **the fire of Gehenom will
have dominion over them and they will be subjected to the nations.'**
Abraham **said to Him, 'May things not come to pass with these two
knots,** the fire of Gehenom and exile. **If it pleases You, let them escape
from the fire of Gehenom and go into exile and become enslaved to**

other nations until they return to You.' The Holy One, blessed be He, answered him, 'So be it then,' and so it was, as it is written, '...Unless their Rock had sold them....' (Deuteronomy 32:30) He asks: "Who is 'their Rock'?" He answers: "Abraham, as it is written, '...Look to the rock from where you are hewn...' (Isaiah 51:1) '...And the Lord had given them up' (Deuteronomy 32:30) refers to the Holy One, blessed be He, who agreed with him."

Fifty days from the Exodus until the Giving of the Torah.

353. אָמַר ר' יְהוּדָה, בְּיוֹמָא דְּנָפָקוּ יִשְׂרָאֵל מִמִּצְרַיִם עַד יוֹמָא דְּאִתְיְהִיבַת אוֹרַיְיתָא, חַמְשִׁין יוֹמִין הֲווֹ. מ"ט אָמַר ר' יְהוּדָה, בְּשׁוּם אִינּוּן שְׁנֵי דְּיוֹבְלָא, דִּכְתִיב וְקִדַּשְׁתֶּם אֵת שְׁנַת הַחֲמִשִּׁים שָׁנָה.

353. Rav Yehuda said, "From the day Israel left Egypt until the day the Torah was given, there were fifty days." He asks: "What was the reason?" Rav Yehuda said, "Because they are the years of Jubilee, which is Binah, as it is written, 'And you shall sanctify the fiftieth year' (Leviticus 25:10), namely the Fiftieth Gate in Binah."

The Exodus came from the side of Jubilee.

354. תָּאנָא, אר"ש, הַהוּא יוֹבְלָא אַפִּיק לוֹן לְיִשְׂרָאֵל מִמִּצְרַיִם. וְאִי תֵּימָא דְּיוֹבְלָא מַמָּשׁ. אֶלָּא מִסִּטְרָא דְּיוֹבְלָא הֲוָה, וּמִסִּטְרָא דְּיוֹבְלָא אִתְּעַר דִּינָא עַל מִצְרָאֵי, וּבְגִינֵי כָּךְ חַמְשִׁין אִלֵּין דְּיוֹבְלָא הֲווֹ.

354. Rav Shimon said, "We have learned that it was the Jubilee that took Israel out of Egypt. If you believe that it is Jubilee itself, namely Binah itself, it is not so. The exodus occurred through the aspect of Jubilee and from the aspect of the same Judgment that was stirred up against the Egyptians. Therefore, those fifty years are the Fifty Gates of Jubilee, which is Binah.

Explanation: It was not Binah Herself that took Israel out of Egypt. Rather, the Nukva of Zeir Anpin elevated and clothed Binah, and became similar to it. Then She took Israel out of Egypt. This is considered from the side of Binah, but not actually Binah.

Fifty mentions of the Exodus in the Torah.

355. תָּאנָא, לָקֳבֵל דָּא, חַמְשִׁין זִמְנִין אִתְּמַר וְאִדְכַּר בְּאוֹרַיְיתָא, נְמוּסִין דְּמִצְרַיִם, וְשִׁבְחֵי אִינּוּן כֻּלְּהוּ, אֲשֶׁר הוֹצֵאתִיךָ. וַיּוֹצִיאֲךָ. כִּי בְּיַד חֲזָקָה הוֹצִיאֲךָ. וְכֻלְּהוּ זִמְנֵי, חַמְשִׁין אִינּוּן, וְלָא יַתִּיר, מִשּׁוּם דְּכֹלָּא בְּיוֹבְלָא אִתְעֲטַּר, וּמִסִּטְרָא דְיוֹבְלָא אָתָא כֹּלָּא. וּבְגִינֵי כַּךְ, אוֹרַיְיתָא דְּאָתֵי מִגְּבוּרָה, אִתְעֲטָּרַת בִּימִינָא. דִּכְתִיב מִימִינוֹ אֵשׁ דָּת לָמוֹ. וְתַנְיָא חֲמִשָּׁא קָלִין הֲווֹ. וְכֻלְּהוּ אִתְחֲזִיאוּ בְּהוֹ, וְאִתְכְּלִילוּ בְּהוֹ, וְאִתְעֲטָּרוּ בְּדָא.

355. "We have learned that corresponding to this were there fifty mentions of the acts of Egypt in the Torah, all of which are praises. For instance, '…who have brought you out of the land of Egypt…' (Exodus 20:2) and '…and brought you out…' (Deuteronomy 4:37) and '…for by strength of hand the Lord brought you out from this place….' (Exodus 13:3) Exactly fifty times and no more, since all is adorned with Jubilee, which is Binah, and everything came from the side of Jubilee. And there are Fifty Gates in Binah. Therefore the Torah, which comes from Gevurah, is crowned by the Right, as it is written, '…from His right hand went a fiery law for them.' (Deuteronomy 33:2) We have also learned that when the Torah was given, there were five voices, Chesed, Gevurah, Tiferet, Netzach, and Hod of Binah, and all of these were seen in them, included in them, and crowned in Binah."

Binah crowned Zeir Anpin when the Israelites received the Torah.

356. אָמַר ר' שִׁמְעוֹן, בְּהַהוּא זִמְנָא דְּקַבִּילוּ יִשְׂרָאֵל אוֹרַיְיתָא, יוֹבְלָא דָּא אַעֲטַּר בְּעִטְרוֹי לְקוּדְשָׁא בְּרִיךְ הוּא, כְּמַלְכָּא דְּאִתְעֲטָּר בְּגוֹ וְחֵילֵיהּ. דִּכְתִיב,

צְאֶינָה וּרְאֶינָה בְּנוֹת צִיּוֹן בַּמֶּלֶךְ שְׁלֹמֹה בַּעֲטָרָה שֶׁעִטְּרָה לּוֹ אִמּוֹ. מַאן אִמּוֹ. דָא יוֹבְלָא. וְיוֹבְלָא אִתְעַטָּר, בְּחֶדְוָה בִּרְחִימוּ בִּשְׁלִימוּ. דִּכְתִיב אֵם הַבָּנִים שְׂמֵחָה. מַאן אֵם הַבָּנִים. אר"ע דָּא יוֹבְלָא.

356. Rav Shimon said, "At the time that Israel received the Torah, that Jubilee, Binah, crowned the Holy One, blessed be He, who is Zeir Anpin, **as a king is crowned in the midst of his hosts, as it is written, 'Go forth, daughters of Zion, and behold King Solomon with the crown with which his mother crowned him....' (Song of Songs 3:11)** He asks: **"Who is 'his mother'?"** He answers: **"It is Jubilee,** for Binah is called Jubilee and she is the Mother of Zeir Anpin, called Solomon. **The Jubilee was crowned with joy, love, and completion, as it is written, '...a joyful mother of children....' (Psalms 113:9)"** He asks: **"Who is the 'mother of children'?"** Rav Shimon said, **"This is Jubilee."**

Father and Mother are Chochmah and Binah.

357. א"ר יְהוּדָה, ע"ד כְּתִיב, יִשְׂמַח אָבִיךָ וְאִמֶּךָ וְתָגֵל יוֹלַדְתֶּךָ. מַאן אָבִיךָ וְאִמֶּךָ. א"ר יְהוּדָה, כְּמָה דְאוּקְמוּהָ בְּסִפְרָא דִּצְנִיעוּתָא, דִּכְתִיב, עֶרְוַת אָבִיךָ וְעֶרְוַת אִמְּךָ לֹא תְגַלֵּה וַוי לְמַאן דְּגַלֵּי עֲרַיְיתְהוֹן.

357. Rav Yehuda said, "Concerning this it is written, 'Let your father and your mother be glad and let her who bore you rejoice.' (Proverbs 23:25) He asks: **"Who are 'your father and your mother'?"** He answers: **"They are as explained in** *Safra deTzni'uta* **(The Concealed Book), relating to the verse, 'The nakedness of your father, or the nakedness of your mother, shall you not uncover....' (Leviticus 18:7) Woe to one who uncovers their nakedness,** which alludes to Chochmah and Binah called Father and Mother (as said in *Safra deTzniuta* 32)."

All the mountains in the world shook.

358. תָּאנָא, א"ר יִצְחָק, בְּשַׁעֲתָא דְקוּדְשָׁא בְּרִיךְ הוּא אִתְגְּלֵי בְּטוּרָא דְסִינַי,
אוֹדַדְעָע טוּרָא. וּבְשַׁעֲתָא דְסִינַי אוֹדַדְעָע, כָּל שְׁאַר טוּרֵי עָלְמָא אוֹדַדְעָעוּ, וַהֲווֹ
סַלְקִין וְנַחְתִּין, עַד דְּאוֹשִׁיט קוּדְשָׁא בְּרִיךְ הוּא יְדוֹי עָלַיְיהוּ, וְאִתְיַישְׁבוּ. וְקַלָא
נַפְקָא וּמַכְרְזָא, מַה לְּךָ הַיָּם כִּי תָנוּס הַיַּרְדֵּן תִּסוֹב לְאָחוֹר הֶהָרִים תִּרְקְדוּ
כְאֵילִם וְגוֹ'.

358. Rav Yitzchak said, "We have learned that at the time that the
Holy One, blessed be He, revealed Himself on Mount Sinai, the
mountain began to shake and all the mountains on Earth trembled
and quaked, and they rose and fell until the Holy One, blessed be
He, stretched out His hand and calmed them. And a Voice was
heard proclaiming: 'What ails you, you sea that you flee? Jordan,
that you are driven back? You mountains, that you skip like rams....'
(Psalms 114:5-6)"

Malchut trembled due to Binah and Zeir Anpin.

359. וְאִינּוּן תָּבְאָן וְאַמְרִין, מִלִּפְנֵי אָדוֹן חוּלִי אָרֶץ. אָמַר ר' יִצְחָק, מִלִּפְנֵי אָדוֹן,
דָּא אִימָּא, דִּכְתִיב אֵם הַבָּנִים שְׂמֵחָה. חוּלִי אָרֶץ, דָּא אִימָּא תַּתָּאָה. מִלִּפְנֵי
אֱלוֹהַּ יַעֲקֹב, דָּא הוּא אַבָּא, דִּכְתִיב, בְּנִי בְכוֹרִי יִשְׂרָאֵל. וְעַל הַאי כְּתִיב
בַּעֲטָרָה שֶׁעִטְרָה לּוֹ אִמּוֹ.

359. "And they answered Him, 'Tremble, you Earth, at the presence
of the Master....' (Psalms 114:7)" Rav Yitzchak said, "'At the
presence of the Master,' refers to Ima, who is Binah, as it is written:
'...a joyful mother of children....' (Psalms 113:9) 'Tremble, you
Earth...' (Psalms 114:7) refers to the Lower Ima, who is Malchut.
'...at the presence of the God of Jacob,' (Ibid.) is Aba, who is Zeir
Anpin, lower Aba, as it is written, '... "Israel is My son, My firstborn"'
(Exodus 4:22), meaning Zeir Anpin that is called 'Israel.' And of that it

is written, 'the crown with which his mother crowned him' (Song of Songs 3:11), 'his mother' being Binah."

Zeir Anpin was crowned with the Upper Three Sefirot.

360. מַהוּ בַּעֲטָרָה. א"ר יִצְחָק, כְּמָה דִּכְתִיב, וְשָׁאוּל וַאֲנָשָׁיו עוֹטְרִים אֶת דָּוִד. מִשּׁוּם דְּמִתְעַטָּר, בְּחִוָּורָא בְּסוּמָקָא וּבִירוֹקָא, בְּכָל גַּוְונִין דְּכֻלְּהוּ כְּלִילָן בֵּיהּ, וְאִסְתַּחֲרָן בֵּיהּ. אָמַר ר' יְהוּדָה, בַּעֲטָרָה שֶׁעֲטָרָה לוֹ אִמּוֹ. מַאן עֲטָרָה. דִּכְתִיב, יִשְׂרָאֵל אֲשֶׁר בְּךָ אֶתְפָּאָר. וּכְתִיב וּבֵית תִּפְאַרְתִּי אֲפָאֵר.

360. He asks: "What is '…the crown (atara; עֲטָרָה) with which his mother crowned him' (Song of Songs 3:11)?" And Rav Yitzchak replies, "This resembles the verse, '…for Saul and his men compassed (otrim; עוֹטְרִים) David and his men round about…' (I Samuel 23:26), which is like encircling, for Zeir Anpin is crowned and surrounded by Ima with white, red, and green, all colors—the secret of the Three Columns—all of which are included and encircled in it." Rav Yehuda asked, "What is the crown in the verse, '…the crown with which his mother crowned him' (Song of Songs 3:11)?" He answers: "It has the same meaning as in, 'Israel, in whom I will be glorified' (Isaiah 49:3) and 'And I will glorify the house of My glory" (Isaiah 60:7), namely the Upper Three Sefirot, which are the glory of Zeir Anpin called Israel and Tiferet."

Black fire on white fire.

361. אָמַר ר' יִצְחָק, אוֹרַיְיתָא אִתְיְהִיבַת בְּאֶשָׁא אוּכְמָא, עַל גַּבֵּי אֶשָׁא חִוָּורָא, לְאַכְלְלָא יְמִינָא בִּשְׂמָאלָא, וּשְׂמָאלָא דְּאִתְחַזָּר יְמִינָא, דִּכְתִיב מִימִינוֹ אֵשׁ דָּת לָמוֹ.

361. Rav Yitzchak said, "The Torah was given in a black fire engraved upon a white fire, so as to include the Right in the Left.

And the Left was returned to the Right, as it is written, '...from His right hand went a fiery law for them.' (Deuteronomy 33:2)"

The smoke on Mount. Sinai had the aromas of the Garden of Eden.

362. א"ר אַבָּא, בְּשַׁעֲתָא דִּתְנָנָא דְּסִינַי הֲוָה נָפִיק, סָלִיק אֶשָּׁא, וּמִתְעַטָּר בְּהַהוּא תְּנָנָא בְּאִתְגַּלְיָיא, כְּאִתְכְּלָא דָּא, וְסָלִיק וְנָחֵית, וְכָל רֵיחִין וּבוּסְמִין דִּבְגִנְתָא דְּעֵדֶן, הֲוָה סָלִיק הַהוּא תְּנָנָא, בְּחֵיזוּ דְּחִוָּור וְסוּמָק וְאוּכָם, הה"ד, מְקֻטֶּרֶת מוֹר וּלְבוֹנָה מִכֹּל אַבְקַת רוֹכֵל.

362. Rav Aba said, "When the smoke came out of Mount Sinai, a fire ascended and was crowned with it openly, and looked like a cluster. And it flared high and dwindled again, and all the aromas of the Garden of Eden were blended in that smoke, having the colors white, red, and black, as it is written, '...perfumed with myrrh and frankincense, with all powders of the merchant.' (Song of Songs 3:6)

The smoke was the revelation of the Shechinah.

363. הַהוּא תְּנָנָא מַאן הֲוָה. אָמַר ר' יִצְחָק, שְׁכִינְתָּא דְּאִתְגַּלֵּי לְתַמָּן, כד"א, מִי זֹאת עוֹלָה מִן הַמִּדְבָּר כְּתִמְרוֹת עָשָׁן. אָמַר ר' יְהוּדָה, לָמָה לָךְ כּוּלֵי הַאי הָא קְרָא שְׁלִים הוּא, דִּכְתִּיב וְהַר סִינַי עָשַׁן כֻּלּוֹ מִפְּנֵי אֲשֶׁר יָרַד עָלָיו יְיָ' בָּאֵשׁ וַיַּעַל עֲשָׁנוֹ כְּעֶשֶׁן הַכִּבְשָׁן. זַכָּאָה עַמָּא דְּיוֹדְמָאן דָּא, וְיָדְעִין דָּא.

363. "What was this smoke?" Rav Yitzchak said, "It was the Shechinah who manifested Herself there, as it is written in the verse, 'Who is this coming out of the wilderness like columns of smoke...' (Song of Songs 3:6), which alludes to the Shechinah." Rav Yehuda said, "Surely you do not have to go to great lengths to learn this, for there is an explicit verse, 'And Mount Sinai smoked in every part because the Lord descended upon it in fire, and the smoke of it ascended like the smoke of a furnace....' (Exodus 19:18) Blessed are the people who saw it and knew it."

21. "The Tablets were the work of God"

A Synopsis

We hear how the Tablets of the Ten Utterances were of sapphire, and the letters were visible on both sides and composed of both black fire and white fire, from the Left and the Right. The friends are in some confusion about whether God made the Tablets specially or whether they were really *just* sapphire as any other sapphire. Rav Shimon says the Tablets were formed of the Supernal dew that flows from Atika Kadisha, and that they pre-existed the creation of the world but were perfected on the Sixth Day of Creation especially for this purpose. The miracle was that one could read one side from the other. We are told that the Torah actually literally restored the souls of Israel after they had flown away at the time the people heard the words of God. The text now turns to the rule of Solomon, during which time the moon was full. When Zedekiah came, the moon waned and remained thus, so Malchut was removed far from Zeir Anpin, and became dark. The moon shone when Israel stood by Mount Sinai, and it shone when Judah was found worthy to receive the Kingdom.

The Tablets were of sapphire.

364. א"ר וַיִּיא, כַּד אִתְגְּלִיפוּ אַתְוָון בְּלוּחֵי אַבְנָא, הֲוֹו מִתְחַזְיָין בִּתְרֵין סִטְרִין, מִסִּטְרָא דָא, וּמִסִּטְרָא דָא, וְלוּחִין מֵאֶבֶן סַנְפִּירִינוֹן הֲוֹו, וְאִתְגְּלִיפוּ וְאִתְוַוּפְיָין בְּאֶשָּׁא חִוּוּרָא, וְאַתְוָון הֲוֹו מֵאֶשָּׁא אוּכָּמָא, וּמִתְגַּלְּפָן בִּתְרֵין סִטְרִין, מִסִּטְרָא דָא וּמִסִּטְרָא דָא.

364. Rav Chiya said, "When the letters were engraved upon the Tablets of stone, they were visible on both sides. The Tablets were of sapphire, engraved and covered with white fire, and the letters were of black fire, and they were engraved upon both sides."

Black and white fire allude to Right and Left.

אָמַר ר' אַבָּא, לוֹחִין הֲווֹ בְּעֵינַיְיהוּ, וְאַתְוָוֹן הֲווֹ טָאסִין, וּמִתְחַזְיָין בִּתְרֵין .365
אֶשִׁין, אֶשָׁא חִוָּורָא, וְאֶשָׁא אוּכְמָא, לְאִתְחֲזָאָה כַּחֲדָא, יְמִינָא וּשְׂמָאלָא,
דִּכְתִיב אֹרֶךְ יָמִים בִּימִינָהּ בִּשְׂמֹאלָהּ וְגוֹ'. וְהָא כְּתִיב מִימִינוֹ אֵשׁ דָּת לָמוֹ.
אֶלָּא מִסִּטְרָא דִּגְבוּרָה הֲוָה, וְאִתְכְּלִילַת בִּימִינָא. וּבְגִין כַּךְ אֶשָׁא חִוָּורָא
וְאֶשָׁא אוּכְמָא.

365. Rav Aba said, "The Tablets remained as they were, that is, complete, without any change. And the letters soared in the air and could be seen with two types of fire, black fire and white fire, to demonstrate the union of the Right and the Left, for white is Right and black is Left, as it is written, 'Length of days is in her right hand and in her left hand are riches and honor.' (Proverbs 3:16)" He asks, "Is it not written, '...from His right hand went a fiery law to them.' (Deuteronomy 33:2)? He answers, "The Torah emanated from the side of Gevurah, which is the Left, and was included with the Right side. Therefore it had in it black and white fire.

The Two Tablets appeared as one.

תָּאנָא, כְּתִיב וְהַלֻּחֹת מַעֲשֵׂה אֱלֹהִים הֵמָּה וְגוֹ', אָ"ר יְהוּדָה, וְהַלֻּחֹת .366
כְּתִיב, חַד. תְּרֵי הֲווֹ וּמִתְחַזְיָין חַד. וְעֶשֶׂר אֲמִירָן מִתְגַּלְּפֵי בְּהוּ. חָמֵשׁ כְּלִילָן
בְּחָמֵשׁ, לְמֶהֱוֵי כֹּלָּא יְמִינָא. מַעֲשֵׂה אֱלֹהִים הֵמָּה וַדַּאי.

366. "As we learned, it says 'The Tablets (*Luchot*) were the work of God....' (Exodus 32:16)" Rav Yehuda said, "It is written *luchot* (לחת), without Vav (ו), namely one (in singular), for they were two but appeared as one. And the Ten Utterances were engraved upon them, one section of five being included in the other section of five, so that all would be in the Right. Surely they were the '...work of God.' (Ibid.)"

Only the Creator judged the case of Rav Shimon.

367. רַבִּי יִצְחָק אָמַר, שֶׁל סַנְפִּירִינוֹן הָווֹ, וּתְרֵין אַבְנִין הָווֹ. וְאַבְנִין הָווֹ סְתִימָאן. נָשִׁיב קוּדְשָׁא בְּרִיךְ הוּא בְּרוּחָא, וְאִתְפָּשָׁטוּ וְאִתְגְּלִיפוּ תְּרֵין לוּחִין. ר' יְהוּדָה אָמַר, כְּעֵין סַנְפִּירִינוֹן הָווֹ. מַשְׁמַע דִּכְתִיב מַעֲשֵׂה אֱלֹהִים הֵמָּה.

367. Rav Yitzchak said, "The Tablets were of sapphire, for there were originally two sapphire stones that were roughhewn, and the Holy One, blessed be He, caused a wind to blow upon them, and they were smoothed and transformed into two Tablets." Rav Yehuda said. "They only looked like sapphire, but were not of real sapphire, **and this is the meaning of the verse that describes them as '…the work of God…" (Exodus 32:16)"** For if they were of sapphire, they would have been like other precious stones and not '…the work of God….' (Ibid.)

God blew upon the stones and they transformed into Two Tablets.

368. אָמַר לֵיהּ, אִי הָכִי, סַנְפִּירִינוֹן דָּא דְּהוּא אַבְנָא טָבָא יַקִּירָא מִשְׁאָר אַבְנִין, לָאו עוֹבָדָא דְּקוּדְשָׁא בְּרִיךְ הוּא אִינּוּן. א"ל, בְּמַאי אוֹקִימְנָא מַעֲשֵׂה אֱלֹהִים הֵמָּה. הֲבָה דַּיְיקָא. אֶלָּא ת"ח, כְּתִיב וְהַלוּחוֹת מַעֲשֵׂה אֱלֹהִים הֵמָּה. הַלּוּחוֹת כְּתִיב, וְלָא כְּתִיב וְהָאֲבָנִים מַעֲשֵׂה אֱלֹהִים הֵמָּה.

368. He said to him, "If this is so, the sapphire—which is a stone more precious than any other—is not the work of God, yet the whole Creation is 'the work of God….' (Exodus 32:16)" **He said to him, "How can we explain the words, '…were the work of God.' (Ibid.)? They were indeed so.** They were a unique 'work of God,' not included in the works of Creation. **Yet come and behold, it is written that 'The Tablets were the work of God.' (Ibid.) It says 'The Tablets…' (Ibid.) not 'The stones were the work of God'** for He blew upon the stones, which were of real sapphire, and they were transformed into Two Tablets, as mentioned above."

God, before Creation, made the Two Tablets.

אָמַר ר' שִׁמְעוֹן, כֹּלָּא חַד הוּא, אֲבָל אִלֵּין תְּרֵין לוּחִין עַד לָא אִתְבְּרֵי .369
עָלְמָא הֲווֹ, וְאִסְתְּלָקוּ בְּעֶרֶב שַׁבָּת, וְעֲבַד לוֹן קוּדְשָׁא בְּרִיךְ הוּא, וְעוֹבָדוֹי הֲווֹ.

369. Rav Shimon said, "**Both are the same,** for both Rav Yosi and
Rav Yehuda's words lead to the same place. **These Two Tablets existed
from before the creation of the world, and they emerged on the eve
of Shabbat. The Holy One, blessed be He, made them, and they
were His handiwork.**"

The Tablets were formed of the Supernal dew of Atika.

מִמַּה אִתְעֲבִידוּ. תָּאנָא, מֵהַהוּא טַלָּא עִלָּאָה, דְּנָגֵיד מֵעַתִּיקָא קַדִּישָׁא. .370
וְכַד נָגֵיד וְאִתְמְשַׁךְ לַחֲקַל דְּתַפּוּחִין קַדִּישִׁין, נָטַל קוּדְשָׁא בְּרִיךְ הוּא תְּרֵין
כְּפּוּרֵי מִנַּיְהוּ, וְאִתְגְּלִידוּ, וְאִתְעֲבִידוּ תְּרֵין אַבְנִין יַקִּירִין. נָשַׁב בְּהוּ, וְאִתְפַּשְׁטוּ
לִתְרֵין לוּחִין, הה"ד, מַעֲשֵׂה אֱלֹהִים הֵמָּה וְהַמִּכְתָּב מִכְתַּב אֱלֹהִים הוּא. כְּמָה
דִּכְתִיב, כְּתוּבִים בְּאֶצְבַּע אֱלֹהִים.

370. He asks: "**Of what were they made?**" He answers: "**We have
learned that they were formed of the Supernal dew that issues from
Atika Kadisha,** which is Keter, **and when it drops on the orchard of
Holy apples,** Malchut, **the Holy One, blessed be He, took two drops,
causing them to solidify and turn into two precious stones. He blew
on them and they became flat like tablets,** as it is written, '…the work
of God, and the writing was the writing of God,' (Exodus 32:16) and
'written with the finger of God….' (Deuteronomy 9:10)

The Finger of God alludes to the Ten Sefirot.

תָּאנָא, אֶצְבַּע אֱלֹהִים. הַהוּא אֶצְבַּע סָלִיק לַעֲשָׂרָה. כְּמָה דְּאִתְּמַר, אֶצְבַּע .371
אֱלֹהִים הִיא. וְכָל אֶצְבַּע וְאֶצְבַּע סָלִיק לַעֲשָׂרָה, עַד דְּאִתְעֲבִיד יְדָא שְׁלֵימָתָא,
דִּכְתִיב וַיַּרְא יִשְׂרָאֵל אֶת הַיָּד הַגְּדוֹלָה.

371. We have learned: '…the finger of God…' (Deuteronomy 9:10) **expanded into ten,** for the ten fingers correspond to the Ten Sefirot and each one of them includes Ten Sefirot, **as it is written, '…written with the finger of God….'** (Deuteronomy 9:10) Each one of the fingers expanded into ten until a complete hand was formed, as it is written: **"And Israel saw that great work (lit. 'hand')…."** (Exodus 14:31) Thus, here also, '…the finger of God…' (Deuteronomy 9:10) is expanded into ten.

The letters of the Tablets were seen from both sides.

372. אָמַר ר' יְהוּדָה, חָרוּת עַל הַלָּחוֹת, נְקִיבָן הֲוֹו אַבְנִין, וְאִתְחֲזִיאוּ לִתְרֵין סִטְרִין, חָרוּת גְּלוּפָא דִּגְלוּפִין. אָמַר ר' אַבָּא, מֵהַאי סִטְרָא אִתְחֲזֵי סִטְרָא אַחֲרָא, וְאִתְקְרֵי מֵהָכָא, מַה דִּכְתִיב בְּסִטְרָא אַחֲרָא.

372. Rav Yehuda said, "'Engraved upon the Tablets;" (Exodus 32:16) the letters on **the stones were pierced so that the writing could be seen** from one side to the other, and the writing **was seen from both sides. '…engraved…'** (Ibid.) means **an engraving of an engraving,** through one side to the other." **According to Rav Aba, from one side you could see the other side and read on this side what is written on the other side.**

The Tablets were miraculously written.

373. רַבִּי אֶלְעָזָר אָמַר, בְּנֵס הֲוֹו כְּתִיבִין, דְּכָל בְּנֵי נָשָׁא, הֲוֹו אַמְרִין וְסָהֲדִין, דְּהָא מִכְתַּב אֱלֹהִים הוּא וַדַּאי, דְּהָא כָּל בְּנֵי עָלְמָא לָא יַכְלִין לְמִנְדַּע לוֹן כְּמָה דַּהֲוֹו.

373. Rav Elazar said, "They were written miraculously so that every man would bear testimony that it was the writing of God, for none of the people in the world could conceive them as they really were."

The five Utterences on the right were able to been seen
from the left, and vice versa.

374. כְּדַעְתַּיְיהוּ דְּאִינּוּן דְּאַמְרִין, נְקִיבִין הֲוֹו, בֵּי כְּתִיב וְרוּת בַּלָּחוֹת, עַל הַלָּחוֹת כְּתִיב. אֶלָּא הָכִי תָּאנָא, חֲמִשָּׁא קָלִין אִינּוּן לִימִינָא, וַחֲמִשָּׁא לִשְׂמָאלָא. וְאִינּוּן דִּשְׂמָאלָא כְּלִילָן בִּימִינָא. וּמַן יְמִינָא, אִתְחֲזוֹן אִינּוּן דִּשְׂמָאלָא, וְהָכָא כֹּלָּא אִיהוּ יְמִינָא, וְאִתְכְּלִילָן אִלֵּין בְּאִלֵּין, מַאן דַּהֲוָה בְּסִטְרָא דָּא, חָמֵי לְסִטְרָא אַחֲרָא, וְקָרֵי לוֹן לְאִינּוּן אַתְוָון. דְּהָא תָּנֵינָן, שְׂמָאלָא אִתְחֲזַר יְמִינָא, דִּכְתִיב מִימִינוֹ אֵשׁ דָּת לָמוֹ, וּבְגִין כַּךְ מִכְתַּב אֱלֹהִים הוּא וַדַּאי.

374. He asks: "According to those who say they were pierced through, why does it not say that the writing was engraved 'on the Tablets' instead of 'upon the Tablets'?" He answers: "We have learned that five sounds were on the right and five on the left, and those of the left were included in the right, and from the right one could see those of the left. And here, upon the Tablets, all was on the right because those five Utterances of the left were included in those of the right. Therefore he who stood at one side could see what was on the other side and read the letters. So the miracle about the Tablets—that one could read one side from the other—does not refer to the front and back but to the right and left side because they were not engraved through; for we have learned that the left turned into the right, as it is written, '… from His right hand went a fiery law for them.' (Deuteronomy 33:2) Therefore, assuredly it was '…the work of God….' (Exodus 32:16)"

From the first Utterance, you could read the sixth Utterance, and so on.

375. הָא כֵּיצַד, מַאן דַּהֲוָה מִסִּטְרָא דָּא, הֲוָה קָרֵי בְּדָא, אָנֹכִי יְיָ' אֱלֹהֶיךָ. וּמֵאֵלֵּין אַתְוָון הֲוָה חָמֵי, וְקָרֵי לֹא תִרְצַח. הֲוָה קָרֵי לֹא יִהְיֶה לָךְ. וַהֲוָה חָמֵי וְקָרֵי, לֹא תִנְאָף. וַהֲוָה קָרֵי לֹא תִשָּׂא אֶת שֵׁם יְיָ' אֱלֹהֶיךָ לַשָּׁוְא. וַהֲוָה חָמֵי וְקָרֵי לֹא תִגְנֹב. וְכֹלָּא מִסִּטְרָא דָּא, וְכַךְ לְכֻלְּהוּ, וּכְדֵין מִסִּטְרָא אַחֲרָא, וְכֻלְּהוּ כְּלִילָן דָּא בְּדָא כה"ג. הה"ד מִכְתַּב אֱלֹהִים הוּא. מִכְתַּב אֱלֹהִים הוּא וַדַּאי.

375. He explains: "Thus, he who stood on one side would read 'I am the Lord your God,' (Exodus 20:2) and out of these letters he could see and read the words, 'You shall not murder,' (Ibid. 13) and he read, 'You shall not have,' (Ibid. 3) and could see and read the words, 'You shall not commit adultery.' (Ibid. 13) He read, 'You shall not take the Name of the Lord your God in vain,' (Ibid. 7) and at the same time he could see and read the words, 'You shall not steal.' (Ibid. 13) And it was thus with all the words from the right side, and in the same way all those from the other side, and they were all included one within the other this way. Of this, it is said, 'the writing of God' for assuredly it was '...the writing of God....' (Exodus 32:16)"

Moses prepared the Israelites with his words.

376. וַיֵּרֶד מֹשֶׁה אֶל הָעָם וַיֹּאמֶר אֲלֵיהֶם. רַבִּי יוֹסֵי אָמַר, מַאי אֲמִירָא דָא דִּכְתִיב וַיֹּאמֶר אֲלֵיהֶם, וְלָא כְּתִיב מַאי קָאָמַר. א"ר יִצְחָק, תָּא חֲזֵי, אָרְחָא דְּעָלְמָא הוּא, כַּד אָתֵי וֶחֱדְוָתָא לְבַר נָשׁ, אוֹ כַּד אָתֵי צַעֲרָא, עַד לָא יָדַע מִנֵּיהּ לָא יָכִיל לְמִסְבַּל, דְּהָא לִבָּא אִתְפָּרוֹ לְשַׁעֲתָא. וְכַד יָדַע מִנֵּיהּ, קָאִים בְּקִיּוּמֵיהּ, וְיָכִיל לְמִסְבַּל. כָּל שֶׁכֵּן הָכָא, דְּהָא מֹשֶׁה אָמַר לוֹן כָּל מַה דַּהֲוָה לְבָתַר, וְאִתְתְּקִיף לַבַּיְיהוּ בְּמִלִּין, וְלָא יָכִילוּ לְמִסְבַּל. כ"ש אִי לָא אָמַר לוֹן בְּיָדִי. וּבג"כ וַיֹּאמֶר אֲלֵיהֶם בְּקַדְמֵיתָא, וְאִתְתַּקַּף לַבַּיְיהוּ. וּלְבָתַר וַיְדַבֵּר אֱלֹהִים.

376. Rav Yosi said, "In the verse 'And Moses went down to the people and said to them' (Exodus 19:25), what was actually said? What he said was not written." Rav Yitzchak explained, "Come and behold, it is the way of the world that when joy or sorrow comes to a person, before he understand it he cannot bear it, for his heart instantly flies out of him. But once he understands it, he is relaxed and can endure it. It is all the more so in this case. When Moses prepared them for that which was about to take place, he strengthened their hearts with his words, for otherwise they would not be able to bear all that was about to come. Therefore it is written, '...And said to them,' ((Ibid.) and right after that, 'And God spoke....' (Exodus 20:1)

The souls of the Israelites flew away to the Throne of Glory.

377. וְעִם כָּל דָּא, לָא יָכִילוּ לְמִסְבַּל, דְּהָא תָּנֵינָן, אָמַר ר' יְהוּדָה אָמַר ר' חִיָּיא אָמַר ר' יוֹסֵי, כַּד שָׁמְעוּ מִלָּה דְּקוּדְשָׁא בְּרִיךְ הוּא, פַּרְחַת נִשְׁמָתַיְיהוּ, וְסַלְקָא נִשְׁמָתַיְיהוּ דְּיִשְׂרָאֵל, עַד כּוּרְסֵי יְקָרָא דִּילֵיהּ, לְאִתְדַּבְּקָא תַמָּן.

377. "Despite all this, they could not endure it since as we have been taught from Rav Yehuda who said in the name of Rav Chiya, in the name of Rav Yosi, 'When they heard the words of the Holy One, blessed be He, their souls flew from them and ascended up to the Throne of Glory so as to cleave to it.'

The Torah returned the souls back to their bodies.

378. אָמְרָה אוֹרַיְיתָא קָמֵיהּ דְּקוּדְשָׁא בְּרִיךְ הוּא, וְכִי לְמַגָּנָא הֲוֵינָא מִתְּרֵי אַלְפֵי שְׁנִין, עַד לָא אִתְבְּרֵי עָלְמָא, לְמַגָּנָא כְּתִיב בָּהּ, וְאִיעַ אִיעַ מִבְּנֵי יִשְׂרָאֵל וּמִן הַגֵּר הַגָּר בְּתוֹכָם וְאֶל בְּנֵי יִשְׂרָאֵל תְּדַבֵּר לֵאמֹר. כִּי לִי בְנֵי יִשְׂרָאֵל עֲבָדִים. אָן אִינּוּן בְּנֵי יִשְׂרָאֵל. בָּה שַׁעֲתָא, אָהַדְּרַת אוֹרַיְיתָא נִשְׁמָתַיְיהוּ דְּיִשְׂרָאֵל, כָּל חַד וְחַד לְאַתְרֵיהּ. אוֹרַיְיתָא אִתְקִיפַת, וַאֲחִידַת בְּהוּ בְּנִשְׁמָתַיְיהוּ, לְאַהֲדְּרָא לְהוּ לְיִשְׂרָאֵל הֲדָ"ה תּוֹרַת יְיָ' תְּמִימָה מְשִׁיבַת נָפֶשׁ. מְשִׁיבַת נֶפֶשׁ מַמָּשׁ.

378. "The Torah said to the Holy One, blessed be He, 'Was it for nothing that I was fashioned two thousand years before the creation of the world? Is it all in vain that in Me it is inscribed, '... "Whatever man there be of the house of Israel, or of the strangers who sojourn among you..." (Leviticus 17:8); 'And you shall speak to the children of Israel, saying...' (Leviticus 24:15); and 'For to Me the children of Israel are servants....' (Leviticus 25:55) 'Where, then, are these children of Israel?' In that moment, the Torah returned their souls to the children of Israel, each one of them to its own place. The Torah strengthened and took hold of the souls and gave them back to Israel, as it is written, 'The Torah of the Lord is perfect, restoring

the soul....' (Psalms 19:8) '...restoring...' (Ibid.) literally, as it
restored the souls of Israel after they flew away from them.

In the days of Solomon, the moon was in its fullness.

379. תָּאנָא, כְּתִיב וַיֵּשֶׁב שְׁלֹמֹה עַל כִּסֵּא יְיָ' לְמֶלֶךְ, כְּמָה דִכְתִיב, שֵׁשׁ מַעֲלוֹת
לַכִּסֵּא. ר' אַבָּא אָמַר, דְּקַיְּימָא סִיהֲרָא בְּאַשְׁלָמוּתָא. דִּתְנֵינָן, בְּיוֹמוֹי דִּשְׁלֹמֹה,
קַיְּימָא סִיהֲרָא בְּאַשְׁלָמוּתָא.

379. "We have learned that the verses, 'Then Solomon sat on the
Throne of the Lord as king...'" (I Chronicles 29:23) and 'The throne
had six steps...' (I Kings 10:19) corresponding to the six Sefirot:
Chesed, Gevurah, Tiferet, Netzach, Hod, and Yesod. Therefore it is
called '...the Throne of the Lord....'" (I Chronicles 29:23) **Rabbi Aba
said, "The moon was then full; as we learned that in the days of
King Solomon, the moon was in its fullness,** meaning that the Nukva
of Zeir Anpin called moon was in her fullness."

Fifteen generations from Abraham to Solomon.

380. אֵימָתַי בְּאַשְׁלָמוּתָא. דְּקַיְּימָא בַּחֲמֵשָׁה עָשָׂר, כְּמָה דִּתְנֵינָן, אַבְרָהָם.
יִצְחָק. יַעֲקֹב. יְהוּדָה. פֶּרֶץ. וְחֶצְרוֹן. רָם. עֲמִינָדָב. נַחְשׁוֹן. שַׂלְמוֹן. בּוֹעַז. עוֹבֵד.
יִשַׁי. דָּוִד. שְׁלֹמֹה. כַּד אָתָא שְׁלֹמֹה, קַיְּימָא סִיהֲרָא בְּאַשְׁלָמוּתָא. הֲדָ"ה, וַיֵּשֶׁב
שְׁלֹמֹה עַל כִּסֵּא יְיָ' לְמֶלֶךְ. וּכְתִיב שֵׁשׁ מַעֲלוֹת לַכִּסֵּא. כֹּלָּא כְּגַוְונָא דִלְעֵילָּא.

380. He asks, "When was the moon, which is Malchut, **in its fullness?"**
He answers, "**When it was established by fifteen** kings, as we learned.
**Abraham. Isaac. Jacob. Judah. Peretz. Chetzron. Ram. Aminadab.
Nachshon. Shalmon. Boaz. Oved. Yishai. David. Solomon. When
Solomon sat on his throne, the moon,** Malchut, **was in its fullness.
Therefore, it is written, 'Then Solomon sat on the Throne of the
Lord as king...'** (I Chronicles 29:23), which is Malchut. **It is also
written, 'The throne had six steps...'** (I Kings 10:19) corresponding

to the six Sefirot of Malchut—Chesed, Gevurah, Tiferet, Netzach, Hod, and Yesod, **everything as Above.**

In the days of Zedekiah, the moon was in its wane.

381. בְּיוֹמוֹי דְּצִדְקִיָּה, קַיְימָא סִיהֲרָא בִּפְגִימוּתָא, וְאִתְפְּגִים. כד"א, וְיָרֵחַ לֹא יַגִּיהַ אוֹרוֹ. דְּתָנֵינָן, בְּיוֹמוֹי דְּצִדְקִיָּה, אִתְפְּגִים סִיהֲרָא, וְאִתְחַשַּׁכוּ אַנְפַּיְיהוּ דְּיִשְׂרָאֵל.

381. "In the days of Zedekiah, the moon, Malchut, was waning and was defective, as it is written, '...and the moon shall not shed her light.' (Isaiah 13:10) Since, as we have learned, in the days of Zedekiah the moon was in its wane and the face of Israel was darkened.

Fifteen generations of waning from Rechavam to Zedekiah.

382. פּוּק וְחַשִׁיב, רְחַבְעָם. אֲבִיָּה. אָסָא. יְהוֹשָׁפָט. יְהוֹרָם. אֲחַזְיָהוּ. יוֹאָשׁ. אֲמַצְיָהוּ. עוּזִיָּהוּ. יוֹתָם. אָחָז. יְחִזְקִיָּהוּ. מְנַשֶּׁה. אָמוֹן. יֹאשִׁיָּהוּ. צִדְקִיָּהוּ. וְכַד אָתָא צִדְקִיָּהוּ אִתְפְּגִים סִיהֲרָא וְקַיְימָא עַל פְּגִימוּתָא. דִּכְתִיב וְאֶת עֵינֵי צִדְקִיָּה עִוֵּר. בֵּיהּ זִמְנָא הִשְׁלִיךְ מִשָּׁמַיִם אֶרֶץ. הַאי אֶרֶץ אִתְעֲבָרָא מִקָּמֵי שָׁמַיִם, וְאִתְרָחֲקַת מִנֵּיהּ, וְאִתְחַשְּׁכָא הַאי אֶרֶץ.

382. "Go and calculate: Rechavam. Aviyah. Asa. Yehoshafat. Yehoram. Achazyahu. Yoash. Amatzyahu. Uziyahu. Yotam. Achaz. Yechizkiyahu. Menasheh. Amon. Josiah. When Zedekiah came, the moon was blemished and stayed lacking, as is written, 'Then he put out the eyes of Zedekiah....' (Jeremiah 52:11) Then 'the Lord... cast down from Heaven, Earth...' (Lamentations 2:1), meaning that the Earth, which is Malchut, **was removed far from Heaven,** which is Zeir Anpin, **and became dark.**"

The moon began to shine when Israel stood by Mount Sinai.

383. תָּאנָא, בְּשַׁעֲתָא דְקַיְימוּ יִשְׂרָאֵל עַל טוּרָא דְסִינַי שָׁארֵי סִיהֲרָא לְאַנְהָרָא, דִּכְתִיב, וַיֵּט שָׁמַיִם וַיֵּרַד. מַהוּ וַיֵּרַד. דְּקָרִיב שִׁמְשָׁא לְגַבֵּי סִיהֲרָא, וְשָׁרֵי לְאַנְהָרָא סִיהֲרָא. דִּכְתִיב אֶל מִזְרָח מַחֲנֵה יְהוּדָה מִזְרָחָה.

383. We have learned that when Israel stood by Mount Sinai, the moon began to shine, as it is written: "He bowed the Heavens also, and came down..." (II Samuel 22:10), meaning that the sun, which is Zeir Anpin and is called Heavens, **approached the moon,** which is Malchut. **And the moon began to shine,** as is expressed in the verse, "And on the east side toward the rising of the sun shall they of the standard of the camp of Judah pitch by their hosts...." (Numbers 2:3) "Judah" is the Chariot of Malchut, and the "east side" signifies shining and Illumination.

Judah received the kingship on Mount Sinai.

384. בְּטוּרָא דְסִינַי, אִתְמָנָא יְהוּדָה, רוֹפִינָס בְּמַלְכוּתָא, דִּכְתִיב, וִיהוּדָה עוֹד רָד עִם אֵל וְעִם קְדוֹשִׁים נֶאֱמָן. מַהוּ וְעִם קְדוֹשִׁים נֶאֱמָן. כַּד אָמַר קֻבָּ"ה לְיִשְׂרָאֵל, וְאַתֶּם תִּהְיוּ לִי מַמְלֶכֶת כֹּהֲנִים וְגוֹי קָדוֹשׁ, נֶאֱמָן הֲוָה יְהוּדָה לְקַבְּלָא מַלְכוּתָא, וְשָׁארֵי סִיהֲרָא לְאַנְהָרָא.

384. On Mount Sinai, Judah was appointed to rule over the kingdom, as it is written, '...But Judah still rules with God, and is faithful with Holy Ones" (Hosea 12:1), "...faithful with Holy Ones..." (Ibid.) means that when the Holy One, blessed be He, said to Israel: "And you shall be to Me a kingdom of priests, and a holy nation..." (Exodus 19:6), Judah was found trustworthy to receive the kingship. **Then the moon,** which is Malchut, **began to shine.**

YOSEF HATZADIK

Vayeshev

10. "And a certain man found him"

A Synopsis

This section addresses the role of Providence in the sale of Joseph to the Egyptians and illustrates our inability to interpret events and their causal relationships as positive or negative, since we are ignorant of their role in God's preordained design.

The Relevance of this Passage

The selling of Joseph into slavery, and his subsequent rise from the status of prisoner to the second in command of Egypt, alludes to our ability to take control over the physical reality and triumph over our most base desires, thereby freeing our souls. The strength to accomplish this is aroused within us through the liberating Light set aflame by these kabbalistic verses. In addition, we become more cognizant of our limited perspectives on life, particularly when hardships strike. Just as Joseph's imprisonment was a dire and tragic predicament that was eventually turned into triumph, our afflictions can be transformed into conquests given the right state of enlightened consciousness. That is, the foresight and wisdom to see beyond the immediate circumstances. Enlightenment is thus awakened in us by the lessons and Light emitted through the luminous letters of the Hebrew language appearing in this passage.

Israel sent Joseph to his brothers to fulfill the
Creator's decree in His covenant with Abraham.

102. וַיִּמְצָאֵהוּ אִישׁ וְהִנֵּה תֹעֶה בַּשָּׂדֶה וַיִּשְׁאָלֵהוּ הָאִישׁ לֵאמֹר מַה תְּבַקֵּשׁ. מַה כְּתִיב לְעֵילָּא, וַיֹּאמֶר יִשְׂרָאֵל אֶל יוֹסֵף הֲלוֹא אַחֶיךָ רֹעִים בִּשְׁכֶם לְכָה וְאֶשְׁלָחֲךָ אֲלֵיהֶם. וְכִי יַעֲקֹב שְׁלֵימָא, דַּהֲוָה רְחֵים לֵיהּ לְיוֹסֵף מִכָּל בְּנוֹי, וְהוּא יָדַע דְּכָל אֲחוֹי הֲווֹ סָנְאִין לֵיהּ, אַמַּאי שַׁדַּר לֵיהּ לְגַבַּיְיהוּ, אֶלָּא אִיהוּ לָא חָשִׁיד עֲלַיְיהוּ,

דַּהֲוָה יָדַע דְּכֻלְּהוּ הֲווֹ זַכָּאִין, וְלָא חָשִׁיד לוֹן, אֶלָּא גְּרֵים קוּדְשָׁא בְּרִיךְ הוּא כָּל
דָּא, בְּגִין לְקַיְּימָא גְּזֵרָה דִּגְזַר בֵּין הַבְּתָרִים.

102. "And a certain man found him, and behold, he was wandering in the field; and the man asked him, saying, 'What are you seeking?'" (Genesis 37:15) It is written earlier: "And Israel said to Joseph, 'Are not your brothers feeding the flock in Shchem? Come, and I will send you to them'...." (Ibid. 13) [He asks:] "Why did the perfected Jacob, who loved Joseph above all his sons and knew that his brothers hated him, send Joseph to them?" He answers: "Because he knew they were righteous, he did not suspect them. Rather, the Holy One, blessed be He, caused all this to fulfill the decree He made to Abraham in the Covenant between the pieces."

The reason the brothers needed to be master over Joseph
before he descended to Egypt.

103. אַשְׁכַּחְנָא בְּסִפְרֵי קַדְמָאֵי, דְּבָעְיָין אִלֵּין בְּנֵי יַעֲקֹב, לְשַׁלְטָאָה עֲלוֹי, עַד לָא
יֵחוֹת לְמִצְרַיִם, דְּאִילוּ הוּא יֵחוֹת לְמִצְרַיִם וְאִינּוּן לָא שָׁלְטוּ בֵּיהּ בְּקַדְמֵיתָא, יָכְלֵי
מִצְרָאֵי לְשַׁלְטָאָה לְעָלְמִין עֲלַיְיהוּ דְּיִשְׂרָאֵל, וְאִתְקַיְּימָא בֵּיהּ בְּיוֹסֵף, דְּאוֹזְדַּבַּן
לְעַבְדָּא, וְאִינּוּן שָׁלְטוּ עֲלוֹי, וְאַף עַל גַּב דְּיוֹסֵף הֲוָה מַלְכָּא לְבָתַר, וּמִצְרָאֵי הֲווֹ
עַבְדִין לֵיהּ, אִשְׁתְּכָחוּ יִשְׂרָאֵל דְּשָׁלְטוּ עַל כֻּלְּהוּ.

103. We have found it stated in ancient books that it was imperative that the sons of Jacob have mastery over Joseph before he descended to Egypt. For if he had gone there before they had dominion over him, the Egyptians would have ruled over Israel forever, and Israel would not have been able to leave. Therefore it came to pass that his brothers were Joseph's masters and sold him as a slave. Thus, when Joseph was later crowned king of Egypt, Israel ruled over them all. Since they obtained mastery over Joseph, their king, by selling him to be a slave, it was as if they ruled over the Egyptians themselves. This weakened the Egyptian power and enabled Israel to be freed from them.

The Shechinah and Israel went into exile when Joseph was sold as a slave.

‏104. תָּא חֲזֵי, דְּיוֹסֵף דְּאִיהוּ בְּרִית עִלָּאָה, כָּל זִמְנָא דְּאִתְקַיַּים בְּרִית, שְׁכִינְתָּא אִתְקַיַּים בַּהֲדַיְיהוּ דְּיִשְׂרָאֵל בִּשְׁלָם, כְּדְקָא יָאוֹת, כֵּיוָן דְּאִסְתַּלָּק יוֹסֵף בְּרִית עִלָּאָה מֵעַלְמָא, כְּדֵין בְּרִית, שְׁכִינְתָּא, וְיִשְׂרָאֵל כֻּלְּהוּ בְּגָלוּתָא נָפְקוּ, וְהָא אוֹקִימְנָא דִּכְתִיב, וַיָּקָם מֶלֶךְ חָדָשׁ עַל מִצְרָיִם אֲשֶׁר לֹא יָדַע אֶת יוֹסֵף, וְכֹלָא הֲוָה מֵעִם קוּדְשָׁא בְּרִיךְ הוּא, כְּדְקָא יָאוֹת.

104. Come and see, Joseph was the Supernal Covenant, Yesod of Zeir Anpin, **and as long as the Covenant,** Joseph, **endured, the Shechinah lived within Israel in peace. Once Joseph, the Supernal Covenant, was gone from the world** and sold as a slave, **the Covenant, the Shechinah, and Israel all went into exile. This has been explained in connection with the verse, "Now there arose a new king over Egypt, who knew not Joseph." (Exodus 1:8)** This indicates that his rank had been revoked and he went into exile. **Everything was from the Holy One, blessed be He, and it happened as it had to.**

Vayeshev

19. "And Joseph was brought down to Egypt..."

A Synopsis

This section begins by interpreting the phrasing of the title quotation as indicating God's approval of this act; it was necessary in order to fulfill His announcement to Abraham. A discussion follows concerning the legions of angels who sing praises to the glory of God throughout the night. It is the role of the children of Israel to offer praises to God through litanies three times daily. In this way, God is glorified both day and night, from Above and Below. Rav Shimon next offers two explanations of the phrase, "who commands the sun," in the context of Jacob and Joseph. One explanation interprets this as an allusion to Joseph, when he was sold. The other understands it to be concerned with Jacob, when his sons showed him evidence of Joseph's death.

The Relevance of this Passage

In the course of spiritual development, we sometimes have to fail so as to build a greater vessel that can hold all the Light that awaits us as we ascend to the next level. This is what happened to Joseph when he was "brought down to Egypt." Egypt is a code word for darkness and disconnection from the Light of the Creator. Reading these passages helps attune us to the angelic hierarchies and the spiritual energy forces they transmit. These forces give us power to rise when we fall, strength to stand after we stumble—and this serves to increase the size of our vessel so that we can receive even greater Light in our lives. These verses also help us expand our vessel so that it is not necessary for us to fall quite so far down or to stumble quite so often.

Joseph was brought down to Egypt to fulfill the Creator's decree.

195. וְיוֹסֵף הוּרַד מִצְרָיְמָה וַיִּקְנֵהוּ פּוֹטִיפַר וְגו'. מַאי הוּרַד. דְּאִסְתַּכַּם קוּדְשָׁא בְּרִיךְ הוּא בְּהַהוּא עוֹבָדָא, לְקַיְּימָא גְּזֵרָה דִּילֵיהּ דַּגְזַר בֵּית הַבְּתָרִים, דִּכְתִיב יָדֹע תֵּדַע כִּי גֵּר יִהְיֶה זַרְעֲךָ וְגו'. וַיִּקְנֵהוּ פּוֹטִיפַר לְסִטְרָא וְחַטָּאָה קָנָה לֵיהּ.

195. [He asks:] "In the verse, 'And Joseph was brought down to Egypt; and Potifar bought him...' (Genesis 39:1) why is it written, 'was brought down' rather than 'went down to Egypt'?" He answers: "The Holy One, blessed be He, consented to the act of selling Joseph to Egypt, so that the decree He made between the pieces would be fulfilled, as it is written, 'Know surely that your seed shall be a stranger....' (Genesis 15:13) Therefore it says 'was brought down,' meaning from Heaven's decree he was brought down. '...and Potiphar bought him...' (Genesis 39:1) to commit sin with him, namely sodomy."

Seven stars correspond to the Seven Sefirot.

196. פָּתַח וַאֲמַר, הָאוֹמֵר לַחֶרֶס וְלֹא יִזְרָח וּבְעַד כּכָבִים יַחְתֹּם. תָּא וְחֲזֵי שִׁבְעָה כֹּכְבַיָּא עֲבַד קוּדְשָׁא בְּרִיךְ הוּא בִּרְקִיעָא, וְכָל רְקִיעָא וּרְקִיעָא, אִית בֵּיהּ כַּמָּה שַׁמָּשִׁין מְמַנָּן, לְשַׁמָּשָׁא לֵיהּ לְקוּדְשָׁא בְּרִיךְ הוּא.

196. He opened and said: "'Who commands the sun, and it rises not; and seals up the stars.' (Job 9:7) Come and see: the Holy One, blessed be He, made seven stars in the Firmament, corresponding to the Seven Sefirot: Chesed, Gevurah, Tiferet, Netzach, Hod, Yesod, and Malchut. Each Firmament contains numerous attendants who serve the Holy One, blessed be He.

Each appointee has a specific task.

197. בְּגִין דְּלֵית לָךְ שַׁמָּשָׁא, אוֹ מְמַנָּא, דְּלֵית לֵיהּ פּוּלְחָנָא וְשִׁמוּשָׁא לְמָארֵיהּ, וְקַיְימֵי כָּל חַד וְחַד, עַל הַהוּא שִׁמוּשָׁא דְּאִתְפַּקְדָא בֵּיהּ, וְכָל חַד יָדַע עֲבִידְתֵּיהּ לְשַׁמָּשָׁא.

197. "There is no attendant or appointee who does not have a specific task and service to perform for the Holy One, blessed be He, and each knows his own task to perform.

All powers, stars, and constellations sing praises to the Creator.

198. מִנְּהוֹן מְשַׁמְּשֵׁי בִּשְׁלִיחוּתָא דְמָרֵיהוֹן, וְאִתְפַּקְדָן בְּעַלְמָא עַל כָּל עוֹבָדֵיהוֹן דִּבְנֵי נָשָׁא, וּמִנְּהוֹן דְּקָא מְשַׁבְּחִין לֵיהּ, וְאִינּוּן אִתְפַּקְדָן עַל שִׁירָתָא, וְאַף עַל גַּב דְּאִינּוּן אִתְפַּקְדָן בְּהַאי, לֵית לָךְ כָּל חֵילָא בִּשְׁמַיָּא, וְכֹכְבִין וּמַזָּלֵי, דְּכֻלְּהוּ לָא מְשַׁבְּחָן לֵיהּ לְקוּדְשָׁא בְּרִיךְ הוּא.

198. "Some act as their Master's messengers, appointed in this world to oversee the deeds of humanity. There are those who sing chants and hymns before Him, and even those who are in charge of poetry; there is no power, no star nor constellation that does not praise the Holy One, blessed be He.

At night, three legions of angels are appointed over song.

199. דְּהָא בְּשַׁעֲתָא דְּעָאל לֵילְיָא, כְּדֵין אִתְפַּרְשָׁן תְּלַת סִטְרִין מַשִׁרְיָין, לִתְלַת סִטְרֵי עַלְמָא, וּבְכָל סִטְרָא וְסִטְרָא, אֶלֶף אַלְפִין, וְרִבּוֹא, וְכֻלְּהוּ מְמַנָּן עַל שִׁירָתָא.

199. "For when night falls, three legions are divided into the three directions of the world, each and every side containing thousands and tens of thousands of angels, who are appointed over song.

The angels from the south sing praises in the morning.

200. תְּלַת מַשִׁירְיָין אִינּוּן, וְחַד חֵיוְתָא קַדִּישָׁא מְמַנָּא עֲלַיְיהוּ, וְקָיְימָא עֲלַיְיהוּ, וְכֻלְּהוּ קָא מְשַׁבְּחָן לֵיהּ לְקוּדְשָׁא בְּרִיךְ הוּא, עַד דְּאָתֵי צַפְרָא, כַּד אָתֵי צַפְרָא, כָּל אִינּוּן דִּבְסְטַר דָּרוֹם, וְכָל כֹּכְבַיָּא דִּנְהָרֵי, כֻּלְּהוּ מְשַׁבְּחָן, וְאָמְרֵי שִׁירָתָא לְקוּדְשָׁא בְּרִיךְ הוּא, כד"א, בְּרָן יַחַד כֹּכְבֵי בֹקֶר וַיָּרִיעוּ כָּל בְּנֵי אֱלֹהִים. בְּרָן יַחַד כֹּכְבֵי בֹקֶר, אִלֵּין כֹּכְבַיָּא דִּבְסְטַר דָּרוֹם, כד"א וַיַּשְׁכֵּם אַבְרָהָם בַּבֹּקֶר. וַיָּרִיעוּ כָּל בְּנֵי אֱלֹהִים, אִלֵּין אִינּוּן, דִּבְסְטַר שְׂמָאלָא, דְּאִתְכְּלִילוּ בִּימִינָא.

200. "There are three legions of angels **and one Living Creature,** the Nukva, **who stands in charge of them. They all praise the Holy One, blessed be He, until morning comes. When morning comes, those of the south side and the luminous stars,** the angels, **praise and recite poetry before the Holy One, blessed be He; as it is written, 'When the morning stars sang together, and all the sons of God (Elohim) shouted for joy.' (Job 38:7) '...The morning stars' (Ibid.) are the stars on the south side,** namely Chesed, **as it is written, 'And Abraham went early in the morning....' (Genesis 19:27) '...all the sons of God (Elohim) shouted for joy' (Job 38:7) refers to the stars on the Left Column, which are included within the Right.**

Israel praise the Creator three times a day.

201. וּכְדֵין צַפְרָא נָהֵיר, וְיִשְׂרָאֵל נָטְלֵי שִׁירָתָא, וּמְשַׁבְּחָן לֵיהּ לְקוּדְשָׁא בְּרִיךְ הוּא, בִּימָמָא, תְּלַת זִמְנִין בִּימָמָא, לָקֳבֵל תְּלַת זִמְנִין דְּלֵילְיָא, וְקָיְימִין אִלֵּין לָקֳבֵיל אִלֵּין, עַד דְּיִסְתַּלַּק יְקָרָא דְּקוּדְשָׁא בְּרִיךְ הוּא, בִּימָמָא וּבְלֵילְיָא כִּדְקָא יָאוֹת, וְקוּדְשָׁא בְּרִיךְ הוּא אִסְתַּלַּק בְּהוּ בְּשִׁית אִלֵּין.

201. "When daylight breaks, **Israel sing the praises of the Holy One, blessed be He, three times a day, corresponding to the three night** watches. **They stand before each other until the glory of the Holy One, blessed be He, is duly risen day and night. The Holy**

One, blessed be He, ascends by means of these six, namely three in
the day and three at night.

Nukva gives nourishment to the legions Above and Israel Below.

202. הַהוּא חֵיוָתָא קַדִּישָׁא, דְּקַיְּימָא עֲלַיְיהוּ לְעֵילָא, קַיְּימָא עַל יִשְׂרָאֵל לְתַתָּא,
בְּגִין לְאַתְקָנָא כֹּלָּא כְּדְקָא יָאוֹת, מַה כְּתִיב בָּהּ, וַתָּקָם בְּעוֹד לַיְלָה וַתִּתֵּן טֶרֶף
לְבֵיתָהּ וְחֹק לְנַעֲרוֹתֶיהָ. וַתִּתֵּן טֶרֶף לְבֵיתָהּ אִלֵּין אִינוּן מַשִׁירְיָין דִּלְעֵילָא, וְחֹק
לְנַעֲרוֹתֶיהָ, אִלֵּין מַשִׁירְיָין דְּיִשְׂרָאֵל לְתַתָּא, וּבְגִין כָּךְ יְקָרָא דְּקוּדְשָׁא בְּרִיךְ הוּא
אִסְתַּלַּק מִכָּל סִטְרִין, מֵעֵילָא וּמִתַּתָּא. וְעַל דָּא כֹּלָּא הוּא בִּרְשׁוּתֵיהּ קַיְּימָא,
וְכֹלָּא אִיהוּ בִּרְעוּתֵיהּ.

202. "The Living Creature, the Nukva, who stands above them, also
stands on Israel Below to properly fix everything." [He asks:] "What
is written about her?" [He answers:] "'She rises also while it is yet
night, and gives food to her household, and a portion to her maidens.'
(Proverbs 31:15) '…and gives food to her household…' (Ibid.) refers
to the three legions Above and '…a portion to her maidens' (Ibid.)
alludes to the camps of Israel Below. Therefore the glory of the Holy
One, blessed be He, is extolled on every side, Above and Below; thus
everything stands in His domain and His will."

The sun and stars stopped shining due to the sale of Joseph.

203. הָאוֹמֵר לַחֶרֶס וְלֹא יִזְרָח. רַבִּי שִׁמְעוֹן אֲמַר, דָּא יוֹסֵף. וּבְעַד כּוֹכָבִים
יַחְתּוֹם, אִלֵּין אִינּוּן אֲחוֹי, דִּכְתִיב בְּהוֹ, וְאַחַד עָשָׂר כּוֹכָבִים מִשְׁתַּחֲוִים לִי.
דָּבָר אַחֵר הָאוֹמֵר לַחֶרֶס, דָּא יַעֲקֹב, בְּשַׁעֲתָא דַּאֲמָרוּ לוֹ הַכֵּר נָא. וְלֹא יִזְרָח,
בְּשַׁעֲתָא דְּאִסְתַּלְּקַת שְׁכִינְתָּא מִנֵּיהּ. וּבְעַד כּוֹכָבִים יַחְתּוֹם, בְּגִין בְּנוֹי, אִתְחַזַּם
וְאִסְתִּים נְהוֹרָא דִּלֵיהּ, שִׁמְשָׁא אִתְחַשַּׁךְ, וְכֹכְבַיָּא לָא נְהִירוּ, בְּגִין דְּיוֹסֵף
אִתְפָּרַשׁ מֵאֲבוֹי. וְתָא חֲזֵי מֵהַהוּא יוֹמָא דְּהַהוּא עוֹבָדָא דְּיוֹסֵף, אִתְפָּרַשׁ יַעֲקֹב
מִשִׁמּוּשָׁא דְּעַרְסָא, וְאִשְׁתָּאַר אֲבֵלָא, עַד הַהוּא יוֹמָא דְּאִתְבַּשַּׂר בְּשׂוֹרָה דְּיוֹסֵף.

203. [Concerning,] "...who commands the sun, and it rises not...." (Job 9:7), Rav Shimon says this refers to Joseph when he was sold into Egypt. "...and seals up the stars" (Ibid.) are his brothers, about whom it is written: "...and the eleven stars bowed down to me." (Genesis 37:9) In another explanation, "...who commands the sun..." (Job 9:7) refers to Jacob at the time he was told, "...know now whether it be your son's coat or not." (Genesis 37:32) "...and it rises not..." (Job 9:7) means when the Shechinah was gone from him; "...and seals up the stars" (Ibid.) means his sons, as his Light was sealed and closed upon him because of them. The sun darkened and the stars did not shine because Joseph was separated from his father. Come and see, from the day Joseph was sold, Jacob abstained from marital intercourse and remained in mourning until he heard the good tidings of Joseph.

VAYESHEV

20. "And the Lord was with Joseph"

A Synopsis

Rav Yosi quotes the verse, "For the Creator loves justice," so as to lead a discussion on the protection that God offers the righteous. Through the examples of David and Joseph, both of whom walked "through the valley of the shadow of death," we are shown that God never abandons the righteous. In His mercy, He even guards the wicked, who, we learn, receive blessings and are sustained by the spiritual elevation of the righteous. Ultimately, though, we see that fortunate, indeed, are the righteous in this world and in the World to Come.

The Relevance of this Passage

Kabbalistically, Mercy represents the concept of time. Time is defined as the distance between cause and effect; the separation between action and reaction; the space between deed and dividend; the span between a person's behavior and the inevitable repercussion; the divide between crime and consequence. Within this gap, it is hoped that a person becomes enlightened to the senselessness of negative ways and recognizes the rewards of spiritual growth and positive, unselfish behavior. Time, however, can cause us to mistakenly believe that goodness goes unrewarded, while the wicked go unpunished. Yet time merely creates a delay—a window of opportunity in which our free will can earn us fulfillment, transformation, and recognition of the cause-and-effect principle that is at work in our world. Without time, a person would be instantly punished the moment he sinned. The wicked would be obliterated the moment they transgressed. They would lose the opportunity to change their ways and partake of the endless fulfillment in the World to Come. Mercy [time] is awarded to the wicked in the merit of the righteous who love humanity unconditionally. Awareness and a deeper understanding of mercy and the cause-and-effect principle are aroused within us through

the merit of the righteous, whose spiritual power surges through
this passage.

The Creator does not forsake the Righteous.

‏204. וַיְהִי ה' אֶת יוֹסֵף וַיְהִי אִישׁ מַצְלִיחַ וַיְהִי בְּבֵית אֲדוֹנָיו וגו'. רִבִּי יוֹסֵי פָּתַח,‏
‏כִּי ה' אֹהֵב מִשְׁפָּט וְלֹא יַעֲזֹב אֶת חֲסִידָיו לְעוֹלָם נִשְׁמָרוּ. הַאי קְרָא אוּקְמוּהָ‏
‏בְּאַבְרָהָם, אֶת חֲסִידָיו, וַחֲסִידוֹ כְּתִיב, וְהָא אִתְּמָר.‏

204. "And the Lord was with Joseph, and he was a successful man;
and he was in the house of his master the Egyptian." (Genesis 39:2)
Rav Yosi opened the discussion with the verse, "'For the Lord
loves justice, and forsakes not His pious ones; they are preserved
forever....' (Psalms 37:28) It has been explained that this refers
to Abraham because 'His pious ones (*chasidav*; ‏וַחֲסִידָיו‏)' (Ibid.) is
spelled 'pious one (*chasido*; ‏וַחֲסִידוֹ‏)' in the singular, as has already
been explained.

Wherever the Righteous go the Shechinah follows.

‏205. תָּא וַחֲזֵי, בְּכָל אֲתַר דְּצַדִּיקַיָּא אָזְלֵי, קוּדְשָׁא בְּרִיךְ הוּא נָטִיר לוֹן, וְלָא‏
‏שָׁבֵיק לוֹן. דָּוִד אָמַר, גַּם כִּי אֵלֵךְ בְּגֵיא צַלְמָוֶת לֹא אִירָא רָע כִּי אַתָּה עִמָּדִי‏
‏שִׁבְטְךָ וּמִשְׁעַנְתֶּךָ וגו', בְּכָל אֲתַר דְּצַדִּיקַיָּא אָזְלֵי, שְׁכִינְתָּא אָזְלָא עִמְּהוֹן, וְלָא‏
‏שָׁבֵיק לוֹן.‏

205. "Come and see, wherever the Righteous go, the Holy One,
blessed be He, protects them and never abandons them. As David
said, 'Even though I walk through the valley of the shadow of death,
I will fear no evil: for You are with me; Your rod and Your staff....'
(Psalms 23:4) For wherever the Righteous go the Shechinah goes
with them and never leaves them.

The Shechinah ensured that Joseph was successful in everything he did.

‏206. יוֹסֵף אָזַל בְּגֵיא צַלְמָוֶת, וְנָחֲתוּ לֵיהּ לְמִצְרַיִם, שְׁכִינְתָּא הֲוַת עִמֵּיהּ, הה"ד, וַיְהִי ה' אֶת יוֹסֵף, וּבְגִין דַּהֲוַת עִמֵּיהּ שְׁכִינְתָּא, בְּכָל מַה דַּהֲוָה עָבֵיד, הֲוָה מַצְלַח בִּידֵיהּ. דַּאֲפִילוּ מַאי דַּהֲוָה בִּידֵיהּ, וַהֲוָה תָּבַע לֵיהּ מָארֵיהּ בְּגַוְונָא אָחֲרָא, הֲוָה מִתְהַפֵּךְ בִּידֵיהּ, לְהַהוּא גַּוְונָא דִּרְעוּתָא דְּמָארֵיהּ הֲוָה רָעֵי בֵּיהּ, כד"א וַיַּרְא אֲדֹנָיו כִּי ה' אִתּוֹ וְכָל אֲשֶׁר הוּא עוֹשֶׂה ה' מַצְלִיחַ בְּיָדוֹ, מַצְלִיחַ בְּיָדוֹ וַדַּאי, כִּי ה' אִתּוֹ.

206. "When Joseph walked the valley of the shadow of death and was brought down to Egypt, the Shechinah was with him, as it is written, 'And the Lord was with Joseph....' (Genesis 39:2) Because the Shechinah was with him, whatever he did in his hand prospered. If he had something in his hand but his master asked for something else, what was in his hand would turn into that which his master wanted, as it is written, 'And his master saw that the Lord was with him, and that the Lord made all that he did prosper in his hand.' (Genesis 39:3) Assuredly, it '...did prosper in his hand...' (Ibid.) for the Lord was with him.

The Holy One, blessed by He, protects the Righteous
and the wicked for the sake of the Righteous.

‏207. תָּא חֲזֵי, וַיַּדַע אֲדֹנָיו כִּי ה' אִתּוֹ לָא כְּתִיב, אֶלָּא וַיַּרְא אֲדֹנָיו, דְּהָא בְּעֵינוֹי הֲוָה חָמֵי, עוֹבָדָא דְּנִסִּין בְּכָל יוֹמָא, דְּקוּדְשָׁא בְּרִיךְ הוּא עָבֵיד בִּידֵיהּ. וְעַל דָּא וַיְבָרֶךְ ה' אֶת בֵּית הַמִּצְרִי בִּגְלַל יוֹסֵף. קוּדְשָׁא בְּרִיךְ הוּא נָטֵיר לוֹן לְצַדִּיקַיָּא, וּבְגִינְהוֹן נָטַר לוֹן לְרַשִׁיעַיָּא, דְּהָא רַשִׁיעַיָּא מִתְבָּרְכִין בְּגִינְהוֹן דְּצַדִּיקַיָּא. כְּגַוְונָא דָא, כְּתִיב וַיְבָרֶךְ ה' אֶת בֵּית הַמִּצְרִי עוֹבֵד אֱדוֹם הַגִּתִּי בַּעֲבוּר אֲרוֹן הָאֱלֹקִים.

207. "Come and see, it is not written, 'And his master knew that the Lord was with him,' but rather 'And his master saw....' (Genesis 39:3) This teaches us that he saw with his own eyes the miracles that the Holy One, blessed be He, performed by His hand. Therefore '...the

Lord blessed the Egyptian house for Joseph's sake....' (Genesis 39:5) The Holy One, blessed be He, preserves the righteous. For their sakes, He also protects the wicked as they are blessed for the sake of the Righteous, as it is written, '..."The Lord has blessed the house of Oved Edom... because of the Ark of God"....' (II Samuel 6:12)

The Righteous are not saved by their own merits.

208. צַדִּיקַיָּא, אָחֳרָנִין מִתְבָּרְכִין בְּגִינַיְיהוּ, וְאִינוּן לָא יָכְלוּ לְאִשְׁתְּזָבָא בְּזְכוּתַיְיהוּ, וְהָא אוֹקִמוּהָ. יוֹסֵף אִתְבָּרֵךְ מָארֵיהּ בְּגִינֵיהּ, וְאִיהוּ לָא יָכִיל לְאִשְׁתְּזָבָא בְּזְכוּתֵיהּ מִנֵּיהּ, וּלְנָפְקָא לְחֵירוּ.

208. "Other people are blessed for the sake of the Righteous but they themselves cannot be saved by their own merits. This has been explained: Joseph's master has been blessed for his sake, yet Joseph could not be saved by his merits and gain his freedom.

The Creator protects the righteous in both worlds.

209. וּלְבָתַר אָעֵיל לֵיהּ בְּבֵית הַסֹּהַר, כד"א עִנּוּ בַכֶּבֶל רַגְלוֹ בַּרְזֶל בָּאָה נַפְשׁוֹ, עַד דִּלְבָתַר קוּדְשָׁא בְּרִיךְ הוּא אַפִּיק לֵיהּ לְחֵירוּ, וְשַׁלְטֵיהּ עַל כָּל אַרְעָא דְּמִצְרָיִם. וּבְגִין כָּךְ כְּתִיב, וְלֹא יַעֲזֹב אֶת וַחֲסִידָיו לְעוֹלָם נִשְׁמָרוּ, וַחֲסִידוֹ כְּתִיב וְאִתְּמַר, וְקוּדְשָׁא בְּרִיךְ הוּא אָגֵין עֲלַיְיהוּ דְּצַדִּיקַיָּא, בְּעַלְמָא דֵין וּבְעַלְמָא דְּאָתֵי, דִּכְתִיב וְיִשְׂמְחוּ כָל חוֹסֵי בָךְ לְעוֹלָם יְרַנֵּנוּ וְתָסֵךְ עָלֵימוֹ וְיַעְלְצוּ בָךְ אוֹהֲבֵי שְׁמֶךָ.

209. "He was later put in prison, as it is written, 'Whose foot they hurt with fetters; he was laid in iron.' (Psalms 105:18) Until afterwards the Holy One, blessed be He, set him free and made him ruler over Egypt. Therefore, it is written, 'For the Lord loves justice, and forsakes not His pious ones; they are preserved forever....' (Psalms 37:28) '...pious ones... (*chasidav*; plural) ' (Ibid.) is spelled to read 'pious one (*chasido*; singular),' as was explained. The Holy

One, blessed be He, protects the Righteous in this world and in the World to Come, as it is written, 'But let all those that put their trust in You rejoice, let them ever shout for joy, because You do defend them; and let those who love Your Name be joyful in You.' (Psalms 5:12)"

VAYESHEV

21. "His master's wife cast her eyes"

A Synopsis

This section pointedly reminds us that we must constantly be on guard to avoid being led astray by the Evil Inclination. As the Accusers assail man daily, he must cleave to the dimension and Sefirah known as Gevurah to become mightier than the Evil Inclination. As the friends point out, Joseph exemplifies this endeavor. He exposed himself to unfounded accusations because of the enormous care he took over his personal appearance. The friends next address the importance of guarding and preserving the Holy Covenant. The Covenant, we are told, upholds Heaven and Earth. When it is properly guarded, God showers the world with blessings, but if God's Judgment finds the world full of wicked people, Heaven and Earth will dry up and their natural, life-sustaining functions will cease.

The Relevance of this Passage

A reading of this section strengthens our resistance to evil and vain impulses, and steels our resolve to pursue positive change, for the sake of our soul and for all humankind. The collective intolerant, self-centered actions of man can become so great that they create a mass of negativity that literally blocks the Light from flowing into our world. Our connection to this passage helps dissolve this blockage, to allow the penetration of the Light.

One needs to be cautious of the Evil Inclination.

210. וַיְהִי אַחַר הַדְּבָרִים הָאֵלֶּה וַתִּשָּׂא אֵשֶׁת אֲדֹנָיו אֶת עֵינֶיהָ אֶל יוֹסֵף. רִבִּי חִיָּיא פָּתַח וְאָמַר, בָּרְכוּ ה' מַלְאָכָיו גִּבּוֹרֵי כֹחַ עוֹשֵׂי דְבָרוֹ לִשְׁמוֹעַ בְּקוֹל דְּבָרוֹ. תָּא חֲזֵי, כַּמָּה אִצְטְרִיךְ לֵיהּ לְבַר נָשׁ לְאִסְתַּמְּרָא מֵחוֹבוֹי, וּלְמֵיהַךְ בְּאָרַח

מִתְתַּקְנָא, בְּגִין דְּלָא יִסְטֵי לֵיהּ הַהוּא יֵצֶר הָרָע, דְּאִיהוּ מְקַטְרְגָא לֵיהּ כָּל יוֹמָא וְיוֹמָא, כְּמָה דְאִתְּמָר.

210. "And it came to pass after these things that his master's wife cast her eyes upon Joseph." (Genesis 39:7) Rav Chiya began the discussion with the verse, "'Bless the Lord, you angels of His, you mighty in strength who perform His bidding, listening to the voice of His word.' (Psalms 103:20) Come and see, a man should be very careful to avoid sinning and should walk the path of righteousness so as not to be led astray by the Evil Inclination, who daily brings accusations against him.

One needs to cleave to Might to be stronger
than the mighty Evil Inclination.

211. וּבְגִין דְּאִיהוּ מְקַטְרְגָא לֵיהּ תָּדִיר, בָּעֵי בַּר נָשׁ לְאִתְתַּקְפָא עֲלֵיהּ, וּלְאַסְתַּלְקָא עֲלֵיהּ, בַּאֲתַר תַּקִּיפוּ, דְּבָעֵי לְמֶהֱוֵי גְּבַר עֲלֵיהּ, וּלְאִשְׁתַּתְּפָא בַּאֲתַר הַגְּבוּרָה, בְּגִין דְּכַד בַּר נָשׁ אִתְקַף עֲלֵיהּ, כְּדֵין אִיהוּ בִּסְטַר גְּבוּרָה, וְאִתְדַּבַּק בֵּיהּ לְאִתְתַּקְפָא, וּבְגִין דְּהַהוּא יֵצֶר הָרָע תַּקִּיף, בָּעֵי בַּר נָשׁ דִּיהֵא תַּקִּיף מִנֵּיהּ.

211. "Because the Evil Inclination constantly accuses him, it behooves a man to overcome it and stand firmly so that the Evil Inclination cannot move him. **Man must be mightier than it and be attached to the place of Might (Gevurah), for when man overpowers it, he cleaves to the side of Gevurah and is strengthened. Because the Evil Inclination is mighty, it behooves a man to be mightier.**

One who overcomes his Evil Inclination is mighty in strength.

212. וְאִלֵּין בְּנֵי נָשָׁא דְּאִתְתַּקְפוּ עֲלֵיהּ, אִקְרוּן גִּבּוֹרֵי כֹחַ, לְאִשְׁתַּכְחָא זִינָא עִם זִינֵיהּ, וְאִלֵּין אִינוּן מַלְאָכָיו דְּקוּדְשָׁא בְּרִיךְ הוּא, דְּאַתְיָין מִסִּטְרָא דִּגְבוּרָה קַשְׁיָא, לְאִתְתַּקְפָא עֲלֵיהּ, גִּבּוֹרֵי כֹחַ עוֹשֵׂי דְבָרוֹ. בָּרְכוּ ה' מַלְאָכָיו, כְּיוֹסֵף, דְּאִקְרֵי צַדִּיק וְגִבּוֹר בְּרִית הַקַּדִּישָׁא דְּאִתְרְשִׁים בְּגַוֵּיהּ.

212. "Therefore, those who overcome it are called 'mighty in strength,' since they are with their own kind for by overcoming the mighty one, they become as mighty as it. **These are the angels of the Holy One, blessed be He,** namely the Righteous, **who come from the side of Strong Might to overcome** the Evil Inclination. They are called the **'...mighty in strength who perform His bidding....'** (Psalms 103:20) 'Bless the Lord, you angels of His...' (Ibid.) such as Joseph, who was called 'Righteous' and 'Mighty' and preserved the Holy Covenant, which was imprinted upon him."

Joseph left room for the Evil Inclination to enter.

213. רִבִּי אֶלְעָזָר אָמַר, וַיְהִי אַחַר הַדְּבָרִים הָאֵלֶּה, מַאי הִיא, הָא אוּקְמוּהָ, אֲתַר דָּא דְּיֵצֶ"ר מְקַטְרְגָ, דְּאִיהוּ דַרְגָּא אַחַר הַדְּבָרִים. בְּגִין דְּיוֹסֵף יְהַב לֵיהּ דּוּכְתָּא לְקַטְרְגָא, דַּהֲוָה יוֹסֵף מְסַלְסֵל בִּשְׂעָרֵיהּ, וְאַתְקִין גַּרְמֵיהּ, וְקַשִּׁיט לֵיהּ, כְּדֵין אִתְיְהֵיב דּוּכְתָּא לְיֵצֶ"ר לְקַטְרְגָא, דַּאֲמַר וּמַה אֲבוֹי דְּאִיהוּ מִתְאַבֵּל עֲלֵיהּ, וְיוֹסֵף מְקַשִּׁיט גַּרְמֵיהּ, וּמְסַלְסֵל בִּשְׂעָרֵיהּ, כְּדֵין אִתְגְּרֵי בֵּיהּ דּוּבָּא וְקַטְרִיג לֵיהּ.

213. **Rav Elazar asks, "What is** the meaning of the verse, **'And it came to pass after these things....'** (Genesis 39:7)? He says: "It has been explained that the place from which the Evil Inclination brings forth accusations is the grade** called '...after these things....' (Ibid.) Malchut is called 'things' (*devarim*) as She is the final level of Holiness, beyond which is the Evil Inclination and Klipot, and therefore '...after these things...' (Ibid.) refers to the Evil Inclination. **This was because Joseph gave it an opening for accusations.** The Evil Inclination **said: 'Joseph's father was mourning over him, and Joseph adorned himself and curled his hair.' Thus the bear,** namely Potiphar's wife, **aroused against him, and it assailed him."**

The Heavens and the Earth stop performing due to sins of men.

214. וַיְהִי אַחַר הַדְּבָרִים הָאֵלֶּה. תָּא חֲזֵי, בְּזִמְנָא דְּקוּדְשָׁא בְּרִיךְ הוּא אַשְׁגַּח בֵּיהּ
בְּעַלְמָא, לְמֵידַן יָתֵיהּ, וְאַשְׁכַּח חַיָּיבִין בְּעַלְמָא, מַה כְּתִיב, וְעָצַר אֶת הַשָּׁמַיִם
וְלֹא יִהְיֶה מָטָר וְהָאֲדָמָה לֹא תִתֵּן אֶת יְבוּלָהּ, וּכְדֵין וַאֲבַדְתֶּם מְהֵרָה, דְּהָא
בְּגִין חוֹבִין דִּבְנֵי נָשָׁא, שְׁמַיָּא וְאַרְעָא אִתְעַצָּרוּ, וְלָא נָהֲגֵי נִמּוּסֵיהוֹן כִּדְקָא יָאוֹת.

**214. "And it came to pass after these things…." (Genesis 39:7) [He
says:] "Come and see, when the Holy One, blessed be He, inspects
the world to judge it and finds wicked people therein, then 'He shut
up the Heavens, that there be no rain, and that the land yield not
its fruit…' (Deuteronomy 11:17) and then '…you perish quickly….'
(Ibid.) Because of the sins of men, the Heavens and Earth halt, and
their rules no longer function properly.**

Being false with the Covenant is like serving other gods.

215. וְתָא חֲזֵי, אִינּוּן דְּלָא נָטְרוּ לְהַאי קְיָימָא דְּקוּדְשָׁא, גָּרְמֵי פְּרִישׁוּ בֵּין יִשְׂרָאֵל
לַאֲבוּהוֹן דְּבִשְׁמַיָּא, בְּגִין דִּכְתִיב וְסַרְתֶּם וַעֲבַדְתֶּם אֱלֹהִים אֲחֵרִים וְהִשְׁתַּחֲוִיתֶם
לָהֶם, וּכְתִיב וְעָצַר אֶת הַשָּׁמַיִם וְלֹא יִהְיֶה מָטָר. דְּהַאי אִיהוּ כְּמַאן דְּסָגִיד
לֵאלָהָא אָחֳרָא, דִּמְשַׁקֵּר בְּהַאי אֶת קְיָימָא קַדִּישָׁא.

**215. "Come and see, those who do not keep the Holy Covenant
cause separation between the children of Israel and their Father
in Heaven. For it is written, 'And you turn aside, and serve other
gods, and worship them… and then the Lord's anger be inflamed
against you and He shut up the Heavens, that there be no rain….'
(Deuteronomy 11:16-17) He who guards not the Covenant is equal to
a person who serves other gods, for he is false to the Holy Covenant.**

When the Covenant is kept, the Creator bestows blessings to the world.

216. וְכַד קְיָימָא קַדִּישָׁא אִתְנְטֵיר בְּעַלְמָא כִּדְקָא יָאוֹת, כְּדֵין קוּדְשָׁא בְּרִיךְ הוּא יָהִיב בִּרְכָאן לְעֵילָא, לְאִתְרַקָא בְּעַלְמָא, כד"א, גֶּשֶׁם נְדָבוֹת תָּנִיף אֱלֹהִים נַחֲלָתְךָ וְנִלְאָה אַתָּה כוֹנַנְתָּהּ. גֶּשֶׁם נְדָבוֹת, דָּא גֶּשֶׁם דִּרְעוּתָא, כַּד אִתְרְעֵי קוּדְשָׁא בְּרִיךְ הוּא בִּכְנֶסֶת יִשְׂרָאֵל, וּבָעֵי לַאֲרָקָא לָהּ בִּרְכָאן, כְּדֵין נַחֲלָתְךָ וְנִלְאָה אַתָּה כוֹנַנְתָּהּ.

216. "When the Holy Covenant is well kept in the world, the Holy One, blessed be He, pours blessings from Above, which are showered over the world, as it is written, 'You released a bountiful rain, God; when Your own land languished, You sustained it.' (Psalms 68:10) The '…bountiful rain…' (Ibid.) is a rain of favor that pours when the Holy One, blessed be He, is favorable toward the Congregation of Israel and desires to pour blessings upon them. Then, '…when Your own land languished, You sustained it.' (Ibid.)

Israel and the Congregation of Israel are in need for favorable rain.

217. נַחֲלָתְךָ: אִינוּן יִשְׂרָאֵל, דְּאִינוּן אַחֲסַנְתֵּיהּ דְּקוּדְשָׁא בְּרִיךְ הוּא, כד"א, יַעֲקֹב חֶבֶל נַחֲלָתוֹ. וְנִלְאָה: דָּא כְּנֶסֶת יִשְׂרָאֵל, דְּאִיהִי נִלְאָה בְּאַרְעָא אָחֳרָא, דְּאִיהִי צַחֲיָא לְמִשְׁתֵּי, וּכְדֵין אִיהִי נִלְאָה. וְכַד הַהוּא גֶּשֶׁם דִּרְעוּתָא אִתְיְהִיב, כְּדֵין אַתָּה כוֹנַנְתָּהּ.

217. "'…Your own land…' (Ibid.) is Israel, the inheritance of the Holy One, blessed be He, as it is written, 'Jacob is the lot of His inheritance.' (Deuteronomy 32:9) The '…languished…' (Psalms 68:10) is the Congregation of Israel who languishes in a strange land. It is thirsty for water but cannot quench its thirst and is thus weary. With favorable rain then, '…You sustained it.' (Ibid.)

The entire existence depends on the Covenant.

218. וְעַל דָּא, שְׁמַיָּא וְאַרְעָא, וְכָל חֵילֵיהוֹן, כֻּלְּהוּ קָיְימִן עַל קְיוּמָא דָא, דִּכְתִיב אִם לֹא בְּרִיתִי יוֹמָם וָלַיְלָה חֻקּוֹת שָׁמַיִם וָאָרֶץ לֹא שָׂמְתִּי. וּבְגִין כָּךְ, בָּעֵי לְאִזְדַּהֲרָא בְּדָא, וְהָא אוּקְמוּהָ. וּבְגִין כָּךְ כְּתִיב, וַיְהִי יוֹסֵף יְפֵה תֹאַר וִיפֵה מַרְאֶה, וּבַתְרֵיהּ כְּתִיב וַתִּשָּׂא אֵשֶׁת אֲדֹנָיו אֶת עֵינֶיהָ אֶל יוֹסֵף.

218. "Thus the Heavens, the Earth, and all their legions are all established on the principles of the Covenant, as it is written, 'If My Covenant be not day and night, it were as if I had not appointed the ordinances of Heaven and Earth.' (Jeremiah 33:25) We should guard it, as has already been explained. It is therefore first written, 'And Joseph was of beautiful form and fair to look upon...' (Genesis 39:6) and then, '...his master's wife cast her eyes upon Joseph...' (Genesis 39:7), which means that because he was not on his guard but adorned himself by curling his hair, and was good-looking and well-favored, his master's wife cast her eyes upon him."

MIKETZ

5. "Since God has shown you all this"

A Synopsis

Here the Zohar speculates on the hidden meaning of Joseph's successful interpretation of Pharaoh's dream, and the resulting prosperity for both himself and the people of Israel. The friends compare Joseph's experience to that of Daniel in Babylon. They proceed to describe Joseph's work as Pharaoh's Minister of Agriculture and Minister of Finance, and praise his wisdom and discretion in both posts. An interesting passage concerns God's ability to create demand so as to benefit those who are able to supply.

The Relevance of this Passage

A reading of this section helps us to recognize the links between cause and effect, and to govern our actions accordingly. In this way, when life makes demands on us, we can know they are only for our benefit.

Joseph desired the Shechinah, and thus ruled the world.

‏77. תָּא חֲזֵי, יוֹסֵף זָכָה בְּהַאי עָלְמָא, וְזָכָה בְּעָלְמָא דְאָתֵי, בְּגִין דִּבְעָא לְאִתְאַחֲדָא בְּאִשָּׁה יִרְאַת יְיָ, כד"א וְחָטָאתִי לֵאלֹהִים, וּבְגִין כָּךְ זָכָה לְמִשְׁלַט בְּהַאי עָלְמָא, וְזָכָה לוֹן לְיִשְׂרָאֵל.‏

77. **Come and see, Joseph merited this world and merited the World to Come because he wished to be united with "...the God-fearing woman..."** (Proverbs 31:30), **the Nukva, the secret of this world, as it is written: "...and sin against God (Elohim)"** (Genesis 39:9), the Nukva called God. **He, therefore, deserved to be ruler over this world and to cause Israel to acquire merit.**

Joseph is Yesod, the gatherer.

78. מַה כְּתִיב וַיְלַקֵּט יוֹסֵף אֶת כָּל הַכֶּסֶף, וְהָכֵי אִתְחֲזֵי, דְּהָא הַהוּא נָהָר דְּנָגֵיד
וְנָפִיק, אִיהוּ לָקֵיט כֹּלָּא, וְכָל עוּתְרָא בֵּיהּ קָיְימָא. וְדָא הִיא רָזָא דִכְתִיב, וַיִּתֵן
אֹתָם אֱלֹהִים בִּרְקִיעַ הַשָּׁמַיִם, וְכֹלָּא אִיהוּ כִּדְקָא יָאוֹת, וַדַּאי יוֹסֵף בָּעֵי לְמִשְׁלַט
עַל מַלְכוּתָא.

78. It is written: "And Joseph gathered all the money..."
(Genesis 47:14) as it should be because that river that flows
from Eden, which is Yesod called Joseph, **gathers everything,** as
he is composed of and receives from all the Sefirot, **and all wealth is
found in it.** This is the secret of the verse, **"And God set them in
the Firmament of Heaven..."** (Genesis 1:17), as Yesod is called
Firmament, and it shines on the Earth, the secret of the Nukva. **All is
as it should be, for surely Joseph,** the secret of Yesod, **should rule over
the Kingdom (Malchut),** the Nukva, and bestow abundance upon Her.

The Creator made the Righteous rule so that the world is sustained.

79. וְתָא חֲזֵי, כְּתִיב וַיַּרְכֵּב אוֹתוֹ בְּמִרְכֶּבֶת הַמִּשְׁנֶה, מַאן מִרְכֶּבֶת הַמִּשְׁנֶה.
קוּדְשָׁא בְּרִיךְ הוּא עָבֵיד לֵיהּ לַצַּדִּיק שַׁלִּיטָא, בְּגִין דְּהָא מִנֵּיהּ אִתְזַן עַלְמָא,
וְאִצְטְרִיךְ לְאִתְזָנָא, וְקוּדְשָׁא בְּרִיךְ הוּא אִית לֵיהּ רְתִיכָא עִלָּאָה, וְאִית לֵיהּ
רְתִיכָא תַּתָּאָה, רְתִיכָא תַּתָּאָה אִיהִי מִרְכֶּבֶת הַמִּשְׁנֶה, וְיוֹסֵף צַדִּיק אִקְרֵי וְלֵיהּ
אִתְחֲזֵי לְמֶהֱוֵי רָכֵיב עַל מִרְכֶּבֶת הַמִּשְׁנֶה אֲשֶׁר לוֹ לְקוּדְשָׁא בְּרִיךְ הוּא, וְכֹלָּא
אִיהוּ בְּרָזָא עִלָּאָה, לְמֶהֱוֵי כְּגַוְונָא דִּלְעֵילָא.

79. Come and see, it is written: **"And he made him ride in the second
chariot which he had...."** (Genesis 41:43) He asks: **"What is the
second chariot?"** He replied: **"The Holy One, blessed be He, made
the Righteous to rule, because the world,** the Nukva, **is sustained by
him, and** from him **it needs to be sustained. The Holy One, blessed
be He, has an Upper Chariot**—Chesed, Gevurah, Tiferet, and Malchut
above the chest of Zeir Anpin—**and a Lower Chariot**—the secret of

the Nukva. **The Lower Chariot is called the Second Chariot, and Joseph who is called Righteous,** namely Yesod, **is worthy of riding the second chariot of the Holy One, blessed be He, as everything is in the likeness of the world Above."**

Avrech is the giver of abundance to which everyone kneels.

80. תָּא חֲזֵי, וַיִּקְרְאוּ לְפָנָיו אַבְרֵךְ, מַאי אַבְרֵךְ. קְשִׁירוּ דְּאִתְקְשַׁר שִׁמְשָׁא
בְּסִיהֲרָא, וְכֹלָּא כְּרָעִין לְקָבֵל אֲתַר דָּא. וְנָתוֹן אוֹתוֹ עַל כָּל עַלְמָא, וְכֻלְּהוּ אוֹדָן
לְגַבֵּיהּ, וּבְגִין דָּא כֹלָּא בְּרָזָא עִלָּאָה אִיהוּ.

80. Come and see, "…and they cried before him 'Avrech'…." (Genesis 41:43) He asks: **"What is an Avrech?"** He answers: **"It is the connection between the sun and the moon,** the secret of Yesod, which joins Zeir Anpin and the Nukva. **Everybody kneels to that place,** for bowing during prayer alludes to Yesod, who is called blessed (*baruch*). He was called Avrech because of the kneeling, which is derived from the verse, 'And he made his camels kneel (*vayavrech*)…' (Genesis 24:11), '… **and he set him over…'** (Genesis 41:43) **the whole world,** the Nukva, **and all the inhabitants of the world are thankful** for the plenty he pours on them. **Thus, everything is in the Supernal secret."**

What happens Below is in the likeness of Above.

81. תָּא חֲזֵי, קוּדְשָׁא בְּרִיךְ הוּא עָבַד מַלְכוּתָא דְּאַרְעָא, כְּעֵין מַלְכוּתָא
דִּרְקִיעָא, וְכֹלָּא דָּא כְּגַוְונָא דָּא. וְכָל מַה דְּאִתְעֲבֵיד בְּאַרְעָא קָיְימָא קַמֵּי
קוּדְשָׁא בְּרִיךְ הוּא בְּקַדְמֵיתָא. תָּא חֲזֵי, מַלְכוּתָא קַדִּישָׁא, לָא קָבֵיל מַלְכוּתָא
שְׁלֵימָתָא, עַד דְּאִתְחַבַּר בַּאֲבָהָן, בְּגִין דְּקוּדְשָׁא בְּרִיךְ הוּא עָבַד לָהּ לְמַלְכוּ
עִלָּאָה, לְאִתְנַהֲרָא מֵרָזָא דַּאֲבָהָן.

81. Come and see, the Holy One, blessed be He, created the Kingdom of the Earth in the likeness of the Kingdom of Heaven. Thus the one resembles the other, for whatever is on Earth has a counterpart root in Heaven. **Everything that happens on Earth was first in front of the Holy One, blessed be He,** in Heaven. **Come and see, the Holy Malchut did not receive Complete Kingdom until it was united with the Patriarchs, for the Holy One, blessed be He, made the Upper Malchut so it would shine from the secret of the Patriarchs.**

Joseph was sent to Egypt to collect all the money of the world.

82. וְכַד יוֹסֵף הַצַּדִּיק נָוַת לְמִצְרַיִם בְּקַדְמֵיתָא, אִיהוּ מָשִׁיךְ לָהּ לִשְׁכִינְתָּא לְבָתַר עֲמֵיהּ, דְּהָא שְׁכִינְתָּא לָא אָזְלָא אֶלָּא בַּתְרָא דְּצַדִּיק, וּבְגִין כָּךְ אִתְמְשַׁךְ יוֹסֵף לְמִצְרַיִם בְּקַדְמֵיתָא, וְנָטִיל כָּל עוֹתְרָא דְּעַלְמָא כִּדְקָא יָאוֹת, וּלְבָתַר נָחֲתַת שְׁכִינְתָּא לְמִצְרַיִם, וְכֻלְּהוּ שִׁבְטִין בַּהֲדָהּ.

82. After Joseph the Righteous went down to Egypt, he drew the Shechinah to him, for the Shechinah follows only the Righteous. Therefore Joseph first went down to Egypt and received all the wealth of the world as is fit, and then the Shechinah went down to Egypt with all the Tribes.

Joseph merited the Upper and Lower Kingdom
because he guarded the Covenant.

83. וּבְגִינֵי כָּךְ, יוֹסֵף דְּנָטַר לֵיהּ לַבְּרִית, זָכָה לְאִתְעַטְּרָא בְּאַתְרֵיהּ, וְזָכָה לְמַלְכוּתָא דִּלְעֵילָּא, וּלְמַלְכוּתָא דִּלְתַתָּא, וְעַל דָּא כָּל מַאן דְּנָטַר בְּרִית קַדִּישָׁא, כְּאִילּוּ קַיֵּים אוֹרַיְיתָא קַדִּישָׁא כּוּלָהּ, דְּהָא בְּרִית שָׁקִיל כְּכָל אוֹרַיְתָא.

83. Because of this, Joseph who kept the Holy Covenant merited to be adorned in his place, namely to become a Chariot to Yesod of Zeir Anpin, **and attained the Upper Kingdom and the Lower Kingdom. Therefore whoever guards the Holy Covenant is considered to be observing the Holy Torah in its entirety, for the Covenant corresponds to the whole Torah.**

MIKETZ

7. "And Joseph was the governor of the land"

A Synopsis

This passage speculates on the secret meanings of Joseph's triumph in Egypt. It tells us that his victory was also one against the hidden powers of evil on the Left, namely the Evil Inclination.

The Relevence of this Passage

Egypt is a metaphor for the human ego, our Evil Inclination, which is rooted in the Left Column. Strength and discipline to triumph over egocentric desires and evil tendencies are summoned forth in our souls as we scan the Hebrew Letters of this passage.

When the Creator desires an individual, He raises him above all people.

106. וְיוֹסֵף הוּא הַשַּׁלִּיט עַל הָאָרֶץ וְגוֹ', ר' יֵיסָא פָּתַח וַאֲמַר, וְעַתָּה יָרוּם רֹאשִׁי עַל אוֹיְבַי סְבִיבוֹתַי וְאֶזְבְּחָה בְאָהֳלוֹ זִבְחֵי תְרוּעָה אָשִׁירָה וַאֲזַמְּרָה כַיי'. תָּא וְחֲזֵי, כַּד קוּדְשָׁא בְּרִיךְ הוּא אִתְרְעֵי בֵּיה בְּבַר נָשׁ, זָקִיף לֵיה עַל כָּל בְּנֵי עָלְמָא, וְעָבֵיד לֵיה רֵישָׁא דְכֹלָּא, וְכֻלְּהוּ שַׂנְאוֹי אִתְכַּפְיָין תְּחוֹתוֹי.

106. "And Joseph was the governor of the land...." (Genesis 42:6) Rav Yesa opened the discussion with the verse: "'And now shall my head be lifted up above my enemies round about me, therefore I will offer in His Tabernacle sacrifices with trumpet sound; I will sing, and I will make melody to the Lord.' (Psalms 27:6) Come and see, when the Holy One, blessed be He, desires an individual, He raises him above all the people of the world and makes him ruler over them. All his enemies are subdued under him.

David and Joseph were both rejected by their brothers.

107. דָּוִד מַלְכָּא, שָׂנְאוּ לֵיהּ אֲחוֹי, דָּחוֹ לֵיהּ מִנַּיְיהוּ, קוּדְשָׁא בְּרִיךְ הוּא אָרִים לֵיהּ, עַל כָּל בְּנֵי עַלְמָא, אָתָא וַחֲמוֹי עָרַק מִקַּמֵּיהּ, קוּדְשָׁא בְּרִיךְ הוּא אָרִים לֵיהּ, עַל כָּל מַלְכוּתֵיהּ, וְכֻלְּהוּ הֲווֹ כָּרְעִין וְסָגְדִין קַמֵּיהּ. וְיוֹסֵף דָּחוֹ לֵיהּ אֲחוֹי, לְבָתַר כֻּלְּהוּ כָּרְעוּ וְסָגְדוּ קַמֵּיהּ, הַהֲ"ד וַיָּבֹאוּ אֲחֵי יוֹסֵף וַיִּשְׁתַּחֲווּ לוֹ אַפַּיִם אָרְצָה.

107. "King David was hated and rejected by his brothers, and the Holy One, blessed be He, raised him above all the people of the world. He fled from Saul, his father-in-law, and the Holy One, blessed be He, raised him above all kingdoms, and everyone bowed and knelt before him. Joseph was rejected by his brothers, and afterwards they all knelt and prostrated themselves before him, as it is written, '…And Joseph's brothers came, and bowed themselves down before him with their faces to the earth.' (Genesis 42:6)"

Ve'ata is male and female together.

108. דָּבָר אַחֵר, וְעַתָּה יָרוּם רֹאשִׁי, מַאי וְעַתָּה, כְּמוֹ וְאַתָּה. ר' יְהוּדָה אָמַר, הָא אִתְּמַר, עֵת דְּאִיהוּ דַרְגָּא עִלָּאָה, וּמַאן אִיהוּ הַהוּא עֵת. דָּא ה"א, וְאִקְרֵי עַתָּה, וְעַתָּה: דָּא אִיהוּ וּבֵי דִינֵיהּ.

108. Another explanation for "And now (ve'ata; וְעַתָּה) shall my head be lifted up…." (Psalms 27:6) He asks: "What is the meaning of ve'ata?" He answers: "It is like 'and you (ve'ata; וְאַתָּה).'" Just as ve'ata (וְאַתָּה) is the Name of the Shechinah, so is ve'ata (וְעַתָּה) the Name of the Shechinah. This means that [King David] prayed to the Shechinah to lift his head. **Rav Yehuda said: "We have learned that et (time; עֵת) is a Supernal grade."** [He asks:] **"What is the et here?"** [He answers:] "It is the Hei (ה) of the Name Yud-Hei-Vav-Hei (יהוה), namely the Shechinah **called ata (now; עַתָּה).** Ve'ata (and now; וְעַתָּה) with the letter Vav (ו) **refers to Him,** Zeir Anpin, **and His Court of Judgment,** the Nukva. The Vav of ve'ata alludes to Zeir Anpin.

A head above all other ministers.

109. יָרוּם רֹאשִׁי, לְאַרְמָא לָהּ, בִּיקָרָא וּמַלְכוּתָא. עַל אוֹיְבַי סְבִיבוֹתַי, אִלֵּין שְׁאָר מַלְכֵי אַרְעָא. וְאֶזְבְּחָה בְאָהֳלוֹ, דָּא יְרוּשָׁלַם, בְּאָהֳלוֹ דָּא אֹהֶל מוֹעֵד. וְבֹחֵי תְרוּעָה, לְמִשְׁמַע כָּל עַלְמָא. אָשִׁירָה וַאֲזַמְּרָה, מֵהַהוּא סִטְרָא דִּתְרוּעָה הִיא, דְּהָא מִתַּמָּן, מֵהַהוּא סִטְרָא דִּתְרוּעָה, הִיא אַתְיָא שִׁירָה וְתוּשְׁבַּחְתָּא.

109. "And now shall my head be lifted up…." (Psalms 27:6), [namely] to lift my head in dignity and dominion; "…above my enemies round about me…" (Ibid) refers to the other kings of the land. "… therefore I will offer in His Tabernacle…" refers to Jerusalem; "… in His Tabernacle (בָּאָהֳלוֹ)…." (Ibid.) spelled with **Vav** (ו) alludes to the Tent of Meeting; "…sacrifices with trumpet sound…" (Ibid.) that will sound throughout the world; "…I will sing, and I will make melody…" (Ibid.) from the side of the trumpet sound (teru'ah), for from there, song and melody arise.

The Congregation of Israel above Esau and his ministers.

110. דָּבָר אַחֵר, וְעַתָּה יָרוּם רֹאשִׁי, דָּא כְּנֶסֶת יִשְׂרָאֵל. עַל אוֹיְבַי סְבִיבוֹתַי, דָּא עֵשָׂו וְכָל אַפַּרְכִין דִּילֵיהּ. וְאֶזְבְּחָה בְאָהֳלוֹ, אִלֵּין יִשְׂרָאֵל. וְבֹחֵי תְרוּעָה, דִּכְתִיב וְבֹחֵי אֱלֹקִים רוּחַ נִשְׁבָּרָה, בְּגִין לְאַעְבָּרָא דִינָא מֵעַלְמָא. אָשִׁירָה וַאֲזַמְּרָה, לְאוֹדָאָה וּלְשַׁבְּחָא לְקוּדְשָׁא בְּרִיךְ הוּא, בְּלָא פָּסִיקוּ לְעוֹלָם.

110. According to another explanation, "And now shall my head be lifted up…" (Psalms 27:6) refers to the Congregation of Israel, namely the Nukva called *ata* (now; עֵתָּה), as mentioned earlier, "… above my enemies round about me…" (Ibid.) refers to Esau and his ministers. "…I will offer in His Tabernacle…" (Ibid.), namely in the midst of Israel "…sacrifices with trumpet sound (*teru'ah*)…" (Ibid.) as it is written: "The sacrifices of God are a broken spirit…" (Psalms 51:19), so as to remove Judgment from the world. "…I will

sing, to make melody..." (Psalms 27:6), namely **to thank and praise the Holy One, blessed be He, continuously, forever.**

The Torah lifts the Good Inclination over the Evil Inclination.

111. דָּבָר אַחֵר, וְעַתָּה יָרוּם רֹאשִׁי, בְּכֹלָּא, יֵצֶר טוֹב עַל יֵצֶר רָע, דִּכְתִיב עַל אוֹיְבַי סְבִיבוֹתַי, דָּא יֵצֶר הָרָע, דְּאִיהוּ סַחֲרָנֵיהּ דְּבַר נָשׁ, וְאִיהוּ שָׂנְאֵיהּ בְּכֹלָּא. וְאֶזְבְּחָה בְאָהֳלוֹ זִבְחֵי תְרוּעָה, דָּא אוֹרַיְיתָא, דְּאִתְיְהִיבַת מִסִּטְרָא דְּאֶשָׁא, כִּדְכְתִיב מִימִינוֹ אֵשׁ דָּת לָמוֹ, דְּהָא בְּגִין אוֹרַיְיתָא, יָרוּם רֵישֵׁיהּ, וְאִתְכַּבָּרוּ כָּל שַׂנְאוֹי קָדָמוֹי, כִּדְכְתִיב תַּכְרִיעַ קָמַי תַּחְתָּי.

111. Another explanation of "And now shall my head be lifted up..." (Psalms 27:6) is that my head is an allusion to the Good Inclination. He prayed **that in every respect the Good Inclination** shall be lifted **above the Evil Inclination, as it is written: "...above my enemies round about me..."** (Ibid.), which is an allusion to the Evil Inclination that surrounds and hates man. "...I will offer in His tabernacle sacrifices with trumpet sound..." (Ibid.) refers to the study of **the Torah, which** was given from the side of fire, as it is written: "...from His right hand went a fiery law for them." (Deuteronomy 33:2) Through the Torah shall his head be lifted up and his enemies subjugated before him, as it is written: "...You have subdued under me those who rose up against me." (Psalms 18:40)

The Patriarchs and King David were the four legs of the Throne.

112. דָּבָר אַחֵר וְעַתָּה יָרוּם רֹאשִׁי, לְאִתְכְּלָלָא בַּאֲבָהָן, דְּהָא דָוִד מַלְכָּא, אִית לֵיהּ לְאִתְדַּבְּקָא בַּאֲבָהָן, וּכְדֵין יִתְרוֹמֵם וְסָלִיק לְעֵילָא, וְאִיהוּ בְּחַד קְשׁוּרָא בְּהוֹ. עַל אוֹיְבַי סְבִיבוֹתַי, אִלֵּין אִינוּן דְּבִסְטַר שְׂמָאלָא, כֻּלְּהוּ מָארֵי דִינִין, דְּמִתְכַּנְּנִין לְחַבָּלָא, וּכְדֵין שְׂמָשָׁא אִתְחַבַּר בְּסִיהֲרָא, וַהֲוֵי כֹּלָּא חַד.

112. Another explanation of the verse, "And now shall my head be lifted up..." (Psalms 27:6) is that it means that **I shall be included**

with the Patriarchs, which are Chesed-Gevurah-Tiferet of Zeir Anpin, **for King David was able to cleave to the Patriarchs, as he unites with them** in the secret of the fourth leg, **and then he will be lifted and ascend Above,** namely above the chest of Zeir Anpin, **and be bound to them. "…above my enemies round about me…"** (Ibid.) **refers to those of the Left Column; all of them accusers intent upon destruction.** When he is lifted above them, **the sun,** Zeir Anpin, **is united with the moon,** the Nukva, **and all becomes one.**

Joseph is Yesod that rules over and nourishes Malchut.

113. תָּא חֲזֵי, כְּתִיב וְיוֹסֵף הוּא הַשַּׁלִּיט עַל הָאָרֶץ, דָּא שִׁמְשָׁא דְּשַׁלִּיט בְּסִיהֲרָא, וְנָהִיר לָהּ, וְזָן לָהּ. הוּא הַמַּשְׁבִּיר לְכָל עַם הָאָרֶץ, דְּהָא הַהוּא נָהָר דְּנָגֵיד וְנָפֵיק, מִנֵּיהּ אִתְזָנוּ כֻּלְּהוּ, וּמֵהַתַּמָּן פָּרְחִין נִשְׁמָתִין לְכֹלָּא, וּבְגִין דָּא כֻּלְּהוּ סָגְדִין לְגַבֵּיהּ דְּהַהוּא אֲתַר, דְּהָא לֵית לָךְ מִלָּה בְּעָלְמָא, דְּלָא תַּלְיָא בְּמַזְּלָא וְאוֹקְמוּהָ.

113. Come and see, it is written: "And Joseph was the governor of the land…." (Genesis 42:6) Joseph **is the sun,** Zeir Anpin, for Joseph is Yesod of Zeir Anpin, **which rules over the moon,** the Nukva, **shining upon and sustaining her. "…and it was he who dispensed rations to all the people of the land…"** (Ibid.) as the river that flows **and comes out** from Eden, Yesod called Joseph, **supplies everyone with nourishment. From there souls fly to everyone. Therefore everyone bows before that place, for there is nothing in the world that does not depend upon Mazal,** Yesod, **as has already been explained.**

MIKETZ

11. "And took from them Shimon"

A Synopsis

This passage comments on the mercy Joseph shows his brothers. The commentators assert that even idolaters are not punished if they live in peace. The secret meaning of Circumcision and its relation to the Covenant are also discussed. Whoever is charitable in this world is free of Harsh Judgment in the next. Thus, like Joseph, we are encouraged to turn the other cheek and leave vengeance to the Lord.

The Relevence of this Passage

Judgments decreed against us are measured and meted out in accordance to the degree and severity of the judgments we pass on our friends and foes. Trust in the Creator encompasses certainty in the laws of cause and effect, which dictate that all our enemies will be correctly judged without our having to participate in the correction process. A person who has attained spiritual enlightenment accepts any wrongs committed against him as payment for negative actions he may have committed in the past. This wise perspective is stimulated by the Divine Light of this Hebrew script.

There is not a word in the Torah that does not contain secrets.

177. תָּא חֲזֵי, כָּל דָּא דְּיוֹסֵף עִם אֲחוֹי, וְכָל הַנֵּי מִילֵי, אַמַאי אִצְטְרִיךְ, אֶלָּא אוֹרַיְיתָא דִּקְשׁוֹט, אִיהִי אוֹרַיְיתָא, וְכָל אָרְחָתָא אָרְחִין קַדִּישִׁין, וְלֵית לָהּ מִלָּה בְּאוֹרַיְיתָא דְּלָאו אִית בָּהּ רָזִין עִלָּאִין וְקַדִּישִׁין, וְאָרְחִין לִבְנֵי נָשָׁא לְאִתְתַּקְפָא בְּהוֹ.

177. [He asks:] **"Come and see, why was all that passed between Joseph and his brothers** recorded in the Torah?" He answers: **"The Torah is of truth; all her ways are Holy. There is not one word in the**

Torah that does not contain Holy and Supernal secrets and ways in which humanity can be strengthened."

The way of Torah is love over hate, Right over Left.

178. פָּתַח וַאֲמַר, אַל תֹּאמַר אֲשַׁלְּמָה רָע וגו'. תָּא חֲזֵי, קוּדְשָׁא בְּרִיךְ הוּא עֲבֵיד לֵיהּ לְבַר נָשׁ, לְאִתְתַּקְּפָא בָּהּ בְּאוֹרַיְיתָא, וּלְמֵיהַךְ בְּאֹרַח קְשׁוֹט, וְלִסְטַר יְמִינָא, וְלָא יָהַךְ לִסְטַר שְׂמָאלָא. וּבְגִין דְּבָעֵי לְהוֹ לְמֵיהַךְ לִסְטַר יְמִינָא, אִית לוֹן לְאַסְגָּאָה רְחִימוּ דָּא עִם דָּא, וְלָא יְהֵא דְּבָבוּ דָּא עִם דָּא, בְּגִין דְּלָא לְאַכְחֲשָׁא יְמִינָא, דְּאִיהוּ אֲתַר דְּיִשְׂרָאֵל מִתְדַּבְּקָן בֵּיהּ.

178. He opened the discussion with the verse: "'Do not say, "I will repay evil"....' (Proverbs 20:22) Come and see, the Holy One, blessed be He, created man so he would strengthen himself in the Torah and walk the Way of Truth, staying on the Right Column and avoiding the Left. Because people should walk on the Right Column, they have to increase love between them, as love is of the Right Column, and avoid hatred among them, as hatred is of the Left Column, so as not to weaken the Right, which is the place to which Israel cleave.

The Evil Inclination becomes whole by our misdeeds.

179. וְתָא חֲזֵי, בְּגִין כָּךְ אִיהוּ יֵצֶר טוֹב וְיֵצֶר רָע, וְיִשְׂרָאֵל בָּעְיִין לְאִתְתַּקְּפָא לְיֵצֶר טוֹב עַל יֵצֶר רָע, בְּאִינוּן עוֹבָדִין דִּכְשָׁרָן, וְאִי סָטֵי בַּר נָשׁ לִשְׂמָאלָא, כְּדֵין אִתְתַּקַּף יֵצֶר רָע עַל יֵצֶר טוֹב, וּמַאן דַּהֲוָה פָּגֵים, אַשְׁלִים לֵיהּ בְּחֶטְאוֹי, דְּהָא לָא אִשְׁתְּלִים דָּא מְנֻוְּלָא, אֶלָּא בְּחֶטְאִין דִּבְנֵי נָשָׁא.

179. "Come and see, for this purpose, the Good Inclination and the Evil Inclination exist. Israel should make the Good Inclination master over the Evil through good deeds. If a person veers to the Left, the Evil Inclination overpowers the good, and the one that was

defective, the Evil Inclination, **is made whole through his sin, for this ugly one only becomes whole through people's sins.**

One needs to be careful to keep the Evil lacking and the Good whole.

180. וּבְגִין כָּךְ בָּעֵי בַּר נָשׁ לְאִזְדַּהֲרָא, דְּלָא יִשְׁתְּלִים הַהוּא יֵצֶר רַע בְּחֶטְאוֹי, וְיִסְתַּמַּר תָּדִיר, דְּהָא יֵצֶר טוֹב בָּעֵי לְאַשְׁלָמָא לֵיהּ בִּשְׁלִימוּת תָּדִיר, וְלֹא יֵצֶר הָרָע. וּבְגִין כָּךְ אַל תֹּאמַר אֲשַׁלְּמָה רַע הַוֵה אֶל ה' וְיֹשַׁע לָךְ.

180. "One should therefore be careful lest the Evil Inclination be made whole through his sins. He should always be guarded, for we need to always wholly complete the Good Inclination instead of the Evil Inclination. Therefore 'Do not say, "I will repay (also 'complete') evil"...' (Proverbs 20:22) because through hatred you shall increase the power of the Left and complete the Evil Inclination. **Only say, '...wait on the Lord, and He will save you.' (Ibid.)"**

We must not reward evil with evil.

181. דָּבָר אַחֵר אַל תֹּאמַר אֲשַׁלְּמָה רַע, כִּדְכְתִיב וּמְשַׁלֵּם רָעָה תַּחַת טוֹבָה, לְמֵעַן דְּשַׁלֵּים לֵיהּ טוֹבָה, דְּלֹא יַשְׁלֵים לֵיהּ רַע, בְּגִין דִּכְתִיב מֵשִׁיב רָעָה תַּחַת טוֹבָה לֹא תָמוּשׁ רָעָה מִבֵּיתוֹ, אֲפִילוּ לְמַאן דְּאַשְׁלִימוּ לֵיהּ בִּישִׁין, לָא אִית לֵיהּ לְאַשְׁלָמָא בִּישָׁא, וְכַד הַהוּא בִּישׁוּ דְּשַׁלִּימוּ לֵיהּ, אֶלָּא הַוֵה לַהּ וְיֹשַׁע לָךְ.

181. Another explanation of the verse, "Do not say, 'I will repay evil'..." (Proverbs 20:22) is that it has the same meaning as the verse, "...whoever rewards evil for good." (Proverbs 17:13) One should not repay a person who did him good with evil because "... whoever rewards evil for good, evil shall not depart from his house." (Proverbs 17:13) But even if a person caused him evil, he must not reward evil with evil but "wait on the Lord, and He will save you." (Proverbs 20:22)

Joseph did not repay his brothers evil.

182. וְהַאי קְרָא אוּקְמוּהָ, בְּיוֹסֵף זַכָּאָה, דְּלָא בָּעָא לְאַשְׁלְמָא בִישָׁא לַאֲחוֹי, בְּשַׁעְתָּא דְּנָפְלוּ בִּידוֹי. הֲוָה כַּהּ' וְיוֹשַׁע לָךְ, בְּגִין דְּהוּא הֲוָה דָחֵיל לְקוּדְשָׁא בְּרִיךְ הוּא, דִּכְתִיב זֹאת עֲשׂוּ וִחְיוּ וְגוֹ', וְאִיהוּ תָּדִיר הֲוָה מְחַכֶּה לְקוּדְשָׁא בְּרִיךְ הוּא.

182. This verse has been explained in relation to Joseph the Righteous, who did not wish to repay his brothers with evil when they fell into his hands, as it is written: "Do not say, I will repay evil; but wait on the Lord, and He will save you." (Proverbs 20:22) For he feared the Holy One, blessed be He, as it is written: "...'This do, and live, I fear God.'" (Genesis 42:18) He always waited on the Holy One, blessed be He.

Joseph knew how to draw out the deep meanings of the Creator's decree.

183. ר' אַבָּא פָּתַח וַאֲמַר, מַיִם עֲמוּקִים עֵצָה בְּלֵב אִישׁ וְאִישׁ תְּבוּנָה יִדְלֶנָּה. מַיִם עֲמוּקִים עֵצָה בְּלֵב אִישׁ, דָּא קוּדְשָׁא בְּרִיךְ הוּא, בְּגִין דְּאִיהוּ עָבֵיד עֵצוֹת, דְּאַיְיתֵי טַעֲמִין לְגַלְגְּלָא גִּלְגּוּלִין עַל עַלְמָא עַל יָדָא דְּיוֹסֵף, לְקַיְימָא הַהוּא גְּזֵרָה, דִּגְזַר כַּפְנָא עַל אַרְעָא. וְאִישׁ תְּבוּנָה יִדְלֶנָּה, דָּא יוֹסֵף, דְּגַלֵּי אִינּוּן עֲמִיקִין, דִּגְזַר קוּדְשָׁא בְּרִיךְ הוּא עַל עַלְמָא.

183. Rav Aba opened with the verse: "'Counsel in the heart of man is like deep water; but a man of understanding will draw it out.' (Proverbs 20:5) 'Counsel in the heart of man is like deep water...' (Ibid.) refers to the Holy One, blessed be He, who gave counsel by bringing about events through the hands of Joseph to fulfill the decree of famine upon the world. '...but a man of understanding will draw it out...' (Ibid.) refers to Joseph, who revealed the deep meanings of the decree of the Holy One, blessed be He, over the world through the interpretation of the dream.

Joseph acted kindly toward his brothers.

184. תָּא חֲזֵי, יוֹסֵף לֹא דַּי לֵיהּ דְּאִיהוּ לָא שַׁלִּים בִּישָׁא לַאֲחוֹי, אֶלָּא דַּעֲבַד עִמְּהוֹן טִיבוּ וּקְשׁוֹט, וְכָךְ אָרְחַיְיהוּ דְּזַכָּאֵי תָּדִיר, בְּגִין דָּא קוּדְשָׁא בְּרִיךְ הוּא וְחָיֵיס עֲלַיְיהוּ תָּדִיר, בְּעָלְמָא דֵּין וּבְעָלְמָא דְּאָתֵי.

184. "Come and see, Joseph not only abstained from causing evil to his brothers but he did kindness and truth by them. This is always the way of the Righteous. Therefore the Holy One, blessed be He, always has compassion for them in this world and the World to Come."

Judah approached Joseph, and Joseph revealed himself to the brothers.

185. מַיִם עֲמוּקִים עֵצָה בְלֶב אִישׁ, דָּא יְהוּדָה, וְהָא אוּקְמוּהָ, בְּשַׁעְתָא דְּאִתְקְרִיב לְגַבֵּיהּ דְּיוֹסֵף, עַל עִסְקָא דְּבִנְיָמִין. וְאִישׁ תְּבוּנָה יִדְלֶנָּה דָּא יוֹסֵף.

185. "Counsel in the heart of man is like deep water..." (Proverbs 20:5) refers to Judah, as we explained, when he approached Joseph on behalf of Benjamin. The phrase, "...a man of understanding will draw it out..." (Ibid.) refers to Joseph when he made himself known to his brothers.

Rav Aba witnessed two miracles happen to a man.

186. ר' אַבָּא הֲוָה יָתִיב אַתַּרְעָא דְּאַבָּבָא דְּלוֹד, חָמָא חַד בַּר נָשׁ דַּהֲוָה אָתֵי, וְיָתִיב בְּחַד קוּלְטָא דִּתְּלָא דְּאַרְעָא, וַהֲוָה לָאֵי מֵאָרְחָא, וְיָתִיב וְנָאִים תַּמָּן, אַדְהָכֵי חָמֵי חַד חִוְיָא, דַּהֲוָה אָתֵי לְגַבֵּיהּ, נָפַק קוּסְטְפָא דְּגוּרְדְּנָא, וְקָטִיל לֵיהּ לְחִוְיָא. כַּד אִתְּעַר הַהוּא בַּר נָשׁ, חָמָא הַהוּא חִוְיָא לְקִבְלֵיהּ, דַּהֲוָה מִית, אוֹזְדַּקַּף הַהוּא בַּר נָשׁ, וְנָפַל הַהוּא קוּלְטָא לְעוֹמְקָא דִּתְחוֹתוֹי וְאִשְׁתֵּזִיב.

186. Rav Aba sat at the gate of the city Lod. He saw a man sitting on a ledge protruding from a mountainside. He was weary from the

road, so he sat down and slept. While he was sleeping, he saw a
snake coming toward him. A reptile emerged and killed the snake.
When the man awoke, he saw the dead snake. He stood up, and the
ledge that had been torn from the mountain **fell to the valley below.**
Thus, he was saved, for had he risen a moment later, he would have
fallen together with the ledge into the valley and been killed.

The miracles were not just chance.

187. אָתָא ר' אַבָּא לְגַבֵּיה, אָמַר לוֹ אֵימָא לִי מָאן עוֹבָדָךְ, דְּהָא קוּדְשָׁא בְּרִיךְ
הוּא רָחֵישׁ לָךְ אִלֵּין תְּרֵין נִסִּין, לָאו אִינוּן לְמַגָּנָא.

**187. Rav Aba came to him and said: "What have you done that the
Holy One, blessed be He, performed two miracles for you** —saving
you from the snake and from the ledge that fell—**for these events did
not happen without reason."**

Not going to sleep without forgiving all those who hurt you.

188. אָמַר לוֹ הַהוּא בַּר נָשׁ, כָּכָל יוֹמַאי לָא אַשְׁלֵים לִי בַּר נָשׁ בִּישָׁא בְּעָלְמָא,
דְּלָא אִתְפַּיַּיסְנָא בַּהֲדֵיהּ, וּמָחֵילְנָא לֵיהּ. וְתוּ, אִי לָא יָכֵילְנָא לְאִתְפַּיְּיסָא בַּהֲדֵיהּ,
לָא סָלֵיקְנָא לְעַרְסִי, עַד דְּמָחֵילְנָא לֵיהּ, וּלְכָל אִינּוּן דִּמְצַעֲרוּ לִי, וְלָא וַיְּישְׁעָנָא
כָּל יוֹמָא לְהַהוּא בִּישָׁא דְּאַשְׁלֵים לִי. וְלָאו דִּי לִי דָּא, אֶלָּא דְּמֵהַהוּא יוֹמָא
וּלְהָלְאָה, אִשְׁתַּדְלְנָא לְמֶעְבַּד עִמְּהוֹן טָבָא.

**188. The man said: "In all my days, I forgave and made peace with
any man who did evil by me. If I could not make peace with him,
I did not sleep on my bed before forgiving him and all those who
grieved me. Thus I did not harbor hatred all that day for the harm
he did me. Not only that, but also from that day on I strived to do
kindness by them."**

Greater than Joseph.

189. בָּכָה ר' אַבָּא וַאֲמַר, יַתִּיר עוֹבָדוֹי דְּדֵין בְּיוֹסֵף, דְּיוֹסֵף הֲווֹ אֲחוֹי וַדַּאי, וַהֲוָה לֵיהּ לְרַחֲמָא עֲלוֹי, אֲבָל מַה דַּעֲבֵיד דָּא, יַתִּיר הוּא בְּיוֹסֵף, יָאוֹת הוּא דְקוּדְשָׁא בְּרִיךְ הוּא יַרְוֵויש לֵיהּ נִיסָא עַל נִיסָא.

189. Rav Aba wept and said: "This man's deeds exceed those of Joseph. As for Joseph, those who injured him **were his brothers.** Assuredly, he should have pitied them **from brotherhood. But this one behaved so** to any man, **thus he is greater than Joseph and is worthy to have the Holy One, blessed be He, perform one miracle after the other for his sake.**"

Vayechi

77. "Joseph is a fruitful bough"

A Synopsis
The Zohar offers a complex discourse concerning the exact makeup of the great spiritual channel Joseph.

The Relevence of this Passage
Joseph is considered to be the Foundation of our physical world. Within the structure of the Ten Sefirot, Joseph corresponds to the dimension of Yesod, the doorway through which all the energy of the Upper Worlds enters our material realm. Joseph also corresponds to sustenance. Therefore in this passage, we draw the power of good fortune, and we strengthen our soul's connection to the true foundation of all spirituality.

Yesod Above and Yesod Below.

770. סִיּוּמָא דְגוּפָא, דָא דִכְתִיב בֵּן פּוֹרָת יוֹסֵף בֵּן פּוֹרָת עֲלֵי עָיִן, אַמַּאי תְּרֵי זִמְנֵי. אֶלָּא בֵּן פּוֹרָת לְעֵילָא. בֵּן פּוֹרָת לְתַתָּא. וְאַמַּאי לָאו אִיהוּ בֵּן פּוֹרָת לְתַתָּא, בְּתִקּוּנֵי מַטְרוֹנִיתָא. בְּגִין דִּבְנוֹת צַעֲדָה, לְמֶהֱוֵי עֲלֵי שׁוּר, דְּבָעֲיִין בָּנוֹת לְתִקּוּנָהָא וְלָא בָּנִים. כד"א רַבּוֹת בָּנוֹת עָשׂוּ חָיִל וְגו'. רַבּוֹת בָּנוֹת עָשׂוּ חָיִל, אִלֵּין תְּרֵיסַר שִׁבְטִין.

770. The ending of the body, Yesod, **is referred to in the verse, "Joseph is a fruitful bough, a fruitful bough by a well...." (Genesis 49:22)** He asks: **"Why does it say 'a fruitful bough' twice?"** He answers: **"There is a fruitful bough Above,** the aspect of Yesod above the chest, **and a fruitful bough Below,** the aspect of Yesod below the Chest." [He asks:] **"Why is there no fruitful bough Below among the corrections of the Matron,** namely among the Twelve Tribes, the secret of the twelve cattle, which support the Matron above?" He replies: **"Because '...the**

daughters advanced upon the wall' (Genesis 49:22), which means that daughters are used as Her corrections, namely Female aspects, which are the secret of the Twelve Tribes, and not sons. And Joseph is Yesod, which is a son, namely Male. As the verse says, "Many daughters have done virtuously…." (Proverbs 31:29) "Many daughters have done virtuously…" (Ibid.) are the Twelve Tribes, who are established to be a Throne under the Nukva. Thus, the verse ends with "but you excel (lit. 'rises above') them all." (Ibid.)

The Holy Kingdom is not complete until Binah builds it.

771. תָּא חֲזֵי, מַלְכוּתָא קַדִּישָׁא, לָא קַבִּיל מַלְכוּתָא קַדִּישָׁא שְׁלֵימָתָא, עַד דְּאִתְחַבַּר בַּאֲבָהָן, וְכַד אִתְחַבַּר בַּאֲבָהָן, אִתְבְּנֵי בִּנְיָינָא שְׁלֵימָא מֵעָלְמָא עִלָּאָה, דְּאִיהוּ עָלְמָא דִּדְכוּרָא, וְעָלְמָא עִלָּאָה אִקְרֵי ז' שְׁנִין, בְּגִין דְּכָלְהוּ ז' שְׁנִין בֵּיהּ.

771. Come and see, the Holy Malchut does not attain perfection as Holy Malchut, until it is united with the Patriarchs, who are Chesed-Gevurah-Tiferet that are above the chest of Zeir Anpin. When it joins them, the Kingdom was transformed into a complete building through the Upper World, which is the world of the Male, namely Binah, since then Chesed-Gevurah-Tiferet of Zeir Anpin receive from the Right Column of Binah and Malchut from the Left Column of Binah. The Supernal World is called "seven years" since it includes all seven years, as Binah includes within her all the Seven Sefirot: Chesed, Gevurah, Tiferet, Netzach, Hod, Yesod, and Malchut, which are called seven years.

The seven years allude to the Upper World, Binah.

772. וְסִימָנֵיךְ וַיִּבְנֵהוּ שֶׁבַע שָׁנִים, דָּא עָלְמָא עִלָּאָה, וְלָא כְּתִיב בְּשֶׁבַע שָׁנִים, כד"א כִּי שֵׁשֶׁת יָמִים עָשָׂה ה' אֶת הַשָּׁמַיִם וְאֶת הָאָרֶץ, וְלָא כְּתִיב בְּשֵׁשֶׁת וּכְתִיב אֵלֶּה תוֹלְדוֹת הַשָּׁמַיִם וְהָאָרֶץ בְּהִבָּרְאָם: בְּאַבְרָהָם. וְאַבְרָהָם, ז' יָמִים אַחֲרֵי, וּבֵיהּ אִתְבְּנֵי עָלְמָא עִלָּאָה, וְאִלֵּין אִקְרוּן עָלְמָא דִּדְכוּרָא.

772. This is indicated by: "...And he built it seven years." (I Kings 6:38) This is the Upper World, Binah, which includes seven years. It therefore does not say "in seven years," but "seven," as in, "...For six days the Lord made Heaven and Earth..." (Exodus 31:17), instead of "in six days." This means that the Six Days—Chesed, Gevurah, Tiferet, Netzach, Hod, and Yesod—made Heaven and Earth; here also it means that the seven years, Binah, built it. It is written: "These are the generations of the Heaven and of the Earth when they were created (behibaram; בהבראם)..." (Genesis 2:4), which are the letters of "be'Avraham (באברהם; by Abraham)," since Abraham, who is Chesed, is called "seven days," and by him the Upper World, Binah, was built. They are called the "world of the Male."

Explanation: Chesed includes all Seven Sefirot, and its place is above the chest of Zeir Anpin, which is the place of the Four Legs of the Throne—Chesed, Gevurah, Tiferet, and Malchut—for Binah that is above them. Therefore, it is considered as if they build Binah because Binah depends on them.

Seven Above and Seven Below.

773. כְּגַוְונָא דָא לְתַתָּא, אִית ז' שְׁנִין, רָזָא דְעָלְמָא תַּתָּאָה, וְרָזָא דָא, דִּכְתִיב ז' יָמִים וְז' יָמִים י"ד יוֹם. דְּכֵיוָן דַּאֲמַר שִׁבְעַת יָמִים וְשִׁבְעַת יָמִים, לָא יַדְעָא דְּאַרְבֵּיסַר אִינוּן. אֶלָּא, לְאַחֲזָאָה עַלְמָא עִלָּאָה, וְעַלְמָא תַּתָּאָה. וְאִינוּן שִׁבְעַת יָמִים וְשִׁבְעַת יָמִים. אִלֵּין דְּכוּרִין, וְאִלֵּין נוּקְבִין. אִלֵּין נוּקְבֵי הַאי עַלְמָא עַלַיְיהוּ, דִּכְתִיב רְבוֹת בָּנוֹת עָשׂוּ חָיִל, אִלֵּין תְּרֵיסַר שְׁבָטִין, דְּאִינּוּן עָשׂוּ חָיִל, כִּדְכְתִיב כָּל הַפְּקוּדִים לְמַחֲנֵה יְהוּדָה וְגוֹ', וְכֵן כֻּלְהוּ.

773. Likewise there are seven years Below, Chesed, Gevurah, Tiferet, Netzach, Hod, Yesod, and Malchut divided among the Twelve Tribes, the secret of the Lower World, the Nukva. This is the secret meaning of the words, "...seven days and seven days, fourteen days." (I Kings 8:65) He asks: "From '...seven days and seven days...' (Ibid.)

do I not know they amount to fourteen, why add 'fourteen days'?" He answers: "Their purpose is to indicate the Upper and Lower Worlds, which are seven days and seven days, alluded to by the fourteen days. Those of the Upper World are Males and those of the Lower World are Females. This world, the Nukva, is above the Females, Chesed, Gevurah, Tiferet, Netzach, Hod, and Yesod that are divided to twelve, as it is written, 'Many daughters have done virtuously....' (Proverbs 31:29) This refers to the Twelve Tribes that 'have done virtuously,' (Ibid.) as it says '...all that were numbered in the camp of Judah...' (Numbers 2:9) and the others multiplied exceedingly." Thus the verse ends with "...but you rise above them all," (Proverbs 31:29) since the Nukva is above them all.

The head of each camp is called the Great Living Creature,
and those who camp by them are called the Small Living Creatures.

774. וְאִי תֵימָא רַבּוֹת, וְהָא תְּרֵיסַר אִינּוּן, וְלָא יַתִּיר, בַּר הַהוּא וַזִּיל דְּעָבְדוּ, מַאי רַבּוֹת. אֶלָּא כְּמָה דִּכְתִיב, זַעֲקַת סְדוֹם וַעֲמוֹרָה כִּי רַבָּה, כְּמוֹ גָּדְלָה. וְכֵן רַבּוֹת גְּדוֹלוֹת, עִלָּאִין, וְרַבְרְבִין עַל כֹּלָּא. וְאִלֵּין אִקְרוּן חַיּוֹת גְּדוֹלוֹת. עָשׂוּ וָזִיל, הַהוּא וַזִּיל דְּעָבְדוּ דִּסְמִיכִין עָלַיְיהוּ, אִקְרוּן חַיּוֹת קְטַנּוֹת, עִם גְּדוֹלוֹת, לְאִתְחַבְּרָא כַּחֲדָא, לְאִתְתַּקְנָא בְּהוֹ מַטְרוּנִיתָא, לְמֶהֱוֵי בְּהוֹ עִלָּאִין וְתַתָּאִין, כְּד"א לִוְיָתָן זֶה יָצַרְתָּ לְשַׂחֶק בּוֹ, בְּגִינֵי כָךְ רַבּוֹת בָּנוֹת עָשׂוּ וָזִיל.

774. He asks: "You may say that the verse says '...many...' (Proverbs 31:29) yet they are but twelve? Besides that virtuous deed they did, for each multiplied, as hinted with the words '...have done virtuously...' (Ibid.) what is '...many (rabot) daughters...'?" He answers: "Like in the verse, '...because the cry of Sodom and Amorah is great (rabah)...' (Genesis 18:20), '...many...' (Proverbs 31:29) means that they are great above all and greater than all. These are the Great Living Creatures. They '...have done virtuously...' (Ibid.) as each tribe multiplied exceedingly. 'And those that encamp by him...' (Numbers 2:5), Issachar and Zebulun by the standard of Judah, and so

on, are called Small Living Creatures, which join as one [with] the Great Living Creatures, Judah, Reuben, Ephraim, and Dan so that the Matron, the Nukva, will be established through them. The Upper and Lower will rejoice in them. Therefore it says, 'There… is the Leviathan, whom You have made to play therein.' (Psalms 104:26) The Leviathan is the connection between the Small and Great Living Creatures. Therefore 'Many daughters have done virtuously….' (Proverbs 31:29)

Joseph, who is Yesod, cannot bear the arrows of love of Nukva.

775. וְעַל דָּא בָּנוֹת צָעֲדָה עֲלֵי שׁוּר. בָּנוֹת צָעֲדָה, צְעָדוֹת מִבָּעֵי לֵיהּ, אֶלָּא הַהוּא עַיִן דִּכְתִיב לְעֵילָא, וּמַאן אִיהוּ, עַיִן מִשְׁפָּט, וְאִיהוּ קָאִים עֲלֵי עַיִן, וְאִיהוּ עַיִן, צָעֲדָה, וּפָסְעַת לְמֵיטַל בָּנוֹת לְתִקּוּנָהָא, וְהַיְינוּ בָּנוֹת צָעֲדָה, וְלָא בָּנִים, בָּנוֹת צָעֲדָה, אִסְתַּכְּלַת לְתִקּוּנָהָא, וְלָא בָנִים. וַיְמָרַרֻהוּ וָרֹבּוּ, בְּאִסְתַּכְּלוּתָא דִּרְחִיזוּ לְגַבֵּיהּ, כִּדְכְּתִיב הָסֵבִּי עֵינַיִךְ מִנֶּגְדִּי שֶׁהֵם הִרְהִיבֻנִי. וְעַל דָּא וַיִּשְׂטְמֻהוּ בַּעֲלֵי חִצִּים.

775. "Hence '…the daughters advanced upon the wall.' (Genesis 49:22)" He asks: "It says '…daughters advanced (tza'ada, singular)…' (Ibid.); it should have said tza'adot (plural)?" He answers: "This is the reflection of that which is written above '…a fruitful bough by a well…' (Ibid.)" [He asks:] "What is this well?" [He answers:] "It is the Well of Justice, the Nukva, Who receives Justice, Tiferet. He, Joseph, Yesod, stands and gives to the well, the Nukva, and that well advances to take daughters for its adornment. '…the daughters advanced…' (Ibid.); the Nukva advanced with daughters but not with sons, as daughters are worthy to establish Her but sons are not. 'They fiercely attacked him…' (Genesis 49:23) by looking lovingly at him, as it is written, 'Turn away your eyes from me, for they have overcome me…' (Song of Songs 6:5), meaning for they burn me with your love's flame. Here too, he could not suffer the Nukva's arrows of love. This is the meaning of 'They fiercely attacked him…'

(Genesis 49:23) **and '…the archers hated him'** (Genesis 49:23), **so that he could not tolerate it."**

Explanation: Nukva is built by the Left Column, and therefore her eyes sway Zeir Anpin toward the Judgments of the Left, and since [Zeir Anpin] is from the aspect of the Central Column he cannot bear it. So too, Yosef, who is Yesod, is the aspect of the Central Column that does not veer Right nor Left. Therefore, he too, cannot tolerate the arrows of love of the Nukva, which represent the awakening of the Left.

Nukva is Joseph's spouse who clothes Him in strength.

776. וַתֵּשֶׁב בְּאֵיתָן קַשְׁתּוֹ דָּא קֶשֶׁת. מַה קֶשֶׁת. דָּא בַּת זוּגוֹ. בְּאֵיתָן: תּוּקְפָּא אַלְבֵּישַׁת עָלוֹי, דְּלָא אַחְלָשַׁת חֵילָא, דְּהָא יָדְעַת דְּיוֹסֵף לָא יִסְטֵי בְּהַהוּא דַרְגָּא, דְּאִת קַיָּימָא דִּילֵהּ, לִימִינָא וְלִשְׂמָאלָא.

776. "But his bow abode in strength…." (Genesis 49:24) The bow is the Nukva. He asks: **"Why say '…his bow…'** (Ibid.) when it should have been 'but the bow abode…'?" He answers: **"It is Joseph's spouse,** and therefore it says 'his bow.' **'…in strength…'** (Ibid.) **means that she clothed him in strength and might, and so his strength will not be weakened** due to his union with her, **since she knew that Joseph would not turn aside within his grade;** namely he would not turn, due to the union, to the Left grade, the place of Judgments, **since his Sign of the Covenant is to the Right and Left** together."

Joseph's hands were made precious by the Nukva.

777. וַיָּפֹזוּ, מַאי וַיָּפֹזוּ. אֶלָּא כְּדִכְתִיב הַנֶּחֱמָדִים מִזָּהָב וּמִפַּז רָב. וּכְתִיב וּתְמוּרָתָהּ כְּלִי פָז. אִתְיַיקְּרוּ דְּרוֹעוֹי בְּמַרְגָּלִיתָא עִלָּאָה. מִיְדֵי אֲבִיר יַעֲקֹב, מֵאִינּוּן תְּרֵין סִטְרִין, דְּאִתְתְּקִיף בְּהוֹ יַעֲקֹב. מִשָּׁם רוֹעֶה אֶבֶן יִשְׂרָאֵל, מִתַּמָּן אִתָּן הַהוּא אֶבֶן יְקָרָא, כִּדְקָאָמְרָן. תּוּ, מֵאִינּוּן תְּרֵיסַר סִטְרִין, אִתָּן הַהוּא אֶבֶן יְקָרָא, דְּאִינּוּן

צָפוֹן וְדָרוֹם, וְהִיא אִתְיַהֲבַת בֵּינַיְיהוּ, וְאִתְבָּרְכָא מִנַּיְיהוּ, וְאִתְּזָנָא מִנְהוֹן עַל יְדָא דְצַדִּיק.

777. [He asks:] "What do the words '...were made supple (vayafozu; וַיָּפֹזוּ)...' (Genesis 49:24) mean?" He answers: "As it says, 'They are more desirable than gold, even much fine gold (paz; פָּז)...' (Psalms 19:11) and '...nor shall it be valued with pure gold (paz; פָּז)....' (Job 28:17) Here too, vayafozu (וַיָּפֹזוּ) is derived from paz (פָּז), fine gold and preciousness, **as his hands were made precious by the Supernal Gem,** the Supernal Nukva above the chest, for he received abundance from being united with her. He received this '...by the hand of the Mighty One of Jacob...' (Genesis 49:24) from the two sides, Right and Left**, with which Jacob was strengthened. '...from thence he fed the Stone of Israel' (Ibid.),** from thence that Precious stone, the Nukva, **was fed, like we said. We should further explain that the Precious Stone was fed by the twelve sides, north and south,** which are the hands of Jacob, for there are Chesed, Gevurah, Tiferet, Netzach, Hod, and Yesod to the north and Chesed, Gevurah, Tiferet, Netzach, Hod, and Yesod to the south; altogether twelve. The Nukva **is put in their midst to be blessed by them, nourished by them through** that **Righteous,** which is Joseph."

Three questions regarding the wording of Joseph's blessing.

778. תָּא חֲזֵי, לְיוֹסֵף אִתּוֹסַף לֵיהּ בִּרְכָה אַחֲרָא, כְּד"א מֵאֵל אָבִיךָ וְיַעְזְרֶךָּ וְגו', הַאי קְרָא קַשְׁיָא, מֵאֵל אָבִיךָ, אֵל אָבִיךָ יַעְזְרֶךָ מִבָּעֵי לֵיהּ. מַאי מֵאֵל אָבִיךָ וּלְבָתַר יַעְזְרֶךָּ. וְאֵת שַׁדַּי, וְאֵל שַׁדַּי מִבָּעֵי לֵיהּ, כְּמָה דִכְתִיב וְאֵל שַׁדַּי יִתֵּן לָכֶם רַחֲמִים לִפְנֵי הָאִישׁ. וִיבָרְכֶךָּ, יְבָרֶכְךָ מִבָּעֵי לֵיהּ.

778. Come and see, Joseph was bestowed yet another blessing: "By the God (El) of your father, and He shall help you; and by *Shadai* (ve'et *Shadai*), and He shall bless you." (Genesis 49:25) [He asks:] "**This verse is hard to understand,** since it says 'By the God (El) of your father...'

(Ibid.) when it should have been 'the God (El) of your father help you.' It says '…by Shadai (et Shadai)…' (Ibid.) instead of El as in 'And El Shadai give you Mercy before the man….' (Genesis 43:14) '…and He shall bless you' (Genesis 49:25) should have been 'El Shadai shall bless you.'"

Joseph inherited Zeir Anpin and Nukva, Above and Below.

779. אֶלָּא אַחְסִין לֵיהּ לְעֵילָּא וְתַתָּא. אַחְסִין לֵיהּ לְעֵילָּא, בְּאֵל אָבִיךָ, דְּאִיהוּ אַחְסָנָא עִלָּאָה, אֲתַר דְּאִקְרֵי שָׁמַיִם. וְיַעֲזֶרֶךָ, בְּגִין דְּלָא יַחֲלִיף הַאי אֲתַר, לַאֲתַר אָחֳרָא, וְסִיּוּעָא דִּילֵיהּ לֶהֱוֵי מֵאֲתַר דָּא, וְלָא מֵאַחֳרָא.

779. He answers: "He inherited both Above in Zeir Anpin and Below in the Nukva. He inherited Above, as it says '…by the God (El) of your father…' (Genesis 49:25) which is the Supernal Inheritance, a place called Heaven, namely Zeir Anpin, the Chariot Jacob, "…and He shall help you…' (Genesis 49:25); [meaning] He shall not exchange it for another place, and His help shall be from this place and no other."

Ve'et shadai refers to both Zeir Anpin and Nukva—
day in night, night in day.

780. וְאֵת שַׁדַּי, מַהוּ וְאֵת שַׁדַּי, אֶלָּא, אִיהוּ דַּרְגָּא אָחֳרָא תַּתָּאָה, דְּהָא תָּנִינָן, בְּכָל אֲתַר אֶת ה', דָּא שְׁכִינְתָּא, כְּמוֹ וָאֵרֶא אֶת ה', אֶת לְרַבּוֹת. וְאֵת לְאַכְלְלָא יוֹם בְּלֵילְה, וְלֵילְה בְּיוֹם, כִּדְכְתִיב וְאֵת שַׁדָּ"י, דְּהָא מִתַּמָּן נָפְקִין בִּרְכָאן לְבָרְכָא עָלְמִין.

780. [He asks:] "What is the meaning of: '…and by Shadai (ve'et Shadai)…' (Genesis 49:25); should it not have been El Shadai as asked above?" [He answers:] "But this is another Lower grade, as we have learned that uniformly 'et HaShem (the Lord)' is the Shechinah, as in 'I saw the Lord (Va'ere et Adonai)…' (Ezekiel 6:1); Et includes the Shechinah. Ve'et alludes to Zeir Anpin, thus comprising day, Zeir

Anpin, **in night, and night in day, as it is written, 'and** *Shadai (ve'et shadai)'* **(Genesis 49:25) with Vav (and; ו), since from thence blessings issue into the world.**

Et (Alef-Tav) contains all 22 letters.

781. תּוּ, אַמַּאי לָא קָאֲמַר וְאֵל שַׁדַּי, דְּהָא ה"נ מַשְׁמַע כְּדְקָאֲמְרִינָן, דִּכְתִיב וְאֵל שַׁדַּי יִתֵּן לָכֶם רַחֲמִים, כֹּלָּא אֲתַר וַד הוּא, אַמַּאי עָבַק ל' וְכָתַב ת'. אֶלָּא רָזָא אִיהוּ, דְּכַד אִינּוּן שְׁבִילִין נָפְקִין מֵעֵילָּא, כָּלְלָא דְּאוֹרַיְיתָא, אַחְסִין עֲמַיִם, כְּד"א אֵת הַשָּׁמַיִם, כְּלָּלָא דְּכ"ב אַתְוָון. וּמֵהָכָא נָפְקֵי לְתוֹרָה שֶׁבְּעַ"פ דְּאִקְרֵי אֶרֶץ, כְּדְקָאֲמְרִינָן וְאֵת הָאָרֶץ, כְּלָּלָא דְּכ"ב אַתְוָון. וְשָׁמַיִם כָּלִיל כֹּלָּא כַּחֲדָא, וּכְדֵין מִתְעַטְּרָא סִיהֲרָא בְּכֹלָּא, וְיַתְבָא בְּאַשְׁלָמוּתָא, וּבִרְכָאן נָגְדִין כְּדֵין מִתַּמָּן, וְעַל דָּא וְאֵת שַׁדָּי.

781. "We should explain further why it does not say '…and *El Shadai'* **seeing that it has the same meaning as we said** that it too, alludes to the Nukva, also called *El Shadai*, **as it is written, 'and** *El Shadai* **gives you mercy….' (Genesis 43:14) All is the same** since 'and *El Shadai*' refers to the Nukva as in '…and *Shadai (ve'et Shadai)*….' (Genesis 49:25)" [He asks:] **"Why then omit the Lamed (אֵל) and replace it with Tav (אֵת)?"** He answers: **"It is a secret, for when these paths come from Above,** namely the 22 Hebrew letters, from which every perfection is supplied, **which are the entirety of the Torah,** namely all the abundance of Zeir Anpin, **the Heaven,** Zeir Anpin, **inherits them, as it is written, '…the Heaven (et hashmayim; אֵת הַשָּׁמַיִם)…' (Genesis 1:1);** *Et* (Alef–Tav; אֵת) **including all the 22 letters** from Alef to Tav. **From here, they depart to the Oral Torah, called Earth,** namely the Nukva, **as it says '…and the Earth (ve'et ha'aretz; וְאֵת הָאָרֶץ)…' (Ibid.),** *Et* (Alef–Tav; אֵת) **including the 22 letters** received by the Nukva. At first, **Heaven,** Zeir Anpin, **includes them all as one, and then the moon,** the Nukva, **is adorned by them all;** namely she receives them from Zeir Anpin and dwells in perfection. Blessings are then drawn from there, and thus it says '…and *Shadai (ve'et Shadai;* וְאֵת שַׁדָּי)…' (Genesis 43:14) indicating the Great Perfection of the entirety of the 22 letters in the Nukva, where all blessings issue, as explained.

Vav always refers to an addition and sustainment.

782. וִיבָרְכֶךָ, בְּגִין דְּיֶהֱא לֵיהּ קִיּוּם תָּדִיר וְיַתִּיר, דְּהָא בְּכָל אֲתַר דְּאִית בֵּיהּ וָא"ו, תּוֹסֶפֶת אִית לֵיהּ, וְקִיּוּמָא. עַד כָּאן כְּלַל, וּלְבָתַר עָבֵיד פְּרָט, דִּכְתִיב בִּרְכוֹת שָׁמַיִם וְגו'.

782. "…and (*ve*; ו) He shall bless you…" (Genesis 49:25) is spelled with Vav (ו) so that there will be further lasting prevalence to the blessings. For wherever there is Vav (ו), it is an indication of an increase and maintenance. Up to this point, it was said in general. Now he gives details, as it is written: "blessings of Heaven…." (Ibid.), meaning that until here the blessings from Zeir Anpin and from Nukva are hinted in a general way. "…by the God (El) of your father…" (Ibid.) alludes to Zeir Anpin, "…and by *Shadai*…" (Ibid.) alludes to Nukva. Afterwards, the verse details them. "…blessings of heaven above…" (Ibid.) is for Zeir Anpin, "…and blessings of the deep…" (Ibid.) is for Nukva.

Joseph (Yesod) inherited all the blessings from the Patriarchs.

783. בִּרְכוֹת אָבִיךָ גָּבְרוּ עַל בִּרְכוֹת הוֹרַי. בִּרְכוֹת אָבִיךָ גָּבְרוּ וַדַּאי, דְּהָא יַעֲקֹב אַחְסִין שְׁבָחָא דְּכֹלָּא, יַתִּיר מֵאֲבָהָן, דְּהָא הוּא שְׁלִים בְּכֹלָּא. וְכֹלָּא יָהַב לֵיהּ לְיוֹסֵף, מ"ט. בְּגִין דְּהָכֵי אִתְחֲזֵי, דְּהָא צַדִּיק כֹּלָּא נָטִיל, וְאַחְסִין כֹּלָּא כַּחֲדָא, וְכָל בִּרְכָאן בֵּיהּ שַׁרְיָין. הוּא אָרִיק בִּרְכָאן מֵרֵישָׁא לְעֵילָא, וְכָל שַׁיְיפֵי גוּפָא כֻּלְּהוּ אִתְתַּקְּנָן, לְאַרְעָא בֵּיהּ בִּרְכָאן, וּכְדֵין אִתְעֲבֵיד נָהָר דְּנָפִיק מֵעֵדֶן.

783. "The blessings of your father have surpassed the blessings of my ancestors…." (Genesis 49:26) The blessings of your father, Jacob, the Central Column, have surely surpassed the blessings of Abraham and Isaac, since Jacob inherited more praises than the Patriarchs,

he being perfect in all. The two Columns, Right and Left, which are Abraham and Isaac, are incomplete until the Central Column, Jacob, comes and mediates between them. Therefore he inherits all the Mochin that are in the two Columns, Right and Left. He gave it all to Joseph. Why? Because this is appropriate, since the Righteous, Yesod, namely Joseph, takes all and inherits all together, meaning that he receives from all the Sefirot of Zeir Anpin together, and all blessings dwell in him. He draws the blessings from the Head Above, the Upper Three [Sefirot] of Zeir Anpin, and all the members of the Body, Chesed, Gevurah, Tiferet, Netzach, Hod, and Yesod of Zeir Anpin prepare to pass the blessings to Yesod, and then Yesod turns into a "...river that flows from Eden...." (Genesis 2:10)

All the Sefirot link in delight and flow to Yesod.

784. מַאי מֵעֵדֶן, אֶלָּא, בְּכָל שַׁעֲתָא דְּכָל שַׁיְיפִין יָתְבִין בְּקִשׁוּרָא חֲדָא, וְאִינוּן בְּעֵדוּנָא דְּתִיאוּבְתָּא מֵרֵישָׁא לְעֵילָּא וּלְתַתָּא, וְכֻלְּהוּ מֵעֵדוּנָא וְתִיאוּבְתָּא דִּלְהוֹן, מְרִיקִין בֵּיהּ, וְאִתְעֲבִיד נָהָר דְּנָגֵיד וְנָפִיק מֵעֵדֶן וַדַּאי. תּוּ מֵעֵדֶן מֵחָכְמָה עִלָּאָה, נָגֵיד כֹּלָּא לְאִתְמַשְׁכָא, וְעָבֵיד נַהֲרָא, וְאִתְמַשְׁכָא עַד דְּמָטֵי לְהַאי דַּרְגָּא, וּכְדֵין כֹּלָּא בְּבִרְכָאן, וְכֹלָּא חַד.

784. He asks: "What is the meaning of '...from Eden...' (Genesis 2:10)?" He answers: "As long as all the limbs are linked together in delight and desire from the abundance of the Head Above and from Below, and they all pour upon Yesod their delight and desire surely becomes a river that flows and comes out from Eden, for eden (עדן) comes from idun (delight; עידון) and pleasure. We should further explain that the word '...from Eden...' (Ibid.) means that from Supernal Chochmah called Eden, everything flows and turns into a river, which pours down until it reaches the grade of Yesod, and then all the Sefirot of Zeir Anpin are blessed, and all is one."

All the Sefirot desire the Upper and Lower Female.

785. עַד תַּאֲוַת גִּבְעוֹת עוֹלָם, תֵּיאוּבְתָּא דְּאִינּוּן גִּבְעוֹת עוֹלָם. וּמַאי נִינְהוּ. תְּרֵי נוּקְבֵי, חַד לְעֵילָא, וְחַד לְתַתָּא, דְּכָל חַד אִקְרֵי עוֹלָם. וְתֵיאוּבְתָּא דְּכָל שַׁיְיפֵי גּוּפָא, בְּאִינּוּן תְּרֵין אִמָּהָן. תֵּיאוּבְתָּא לְיַנְקָא מֵאִמָּא עִלָּאָה. תֵּיאוּבְתָּא לְאִתְקַשְּׁרָא בְּאִמָּא תַּתָּאָה. וְתֵיאוּבְתָּא דְּכֹלָּא חַד, בְּגִין כָּךְ כֻּלְּהוּ, תִּהְיֶינָה לְרֹאשׁ יוֹסֵף וְגוֹ', לְאִתְבָּרְכָא הַהוּא דַּרְגָּא דְּצַדִּיק, וּלְנַטְלָא כֹּלָּא, כִּדְקָא חֲזֵי.

785. "To the utmost bound (also 'desires') of the everlasting hills (givot olam, lit. hills of the world)…" (Genesis 49:26) means the passion for those hills of the world. [He asks:] "What are they?" [He answers:] "They are the two Females, one Above, Binah, and one Below, the Nukva of Zeir Anpin, each called 'World.' The desire of all the members of the Body, all the Sefirot of Zeir Anpin, is for these two Mothers. They desire to suckle from the Upper Mother, Binah, and desire to be attached to the Lower Mother, the Nukva. The desire of all is one, and therefore '…they shall be on the head of Joseph…' (Ibid.), who is Yesod, as that grade of the Righteous, Yesod, will be blessed and receive them all as befits."

A righteous individual is one who safeguards the level of Yesod.

786. זַכָּאִין אִינּוּן דְּאִקְרוּן צַדִּיקִים, דְּהָא צַדִּיק לָא אִקְרֵי, אֶלָּא מַאן דְּנָטֵיר הַאי דַּרְגָּא, הַאי אָת קַיָּימָא קַדִּישָׁא. זַכָּאִין אִינּוּן בְּעַלְמָא דֵין, וּבְעַלְמָא דְּאָתֵי. נָפְקוּ מִן מְעַרְתָּא, אֲמַר ר' שִׁמְעוֹן, כָּל חַד וְחַד לֵימָא מִלָּה, וְגֵיהַךְ בְּאָרְחָא.

786. Happy are those who are called Righteous, for no one is called Righteous except those who keep the grade of the Sign of the Holy Covenant. They are happy in this world and in the World to Come. They came out of the cave (mentioned in verse 730). Rav Shimon said: "Let each of us discourse as we walk."

NINTH OF AV

Vayishlach

7. The sinew of the vein

A Synopsis

Rav Chiya opens a discussion on the significance of the sinew of
Jacob's thigh, which we can now identify as the sciatic nerve. Had
the sinew not failed Jacob on the night he struggled with Esau's
minister, Jacob would have prevailed over Esau's power completely,
both Above and here Below. Rav Shimon then explains that because
the energy of Jacob's thigh was broken, the strength of the upholders
of the Torah was diminished. As a result, none of the prophets,
except Moses, were able to retain their faculties unimpaired when
receiving divine messages. Thus it is incumbent on the children of
Israel to preserve the sinew of the thigh vein. The dark side controls
the sciatic nerve in all creatures, including cows, so that none may be
defiled by eating or benefiting from it in other ways. In addition, we
learn, the children of Israel are responsible for preserving the power
of the Torah by supporting those who toil in it.

The Relevance of this Passage

The sciatic nerve affects the lower back and extends down through
the thigh, which supports and upholds the body. The thigh
corresponds to the students of a righteous sage who support their
master, or to benefactors who financially assist those who engage in
Torah study and the revelation of spiritual Light. When the dark
side seeks to penetrate an individual, it will often attack supporting
elements that are not as strong as the person himself. The Evil
Inclination will strike first at our vulnerabilities and weaknesses.
These verses fortify our defenses. In addition, we arouse great
spiritual Light to strengthen those who support the righteous in
their endeavor to reveal the Light of the Torah to all the world.

No benefit can be derived from the sinew of the vein.

.99. עַל כֵּן לֹא יֹאכְלוּ בְנֵי יִשְׂרָאֵל אֶת גִּיד הַנָּשֶׁה וגו', כִּי נָגַע בְּכַף יֶרֶךְ יַעֲקֹב בְּגִיד הַנָּשֶׁה, דַּאֲפִילוּ בַּהֲנָאָה אָסִיר, וַאֲפִילוּ לְיַהֲבֵיהּ לְכַלְבָּא. וְאַמַּאי אִקְרֵי גִּיד הַנָּשֶׁה. כְּלוֹמַר, גִּיד דְּאִיהוּ מְנַשֶּׁה לִבְנֵי נָשָׁא, מִפּוּלְחָנָא דְּמָארֵיהוֹן, וְתַמָּן הוּא יֵצֶר הָרָע רְבִיעַ.

99. "Therefore the children of Israel eat not of the sinew of the vein... because he touched the hollow of Jacob's thigh in the sinew of the vein." (Genesis 32:33) **It is forbidden to enjoy it or even to give it to a dog.** He asks: **"Why is it called the 'sinew of the vein'** (*gid hanashe*)?" He answers: **"It is as if to say, it is a sinew that seduces** (*menasheh*) **men from serving their Master. There lies the Evil Inclination.**

Jacob was complete and strong, except in the sinew of the vein.

.100. וְכֵיוָן דְּאִתְדַּבַּק עִם יַעֲקֹב, לָא אַשְׁכַּח אֲתַר דְּיָכֵיל לְאִתְגַּבְּרָא עֲלֵיהּ דְּיַעֲקֹב, בְּגִין דְּכָל שַׁיְיפֵי גוּפָא סַיְיעֵי לְיַעֲקֹב, וְכֻלְּהוּ הֲווֹ תַּקִּיפִין, וְלָא הֲווֹ בְּהוֹן חוּלְשָׁא, מַה עֲבַד, וַיִּגַּע בְּכַף יְרֵכוֹ בְּגִיד הַנָּשֶׁה, בְּזִינֵיהּ, בְּיֵצֶר הָרָע דְּאִיהוּ זִינֵיהּ וְאַתְרֵיהּ, וּמִתַּמָּן אָתֵי יֵצֶר הָרָע עַל בְּנֵי נָשָׁא.

100. **"When the angel wrestled with Jacob, he could not find a weak place in his body through which to overcome Jacob because the parts of his body were all strong and without weakness,** and the Klipah takes hold only in a place of lack and weakness." [He asks:] **"What did he do then?"** [He answers:] **"'...he touched the hollow of his thigh...'** (Genesis 32:33) the sinew of the vein, **his own kind,** namely **the Evil Inclination that is his own kind, and** there is the **place** of the Evil Inclination. **From there the Evil Inclination comes to people.**

Every animal part we eat strengthens or weakens
our corresponding body part.

‫101. וּבְגִין כָּךְ אָמְרָה אוֹרַיְיתָא לֹא יֹאכְלוּ בְּנֵי יִשְׂרָאֵל אֶת גִּיד הַנָּשֶׁה. כְּמָה‬
‫דְּאָמְרוּ וַחֲבֵרַיָּא, בְּשַׁיְיפִין דְּבַר נָשׁ, דְּרַמְזִין לְעֵילָּא, אִי טַב טַב, וְאִי בִּישׁ בִּישׁ,‬
‫וּבְגִין כָּךְ, כָּל שַׁיְיפָא מִתְתָּקַף שַׁיְיפָא, וַדַּאי גִּיד הַנָּשֶׁה מִתְתָּקַף לְיֵצֶר הָרָע, דְּהוּא‬
‫זִינֵיהּ, וּבְנֵי יִשְׂרָאֵל לָא יֹאכְלוּ לֵיהּ, דְּלָאו אִינּוּן מִסִּטְרֵיהּ וּמִזִּינֵיהּ, אֲבָל עַמִּין‬
‫עע״ז, יֹאכְלוּ לֵיהּ, דְּאִיהוּ מִסִּטְרָא וּמִזִּינָא דְּמַלְאָכָא דִּלְהוֹן, דְּאִיהוּ סמא״ל,‬
‫בְּגִין לְתַקְּפָא לִבְהוֹן.‬

101. "For that reason the Torah reads, 'Therefore the children of Israel eat not of the sinew of the vein….' (Genesis 32:33)" The friends said that a man's body parts allude to higher places. If the member **is good,** it draws **goodness; if it be evil,** it draws **evil. Thus each** animal **member** we eat **strengthens the** corresponding **member** of the man who eats it. **Assuredly, the sinew of the vein strengthens the Evil Inclination, which is its own kind, and therefore the children of Israel do not eat it. But the heathen nations may eat it, as they are of the side and kind of their angel Sama"el, for it strengthens their hearts.**

248 limbs corresponding to 248 Positive Precepts.

‫102. בְּגִין דְּאִית בְּבַר נָשׁ, רמ״ח שַׁיְיפִין, לָקֳבֵל רמ״ח פָּקוּדִין דְּאוֹרַיְיתָא,‬
‫דְּאִינּוּן לְמֶעְבַּד אִתְיְהֲבוּ, וְלָקֳבֵל רמ״ח מַלְאָכִין, דְּאִתְלַבַּשַׁת בְּהוֹן שְׁכִינְתָּא,‬
‫וּשְׁמָא דִּלְהוֹן כִּשְׁמָא דְּמָארֵיהוֹן.‬

102. Man has 248 members in his body corresponding to the 248 Positive Precepts in the Torah that are meant to be performed, and corresponding to the 248 Angels, with whom the Shechinah is clothed, and their Names are like the Name of their Master.

365 sinews corresponding to the 365 Negative Precepts.

103. וְאִית בְּבַר נָשׁ עס"ה גִּידִין, וּלְקַבְלֵהוֹן עס"ה פִּקּוּדִין, דְּלָאו אִינּוּן, אִתְיְהִיבוּ לְמֶעְבַּד, וְלָקֳבֵל עס"ה יוֹמֵי שַׁתָּא, וְהָא תִּשְׁעָה בְּאָב חַד מִנַּֽיְהוֹן, דְּאִיהוּ לָקֳבֵל סמא"ל, דְּאִיהוּ חַד מֵאִינּוּן עס"ה מַלְאָכִין, וּבג"כ אָמְרָה אוֹרַיְיתָא, לֹא יֹאכְלוּ בְּנֵי יִשְׂרָאֵל אֶת גִּיד הַנָּשֶׁה, א"ת לְאַסְגָּאָה תִּשְׁעָה בְּאָב, דְּלָא אָכְלִין בֵּיהּ, וְלָא שָׁתִין.

103. There are 365 sinews, corresponding to 365 Negative Precepts that are not to be done, and the sinew of the vein is one of them. **They correspond to the 365 days of the year,** namely together with the ten days of Teshuvah, **the Ninth of Av being one of them. It corresponds to** the angel **Sama"el, who is one of the 365 angels** ruling over the 365 days of the year. The Ninth of Av is one of the days of the year, and the sinew of the vein is one of the 365 sinews. Both belong to the same category. **Therefore the Torah said, "Therefore the children of Israel eat not of the (et) sinew of the vein...." (Genesis 32:33) The particle et (the) here includes the Ninth of Av, when it is forbidden to eat and drink,** being in the same category as the sinew of the vein.

The Ninth of Av corresponds to the sinew of the vein.

104. וּבְגִין כָּךְ חָזָא קוּדְשָׁא בְּרִיךְ הוּא כֹּלָּא, וְרַמְזוּ בְּהוֹן רֶמֶז לְיַעֲקֹב, וַיֵּאָבֵק אִישׁ עִמּוֹ, בְּכָל יוֹמֵי שַׁתָּא, וּבְכָל שַׁיְיפִין דְּיַעֲקֹב, וְלָא אַשְׁכַּח בַּר הַהוּא גִּיד הַנָּשֶׁה, מִיָּד תְּשַׁע וֵאלֵיהּ דְּיַעֲקֹב, וּבְיוֹמֵי שַׁתָּא אַשְׁכַּח יוֹם תִּשְׁעָה בְּאָב, דְּבֵיהּ אִתְתַּקַּף וְאִתְגְּבַר דִּינָא עֲלָנָא, וְאִתְחֲרַב בֵּי מַקְדְּשָׁא, וְכָל מַאן דְּאָכִיל בְּתִשְׁעָה בְּאָב, כְּאִילּוּ אָכִיל גִּיד הַנָּשֶׁה. ר' חִיָּיא אָמַר, אִלְמָלֵא לָא אִתְחַלַּשׁ חֵילָא דָא דְּיַעֲקֹב, הֲוָה אִתְקַיַּים יַעֲקֹב לְגַבֵּיהּ, וְאִתְבַּר חֵילָא דְּעֵשָׂו, לְעֵילָא וְתַתָּא.

104. Therefore the Holy One, blessed be He, saw it all, and there is a hint to Jacob in the verse, **"...and there wrestled a man with him," (Genesis 32:26), meaning with all the days of the year and with all of Jacob's members but found** no place to hold on to **but the sinew of the**

vein. Immediately, Jacob's strength diminished. Among the days of
the year he found the Ninth of Av, on which day Sama"el prevailed,
and our decree was sentenced, and the Temple was destroyed. He
who eats on the Ninth of Av, it is as if he eats the sinew of the vein.
Rav Chiya said: "Had the strength of Jacob's thigh not weakened,
Jacob would have prevailed, and Esau's power would have been
broken Above and Below."

Only Moses was strong enough to have clear prophecy.

105. רַבִּי שִׁמְעוֹן פָּתַח וַאֲמַר, כְּמַרְאֵה הַקֶּשֶׁת אֲשֶׁר יִהְיֶה בֶעָנָן בְּיוֹם הַגֶּשֶׁם כֵּן
מַרְאֵה הַנֹּגַהּ סָבִיב הוּא מַרְאֵה דְּמוּת כְּבוֹד יְיָ' וָאֶרְאֶה וָאֶפֹּל עַל פָּנַי וְגוֹ'. הַאי
קְרָא אִתְּמַר. אֲבָל תָּא חֲזֵי, דְּהָא כְּתִיב וְלֹא קָם נָבִיא עוֹד בְּיִשְׂרָאֵל כְּמֹשֶׁה.
מַה בֵּין מֹשֶׁה לִשְׁאָר נְבִיאֵי עָלְמָא. מֹשֶׁה אִסְתַּכַּל בְּאַסְפַּקְלַרְיָאה דְּנָהֲרָא,
שְׁאָר נְבִיאֵי, לָא הֲווֹ מִסְתַּכְּלֵי, אֶלָּא בְּאַסְפַּקְלַרְיָאה דְּלָא נָהֲרָא. מֹשֶׁה הֲוָה
שָׁמַע וְקָאִים עַל רַגְלוֹי, וְחֵילֵיהּ אִתְתַּקַּף, וַהֲוָה יָדַע מִלָּה עַל בּוּרְיֵיהּ, כְּמָה
דִּכְתִיב וּמַרְאֶה וְלֹא בְחִידֹת. שְׁאָר נְבִיאֵי, הֲווֹ נָפְלֵי עַל אַנְפַּיְיהוּ, וְאִתְחֲלַשׁ
חֵילָא דִּלְהוֹן, וְלָא הֲווֹ יָכְלֵי לְקַיְּימָא עַל בּוּרְיֵיהּ דְּמִלָּה, מַאן גָּרַם לוֹן דָּא, בְּגִין
דִּכְתִיב, כִּי נָגַע בְּכַף יֶרֶךְ יַעֲקֹב וְהוּא צֹלֵעַ עַל יְרֵכוֹ.

105. Rav Shimon opened and said: "'As the appearance of the [rain]
bow that is in the cloud on the day of rain, so was the appearance of
the brightness round about. This was the appearance of the likeness
of the glory of the Lord. And when I saw it, I fell upon my face....'
(Ezekiel 1:28) We have already studied this verse, yet come and see,
it is written, 'Never again did there arise in Israel a prophet like
Moses....' (Deuteronomy 34:10)" He asks: "What is the difference
between Moses and the other prophets?" He answers: "Moses looked
into a clear mirror, Zeir Anpin; the other prophets beheld only a
clouded mirror, the Nukva. Moses heard the prophecy standing, and
his power was strengthened. He understood the matter thoroughly,
as it is written, '...in vision and not in riddles....' (Numbers 12:8)
The other prophets fell upon their faces at the time of prophecy, and

became weak because they could not understand it clearly. This was because '...he touched the hollow of Jacob's thigh...' (Genesis 32:26) '...and he limped upon his thigh....' (Genesis 32:32) Prophecy is from Netzach and Hod of Zeir Anpin, which are the secret of the two thighs. Since the thigh was damaged, their prophecy was not clear as it ought to be.

Only Obadiah, who came from Esau, was able to prophesy about Esau.

106. וְכָל אִינוּן נְבִיאִין, לָא יָכִילוּ לְקָיְימָא, עַל מַה דְּזַמִּין קוּדְשָׁא בְּרִיךְ הוּא לְמֶעְבַּד לֵיה לְעֵשָׂו, בַּר עוֹבַדְיָה נְבִיאָה, דַּהֲוָה גִּיּוֹרָא, דְּאָתֵי מִסִּטְרָא דְּעֵשָׂו, דָּא קָאִים בְּקִיּוּמֵיה עֲלֵיה דְּעֵשָׂו, וְלָא אִתְחַלַּשׁ וֵזִילֵיה.

106. "No prophet knew what the Holy One, blessed be He, was destined to do to Esau, except the prophet Obadiah, who was a convert from the side of Esau. He understood clearly what pertained to Esau, yet his strength did not diminish, as recorded in the book of Obadiah.

The prophets had unclear vision because
"he touched the hollow of Jacob's thigh."

107. וְע"ד כָּל שְׁאָר נְבִיאֵי, אִתְחַלַּשׁ תּוּקְפַּיְיהוּ, וְלָא הֲוֹו יָכְלִין לְאִתְקָיְימָא, לְקַבְּלָא מִלָּה עַל בּוּרְיֵיה כַּדְקָא יָאוֹת, מַאי טַעְמָא, בְּגִין כִּי נָגַע בְּכַף יֶרֶךְ יַעֲקֹב בְּגִין הַנָּשֶׁה, דְּנָסִיב וְשָׁאִיב כָּל חֵילָא דְּיַרְכָא, וְעַל דָּא אִתְבַּר חֵילָא דְּיַרְכָא, וְאִשְׁתְּאַר צוֹלֵעַ עַל יְרֵכוֹ, דְּהָא כָּל נְבִיאִין דְּעָלְמָא, לָא יָכִילוּ לְאַדְבְּקָא וּלְקָיְימָא בֵּיה. תָּא חֲזֵי, נְבִיאִין כֻּלְּהוּ, בַּר מֹשֶׁה, לָא קָיְימוּ בְּתוּקְפַּיְיהוּ כַּדְקָא חָזֵי.

107. "This is why the other prophets were weakened and could not perceive and grasp the prophecy as they ought. The reason is that '...he touched the hollow of Jacob's thigh in the sinew of the vein....' (Genesis 32:33) He drew and sucked away the power of the thigh. The power of the thigh broke, leaving him limping on his thigh, and

all the prophets in the world became limited in their conception and understanding. Come and see, all the prophets except Moses did not understand things clearly.

The Torah is diminished and forgotten when
Torah Scholars have no support.

108. וּמַאן דְּלָעֵי בְּאוֹרַיְיתָא, וְלֵית מַאן דְּסָמִיךְ לֵיהּ, וְלָא אִשְׁתְּכַח מַאן דְּאַטֵּיל מִכְּלֵי לְכִיסֵיהּ לְאַתְתַּקְפָּא, עַל דָּא, אוֹרַיְיתָא קָא מִשְׁתַּכְחָא בְּכָל דָּרָא וְדָרָא, וְאִתְחַלַּשׁ תּוּקְפָּא דְּאוֹרַיְיתָא כָּל יוֹמָא וְיוֹמָא, בְּגִין דְּלֵית לוֹן לְאִינוּן דְּלַעְאָן בָּהּ, עַל מַה דְּסָמְכִין, וּמַלְכוּ חַיָּיבָא אִתְתַּקַּף בְּכָל יוֹמָא וְיוֹמָא. ת"ח, כַּמָּה גָּרִים חוֹבָא דָּא, וּבְגִין דְּלֵית מַאן דְּאַסְמִיךְ לְאוֹרַיְיתָא כִּדְקָא יָאוֹת, אִינּוּן סָמְכִין חַלָּשִׁין, וְגָרְמִין לְאַתְתַּקְפָּא, לְהַהוּא דְּלֵית לֵיהּ שׁוֹקִין וְרַגְלִין לְקָיְימָא עֲלַיְיהוּ.

108. "He who studies Torah and has no one to support him, and finds no one to give money to his pocket for his needs **and thereby strengthen him, due to this, the Torah is forgotten in every generation and its power is diminished every day because those who deal with the Torah have nothing to support themselves with.** The secret of, '...he limped upon his thigh...' (Genesis 32:32) is that no one gives support and strength for the Torah Scholars to be able to deal with the Torah. Therefore **the evil kingdom grows stronger every day. Come and see how much this sin caused. Because there is no one to support the Torah,** Zeir Anpin, **properly, the supports** of Zeir Anpin **are weakened,** that is, Netzach and Hod of Zeir Anpin called 'supports,' **and as a result, he who has no legs or thighs on which to stand,** the primordial serpent, **is thereby strengthened.**"

When Israel does not want to support the Torah,
they give legs to the serpent.

109. פָּתַח וַאֲמַר, וַיֹּאמֶר יי' אֱלֹהִים אֶל הַנָּחָשׁ כִּי עָשִׂיתָ זֹּאת אָרוּר אַתָּה מִכָּל הַבְּהֵמָה וְגו', עַל גְּחוֹנְךָ תֵלֵךְ. מַאי עַל גְּחוֹנְךָ תֵלֵךְ. דְּאִתְחַבְּרוּ סַמְכִין דִּילֵיהּ,

וּקְצִיצוּ רַגְלוֹי, וְלֵית לֵיהּ עַל מַה דְּקָאִים. כַּד יִשְׂרָאֵל לָא בָּעָאן לְסַמְכָא לֵיהּ לְאוֹרַיְיתָא, אִינוּן יָהֲבִין לֵיהּ, סָמְכִין וְשׁוֹקִין, לְקָיְימָא וּלְאִתְתַּקְּפָא בְּהוֹ.

109. He opened and said: "'And the Lord God said to the serpent, "Because you have done this, you are cursed above all animals... upon your belly shall you go...."' (Genesis 3:14)" He asks: "What is the meaning of, '...upon your belly shall you go...' (Ibid.)?" He answers: "**Its supports were broken. Its legs were cut off, and it had nothing to stand on. Thus when Israel do not want to support the Torah,** namely fund the Torah Scholars who deal with the Torah, as mentioned, **they give** the serpent **supports and legs to stand on and be strengthened by** because the Other Side is built by the lacks in holiness.

When the voice of Torah is interrupted, the hands of Esau strengthen.

110. תָּא חֲזֵי, כַּמָּה עֲקִימוּ וְזַכִּימוּ, אִתְחֲזַּם בְּהַהוּא לֵילְיָא, הַהוּא דְּרָכֵיב נָחָשׁ, לְקָבְלֵיהּ דְּיַעֲקֹב, דְּהָא אִיהוּ הֲוָה יָדַע, דִּכְתִיב הַקּוֹל קוֹל יַעֲקֹב וְהַיָּדַיִם יְדֵי עֵשָׂו, וְאִי פָּסִיק קָלָא דְּיַעֲקֹב, כְּדֵין וְהַיָּדַיִם יְדֵי עֵשָׂו, בְּגִין כָּךְ, אִסְתַּכַּל לְכָל סִטְרִין, לְאַבְאָשָׁא לֵיהּ לְיַעֲקֹב, וּלְאַפְסָקָא קָלֵיהּ.

110. "**Come and see, how much deceit and crookedness did that rider of the serpent,** Sama"el, **employ against Jacob that night. He** knew well the verse, '...**"The voice is Jacob's voice, but the hands are the hands of Esau"** (Genesis 27:22), which means that **if the voice of Jacob,** the voice of Torah, **is interrupted,** power is transferred to **the hands of Esau. He therefore searched on every side to harm Jacob and stop the voice** of his Torah.

Esau's angel attacked the thigh of Jacob, which was the support of the Torah.

111. וְחָמָא לֵיהּ תַּקִּיף בְּכֹלָּא. דְּרוֹעִין מִסִּטְרָא דָא וּמִסִּטְרָא דָא, דְּאִינוּן תַּקְפִין. גּוּפָא, דְּאִתְתַּקַּף בֵּינַיְיהוּ, וְחָמָא תּוּקְפָּא דְּאוֹרַיְיתָא, וְאִתְתַּקַּף בְּכֹלָּא, כְּדֵי חֲרָא כִּי לֹא יָכוֹל לוֹ. מָה עֲבַד, מִיָּד וַיִּגַּע בְּכַף יְרֵכוֹ, דְּאִתְחֲזַּם לְקָבְלֵיהּ, אָמַר כֵּיוָן

דְּאִתְבְּרוּ סָמְכִין דְּאוֹרַיְיתָא, מִיָּד אוֹרַיְיתָא לָא אִתְתַּקַּף, וּכְדֵין יִתְקַיַּים מַה
דַּאֲמַר אֲבוּהוֹן, הַקּוֹל קוֹל יַעֲקֹב וְהַיָּדַיִם יְדֵי עֵשָׂו. וְהָיָה כַּאֲשֶׁר תָּרִיד וּפָרַקְתָּ
עֻלּוֹ מֵעַל צַוָּארֶךָ.

111. "He found him strong in every respect; he saw that **his arms
are strong on this side and that side,** Chesed and Gevurah called
Abraham and Isaac; he saw **the body,** the secret of Jacob, who connects
the two arms, **strengthened between them. He saw the power of his
Torah strong** in every respect **and was afraid lest he would not prevail
against him. What did he do? Immediately, '...he touched the hollow
of Jacob's thigh...' (Genesis 32:26),** namely the supports of the Torah.
He employed cunning against him, saying: 'Now that the supports
of the Torah are broken, the Torah can no longer be strong, and
their father's words shall be fulfilled,' '..."The voice is Jacob's voice,
but the hands are the hands of Esau,"' (Genesis 27:22) and '...and
it shall come to pass when you shall have the dominance, that you
shall break his yoke from off your neck.' (Genesis 27:40)

When there is no support, there is no voice of Jacob.

112. וּבְדָא אִתְחַכַּם לְקָבְּלֵיהּ דְּיַעֲקֹב, דְּהָא בְּגִין דְּיִתְּבַר וֵילָא דְאוֹרַיְיתָא, אָזֵיל
וְאִתְתַּקַּף עֵשָׂו. וְכַד חָמָא דְלָא יָכֵיל לָהּ לְאוֹרַיְיתָא, כְּדֵין חָלִישׁ תּוּקְפָּא, דְּאִינּוּן
דְּסָמְכִין לָהּ, וְכַד לָא יִשְׁתַּכְחוּן מַאן דְּסָמְיךְ לְאוֹרַיְיתָא כְּדֵין לָא יְהֵא קוֹל קוֹל
יַעֲקֹב, וִיהוֹן יָדַיִם יְדֵי עֵשָׂו.

112. "He acted craftily against Jacob, for in order to break the
power of the Torah, Esau grew stronger. When he saw he could not
hurt the Torah, he weakened those who supported the students of
Torah. For when there is no support to be found for the students of
the Torah, there will be none of '...Jacob's voice...' (Genesis 27:22)
but there will be '...the hands of Esau.' (Ibid.)

Jacob alludes to deceit, and Israel alludes to pride and might.

113. וְכַד וָזָמָא יַעֲקֹב הָכֵי, כַּד סָלֵיק צַפְרָא, אִתְקֵיף בֵּיהּ, וְאִתְגַּבַּר עֲלֵיהּ, עַד דְּאִיהוּ בְּרִיךְ לֵיהּ, וְאוֹדֵי לֵיהּ עַל אִינוּן בִּרְכָאן, וַאֲמַר לֵיהּ, לֹא יַעֲקֹב יֵאָמֵר עוֹד שִׁמְךָ כִּי אִם יִשְׂרָאֵל, לָאו יַעֲקֹב בַּעֲקִימוּ, אֶלָּא בְּגֵאֲוָתָא וְתוֹקְפָּא, דְּלֵית מַאן דְּיָכֵיל לָךְ.

113. "When Jacob saw this, he struck and overpowered him at dawn, until he blessed him and confirmed to him the blessings, saying: '..."Your name shall no more be called Jacob, but Israel..."'** (Genesis 32:29)** This means, your name is **no longer Jacob, which indicates deceit**—as it is written, "'...for he has supplanted (*ya'akveni*) me these two times...'" (Genesis 27:36)—**but** Israel, which means **with pride and might, for no one can prevail against you.** For the name Israel indicates pride and authority, as it is written, "'...for you have contended (*sarita*) with gods and with men, and have prevailed.'" (Genesis 32:29)

The sinew of the vein will be corrected in the Future to Come.

114. וְתָא חֲזֵי, מֵהַאי נָחָשׁ, כַּמָּה חֲיָלִין מִתְפָּרְשָׁן לְכָל סְטַר, וְאִשְׁתַּכְּחוּ בְּעָלְמָא לְגַבֵּי בְּנֵי נָשָׁא. וּבְעֵינָן לְקַיְּימָא לְהַהוּא גִּיד הַנָּשֶׁה, דְּאַף עַל גַּב דְּקָרֵיב בֵּיהּ הַהוּא דְּרָכֵיב עַל חִוְיָא, קַיָּים אִיהוּ, וְאִתְקַיַּים בְּגַוְון וְלָא אִתָּבַר.

114. "Come and see, from this serpent many armies are released to all sides, and they are found in the world among people. It is incumbent upon us then to maintain the sinew of the vein because although the rider of the serpent, Sama"el, **approached it, it exists, and it stands in its color and is not broken."**

To explain these words we need to explain the entirety of this article. It is known that 320 Sparks fell at the Shattering of the Vessels in the World of Nekudim, which are Ten Sefirot that each had 32 Aspects shattered.

Namely there are eight kings—Da'at, Chesed, Gevurah, Tiferet, Netzach, Hod, Yesod, and Malchut—and each contain four Aspects, which are Chochmah, Binah, Tiferet, and Malchut, thus 32. And ten times 32 is 320. The first nine Sefirot in them are sorted and corrected by the Emanator, Who established from them the Four Worlds: Atzilut, Briyah, Yetzirah, and Asiyah, and also through the Righteous fulfilling the Torah and Precepts. They are nine times 32, which equals 288.

But their last Sefirah, Malchut, which also contains 32 Aspects, remained unrefined among the Klipot, and we cannot refine or correct it during the 6,000 years. Therefore it is called the Heart (*lev*; 32) of Stone, for it is prohibited to sort from it. Only by properly being careful to just sort out the 288 sparks during the 6,000 years does it get refined automatically without any action from Below. Then it is said about it: "...I will remove the heart (*lev*; 32) of stone from your body..." (Ezekiel 36:26), which are the 32 Aspects that are in the mentioned Vessel of Malchut that shattered and clothed in the Klipot, Whose correction is only in the hands of the Emanator and not in the hands of man.

It is also known that in everything there is World, Year, and Soul. Therefore within this Aspect of the Heart of Stone there is also World, Year, and Soul. In the aspect of World it is the Primordial Serpent that Sama"el rides on, in the aspect of Year it is the Ninth of Av, and in the aspect of Soul it is the secret of the sinew of the vein. This is the secret of "And when he saw that he did not prevail against him..." (Genesis 32:26) because Jacob was complete with all 288 Sparks, as he had already completely corrected them, then "...he touched the hollow of his thigh, in the sinew of the vein..." (Ibid.) since it had not been sorted yet, as mentioned. Therefore, "...and the hollow of Jacob's thigh was put out of joint..." (Ibid.) because just like Sama"el has the power to ride on the serpent, so does he have the power over the sinew of the vein for they are the same Aspect, one in World and one in Soul.

In verse 104, this is: **"...and there wrestled a man with him"** (Genesis 32:26), **with all the days of the year and with all of Jacob's members,** namely in the Aspect of Year and in the Aspect of Soul **but found nothing except the sinew of the vein. Among the days of the year he found the Ninth of Av,** as the sinew of the vein is the Aspect of the Heart of Stone in the Soul, and the Ninth of Av is the Aspect of the Heart of Stone of the Year, as they have not yet been sorted from the Klipot, and therefore he [the Serpent] latches onto them. Thus **He who eats on the Ninth of Av, it is as if he eats the sinew of the vein** because eating is the secret of sorting out from the Klipot, and since the sinew of the vein is the Aspect of the Heart of Stone, the verse says: "Therefore, the children of Israel do not eat the sinew of the vein..." (Genesis 33:33) for it is prohibited to sort it by means of man, as mentioned. For this reason it is prohibited to eat on the Ninth of Av, since on this day, which is the Aspect of the Heart of Stone, sorting is prohibited. Thus the prohibition of the sinew of the vein and the prohibition of eating on the Ninth of Av is one matter.

This is why it says here (verse 114): **"It is incumbent upon us, then, to maintain the sinew of the vein."** In other words, though it is prohibited to sort it and eat it, since the Klipot are attached to it, we are nevertheless commanded to maintain it until the Future to Come, when it will be corrected by the Emanator **"because although the rider of the serpent approached it, it exists,"** even though Sama"el latches onto it, it does not get nullified by this, **"and it stands in its color and is not broken."** Even though it has no correction in its essence, it nevertheless has a correction in its color. Its color, which is black, is composed of the Three Colors of Holiness that are in the first nine Sefirot, and it receives from them an Illumination and correction so that it can be maintained in a way that it can be fit to be sorted in the future.

Refraining from eating the sinew of the vein breaks Satan's power.

115. וְחֵילָא בְּעֵינָן לְאִתְתַּקְּפָא בְּעָלְמָא, וּלְאַחֲזָאָה כִּי שָׂרִיתָ עִם אֱלֹהִים וְעִם אֲנָשִׁים וַתּוּכָל. וְכַד חָמֵי, דְּהָא לָא אִתְּבַר, וְלָא אִתְאֲכִיל הַהוּא אֲתַר, כְּדֵין אִתְּבַר חֵילֵיהּ וְתוּקְפֵּיהּ, וְלָא יָכִיל לְאַבְאָשָׁא לִבְנוֹי דְּיַעֲקֹב. וְעַל דָּא, לָא בְּעֵינָן לְמֵיהַב דּוּכְתָּא לִבְרִיָּיתָא דְּעָלְמָא, לְמֵיכַל לֵיהּ, וְלָא לְאִתְהֲנָאָה מִנֵּיהּ כְּלָל.

115. **It behooves us to increase the power** of Holiness **in the world and to show that "…you have contended with gods and with men, and have prevailed." (Genesis 32:29) When he sees that** the sinew of the vein **is intact,** as Light is drawn on it to preserve it, **and the place is not consumed,** that is, if people refrain from eating it, which means "sorting," as mentioned in the previous paragraph, **then the power and vigor** of Sama"el **is broken, and he is unable to harm the children of Jacob. Thus we do not need to give room for the inhabitants of the world to eat the sinew of the vein and enjoy it.**

No enjoyment may be derived from an unholy place.

116. ר' יֵיסָא סָבָא דָּרַשׁ, כִּי נָגַע בְּכַף יֶרֶךְ יַעֲקֹב. כְּתִיב הָכָא כִּי נָגַע בְּכַף, וּכְתִיב הָתָם, כָּל הַנּוֹגֵעַ בְּמֵת בְּנֶפֶשׁ הָאָדָם וְגו'. מַה לְּהַלָּן מְסָאֲבָא, אוֹף הָכָא נָמֵי מְסָאֲבָא, דְּסָאִיב הַהוּא אֲתַר, וּמֵאֲתַר מְסָאֲבָא, לֵית לָן לְאִתְהֲנָאָה מִנֵּיהּ כְּלָל, כ"ע בַּאֲתַר דְּקָרִיב הַהוּא סְטַר מְסָאֲבָא, וְאוֹרַיְיתָא לָא קָאָמַר, אֶלָּא כִּי נָגַע, וּכְתִיב וַיִּגַּע בְּכַף יְרֵכוֹ, כד"א אֲשֶׁר יִגַּע בּוֹ הַטָּמֵא יִטְמָא, בְּרִיךְ רַחֲמָנָא, דְּיָהֵיב אוֹרַיְיתָא לְיִשְׂרָאֵל, לְמִזְכֵּי בָּהּ בְּעָלְמָא דֵּין וּבְעָלְמָא דְּאָתֵי, כְּמָה דִּכְתִיב אֹרֶךְ יָמִים בִּימִינָהּ בִּשְׂמֹאלָהּ עֹשֶׁר וְכָבוֹד.

116. **Rav Yesa Saba explained that the verse, "…touched the hollow of Jacob's thigh…" (Genesis 32:26) is similar to the verse, "Whoever touches the dead body of any man that has died…." (Numbers 19:13) Both refer to impurity because** Sama"el **has defiled that place,** the sinew of the vein, **and no enjoyment may be derived from an unholy place, particularly if the Side of Defilement,** Sama"el, **has touched**

the place. The Torah does not add more than, "...for he touched..." (Genesis 32:26) as in, "...he touched the hollow of Jacob's thigh..." (Ibid.), which is similar to, "And whatever the unclean person touches shall be unclean...." (Numbers 19:22) Therefore we learn that Sama"el defiled this place by touching it. **Blessed be the Merciful One who gave the Torah to Israel, to merit this world and the World to Come, as it is written: "Length of days in her right hand; and in her left hand are riches and honor." (Proverbs 3:16)**